IFIP Advances in Information and Communication Technology 580

Editor-in-Chief

Kai Rannenberg, Goethe University Frankfurt, Germany

Editorial Board Members

IFIP – The International Federation for Information Processing

IFIP was founded in 1960 under the auspices of UNESCO, following the first World Computer Congress held in Paris the previous year. A federation for societies working in information processing, IFIP's aim is two-fold: to support information processing in the countries of its members and to encourage technology transfer to developing nations. As its mission statement clearly states:

> *IFIP is the global non-profit federation of societies of ICT professionals that aims at achieving a worldwide professional and socially responsible development and application of information and communication technologies.*

IFIP is a non-profit-making organization, run almost solely by 2500 volunteers. It operates through a number of technical committees and working groups, which organize events and publications. IFIP's events range from large international open conferences to working conferences and local seminars.

The flagship event is the IFIP World Computer Congress, at which both invited and contributed papers are presented. Contributed papers are rigorously refereed and the rejection rate is high.

As with the Congress, participation in the open conferences is open to all and papers may be invited or submitted. Again, submitted papers are stringently refereed.

The working conferences are structured differently. They are usually run by a working group and attendance is generally smaller and occasionally by invitation only. Their purpose is to create an atmosphere conducive to innovation and development. Refereeing is also rigorous and papers are subjected to extensive group discussion.

Publications arising from IFIP events vary. The papers presented at the IFIP World Computer Congress and at open conferences are published as conference proceedings, while the results of the working conferences are often published as collections of selected and edited papers.

IFIP distinguishes three types of institutional membership: Country Representative Members, Members at Large, and Associate Members. The type of organization that can apply for membership is a wide variety and includes national or international societies of individual computer scientists/ICT professionals, associations or federations of such societies, government institutions/government related organizations, national or international research institutes or consortia, universities, academies of sciences, companies, national or international associations or federations of companies.

More information about this series at http://www.springer.com/series/6102

Marko Hölbl · Kai Rannenberg ·
Tatjana Welzer (Eds.)

ICT Systems Security and Privacy Protection

35th IFIP TC 11 International Conference, SEC 2020
Maribor, Slovenia, September 21–23, 2020
Proceedings

 Springer

Editors
Marko Hölbl (ID)
University of Maribor
Maribor, Slovenia

Kai Rannenberg
Goethe University Frankfurt
Frankfurt, Germany

Tatjana Welzer
University of Maribor
Maribor, Slovenia

ISSN 1868-4238   ISSN 1868-422X (electronic)
IFIP Advances in Information and Communication Technology
ISBN 978-3-030-58203-6   ISBN 978-3-030-58201-2 (eBook)
https://doi.org/10.1007/978-3-030-58201-2

This Springer imprint is published by the registered company Springer Nature Switzerland AG
The registered company address is: Gewerbestrasse 11, 6330 Cham, Switzerland

Preface

In these challenging times caused by the COVID-19 situation, we are honored to bring you this collection of the best papers submitted to the 35th IFIP International Conference on ICT Systems Security and Privacy Protection, which was held in Maribor, Slovenia, September 21–23, 2020. IFIP SEC conferences are the flagship events of the International Federation for Information Processing (IFIP) Technical Committee 11 on Information Security and Privacy Protection in Information Processing Systems (TC-11).

The 2020 edition of the IFIP SEC proceedings includes 29 high-quality papers covering a wide range of research areas in the information security field. They were authored by researchers from 19 different countries. The selection of papers was a highly challenging task: 149 received submissions were evaluated based on their significance, novelty, and technical quality. Each paper received at least three, but most of them four reviews by members of the Program Committee. The Program Committee meetings were held electronically, with intensive discussions over a period of three weeks. Of the papers submitted, 29 were selected for presentation at the conference, leading to an acceptance rate of 19.5%.

We want to express our appreciation to all the contributors who helped to make IFIP SEC 2020 a success. There is a long list of people who volunteered their time and energy to put together the conference and who deserve acknowledgement. We want to thank the members of the Program Committee and the external reviewers, who devoted significant amounts of their time to evaluate all the submissions. Special thanks go to the keynote speakers Elisa Bertino from Purdue University West Lafayette, USA, and Stanka Šalamun and Mitja Kolšek from 0patch by ACROS Security, Slovenia, who accepted our invitation to present their insights at the conference.

Further individuals who deserve special thanks and without whom the current program and success of the conference would not have been possible include: the organizing chair Lili Nemec Zlatolas and the members of the Organizing Committee Borut Zlatolas, Luka Hrgarek, and Marko Kompara, all from the University of Maribor, Faculty of Electrical Engineering and Computer Science. They kept all things smooth and flowing, even after the delays caused by the pandemic. The IFIP SEC and WISE had to be postponed without clear information on when public events like it could be safely held again. The IFIP Summer School, which was being organized separately, also got postponed and found a new home at IFIP SEC 2020. Due to the constant changes in local regulation, the questionable safety of international travel and uncertainty regarding the future spread of the disease, the decision was made to hold the conference virtually, despite the best efforts to have it in Maribor, Slovenia. Special recognition goes to Hotel City Maribor and the Maribor Convention Bureau, who were very accommodating and understanding regardless of the economic impact of the unfortunate situation, and we express our regret to the participants, for missing the opportunity to see the beauty Slovenia has to offer.

We also acknowledge the institutional support for IFIP SEC 2020, which came from the University of Maribor, Faculty of Electrical Engineering and Computer Science, Institute of Informatics. Without this support, it would not have been possible to organize the conference.

Last but certainly not least, we thank all the authors who submitted papers and all the conference's attendees who coped with the changing circumstances in a kind and flexible manner.

We hope you find the proceedings of IFIP SEC 2020 interesting, stimulating, and inspiring for your future research regardless of the challenging times in which the conference took place.

July 2020   Marko Hölbl
                                                             Kai Rannenberg
                                                             Tatjana Welzer

Organization

General Chair

Tatjana Welzer   University of Maribor, Slovenia

Program Committee Chairs

Marko Hölbl   University of Maribor, Slovenia
Kai Rannenberg   Goethe University Frankfurt, Germany

Organizing Chair

Lili Nemec Zlatolas   University of Maribor, Slovenia

Program Committee

Rose-Mharie Åhlfeldt   University of Skövde, Sweden
Raja Naeem Akram   Royal Holloway, University of London, UK
Vijay Atluri   Rutgers University, USA
Man Ho Au   The University of Hong Kong, China
Gergei Bana   University of Missouri, USA
Joao Paulo Barraca   University of Aveiro, Portugal
Pedro Brandão   University of Porto, Portugal
Dagmar Brechlerova   EuroMISE Prague, Czech Republic
Ricardo Chaves   IST, INESC-ID, Portugal
Michal Choras   ITTI Ltd., Poland
K. P. Chow   The University of Hong Kong, China
Nathan Clarke   University of Plymouth, UK
Miguel Correia   Universidade de Lisboa, Portugal
Nora Cuppens-Boulahia   Polytechnique Montréal, Canada
Paolo D'Arco   Università di Salerno, Italy
Ed Dawson   QUT, Australia
Sabrina De Capitani di   Università degli Studi di Milano, Italy
  Vimercati
Bart De Decker   Katholieke Universiteit Leuven, Belgium
Nicola Dragoni   Technical University of Denmark, Denmark
Nicolás Emilio Daz Ferreyra   University of Duisburg-Essen, Germany
Isao Echizen   National Institute of Informatics, Japan
Simone Fischer-Hübner   Karlstad University, Sweden
Sara Foresti   Università degli Studi di Milano, Italy
Steven Furnell   University of Plymouth, UK
Chaya Ganesh   Aarhus University, Denmark

Sergio Nunes	ISEG - School of Economics and Management, Portugal
Balaji Palanisamy	University of Pittsburgh, USA
Brajendra Panda	University of Arkansas, USA
Sebastian Pape	Goethe University Frankfurt, Germany
Stefano Paraboschi	Università di Bergamo, Italy
Miguel Pardal	Universidade de Lisboa, Portugal
Gilbert Peterson	US Air Force Institute of Technology, USA
António Pinto	ESTG, P.Porto, Portugal
Rami Puzis	Ben-Gurion University of the Negev, Israel
Arun Raghuramu	Forescout Technologies Inc., USA
Carlos Rieder	Isec AG, Switzerland
Juha Röning	University of Oulu, Finland
Elham Rostami	Örebro University, Sweden
Reyhaneh Safavi-Naini	University of Calgary, Canada
Pierangela Samarati	Università degli Studi di Milano, Italy
Damien Sauveron	Université de Limoges, France
Ingrid Schaumüller-Bichl	Upper Austrian University of Applied Sciences Campus Hagenberg, Austria
Jetzabel Maritza Serna Olvera	Universitat Politècnica de Catalunya, Spain
Paria Shirani	Concordia University, Canada
Nicolas Sklavos	University of Patras, Greece
Daniel Slamanig	AIT Austrian Institute of Technology, Austria
Kane Smith	University of North Carolina at Greensboro, USA
Agusti Solanas	Rovira i Virgili University, Spain
Teodor Sommestad	Swedish Defence Research Agency (FOI), Sweden
Chunhua Su	Osaka University, Japan
Shamik Sural	Indian Institute of Technology, India
Kerry-Lynn Thomson	Nelson Mandela University, South Africa
Muhamed Turkanović	University of Maribor, Slovenia
Rossouw Vonsolms	Nelson Mandela University, South Africa
Jozef Vyskoc	VaF, Slovakia
Ding Wang	Peking University, China
Lingyu Wang	Concordia University, Canada
Edgar Weippl	University of Vienna, SBA Research, Austria
Vladimir Zadorozhny	University of Pittsburgh, USA
Filip Zagorski	Wroclaw University of Technology, Poland
Yuexin Zhang	Swinburne University of Technology, Australia
André Zúquete	University of Aveiro, Portugal

Additional Reviewers

Mohiuddin Ahmed
Marios Anagnostopoulos
Arash Atashpendar
Sebastian Berndt
Olivier Blazy
Rohit Chadha
Aveek Kumar Das
Tiago Dias
Rong Huang
Vincenzo Iovino
Andreas Jakoby
Manfred Jeusfeld
Jan Kalbantner
Kallol Krishna Karmakar
Joakim Kävrestad
Mathieu Klingler
Vasileios Kouliaridis
Chengjun Lin
Chao Lin
Chang Liu
Francesco Mercaldo
Louis Moreau
Hong-Huy Nguyen
Wojciech Niewolski
Fahad Nife
Jianting Ning
Marcus Nohlberg

Tomasz Nowak
Tomás Oliveira E Silva
Oleksii Osliak
Ali Padyab
Bernardo Portela
Nektaria Potha
Andreas Put
Sebastian Ramacher
Musa Samaila
Benjamin Semal
Mariusz Sepczuk
Bernardo Sequeiros
Mina Sheikhalishahi
João Marco Silva
Tiago Simões
Marjan Skrobot
Eva Söderström
Patryk Szewczyk
Florian Thaeter
Ngoc Dung Tieu
Ganbayar Uuganbayar
Benito van der Zander
Weizheng Wang
S. J. Yang
Wenjie Yang
Xu Yang
Kai Zhu

Contents

Channel Attacks

Leaky Controller: Cross-VM Memory Controller Covert Channel
on Multi-core Systems.   3
   Benjamin Semal, Konstantinos Markantonakis, Raja Naeem Akram,
   and Jan Kalbantner

Evaluation of Statistical Tests for Detecting Storage-Based
Covert Channels.   17
   Thomas A. V. Sattolo and Jason Jaskolka

IE-Cache: Counteracting Eviction-Based Cache Side-Channel Attacks
Through Indirect Eviction   32
   Muhammad Asim Mukhtar, Muhammad Khurram Bhatti,
   and Guy Gogniat

Connection Security

Refined Detection of SSH Brute-Force Attackers Using Machine Learning. . .   49
   Karel Hynek, Tomáš Beneš, Tomáš Čejka, and Hana Kubátová

MultiTLS: Secure Communication Channels with Cipher Suite Diversity . . .   64
   Ricardo Moura, David R. Matos, Miguel L. Pardal, and Miguel Correia

Improving Big Data Clustering for Jamming Detection in Smart Mobility . . .   78
   Hind Bangui, Mouzhi Ge, and Barbora Buhnova

Human Aspects of Security and Privacy

Assisting Users to Create Stronger Passwords Using
ContextBased MicroTraining   95
   Joakim Kävrestad and Marcus Nohlberg

Facilitating Privacy Attitudes and Behaviors with Affective Visual Design. . .   109
   Agnieszka Kitkowska, Yefim Shulman, Leonardo A. Martucci,
   and Erik Wästlund

Privacy CURE: Consent Comprehension Made Easy.   124
   Olha Drozd and Sabrina Kirrane

Detecting Malware and Software Weaknesses

JavaScript Malware Detection Using Locality Sensitive Hashing   143
  Stefan Carl Peiser, Ludwig Friborg, and Riccardo Scandariato

RouAlign: Cross-Version Function Alignment and Routine Recovery
with Graphlet Edge Embedding   155
  Can Yang, Jian Liu, Mengxia Luo, Xiaorui Gong, and Baoxu Liu

Code Between the Lines: Semantic Analysis of Android Applications   171
  Johannes Feichtner and Stefan Gruber

System Security

IMShell-Dec: Pay More Attention to External Links in PowerShell   189
  RuiDong Han, Chao Yang, JianFeng Ma, Siqi Ma, YunBo Wang,
  and Feng Li

Secure Attestation of Virtualized Environments   203
  Michael Eckel, Andreas Fuchs, Jürgen Repp, and Markus Springer

Network Security and Privacy

Security and Performance Implications of BGP Rerouting-Resistant Guard
Selection Algorithms for Tor   219
  Asya Mitseva, Marharyta Aleksandrova, Thomas Engel,
  and Andriy Panchenko

Actively Probing Routes for Tor AS-Level Adversaries with RIPE Atlas   234
  Wilfried Mayer, Georg Merzdovnik, and Edgar Weippl

Zeek-Osquery: Host-Network Correlation for Advanced Monitoring
and Intrusion Detection   248
  Steffen Haas, Robin Sommer, and Mathias Fischer

Access Control and Authentication

Revisiting Security Vulnerabilities in Commercial Password Managers   265
  Michael Carr and Siamak F. Shahandashti

Evaluation of Risk-Based Re-Authentication Methods   280
  Stephan Wiefling, Tanvi Patil, Markus Dürmuth, and Luigi Lo Iacono

Fuzzy Vault for Behavioral Authentication System   295
  Md Morshedul Islam and Reihaneh Safavi-Naini

Crypto Currencies

Improvements of the Balance Discovery Attack on Lightning Network
Payment Channels.   313
    Gijs van Dam, Rabiah Abdul Kadir, Puteri N. E. Nohuddin,
    and Halimah Badioze Zaman

CCBRSN: A System with High Embedding Capacity for Covert
Communication in Bitcoin   324
    Weizheng Wang and Chunhua Su

Privacy-Friendly Monero Transaction Signing on a Hardware Wallet.   338
    Dusan Klinec and Vashek Matyas

Privacy and Security Management

A Matter of Life and Death: Analyzing the Security
of Healthcare Networks   355
    Guillaume Dupont, Daniel Ricardo dos Santos, Elisa Costante,
    Jerry den Hartog, and Sandro Etalle

Establishing a Strong Baseline for Privacy Policy Classification   370
    Najmeh Mousavi Nejad, Pablo Jabat, Rostislav Nedelchev,
    Simon Scerri, and Damien Graux

Cross-Platform File System Activity Monitoring and Forensics –
A Semantic Approach   384
    Kabul Kurniawan, Andreas Ekelhart, Fajar Ekaputra,
    and Elmar Kiesling

Machine Learning and Security

A Correlation-Preserving Fingerprinting Technique for Categorical
Data in Relational Databases   401
    Tanja Sarcevic and Rudolf Mayer

FDFtNet: Facing Off Fake Images Using Fake Detection
Fine-Tuning Network   416
    Hyeonseong Jeon, Youngoh Bang, and Simon S. Woo

Escaping Backdoor Attack Detection of Deep Learning   431
    Yayuan Xiong, Fengyuan Xu, Sheng Zhong, and Qun Li

Author Index   447

Channel Attacks

Leaky Controller: Cross-VM Memory Controller Covert Channel on Multi-core Systems

Benjamin Semal[(✉)], Konstantinos Markantonakis, Raja Naeem Akram, and Jan Kalbantner

Royal Holloway University of London, Egham, UK
benjamin.semal.2018@live.rhul.ac.uk

Abstract. Data confidentiality is put at risk on cloud platforms where multiple tenants share the underlying hardware. As multiple workloads are executed concurrently, conflicts in memory resource occur, resulting in observable timing variations during execution. Malicious tenants can intentionally manipulate the hardware platform to devise a covert channel, enabling them to steal the data of co-residing tenants. This paper presents two new microarchitectural covert channel attacks using the memory controller. The first attack allows a privileged adversary (i.e. process) to leak information in a native environment. The second attack is an extension to cross-VM scenarios for unprivileged adversaries. This work is the first instance of leakage channel based on the memory controller. As opposed to previous denial-of-service attacks, we manage to modulate the load on the channel scheduler with accuracy. Both attacks are implemented on cross-core configurations. Furthermore, the cross-VM covert channel is successfully tested across three different Intel microarchitectures. Finally, a comparison against state-of-the-art covert channel attacks is provided, along with a discussion on potential mitigation techniques.

Keywords: Covert channel · Memory controller · DRAM · Microarchitectural attack · Cross-VM

1 Introduction

The cloud computing model allows on-demand access to what seems an unlimited pool of storage and computing resource. In order to cope with the elastic demands of its customers, cloud providers rely on multi-tenancy. Infrastructure-as-a-service provides the service users with a virtual environment which maps dynamically to physical resource. These virtual machines (VMs) are co-located on a shared hardware platform, and separated virtually by the hypervisor. Thus, data confidentiality and integrity is enforced at the software level. Yet, because the underlying hardware is common to multiple VMs, attackers are left with means to exploit functional and timing vulnerabilities at the hardware level.

© IFIP International Federation for Information Processing 2020
Published by Springer Nature Switzerland AG 2020
M. Hölbl et al. (Eds.): SEC 2020, IFIP AICT 580, pp. 3–16, 2020.
https://doi.org/10.1007/978-3-030-58201-2_1

The functional behaviour of a system is usually well understood by designers. For example, the seL4 micro-kernel has been proposed as a general purpose solution, providing strong assurance of confidentiality, availability, and integrity enforcement from a functional perspective [11]. The identification of hidden leakage channels works by analyzing the system's resources or source-code. Yet, these identification methods rarely account for the system's temporal behaviour. Murray et al. [18] highlighted that seL4 micro-kernel formal proofs completely omit timing channels. *Microarchitectural timing attacks* aim at recovering data that is dependent on the timing behaviour of an application. More specifically, two processes can exploit timing variations to encode and leak sensitive data across isolation boundaries. *Covert channel attacks* employ this mechanism to violate information flow policies such as in cloud computing.

Cloud providers commonly disable support for simultaneous multi-threading [14] as well as memory deduplication [4], thus hindering a large range of microarchitectural timing attacks. Multiple academic proposals address the mitigation of timing channels in the cache memory [5,8,10,12,20,21,25,29]. Other internal (memory controller, on-chip memory bus) and external (DRAM) resource remain shared among cores, and processors. The sharing of these components has been exploited to design denial-of-service [17,33], covert and side-channel attacks [22,27]. Wang et al. [26] previously proposed a simulated version of memory controller-based leakage channels. In this paper, we present for the first time a practical implementation in both native and virtualized environments. Both attacks work in cross-core configuration, i.e. sender and receiver execute on different physical cores. We test our cross-VM covert channel attack on three different Intel microarchitectures, namely Ivy Bridge, Broadwell, and Skylake. The channel capacity is systematically evaluated and results are discussed against state-of-the-art covert channel attacks.

Contributions. This paper makes the following contributions:

1. We present two microarchitectural covert channel attacks using the memory controller channel scheduler. The first one is *privileged* and is tested in a native environment. The second one is *unprivileged* and can work under both native and virtualized configurations.
2. We evaluate the proposed covert channels under the binary symmetric model. Results of our experiments are reported in Table 3. A discussion of our memory controller-based covert channel against state-of-the-art covert is provided. We also discuss potential mitigation strategies.

Outline. The remainder of the paper is organized as follows. Section 2 provides background on the memory controller and the DRAM organization. In Sect. 3, we present a new memory controller native, privileged covert channel attack. In Sect. 4, we describe a memory controller cross-VM, unprivileged covert channel. In Sect. 5, we evaluate the capacity of both covert channels under the binary symmetric model. Section 6 reviews related works. Section 7 examines potential mitigation strategies. Finally, we conclude in Sect. 8.

2   Background

The (integrated) memory controller handles memory accesses to DRAM. Such access occurs when the data requested by a CPU is not contained in the cache(s). Before serving a memory access, the memory controller must translate the requested data's physical address into a DRAM map. A map is a selection of channel, rank, bank, row, and column. The physical-to-DRAM address translation is performed according to DRAM addressing functions. Once the DRAM map is recovered, the request is then buffered according to the bank and channel that it targets.

The memory controller contains storage and scheduling resources to arbitrate memory accesses (see Fig. 1). First, a request is stored in the buffer matching the DRAM bank that it targets. Then, the bank scheduler will prioritize one request or another, according to pre-determined scheduling algorithm. Once a request wins bank arbitration, it is rescheduled by a channel scheduler. Again, the scheduling algorithm determines priorities. Usually, requests that target open-pages are served first, so as to mitigate the latency incurred by updating a row-buffer.

The memory controller's page policy dictates the aliveness of data in the row-buffer. If a close-page policy is enforced, the row-buffer will systematically be cleared after serving a request. Thus, each memory access results in a row-miss, preventing timing variations, but globally slowing down the execution of programs. If an open-page policy is enforced, the row-buffer will retain data until it must be updated with a new row. Thus, it allows the occurrence of row-hits, reducing the global execution time of programs, but introducing exploitable timing variations.

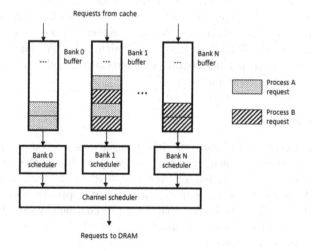

Fig. 1. Organization of a memory controller.

Several sources of contention exist in the memory controller. First, delays can be caused via the bank scheduler, as requests from different processes are mixed in the same bank buffer. If process A is the only one requesting data in a bank, its memory accesses will be served immediately. However, if another process B starts requesting data in the same bank as process A, requests of A and B will compete for scheduling. Because the load on the bank scheduler increases, requests of process A can be delayed.

Second, delays can be caused via the channel scheduler, since it arbitrates requests for several banks. If there are no other requests then for bank i, these will systematically win arbitration and be served immediately. However, if other requests for bank j, with $j \neq i$, compete for access to the channel, the load on the channel scheduler will increase, resulting in requests for bank i to be delayed.

Finally, contention can be caused via the DRAM row-buffer, as long as the memory controller has an open-page policy. Within the same bank, if there are no other requests then for row m, these will systematically result in row-hits. However, if other requests in row n interfere, with $m \neq n$, the row-buffer will alternatively be updated with rows m and n, resulting in frequent row-misses.

3   A Privileged Native Covert Channel

This section presents the basic concept to generating contention via the channel scheduler through a privileged covert channel in a native environment[1].

3.1   Threat Model

The threat model assumes two processes, a *receiver* and a *sender*, who want to share information illegitimately. The security policy forbids these two entities from communicating directly. The sender possesses sensitive information and intends to transmit this information to the receiver. Entities each have their own address space, which is dissociated in physical memory. They are running on different cores. Both entities require root privileges, and have knowledge of the DRAM addressing functions.

3.2   Principle

The proposed covert channel exploits timing variations upon uncached memory accesses. The receiver and sender both occupy space in N, the set of DRAM banks served by a single channel. The receiver "listens" to the channel by continuously performing uncached memory accesses at a pre-determined address, i.e. bank i with $i \in N$. The sender writes on the channel by creating conflicts on the resource involved in the memory accesses of the receiver. The sender generates bit values as follows,

---

[1] The source code of our native covert channel is available at https://github.com/bsepage/mc2c.git.

- A zero is written by performing uncached memory accesses in bank j, with $j \neq i$ and $j \in N$. Because the channel scheduler only serves banks i and j, contention is negligible. Thus, the receiver's memory access in bank i will result in a "normal" latency, which is interpreted as a zero.
- A one is written by performing uncached memory accesses in all the banks comprised in N, except for bank i. This operation causes the channel scheduler to serve requests for every bank within N, which generates an observable contention. Thus, the receiver's memory access in bank i will increase in latency, which is interpreted as a one.

Table 1 summarizes how bit values are encoded and decoded across the covert channel. A **Read** (a) operation consists in performing an uncached memory access in bank a. A **Probe** (a) operation is equivalent, at the exception that the elapsed time of the operation is returned to its caller. In order to write a zero, the sender needs to perform memory accesses in a different bank than the receiver. Doing so prevents interference from the DRAM row-buffer. Indeed, if both entities were to read from the same bank, they would most likely read from different rows (a bank contains thousands of rows). As a result, reading alternatively from the sender's row and the receiver's row would cause the row-buffer to be systematically updated. Thus, memory accesses would result in a majority of row-misses, and dramatically increase in latency. Because our attack exploits exclusively the memory controller, such interference is undesirable. Furthermore, it is preferable to keep the sender active upon sending a zero, in order to compensate the effect of other microarchitectural components (e.g. memory bus). Our objective is to demonstrate the vulnerability in the memory controller, therefore we need to isolate its effect from other sources of contention.

Table 1. Modulating the load on the memory controller channel scheduler. Banks i, j, and k belong to N, the set of banks served by a single channel.

Receiver	Sender	Bit value
Probe (i)	**Read** $(j \mid j \neq i)$	0
Probe (i)	**Read** $(k = 0, \ldots, k = N - 1 \mid k \neq i)$	1

3.3 Design Considerations

The native, privileged covert channel works in two phases. First, each entity must identify a virtual address which maps to the desired DRAM bank(s). Then, both processes synchronize to exchange information covertly.

In the first phase, processes read the restricted */proc/self/pagemap* page translation table to compute the pointer's physical address. Physical-to-DRAM address translation (channel, rank, bank, row, column) requires knowledge of the DRAM addressing functions. These vary from one processor to another, and must be reverse-engineered if not disclosed by the manufacturer[2]. The DRAM address mapping was computed with the reverse engineering tool first presented in [22]. Prior to launching the covert channel, entities can decide on which DRAM banks to use specifically.

In the second phase, entities use the operating system wall-clock to synchronize. The `clflush` instruction is used to flush the cache upon each memory access, so as to force the request to be served from DRAM. Because an uncached memory access is higher in latency than a cached one, the `cpuid` instruction is used to prevent out-of-order execution of the time-stamp reads. Finally, time-stamps are read with the `rdtsc` and `rdtscp` instructions.

4   An Unprivileged Cross-VM Covert Channel

In this section, we present a cross-VM covert channel using the memory controller. We present a strategy to discard root privileges, as well as the necessity to learn the DRAM addressing functions.

4.1   Threat Model

Consider two application processes, a *trojan* and a *spy*, running in concurrent VMs. The hardware platform features a multi-core processor, such that the hypervisor schedules each VM on a different core. The security policy enforced ensures memory isolation, access control, and does not present any software vulnerability. The *trojan* transmits a bitstream across the covert channel, and the *spy* captures the data by probing memory accesses in its own address space (see Fig. 2).

Such a scenario is plausible if the adversary can infect a software with a malicious code. The (accidental) compromising of open-source software has been demonstrated, for instance, with the infection of the OpenSSL cryptographic library in 2014 (Heartbleed) [6]. Compromising of corporate software has also occurred, for example, with the multiple WhatsApp bugs [1,3]. Furthermore, whether it is open-source or proprietary, the software supply chain involves a growing number of developers and corporations. It is hard (if not impossible) for users to control that the different parties involved in the development process apply suitable security practices (e.g. a code is reviewed by a different person than its developer). Therefore, it is reasonable to assume that commercial and open-source software are not immune to malicious insiders.

With regards to the co-location problem, previous studies have shown that it is possible to create a topology of the data centre's network [24,32], even when network isolation countermeasures are employed (e.g. virtual private clouds). As a result, an attacker is capable of co-locating itself with the victim instance on a shared hardware platform.

---

[2] DRAM addressing functions on the Ivy Bridge test platform (see Table 2): $BA0 = b_{13} \oplus b_{17}$; $BA1 = b_{14} \oplus b_{18}$; $BA2 = b_{16} \oplus b_{20}$; and $Rank = b_{15} \oplus b_{19}$.

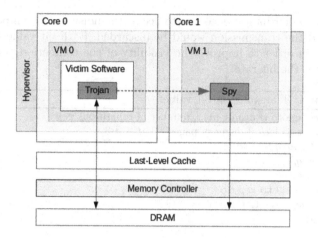

Fig. 2. Cross-VM covert channel.

4.2   Loosing Privileges and Principle

In Sect. 3, the channel scheduler covert channel is limited to a privileged adversary model. Indeed, an unprivileged attacker is unable to read the */proc/self/- pagemap* file, which is necessary for virtual-to-physical address resolution. Yet, the attacker needs to find addresses in its virtual address space which map to different DRAM banks.

Rather than searching for specific banks in a process' address space, we mapped several virtual pages, and observed how these were spread across physical memory. We iterated through the pages, and translated each virtual pointer into a physical address. These addresses were then converted into bank addresses, according to the platform's DRAM addressing functions. The following observations were made,

1. A single (page-aligned) virtual page is mapped to a single bank.
2. Different virtual pages tend to be mapped to different DRAM banks.

These observations suggest that the sending-end only requires to declare several virtual pages, and that each page will map to a different bank. However, there is a probability that one page will be mapped to the same bank as the one accessed by the receiving-end. Such scenario would cause row-buffer conflicts to occur. Accessing different rows triggers row-buffer updates, which would add a significant delay into the receiver's accesses.

By using a smaller amount of memory pages, the probability of having pages mapped in the same bank is reduced. The proposed methodology is detailed in Algorithm 1. The sending-end is designed such that it uses only 3 pages. Upon writing a one, the sender performs accesses in 3 different banks. Thus, the channel scheduler serves accesses in 4 different banks at once (3 for the sender and 1 for the receiver). Upon writing a zero, the sender performs accesses in 1 single page. Thus, the channel scheduler serves accesses in 2 different banks at once. If a row-buffer interference was to occur, the noise would tamper with the bitstream and the transmission would be discarded. Each bit value is repeated several times in order to improve the visibility of the contention. The value of *rep* determines the bit rate.

Algorithm 1: Transmitting bit values

---

input: message to transmit *msg*, number of repetitions *rep*
init   : map and lock 3 memory pages *P1*, *P2*, *P3*
for $i \leftarrow 0$ **to** *msg_len* **do**
    $bit \leftarrow msg[i]$;
    if *bit* **then**
        for $j \leftarrow 0$ **to** *rep* **do**
            | *access*(*P1*, *P2*, *P3*);
        end
    else
        for $j \leftarrow 0$ **to** *rep* **do**
            | *access*(*P1*, *P1*, *P1*);
        end
    end
end

Figure 3 shows the latency of the receiver's memory accesses, with the sender alternatively being active and inactive. The latency graph shows that when the sender is active, the receiver presents an overhead of 6.5 CPU cycles on its accesses. The timing variation indicates that the proposed strategy is valid for creating a covert channel. This new approach has the benefit that it completely discards the virtual-to-bank address translation procedure. Therefore, the attacker neither requires privileges, nor knowledge of the platform's DRAM addressing functions. In this configuration, the attack can be applied to virtual environments, where physical addresses are virtualized by the hypervisor.

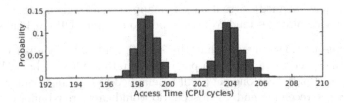

Fig. 3. Effect of active sender upon latency of receiver's memory accesses (Ivy Bridge setup).

4.3   Design Considerations

The cross-VM, unprivileged covert channel also works in two phases. In the first phase, the trojan maps and locks memory pages without reverse-engineering their physical location. We note that spy and trojan no longer require agreeing on specific DRAM banks. In the second phase, entities read or probe their memory accesses to encode and decode bit values. Probing and accessing is performed using the `clflush`, `cpuid`, `rdtsc`, and `rdtscp` instructions.

5   Characterizing the Channel Capacity

This section details our testing environment and provides an evaluation of both covert channel attacks.

5.1   Experimental Setup

The experimental setups used for characterizing the channel capacity and noise ratio are presented in Table 2. The Kernel Virtual Machine [2] hypervisor is used to manage virtual machines, and each VM is operated by a Debian distribution (Linux kernel version 4.19.0). All setups feature a dual-core processor, allowing us to lock the *trojan* and *spy* VMs onto different cores. The `virsh edit` command is used to assign a specific `cpuset` to the `vcpu` attribute. All our setups feature 16 DRAM banks. Note that a commercial infrastructure- or platform-as-a-service server system will likely feature greater amounts of DRAM, i.e. the occurrence of row-buffer interference will drop accordingly. Therefore, the proposed setup represents a worst-case scenario for the attacker.

Table 2. Experimental setups.

Setup	Processor	CPU frequency	Memory	#DRAM banks
Ivy Bridge	Intel i5-3210M	2.5 GHz	1×4 GB DDR3	16
Broadwell	Intel i7-5500U	2.4 GHz	1×8 GB DDR3	16
Skylake	Intel i5-6300U	2.4 GHz	1×8 GB DDR4	16

5.2   Evaluation

In order to evaluate the effective capacity, we model our covert channel as a binary symmetric channel. Under the binary symmetric model, and given a bit error probability p, the probability of correctly transmitting a bit is $1 - p$. Therefore, if $p = 0.5$, it is assumed that the channel has reached maximum entropy, i.e. the probabilities of a bit being erroneous (p) and correct ($1 - p$) are equal. The binary entropy $H_2(p)$ is defined as follows,

$$H_2(p) = -p \log_2 p - (1 - p) \log_2(1 - p) \tag{1}$$

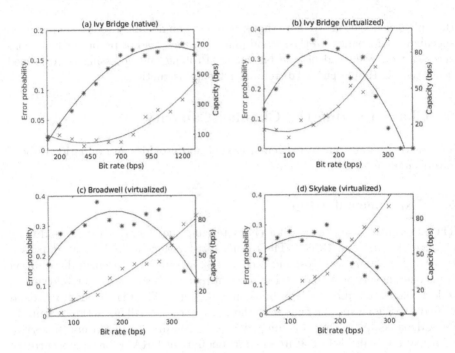

Fig. 4. Effective capacity and error probability measured against raw bit rate.

The channel capacity $C(p, r)$, defined as the quantity of information that can be transmitted reliably, is a function of the entropy $H_2(p)$ and the raw bit rate r,

$$C(p, r) = r(1 - H_2(p)) \tag{2}$$

Figure 4 compares the effective capacity and error probability against a raw bit rate ranging from 100 to 1300 bps for the native scenario (Fig. 4.a), and from 50 to 350 bps for the virtualized scenarios (Fig. 4.b, 4.c, and 4.d). Measures were taken by sending a fixed-size message and counting the number of bit flips on the receiving-end. The error probability p was then calculated as the number of bit flips divided by the number of bits sent. The capacity $C(p, r)$ was computed with Eqs. (1) and (2).

In the native scenario (Fig. 4.a), the error probability stays below 0.1 for bit rates of up to 1250 bps. The channel capacity reaches up to 729 bps, with an error probability of 6.25%. In the virtualized scenarios, the Ivy Bridge (Fig. 4.b), Broadwell (Fig. 4.c), and Skylake (Fig. 4.d) setups respectively achieve a maximum capacity of 90, 95, and 69 bps. The error probability remains below 0.1 for a raw bit rate of up to 175 bps across the three setups. Results are reported in Table 3.

Virtualization has a significant impact on the effective channel capacity, as it brings additional sources of noise. First, sender and receiver compete with each other to be scheduled by the hypervisor. Second, the sender and receiver

Table 3. Experimental results.

Setup	Environment	Bit rate	Error rate	Capacity
Ivy Bridge	Native	1100 bps	6.25%	729 bps
Ivy Bridge	Virtualized	150 bps	7.8%	90 bps
Broadwell	Virtualized	150 bps	7%	95 bps
Skylake	Virtualized	100 bps	5.6%	69 bps

are not able to use the operating system wall-clock to synchronise, as they run in separate VMs. The receiver might sample at a different rate than the sender can transmit, with the bias increasing over time. Third, programs executing concurrently (e.g. hypervisor) can alter the state of the channel scheduler, bank scheduler, or row-buffer. We note that our implementation is free from any fault recovery technique.

6   Discussion and Related Work

At the highest level, simultaneous multi-threading (SMT) allows concurrent threads to share execution units and CPU caches. Percival [21] demonstrated a covert channel between two threads, based on contention within the L1-D and L2 caches. Shortly after, Wang and Lee [28] designed a covert channel that leverages contention on multipliers. More recently, Sullivan et al. [23] demonstrated a high-speed covert channel between two hyperthreads in Amazon EC2 and Google Compute Engine instances. In a virtualized environment, core-level co-residency is hard to achieve as VMs tend to be isolated onto different cores. Furthermore, this class of covert channels is only relevant to cloud platforms where hyperthreads are enabled.

Other works proposed exploiting the LLC cache as it is fast and shared among cores. Xu et al. [31] proposed exploiting conflict in the LLC. They used a covert channel to achieve co-location in an Amazon EC2 setting. Further works followed based upon the *Prime+Probe* [13,15,19] or *Flush+Flush* technique [9]. Maurice et al. [16] implemented a robust covert channel capable of establishing a rogue SSH connection across Amazon EC2 instances. A number of academic works have been proposed in order to tackle timing vulnerabilities emanating from the cache, including hardware cache partitioning [12,20,21,29], software cache partitioning [5,8,10], and noise injection [25,29]. It is difficult to assess whether these covert channels could bypass such countermeasures, and calls for further analysis.

Wu et al. [30] exploited the memory bus as a high-bandwidth covert channel medium. Their Amazon EC2 experiment achieves an effective capacity of 340 bps, with the use of a robust communication protocol. In order to prevent timing channels over the on-chip memory bus (or network), Wang and Suh [27] proposed two approaches. The first one consists in prioritizing traffic from high-security domains over lower ones, thus isolating sensitive software from a potential spy.

The second one consists in assigning separate hardware resources to different security domains, thus inhibiting timing channels on the memory bus.

Pessl et al. [22] built a high-speed covert channel based on the DRAM row-buffer. Their channel reaches up to 596 kbps in virtualized environment. Mitigating row-buffer covert channels could be achieved by enforcing a close-page policy on the memory controller. As a result, every memory access would result in a row-miss, thus inhibiting the timing channel. Furthermore, authors relied on a privileged adversary model, and both entities need to undergo an initialization phase in order to agree on a specific DRAM bank. This agreement cannot be performed online without incurring additional memory usage side-effects. We propose an alternative to the row-buffer exploitation, with a weaker adversary model and less operational constraints.

The vulnerability of the memory controller was previously demonstrated by Moscibroda et al. [17]. Their work shows that by combining all timing channels detailed in Sect. 2, a malicious process can slowdown the execution of a concurrent process by a factor of 190%. It is worth noting that their denial-of-service attack exploits both the memory controller, and the DRAM row-buffer. Furthermore, they do not address the problem of encoding and decoding information across virtual machines via the channel scheduler.

7 Mitigation

Memory controller-based (and DRAM row-buffer covert channels) rely on uncached memory accesses. Therefore, one countermeasure consists in disabling or restricting access to the `clflush` instruction. This mitigation technique would require architectural changes, thus adding in complexity. However, it would go a long way to making shared platforms resilient against this class of microarchitectural covert channels.

Auditing-based techniques have been proposed in the past [7,9]. The systematic flushing of the cache causes a very high number of cache misses, which can be monitored in order to detect abnormal behaviours. However, auditing usually results in high numbers of false positives. Further work is required to assess whether this is a suitable approach.

Wang et al. [26] proposed an alternative hardware design of a memory controller. They achieve temporal isolation between different security domains, at the cost of a memory latency ranging from 60% to 150%. So far, there haven't been any countermeasures relying on spatial isolation, or noise injection.

8 Conclusion and Further Work

In this paper, we presented two instances of microarchitectural covert channel attacks using the memory controller channel scheduler. The first attack is privileged and was tested in a native environment. It achieved a capacity of up to 729 bps (raw bit rate of 1100 bps). The second attack is unprivileged and was tested in a virtualized environment. It achieved a capacity of up to 95 bps (raw bit rate of 150 bps). In further work, we aim to develop countermeasures to prevent exploitation of the memory controller and the DRAM row-buffer resource. We also intend to expand the study to multi-processor x86-64 server platforms, as well as investigating mechanism for bi-directional communication.

References

1. Hackers used WhatsApp 0-day flaw to secretly install spyware on phones. https://thehackernews.com/2019/05/hack-whatsapp-vulnerability.html. Accessed 18 Feb 2020
2. Kernel virtual machine. https://www.linux-kvm.org. Accessed 18 Feb 2020
3. New WhatsApp bug could have let hackers secretly install spyware on your devices. https://thehackernews.com/2019/11/whatsapp-hacking-vulnerability.html. Accessed 18 Feb 2020
4. Base, V.K.: Security considerations and disallowing inter-virtual machine transparent page sharing. VMware Knowl. Base **2080735** (2014)
5. Cock, D., Ge, Q., Murray, T., Heiser, G.: The last mile: an empirical study of timing channels on sel4. In: Proceedings of the 2014 ACM SIGSAC Conference on Computer and Communications Security, pp. 570–581. ACM (2014)
6. Durumeric, Z., et al.: The matter of heartbleed. In: Proceedings of the 2014 Conference on Internet Measurement, pp. 475–488. ACM (2014)
7. Ge, Q., Yarom, Y., Cock, D., Heiser, G.: A survey of microarchitectural timing attacks and countermeasures on contemporary hardware. J. Cryptogr. Eng. **8**(1), 1–27 (2018)
8. Godfrey, M.M., Zulkernine, M.: Preventing cache-based side-channel attacks in a cloud environment. IEEE Trans. Cloud Comput. **2**(4), 395–408 (2014)
9. Gruss, D., Maurice, C., Wagner, K., Mangard, S.: Flush+Flush: a fast and stealthy cache attack. In: Caballero, J., Zurutuza, U., Rodríguez, R.J. (eds.) DIMVA 2016. LNCS, vol. 9721, pp. 279–299. Springer, Cham (2016). https://doi.org/10.1007/978-3-319-40667-1_14
10. Kim, T., Peinado, M., Mainar-Ruiz, G.: STEALTHMEM: system-level protection against cache-based side channel attacks in the cloud. In: The 21st USENIX Security Symposium, pp. 189–204 (2012)
11. Klein, G., et al.: Comprehensive formal verification of an OS microkernel. ACM Trans. Comput. Syst. (TOCS) **32**(1), 2 (2014)
12. Liu, F., et al.: Catalyst: defeating last-level cache side channel attacks in cloud computing. In: 2016 IEEE International Symposium on High Performance Computer Architecture (HPCA), pp. 406–418. IEEE (2016)
13. Liu, F., Yarom, Y., Ge, Q., Heiser, G., Lee, R.B.: Last-level cache side-channel attacks are practical. In: 2015 IEEE Symposium on Security and Privacy, pp. 605–622. IEEE (2015)
14. Marshall, A., et al.: Security best practices for developing windows azure applications, p. 42. Microsoft Corp (2010)
15. Maurice, C., Neumann, C., Heen, O., Francillon, A.: C5: cross-cores cache covert channel. In: Almgren, M., Gulisano, V., Maggi, F. (eds.) DIMVA 2015. LNCS, vol. 9148, pp. 46–64. Springer, Cham (2015). https://doi.org/10.1007/978-3-319-20550-2_3
16. Maurice, C., et al.: Hello from the other side: SSH over robust cache covert channels in the cloud. In: NDSS, vol. 17, pp. 8–11 (2017)

17. Moscibroda, O., Mutlu, T.: Memory performance attacks: denial of memory service in multi-core systems. In: 16th USENIX Security Symposium (2007)
18. Murray, T., et al.: seL4: from general purpose to a proof of information flow enforcement. In: 2013 IEEE Symposium on Security and Privacy, pp. 415–429. IEEE (2013)
19. Oren, Y., Kemerlis, V.P., Sethumadhavan, S., Keromytis, A.D.: The spy in the sandbox: practical cache attacks in Javascript and their implications. In: Proceedings of the 22nd ACM SIGSAC Conference on Computer and Communications Security, pp. 1406–1418. ACM (2015)
20. Page, D.: Partitioned cache architecture as a side-channel defence mechanism (2005)
21. Percival, C.: Cache missing for fun and profit (2005)
22. Pessl, P., Gruss, D., Maurice, C., Schwarz, M., Mangard, S.: DRAMA: exploiting DRAM addressing for cross-CPU attacks. In: 25th USENIX Security Symposium, pp. 565–581 (2016)
23. Sullivan, D., Arias, O., Meade, T., Jin, Y.: Microarchitectural minefields: 4K-aliasing covert channel and multi-tenant detection in IaaS clouds. In: NDSS (2018)
24. Varadarajan, V., Zhang, Y., Ristenpart, T., Swift, M.: A placement vulnerability study in multi-tenant public clouds. In: 24th USENIX Security Symposium, pp. 913–928 (2015)
25. Vattikonda, B.C., Das, S., Shacham, H.: Eliminating fine grained timers in xen. In: Proceedings of the 3rd ACM Workshop on Cloud Computing Security Workshop, pp. 41–46. ACM (2011)
26. Wang, Y., Ferraiuolo, A., Suh, G.E.: Timing channel protection for a shared memory controller. In: 2014 IEEE 20th International Symposium on High Performance Computer Architecture (HPCA), pp. 225–236. IEEE (2014)
27. Wang, Y., Suh, G.E.: Efficient timing channel protection for on-chip networks. In: 2012 IEEE/ACM Sixth International Symposium on Networks-on-Chip, pp. 142–151. IEEE (2012)
28. Wang, Z., Lee, R.B.: Covert and side channels due to processor architecture. In: 22nd Annual Computer Security Applications Conference (ACSAC 2006), pp. 473–482. IEEE (2006)
29. Wang, Z., Lee, R.B.: New cache designs for thwarting software cache-based side channel attacks. ACM SIGARCH Comput. Archit. News **35**(2), 494–505 (2007)
30. Wu, Z., Xu, Z., Wang, H.: Whispers in the hyper-space: high-bandwidth and reliable covert channel attacks inside the cloud. IEEE/ACM Trans. Network. **23**(2), 603–615 (2014)
31. Xu, Y., Bailey, M., Jahanian, F., Joshi, K., Hiltunen, M., Schlichting, R.: An exploration of L2 cache covert channels in virtualized environments. In: Proceedings of the 3rd ACM Workshop on Cloud Computing Security Workshop, pp. 29–40. ACM (2011)
32. Xu, Z., Wang, H., Wu, Z.: A measurement study on co-residence threat inside the cloud. In: 24th USENIX Security Symposium, pp. 929–944 (2015)
33. Zhang, T., Zhang, Y., Lee, R.B.: Memory dos attacks in multi-tenant clouds: severity and mitigation. arXiv preprint arXiv:1603.03404 (2016)

Evaluation of Statistical Tests for Detecting Storage-Based Covert Channels

Thomas A. V. Sattolo[ID] and Jason Jaskolka[✉][ID]

Systems and Computer Engineering, Carleton University,
Ottawa, ON K1S 5B6, Canada
{thomas.sattolo,jason.jaskolka}@carleton.ca

Abstract. Individuals and organizations are more aware than ever of the importance and value of preserving the confidentiality and privacy of sensitive information. However, detecting the leakage of sensitive information in networked systems is still a challenging problem, especially when adversaries use covert channels to exfiltrate sensitive information to unauthorized parties. Presently, approaches for detecting timing-based covert channels have been studied more extensively than those for detecting storage-based covert channels. In this paper, we evaluate the effectiveness of a selection of statistical tests for detecting storage-based covert channels. We present the results of several experiments which show that complexity-based tests are effective at detecting storage-based covert channels when information is embedded into network packet header fields that are not expected to follow a particular pattern, such as the IP Identification and Time-to-Live. These results can help to guide the construction of practical detection platforms capable of effectively detecting the leakage of sensitive information via storage-based covert channels.

Keywords: Covert channel · Detection · Statistical tests · Storage

1 Introduction and Motivation

Data breaches are an ever-growing problem and detecting them is both challenging and valuable as the average total cost of a data breach is now $3.68 million [21]. One of the ways an adversary may seek to avoid detection is by using a covert channel to exfiltrate data from the network.

A covert channel is a means of communication that purports to be difficult for a third-party observer to detect [15]. In the field of information technology, a variety of covert channels have been devised to enable communication between computers without alerting the network owner. Covert channels can be divided into two major categories: timing-based channels and storage-based channels. Timing-based covert channels operate by altering the timing of otherwise legitimate network traffic so that the arrival times of packets encode secret

This research was supported by the Natural Sciences and Engineering Research Council of Canada (NSERC) grant RGPIN-2019-06306.

information. For example, sending two packets in quick succession could represent bit '0' and a long gap between subsequent packets could represent bit '1'. Storage-based covert channels, on the other hand, operate by hiding data in unused fields of RFC-defined network protocols like IP and TCP.

At present, the literature on detecting timing-based covert channels is much more extensive than that on detecting storage-based covert channels. This paper aims to narrow this gap by taking several techniques that have been used successfully to detect timing-based channels, and evaluating their effectiveness for detecting storage-based channels. This is part of an overarching goal to develop methods to detect storage-based covert channels in real-time by observing network traffic. This will necessarily involve computationally efficient statistical tests to distinguish covert channels from ordinary network traffic.

The remainder of this paper is organized as follows. Section 2 provides a short overview of related work. This is followed by a categorization of the tests to be studied in Sect. 3. Next, the experimental methodology is detailed in Sect. 4 and the results are reported in Sect. 5. These results are discussed in Sect. 6 and, lastly, Sect. 7 concludes and highlights future work.

2 Related Work

When identifying the existence of covert channels in computer systems, particularly those which use network protocols as covert message carriers, anomaly detection has been among the most popular detection mechanisms. Anomaly detection refers to the detection of patterns in a given data set that do not conform to what is considered normal behaviour. Anomaly detection techniques are usually used in conjunction with machine learning and statistical approaches.

As previously indicated, much of the existing work on detecting covert channels has focused on timing-based covert channels. Cabuk et al. [3,4] and Gianvecchio and Wang [8] proposed a variety of statistical tests focussed on detecting timing-based covert channels. Naik et al. [20] proposed an entropy-based approach for detecting timing-based channels. Similarly, Li et al. [19] proposed yet more tests for detecting timing-based channels and combined them into a random forest classifier. Crespi et al. [6] studied different statistical anomaly detection methods, commonly used in network traffic analysis, to detect timing-based covert channels.

While there has been a focus on timing-based channels, approaches for storage-based covert channels have also been proposed. Sohn et al. [23] proposed an offline covert channel detection technique using a support vector machine to search for anomalies in the header fields of network packets. A similar technique was proposed by Tumoian and Anikeev [24] involving the interception of all TCP traffic and a model of the initial sequence number generation. The idea uses a neural network to create a model using only the intercepted TCP traffic without any knowledge of the data generation algorithm in an attempt to identify anomalies in the initial sequence numbers of the intercepted TCP segments. Berk et al. [1,2] investigated a methodology for detecting such channels based on a statistical measure of how well the capacity of a given channel is achieved. Jadhav and Kattimani [13] proposed a statistical detection method involving the capture of TCP segments from active network streams and analyzing the covert channel vulnerable fields of TCP headers. Zhai et al. [25] proposed a method based on a TCP Markov model and the Kullback-Leibler divergence [17] to verify the existence of anomalies in the TCP Flags field. Zhao and Shi [26] aimed to detect the existence of covert information embedded in TCP Initial Sequence Numbers using phase-space reconstruction to represent the dynamic nature of initial sequence numbers by building a four-dimensional space of the one dimensional initial sequence numbers.

Besides these, Gunadi and Zander [9–12] built an entire covert channel detection system covering aspects of both timing-based and storage-based channels. That said, their system considers far fewer tests than what we describe in this paper and it does not focus on analyzing which tests are most effective for detecting storage-based covert channels.

3   Test Classification

Statistical tests previously used to detect timing-based covert channels can be classified into two general categories: *Complexity Tests* and *Distributional Tests*.

3.1   Complexity Tests

Complexity tests attempt to measure the extent to which a stream of data is random or predictable and they work if the information transmitted via a covert channel is systematically different from normal network traffic in this way. This works with timing-based covert channels [4,8,12], and the concept should extend to storage-based covert channels, with some caveats. Firstly, it is not necessarily the case that traffic becomes less random when used as a covert channel[1]. This ought to be the case with some fields of network packet headers such as TCP Sequence numbers and IP Identification numbers that can be expected to be random under normal circumstances, but not with others such as IP Flags that would usually just be the same for most packets. The latter, of course, become more random once they have covert information stored in them. It should be possible to determine thresholds—ones that are different for each field—that will separate normal traffic from that when a covert channel is being used.

There are many ways to measure the complexity of a stream of data and thus there are many potential complexity tests to consider. Nonetheless, they can be divided into two types: compressibility-based tests and entropy-based tests.

The compressibility of a stream of data can be used as measure of its randomness—more compressible data is less random. This randomness, in turn,

---

[1] This is the case with timing-based covert channels because normal inter-packet delays are essentially random and those of covert channels cluster at either of the values used as symbols in the communication.

is informative as to the likelihood that the stream is being used as a covert channel. This technique was used by Cabuk et al. [4] to detect timing-based covert channels. They examined a covert channel created using the arrival times of IP packets; messages were sent by alternating long and short delays between packets to represent binary digits. They found that the arrival time pattern of this traffic could be separated from normal traffic because it was more compressible than normal, unaltered traffic.

Entropy is a measure of the information contained in data. As such, it is the most direct tool to search for covert information. Both unused network protocol fields and the covert messages that people may send contain some information, but there is no particular reason for them to contain the same amount of information per byte sent. If these happen to differ, measuring the entropy of unused network protocol fields has the potential to reveal covert channels if they exist.

All of the complexity tests evaluated in our experiments are ultimately based on either compressibility or entropy.

3.2   Distributional Tests

Much of the work of statistical science is to quantify the extent to which two or more entities are different in a world of limited observations. Fundamentally, this is the same as the task of identifying a covert channel so it stands to reason that the huge body of work that exists in statistics would be useful for detecting covert channels. In the literature, several different statistical features—ones that have nothing to do with entropy or compressibility—of inter-packet delay data have been used successfully to detect timing-based covert channels [3,12,19].

However, there is reason to believe that the usefulness of these tests will not transfer to storage-based covert channels. Underlying the logic of these distributional tests is the assumption that the data provided to them is measuring something; they involve ordinal comparisons between the elements in putative covert channels. This makes sense for timing-based covert channels where each element is an inter-packet delay, measured in seconds, and ordering inter-packet delays is obviously meaningful. The same cannot be said of storage-based covert channels, where each element is just the data observed in a network protocol header field. These are not measuring anything, are dimensionless, and ordering them in any way is spurious.

In spite of this, the applicability of distributional tests to storage-based covert channels cannot be so easily dismissed. Distributional tests seem less likely than complexity tests to transfer to storage-based covert channels, but abstract reasoning is no match for experiment, so a range of distributional tests will be considered and evaluated in our study.

4   Experimental Setup and Approach

4.1   Tests Included in the Experiments

Below is a brief overview and rationale for including the statistical tests that are considered in our experiments.

Complexity Tests

LZMA Compression (LZMA): The Lempel-Ziv Markov Chain compression algorithm is a widely used algorithm that offers a high compression ratio at the price of relatively low compression speed [5]. The compression ratio is what is reported as the output of the test. As with all the compression algorithms among the tests considered in our experiments, the rationale for studying LZMA to detect storage-based covert channels comes from [4].

LZ77 Compression (LZ77): Since the overall performance (compression ratio) of the compression is not directly relevant to the purpose of our experiments—all that matters is the difference between how it compresses covert channel traffic versus innocent traffic—it is worthwhile to test a simpler compression algorithm such as Lempel-Ziv 77 [27].

LZ78 Compression (LZ78): Lempel and Ziv also proposed another simple compression algorithm known as Lempel-Ziv 78 [28]. For the same reasons to consider LZ77 in our study, we also consider LZ78.

Lempel-Ziv Complexity (LZC): As precursor to their publications on practical compression algorithms, Lempel and Ziv studied a complexity measure for strings related to the number of distinct substrings and their abundance within the original string [18]. Seeing as the compression ratio given by LZ77 or LZ78 is expected to be a useful test, is only natural to also include a related idea that is meant specifically to be a complexity measure.

First-Order Entropy (FOE): Entropy is generally calculated based on a probability mass function. From any given sequence of values one can compute a histogram (i.e., count the occurrences of every unique value); this histogram can then be taken as an approximation of the probability mass function for the process generating the sequence and one can compute the resulting entropy. The result of approximating entropy in this way is termed first-order entropy and was used to detect timing-based covert channels in [9,19].

Corrected Conditional Entropy (CCE): The entropy rate of a sequence is only truly defined for sequences of infinite length. Of course, this means that the entropy rate of any empirically obtained sequence cannot be computed so it must be estimated. Corrected Conditional Entropy is one method to produce such an estimate [22]. It was first imported into the field of covert channels by Gianvecchio and Wang [8].

Repetition (REP): This test simply counts the fraction of elements in a trace that are unique. This test is considered not so much a practical test, but rather as a "sanity check" that the other tests considered in our study are not performing worse than such a simple and easily computable measure.

Distributional Tests

Autocovariance: This is a measure of how similar a sequence is to itself at other points in the series. It was used to detect timing-based covert channels by Gunadi and Zander [9], as well as Li et al. [19].

Kolmogorov-Smirnov Test: This is a statistical test used determine whether two empirical cumulative distribution functions were sampled from the same source. It has also been used in [9,19] to detect timing-based covert channels.

Wilcoxon Signed Rank: This is a statistical test that compares the rank of two sequences to assess their similarity. It was used by Li et al. [19] for timing-based covert channel detection.

Spearman Correlation: The correlation between the rank of two sequences can be used a measure of the similarity of these two sequences. This is known as Spearman Correlation. It has been used to detect timing-based channels in [19].

Regularity: This is a metric proposed by Cabuk et al. [3] specifically to detect timing-based covert channels. It effectively measures how much the standard deviation of a sequence changes over time.

4.2   Building the Dataset

To build the dataset for our experiments, we needed samples of network traffic with and without information covertly embedded into them. Samples of real normal network traffic were acquired from the Malware Capture Facility Project at the Czech Technical University in Prague [7].

To generate network traffic with covert information, we chose to build a storage-based covert channel embedding bits into the Identification (ID) field of the IP header. The purpose of this field is to identify packets that have been fragmented when the fragments are to be reconstructed. But today, networks tend to have large enough maximum transmissible units that IP packets do not need to be fragmented and these packets are usually sent with IP Flags set to "Don't fragment." Because of this, the ID field is rarely payed any attention, making it a good place to inject covert information. Furthermore, the field is included in every IP packet and is not expected to follow any particular pattern (unlike TCP Sequence numbers), so new covert information can be included in every packet sent. The field is 16 bits long, so a covert channel could transmit up to two bytes per packet.

For our experiments, a covert message had to be selected. The covert message ought to be something that any test would view as similar to real human communication. Text from a novel is appropriate for this purpose, and we chose to use the first few paragraphs of *Pride and Prejudice* by Jane Austen.

To create test data, the IP ID fields were extracted from each of the IP headers. Bits from the message were embedded into the these IP ID fields by replacing the least significant bits of the field with bits from the message[2]. The

---

[2] A similar process can be adopted for other header fields of network packets.

number of bits replaced was varied between 1 and 16, i.e., between changing just one bit of the field, and replacing them completely. Henceforth, the sequence of IP ID values extracted from the network before the message is embedded will be referred to as the *carrier*; once these carriers have message bits embedded into them they will be known as *traces*. Each 16-bit IP ID value (with or without message bits embedded) that form the traces/carrier will be known as an *element*. Note that to create the traces, the least significant bits of the carriers were replaced completely (i.e., AND-ed with zeroes and then OR-ed with the message bits). Using an exclusive-or operation to embed information does not work in this case because the message recipient does not know the value of the field in the carrier and so cannot recover the message if it is embedded via exclusive-or. For example, to embed the first two bits of the word "The" into the IP ID value 0x154A8FE0E, we set the two least significant bits to zero to get 0x154A8FE0C and OR that with '01'—the first two bits of 0x54, the value of 'T' in ASCII—to get 0x154A8FE0D. The result of this process is a set of 16 different traces, one for each number of bits. To ensure that comparisons between them are valid, all 16 traces are of the same length and they all contain the entire message. This requires that all traces except the 1-bit trace contain IP ID fields with no message content.

4.3   Conducting the Experiments

The code for generating the datasets and conducting our experiments is available at: `gitlab.com/CyberSEA-Public/CCStatTests`. The experiments are done in iterations. On each iteration the IP ID field is extracted from a certain number of different packets creating a carrier. The message is then embedded, creating 16 traces and the tests are applied to each trace. The result is one value per test per trace. The test is also applied to the carrier independently of the tests on the traces.

In the next iteration each of these tests is repeated. In total, 1000 iterations are performed and we calculate the mean and standard deviation for each trace/carrier. This whole process is repeated 3 times so as to vary the size of the message. Tests with 256, 16 and 1 byte messages are performed.

In addition to the repeated iterations and different message sizes, the process was repeated with the message encrypted. The Rijndael cipher of the Advanced Encryption Standard (AES) is the current state-of-the-art, so this is what we used. However, AES uses a block cipher with 16-byte blocks such that the smallest message that can be encrypted is 16 bytes long[3]. Consequently a stream cipher that can encrypt a single byte was used for the 1-byte messages, namely the Salsa20 cipher. This limitation is the reason for using 16 bytes as the second smallest message size in our experiments.

---

[3] Padding the message would complicate interpretation of the results.

5 Experimental Results

5.1 Results for Tests Used in Isolation

The results of each experiment are presented here as a series of tables. First Tables 1, 2 and 3 present the effect size for every trace for each message size for each test in our experiments. More specifically, they show the difference between the mean of the test's output on the traces and the mean output on the carrier. This difference is presented in units of the joint standard deviation of the carrier and trace outputs (i.e., the square root of the mean of the two variances). This is known as the *effect size* and it measures how clearly the test can distinguish each trace from the carrier.

The first thing to note is that complexity tests perform much better than distributional tests. No distributional test ever produced an effect size greater than 0.00189 (see Table 1) and, excluding the 1-byte messages (Table 3), all the complexity tests results are at least 0.445 (Table 1)—a difference of more than 2 orders of magnitude. If we go further and exclude Corrected Conditional Entropy on 256-byte messages the weakest results for a complexity test is much larger still at 2.58 (Table 2). As for the 1-byte messages, several test results were undefined (denoted by ⊥). This means that the difference in the mean and joint standard deviations were both zero, i.e., the test result was the same for every iteration for both the carrier and at least one trace. In context, this means the test fails to differentiate the traces from the carrier, so ⊥ is roughly equivalent to 0. That this is the result for many of the complexity tests means that a 1-byte message is not sufficient for them to usefully detect covert channels; even the tests that avoid this issue do not produce large effects.

Next, it is interesting to note that 1-bit traces are generally the least different from the carrier. The only exceptions to this, besides the distributional tests and the 1-byte message table where the tests are not effective, are some of the LZ77 results. Moreover, encryption made little difference and, counterintuitively, the tests mostly did better when the message was encrypted. This improvement is nonetheless quite small; LZ77 was affected the most and even it has a large effect everywhere (except on 1-byte messages) regardless of encryption.

One of the most interesting things about the result is that Repetition outperformed both First-Order Entropy and Corrected Conditional Entropy. This is odd because these both rely heavily on counting unique elements. The main difference is that entropy does so in a way that properly reflects the information contained in the traces and takes into account elements that are repeated more than once, whereas Repetition is ad hoc and should not be expected to be very meaningful. Nevertheless, Repetition performs better and is certainly more efficient than either of the entropy-based tests: the computations required for Repetition are a strict subset of those required for First-Order Entropy which are themselves a strict subset of those for Corrected Conditional Entropy.

As for the compression-based tests and Lempel-Ziv Complexity, all of them perform similarly and on par with Repetition on 256-byte messages. On 16-byte messages, LZ77 is notably worse and LZ78 is notably better, but all are

Table 1. Effect sizes for 256-byte messages in an IP ID covert channel

	1-bit trace		Minimum		Min. index	
Encrypted?	Y	N	Y	N	Y	N
LZMA Compression	2.95	3	2.95	3	1	1
LZ77 Compression	6.3	4.62	3.59	3.55	3	2
LZ78 Compression	3.56	3.25	3.56	3.25	1	1
Lempel-Ziv Complexity	5.04	4.28	5.04	4.28	1	1
First-Order Entropy	3.37	3.13	3.37	3.13	1	1
Corr. Cond. Entropy	0.445	0.449	0.445	0.449	1	1
Repetition	4.58	3.94	4.58	3.94	1	1
Autocovariance	3.08e−08	9.12e−07	3.08e−08	4.23e−07	1	3
Kolm.-Smirnov Test	0.00189	0.00184	0.00189	0.00184	1	1
Wilcoxon Signed Rank	1.26e−05	2.53e−05	1.26e−05	2.53e−05	1	1
Spearman Correlation	3.46e−06	1.31e−05	3.46e−06	1.31e−05	1	1
Regularity	8.77e−07	3.82e−06	8.77e−07	3.82e−06	1	1

Table 2. Effect sizes for 16-byte messages in an IP ID covert channel

	1-bit trace		Minimum		Min. index	
Encrypted?	Y	N	Y	N	Y	N
LZMA Compression	4.87	4.76	4.87	4.76	1	1
LZ77 Compression	3.24	3.15	2.58	3.15	2	1
LZ78 Compression	6.9	5.98	6.9	5.98	1	1
Lempel-Ziv Complexity	4.25	4.05	4.25	4.05	1	1
First-Order Entropy	6.24	5.55	6.24	5.55	1	1
Corr. Cond. Entropy	2.64	2.63	2.64	2.63	1	1
Repetition	8.25	6.7	8.25	6.7	1	1
Autocovariance	6.88e−07	1.19e−06	6.88e−07	1.19e−06	1	1
Kolm.-Smirnov Test	0.000624	0.00125	0.000624	0.00125	1	1
Wilcoxon Signed Rank	3.95e−06	8.82e−05	3.95e−06	8.82e−05	1	1
Spearman Correlation	0.00109	0.000826	0.00109	0.000826	1	1
Regularity	⊥	⊥	⊥	⊥	⊥	⊥

outperformed by Repetition. This analysis tentatively pinpoints Repetition as the best test overall with LZ78 close behind, but there is no clear winner.

5.2 Results for Tests Used in Combination

Tests need not be used in isolation of each other and it is of interest to determine how they perform together. To do this, we show the correlation between the

Table 3. Effect sizes for 1-byte messages in an IP ID covert channel

	1-bit trace		Minimum		Min. index	
Encrypted?	Y	N	Y	N	Y	N
LZMA Compression	⊥	⊥	⊥	⊥	⊥	⊥
LZ77 Compression	⊥	⊥	⊥	⊥	⊥	⊥
LZ78 Compression	0.135	0.165	0.135	0.165	1	1
Lempel-Ziv Complexity	0.0164	0.0106	0.0164	0.0106	1	1
First-Order Entropy	0.139	0.169	0.139	0.169	1	1
Corr. Cond. Entropy	0.139	0.171	0.139	0.171	1	1
Repetition	0.139	0.169	0.139	0.169	1	1
Autocovariance	3.32e−06	3.45e−07	6.66e−07	3.45e−07	2	1
Kolm.-Smirnov Test	0.00157	0	0	0	2	1
Wilcoxon Signed Rank	0	0	0	0	1	1
Spearman Correlation	0.000775	0.000996	9.73e−05	9.73e−05	7	7
Regularity	⊥	⊥	⊥	⊥	⊥	⊥

Table 4. Correlation for 1-bit traces of 256-byte messages in an IP ID covert channel

	LZMA	LZ77	LZ78	LZC	FOE	CCE	REP
LZMA	1	0.25	0.23	0.19	0.18	0.18	0.16
LZ77	0.25	1	0.66	0.76	0.68	0.13	0.65
LZ78	0.23	0.66	1	0.87	0.94	0.15	0.94
LZC	0.19	0.76	0.87	1	0.92	0.17	0.94
FOE	0.18	0.68	0.94	0.92	1	0.14	0.99
CCE	0.18	0.13	0.15	0.17	0.14	1	0.14
REP	0.16	0.65	0.94	0.94	0.99	0.14	1

results of the tests across iterations in Tables 4 and 5. Because, in the previous section, the 1-bit traces were the hardest to detect, we restrict our analysis here to those and because encryption had no significant impact, we no longer keep it in our consideration. We also do not continue to analyze distributional tests and 1-byte messages, having concluded that a storage-based covert channel detector based on these ideas is not effective. To be clear, what is being compared is the correlation across all iterations in the difference between the output of the tests for 1-bit traces and the carrier.

Surprisingly, the compression-based tests are not clearly more correlated with each other than with the entropy-based ones. The general trend is that tests are moderately correlated with each other. There are, however, some definite outliers. First of all, First-Order Entropy and Repetition are very strongly correlated; this diminishes First-Order Entropy as a contender because Repetition

Table 5. Correlation for 1-bit traces of 16-byte messages in an IP ID covert channel

	LZMA	LZ77	LZ78	LZC	FOE	CCE	REP
LZMA	1	0.65	0.59	0.71	0.59	0.19	0.58
LZ77	0.65	1	0.50	0.71	0.51	0.064	0.51
LZ78	0.59	0.50	1	0.69	0.97	0.20	0.97
LZC	0.71	0.71	0.69	1	0.70	0.11	0.70
FOE	0.59	0.51	0.97	0.70	1	0.18	1
CCE	0.19	0.064	0.20	0.11	0.18	1	0.18
REP	0.58	0.51	0.97	0.70	1	0.18	1

outperforms it and gives very similar results from one iteration to the next. Secondly, Corrected Conditional Entropy and LZMA Compression have relatively weak correlation with the other tests. The weakness of these correlations suggest that two tests could be combined to make a more effective detector. In fact, except for First-Order Entropy and Repetition, any number of the tests could be combined because their correlations are not close to perfect.

5.3 Logistic Regression Detector

In this section, we evaluate the performance of covert channel detectors that use the tests evaluated herein. The algorithm used to create the detector is a simple logistic regression classifier. This technique takes in negative and positive examples and returns a model that estimates the probability that a certain sample is positive based on its Euclidean distance from a line—the number of tests determines the dimensionality of the space in which the linear classifier exists. In this instance, the positive examples are the test results for the 1-bit traces and the negative examples are the test results for the carrier. The examples are split into a training set and a test set so that the model can be evaluated on examples it has not yet seen. 70% of examples are in the training set leaving 30% for the test set. There are 2000 examples in total; two—a negative and a positive—for each of the 1000 iterations. This yields a training set of 1400 examples and a test set of 600 examples; both are balanced (i.e., they contain roughly the same number of positive and negative examples). All this is repeated for four message sizes: 256, 64, 16, and 4 bytes. The creation of the classifier was repeated 1000 times, randomizing the examples that were included in the test set in order to average out any effect of how the dataset is split; both the mean and the standard deviation are reported.

The accuracy of the classifier for an IP ID covert channel is presented in Table 6. Each column represents the accuracy for a different message size while each row except for the last represents the accuracy of a detector that uses only one of the complexity tests. The bottom row (All) shows the accuracy of a detector using all the tests together. The first thing to note about the results is that a detector using just one of these tests works very well: most of the detectors

Table 6. Detector accuracy for IP ID covert channel for various message sizes

Message size	256 bytes	64 bytes	16 bytes	4 bytes
LZMA	0.950 ± 0.0086	0.966 ± 0.0066	0.985 ± 0.0040	0.526 ± 0.038
LZ77	0.998 ± 0.0013	0.995 ± 0.0023	0.973 ± 0.0054	0.908 ± 0.0099
LZ78	0.976 ± 0.0056	0.992 ± 0.003	0.997 ± 0.0021	0.945 ± 0.0093
LZC	0.966 ± 0.11	0.995 ± 0.0024	0.969 ± 0.0061	0.74 ± 0.015
FOE	0.982 ± 0.0046	0.995 ± 0.0027	0.997 ± 0.0017	0.984 ± 0.012
CCE	0.996 ± 0.002	0.998 ± 0.0015	0.930 ± 0.0086	0.982 ± 0.0046
REP	0.984 ± 0.0043	0.995 ± 0.0024	0.999 ± 0.0013	0.953 ± 0.021
All	0.992 ± 0.0038	0.995 ± 0.0025	0.991 ± 0.0038	0.982 ± 0.0045

are greater than 90% accurate even for messages as small as 4 bytes and some are greater than 95% accurate. For messages of 16 bytes or more, the accuracy climbs to over 99% in most cases. The second thing to note is that the detector using all the tests does not outperform those that use just one test. Given this, it seems that combining more than one of the tests to create a more effective detector just leads to unnecessary complexity in the detector design.

6 Discussion

Having performed this experiment on storage-based covert channels using the IP ID field it seemed natural to investigate covert channels using other fields such as TCP Initial Sequence Numbers (ISN). This was done to underwhelming results as shown in Table 7. Effect sizes for complexity tests were generally less than 0.01 and the resulting logistic regression detector was no better than chance. The likely reason for this is that TCP ISNs can be truly random—no vestigial need to be unique in order to reconstruct fragmented IP packets unlike IP ID. The small fragments of messages that we embed are also very close to random,

Table 7. Detector accuracy for TCP ISN covert channel for various message sizes

Message bytes	256 bytes	64 bytes	16 bytes	4 bytes
LZMA	0.415 ± 0.061	0.412 ± 0.062	0.408 ± 0.064	0.407 ± 0.069
LZ77	0.415 ± 0.06	0.412 ± 0.063	0.410 ± 0.063	0.403 ± 0.064
LZ78	0.412 ± 0.063	0.408 ± 0.064	0.409 ± 0.064	0.412 ± 0.063
LZC	0.412 ± 0.063	0.411 ± 0.065	0.404 ± 0.075	0.392 ± 0.087
FOE	0.414 ± 0.061	0.411 ± 0.062	0.410 ± 0.065	0.413 ± 0.066
CCE	0.410 ± 0.065	0.400 ± 0.078	0.430 ± 0.098	0.417 ± 0.075
REP	0.414 ± 0.061	0.408 ± 0.068	0.412 ± 0.063	0.409 ± 0.064
All	0.415 ± 0.059	0.384 ± 0.071	0.403 ± 0.097	0.378 ± 0.089

so tests relying on information content cannot distinguish the two. This observation reveals something of a trade-off in how systems should choose their TCP ISNs. The conventional wisdom is that they should be truly random so as to make it difficult for an attacker to spoof a connection, but doing this creates an opportunity for a nearly undetectable covert channel (at least by the statistical tests considered in this paper). That said, this is not much of a trade-off because almost any system will have much greater exposure from spoofed connections than from covert channels.

Despite this, there is still a reason why an attacker might use an IP ID covert channel and thus why one might want to detect them. Most obviously there is bandwidth: machines send out one IP ID per IP packet but only one TCP ISN per TCP connection and, since one TCP connection generally comprises many packets, many more IP IDs are transmitted than TCP ISNs. For instance, the dataset used in this paper contains 76 times more IP IDs than TCP ISNs. Furthermore, using TCP ISN requires more access to the machine than IP IDs. With IP IDs an attacker can just change what IP IDs the machine sends and if the packet is never fragmented (the usual case) no one is likely to notice; with TCP ISN the attacker would not only have to change what is sent, but also what sequence number the machine expects to receive for subsequent segments.

This limited transferability does not mean that the statistical tests evaluated in this paper are specific to IP ID covert channels. IP Time-to-Live (TTL) is another network protocol field that can be used to build a covert channel, and was one of many studied by Gunadi and Zander [10]. Using the same methodology as above, we trained a classifier to detect IP TTL covert channels. The results are presented in Table 8 and are similar to those for IP ID covert channels. Note that for IP TTL it was the 8-bit traces that were hardest to classify (i.e., produced the smallest effect sizes), and therefore it is the accuracy on those that are presented in Table 8.

Table 8. Detector accuracy for IP TTL covert channel for various message sizes

Message size	256 bytes	64 bytes	16 bytes	4 bytes
LZMA	0.975 ± 0.0072	0.921 ± 0.015	0.897 ± 0.028	0.787 ± 0.014
LZ77	0.924 ± 0.0098	0.906 ± 0.01	0.921 ± 0.0092	0.919 ± 0.0096
LZ78	0.669 ± 0.18	0.636 ± 0.18	0.895 ± 0.014	0.854 ± 0.012
LZC	1 ± 0	1 ± 0.00097	0.986 ± 0.0065	0.936 ± 0.0082
FOE	0.562 ± 0.22	0.497 ± 0.14	0.776 ± 0.019	0.836 ± 0.014
CCE	0.998 ± 0.0017	0.976 ± 0.0062	0.897 ± 0.013	0.810 ± 0.019
REP	0.746 ± 0.24	1 ± 0.00067	0.997 ± 0.0019	0.955 ± 0.007
All	1 ± 0	1 ± 0.00087	0.988 ± 0.0039	0.942 ± 0.0088

7 Concluding Remarks

This paper evaluated the effectiveness and applicability of several statistical tests to detect storage-based covert channels. The tests were selected based on their past success in being effective to detect timing-based covert channels. In particular, we conducted several experiments on sequences of IP IDs with and without information embedded into them. The results of the experiments show that complexity tests are much more effective that distributional tests for detecting storage-based covert channels. Many of the tests were determined to be able to detect covert channels on their own and combining multiple tests into a multi-dimensional classifier did not bring any significant improvement which means that simple covert channel detectors can be built using a single test.

In our ongoing and future work, we seek to build off of the results presented in this paper by exploring the practicality and effectiveness of more techniques for detecting storage-based covert channels such as those in [14,16]. The goal is to adapt a collection of these tests into a high-performance platform to create a practical real-time storage-based covert channel detector.

References

1. Berk, V., Giani, A., Cybenko, G.: Covert channel detection using process query systems. In: 2nd Annual Conference for Network Flow Analysis, September 2005
2. Berk, V., Giani, A., Cybenko, G.: Detection of covert channel encoding in network packet delays. Technical report TR2005-536, Dartmouth College, Hanover, NH, USA, August 2005
3. Cabuk, S., Brodley, C.E., Shields, C.: IP covert timing channels: design and detection. In: 11th ACM Conference on Computer and Communications Security, pp. 178–187. ACM (2004)
4. Cabuk, S., Brodley, C.E., Shields, C.: IP covert channel detection. ACM Trans. Inf. Syst. Secur. **12**(4), 22 (2009)
5. Collin, L.: A quick benchmark: Gzip vs. Bzip2 vs. LZMA (2005). https://tukaani.org/lzma/benchmarks.html. Accessed 22 Oct 2019
6. Crespi, V., Cybenko, G., Giani, A.: Engineering statistical behaviors for attacking and defending covert channels. IEEE J. Sel. Top. Signal Process. **7**(1), 124–136 (2013)
7. Garcia, S.: Normal captures (2017). https://stratosphereips.org. Malware Capture Facility Project
8. Gianvecchio, S., Wang, H.: An entropy-based approach to detecting covert timing channels. IEEE Trans. Dependable Secure Comput. **8**(6), 785–797 (2010)
9. Gunadi, H., Zander, S.: Bro covert channel detection (BroCCaDe) framework: design and implementation. Technical report 20171117B, Murdoch University (2017)
10. Gunadi, H., Zander, S.: Bro covert channel detection (BroCCaDe) framework: scope and background. Technical report 20171117A, Murdoch University (2017)
11. Gunadi, H., Zander, S.: Extending bro covert channel detection (BroCCaDe) with new plugins. Technical report 20171207A, Murdoch University (2017)
12. Gunadi, H., Zander, S.: Performance evaluation of the bro covert channel detection (BroCCaDe) framework. Technical report 20180427A, Murdoch University (2018)

13. Jadhav, M., Kattimani, S.: Effective detection mechanism for TCP based hybrid covert channels in secure communication. In: 2011 International Conference on Emerging Trends in Electrical and Computer Technology, pp. 1123–1128 (2011)
14. Jaskolka, J.: Modeling, analysis, and detection of information leakage via protocol-based covert channels. Master's thesis, McMaster University, Hamilton, ON, Canada, September 2010
15. Jaskolka, J., Khedri, R.: Exploring covert channels. In: 44th Hawaii International Conference on System Sciences, pp. 1–10, January 2011
16. Jaskolka, J., Khedri, R., Sabri, K.: A formal test for detecting information leakage via covert channels. In: 7th Annual Cyber Security and Information Intelligence Research Workshop, pp. 1–4, October 2011
17. Kullback, S., Leibler, R.: On information and sufficiency. Ann. Math. Stat. **22**(1), 79–86 (1951)
18. Lempel, A., Ziv, J.: On the complexity of finite sequences. IEEE Trans. Inf. Theory **22**(1), 75–81 (1976)
19. Li, Q., Zhang, P., Chen, Z., Fu, G.: Covert timing channel detection method based on random forest algorithm. In: 17th IEEE International Conference on Communication Technology, pp. 165–171 (2017)
20. Naik, B., Boddukolu, S., Sujatha, P., Dhavachelvan, P.: Connecting entropy-based detection methods and entropy to detect covert timing channels. In: Meghanathan, N., Nagamalai, D., Chaki, N. (eds.) Advances in Computing and Information Technology. AISC, vol. 176, pp. 279–288. Springer, Heidelberg (2012). https://doi.org/10.1007/978-3-642-31513-8_29
21. Ponemon Institute: 2018 cost of a data breach study: global overview. Technical report, IBM Security (2018)
22. Porta, A., et al.: Measuring regularity by means of a corrected conditional entropy in sympathetic outflow. Biol. Cybern. **78**(1), 71–78 (1998)
23. Sohn, T., Seo, J.T., Moon, J.: A study on the covert channel detection of TCP/IP header using support vector machine. In: Qing, S., Gollmann, D., Zhou, J. (eds.) ICICS 2003. LNCS, vol. 2836, pp. 313–324. Springer, Heidelberg (2003). https://doi.org/10.1007/978-3-540-39927-8_29
24. Tumoian, E., Anikeev, M.: Network based detection of passive covert channels in TCP/IP. In: 30th IEEE Conference on Local Computer Networks, pp. 802–807 (2005)
25. Zhai, J., Liu, G., Dai, Y.: A covert channel detection algorithm based on TCP Markov model. In: 2nd International Conference on Multimedia Information Networking and Security, pp. 893–897 (2010)
26. Zhao, H., Shi, Y.: A phase-space reconstruction approach to detect covert channels in TCP/IP protocols. In: 2010 IEEE International Workshop on Information Forensics and Security, pp. 1–6 (2010)
27. Ziv, J., Lempel, A.: A universal algorithm for sequential data compression. IEEE Trans. Inf. Theory **23**(3), 337–343 (1977)
28. Ziv, J., Lempel, A.: Compression of individual sequences via variable-rate coding. IEEE Trans. Inf. Theory **24**(5), 530–536 (1978)

IE-Cache: Counteracting Eviction-Based Cache Side-Channel Attacks Through Indirect Eviction

Muhammad Asim Mukhtar[1]($\boxtimes$), Muhammad Khurram Bhatti[1], and Guy Gogniat[2]

[1] Information Technology University, Lahore, Pakistan
{asim.mukhtar,khurram.bhatti}@itu.edu.pk
[2] Université Bretagne Sud, Lorient, France
guy.gogniat@univ-ubs.fr

Abstract. Protecting critical information against eviction-based cache side-channel attacks has always been challenging. In these attacks, attacker reveals secrets by observing cache lines evicted by the co-running applications. A precondition for such attacks is that the attacker needs a set of cache lines mapped to memory addresses belonging to victim, called *eviction set*. Attacker learns eviction set by loading the cache lines at random and then it observes their evictions as a result of victim access. We have found that the relation between the incoming memory location and the resulting evicted cache line eases the learning of an eviction set. In this paper, we propose *Indirect Eviction Cache (IE-Cache)* that is based on the principle of indirect eviction to harden the building of eviction set. In an eviction process of IE-Cache, incoming memory triggers series of replacements based on the cached memory addresses and a secure-indexing function, and the last replaced cache line is evicted. This increases the set size and introduces non-evicting cache lines in the eviction set. Through experimental results, we have shown that a 4-way set associative IE-Cache having 1MB and up to 3 replacements per eviction would require an attacker to generate $\approx 2^{59}$ memory accesses to learn an eviction set with 99% confidence. Moreover, it achieves 1–3% speedup compared to set-associative cache with a random-replacement policy on PARSEC benchmarks.

Keywords: Cache-based side-channel attack · Randomization · Encrypted cache space · Prime+Probe attack

1 Introduction

Caches are main component of modern computer systems that bridge the performance gap between processor and main memory. Caches are usually shared among applications for efficient utilization of cache space. However, this sharing turns out to be a high-security threat. In particular, the eviction behavior of

© IFIP International Federation for Information Processing 2020
Published by Springer Nature Switzerland AG 2020
M. Hölbl et al. (Eds.): SEC 2020, IFIP AICT 580, pp. 32–45, 2020.
https://doi.org/10.1007/978-3-030-58201-2_3

shared cache lines can reflect the secrets of secure applications to other applications. Eviction behavior can be extracted from the cache using eviction based cache side-channel attacks, which initialize cache lines in such state that victim access of interest (or secure dependent memory access) has to evict attacker's cache line. In the past few decades, the research on eviction-based cache-side channel attacks mainly focused on extracting secret keys of cryptographic algorithms [1–4]. Recent advancements in such attacks (Spectre [5] and Meltdown [6]) extend the security threat that these attacks can read all unauthorized memory space.

To mitigate these attacks, state-of-the-art hardware-based countermeasures have been proposed in past few decades [7–12], which can broadly fall into two categories partition-based and randomization-based solutions. Partition-based solutions divide the cache among applications to make eviction behavior independent among applications. However, efficient partitioning of cache among applications is NP-Hard problem [13]. Moreover, increasing-trend of a number of cores on-chip is pushing computer architecture toward cache scalability, therefore, partitioning the already low capacity cache for security exaggerates the cache scalability requirement. On the other side, randomization-based solutions can mitigate without limiting the cache space among applications. These solutions randomize the memory-to-cache mapping to increase the attacker's difficulty in finding all memory addresses that would contend with victim memory addresses, also called an eviction set. Unfortunately, existing randomized based solutions are limited in the scope of security. Such as a recently proposed solution called as ScatterCache [14] claimed that building eviction set requires 38 h but research work by [15] has proved that advanced profiling techniques can be used to reduce 38 h to less than 5 min. Currently, there is no countermeasure that achieves security against eviction-based cache attacks with preserving the sharing feature of the cache. The goal of this paper is to propose a countermeasure while preserving the sharing feature because shared caching naturally adjusts the allocation for each application dynamically and does not need extensive profiling of all applications before allocating cache locations as it is required in case of cache partitioning.

To mitigate the eviction-based cache side-channel attacks in a shared cache, the key challenge is to make attacker unable to build an eviction set. In conventional caches, on the insertion of a new memory block, the incoming block replaces one cache line preferred by replacement policy (or colliding cache line) and then the replaced cache line is evicted from the cache (or evicting cache line). We provide key insight that the building of an eviction set becomes impractical if the colliding and evicting caches lines are different. To propose a solution based on this insight, we present a novel cache architecture, called *IE-Cache*. In an eviction process, incoming memory address replaces one of the cache lines at random, and then the replaced cache line replaces another cache line. This repeats until replacement limit is achieved and the last replaced cache line is evicted. This introduces multiple cache lines in between the incoming address and evicting cache line, yielding benefits in two ways regarding the eviction set.

First, it increases the size of the eviction set. Secondly, the eviction set includes cache lines that do not evict as a result of accommodating the incoming address, we call as non-evicting cache lines of eviction set, finding these cache lines without the side information (eviction behavior) enormously increased the complexity of building eviction set by the attacker. We are saying non-evicting with respect to one address but it may evict by another address. We have shown experimentally that it is impractical for the attacker to find all memory addresses that directly and indirectly collide with the victim's access. The contributions of this paper are as follows:

- We propose a countermeasure that mitigates eviction based cache side-channel attacks in a novel way by making the indirect relation between incoming address and evicting cache lines.
- We have experimentally analyzed the security of IE-Cache by demonstrating that it is impractical to build the eviction set by the attacker. This inhibits the attacker to launch eviction-based cache attacks.
- We evaluate the performance impact of IE-Cache in comparison with the set-associative cache architecture having random replacement policy while running PARSEC benchmark using *zsim* simulator [16].

The rest of the paper is organized as follows. Section 2 gives the necessary background. Section 3 presents the IE-Cache. Sections 4 and 5 present the security and performance evaluation of the IE-Cache respectively. Section 6 concludes the paper.

2   Background

In this section, we provide the background on eviction-based cache attacks and Prime+Probe attack.

2.1   Eviction-Based Cache Attacks

Various eviction-based cache side-channel attacks have been proposed in the literature [1–4]. In these attacks, an adversary finds cache lines that are mapped to victim application and initializes them in an interesting state. Then observes whether the initialized state is changed or not after the victim execution, which results in the extraction of victim secrets in the form of victim accesses. In Prime+Probe attack [3], an adversary loads the cache lines and observes evictions of loaded cache lines by the victim's memory accesses. Evict+Reload attack [2] is similar to Prime+Probe attack except it can only be launched if adversary and victim share memory lines. Flush+Reload attack [4] is similar to Evict+Reload attack except an adversary makes a cache state by flushing instead of loading cache lines. The Flush+Flush [1] attack is a variant of Flush+Reload attack in which an adversary observes the state of cache lines by measuring the time to flush the cache lines instead of reading the memory lines. Evict+Reload, Flush+Reload and Flush+Flush attacks can be successfully launched if the memory deduplication feature is enabled in the system. However, the memory deduplication feature is usually disabled in shared computing environments such as cloud computing [17]. Prime+Probe attack is not dependent on memory deduplication and requires commonly used instructions such as *mov* and *rdtsc* instructions. Mitigation of Prime+Probe attack is difficult because it can be launched through any instruction that can load the cache such as *mov*, *add*, *jmp*, etc. It is impossible to disable all these instructions, therefore, major modifications are required in the computing stack to mitigate the Prime+Probe attack.

2.2 Prime+Probe Attack

Memory accesses can be backtracked to secure information of application. Prime+ Probe attack enables an application to extract secret dependent memory accesses of co-running applications by observing the eviction of cache lines. In this attack, the attacker reserves all cache lines where victim memory location of interest can reside in the cache. If victim accesses that memory location, it will evict one of the attacker cache lines, revealing its memory access to the attacker by the action of eviction. However, for a successful attack, the attacker requires memory addresses (or colliding addresses) that share the cache lines with the targeted victim address. In conventional caches like set-associative cache, the mapping of memory-to-cache is static and well-studied in research. Finding colliding addresses in such caches only depends on the indexing bits (specified by the designer) of the memory address that all memory addresses having the same indexing bits will collide in the cache. However, the adversarial effort to learn the colliding addresses has greatly increased in caches that define the mapping of memory-to-cache at run-time and change it over time. The attacker has to find colliding addresses on each change of memory-to-cache mapping through extensive experiments. For finding colliding addresses in such caches, the attacker goes through the following steps.

- The attacker randomly chooses N memory addresses and loads them into the cache by accessing them. As attacker has randomly chosen the memory addresses, there is a possibility that these memory addresses collide with each other and cause eviction of group members. To eliminate self-collisions in group G, attacker reads the accessed memory addresses again and observes there access latency. If attacker observes a longer time it means that memory address is evicted because of self-collision and needs removal from the group. Attacker iterates the action of accessing and removing memory addresses until all memory access results shorter time. Let n_{rmv} indicates the number of iterations required to eliminate self-collisions. The attacker now has a set of G' $\leq$ G addresses, which are guaranteed to reside at a different location in the cache.
- The attacker calls the victim to access memory, expecting an eviction by victim access if correctly sampled G' memory addresses.

– After that attacker accesses G' addresses again and measures their memory access latency to observe the eviction. Attacker will find the colliding address in case of longer access time is observed.

Then attacker repeats the above steps until enough addresses are obtained for the attack, which also depends on the parameter of cache architecture. Note that after the first iteration, the victim access of interest is in the cache and need to be evicted before next iteration. Therefore, an attacker has to access many different memory addresses to ensure the eviction of victim cache line.

3   IE-Cache - Proposed Cache

The objective of IE-Cache is to eliminate the direct eviction of cache line as a result of inserting new memory location to counter eviction-based cache side-channel attacks. We consider that an adversary has access to all user-level instructions except those which are related to cache management such as $clflush$ and $prefetchtx$. Flush+Flush and Flush+Reload attacks cannot be launched because of non access to $clflush$ instruction. Moreover, physical attacks are not considered in the threat model of IE-Cache. In addition to achieving security, we also focus to retain the fundamental design features of cache such as transparent to the user and less reliance on OS. In the following section, we discuss the design and working of IE-Cache.

3.1   IE-Cache: High Level Design

IE-Cache is inspired form Zcache architecture [18], which is proposed to improve the performance by increasing the associativity without increasing the physical ways. However, Zcache is also vulnerable to cache-based side-channel attacks. We have replaced the static hash function with the cipher function to make it resilient to cache-based side-channel attacks.

Figure 1a illustrates the high-level design of IE-Cache with 8 cache lines and 3 ways. IE-Cache employs key-based indexing function for each way. These functions use multiple keys - one for secure and other for a non-secure domain. One bit is added in each cache line to distinguish the secure and non-secure cached data. IE-cache performs eviction of cache line in multiple steps. First, it searches cache lines for eviction in multiple levels. Then it selects the candidate using random replacement policy and evicts it. lastly, it relocates the cache lines to accommodate the incoming block. Figure 1c illustrates the eviction process for the accommodation of non-secure memory block (Y) in IE-Cache having 2 levels of search. In first level, Incoming memory block belonging to a non-secure domain (Y) selects the replacement cache lines (or candidates) using the non-secure key, let say, it selects E (non-secure), A (secure) and C (non-secure). Then in second level, the selected candidates further selects the cache lines using their domain specific key shown in the second level of Fig. 1c. Random replacement policy chooses a candidate for eviction from last level of search and evicts it. Lastly,

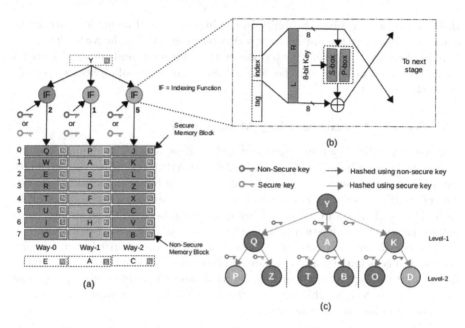

Fig. 1. High level design of IE-Cache (a) Cache architecture (b) Indexing function (c) Replacement candidates tree

series of relocation happens to maintain the cache organization. Let us consider that random replacement policy selects T for eviction then A will be relocated to T and Y will be added to A location. There are two important points here. First, A is moved to other location of its own interest and can become a member of other cache set, which also means even if Y is evicted and requested again for accommodation in the cache, it is not necessary that A is again a member of Y. Second, as the key is managed by hardware and kept secret, an adversary does not know the relation among cache lines and results in unknown evictions. If adversary tries to find a set of memory addresses that can cause eviction of desired cache line using random evictions, then he finds the evicting cache lines belongs to last level only. To find the intermediate level cache lines, attacker requires to generate large number of memory accesses to find one non-evicting cache line, which we have analyzed in the Sect. 4.

3.2 Suitable Indexing Function

The main objective of the indexing functions in IE-Cache is to achieve sufficient pseudo-random permutation with low latency. We observe that different indexing functions (i.e. QARMA and DES) used in previous randomization-based countermeasures [14,19] can fulfill our objectives, and the scope of security of these countermeasures are limited because of the direct eviction but not because of indexing functions used in them. Therefore, these indexing functions can also be used in IE-Cache. We find block cipher used in CEASER [19] most suitable for

IE-Cache because it gives flexibility in the input size and incurs low latency of about one or two cycles. For demonstration purpose, 8MB cache with 4 ways, we have implemented cipher having 3 stages with 16-bit input and output. Figure 1b shows one stage of DES. For the detailed implementation of cipher, we recommend the reader to see [19].

3.3   Security Domain and Key Management

The concept of hardware managed key and creation of security domain are not new as these are already in Intel SGX [20] and ARM TrustZone [21] architectures. These processors are also vulnerable to cache-based side-channel attack. Therefore, IE-Cache suits for such architectures that already have a secure bit in cache lines and hardware managed key mechanism because these architectures require localized modification if IE-Cache is integrated into such platforms.

The key in our IE-Cache plays a crucial role in the security, therefore, its confidentiality is important. We ensure this confidentiality in our design by mandating that the key is fully managed by hardware. There must not be any way to configure or retrieve this key in software. Each time the system is powered up, a new random key is generated.

3.4   Increased Complexity of Prime+Probe

IE-Cache makes both profiling and exploitation steps of Prime+Probe harder by increasing the eviction set size and introducing the non-evicting members in the eviction set.

In the eviction process of IE-Cache, cache lines are selected in multiple levels such that the number of cache lines increases exponentially from one level to the next. For example, for 4 ways and 2 levels, cache lines selected in first and second levels are 4 and 12 respectively. For a successful Prime+Probe attack, the attacker needs to fill all 16 cache lines to observe the eviction. However, because of the random replacement policy, the attacker cannot guarantee the memory access will be placed in the targeted cache line. In case of memory accessed by attacker is placed at the cache line other than the targeted one, attacker has two options to fill the cache line 1) attacker flushes the cache and accesses the same memory address again or 2) attacker accesses another memory address that can be placed in the cache line. Because of no access to flush instruction, the attacker has to indirectly flush using random memory accesses, which is costly. Therefore, the attacker has to adopt the second option and needs to access multiple memory addresses to ensure the filling of the targeted cache line. We analyze the expected number of memory addresses required by the attacker using bins and balls analysis that how many throws are required to fill the interested bin with at least one ball with 99% confidence. Considering IE-Cache having 4-ways and 2 levels, this analysis results that the attacker requires 16 memory addresses to ensure filling of one cache line and 64 memory addresses for four cache lines. Accessing these memory addresses by the attacker will ensure filling of cache lines belonging to the first level of the tree but which four memory addresses have successfully been placed in the targeted cache lines are unknown to the attacker. Therefore, to observe the victim access, the attacker has to load all those cache lines that can be selected by 64 memory addresses on the second level of the tree, so that relocation from the first level to second level causes eviction. As each cache line related to the first level selects 3 cache lines on the next level in IE-Cache having 4 ways, total possible cache lines selected by 64 cached memory addresses are 192 at the second level. The attacker needs 16 memory addresses (using the same bin and ball analysis) to ensure filling of each 192 cache lines, which means 3072 memory addresses are required to fill the second level. This concludes that the eviction set size is 3136 cache lines for IE-Cache having 4 ways and 2 levels in which the number of evicting (first level) and non-evicting (second level) cache lines are 64 and 3072. The attacker in profiling steps needs to find 3136 memory addresses against one victim's memory access. Also in exploitation step attacker needs to load 3136 memory addresses, yielding difficulties for the attacker in two ways. First, attack resolution decreases enormously because of too many memory loads are needed. Second, given that the cache line is of 64 bytes, 3136 cache lines cover 196 KB scattered memory space, hence it is difficult to identify the victim's memory access in case of concurrent processing of multiple applications. Figure 2 shows the number evicting and non-evicting addresses in an eviction set for a varied number of ways and levels of IE-Cache.

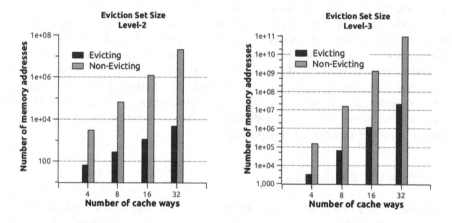

Fig. 2. Eviction set size for varied number of ways and levels of IE-Cache

Finding non-evicting members of the eviction set is another difficulty for the attacker. Victim memory access causes eviction from the last level and relocates the cache lines belonging to upper levels. As the non-evicting cache line does not evict as a result of victim access, there is no direct information to an attacker via timing channel. However, we find that the attacker can use indirect timing analysis to know the relation between non-evicting and evicting cache lines. For example in Fig. 1c, eviction of P (evicting cache line) is dependent on the presence of Q (non-evicting cache line) in the cache, which means that P will not evict if Q is not in the cache. In the profiling step, let say that the attacker has successfully found the P using profiling technique discussed in Sect. 2.2, the attacker knows that Q is also in group G' (set of randomly selected non-colliding memory address). To find Q, the attacker access all memory addresses belonging to G' group again except the one randomly selected address (expecting a Q). Then the attacker calls victim to access memory, aiming that the cache line P will not evict if randomly taken out address is Q. After this, the attacker accesses P again while measuring its time to know the eviction. The attacker will observe the eviction of P on taken out candidate multiple times that the random replacement policy at-least selects P once for eviction if the taken out candidate is not Q. If the attacker finds that taken out member has reduced the probability of eviction of P in multiple runs, the attacker expects taken out member is Q. In case of more levels, for example for three levels, evicting member depends on two non-evicting members, hence, the attacker has to observe eviction of interested last level cache lines by taking out all possible pairs formed in G' group. This greatly increases the time to find non-evicting cache lines as attacker needs $\approx 2^{27}$ years to finds one eviction set for IE-Cache having 4 ways, 3 levels and 2^{12} cache lines per way. Note that the attacker has to flush and place the group members again in cache for observing the eviction behavior on the next taken out member. Placing of non-colliding group members again in cache becomes difficult because there is a probability that two addresses that do not collide in one arrangement of placement may collide in other. Accessing the same memory again does not guarantee the placement in the same cache way as placed in the previous turn because of random replacement policy. Therefore, ensuring the placement of all group members in the cache, attacker has to access all group members multiple times while measuring their access latency. If attacker finds any access with longer latency, it has to repeat the action of flush and placing members again, aiming to place in such arrangement that group members do not cause self evictions. Let n_{pl} indicate the number of iteration required to place the non-colliding member of group in the cache.

4   Security Evaluation

For security evaluation, we have built the python model of IE-Cache and have considered the following assumptions. First, the cache has a random replacement policy and fills the invalid location with high priority. Second, the mapping from memory address to output indices is pseudo-random. Lastly, attacker and victim processes are executing only. We have taken this assumption in favor of the attacker.

We have verified the security of IE-Cache by analyzing the number of attacker and victim memory accesses needed to build an eviction set for Prime+Probe attack as discussed in Sect. 2.2). As victim memory access results in eviction of cache lines belonging to last level in IE-Cache, profiling discussed in Sect. 2.2 can only find the evicting cache lines belonging to an eviction set. For non-evicting cache lines in an eviction set, we used the method discussed in Sect. 3.4. We

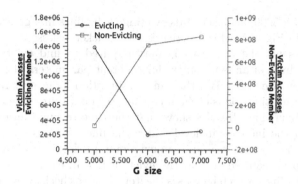

Fig. 3. Victim accesses required to find evicting and non-evicting cache lines of an eviction set of IE-Cache having 4 ways, 2^{11} lines and 2 levels.

experimentally obtained the attacker and victim accesses to find evicting and its non-evicting member averaged over 100,000 simulator runs. Then we multiplied the accesses obtained for one evicting and non-evicting member with the total number of respective members (shown in Fig. 2) in an eviction set. Figure 3 shows the victim accesses and attacker accesses per victim access for IE-Cache having 4 ways, 2^{11} cache lines and 2 levels. As the group size increases, results indicate that the victim accesses become less to find evicting cache line, making it easy for the attacker. However, victim accesses become greater to find non-evicting cache line, making it harder for the attacker. This inverse effect indicates that advanced profiling fails in the case of IE-Cache.

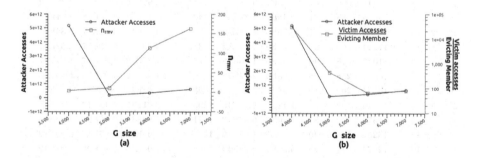

Fig. 4. Attacker accesses required to find evicting cache lines against (a) n_{rmv} and (b) Victim calls required to find evicting cache lines.

Figure 4 shows the attacker accesses required to find evicting cache lines versus different parameters for IE-Cache having 4 ways, 2^{11} cache lines and 2 levels. Figure 4a shows that the group size of 5000 requires less number of attacker accesses as compared to other sizes. We have observed that the iteration required to eliminate the self collisions increases if group size becomes larger than 5000 (shown in Fig. 4a), which increases the attacker accesses. Inversely, for group size smaller than 5000, attacker finds evicting cache lines in a greater number of turns (shown in Fig. 4b), which increases the attacker accesses.

Table 1 presents the adversarial effort required to find evicting and non-evicting cache lines of an eviction set for different parameters of IE-Cache. For time calculation, we had taken the same assumption as in research work [14], i.e, 9.5ns cache hit time, 50ns cache miss time, 0.5 ms victim execution time and 3.6 ms cache flush time. Results show that the time to build an eviction set is increased with the increase in level and cache lines. This is because the non-evicting cache lines are increased in an eviction set. Moreover, results show that a bigger group is required to find the evicting line in caches having a greater number of cache lines, which increases the iterations to check evictions of evicting members against non-evicting members and yields increase in time.

Table 1. Adversarial effort to find eviction set in 4 way IE-Cache having different levels and cache lines. CL = number of cache lines, L = number of levels, G = size of randomly sampled memory addresses, G' = non-colliding member of group, n_{rmv} = turns required to find non-colliding addresses, n_{pl} = number of turn required to place non-colliding members in cache, avg_v = average victim access and avg_a = average attacker accesses per victim access.

CL	L	G (k)	G'	n_{rmv}	n_{pl}	Evicting			Non-evicting		
						avg_v	avg_a	Time (hr)	avg_v	avg_a	Time (hr)
2^{11}	2	7	5720	163	64	2.46E5	5.98E11	22	2.53E12	1.07E16	2.69E06
		6	5582	113	28	1.97E5	3.33E11	13	2.30E12	3.33E15	2.43E06
		5	4993	11	3	1.36E6	1.77E11	7	5.42E10	1.17E12	5.95E04
		4	4000	4	1	9.26E7	5.07E12	213	1.08E10	2.82E11	1.29E04
2^{11}	3	8	6945	90	67	1.06E7	9.58E12	191	4.99E16	1.28E16	2.32E12
		7	6866	73	21	2.48E7	7.37E12	342	1.12E18	1.66E18	1.21E12
2^{12}	2	16	11497	430	71	3.96E5	2.82E12	58	5.13E13	4.06E17	5.84E07
		15	11224	367	61	2.15E5	1.64E12	34	3.23E13	2.45E17	3.67E07
		14	11035	318	49	1.69E5	1.20E12	25	1.56E13	1.39E17	1.91E07
		13	10893	218	38	2.95E5	2.24E12	46	1.26E12	1.22E16	1.43E06
		12	10542	205	10	4.64E5	2.99E12	63	7.82E11	5.86E15	8.88E05
2^{12}	3	16	13446	154	56	1.12E7	5.71E13	293	5.71E17	1.13E17	6.79E12
		15	13554	142	84	1.46E7	6.69E13	1121	9.82E18	2.96E21	1.34E13
		14	13292	144	40	3.10E7	1.93E13	1336	2.05E18	2.67E18	2.40E12
		13	12974	17	25	5.85E7	8.28E13	1657	1.94E18	3.95E20	2.27E12

5   Performance Evaluation

We have used micro-architecture simulator, *zsim* [16], for performance evaluation of IE-Cache. Table 2 shows the configuration used in our experimental setup. A 4-way IE-Cache is introduced at the L3 in the cache hierarchy and it is designed for a different level-of-search, i.e. 2 and 3 levels. We have evaluated the IE-Cache for each level-of-search against baseline architecture by executing 11 workloads of PARSEC using *medium* input set. In each run, we have taken one program at random for each domain (secure and non-secure). We have calculated the weighted speedup metric, which is a sum of ratios of the program's IPC executing in a group to its IPC when it is executing in isolation, and normalized it to baseline architecture.

Table 2. Baseline configuration

Core	4 cores, 2.2 GHz, OoO model
L1 cache	Private, 32 kB, 8-way set associative, split D/I
L2 cache	Private, 256 kB, 8-way set associative
L3 cache	Shared, 1 MB, 16-way set associative or 4-way IE-Cache
Memory	200-cycle latency, 8 GB/s peak memory BW

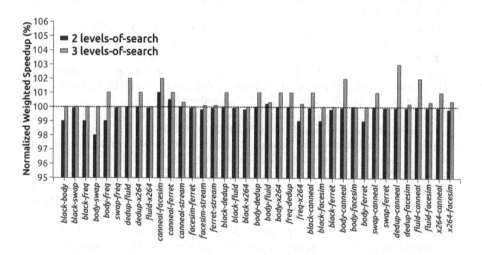

Fig. 5. Normalized Performance of IE-Cache with 2 and 3 levels

Figure 5 shows the normalized weighted speed up metric of IE-Cache. In this figure, a bar higher than 100% indicates performance improvement of IE-Cache as compared to baseline architecture. Results in Fig. 5 show that IE-Cache with 3 levels-of-search outperforms 1%–3%. This performance is improved because of the scattered mapping of memory to cache lines and increased cache associativity. Workload *canneal* and *dedup*, which frequently use L3 cache, shows an improvement of about 3% because of the increased associativity of IE-Cache. IE-Cache with 2 levels-of-search shows low performance on some of the load because of low associativity as compared to baseline.

6   Conclusion

This paper proposes a novel way to mitigate eviction-based cache side-channel attacks while retaining the shared feature of the cache. We have modified the relation between the incoming memory address and evicting cache line that introduces non-evicting members in the eviction set, which are harder to learn by collisions. The attacker has to generate at least $\approx 2^{59}$ memory accesses to find an eviction set. This takes about $\approx 2^{27}$ years to find one eviction set. Moreover, IE-Cache provides strong security with 1–3% improvement in performance.

References

1. Gruss, D., Maurice, C., Wagner, K., Mangard, S.: Flush+Flush: a fast and stealthy cache attack. In: Caballero, J., Zurutuza, U., Rodríguez, R.J. (eds.) DIMVA 2016. LNCS, vol. 9721, pp. 279–299. Springer, Cham (2016). https://doi.org/10.1007/978-3-319-40667-1_14
2. Lipp, M., Gruss, D., Spreitzer, R., Maurice, C., Mangard, S.: Armageddon: cache attacks on mobile devices. In: 25th USENIX Security Symposium, Austin, TX, pp. 549–564. USENIX Association (2016)
3. Liu, F., Yarom, Y., Ge, Q., Heiser, G., Lee, R.B.: Last-level cache side-channel attacks are practical. In: 2015 IEEE Symposium on Security and Privacy, pp. 605–622, May 2015
4. Yarom, Y., Falkner, K.: Flush+reload: a high resolution, low noise, L3 cache side-channel attack. In: 23rd USENIX Security Symposium (USENIX Security 2014), San Diego, CA, pp. 719–732. USENIX Association (2014)
5. Kocher, P., et al.: Spectre attacks: exploiting speculative execution. In: 40th IEEE Symposium on Security and Privacy (S&P 2019) (2019)
6. Lipp, M., et al.: Meltdown: reading kernel memory from user space. In: 27th USENIX Security Symposium (USENIX Security 2018) (2018)
7. Kim, T., Peinado, M., Mainar-Ruiz, G.: STEALTHMEM: system-level protection against cache-based side channel attacks in the cloud. In: Presented as Part of the 21st USENIX Security Symposium (USENIX Security 2012), Bellevue, WA, pp. 189–204. USENIX (2012)
8. Kiriansky, V., Lebedev, I., Amarasinghe, S., Devadas, S., Emer, J.: DAWG: a defense against cache timing attacks in speculative execution processors. In: 2018 51st Annual IEEE/ACM International Symposium on Microarchitecture (MICRO), pp. 974–987, October 2018
9. Kong, J., Aciicmez, O., Seifert, J.-P., Zhou, H.: Deconstructing new cache designs for thwarting software cache-based side channel attacks. In: Proceedings of the 2Nd ACM Workshop on Computer Security Architectures, CSAW 2008, pp. 25–34. ACM (2008)
10. Liu, F., Wu, H., Mai, K., Lee, R.B.: Newcache: secure cache architecture thwarting cache side-channel attacks. IEEE Micro 36(5), 8–16 (2016)
11. Liu, F., et al.: Catalyst: defeating last-level cache side channel attacks in cloud computing, March 2016
12. Liu, F., et al.: Catalyst: defeating last-level cache side channel attacks in cloud computing. In: 2016 HPCA, pp. 406–418, March 2016

13. Fiore, U., Florea, A., Gellert, A., Vintan, L., Zanetti, P.: Optimal partitioning of LLC in CAT-enabled CPUs to prevent side-channel attacks. In: Castiglione, A., Pop, F., Ficco, M., Palmieri, F. (eds.) CSS 2018. LNCS, vol. 11161, pp. 115–123. Springer, Cham (2018). https://doi.org/10.1007/978-3-030-01689-0_9
14. Scattercache: thwarting cache attacks via cache set randomization. In: 28th USENIX Security Symposium, Santa Clara, CA. USENIX Association (2019)
15. Purnal, A., Verbauwhede, I.: Advanced profiling for probabilistic prime+probe attacks and covert channels in scattercache. arXiv, abs/1908.03383 (2019)
16. Sanchez, D., Kozyrakis, C.: ZSim: fast and accurate microarchitectural simulation of thousand-core systems. ACM SIGARCH Comput. Architect. News **41**, 475 (2013)
17. Vañó-García, F., Marco-Gisbert, H.: Slicedup: a tenant-aware memory deduplication for cloud computing. In: UBICOMM International Conference on Mobile Ubiquitous Computing, Systems, Services and Technologies, UBICOMM 2018, United States, pp. 15–20. IARIA, November 2018
18. Sanchez, D., Kozyrakis, C.: The ZCache: decoupling ways and associativity. In: 2010 43rd Annual IEEE/ACM International Symposium on Microarchitecture, pp. 187–198, December 2010
19. Qureshi, M.K.: CEASER: mitigating conflict-based cache attacks via encrypted-address and remapping, pp. 775–787, October 2018
20. McKeen, F., et al.: Intel® software guard extensions support for dynamic memory management inside an enclave. In: HASP, pp. 10:1–10:9. ACM, New York (2016)
21. Li, W., Xia, Y., Chen, H.: Research on arm trustzone. GetMobile Mob. Comput. Commun. **22**(3), 17–22 (2019)

Connection Security

Refined Detection of SSH Brute-Force Attackers Using Machine Learning

Karel Hynek[1,2]([⊠]), Tomáš Beneš[1,2], Tomáš Čejka[2], and Hana Kubátová[1]

[1] FIT CTU, Prague, Czech Republic
{hynekkar,benesto3,kubatova}@fit.cvut.cz
[2] CESNET a.l.e., Prague, Czech Republic
{hynekkar,tomas.benes,cejkat}@cesnet.cz

Abstract. This paper presents a novel approach to detect SSH brute-force (BF) attacks in high-speed networks. Contrary to host-based approaches, we focus on network traffic analysis to identify attackers. Recent papers describe how to detect BF attacks using pure Net-Flow data. However, our evaluation shows significant false-positive (FP) results of the current solution. To overcome the issue of high FP rate, we propose a machine learning (ML) approach to detection using specially extended IP Flows. The contributions of this paper are a new dataset from real environment, experimentally selected ML method, which performs with high accuracy and low FP rate, and an architecture of the detection system. The dataset for training was created using extensive evaluation of captured real traffic, manually prepared legitimate SSH traffic with characteristics similar to BF attacks, and, finally, using a packet trace with SSH logs from real production servers.

Keywords: SSH · Brute-force · Attack · Security · Network · Monitoring · Malicious · Flow · AdaBoost · Decision tree · Classification

1 Introduction

A brute-force (BF) is a common type of attack that may lead to intrusion and taking control by an attacker. A study [20] published by Ponemon Institute in 2014 claims that 51% of interviewed companies experienced SSH related adverse events. Unfortunately, the situation has not changed dramatically to this day based on recent annual security reports by Cisco [8] mentioning BF attacks.

Detection of incoming BF attacks against own server can be easily performed using server logs. However, our scope of interest is rather a detection of sources of attacks at the network level. Accurately detected attacks against a remote server originating in the operated network infrastructure are usually an indicator of compromise, i.e., valuable information about suspicious behavior.

More sophisticated attacks are performed according to "low and slow" tactic [14] to be hidden from detection systems. It usually includes a large

© IFIP International Federation for Information Processing 2020
Published by Springer Nature Switzerland AG 2020
M. Hölbl et al. (Eds.): SEC 2020, IFIP AICT 580, pp. 49–63, 2020.
https://doi.org/10.1007/978-3-030-58201-2_4

coordinated botnet attacking multiple various targets, so the number of repeated attempts from a single IP address against a single server can be very low. The attacking IPs therefore surpass the host-based solutions because their individual contribution does not reach thresholds for blocking. Contrary, it is possible to detect such attacks on the ISP (Internet Service Provider) level, which is our goal, because the attackers' traffic targeting multiple victims is observable.

At the ISP level (in high-speed networks), the packet-based monitoring and traffic analysis is very resource-intensive. Therefore in practice, a flow-based monitoring is used. That means aggregated information about communicating parties is represented by IP flow records, usually in the NetFlow or IPFIX format [9,21]. Even though SSH traffic is encrypted, some published papers show that it is possible to detect BF attacks that use this encrypted protocol (e.g., [16]). Based on our experience, the accuracy of the detection system, which uses traditional IP flows, is limited due to false-positive alerts. For example, our instance of the NEMEA SSH brute-force detector [6,19] (based on the SSHCure [12] algorithm), reported several hosts from the monitored infrastructure as attackers. However, these hosts did not show any other signs of infection or misbehavior.

During the analysis of the relevant traffic, we discovered that it comes from automated tools (e.g., monitoring) and causes false-positive alerts. The tools produce multiple SSH connections periodically with a few seconds/minutes interval, each containing a single command. Despite successful authentication (usually by a public key), the observed IP flows can be easily misinterpreted as BF attacks.

Existing IP Flow-based detection algorithms suffer from the same issues with misinterpreted legitimate traffic, since the traditional IP flow data indeed do not contain information that would distinguish such automated traffic from BF attacks. A typical workaround solution can be a change of threshold values to filter out these connections or to use some whitelisting. Unfortunately, both solutions have disadvantages: a higher value of thresholds decreases detector's sensitivity, and the whitelisting is complicated to maintain. Therefore, we designed a better detector based on machine-learning (ML) and extended IP flow-like data.

Recent papers describe extended IP Flow records (e.g., [5,13,27]) with additional information extracted from unencrypted protocol headers up to application layer (L7). Encryption decreases visibility into the traffic and prevents the extraction of the L7 information. However, the behavior of applications discloses information even in the encrypted traffic, as Anderson et al. described in [3].

Compared to the traditional IP Flow data representing one-directional "connections", modern monitoring systems are able to pair both directions into so called *biflow* records. Additionally, Joy exporter [4] adds various additional traffic features at the packet level (such as length and inter-packet gaps of individual packets). The whole feature vectors can be afterward used as an input for ML models—Anderson et al. focus on the detection of malware traffic.

Our paper focuses on addressing false-positives issues in prior works. We have decided to design a detection mechanism using extended IP flows with a minimal subset of the packet-level features created by Joy exporter. The additional information in IP flows should make the resulting model resilient against false-positive detection and more accurate. In contrast to the model, that uses traditional IP flows only, our approach can distinguish between automated traffic from BF attacks, because it takes advantage of additional information such as individual packets length.

To reach our goal, we have worked on the following contributions:

- We have created an annotated training and testing dataset using manually created traffic and automatically captured real traffic of SSH protocol. It contains legitimate flows and BF attacks. The dataset consists of over 30,000 extended biflow records of SSH, about half of them are BF attacks,
- We have experimentally evaluated over 70 traffic features and several ML models to select a suitable subset of (11) features, and a feasible model that achieves the best results. This demonstrates that a small number of extracted traffic features can provide very good accuracy of BF attacks detection.
- We have described an architecture of a detection system consisting of data preprocessing, ML-based detector, and a knowledge base storage for postprocessing and filtering detected raw events. According to our experiments, the system performs better than the detection based on pure IP flow data.

This paper is divided as follows. Section 2 describes the related work of SSH BF attacks detection. Section 3 describes the ML method we used. Section 4 describes the obtaining and labeling our dataset. Section 5 contains results of our experiments. Section 6 concludes this work.

2   Related Work

There are many published approaches to the detection of SSH BF attacks. We can classify them as *host-based* and *network-level*. A host-based detection and prevention can be performed either by an application natively, or by external software that does an automatic analysis of the system logs and mitigation of the suspicious traffic using, e.g., host's firewall. A well-known example of this approach is Fail2Ban [11]. This solution usually is not capable of detecting coordinated attacks from many hosts (botnet).

Analysis of SSH brute-force traffic in [1] describes that attacks from botnets are well-coordinated, and dictionaries are efficiently distributed among bots. This main disadvantage of the host-based approach can be solved by a special architecture described in [25]. The proposed architecture shares information between involved hosts to detect or prevent SSH brute-force attacks. However, the proposed solution has only been simulated with a handful of servers and does not provide any comparison with the real-world environment. It also does not provide any consideration for drawbacks associated with communication between large amounts of hosts.

The *network-level* approach depends on observation points. However, it is not affected by any of these disadvantages. On the other hand, it has to deal with a massive amount of data. Therefore, Jonker et al. published a study where they described a specific characteristic of an SSH brute-force attack [15]. They analyzed flat traffic showing that the BF attack has a specific number of packets and duration. Based on these observations, the BF attacks can be detected on network-level only from aggregated data.

The paper [12] proposed an IP Flow-based intrusion detection system for SSH attack called SSHCure. It uses *packet per flow* (PPF) metric and a *minimal number of flows* within a 1 or 5-min window. The authors build the algorithm on the assumption published in [24] regarding 3 phases of BF attacks:

1. **Scan Phase** – The attacker scans an IP address block to find out a host with running SSH server.
2. **Brute-force Phase** – The attacker is trying to login to a smaller subset of IP addresses using the brute-force attack.
3. **Die-off Phase** – After the successful break-in, there is still traffic from the attacker, but it is much smaller. This residual traffic represents commands executed on the victim machine.

Nowadays, the first Scan Phase can be skipped by attackers, since targets can be found using scanner services like Shodan [23] or Censys [7]. This kind of specialized search engine is designed to scan and gather information about devices and systems accessible from the Internet. With a simple query, we can obtain thousands of IP addresses with the open SSH port.

The SSHCure solves the scenario by allowing attackers to enter the Brute-force Phase without passing through the Scan Phase. The paper [12] presented 98.4% accuracy of the detector without false-positives. It is worth noting that the algorithm was validated on a dataset with only 130 attacks, where all of the attackers performed the Scan Phase.

A different solution, proposed in [22], combines extended flow with ML techniques. The authors defined a new structure called *sub-flow*, which is an ordered sequence of packet sizes of one IP flow. The *sub-flow* is than used in the clustering algorithm for the detection of the SSH authentication protocol and specific authentication packets. This information is then processed along with the inter-arrival time of authentication packets and compared with the predefined threshold. They achieved very high precision with 99% of successfully detected attacks.

The advanced ML detection methods were studied in [17]. The authors extracted 18 features from an aggregated extended flow. The aggregated flow is a set of flows with the same source IP, destination IP, and destination port observed within a 5-min time window. Using the aggregated flows, they avoided the problem of similarity between failed login produced by legitimate users and brute-force attacks. They separated those classes by the number of BF suspicious flows within the time window.

Features extracted from aggregated flows are then used as input for Naive Bayes, K-NN (exactly 5-NN), and C4.5 decision tree algorithm. All algorithms classified with similar precision with AUC metric around 0.995 on a dataset with around 1,000 aggregated flows. This study proved that the ML detector works sufficiently even with a straightforward algorithm such as a decision tree.

Automated tools that use SSH as a transport protocol (e.g., Zabbix, git, rsync, ansible) can create many independent connections having very similar flow features as BF attacks. Based on our experience, detection presented in [22] and [17] would very likely suffer from the high amount of false-positive detection results. The detection models presented in prior works depend on thresholding suspicious connections identified by standard side-channel features (average inter-packet time, average packet size and so on), and they do not take advantage of the knowledge of SSH protocol auth phase. Therefore, the short and periodic SSH connections are nearly indistinguishable from unsuccessful logins. Although, in the case of [17], extension of the feature set with the information that we present in the following sections will help to separate successful logins from unsuccessful ones. However, even with this modification, we doubt that the same ML-based threshold model would be transferable to other networks since it is data-dependent, and the thresholds are tuned for one particular network traffic.

3 Our Approach

This paper proposes a *network-level* detection architecture to decrease the number of false-positives with the same or higher level of sensitivity, i.e., more accurate. It uses extended IP Flow features provided by the Joy exporter and ML algorithm to distinguish successful and unsuccessful logins. The extended IP flows are obtained from backbone network traffic. The main advantage here is the detection of attackers using the "low and slow" tactic.

The results (identified login failures) are afterward processed by a threshold filter, like in host-based solutions. This allows tuning for the policies of the target network. Contrary to [17], our ML-based algorithm uses protocol-dependent features only, therefore, it is easily transferable to different networks.

The architecture consists of four parts shown in Fig. 1 (inside a dashed border), which will be explained in more detail in the following sections.

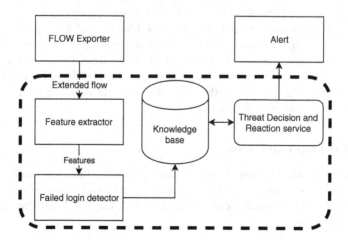

Fig. 1. Overview of the SSH brute-force attack detector

3.1 Feature Extractor

The Feature extractor processes extended IP Flows and converts them into a table of features to be usable by ML. The main idea is that the used exporter (Cisco Joy in our case) provides information about every length of packet, but does not provide aggregated statistical features like mean values that we need for the ML method. The Feature extractor takes extended flow as input and calculates the required features for the Failed login detector.

The feature selection is one of the most important parts because the feature set affects the accuracy of the ML classifier. During our analysis, we started with a set of over 70 features. Our deployment target is a high-speed network, where a high number of extracted characteristics is impractical because every single feature extraction consumes many resources. We needed to balance the accuracy and computational complexity of obtaining features.

We successfully reduced the set by removing features with low information gain ratio. Then we continued with a reduction based on performance, and we ended up with 11 selected features that achieved excellent results among multiple ML algorithms while being easily extracted. The final set of features with a description is shown in Table 1.

The feature set includes the length of four specific packets from 9th to 12th positions (only SSH protocol packets are counted, TCP control packets or possible re-transmissions are filtered out by the flow exporter). These packets have been chosen based on our knowledge of the SSH protocol and experimental evaluation of the feature set during its selection. These packets (usually with the same size) carry a response of an SSH server to unsuccessful login attempts. The first packets belong to the SSH handshake (which is not relevant for the detection), and the authentication process starts from the 9th packet (shown in Fig. 2). Repeated attempts to log into a target server can be observed within one flow by significant similarity of the sizes of the server response packets included in the feature set. To best of our knowledge, there is none prior work that uses these features to distinguish between BF attack and benign traffic.

Our original feature set included also used version of SSH protocol, client name, supported cipher-suites, and other clients related information. According to our results, these features do not improve brute-force attack detection. We found out that the attackers are using clients like *OpenSSH, PUTTY, libssh* that are also present in the benign traffic. Therefore, the information gain ratio value of client-related features is lower than 0.3.

3.2 Failed Login Detector

The detector is an ML-based model that performs binary classification on extracted features. The goal is to classify each flow as a successful or a failed login attempt. The classification results of individual flows are then stored in the Knowledge base.

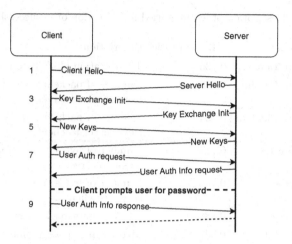

Fig. 2. Conversation diagram of SSH handshake [10, 28].

3.3 Knowledge Base

The knowledge base is the long term memory of the detector. It covers all information about authentication attempts observed during at least 24 h in the past. The source IP, destination IP, timestamp, and type of login are stored and used for attack detection in Threat decision and reaction service.

3.4 Threat Decision and Reaction Service

The Threat Decision and Reaction service processes stored login reports and decides whether to send an alert. Unlike the traditional host-based solutions, the flows obtained from backbone traffic gives us information about multiple victims of a single IP address. This fact gives us a higher probability of detecting "low and slow" attacks of botnets. The overall and complex information about failed login gives us also other possibilities. For example, when one IP address is constantly failing to log in to multiple servers and suddenly succeeds, it might be an indicator of a possible break-in.

This part can also mitigate potential imprecision of ML-based Failed login detector. The probability of misclassification multiple times in a row is very low. Therefore the false classifications are not going to reach the threshold value. The possible false negatives will only cause increased latency of the attack detection by a negligible number of attempts.

4 Dataset Creation

The most important premise to create a good ML model is a proper dataset. The quality of the model is directly linked with the quality of information contained in the dataset. Due to the lack of useful public datasets available online, we

Table 1. Description of features used for detection of unsuccessful login.

Num.	Name	Inf. Gain ratio	Description
1	duration	0.836	The duration of TCP connection
2	numPktsIn	0.666	Number of packets transferred from client to server
3	numPktsOut	0.754	Number of packets transferred from server to client
4	bytesIn	0.758	Number of bytes transferred from client to server
5	bytesOut	0.756	Number of bytes transferred from server to client
6	avgIpt	0.888	Average inter-packet time
7	medIpt	0.942	Median inter-packet time
8	dp9bytes	0.837	The length of 9th packet in flow
9	dp10bytes	0.868	The length of 10th packet in flow
10	dp11bytes	0.837	The length of 11th packet in flow
11	dp12bytes	0.754	The length of 12th packet in flow

have decided to create our own, which should contain malicious and benign SSH traffic. There are two methods on how to create a dataset of SSH traffic with correct labeling.

The first method is to generate malicious traffic ourselves, which can be easily labeled afterward. There are several popular tools to perform a brute-force attack on an SSH server such as THC HYDRA [26] or NCrack [18]. Every tool has a wide variety of options on how to change the characteristics of the attack. Generating malicious traffic from these tools with multiple settings is an extremely time-consuming process. Additionally, resulted dataset would contain only specific kind of brute-force traffic that may not correspond to a real network.

The second method is to use existing traffic from a public server, which is very likely already enduring some form of SSH brute-force attacks. The main downside is that we expose our production server to a potential risk of a successful attack. We did not want to use a custom honeypot or testing server because the resulting dataset would not have the same variety of incoming traffic. Therefore we used Fail2Ban. Contrary to the default behavior that blocks the traffic from an attacker completely, we have prepared an action script to redirect it into an isolated SSH service acting like a honeypot[1].

Our aim was to simulate the same service like the original server (e.g., use of the same certificates), so the attacker should not be able to recognize a change. However, the honeypot has disallowed all user accounts, so it is ensured that every login fails, and we can capture traffic of attacks without interruption. The architecture of the described data capture is depicted in Fig. 3.

---

[1] https://github.com/CESNET/traffic-datasets/tree/master/ssh/f2b.

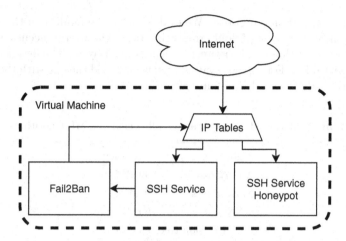

Fig. 3. Architecture of our data collection machine

The captured traffic in PCAP was converted by Joy exporter into extended IP flows. We use the ML approach to detect unsuccessful login so that we could annotate each flow record from the server access log.

Using this method, we created a dataset (*dataset1*) of 35,000 labeled SSH flows, from which 22,000 were malicious, and 13,000 were benign. This dataset represents a realistic traffic that has a slightly higher number of malicious login attempts, which is a similar characteristic as in the real environment. We could not use the exact ratio as it is observed in backbone network because the number of malicious attempts would be very high compared to the number of successful logins.

The dataset is composed of Brute-Force attacks, SSH interactive sessions (authentication by password or public key), file transfer, monitoring by Zabbix, etc. The main advantage of this method is the richness of real attack traffic, which is not restricted to a set of given tools, and easy setup of the traffic capture, which can be deployed on many machines.

Our dataset also covers the main variability in the ssh authentication phase by containing connections encrypted by multiple block and also stream ciphers. Unexpectedly, according to our experiments, the behavior of the server in the authentication phase does not differ between various implementations.

5   Validation and Experimental Results

This section describes the results of our measurements of the ML-based Failed Login detector and the overall accuracy of proposed detection architecture.

5.1   Accuracy of Failed Login Detector

We have considered five ML methods for the flow classification, which are fast and lightweight. They were Ada-Boosted Random tree, Naive Bayes, 5-NN, C4.5

Decision tree, and Random Forest. We evaluated all the models on the *dataset1* (described in Sect. 4) using 5-fold cross-validation. The overall accuracy is very similar across all evaluated algorithms (except Naive Bayes). The detailed results are shown in Table 2. For further evaluations, we selected the one with the highest accuracy, the Ada-Boosted Random tree.

Table 2. Measured accuracy across all considered ML algorithms.

Algorithm	Accuracy
Ada-Boosted tree	99.47%
Naive Bayes	92.09%
5-NN	99.39%
C4.5 Decision tree	99.46%
Random forest	99.38%

The Ada-boost used ten iterations of creating decision trees with a maximal depth of 10, applied pruning, and minimal leaf size of 2. These parameters provide a good balance between accuracy and possible over-fitting.

The trained model achieved an accuracy of 99.47% with a pessimistic AUC value of 0.998. Detailed classification results are displayed in form of confusion matrix in Table 3.

Table 3. Failed login detector confusion matrix.

		Ground truth		Class precision
		Successful login	Failed login	
Classified as	Successful login	13,318	130	99.03%
	Failed login	56	21,698	99.74%
Class recall		99.58%	99.40%	

5.2 Accuracy of the Whole Architecture

The results of the ML method are further filtered by the Threat Decision and Reaction service (as it was mentioned in Sect. 3.4). It triggers an alert only when a several consecutive failed login attempts from a single IP address exceeds a threshold, which was set to 3 in our experiments because it is the default threshold value in Fail2Ban [11]. Therefore, occasional false-positive results of the ML detection usually do not result in an alert. When the detector is evaluated as a whole, including the thresholding, the overall precision on the primary dataset is 100% with no false positives.

For that reason, we decided to make an additional dataset (*dataset2*) to evaluate the system on real data further. For this dataset, we captured 86,000 bidirectional SSH flows (from 564 clients) from the backbone traffic (peering link between CESNET2 and GÉANT). Table 4 shows overall number of flow classification. We can see that the vast majority of login is marked as unsuccessful and originate from a relatively small number of IP addresses.

Creating *dataset2* is equivalent to deployment on the real network, but the offline evaluation has the advantage of the possibility of a detailed examination of detected anomalies and misclassifications.

Table 4. The overall number of login classification in *dataset2*. The IP address is counted as unsuccessful, when we detected at least one unsuccessful login.

	Marked as unsuccessful login	Marked as successful login	Total
Flows	85,322	538	85,860
IP addresses	463	101	564

Table 5 shows the number of detected brute-force attackers (IP addresses) in the *dataset2* compared to the NEMEA SSH brute-force detector [6,19], which is based on the SSHCure algorithm [12]. We can see, that ML detector is much more sensitive and detected around 40% more attackers than the NEMEA detector.

Table 5. Number of detected brute-force attackers from our evaluation datasets

		NEMEA		Total
		Detected	Not detected	
ML	Detected	315	129	444
	Not detected	3	—	3
Total		318	129	447

Table 6 shows several statistics of our evaluation of the results of the detection. Since the higher sensitivity can increase the number of false-positives, we checked the traffic from the dataset2 and the results of ML-based and traditional detection. To evaluate the false-positive rate, we used AbuseIPDB [2], which provides a list of IP addresses associated with malicious activity. It can be observed that most of the IP addresses detected by the evaluated detectors are listed on AbuseIPDB as malicious. We considered these as true-positives. The remaining ones are possibly false-positives. Since there are only 8 of them, we can investigate them manually.

All three attackers that were detected by NEMEA and not detected by our ML-based method are false-positives. In this case, a simple investigation based

Table 6. The number of IP addresses detected as attackers which are also listed on AbuseIPDB. The last column shows results of our investigation of those not listed.

	Listed on AbuseIPDB	Not listed	Confirmed FPs
Detected by both detectors	314	1	0
Detected by ML only	125	4	2
Detected by NEMEA only	0	3	3

on reverse DNS query revealed that these hosts use SSH legitimately for periodic remote access to other servers (e.g., because of monitoring).

The classification of four IP addresses that were not reported on AbuseIPDB but were detected by our method was much more difficult. We marked 2 of them as attackers because they performed a lot of short connections to multiple destinations within one second. The classification of the other two IP addresses was much more difficult. One of them performed short connections with a 5 min interval from different SSH clients (PUTTY, openSSH1.2 and so on) to multiple IP addresses. The other IP address irregularly shortly connected to one host. Even though we found the behavior highly suspicious, we marked those cases as false-positives.

The last candidate for false-positive IP address detected by both detectors was, according to the SSH-client field, a Raspberry Pi. It was connecting to multiple IP addresses every 10 min (default ban time for Fail2Ban). Based on our experience and similarity to other attacks, we marked it as a brute-force attack.

Table 7. The number of reported attackers and false positives for both detectors

	Total reported attackers	False positives
Detected by NEMEA	318	3 (0.94%)
Detected by ML	444	2 (0.45%)

The summary of the results per detector is shown in Table 7. We can observe that the new ML-based approach allows detecting significantly more attackers, while also slightly reducing the false positive rate.

Besides *dataset1* and *dataset2*, we evaluated both detection algorithms using specific traffic samples of a legitimate communication. The samples were generated as a traffic from a robot accessing a server via SSH every second performing a single command. The NEMEA detector, i.e., detection based on pure IP flows misclassified this type of traffic as brute-force attacks, meanwhile, our ML-based detection results were correct.

Although our detector achieved excellent results, the amount of reduction of false positives is smaller than we have expected. However, the overall results show that the ML-based algorithm performs much better than the traditional one with almost a third more detected attackers. The active protective systems that use our detector are going to detect more attackers and lower the risk of a successful attack.

6   Conclusion

Brute-force (BF) attacks are a prevalent type of malicious traffic that can be observed by monitoring systems. Successful attacks belong to high severity adverse events. Additionally, it is a typical activity of malware. Therefore, it is essential to focus on their accurate detection.

Modern monitoring systems for high-speed networks use IP flows to represent the observed traffic, and there are published works that describe how to detect BF attacks based on this aggregated information. Some relevant related works and their benefits/drawbacks were described in Sect. 2. However, after using a flow-based detection algorithm on a real network, we have discovered a significant number of cases where some types of legitimate traffic were misclassified as attacks, which caused false alerts.

Our motivation was to find an improved approach to BF attacks detection at the network level. The aim was to preserve or improve accuracy and decrease the number of false-positive results (without any need for whitelisting or other exceptions that must be maintained). Specifically, our presented detection method focuses on better recognition of legitimate SSH traffic with successful authentication. Contrary to the existing IP flow-based systems, we have designed and evaluated a detection architecture based on machine learning.

To achieve our goal, we have created a large annotated *dataset1* for training and evaluation that contains legitimate communication over SSH (including traffic of automated tools that can cause false-positive alerts due to its flow characteristics) and various BF attacks. Additionally, *dataset2* was prepared using a packet capture of real network traffic to compare the results of the existing non-ML detection and our new ML-based detection. The process of the datasets creation was also described in detail in this paper.

Using the prepared training dataset, which we made publicly available[2], we were able to select 11 traffic features, and train&evaluate several different ML models. Most of them achieved over 99% accuracy of classifying individual flows as successful or failed login attempts. The best model, AdaBoosted tree, which we selected for further experiments, achieved 99.47% accuracy.

When the classified flows are fed into the threshold based detector, the whole system achieves perfect accuracy of detection on *dataset1*, i.e., all BF attackers are successfully reported while there is no false alert.

The method is also successful in real-life comparison. On *dataset2*, which represents real SSH traffic on a large network, it detected about 40% more attackers than an older method implemented in NEMEA, while it also generated less false alerts.

---

[2] https://github.com/CESNET/traffic-datasets/tree/master/ssh/.

As our future work, we want to continue in our investigation of encrypted network traffic and its analysis. Using the IP flows extended by feature vectors that represent packet-level information, we believe it is possible to classify the encrypted traffic and detect a malicious activity of the network hosts.

Acknowledgment. This work was supported by the Grant Agency of the CTU in Prague, grant No. SGS20/210/OHK3/3T/18 funded by the MEYS of the Czech Republic and the project Reg. No. CZ.02.1.01/0.0/0.0/16_013/0001797 co-funded by the MEYS and ERDF.

References

1. Abdou, A.R., Barrera, D., van Oorschot, P.C.: What lies beneath? Analyzing automated SSH Bruteforce attacks. In: Stajano, F., Mjølsnes, S.F., Jenkinson, G., Thorsheim, P. (eds.) PASSWORDS 2015. LNCS, vol. 9551, pp. 72–91. Springer, Cham (2016). https://doi.org/10.1007/978-3-319-29938-9_6
2. AbuseIPDB making the internet safer, one IP at a time, October 2019. https://www.abuseipdb.com/
3. Anderson, B., McGrew, D.: Identifying encrypted malware traffic with contextual flow data. In: ACM Workshop on Artificial Intelligence and Security (2016)
4. Anderson, B., McGrew, D., Perricone, P., Hudson, B.: Joy - a package for capturing and analyzing network flow data and intraflow data, October 2019. https://github.com/cisco/joy
5. Cejka, T., Bartos, V., Truxa, L., Kubatova, H.: Using application-aware flow monitoring for SIP fraud detection. In: Latré, S., Charalambides, M., François, J., Schmitt, C., Stiller, B. (eds.) AIMS 2015. LNCS, vol. 9122, pp. 87–99. Springer, Cham (2015). https://doi.org/10.1007/978-3-319-20034-7_10
6. Cejka, T., et al.: NEMEA: a framework for network traffic analysis. In: 12th International Conference on Network and Service Management (CNSM) (2016)
7. Censys, October 2019. https://censys.io
8. Cisco 2018 annual cybersecurity report, October 2019. https://rfc-editor.org/rfc/rfc3954.txt
9. Claise, B.: Cisco Systems NetFlow Services Export Version 9. RFC 3954, October 2004. https://doi.org/10.17487/RFC3954
10. Cusack, F., Forssen, M.: Generic message exchange authentication for the secure shell protocol (SSH). Technical report, January 2006. https://doi.org/10.17487/rfc4256
11. Fail2ban, October 2019. http://www.fail2ban.org/wiki/index.php/Main_Page
12. Hellemons, L., Hendriks, L., Hofstede, R., Sperotto, A., Sadre, R., Pras, A.: SSHCure: a flow-based SSH intrusion detection system. In: Sadre, R., Novotný, J., Čeleda, P., Waldburger, M., Stiller, B. (eds.) AIMS 2012. LNCS, vol. 7279, pp. 86–97. Springer, Heidelberg (2012). https://doi.org/10.1007/978-3-642-30633-4_11
13. Hendriks, L., et al.: Threats and surprises behind IPv6 extension headers. In: Network Traffic Measurement and Analysis Conference (TMA) (2017)
14. Sadasivam, G.K., Hota, C., Anand, B.: Honeynet data analysis and distributed SSH Brute-force attacks. In: Chakraverty, S., Goel, A., Misra, S. (eds.) Towards Extensible and Adaptable Methods in Computing, pp. 107–118. Springer, Singapore (2018). https://doi.org/10.1007/978-981-13-2348-5_9

15. Jonker, M., Hofstede, R., Sperotto, A., Pras, A.: Unveiling flat traffic on the internet: an SSH attack case study. In: International Symposium on Integrated Network Management (IM) (2015)
16. Najafabadi, M.M., Khoshgoftaar, T.M., Kemp, C., Seliya, N., Zuech, R.: Machine learning for detecting brute force attacks at the network level. In: IEEE International Conference on Bioinformatics and Bioengineering (2014)
17. Najafabadi, M.M., Khoshgoftaar, T.M., Calvert, C., Kemp, C.: Detection of SSH Brute force attacks using aggregated netflow data. In: 14th International Conference on Machine Learning and Applications (ICMLA) (2015)
18. Ncrack - Network authentication cracking tool, October 2019. https://nmap.org/ncrack/
19. NEMEA Bruteforce detector, October 2019. https://github.com/CESNET/Nemea-Detectors/tree/master/brute_force_detector
20. Ponemon 2014 SSH security vulnerability report, October 2019. https://energycollection.us/Energy-Security/Ponemon-2014-SSH.pdf
21. Sadasivan, G., Brownlee, N., Claise, B., Quittek, J.: Architecture for IP flow information export. RFC 5470, March 2009. https://doi.org/10.17487/RFC5470
22. Satoh, A., Nakamura, Y., Ikenaga, T.: SSH dictionary attack detection based on flow analysis. In: 12th International Symposium on Applications and the Internet IPSJ (2012)
23. Shodan, October 2019. https://www.shodan.io
24. Sperotto, A., Sadre, R., de Boer, P.-T., Pras, A.: Hidden Markov model modeling of SSH Brute-force attacks. In: Bartolini, C., Gaspary, L.P. (eds.) DSOM 2009. LNCS, vol. 5841, pp. 164–176. Springer, Heidelberg (2009). https://doi.org/10.1007/978-3-642-04989-7_13
25. Thames, J.L., Abler, R., Keeling, D.: A distributed active response architecture for preventing SSH dictionary attacks. In: IEEE SoutheastCon 2008, pp. 84–89 (2008)
26. THC HYDRA V. Hauser, The Hacker Choice (THC) - Hydra, October 2019. https://www.thc.org/thc-hydra/
27. Velan, P., Čeleda, P.: Next generation application-aware flow monitoring. In: Sperotto, A., Doyen, G., Latré, S., Charalambides, M., Stiller, B. (eds.) AIMS 2014. LNCS, vol. 8508, pp. 173–178. Springer, Heidelberg (2014). https://doi.org/10.1007/978-3-662-43862-6_20
28. Ylonen, T.: The Secure Shell (SSH) Transport Layer Protocol. Technical report, January 2006. https://doi.org/10.17487/rfc4253

MULTITLS: Secure Communication Channels with Cipher Suite Diversity

Ricardo Moura[ID], David R. Matos[ID], Miguel L. Pardal[(✉)][ID],
and Miguel Correia[ID]

INESC-ID, Instituto Superior Técnico, Universidade de Lisboa, Lisbon, Portugal
{ricardo.de.moura,david.r.matos,miguel.pardal,
miguel.p.correia}@tecnico.ulisboa.pt

Abstract. TLS ensures confidentiality, integrity, and authenticity of communications. However, design, implementation, and cryptographic vulnerabilities can make TLS communication channels insecure. We need mechanisms that allow the channels to be kept secure even when a new vulnerability is discovered.

We present MULTITLS, a middleware based on diversity and tunneling mechanisms that allows keeping communication channels secure even when new vulnerabilities are discovered. MULTITLS creates a secure communication channel through the encapsulation of k TLS channels, where each one uses a different cipher suite. We evaluated the performance of MULTITLS and concluded that it has the advantage of being easy to use and maintain since it does not modify any of its dependencies.

Keywords: Secure communication channels · SSL/TLS · Security · Vulnerability-tolerance · Diversity for security · Tunneling

1 Introduction

We are currently living in an increasingly digital age and there have been many cyberattacks that cause increased losses and damage to businesses and Internet users [8]. Secure communication protocols are a fundamental component of distributed systems and digital business because they allow entities to exchange messages through a trusted communication channel over the untrusted public Internet. These channels aim to guarantee confidentiality, integrity and authenticity. Transport Layer Security (TLS) is one of the most commonly used protocols to provide secure communications. It allows server/client applications to communicate over a channel that is designed to prevent eavesdropping, tampering, and message forgery. The most recent version is TLS 1.3 [9].

Protocols that allow secure communications may contain vulnerabilities that make them insecure. Over the years, many vulnerabilities have been discovered and corrected in SSL/TLS. The vulnerabilities with which we are concerned can be divided into three groups: design vulnerabilities, implementation vulnerabilities and cryptographic mechanisms vulnerabilities. Updating the software is

© IFIP International Federation for Information Processing 2020
Published by Springer Nature Switzerland AG 2020
M. Hölbl et al. (Eds.): SEC 2020, IFIP AICT 580, pp. 64–77, 2020.
https://doi.org/10.1007/978-3-030-58201-2_5

advisable in order to fix these vulnerabilities, but sometimes this is not done, e.g., because the update process is inconvenient or time-consuming.

This work explores diversity in communication protocols by using multiple cipher suites. These suites are used for defining a key exchange algorithm, an authentication mechanism, an encryption mechanism, and a message authentication algorithm. Taking into account the existing problems and the objectives defined, the solution found consists in creating several TLS channels, each using a cipher suite different from the other TLS channels, and using tunneling mechanisms to encapsulate each TLS channel within another.

We developed MULTITLS, a middleware that obtains diversity by leveraging tunneling mechanisms. In our implementation, we used *socat*, a tunneling software, and OpenSSL, a TLS implementation, to create multiple TLS channels and encapsulate each one in another. MULTITLS can be run as a shell command and is configured with a parameter k, the *diversity factor* $(k > 1)$. This parameter specifies the number of TLS channels to be created and consequently the number of cipher suites to be used. The cipher suites used by these TLS channels are different from each other to mitigate the vulnerabilities that can be found in each cipher suite. Therefore, the communication channel created by MULTITLS has multiple layers of protection, so that if $k - 1$ of the used cipher suites are vulnerable, communications will remain secure, since there is at least one cipher suite that guarantees the security of communications (confidentiality, integrity, authentication). MULTITLS aims to make progress over VTTLS [5], a vulnerability-tolerant communication protocol also based on diversity and redundancy of cryptographic mechanisms to provide a secure communication channel. However, VTTLS modifies a TLS implementation internally, leading to severe software maintenance challenges.

2   Background and Related Work

Transport Layer Security (TLS) [9] is a security protocol that provides secure communication channels between two entities, server and client. The protocol is structured in two layers: the TLS Record protocol and the TLS Handshake protocol. The TLS Record protocol is used by the TLS Handshake and the application data protocols to provide mechanisms for sending and receiving messages. The TLS Handshake protocol is used to establish or resume a secure session between server and client. A session is established in several steps, each corresponding to a different message and with a specific objective. Following the TLS Handshake protocol, the server and the client can exchange information through the established secure communication channel.

Although the goal of the TLS protocol is to establish a secure communication channel, it may still have unknown vulnerabilities making it insecure and susceptible to attacks.

An example of an attack that exploits a design vulnerability is CRIME (Compression Ratio Info-leak Made Easy) [12]. This vulnerability was found in TLS compression. Using this method, an attacker can brute-force the cookie value by using the responses sent by the server. The Heartbleed vulnerability [3] is a buffer over-read vulnerability that happens when the sender sends a message that specifies a payload size higher than what the real size of the payload. The receiver, upon receiving the message, returns a block of memory where the sent payload begins plus the specified size of the received message, that is, it returns the received payload and dataset with size equal to the size specified in the received message minus the real size of the message.

There are also vulnerabilities in the underlying cryptographic mechanisms used by the TLS protocol. In 2011, Bogdanov et al. [2] published a biclique attack against AES, though only with slight advantage over brute force. The computational complexity of the attack is $2^{126.1}$, $2^{189.7}$ and $2^{254.4}$ for AES128, AES192 and AES256, respectively. Although there is this attack and others, AES is still considered a secure encryption mechanism. MD5 [11] is a hash function, created by Rivest in 1991, that produces a 128 bit hash. In 2005, MD5 was proved not to be collision resistant by Wang and Yu [13], through differential attacks. Differential cryptanalysis, introduced by Biham and Shamir [1], analyzes the differences in input pairs on the differences of the resultant output pairs.

In this work we achieve security through diversity. The term *diversity* describes multi-version software in which redundant versions are purposely made different from between themselves [7]. With diverse versions, one hopes that any faults they contain will be different and show different failure behavior.

vTTLS [5] is a previous work that also uses the diversity approach to solve the limitation of TLS having only one cipher suite negotiated between server and client. It uses the diversity and redundancy of cryptographic mechanisms, keys and certificates. vTTLS was successfully implemented as a fork of OpenSSL version 1.0.2g, but moving to a newer version of OpenSSL requires implementing the diversity features again. Our solution, MULTITLS, is similar to this approach but we do not modify implementations of the tools.

3   MultiTLS

MULTITLS provides secure communication channels with multiple layers through *tunneling* of TLS channels within each other. The term tunneling describes a process of encapsulating entire data packets as the payload within others packets, which are handled properly by the network on both endpoints [6]. MULTITLS provides an increase in security since each of these TLS channels uses a different cipher suite than the others. The reason MULTITLS contributes to increased security is that even when $k-1$ cipher suites become insecure, that is, even when $k-1$ TLS channels become vulnerable, the communication channel created by MULTITLS, which is the combination of the k TLS channels, remains secure since there is still one TLS channel with secure cipher suite. The mechanisms used by MULTITLS allow creating k TLS channels without changing the implementations of the used tools. This approach is an advantage over vTTLS, since it does not require changes to the implementation of TLS. In the following sections, we will discuss the design and implementation of MULTITLS.

3.1   Design

To encapsulate a TLS channel in another TLS channel, we use TUN (network TUNnel) interfaces. This mechanism is a feature offered by some operating systems. Unlike common network interfaces, TUN does not have physical hardware components, that is, it is a virtual network interface implemented and managed by the kernel itself. TUN is a virtual point-to-point network device. Its driver was designed with low level kernel support for IP tunneling. It works at the protocol layer of the network stack. TUN interfaces allow user-space applications to interact with them as if they were a real device, remaining invisible to the user. These applications pass packets to a TUN device, in this case, the TUN interface delivers these packets to the operating system's network stack. Conversely, the packets sent by an operating system to a TUN device are delivered to a user-space application that attaches to the device. Figure 1 shows a practical example in which an application running on two different hosts communicates through TUN interfaces.

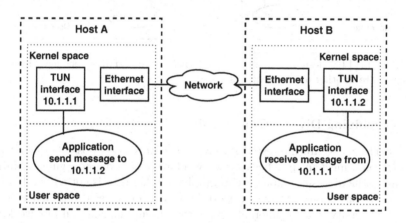

Fig. 1. Example of using TUN interfaces

We create an encapsulation of several tunnels by creating TUN interfaces through others created previously. For each of these interfaces, we can use different TLS implementations running in user space that allow creating a TLS channel that is encapsulated by the tunnel used by the hosts.

Figure 2 presents the architecture of MULTITLS for $k = 2$. This configuration allows an application to communicate over two tunnels, whereas the tunnel between the TUN1 interfaces encapsulates the tunnel between the TUN2 interfaces. In addition, we can see that between the TUN1 interfaces there is a tunnel that crosses two processes that we designate by TLS implementation and whose function is to establish and manage the TLS channel that is encapsulated by the tunnel. To do this, one of these processes will run in server mode and the other in client mode.

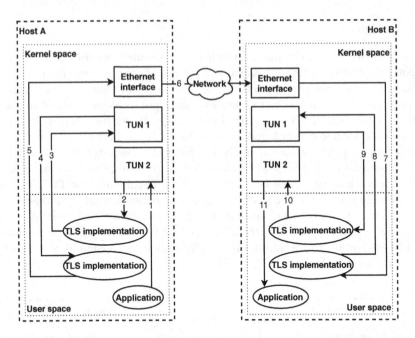

Fig. 2. MULTITLS design with $k = 2$ and the flow of sending messages from one application to another on different hosts

3.2   Combining Diverse Cipher Suites

In MULTITLS, we are interested in having the maximum possible diversity of cryptographic mechanisms, because we want to avoid common vulnerabilities. Evaluating the diversity among cryptographic mechanisms is not trivial. For this purpose, we based our analysis on work by Carvalho [4] regarding heuristics to compare diversity among different cryptographic mechanisms. In our work, we focused on searching for the combination of four cipher suites supported by TLS 1.2 from the OpenSSL 1.1.0g implementation, that guarantees greater diversity.

We began by evaluating the diversity of public key mechanisms. In this case, we observed the various combinations of key exchange and authentication algorithms in cipher suites. The insecure cryptographic mechanisms were discarded as well as the ECDH and DH algorithms since there are the variants of them, ECDHE and DHE, which guarantee perfect forward secrecy. This analysis resulted in the following combinations: ECDHE for key exchange and ECDSA for authentication; RSA for key exchange and authentication; DHE for key exchange and DSS for authentication; ECDHE for key exchange and RSA for authentication; and DHE for key exchange and RSA for authentication. In order to avoid that the key exchange and authentication algorithms are repeated consecutively, we choose the first four combinations of the above list, keeping the presented order, i.e., the first tunnel will use ECDHE for key exchange and ECDSA as authentication algorithm, the second RSA for key exchange and authentication, the third DHE for key exchange and DSS for authentication and the fourth DHE for key exchange and RSA for authentication.

Considering the combination of key exchange and authentication algorithms, we group the supported cipher suites according to this combination. After this step, we chose in each group the cipher suite that maximizes the diversity of the symmetric key algorithms and the hash function between each of the four groups. To measure the diversity of the cryptographic mechanisms, we have taken into account some characteristics such as the origin, i.e., the author or institution that proposed the algorithm, the year in which it was designed, the size of the key in the case of the symmetric key algorithms and the digest size in the case of hash functions and other metrics described in Carvalho's research [4]. We concluded that the combinations of 4 symmetric key algorithms that maximize the diversity itself are:

- ChaCha20 + Camellia 256 + AES256-GCM + AES128CBC
- ChaCha20 + Camellia 256 + AES256-CBC + AES128GCM
- ChaCha20 + Camellia 256 + Camellia128 + AES256-GCM

Regarding hash functions, the variety is greatly reduced since there is only SHA-256 and SHA-384. However, some symmetric key algorithms use operation modes, such as CBC-MAC (CCM mode) and Galois/Counter Mode (GCM), that provide authenticated encryption with associated data (AEAD). It is considered an alternative mechanism which can be used redundantly with HMAC to achieve even higher diversity. In addition, the cipher suites with the ChaCHA20 algorithm use the Poly1305 which is a one-time authenticator. Poly1305 takes a 32-byte one-time key and a message and produces a 16-byte message authentication code (MAC).

From these analyses, the cipher suites selected to be used by default in MultiTLS with $k \leq 4$ are: TLS_ECDHE_ECDSA_WITH_CHACHA20_POLY1305_SHA256, TLS_RSA_WITH_AES_128_CCM_8, TLS_DHE_DSS_WITH_CAMELLIA_256_CBC_SHA256 and TLS_ECDHE_RSA_WITH_AES_256_GCM_SHA 384.

If MultiTLS the user wants to use only 2 tunnels, i.e., k = 2, the first cipher suite shown in the above list is used in the first tunnel and the second cipher suite is used in the second tunnel.

3.3 Running MultiTLS

MultiTLS is implemented as a script in Bash language and can be run as a shell command. Before presenting how MultiTLS creates the secure tunnels, we will first introduce the commands that allow us to create them. The commands available through MultiTLS are:

```
- multitls -s port nTunnels [cert cafile cipher]
- multitls -c port nTunnels IPServer [cert cafile cipher]
```

The flags -s and -c mean that MULTITLS will run as a server or client, respectively. The port argument specifies the port used to establish the last tunnel. In the case of the server, MULTITLS will be listening on that port. In the case of the client, MULTITLS will connect to that port of the machine that has the IP specified in the *IPServer* argument. The *nTunnels* argument specifies the number of tunnels that MULTITLS will create. In addition, we must specify: the path to the file with its certificate and private key in the *cert* argument and the path to the file that contains the peer certificate in the *cafile* argument. The *cipher* argument lets us specify one or more cipher suites. If cipher suites are not specified, the default ones will be used. The arguments between brackets must be specified as many times as the value of the *nTunnels* argument because each tunnel will use a set of keys and ciphers.

3.4   Implementing the Tunnels

The execution of commands provided by MULTITLS allows the creation of TUN interfaces and the creation of the tunnel that encapsulates a TLS channel, as explained in Sect. 3.1. Figure 2 shows the scheme resulting from the execution of the two MULTITLS commands presented in Sect. 3.3.

MULTITLS has as dependencies socat version 1.7.3.2 and OpenSSL version 1.1.0g. Socat is a command line utility[1] that establishes two bidirectional byte streams and transfers data between them. A socat command has the following structure: socat [options] address1 address2, where [options] means that there may be zero or more options that modify the behavior of the program. The specification of the address1 and address2 consists of an address type keyword, for example, TCP4, TCP4-LISTEN, OPENSSL, OPENSSL-LISTEN, TUN; zero or more required address parameters separated by ':' from the keyword and each other; and zero or more address options separated by ','.

The MULTITLS script starts by analyzing the arguments provided by the user. Afterwards, these arguments are used to execute socat commands. MULTI-TLS creates k tunnels running k socat command on the server and k commands on the client. For the establishment of a tunnel using the socat commands, MUL-TITLS executes the following two commands, the first on the server side and the second on the client side:

```
- socat openssl-listen:$port,cert=$cert,cafile=$cafile, \
  cipher=$cipher TUN:$ipTun/24,tun-name=$nameTun,up
- socat openssl-connect:$ipServer:$port,cert=$cert, \
  cafile=$cafile,cipher=$cipher \
  TUN:$ipTun/24,tun-name=$nameTun
```

In the first command, we have the $port argument that represents the port where the socat will be listening, we have the $cert, $cafile and $cipher arguments that have the same meaning as the MULTITLS command arguments. The

---

[1] http://www.dest-unreach.org/socat.

arguments $ipTun and $nameTun are, respectively, the IP of the server in the TUN interface and the name of that, which is created through this command.

In the second command, we have the argument $ipServer that represents the IP of the server, the argument $port that represents the port of the server where the socat connects to establish the communication. We have the $cert, $cafile, and $cipher arguments that have the same meaning as the cert, cafile, and cipher arguments in the MULTITLS commands. The arguments $ipTun and $nameTUN are, respectively, the IP of the client in the TUN interface and its name, which is created through this command.

MULTITLS by default assumes that the IP and names for the TUN interfaces are 10.$k.1.$i and TUN$k, where $k is the tunnel number, $1 \le k \le nTunnels$ and $i has the value 1 if it is the server and 2 if it is the client.

After the establishment of the first tunnel, MULTITLS can create the second tunnel which is encapsulated by the first tunnel, using the previous socat commands in which the value of $ipServer instead of being the real IP of the server is the IP of the TUN interface created on the server to establish the first tunnel, which as previously mentioned is 10.1.1.1, by default. To create more tunnels, the IP of the last TUN interface created on the server side must be specified in the $ipServer argument.

4 Evaluation

The experimental evaluation aims to answer questions about the performance and cost of MULTITLS. We have three experiment sets: performance; comparison with other approaches; and MULTITLS applied to a use case.

4.1 Performance

In this section we want to answer the questions: *What is the cost of adding more tunnels? What is the cost of encrypting messages?* To answer these questions we used two virtual machines running on two different hosts, one playing the role of a server and the other of a client. Both virtual machines used 2 VCPUs, 8 GB of RAM and ran Ubuntu 16 (Xenial).

In the first evaluation, we used the iperf3 tool, version 3.0.11. Iperf3 is a tool used to measure network performance. It has server and client functionality and can create data streams to measure the throughput between the two ends. It supports the adjustment of several parameters related to timing and protocols. The iperf3 output presents the bandwidth, transmission time, and other parameters.

To answer the first question, the first experiment consisted of using the iperf3 tool to measure 100 times the transmission time of 1 MB, 100 MB and 1 GB for each k, considering $k \le 4$. The cipher suites used in this evaluation are the same ones that are defined by default in MULTITLS. The average and the standard deviation of transmission time of 1 MB, 100 MB and 1 GB for each value of k can be seen in Fig. 3.

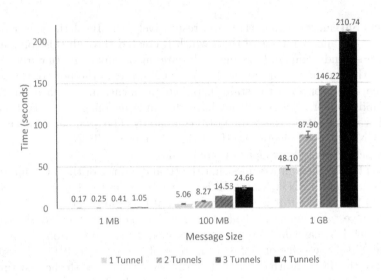

Fig. 3. Comparison between the time it takes to send 1 MB, 100 MB and 1 GB messages in relation to the number of tunnels created.

Figure 4 shows for each message size the overhead of the transmission time for $k = 2$, $k = 3$ and $k = 4$ in relation to $k = 1$. Therefore, we can see that for $k = 2$ and $k = 3$ the cost of having added more tunnels increases as the size of the message to be transmitted also increases. For $k = 4$ the cost of having added more channels decreased as the size of the message to be transmitted increased. We can also observe that the transmission time for k tunnels is less than k times the value of $k = 1$ for each message size, except for $k = 4$, where the overhead exceeds 4 times the value of $k = 1$ and for $k = 3$ in the 1 GB transmission where the time is 3.04 times greater than for $k = 1$.

We can answer the first question that for $k = 2$ the performance of MULTI-TLS is acceptable, since the time of sending messages with $k = 2$ is less than the double of the time of sending messages with $k = 1$. With 3 tunnels, i.e., $k = 3$, for the transfer of 1 GB, the performance of the MULTITLS is poor because the sending time is more than three times the time of $k = 1$, in contrast, to transfer 1 MB and 100 MB the performance is good since the sending time is less than three times the time of $k = 1$.

The second experiment aims to evaluate the cost of encrypting the communication messages. To do this, using the same virtual machines, we performed the same tests we did in the first experiment, however changing the cipher suites by default from MULTITLS to TLS_ECDHE_ECDSA_WITH_NULL_SHA, TLS_RSA_WITH_NULL_SHA256, TLS_RSA_WITH_NULL_SHA and TLS_ECDHE_RSA_WITH_NULL_SHA. Therefore, the messages exchanged by the client and the server were not encrypted. This experiment helps us realize the influence of encrypting the data in the total transmission time of messages with different sizes. Figure 5

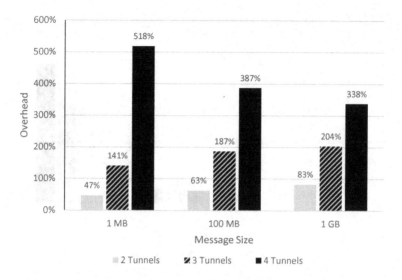

Fig. 4. The overhead of adding more tunnels in relation to k = 1.

shows the average and standard deviation of transmission time of 1 MB, 100 MB, and 1 GB for each value of k.

As with the first experiment, for each message size, the transmission time increases as the number of tunnels increases. However, we verified that the transmission time of 1 MB for all values of k is greater than k times the time of $k = 1$. In the transfer of 100 MB and 1 GB with k tunnels, the transmission time does not exceed k times the value of $k = 1$.

Figure 6 shows the difference between the first and second experiment, for each message size and k. We can see that, for certain message sizes and k, messages sent on the first experiment took less time than messages sent without encryption. However, we can observe that in these cases the average overhead is about −10%, whereas in cases where encrypted communications take longer than unencrypted communications, the average overhead is 35%. Overall, the overhead of encrypting the messages is 13%.

For all this, we can answer the second question: the time to encrypt the messages has a considerable low impact given that it takes 13% more time.

4.2   Comparison with MultiTLS

The purpose of this section is to compare the performance of MULTITLS with other tools and to know which of these approaches performs better.

For this purpose, using the same virtual machines that we used in previous experiments, we use VTTLS to transfer three files each with the size of 1 MB, 100 MB and 1 GB. We ran 100 times the VTTLS for each of these files. In addition to this experience, we also run a file transfer application using a Datagram Transport Layer Security (DTLS) [10] channel implemented through the GnuTLS

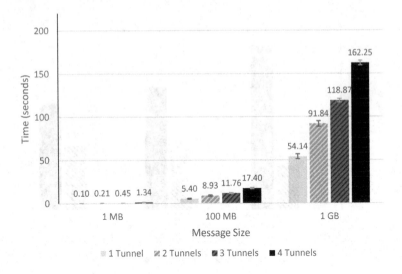

Fig. 5. Comparison between the time it takes to send 1 MB, 100 MB and 1 GB messages in relation to the number of unencrypted tunnels.

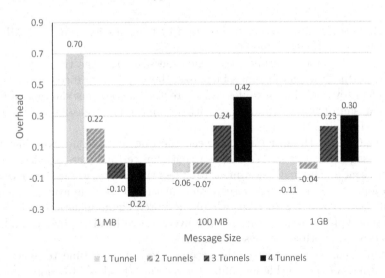

Fig. 6. Difference between first and second evaluation results.

library. This channel used the cipher suite TLS_RSA_AES_128_GCM_SHA256. This application ran over one tunnel created by MULTITLS. DTLS is a communication protocol that provides security, such as TLS, but for datagram-based applications. The purpose of using DTLS is to measure the performance of a channel that uses UDP over TCP, since with MULTITLS communication we have tunnels of several tunnels, that is, TCP over TCP. We run this application

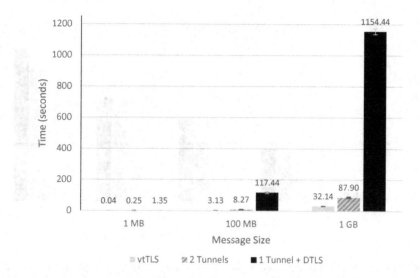

Fig. 7. Time for sending messages with 1 MB, 100 MB and 1 GB in size via VTTLS, 2 MULTITLS tunnels and 1 DTLS communication over 1 MULTITLS tunnel.

100 times for each of the files used in the previous experiment. Besides the diversity of cipher suites used, this experience also shows that it is possible to have a diversity of TLS implementations if the application using MULTITLS uses a library other than OpenSSL.

Figure 7 allows us to compare the average of the results obtained from the two previous experiences with the averages of the results obtained in the first experiment with $k = 2$ once the two previous experiments use approaches in which the messages are encrypted twice such as MULTITLS with two tunnels. In addition, we can also observe the standard deviation in each column. Figure 7 also shows that, of the three approaches, VTTLS is the fastest and the DTLS channel approach is the slowest. The values of the MULTITLS results are closer to the results of the VTTLS than to the DTLS channel approach. However, the transfer time overhead of 1 MB, 100 MB and 1 GB between VTTLS and MULTITLS are, respectively, 525%, 164% and 173%. The DTLS channel approach does not have an expected performance because the server only sends the next fragment after receiving the size of the last fragment sent by it.

4.3   Use Case

Although the use of MULTITLS presents a transfer time overhead in relation to VTTLS, we wanted to know what is the performance of MULTITLS applied in a use case. We use MULTITLS to establish communication between a browser and a proxy, based on the scheme shown in Fig. 2. To do this evaluation, we use two virtual machines, one ran the Squid proxy, version 3.5.12, on a computer

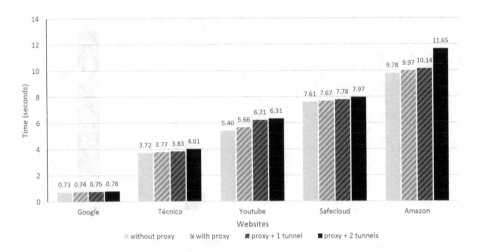

Fig. 8. Time to load sites with: no proxy, with proxy, with proxy using MULTITLS with 1 tunnel and with 2 tunnels.

with Intel Core i5 and 4 GB RAM and the other ran Google Chrome browser, version 66.0.3359.117, on a computer with Intel Core i7 and 8 GB RAM.

In this evaluation we tested four approaches: no proxy, use only the proxy, use the proxy using one and two MULTITLS tunnels. These four approaches allow us to evaluate the cost of using MULTITLS. The evaluation consisted of using the browser to request 30 times certain URLs from Amazon[2], Google[3], SafeCloud[4], Técnico[5] and Youtube[6] websites, for each approach, and recording the load event time that appears on the network tab in the developer tools of the browser. The load event is fired when a resource and its dependent resources have finished loading. The cache was disabled during the experiment.

Figure 8 presents the average of the results obtained with the different approaches for each requested URL. We can observe that the use of MULTITLS in the communication between the browser and the proxy was insignificant. We can conclude that MULTITLS is a tool with good performance in tasks common to the day-to-day of Internet users.

5   Conclusion

We presented MULTITLS, a middleware that allows the creation of a channel of communication through the encapsulation of several secure tunnels in others. It aims to increase security by using the diversity of cipher suites used by the

---

[2] https://www.amazon.com/.

[3] https://www.google.com/.

[4] http://www.safecloud-project.eu/.

[5] https://tecnico.ulisboa.pt/pt/.

[6] https://www.youtube.com/watch?v=oToaJE4s4z0.

tunnels so that if $k-1$ cipher suites become insecure, there is a secure tunnel that makes all communication secure. MULTITLS has the advantage of not modifying any TLS implementation or any of its dependencies.

Acknowledgements. This work was supported by the European Commission through project H2020-653884 (SafeCloud) and by national funds through Fundação para a Ciência e a Tecnologia (FCT) with reference UIDB/50021/2020 (INESC-ID).

References

1. Biham, E., Shamir, A.: Differential Cryptanalysis of the Data Encryption Standard (1993). https://doi.org/10.1007/978-1-4613-9314-6_4
2. Bogdanov, A., Khovratovich, D., Rechberger, C.: Biclique cryptanalysis of the full AES. In: Lee, D.H., Wang, X. (eds.) ASIACRYPT 2011. LNCS, vol. 7073, pp. 344–371. Springer, Heidelberg (2011). https://doi.org/10.1007/978-3-642-25385-0_19
3. Carvalho, M., Demott, J., Ford, R., Wheeler, D.A.: Heartbleed 101. IEEE Secur. Priv. **12**(4), 63–67 (2014)
4. Carvalho, R.J.: Authentication security through diversity and redundancy for cloud computing. Ph.D. thesis, Instituto Superior Técnico, Universidade de Lisboa (2014)
5. Joaquim, A., Pardal, M.L., Correia, M.: Vulnerability-tolerant transport layer security. In: 21st International Conference on Principles of Distributed Systems (OPODIS) (2017)
6. Larson, R., Cockcroft, L.: CCSP : Cisco Certified Security Professional Certification. McGraw-Hill/Osborne, New York (2003)
7. Littlewood, B., Strigini, L.: Redundancy and diversity in security. In: Samarati, P., Ryan, P., Gollmann, D., Molva, R. (eds.) ESORICS 2004. LNCS, vol. 3193, pp. 423–438. Springer, Heidelberg (2004). https://doi.org/10.1007/978-3-540-30108-0_26
8. Nadeau, M.: State of cybercrime 2017: security events decline, but not the impact, July 2017. https://www.csoonline.com/article/3211491/security/state-of-cybercrime-2017-security-events-decline-but-not-the-impact.html#tk.cso_fsb
9. Rescorla, E.: The transport layer security (TLS) protocol version 1.3. RFC 8446, RFC Editor, August 2018
10. Rescorla, E., Modadugu, N.: Datagram transport layer security version 1.2. RFC 6347, RFC Editor, January 2012
11. Rivest, R.: The MD5 Message-Digest Algorithm (RFC 1321) (1992)
12. Rizzo, J., Duong, T.: Crime: compression ratio info-leak made easy. In: ekoparty Security Conference (2012)
13. Wang, X., Yu, H.: How to break MD5 and other hash functions. In: Cramer, R. (ed.) EUROCRYPT 2005. LNCS, vol. 3494, pp. 19–35. Springer, Heidelberg (2005). https://doi.org/10.1007/11426639_2

Improving Big Data Clustering
for Jamming Detection in Smart Mobility

Hind Bangui$^{(\boxtimes)}$, Mouzhi Ge, and Barbora Buhnova

Faculty of Informatics, Masaryk University, Brno, Czech Republic
hind.bangui@mail.muni.cz, mouzhi.ge@muni.cz, buhnova@fi.muni.cz

Abstract. Smart mobility, with its urban transportation services ranging from real-time traffic control to cooperative vehicle infrastructure
systems, is becoming increasingly critical in smart cities. These smart
mobility services thus need to be very well protected against a variety of
security threats, such as intrusion, jamming, and Sybil attacks. One of
the frequently cited attacks in smart mobility is the jamming attack. In
order to detect the jamming attacks, different anti-jamming applications
have been developed to reduce the impact of malicious jamming attacks.
One important step in anti-jamming detection is to cluster the vehicular
data. However, it is usually very time-consuming to detect the jamming
attacks that may affect the safety of roads and vehicle communication in
real-time. Therefore, this paper proposes an efficient big data clustering
model, coresets-based clustering, to support the real-time detection of
jamming attacks. We validate the model efficiency and applicability in
the context of a typical smart mobility system: Vehicular Ad-hoc Network, known as VANET.

Keywords: Smart mobility · Jamming attack · Anti-jamming · Big
data clustering · VANET · Smart city

1 Introduction

Nowadays, smart mobility has become a critical transportation infrastructure [9,38] in smart cities as it provides a variety of mobility services, such
as relieving the traffic congestion in cities and providing better access to public
transport. In [1], smart mobility is described as: "The use of ICT in modern
transport technologies to improve urban traffic". Likewise, in [42], it is defined
as: "local and supra-local accessibility, availability of ICTs, modern, sustain-
able and safe transport systems". Thus, smart mobility can be considered as a
management strategy that produces decisions based on the collected data [9,31]
from vehicle-to-anything communications, such as vehicle-to-vehicle, vehicle-to-
infrastructure, vehicle-to-pedestrian, and infrastructure-to-pedestrian [43]. For
instance, a road infrastructure monitoring system uses e-bikes proposed in [25]
to support municipal transportation activities. Further, an image processing
application based on deep learning has been integrated into e-bikes to facilitate the detection of road anomalies such as litter and damage of roads. It can

© IFIP International Federation for Information Processing 2020
Published by Springer Nature Switzerland AG 2020
M. Hölbl et al. (Eds.): SEC 2020, IFIP AICT 580, pp. 78–91, 2020.
https://doi.org/10.1007/978-3-030-58201-2_6

be seen that smart mobility is a fruitful domain that integrates different up-to-date techniques such as the autonomous driving Internet of Things (IoT) and machine learning. In [21], a vehicular interface notation has been developed to help older customers of smart vehicles to control their driving experience better and improve their cognitive ability. Similarly, in [40], a machine learning system has been proposed to exploit data from autonomous vehicles and external IoT data sources to predict pedestrian's next movement steps using real-time trajectory. The suggested solution ensures safety in urban environments by enhancing autonomous driving efficiently in local public transport services. The recent works indicate that smart mobility is driven by data-intensive processes focused on managing people's mobility and personalizing transport solutions according to the specific needs of cities [8]. On the other hand, smart mobility advances the transport services and quality of citizens' life in smart cities [16,17,29].

Enabling smart mobility in urban environments is, however, challenging because attackers are attempting to access or tamper with valuable mobility data (e.g., personal user information) or disrupt network communication. Since smart mobility generates a massive amount of data, such as sensor data on the road or vehicle communication data, various security applications make use of big data analytics to secure smart mobility applications. There are different prevalent attacks in the smart mobility domain. One of the frequently cited ones is the jamming attack. Jamming attacks can severely influence road safety and vehicle communications.

In order to detect the jamming attacks in smart mobility, different anti-jamming applications have been proposed, which, however, suffer from the inefficiency of the data clustering during the jamming attack detection. In this paper, we, therefore, propose a solution to support the real-time detection of jamming attacks via efficient big data clustering of vehicular data. The solution is mainly based on the coresets technique and Vehicular Ad-hoc Network (VANET) is used as a practical scenario of smart mobility [5,10], where we consider particularly the application of clustering algorithms in anti-jamming detection solutions designed for securing VANET communications.

The remainder of the paper is organized as follows. Section 2 is dedicated to understanding the vulnerability of smart mobility systems by using VANET as an example of smart mobility applications. Then in Sect. 3, we provide an overview of related work concerning anti-jamming applications based on clustering techniques. In Sect. 4, we present a solution that aims at increasing efficiency the clustering process while keeping the quality of analytics. In Sect. 5, we conduct an experiment to show the benefits of the proposed solution. Finally, Sect. 6 concludes the paper and outlines future research.

2 Security in Smart Mobility

Smart mobility intends to control the behavior of smart devices in urban environments by collecting, sharing, and utilizing trace data. Vehicular Ad-hoc Network (VANET) is a typical smart mobility system that can be used to share data within vehicle-to-anything communication. For example, VANET applications such as smart cars are used to support the safety of traffic flows [20,35,39]. The vehicles exchange messages with neighboring vehicles (members of a VANET) and with RSUs (roadside units) to inform them about e.g. their location and speed, and get traffic conditions of the road. However, a malicious attacker may remotely access a target vehicle, possibly tampering with the behavior of the vehicle, such as misinforming the driver.

Constant jamming is one type of jamming attacks that is considered as a severe threat to VANET security [22,39]. In this attack, a jammer regularly sends repeated signals to interfere with the communication between vehicles in the affected network area, where the target vehicles think that the state of the channel is still busy. Consequently, they cannot send or receive packets that can be carrying important information, such as weather and accidents. In other words, when jamming occurs, the sender may send packets. However, the receiver might not be able to receive all the packets sent by the sender. Thus, the failure of receiving or disseminating these packets can lead to the insufficiency of the VANET. Smart mobility systems require the optimized use of detection attack applications to cope with the security and privacy threats.

Several detection attack systems are proposed in the previous literature [19, 39]. Table 1 presents a list of typical attacks in smart mobility. However, developing security and privacy solutions is more challenging in smart mobility infrastructure as data are subject to several malicious attacks causing wrong outcomes (i.e., wrong traffic). Especially, the big data clustering technique is used to facilitate the attack detection. Thus, we focus on examining how big data clustering algorithms in smart mobility [5,10] are investigated to deal with vulnerable attacks. Particularly, it is valuable to study the clustering for detection applications that deal with jamming attacks caused several damages, such as disruption of car-to-car communications.

3   Clustering for Anti-jamming Detection

The concept of big data clustering is very important in smart mobility since it contributes to improving the sustainability, scalability, and reliability of smart mobility systems [5], such as associating mobile nodes into groups, ensuring the stability of channel access management, traffic safety, and QoS Assurance. Many jamming detection approaches in VANET have exploited the advantages of clustering algorithms by collecting jamming measurements and then accurately grouping them into the cluster [6,32]. For example, in [15], a novel jamming detection framework was proposed to detect the presence of a jammer in hierarchical cluster-based wireless sensor networks. The proposed anti-jamming detection method also exploits the benefits of the unsupervised hierarchical algorithm for achieving energy efficiency by re-clustering, overcoming network issues (i.e., reducing the communication overhead), decreasing collision, and improving throughput. Similarly, in [23], a jamming detection solution was developed by leveraging the K-means algorithm, which is one of the most commonly used

Table 1. Cyber attacks in smart mobility

Cyber attacks	Description
Intrusion	Aim at analyzing vehicular data to inspect the abnormal behavior in VANET under different scenarios, and then generate an alarm filtering technique for any detected security anomaly
Misbehavior	Aim at analyzing the behavior of vehicles to detect malicious node that may send incorrect information to other vehicles, and then cause malfunctioning VANET applications
DDoS	Eliminate the DDoS attacks that make the network services unavailable from different locations
Jamming	Eliminate jamming attacks that make physical resources unavailable by interfering with the radio frequencies used by VANET vehicles
Sybil	Aim at detecting the Sybil vehicle attack that can forge different false identities, where each pseudonym acts as a virtual vehicle

partitioned clustering algorithms in Big Data Analytics. This work reflects the benefits of using clustering algorithms in VANETs, where the advantages of k-means are used to differentiate intentional cases from unintentional jamming (Table 2).

The collected jamming measurements are grouped into the interference cluster accurately, and then the specific characteristics of each attack are extracted. Thus, the unsupervised method is aimed at determining whether jamming occurs due to a malicious jammer or whether it is caused unintentionally. Consequently, if jamming is correctly identified as interference, vehicles can preserve their communications either by changing their channel or by temporarily altering their route. Likewise, in [4], a multi-cluster localization (M-cluster) algorithm and an x-rayed jammed-area localization (X-ray) algorithm were successively developed based on fuzzy c-means and K-means to deal with the multi-jammer localization problem in WSNs, which could launch collaborative attacks. In [34], the advantages of K-means were used to predict the number of multiple jamming attackers and ensure the preset functions of VANET. In [33], an anti-jamming method based on fuzzy c-means was proposed to determine the localization and number of jamming attackers. Accordingly, the cluster analysis process simplifies data manipulation by finding similar structures in the data and classifying each object according to its nature. As a result, vehicles can adequately avoid malicious jamming attacks, decrease their collisions, and preserve their communications [27,28,30].

Nevertheless, the existing anti-jamming solutions suffer from efficiency issues due to the growth of smart mobility data and it is time-consuming to perform a computational clustering process.

Table 2. Overview of anti-jamming applications based on Clustering algorithms

Papers	Description	Clustering algorithms used
[23]	Study jamming attack detection in a pair of RF (radio frequency) communicating vehicles	K-means
[26]	Ensure secure communication and defend RF jamming attacks	K-Nearest Neighbors and Random Forests
[15]	Detect jamming attacks	Hierarchical clustering
[6]	Predict jamming attacks	Clusters
[32]	Detect jamming attacks	Clusters
[4]	Detect multi-jammer localization attacks	Fuzzy c-Means, k-means
[34]	Estimate the number of multiple jamming attackers	K-means
[33]	Detect the localization of multiple jamming attackers in VANET	Fuzzy c-Means

Furthermore, vehicles in the smart mobility context are producing big data at a rapid rate in the dynamic urban environment. Thus, the time and cost of the clustering process will increase since they depend on the volume of datasets, which is definitely difficult to be handled in real-time. Yet, the study of data prioritization is required since it aims at serving the real-time Big Data Analytics by selecting the most valuable data from the initial input data [7]. As a result, the anti-jamming applications can detect in real-time viral attacks that cause smart mobility system failures.

4   Coresets-Based Anti-jamming Detection

In this section, we propose a model that aims at minimizing the response time of anti-jamming detection by accelerating the clustering process. Figure 1 presents a general process of attack detection based on the application of data clustering, where a predefined list of features is extracted from vehicular data to detect the characteristics of jamming attacks. The selection of features is according to the context of the proposed anti-jamming solutions, for example, GPS information is used to recognize cases of intentional jamming [33]. After that, the clustering method can be used to analyze vehicular data and classify timely the malicious nodes from benign ones. The coresets can be used to accelerate clustering the big mobility data. In the context of jamming detection, the anti-jamming application is able to deal with the specific characteristics of each jamming attack timely and effectively.

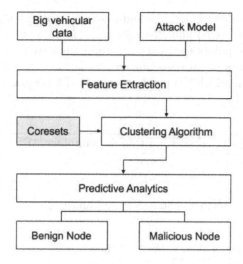

Fig. 1. Coresets-based predictive analytics for attacks in smart mobility

4.1 Coresets

The idea of using approximated data has been investigated in sensor networks [12,14], where coresets are used to extract small data samples that represent the original data approximately, and then solve compression issues of trajectory data in road networks [12–14], such as improving the run-time performance of location-based applications. Moreover, coresets not only can reduce the data scale while keeping the original data distribution [11,24], but also can be used for improving the quality of clustering [18,37]. For Example, ProTraS [37] is a coreset construction algorithm that aims at generating a data sample to deal with big data clustering problems [2,3]. The main idea of ProTraS is to select a representative point based on a probability of cost reduction. Given an $\epsilon > 0$, for each iteration of the algorithm, it adds a new representative into a group of the sample with the highest probability of the cost reduction. When the cost drops below a threshold, which depends on ϵ, the algorithm stops. The algorithm finds the nearest group for points that are not yet assigned to any group of the current sample. The point among them is determined to be the new representative if it is farthest in its group and has the highest probability. That means, the representative selected by ProTraS is the farthest-first traversal item of a given group. As a result, this coreset construction algorithm leads to enhancing the quality of clusters that are required for ensuring the accuracy of the Big Data Analytics outcomes [2,3].

In this work, we aim to investigate the advantages of coresets to optimize the quality of clustering used in anti-jamming detection. Particularly, we use coresets method to deal with the clustering formulation and complexity. We have referred to the coresets technique discussed in [41]. This is an improvement version of the ProTraS algorithm [37] by using a post-processing task. Given a dataset $P = \{x_i\}$, for $i = 1, 2, \ldots, n$ and a given $\epsilon > 0$, the method firstly calls ProTraS to obtain $S = \{y_j\}$ and $P(y_j)$ for $j = 1, 2, \ldots, s$. The method next tries to find some sample points that have low representativeness and remove them from the sample. A point in remaining points is then replicated by the center of the set of patterns which the point represents. The details of the method are given in Algorithm 1.

Algorithm 1. Coresets-based algorithm for sampling [41]

Require: $P = \{x_i\}$, for $i = 1, 2, \ldots, n$, a tolerance $\epsilon > 0$.
Ensure: A sample $S = \{y_j\}$ and $P(y_j)$, for $j = 1, 2, \ldots, s$.

1: Call ProTraS for P and ϵ to obtain $S = \{y_j\}$ and $P(y_j)$.
2: $S' = \emptyset$.
3: **for all** $y_j \in S$ **do**
4:     **if** $|P(y_j)|$ is greater than a threshold **then**
5:         $y_k^* = \arg\min_{y_k \in P(y_j)} \sum_{y_l \in P(y_j)} d(y_k, y_l)$.
6:         $S' = S' \cup \{y_k^*\}$.
7:     **end if**
8: **end for**
9: $S = S'$.
10: **return** S and $P(y_j^*)$, for $j = 1, 2, \ldots, s'$, where $s' \leq s$.

Line 4 determines which sample points will be select into our sample S'. This is performed using a threshold. $|P(y_j)|$ denotes the number of patterns in P with $y_j \in S$ being their representative. A small value of $|P(y_j)|$ means that the representativeness of y_j is low. Accordingly, it is removed from the sample. The value of the threshold should be chosen due to the distribution characteristics of datasets. For $y_j \in S$ that is not removed, line 5 computes the center of the group represented by y_j, to consider replacing it. The center here, denoted by y_k^*, is defined to be the point in $P(y_j)$ such that the total distance to all others in the group is minimized. The set S' including such y_k^* is the output sample of the algorithm.

5   Experiment Evaluation

In the experiment, we focus on examining how the integration of the coreset method [41] can facilitate the analysis process of anti-jamming applications. To do that, we study vehicular data clustering. Then, we present the details of clustering quality evaluation.

5.1   Experimental Setting

The goal of this experiment is to detect the presence of a constant jamming attack. This latter is detected by monitoring the signal power that is reported via the Received Signal Strength Indicator (RSSI), which is an expression of the SNIR (Signal-to-Noise-and-Interference Ratio). In the presence of the malicious attack, the probability of successful message reception is decreased as well as SNIR is decreased too. For achieving this experiment, we have initially referred to a study in [36] that has explored the impact of different jamming attacks, including a constant jamming case, in VANETs. Then, we have selected its dataset[1] that contains traces of 802.11p packets with and without the presence of constant jamming signals.

Table 3 presents the network configuration used for creating a series of constant jamming scenarios. The number of generated packets is 25,000. The vehicular network features used in this experiment are as follows: Node-Id-number, type, vehicle position, GPS-time, speed, time sender, time receiver, RSSI, SNIR, and vehicle heading. For storage and clusters, we used the permanent cloud environment offered by MetaCentrum[2].

Table 3. Experimental parameters

Linkbird	Data Rate	6 Mbps
	Transmit power	17.48 dBm
	Payload length	100 Byte
	Packet generation rate	100 $packets/s$
Constant jamming	Transmit power	16.75 dBm
	Signal duration	64 μ s
	Signal preparation time	10 μ s
General	Center frequency	5.875 GHz

5.2   Clustering Quality Measurement

Our goal in this experiment is to evaluate the representation of clustering sampling yielded from K-means and its improved versions, which are: K-means++ and Fuzzy c-means. We selected k-means as our clustering algorithm, as k-means is a widely used and efficient unsupervised algorithm that uses an iterative method to divide a given dataset into several clusters noted as k. Next, the produced clusters are positioned as points, and all samples are linked with the nearest cluster and adjusted; then, the process overuses the new adjustments until the desired result is achieved. Thus, this algorithm is easy to implement, efficient in terms of its computational costs, and offers easily interpretable clustering results.

On the other hand, since K-means is sensitive to initialization, it is sensitive to the presence of outliers because the "mean" is not a robust statistic value.

---

[1] https://crawdad.org/keyword-vehicular-network.html.

[2] https://www.cerit-sc.cz.

Therefore, k-means may yield poor outcomes and take more processing time. For that reason, we have evaluated the quality of the obtained clusters both with and without the application of the coresets method. We used the improved versions of K-means (i.e., fuzzy c-means) to evaluate how coresets could influence the quality of the clusters by using a list of metrics. For instance, the Dunn index (DI) is used as an internal evaluation metric to determine how well each sample lies within its cluster. A higher DI indicates better clustering. Likewise, we used a second internal metric, named the Davies–Bouldin index (DBI), to evaluate how well the clustering has been done by using the quantities and features inherent to the selected database. A lower DBI indicates better clustering.

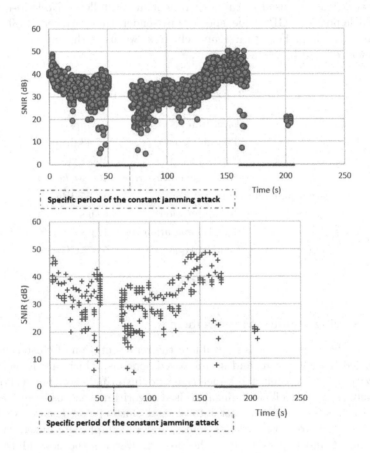

Fig. 2. Before and after using coresets, Sample size = 25,000 and Sample size = 479

5.3   Experimental Results

Figure 2 represented the mapping of the SNIR time evolution. One can see that the sample size is reduced from 25,000 to 479 due to the application of the coreset.

Consequently, the time analysis process is also reduced. Thus, the combination of the coresets with clustering algorithms could help the anti-jamming applications to learn quickly from the approximated data that represent the original data source. As a result, they can detect the presence of constant jamming attacks rapidly.

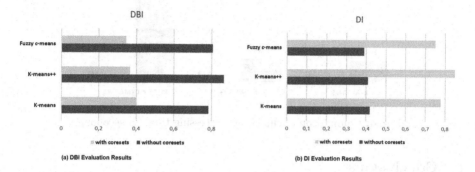

Fig. 3. Clustering evaluation results based on DBI and DI metrics

Meanwhile, the results of internal and external cluster validity indices in Fig. 3 showed that the application of k-means, k-means++, and Fuzzy c-means based on coresets provides promising results compared to their regular application. DBI (Fig. 3a) and DI (Fig. 3b) achieved better values with the coresets compared to the original application of clustering algorithms. Further, DBI and DI reflect how well each sample lies within its cluster. Accordingly, the integration of the coresets with k-means and its improved versions increases the quality of clusters. Besides, K-means shows better efficiency than k-means++ and Fuzzy c-means in term of time. However, we noticed that the application of the coresets supports Fuzzy c-means to proceed quickly compared to its regular time process. Thus, the proposed solution keeps and even significantly improves the quality of the clusters in terms of DBI and DI measurements.

From Fig. 4, one can see that the time of the clustering process is improved on average 132 times across k-means, k-means++, and Fuzzy c-means. Furthermore, all the clustering time is within 1 s, which indicates that the solution can facilitate real-time jamming detection in VANET. In other words, the anti-jamming applications can detect the presence of the viral constant jamming attack and cope with it in real-time, which is a good starting point not only for enhancing the security mechanisms adopted by anti-jamming applications but also for supporting the other detection attack systems based-clustering that have to deal with viral attacks in real-time.

On the other side, the experiment results could be a big motivation for further use of approximated data in smart mobility systems not only for avoiding (or minimizing) the negative impact of malicious attacks, such as damage of personal properties (i.e., cars) and sharing wrong traffic information, but also for supporting the progress of smart mobility applications in urban environments.

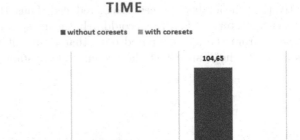

Fig. 4. Comparison of clustering processing time (in seconds)

6   Conclusions

In this paper, we have proposed a model based on the coresets techniques to address the real-time jamming attack detection in smart mobility. Our model demonstrates how to process the big mobility data and use clustering techniques in anti-jamming applications. In order to validate the proposed model, we have conducted an experiment in the VANET setting and our results have shown that the proposed solution can significantly increase the detection efficiency of anti-jamming applications while keeping the clustering quality. With the significant decrease in clustering time, the proposed solution enables the anti-jamming applications to perform real-time jamming detection in smart mobility. Furthermore, our model can also be easily integrated into different smart mobility systems and used to advance the efficiency of other big data applications in the Internet of Vehicles.

As future work, we plan to conduct more experiments with other clustering algorithms, and extend the coresets to detect and discoverer other attacks in smart mobility. Furthermore, we plan to deploy our solution in different real-world scenarios such as the Internet of Vehicles and benchmark the performance of the proposed solution.

Acknowledgements. The work was supported from ERDF/ESF "CyberSecurity, CyberCrime and Critical Information Infrastructures Center of Excellence" (No. CZ.02.1.01/0.0/0.0/16_019/0000822).

References

1. Albino, V., Berardi, U., Dangelico, R.M.: Smart cities: definitions, dimensions, performance, and initiatives. J. Urban Technol. **22**(1), 3–21 (2015)
2. Bangui, H., Ge, M., Buhnova, B.: Exploring big data clustering algorithms for Internet of Things applications. In: IoTBDS, pp. 269–276 (2018)

3. Bangui, H., Ge, M., Buhnova, B.: A research roadmap of big data clustering algorithms for future internet of things. Int. J. Organ. Collective Intell. **9**(2), 16–30 (2019)
4. Cheng, T., Li, P., Zhu, S., Torrieri, D.: M-cluster and x-ray: two methods for multi-jammer localization in wireless sensor networks. Integr. Comput.-Aided Eng. **21**(1), 19–34 (2014)
5. Cooper, C., Franklin, D., Ros, M., Safaei, F., Abolhasan, M.: A comparative survey of VANET clustering techniques. IEEE Commun. Surv. Tutor. **19**(1), 657–681 (2016)
6. Cordero, C.V., Lisser, A.: Jamming attacks reliable prevention in a clustered wireless sensor network. Wirel. Pers. Commun. **85**(3), 925–936 (2015)
7. Darwish, T.S., Bakar, K.A.: Fog based intelligent transportation big data analytics in the internet of vehicles environment: motivations, architecture, challenges, and critical issues. IEEE Access **6**, 15679–15701 (2018)
8. Del Vecchio, P., Secundo, G., Maruccia, Y., Passiante, G.: A system dynamic approach for the smart mobility of people: implications in the age of big data. Technol. Forecast. Soc. Change **149**, 119771 (2019)
9. El-Din, D.M., Hassanien, A.E., Hassanien, E.E.: Information integrity for multi-sensors data fusion in smart mobility. In: Hassanien, A.E., Bhatnagar, R., Khalifa, N.E.M., Taha, M.H.N. (eds.) Toward Social Internet of Things (SIoT): Enabling Technologies, Architectures and Applications. SCI, vol. 846, pp. 99–121. Springer, Cham (2020). https://doi.org/10.1007/978-3-030-24513-9_6
10. Elhoseny, M., Shankar, K.: Energy efficient optimal routing for communication in VANETs via clustering model. In: Elhoseny, M., Hassanien, A.E. (eds.) Emerging Technologies for Connected Internet of Vehicles and Intelligent Transportation System Networks. SSDC, vol. 242, pp. 1–14. Springer, Cham (2020). https://doi.org/10.1007/978-3-030-22773-9_1
11. Feldman, D., Schmidt, M., Sohler, C.: Turning big data into tiny data: constant-size coresets for k-means, PCA and projective clustering. In: Proceedings of the Twenty-Fourth Annual ACM-SIAM Symposium on Discrete Algorithms, pp. 1434–1453. Society for Industrial and Applied Mathematics (2013)
12. Feldman, D., Sugaya, A., Rus, D.: An effective coreset compression algorithm for large scale sensor networks. In: 2012 ACM/IEEE 11th International Conference on Information Processing in Sensor Networks (IPSN), pp. 257–268. IEEE (2012)
13. Feldman, D., Sung, C., Rus, D.: The single pixel GPS: learning big data signals from tiny coresets. In: Proceedings of the 20th International Conference on Advances in Geographic Information Systems, pp. 23–32. ACM (2012)
14. Feldman, D., Xiang, C., Zhu, R., Rus, D.: Coresets for differentially private k-means clustering and applications to privacy in mobile sensor networks. In: 2017 16th ACM/IEEE International Conference on Information Processing in Sensor Networks (IPSN), pp. 3–16. IEEE (2017)
15. Ganeshkumar, P., Vijayakumar, K.P., Anandaraj, M.: A novel jammer detection framework for cluster-based wireless sensor networks. EURASIP J. Wirel. Commun. Netw. **2016**(1), 1–25 (2016). https://doi.org/10.1186/s13638-016-0528-1
16. Ge, M., Bangui, H., Buhnova, B.: Big data for Internet of Things: a survey. Future Gener. Comput. Syst. **87**, 601–614 (2018)
17. Han, J.H., Shin, Y.S., Lee, S.H.: Smart mobility creating smart space: 3D smart aquarium bus. In: 2019 IEEE Transportation Electrification Conference and Expo, pp. 1–5. IEEE (2019)

18. Har-Peled, S., Mazumdar, S.: On coresets for k-means and k-median clustering. In: Proceedings of the Thirty-sixth Annual ACM Symposium on Theory of Computing, pp. 291–300. STOC 2004. ACM, New York (2004). https://doi.org/10.1145/1007352.1007400. http://doi.acm.org/10.1145/1007352.1007400

19. Hasrouny, H., Samhat, A.E., Bassil, C., Laouiti, A.: VANet security challenges and solutions: a survey. Veh. Commun. **7**, 7–20 (2017)

20. Hernafi, Y., Ahmed, M.B., Bouhorma, M.: Smart mobility and driver behavior correlated with vehicular networks under a social perception in smart cities. Int. J. Inf. Sci. Technol. **2**(2), 35–47 (2019)

21. Ikem, C.: Users as programmers: developing a vehicular interface notation for older users of smart vehicles. In: Proceedings of the 1st ACM Workshop on Emerging Smart Technologies and Infrastructures for Smart Mobility and Sustainability, pp. 15–19. ACM (2019)

22. Kalkundri, R.U., Khanai, R., Praveen, K.: Survey on security for WSN based VANET using ECC. Int. Ann. Sci. **8**(1), 30–37 (2020)

23. Karagiannis, D., Argyriou, A.: Jamming attack detection in a pair of RF communicating vehicles using unsupervised machine learning. Veh. Commun. **13**, 56–63 (2018)

24. Karmakar, B., Das, S., Bhattacharya, S., Sarkar, R., Mukhopadhyay, I.: Tight clustering for large datasets with an application to gene expression data. Sci. Rep. **9**(1), 3053 (2019)

25. Katto, J., Takeuchi, M., Kanai, K., Sun, H.: Road infrastructure monitoring system using e-bikes and its extensions for smart community. In: Proceedings of the 1st ACM Workshop on Emerging Smart Technologies and Infrastructures for Smart Mobility and Sustainability, pp. 43–44. ACM (2019)

26. Kosmanos, D., Karagiannis, D., Argyriou, A., Lalis, S., Maglaras, L.: RF jamming classification using relative speed estimation in vehicular wireless networks. arXiv preprint (2018). arXiv:1812.11886

27. Liang, J., Chen, J., Zhu, Y., Yu, R.: A novel intrusion detection system for vehicular ad hoc networks (VANETs) based on differences of traffic flow and position. Appl. Soft Comput. **75**, 712–727 (2019)

28. Liu, X., Xu, Y., Jia, L., Wu, Q., Anpalagan, A.: Anti-jamming communications using spectrum waterfall: a deep reinforcement learning approach. IEEE Commun. Lett. **22**(5), 998–1001 (2018)

29. Matos, A., Pinto, B., Barros, F., Martins, S., Martins, J., Au-Yong-Oliveira, M.: Smart cities and smart tourism: what future do they bring? In: Rocha, Á., Adeli, H., Reis, L.P., Costanzo, S. (eds.) WorldCIST'19 2019. AISC, vol. 932, pp. 358–370. Springer, Cham (2019). https://doi.org/10.1007/978-3-030-16187-3_35

30. Mokdad, L., Ben-Othman, J., Nguyen, A.T.: DJAVAN: detecting jamming attacks in vehicle ad hoc networks. Perform. Eval. **87**, 47–59 (2015)

31. Ning, Z., Xia, F., Ullah, N., Kong, X., Hu, X.: Vehicular social networks: enabling smart mobility. IEEE Commun. Mag. **55**(5), 16–55 (2017)

32. Osanaiye, O., Alfa, A., Hancke, G.: A statistical approach to detect jamming attacks in wireless sensor networks. Sensors **18**(6), 1691 (2018)

33. Pang, L., Chen, X., Shi, Y., Xue, Z., Khatoun, R.: Localization of multiple jamming attackers in vehicular ad hoc network. Int. J. Distrib. Sens. Netw. **13**(8) (2017)

34. Pang, L., Guo, P., Chen, X., Li, J., Xue, Z.: Estimating the number of multiple jamming attackers in vehicular ad hoc network. In: 2017 6th International Conference on Computer Science and Network Technology (ICCSNT), pp. 366–370. IEEE (2017)

35. Pereira, J., Ricardo, L., Luís, M., Senna, C., Sargento, S.: Assessing the reliability of fog computing for smart mobility applications in VANETs. Future Gener. Comput. Syst. **94**, 317–332 (2019)
36. Punal, O., Pereira, C., Aguiar, A., Gross, J.: Experimental characterization and modeling of RF jamming attacks on VANETs. IEEE Trans. Veh. Technol. **64**(2), 524–540 (2014)
37. Ros, F., Guillaume, S.: ProTras: a probabilistic traversing sampling algorithm. Exp. Syst. Appl. **105**, 65–76 (2018). https://doi.org/10.1016/j.eswa.2018.03.052
38. Šemanjski, I., Mandžuka, S., Gautama, S.: Smart mobility. In: 2018 International Symposium ELMAR, pp. 63–66. IEEE (2018)
39. Seuwou, P., Banissi, E., Ubakanma, G.: The future of mobility with connected and autonomous vehicles in smart cities. In: Farsi, M., Daneshkhah, A., Hosseinian-Far, A., Jahankhani, H. (eds.) Digital Twin Technologies and Smart Cities. IT, pp. 37–52. Springer, Cham (2020). https://doi.org/10.1007/978-3-030-18732-3_3
40. Solmaz, G., et al.: Learn from IoT: pedestrian detection and intention prediction for autonomous driving. In: Proceedings of the 1st ACM Workshop on Emerging Smart Technologies and Infrastructures for Smart Mobility and Sustainability, pp. 27–32. ACM (2019)
41. Trang, L.H., Bangui, H., Ge, M., Buhnova, B.: Scaling big data applications in smart city with coresets. In: Proceedings of the 8th International Conference on Data Science, Technology and Applications. Prague, Czech Republic (2019)
42. Vanolo, A.: Smartmentality: the smart city as disciplinary strategy. Urban Stud. **51**(5), 883–898 (2014)
43. Zaffiro, G., Marone, G.: Smart mobility: new roles for telcos in the emergence of electric and autonomous vehicles. In: 2019 AEIT International Conference of Electrical and Electronic Technologies for Automotive (AEIT AUTOMOTIVE), pp. 1–5. IEEE (2019)

Human Aspects of Security and Privacy

Assisting Users to Create Stronger Passwords Using ContextBased MicroTraining

Joakim Kävrestad[(✉)] and Marcus Nohlberg

University of Skövde, Skövde, Sweden
{joakim.kavrestad,marcus.nohlberg}@his.se

Abstract. In this paper, we describe and evaluate how the learning framework ContextBased MicroTraining (CBMT) can be used to assist users to create strong passwords. Rather than a technical enforcing measure, CBMT is a framework that provides information security training to users when they are in a situation where the training is directly relevant. The study is carried out in two steps. First, a survey is used to measure how well users understand password guidelines that are presented in different ways. The second part measures how using CBMT to present password guidelines affect the strength of the passwords created. This experiment was carried out by implementing CBMT at the account registration page of a local internet service provider and observing the results on user-created passwords. The results of the study show that users presented with passwords creation guidelines using a CBMT learning module do understand the password creation guidelines to a higher degree than other users. Further, the experiment shows that users presented with password guidelines in the form of a CBMT learning module do create passwords that are longer and more secure than other users. The assessment of password security was performed using the zxcvbn tool, developed by Dropbox, that measures password entropy.

Keywords: Security training · Passwords · ContextBased MicroTraining · CBMT

1 Introduction

As the digital era continues, almost everyone around the world is becoming ever more present online. As our dependence on digital services increases so does our need for information security, and a key aspect of information security is security behavior including the ability to select good passwords to protect our social media accounts, work accounts, encrypted data and more. However, there is a wealth of papers demonstrating that users tend to select passwords that are easy to guess for an attacker [1–3]. Practitioners, as well as researchers, continuously try to find ways to make users select good passwords, by enforcing complexity rules or using different support systems [4, 5]. Another commonly proposed solution is to use other means of authentication instead of, or in combination with, passwords. Those other means of authentication include one-time passwords, hardware tokens, and password managers, and while the security benefits are undeniable

© IFIP International Federation for Information Processing 2020
Published by Springer Nature Switzerland AG 2020
M. Hölbl et al. (Eds.): SEC 2020, IFIP AICT 580, pp. 95–108, 2020.
https://doi.org/10.1007/978-3-030-58201-2_7

they fail to be widely adopted [6]. A common denominator for why users select not to adopt a more secure behavior is usability, users seem to prefer ease of use over security [7, 8]. As such, a fundamental demand of any security function, especially one designed for the general population, should be usability.

In this paper, we consider a password to be a socio-technical property and argue that a secure password mechanism, for instance, an account registration web site, must not only consider computational security, but also the user. As argued by [9], a password mechanism's effectiveness relies on its ability to make a user select a good password willingly. Yet another important factor in information security is awareness [10]. It is widely believed that users will act more securely if they are aware of the risks of insecure behavior. A common suggestion for how to make users more aware is to train them. In this paper, we propose and analyze how the use of a novel training approach can make users select good passwords during password creation.

The aim of this study is to implement and test how the learning method called ContextBased MicroTraining (CBMT) can assist users in creating stronger passwords. The aim is studied using a two-step method beginning with a survey where participants are asked to create an account. During account creation, the participants are faced with password creation guidelines in different ways and the survey measures how well they learned the password guidelines that were proposed for the survey. The second step involved an experiment were users set to register an account for a local Internet Service Provider were presented with password creating guidelines presented according to the principles of CBMT. The passwords were evaluated and measured against passwords created by a control group that was not faced with any password creation guidelines. The results of this paper will be a demonstration of how CBMT can be implemented. The contexts of passwords were chosen since is easy to measure the effect on passwords strength and passwords are unarguably crucial to security today.

The rest of this paper is structured as follows. Section 2 describes ContextBased MicroTraining (CBMT) and the password creation guidelines that were handed to participants in the study. Section 3 describes the methodology used. Section 4 presented the results of the study before it is concluded in Sect. 5.

2 Background

This research demonstrates how CBMT can be used to train users to select good passwords and measures the effects of using CBMT in a real-world context. Therefore, this chapter is devoted to an explanation of what CBMT is and the theoretical foundation of CBMT. Further, the password guidelines proposed in the CBMT learning modules are explained and motivated.

2.1 CBMT

CBMT is a theoretical framework that outlines how information security training of users can be executed. In essence, CBMT can be summarized as follows [11]:

"CBMT stipulates that training should be delivered in short sequences, in an accessible format, when needed".

On a more practical note, this means that training designed according to the principles of CBMT should be implemented so that it is presented to a computer user when he or she is in a situation where the training is of direct relevance. Further, it should be presented in a way that is easy to understand and short to minimize disruption [12].

The CBMT framework is based on the principle that people need motivation to learn. The idea is that the likelihood that any adult will learn is increased if the knowledge seems meaningful for the learner [13]. This notion is based on the concept of andragogy as presented by Knowles [14]. Knowles [14] argues that adults need the motivation to learn. The foundation in this way of thinking is that the learner will learn better if the knowledge presented seems meaningful. One way to accomplish this is to present knowledge in a context where it is applicable. As discussed by Herrington and Oliver [15], presenting knowledge to learners in a situation where the knowledge is applicable will cause a more meaningful learning experience. This is the first requirement that CBMT tries to facilitate. Also, by providing knowledge to a user when the user needs it brings a reminding effect. In this particular case, a user creating a password will be reminded to select a strong password. As discussed by [16], reminding users to behave in a secure way is likely to be effective in the information security domain.

Further, an obstacle in the sense of providing the computer user with knowledge about information security has been to make the users participate in education. One technique that has gained an increasing interest in recent years is microlearning or similar strategies including nanolearning and micro-training. As described by Wang, Xiao [17], nanolearning is a teaching method where information is presented in short sequences. The idea is to facilitate just-in-time learning meaning that information is provided in small chunks, thus making the time needed to absorb the information short and in an on-demand fashion [18]. As described by Bruck, Motiwalla [19], there has been research showing positive results of microlearning both in terms of learner participation and satisfaction. Microtraining is the second fundamental building block of ContextBased MicroTraining.

CBMT can be described as a framework that describes learning objects from two directions. The first direction concerns the delivery of the learning objects and states that the learning objects should be short sequences delivered in an on-demand fashion. The second direction concerns the content of the learning objects. In this respect, CBMT demands that the information presented in a learning module is of immediate use to the learner and therefore assumes that the information is relevant to the user in the users´ current context. In this respect, CBMT tries to facilitate the concept of "learn by doing" theories that can be summarized as describing that learners learn better when they perform tasks instead of just reading [20]. CBMT is also a learning method that includes aspects of problem-based learning (PBL) in that it is designed to guide the learner through real-world tasks [21]. In summary, the meaningfulness is achieved by the learner doing some task related to his or her situation.

CBMT was first introduced by [22] and [23] who argued that CBMT could be used as an efficient way to counter online fraud. CBMT has been further evaluated in [11] where study participants reported that they perceived CBMT as a good way to learn about security [11]. CBMT has also been used to develop teaching material for technical courses in higher education with success [12].

In this study, CBMT is implemented as a means of teaching users how to create strong passwords at the point of account registration. In essence, a learning module is presented when a user that is creating an account hits the "create password" field. The module contains guidelines for how to create a strong password, as outlined in the next section. The approach, in this case, is inspired by security nudges as described by [24] but attempts to combine passive support with active intervention. At the end of the module, the user is asked to create her password. The steps of the learning module is presented in Fig. 1, below.

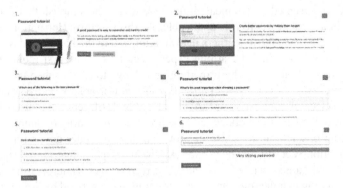

Fig. 1. Implementation of CBMT used in this study

The first part of the learning module presents the user with some fundamental password guidelines. The user may then continue to learn even more. After the second window, the user can test herself by answering three questions about the presented guidelines. An incorrect answer will generate feedback, and a correct answer will allow the user to continue. In the final windows, the user can create her password. A strength meter is also present on the last page. The user may choose to go directly to the last page from the first or second page.

2.2 Password Guidelines

This paper is concerned with teaching users to select good passwords. What a good password actually is, is a question that is debated among scientists as well as practitioners. For instance, as of October 4th 2019, Microsoft suggest long and easy to remember passwords while Apple and Yahoo suggest that a password should include as many different character groups as possible [25–27]. Looking to influential standardizing organizations, NIST now suggest that password guidelines should suggest long passwords that are easy to remember, such as passphrases [28]. On the other hand, ENISA suggest mixing character types [29]. ISO/IEC 27002:2017, as another example, does state that a good password should be easy to remember but does also discourage the use of words in passwords [30].

The password guidelines used in this paper are based on ongoing research into strong and memorable passwords and are based on [31]. They are designed to generate long passwords and read as follows:

- A good password is hard to crack and easy to remember.
- It should consist of at least four words.
- The password should not contain information relating to the password holder.
- Passwords should never be written down.
- A password can be made unique by adding the name of the site or service where it is used to itself.

3   Methodology

This paper seeks to evaluate whether the presented CBMT learning module can assist users in creating stronger passwords. As described by [32], scientific validity is enhanced if a problem is researched from several angles. This study was carried out in two steps beginning with a survey were the participants were asked to create an account and then answer some questions about the password guidelines that was presented to them upon account creation. Then the learning module was implemented on the account creation site of a local ISP. The survey measured how well the users took notice of the presented guidelines and the experiment measured the actual effect the learning module had on password strength. To ensure compliance with ethical guidelines [33], care was taken to ensure that no passwords was disclosed to the researchers or any external party. An overview of the research process is shown in Fig. 2, below.

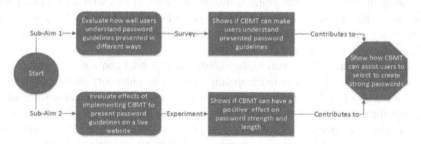

Fig. 2. Research process overview

Throughout the study, two different metrics was used to measure password strength. The first metric was password length in characters. The second metric is called score and is derived from zxcvbn, a password strength estimator developed by Dropbox [34]. According to a large study by [35], zxcvbn was found to be the most accurate password strength estimator. While zxcvbn calculates a number of metrics, the only one used in this paper is called score. The score is a value between 0 and 4 and the scored are described as follows [36]:

- 0# too guessable: risky password. (guesses $< 10^3$)
- 1# very guessable: protection from throttled online attacks. (guesses $< 10^6$)
- 2# somewhat guessable: protection from unthrottled online attacks. (guesses $< 10^8$)
- 3# safely unguessable: moderate protection from offline slow-hash scenario. (guesses $< 10^{10}$)

- 4# very unguessable: strong protection from offline slow-hash scenario. (guesses $\geq 10^{10}$)

The score is based on how many attempts an attacker would have to make to guess a password (entropy). To calculate the entropy, zxcvbn takes several factors into account including:

- Password length, longer passwords mean higher entropy.
- Password complexity, use of different character types mean higher entropy.
- Occurrence of common passwords, use of passwords common in leaked databases mean lower entropy, and use of individual words such as "potato".
- Repeated patterns, repeating patterns such as abcabcbabc mean lower entropy.

The full and exact algorithm used is presented in [36]. Both the score and the password length are considered to be numerical values in all statistical analyses used in this paper. The reminder of this section will detail the survey and the experiment.

3.1 Survey Test

The first part of the study was a survey designed to measure if the participants paid attention to the password creation guidelines presented to them during account creation. The survey itself was not anonymized. Instead, the participants were asked to register an account with their e-mail address and a password of their choosing. They were also told that they would receive personal feedback containing their answers and a summary of the answers from the rest of the population.

The participants were invited to the survey via an e-mail containing a survey link. The survey was distributed to municipalities as well as university staff and students. The link led to a web-based informed consent form where the participants were asked to accept the conditions of the study. Upon accepting the conditions, the participants were randomly assigned to one of three groups; CBMT, TEXT, and LINK. They were then forwarded to the first part of the survey, account creation. During account creation, the participants were asked to register their e-mail and create a password. Password guidelines were shown the participants in the following different ways:

- The CBMT group was shown the CBMT module after clicking on the "select password" box.
- The TEXT-group was given the same guidelines in plain text just above the registration form.
- The LINK-group was shown a link to text-based password guidelines labeled "Click here to learn more about good passwords".

Following registration, the password was analyzed as previously described and the participants were handed questions about demographic aspects including their IT-competence. Following the demographic questions, the participants were given the following questions about the password guidelines that was shown to them during account creation:

- Concerning the password guidelines presented on the previous page, how long passwords were suggested?
- What was suggested as a way to create strong passwords?
- What was described as most important for a password to be secure?
- What was described as most important of the following?
- What tip was given on how to create unique passwords for each of your accounts?

The first question was designed to see if the user's noticed the main point of the guidelines, the password length suggestion of four words. Questions two and three were used to see if the users understood the secondary suggestions, creating long and memorable passwords. The final two questions measured if users noticed tips that were presented at later stages in the guidelines, on how to make passwords even better and unique. In data analysis, two indexes were created. One that reflected how many correct answers each respondent gave to the first three questions and one index of correct answers to all questions. The results for the first question were also analyzed on its own.

For data analysis, the survey data were grouped based on the three test-groups. The participants were further grouped based on their reported IT-competence since previous research suggests that IT-competence is a key factor in security behavior [37]. The Shapiro-Wilks test was used to test whether the generated data were normally distributed [38], and the means and median are reported for the three variables (the first question and the indexes) in all groups. Based on central tendencies observed using descriptive statistics, hypothesis testing was used to evaluate if the tendencies were significant. Because of space limitations, the results are presented in condensed form. The hypotheses were expressed as follows:

H1: Group X scores higher than group Y regarding variable Z
H0: There is no difference between groups X and Z regarding variable Y

Further, Mann-Whitney U-test was used for hypothesis testing. Mann-Whitney U-test was selected in favor of T-test since no samples were normally distributed and are therefore more suitable than T-test [39]. The significance level used in this study is the conventional 95% meaning that results are significant if $p < 0.05$. SPSS was used for statistical analysis.

3.2 Experiment

In the second part of the study, the learning module presented in Sect. 2.1 was implemented on the account registration page of a local ISP. It was implemented so that 50% of the visitors used the learning module when they registered their account and the other 50% was presented with an unmodified version of the registration page. The unmodified registration page does not propose any password guidelines and is displayed in Fig. 3, below.

The password entered during the testing period was analyzed and password length and score were captured. Whether or not the password was created using the learning module was also recorded to allow for analysis of the effects of the learning module. For data analysis, the test data were grouped based on whether the passwords were

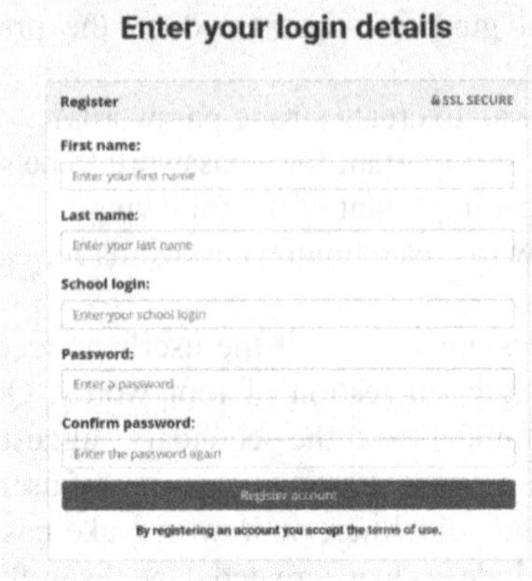

Fig. 3. Unmodified registration page

created using the CBMT module or not. The Shapiro-Wilks test was used to test if the generated data was normally distributed [38], then means and median was reported for the two variables in both groups. Further, Mann-Whitney U-test was used to differences in values between the two groups. Mann-Whitney U-test was used since no samples were normally distributed and are therefore more suitable than T-test [39]. The significance level used in this study is the conventional 95% meaning that results are significant if p < 0.05.

4   Results

This section details the results gathered from the two parts of the study.

4.1   Survey

The survey was completed by 179 participants distributed among the answer groups as follows:

- CBMT: 54
- TEXT: 68
- LINK: 57

61 of the respondents rated the IT-competence as being "IT-professionals", 50 respondents were students, 121 were working and 8 respondents reported having some other occupation. A majority of the respondents were between 20 and 30 years old (120), 31 were between 31 and 40 years and the rest were older. Following the calculations of the indexes, the mean and median values for the different metrics are displayed in Table 1, below. The measures were not normally distributed in any group, mean and median values are displayed once for all respondents and then once for all respondents that did not report being IT-professionals.

Table 1. Mean and median values or metrics from survey

Variable	Group	Mean	Mean_noIT	Median	Median_noIT
Q1	CBMT	0,59	0,69	1	1
Q1	TEXT	0,40	0,38	0	0
Q1	LINK	0,19	0,16	0	0
Index1_3	CBMT	1,61	1,75	1	2
Index1_3	TEXT	1,27	1,20	1	1
Index1_3	LINK	0,77	0,67	1	0
Index1_5	CBMT	2,20	2,44	2	2
Index1_5	TEXT	1,86	1,84	2	2
Index1_5	LINK	1,31	1,18	1	1

As seen in Table 1, the CBMT group has the highest score for all metrics, followed by the group TEXT. The group LINK that only saw a link to password creation guidelines is last in all cases. Furthermore, the values for all metrics in the CBMT group increases when the responses from IT-professionals are disregarded. The same action fields the opposite result in the group TEXT.

Looking at the descriptive statistics in Table 1, the users that were presented with password guidelines using CBMT appears to understand the contents of the guidelines to a higher degree than in the other groups. Mann-Whitney U-test was used to test if the observed tendency is significant. The test was applied pairwise and for the complete answer groups as well as for all respondents except the IT-professionals. The test and results are presented in Table 2, below.

Table 2. Results of Mann-Whitney U-test, results are significant if $p < 0.05$.

Variable	Case	P	P_noit
Q1	CBMT-TEXT	0,033	0,013
Q1	CBMT-LINK	0,000	0,000
Q1	TEXT-LINK	0,014	0,031
Index1_3	CBMT-TEXT	0,087	0,03
Index1_3	CBMT-LINK	0,000	0,000
Index1_3	TEXT-LINK	0,004	0,019
Index1_5	CBMT-TEXT	0,203	0,091
Index1_5	CBMT-LINK	0,000	0,000
Index1_5	TEXT-LINK	0,009	0,019

As seen in Table 2, all test values involving the group LINK are significant, showing that the participants shown a link to password guidelines understands the passwords guidelines to a lower degree than users shown the guidelines in text or using CBMT. Further, the test values for CBMT-TEXT are significant for Q1, showing that the users of CBMT does understand the key part of the guidelines better than the other groups. Further, the value for CBMT-TEXT for Index1_3 is significant if users that consider themselves IT-professionals are disregarded.

In conclusion, the results of the survey show that using CBMT or just plain text to present password guidelines is significantly better than presenting users with a link to the guidelines. Further, the results suggest that CBMT will make the users notice the password guidelines better than presenting the guidelines as text. It is also worth mentioning that the observed results are more significant amongst users that do not consider themselves IT-professionals.

4.2 Experiment

In the experiment, a CBMT module showing the password guidelines was implemented at the account registration page of a local ISP. The passwords created by the users during the experiment were analyzed. A password score and the password length was registered. The passwords were never made available to the researchers but keep confidential by the ISP. During the test period, data was gathered from 124 users that created new accounts. 64 was presented with the CBMT learning module (This group is referred to as CBMT) and 60 was presented with the unmodified registration page (This group is called control). The mean values for password length and score are presented in Table 3, below.

Table 3. Descriptive statistics from experiment data

Variable	Group	Mean	Median	Normality test
Length	CBMT	11.14	11	Not normally distributed
Length	Control	10.52	9.5	Not normally distributed
Score	CBMT	3.06	3	Not normally distributed
Score	Control	2.40	2	Not normally distributed

As seen in Table 1, the values from the CBMT group is higher for password length as well as score. Further, no datasets were normally distributed and thus, the median is the most accurate measure. Reading the median values, the CBMT group scored 1.5 characters higher in password length and 1 higher in password score. The descriptive statistics bring the following hypotheses for testing:

H1: Users presented password guidelines in the form of a CBMT learning module create longer passwords than users not presented with any guidelines.
H2: Users presented password guidelines in the form of a CBMT learning module create passwords with a higher score than users not presented with any guidelines.

The corresponding null hypotheses are that no such difference can be observed. Mann-Whitney U-test was used to test if the observed tendency is significant. The results are presented in Table 4, below.

Table 4. Results of Mann-Whitney U-test, results are significant if $p < 0.05$

Variable	Group	Mean rank	Sum of ranks	P
Length	CBMT	70.15	4489.50	0.013
Length	Control	54.34	3260.50	
Score	CBMT	71.96	4605.50	0.002
Score	Control	52.41	3144.50	

As seen in Table 4, Mean rank and Sum of rank columns indicates that the passwords in the CBMT group are longer and have a higher score. The p-values are below 0.05 in both cases showing that the results are significant. In conclusion, the null hypotheses can be rejected in favor of H1 and H2. Thus, the experiment shows that the users who used CBMT to create passwords created stronger passwords than the users that used the unmodified registration page.

5 Conclusions

This paper presents the learning framework CBMT and analyzes if it can be used to help users create good passwords. The study explores the aim from two different directions; first by using a survey to measure to what degree users understand password creation guidelines presented in different ways and second, by implementing CBMT on the registration page of a local ISP and analyze the actual impact on password strength and length. Length and strength are used as independent measures since it is possible to create a longer password that is computationally weaker than a shorter. The results of the survey suggest that users that are presented with password creation guidelines with CBMT modules do indeed understand the guidelines to a higher degree than if users are presented with the guidelines as text, or with a link to password creation guidelines elsewhere. From the survey data, it is also worth mentioning that presenting password creation guidelines as text is better than a link. Furthermore, the results of the experiment show that using CBMT helps users create passwords that are longer and stronger than if the users are not presented with any password creation guidelines at all. As such, this paper concludes that using CBMT to present password creation guidelines will lead to users creating better passwords and understand the password creation guidelines to a higher degree than if the guidelines are presented in other ways.

This paper shows that CBMT can assist users in the creation of good passwords. However, it is interesting to notice that not even the participants that used CBMT noticed the presented guidelines to a very high degree. Looking at the most emphasized tip, using 4 words as the password only 59% of the respondents in the CBMT group remembered the tip. Looking at the scores for the index of all five questions the mean value in the CBMT group was 2.2 of 5. These numbers suggest that it is hard to make users notice password creation guidelines at all. An explanation could be that users are simply not too concerned with security, or that they do not care about what a certain application proposes.

It is, however, also interesting to see that CBMT has a high impact on password quality. In this particular example, the mean password strength was increased by 1 on a 0–4 scale and the mean password length was increased by 1.5. The increase in password strength has an undeniable and direct effect on security since the passwords are much harder to crack. One explanation as to why the users using CBMT select stronger passwords might be that they understand the password creation guidelines to a greater extent. However, the relatively low scores from the survey suggests that that may not be a complete explanation. Another explanation can be that the CBMT forces the users to integrate with it and thus, reminds them of security.

The implications of this paper are twofold. The paper demonstrates and validates a concrete method for the presentation of password guidelines. The method described in this paper can be implemented by practitioners seeking to increase password security in their organization. The paper also presents a framework for how information security training can be used to improve user's security behavior. As such, the paper contributes to the scientific and practitioner community with new insights into the information security training domain.

Following this study, future projects could further examine the results presented in this paper with more studies using other and larger samples. Another direction for future research could be to analyze how CBMT can be used in other information security contexts to, for instance, assist users in dealing with online fraud, fake news or phishing. It would also be interesting to examine the long term effects of using CBMT. Knowledge retention and organizational security awareness are good starting points. A future study could examine the password culture before, during and after using CBMT for information security training.

References

1. Kävrestad, J., Eriksson, F., Nohlberg, M.: Understanding passwords–a taxonomy of password creation strategies. Inf. Comput. Secur. **27**(3), 453–467 (2019)
2. Wang, C., Jan, S.T., Hu, H., Bossart, D., Wang, G.: The next domino to fall: empirical analysis of user passwords across online services. In: Proceedings of the Eighth ACM Conference on Data and Application Security and Privacy. ACM (2018)
3. Woods, N., Siponen, M.: Too many passwords? How understanding our memory can increase password memorability. Int. J. Hum. Comput. Stud. **111**, 36–48 (2018)
4. Brumen, B.: Security analysis of game changer password system. Int. J. Hum. Comput. Stud. **126**, 44–52 (2019)
5. Shay, R., et al.: Designing password policies for strength and usability. ACM Trans. Inf. Syst. Secur. **18**(4), 1–34 (2016)
6. Petsas, T., Tsirantonakis, G., Athanasopoulos, E., Ioannidis, S.: Two-factor authentication: is the world ready?: Quantifying 2FA adoption. In: Proceedings of the Eighth European Workshop on System Security. ACM (2015)

7. Das, S., Dingman, A., Camp, L.J.: Why Johnny doesn't use two factor a two-phase usability study of the FIDO U2F security key. In: Meiklejohn, S., Sako, K. (eds.) FC 2018. LNCS, vol. 10957, pp. 160–179. Springer, Heidelberg (2018). https://doi.org/10.1007/978-3-662-58387-6_9
8. Whitten, A., Tygar, J.D.: Why Johnny can't encrypt: a usability evaluation of PGP 5.0. In: USENIX Security Symposium (1999)
9. Weirich, D., Sasse, M.A.: Pretty good persuasion: a first step towards effective password security in the real world. In: Proceedings of the 2001 Workshop on New Security Paradigms. ACM (2001)
10. Safa, N.S., Sookhak, M., Von Solms, R., Furnell, S., Ghani, N.A., Herawan, T.: Information security conscious care behaviour formation in organizations. Comput. Secur. **53**, 65–78 (2015)
11. Kävrestad, J., Skärgård, M., Nohlberg, M.: Users perception of using CBMT for information security training. In: Human Aspects of Information Security & Assurance (HAISA 2019) Nicosia (2019)
12. Kävrestad, J., Nohlberg, M.: Using context based micro training to develop OER for the benefit of all. In: Proceedings of the 15th International Symposium on Open Collaboration. ACM (2019)
13. Hedin, A.: Lärande på hög nivå. Uppsala Universitet (2006)
14. Knowles, M.S.: Andragogy in Action: Applying Principles of Adult Learning. Jossey-Bass, San Farancisco (1984)
15. Herrington, J., Oliver, R.: Critical characteristics of situated learning: implications for the instructional design of multimedia (1995)
16. Parsons, K., Butavicius, M., Lillie, M., Calic, D., McCormac, A., Pattinson, M.: Which individual, cultural, organisational and inerventional factors explain phishing resilience? In: Twelfth International Symposium on Human Aspects of Information Security & Assurance, Dundee, Scotland, UK. University of Plymouth (2018)
17. Wang, M., Xiao, J., Chen, Y., Min, W.: Mobile learning design: the LTCS model. In: 2014 International Conference on Intelligent Environments (IE). IEEE (2014)
18. McLoughlin, C., Lee, M.: Mapping the digital terrain: new media and social software as catalysts for pedagogical change. Ascilite Melbourne (2008)
19. Bruck, P.A., Motiwalla, L., Foerster, F.: Mobile learning with micro-content: a framework and evaluation. In: Bled eConference, vol. 25 (2012)
20. Koedinger, K.R., Kim, J., Jia, J.Z., McLaughlin, E.A., Bier, N.L.: Learning is not a spectator sport: doing is better than watching for learning from a MOOC. In: 2015 Proceedings of the Second ACM Conference on Learning@ Scale. ACM (2015)
21. Boud, D., Feletti, G.: The Challenge of Problem-Based Learning. Psychology Press, Routledge (2013)
22. Kävrestad, J., Nohlberg, M.: Online fraud defence by context based micro training. In: HAISA (2015)
23. Werme, J.: Security awareness through micro-training: an initial evaluation of a context based micro-training framework (2014)
24. Furnell, S., Esmael, R., Yang, W., Li, N.: Enhancing security behaviour by supporting the user. Comput. Secur. **75**, 1–9 (2018)
25. Microsoft. Security Identifier (2019). https://docs.microsoft.com/en-us/windows/security/identity-protection/access-control/security-identifiers#security-identifier-architecture. Accessed 2019
26. Yahoo: Password tips (n.d.). https://safety.yahoo.com/Security/STRONG-PASSWORD.html
27. Apple. Security and your Apple ID. (n.d.) https://support.apple.com/en-us/HT201303. Accessed 12 Sept 2019

28. Grassi, P., et al.: NIST special publication 800–63b: digital identity guidelines. National Institute of Standards and Technology (NIST) (2017)
29. ENISA. Authentication Methods (n.d.). https://www.enisa.europa.eu/topics/csirts-in-europe/glossary/authentication-methods. Accessed 04 Oct 2019
30. ISO/IEC, Information technology - Security techniques - Code of practice for information security controls. ISO/IEC (2017)
31. Kävrestad, J., Lennartsson, M., Birath, M., Nohlberg, M.: Constructing secure and memorable passwords. Inf. Comput. Secur. https://doi.org/10.1108/ICS-07-2019-0077
32. Lincoln, Y.S., Guba, E.G.: Naturalistic Inquiry, vol. 75. Sage (1985)
33. Schrittwieser, S., Mulazzani, M., Weippl, E.: Ethics in security research which lines should not be crossed? In: Security and Privacy Workshops (SPW), IEEE (2013)
34. Wheeler, D.L.: zxcvbn: low-budget password strength estimation. In: USENIX Security Symposium (2016)
35. XDCD Carnavalet, Mannan, M.: A large-scale evaluation of high-impact password strength meters. ACM Trans. Inf. Syst. Secur. (TISSEC) 18(1), 1 (2015)
36. Dropbox: Low-Budget Password Strength Estimation (2019). https://github.com/dropbox/zxcvbn. Accessed 07 Oct 2019
37. Siponen, M.T.: Five dimensions of information security awareness. SIGCAS Comput. Soc. 31(2), 24–29 (2001)
38. Mendes, M., Pala, A.: Type I error rate and power of three normality tests. Pak. J. Inf. Technol. 2(2), 135–139 (2003)
39. McKnight, P.E., Najab, J.: Mann-Whitney U test. Corsini Encycl. Psychol. 1 (2010)

Facilitating Privacy Attitudes and Behaviors with Affective Visual Design

Agnieszka Kitkowska[1]([⊠]), Yefim Shulman[2], Leonardo A. Martucci[1],
and Erik Wästlund[1]

[1] Karlstad University, Universitetsgatan 2, Karlstad, Sweden
`agnieszka.kitkowska@kau.se`
[2] Tel Aviv University, Tel Aviv, Israel

Abstract. We all too often must consent to information collection at an early stage of digital interactions, during application sign-up. Paying low attention to privacy policies, we are rarely aware of processing practices. Drawing on multidisciplinary research, we postulate that privacy policies presenting information in a way that triggers affective responses, together with individual characteristics, may influence privacy attitudes. Through an online quasi-experiment ($N = 88$), we investigate how affect, illustration type, personality, and privacy concerns may influence end-users' willingness to disclose information and privacy awareness. Our results partially confirm these assumptions. We found that the affect may have an impact on privacy awareness, and stable psychological factors may influence disclosures. We discuss the applicability of our findings in interface design and in future research.

Keywords: Privacy · Usability · Attitude · Behavior · Affect · Emotion

1 Introduction

Privacy and security breaches are regularly reported in media, but despite their awareness, people may over-disclose their personal information during online interactions [1]. Legal protections have been established, such as the General Data Protection Regulation (GDPR), aiming to improve the current privacy landscape and enhance informed consent as the primary disclosure enabler [11]. Yet, not all of the online services provide appropriate privacy-protective solutions.

The decisions shaping information disclosure usually begin during the sign-up process. At that point, the user must consent to the service providers' data handling practices. However, at that stage, privacy management is not a primary task, and the users may disregard privacy information presented in privacy notices. Current methods of policy display may promote such negligence with inadequate user interface (UI) design—non-transparent and challenging to comprehend [27]. For instance, it is a common practice to collect the consent with affirmative action: a tick of a checkbox approving "understanding" of the hyper linked text of privacy policy.

In search of new ways to overcome issues around consent, and to understand how to make consent more meaningful, we focus on affective states induced with visual design. In this paper, we assess their influence on information disclosure and privacy awareness in the context of the online sign-up process. Moreover, we look into the relationship between individual characteristics, affect, and privacy concerns. Our research objective is to identify how to improve end-users' privacy awareness at an early stage of interaction, and to advance the existing body of knowledge about privacy attitudes and behaviors. Our findings show that affective framing and arousal alter privacy-related attitudes and behaviors. The results also indicate how people may feel hopeless during early-stage interactions, lacking control over their data.

2   Background

The GDPR aims to protect users' privacy and has a direct impact on online companies, providing them with a set of rules regarding data collection and processing practices [11]. Predominantly, online services must deliver to users understandable and transparent information about data provision practices. Further, the GDPR enforces precise requirements regarding informed consent.

We follow the GDPR guidelines and test different designs of the privacy policy providing users with more transparent information. We draw on the definition of transparency and consent being informed by designing structured privacy policy, which emphasizes information collection and processing practices.

2.1   Visual Display, Learning and Attention

Past research has shown that visual stimuli may have an influence on attention and can improve learning [30]. Affective images may impact decisions by effects on the impression formation and decision-making [34]. Further, pictures may have an impact on a performance level; when external representations are available, the effects of the previously viewed visualization decrease, because individuals are less dependent on the existing mental images [30]. The visual design may also affect memory, when it includes animations, anthropomorphic designs, clear layouts such as division into columns and similar [36,38].

In the context of privacy, anthropomorphic designs may increase personal information disclosure [3,25]. Past work demonstrated that text was insufficiently communicating privacy information, and a different approach should be applied to enhance usability [2]. However, alternative design cannot be over-symbolic or cluttered (e.g., unnecessary icons). Moreover, comic strips were found to increase users' attention [37]. Comics convey a message in a way that relates to emotions, enabling a greater understanding of the outlined issues [26].

Past research revealed that the end-user agreements divided into short sections, elicited positive attitudes, increasing comprehension and time of exposure [39]. In our first research question, we aim to investigate privacy design issues:

RQ1: Does different illustration type applied in privacy policies influence privacy awareness and willingness to disclose information?

2.2 Factors Related to Decision-Making

Many factors influence decisions. At times, choices might be rational, e.g., when based on costs and benefits calculus carried out when people possess all the necessary information to compute the optimal outcome(s). Other times, peoples' decisions might be based on simple heuristics enabling effortless decisions, which can be made with limited information and within a short time [18,35].

In this work, we focus on some factors that may influence how people decide upon their privacy, whether their decisions are more or less informed. Particularly, we investigate privacy awareness (defined as participants' ability to recall information presented in the privacy policy); and willingness to disclose (defined as the extent to which users are willing to disclose their personal information to the well-being application service provider).

Affect and Information Processing. One of simple heuristics is the affect heuristic, when people make judgments based on subjective evaluations by adding either positive or negative value to the decision outcome [12]. The *affect-as-information* hypothesis postulates that affective states have cognitive consequences mediated by the subjective experience of affect [6]. Thus, emotions occur, and this feeling has a significant impact on cognitive processing, providing conscious information from unconscious appraisals. Such feelings can guide immediate actions and may create experiences (e.g., liking or disliking), resulting in a higher or lower evaluation of an object. Similarly, the *feelings-as-information* theory proposes that positive affect indicates that a given situation is safe [31]. Positive affect may serve as an incentive to rely on internal thoughts, whereas negative affect should direct attention to new external information, as it indicates whether a situation is safe. In sum, affect relates to recall, thought generation, and processing of new external information. Affective reactions may result from an external stimulus, such as the way information is presented or semantic context, in which the situation takes place.

In the context of privacy, affect may shape risk perceptions [19]. It may have a lasting impact on privacy beliefs (e.g., in an e-commerce environment [22]). Further, negative valence may increase privacy attitude and decrease sharing, while positive valence may increase sharing attitude and decrease privacy attitude [7]. To further examine affect in the context of privacy, we ask the following questions:

RQ2: Do the different designs of privacy policy elicit affective responses?
RQ3: Does affective framing applied in the design of privacy policies influence privacy awareness and willingness to disclose?

Antecedents of Privacy-Related Decision-Making. This research builds on the APCO (Antecedents→ Privacy Concerns→Outcomes) framework [8], because it has been created based on a thorough review of privacy studies from multidisciplinary fields. The APCO framework contains factors active during decision-making processes, enabling a deeper understanding of human aspects of privacy attitudes and behaviors. Following this model, we investigate privacy awareness and willingness to disclose as outcomes, and personality characteristics and privacy concerns as outcomes' antecedents.

Personality traits can influence privacy concerns [24]. The agreeableness, conscientiousness, and imagination can contribute to the formulation of "Concerns for Privacy" [17]. Additionally, personality may influence information disclosure [14]. Past research shows the effects of privacy concerns on disclosure, moderated by psychological biases and mental shortcuts [21,28]. Information disclosure may result from personal concerns, perceived threats, or only from user experience [20]. Considering the APCO model and past research, we raise the following question:

RQ4: Do individual characteristics and privacy concerns influence awareness and willingness to disclose information?

3   Methods

To address our research questions, we developed an online quasi-experiment (the random assignment was present, but the experiment lacked a control group) [32]. The dependent variables were willingness to disclose information, privacy awareness, and affective states (valence & arousal). The two independent variables were the design proprieties: affective framing (positive & negative) and illustration type (anthropomorphic & human). We controlled for the influence of privacy concerns and personality traits.

3.1   Participants

The participants were gathered on Reddit (r/samplesize). The respondents had to be at least 18 years old and fluent in English. Participation in the study was voluntary; no financial compensation was offered. We collected 99 responses. After data screening, the sample size reduced to 88. Almost half of the respondents was females ($N = 40$, 45%), and the majority was between 18–34 years old ($N = 37, 42\%$). Most of the participants completed higher education ($N = 50, 56.\%$). Over half of the participant were from English speaking countries (UK, USA and Canada—$N = 49, 55.6\%$).

3.2   Study Design

Before the study, the respondents had to acknowledge an informed consent form. Majority of questions was mandatory to answer, apart from the demographic questions. To reduce ordering effects, when possible, we implemented question-naires' item randomization. The study consisted of five phases.

Phase 1: Questionnaires. First, we measured *The Big Five* personality traits with the instrument acquired from Donallann et al. [9]. This method is a con-cise instrument validated in past research. The scale contains 20 items (four per each trait: extraversion, agreeableness, conscientiousness, neuroticism, and imagination). Next, the participants were presented with questions measuring their affective states through the "Affective Self Report" (ASR) acquired from Jenkins et al. [15]. The scale consists of ten items measuring the two-dimensional structure of affect: valence & arousal.

Phase 2: Vignette and Interactive Task. We asked the participants to imag-ine that they were signing up for a well-being application, aiming to help with the improvement of their physical and mental well-being. The participants were advised that the app offers social functionality, e.g., sharing, connecting with other users. They were instructed that over the next few pages, they would be exposed to the fictional sign-up form, asking for personal information, such as email address and password, but none of this data would be collected. Next, the participants were prompted to acknowledge the privacy policy. There were four different policy designs (Fig. 1): (1) a positively framed text with anthropomor-phic representation, (2) a positively framed text with human representation, (3) a negatively framed text with anthropomorphic representation, (4) a negatively framed text with human representation. We shortened the policy and struc-tured the text into thematically arranged paragraphs, with a header describing a particular section, e.g., "How we use your data". The Gunning's Fogg text readability score was 12.7, meaning that the text should be understandable by high school seniors [40]. Each privacy policy provided a binary choice: to "Agree" or to "Disagree".

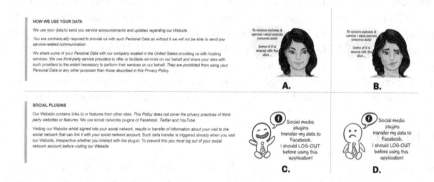

Fig. 1. Examples of the privacy policy sections accompanied by different types of fram-ing. Top row: human like illustration: A. Positive, B. Negative. Bottom row: anthro-pomorphic illustration: C. Positive, D. Negative.

Phase 3: Interactive Task's Exit Questionnaires. We measured the willingness to disclose information with a Likert-type instrument, based on the information disclosure scale proposed by Joinson et al. [16]. The participants were asked to think back about the sign-up process and state which pieces of information they would have disclosed. The scale consisted of 14 items of personal information, e.g., number of sexual partners. The responses scored 1 ("I would disclose") or 0 ("I would not disclose"). We took the 2nd measurement of the affect with the same instrument as in Phase 1, presenting participants with their scores and asking whether they wished to adjust them.

Phase 4: Questionnaires. We measured privacy awareness with a quiz-like questionnaire, assessing how much of the privacy information the participants remembered. We used ten questions related to the text from privacy policies, focusing on the text highlighted by framing images. The participants had a binary choice to select either "True" or "False". To measure privacy concerns, we used an instrument acquired from Malhotra et al. [23], containing six items presenting privacy statements. Participants were asked to declare to what extent they agreed or disagreed with the statements (1 – strongly disagree to 7 – strongly agree). We asked the participants for basic demographic information: gender, age group, nationality, and level of education.

Phase 5: Open-Ended Question. We asked the participants to explain why during the interactive task, they "Agreed", or "Disagreed" with policy. The participants were required to provide an answer.

Ethical Review. The study received ethical approval from the Karlstad University Ethical Review Board. There were no harms or risks associated with the study. We ensured that the data collection and processing was compliant with the GDPR. When possible, we applied data anonymization measures.

Variables in the Model. The between-subject variables were affective framing (AFRM: positive, negative), and illustration type (ILLT: anthropomorphic, human). The four dependent variables were: post-stimulus valence (VALP), post-stimulus arousal (AROP), willingness to disclose (WILD) and privacy awareness (PRAW). The covariates were: pre-stimulus arousal (PRAR) and valence (PREV); conscientiousness (CONS) and neuroticism (NEUR) (extraversion and agreeableness were removed, as they had no effect); privacy concerns (PRIC).

4 Results

The assessment of latent variables collected through self-reported instruments requires checks of validity and reliability. We used qualitative methods to check the face validity. To assess reliability, we applied the Cronbach α estimate, accepting scores higher than 0.7 [13].

Personality Traits. We ran Principal Component Analysis (PCA). Kaiser-Meyer-Olkin (KMO) measure was 0.70, and Bartlett's test for sphericity was significant, $p < 0.001$ [29]. Personality types did not load as expected into five factors [9], but into six factors, with *imagination* loading incorrectly. We removed this trait from further analysis. For each of the remaining constructs, we ran reliability tests, which all scored well, $\alpha > 0.7$.

Affect. We measured valence and arousal with the scale consisting of ten semantic differential items, five per each dimension. For both pre-, and post-stimulus measures, we ran the PCA to check factorability. The KMO scores were satisfying (pre: 0.84, and post: 0.86), and Bartlett's test for sphericity was significant ($p < 0.001$). The scores did not load properly. Hence we removed two items: "Tired-Energetic" and "Indifferent-Curious". We used five items to compute valence, and three to compute arousal.

Table 1. MANCOVA: effects of affective framing and illustration types on the dependent variables: post-stimuli arousal (AROP), post-stimuli valence (VALP), willingness to disclose (WILD), and privacy awareness (PRAW).

	Multivariate		Univariate			
	Wilks's λ	$F(4, 76)$	$F(1, 79)$			
			AROP	VALP	WILD	PRAW
Covariates						
PRAR	0.19	77.21**	79.96**	4.03*	4.70*	1.61
PREV	0.21	70.64**	1.31	85.32**	0.19	3.41
CONS	0.91	1.72	0.54	0.62	2.32	4.2*
NEUR	0.90	2.03	2.24	1.66	5.45*	0.76
PRIC	0.78	5.13*	7.31*	10.02*	11.59*	2.08
Fixed factors						
AFRM	0.87	2.66*	4.74*	3.21	0.90	6.33*
ILLT	0.97	0.54	0.22	0.02	0.06	1.28
AFRM*ILLT	0.91	1.74	4.97*	1.01	0.24	<0.01

Note: Significance values are based on *$p < 0.05$ and **$p < 0.001$.

Willingness to Disclose. The recommended estimate of scale reliability for dichotomous data is KR20 [5]. However, since Cronbach's α is a generalization of KR20, we interpreted its scores. The Cronbach's α was acceptable, 0.90 ($M = 6.68$, $\sigma^2 = 18.05$, $SD = 4.25$).

Privacy Awareness. The privacy awareness scores were measured as dichotomous data (Correct $= 1$, or Incorrect $= 0$). Privacy awareness scale assessed knowledge, not a latent construct; hence, we did not perform reliability checks. We applied an average of scores in further statistical analysis ($M = 0.58$, $SD = 0.13$).

Privacy Concerns. The results of the PCA were satisfying, but Cronbach's α scores for six items scale were below the commonly accepted threshold. We re-ran the analysis and used only four of the scale items (Cronbach's α was satisfactory) to compute the variable.

4.1 Statistical Analysis

We performed a multivariate analysis of covariance (MANCOVA). Before the test, we checked the assumptions (outliers with Mahalanobis distance; linearity; multicollinearity; univariate and multivariate normality; homogeneity and homoscedasticity). Next, we ran the final model and reevaluated homogeneity with a Box's test of equality of covariance matrices ($p = 0.15$) and Levene's tests of equality of variances ($p > 0.05$). The results of MANCOVA, using the Wilk's Lambda as a criterion, are presented in Table 1.

Effects of Covariates. PRAR ($\eta_p^2 = 0.80$), PREV ($\eta_p^2 = 0.78$), and PRIC ($\eta_p^2 = 0.21$) were the significant adjustors of the combined dependent variables.

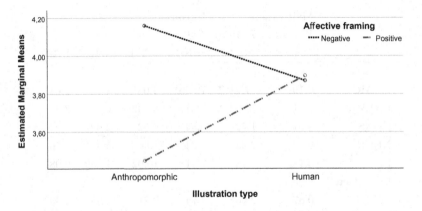

Fig. 2. Estimated marginal means for post-stimulus arousal (AROP). Covariates appearing in the model are evaluated at the following values: PRAR $= 3.58$, PREV $= 4.50$, PRIC $= 4.57$, CONS $= 12.52$, NEUR $= 11.32$.

Table 2. Significant correlations between covariates and outcome variables ($p < 0.01$).

	VALP	AROP	WILD
Pre-stimuli valence	0.77		
Pre-stimuli arousal	−0.33	0.84	
Privacy concerns	—	0.27	−0.38

We used individual ANCOVAs to examine their effect. PRAR was a significant adjustor of AROP ($\eta_p^2 = 0.50$), VALP ($\eta_p^2 = 0.05$), and WILD ($\eta_p^2 = 0.05$).

PREV had a significant influence on VALP ($\eta_p^2 = 0.52$). Some of these variables correlated significantly (Table 2). PRIC significantly influenced AROP ($\eta_p^2 = 0.08$), VALP ($\eta_p^2 = 0.11$), and WILD ($\eta_p^2 = 0.13$), with some correlating significantly (Table 2). Finally, there were significant effects of NEUR on WILD, and of CONS on PRAW; however, no significant correlations between these variables suggest that they might be weak influences of privacy decisions.

Effects of Independent Variables. After estimating out the covariates, AFRM had a significant effect on combined dependent variables ($\eta_p^2 = 0.12$) particularly on AROP ($\eta_p^2 = 0.06$). There was a difference in means of the two levels of AFRM on arousal ($p < 0.05$). The scores for post-stimuli arousal were higher among the participants assigned to negative ($M = 4.01,\ SD = 0.11$), than to positive ($M = 3.67,\ SD = 0.10$) stimulus. Although the effect of AFRM on VALP was not significant, valence scores were higher after exposure to positive ($M = 4.30,\ SD = 0.11$), than to negative ($M = 4.00,\ SD = 0.12$) stimulus.

AFRM had a significant influence on PRAW ($\eta_p^2 = 0.07$). The participants exposed to the negative stimulus scored higher ($M = 0.62,\ SD = 0.01$), than those exposed to the positive stimulus ($M = 0.55,\ SD = 0.01$).

There was a significant interaction effect between AFRM and ILLT on post-stimulus arousal—$\eta_p^2 = 0.60$ (Fig. 2). The arousal's mean was higher for the anthropomorphic negative affective state ($M = 4.16,\ SD = 0.16$), than for human negative affective state ($M = 3.87,\ SD = 0.16$). This effect was reversed for arousal means of the positive anthropomorphic design being lower ($M = 3.45,\ SD = 0.16$) than of the positive human design ($M = 3.89,\ SD = 0.15$).

Table 3. The main reasons for selecting "Disagree" and "Agree" with privacy policy [*Reason*(frequency of appearance)].

Disagree	*Lack of control*(13), *Social media*(7), *Unacceptable*(7), *Trust*(6), *Necessity of collection*(5), *Personal information*(4), *Fairness*(4), *Emotional response*(4), *Protection*(3), *Usability*(3), *Health information*(3), *Pictures help*(2), *Unauthorized sharing*(2), *Tracking*(1), *Legal requirement*(1), *Manipulation*(1)
Agree	*Lack of choice*(28), *Want to use app*(18), *Habit*(14), *Trust*(10), *Don't care*(8), *Not worse than others*(6), *Control*(5), *Somewhat clear*(4), *I can handle privacy*(4), *Protection*(3), *Legal requirement*(2), *Sunk cost*(2), *Consent if changes*(2), *Social media*(2), *Health*(1), *Underwhelming*(1), *Pictures help*(1)

4.2 Exploratory Findings

In the open-ended question, we asked participants why they "Agreed" (AGR) or "Disagreed" (DIS) with the privacy policy. Only 23 participants selected to disagree, and we did not find any significant associations between agreement with policies and the policy design.

All cases where participants stated that they had selected an option only to pursue the study were removed from the analysis, resulting in $N = 77$ answers (DIS $N = 22$, AGR $N = 55$). Two researchers read through the answers and, in a systematic manner, identified justification of the participants' choices, tagging them with a theme word. The tags were discussed and combined (Table 3).

Disagreeing. Sixteen reasons surfaced during the analysis of answers from the respondents who disagreed. The most frequent reason related to the *lack of control*; sharing personal data with *social media* platforms was the second most frequent. For instance, "The lack of control over personal data shared with third parties as well as the catch-22 of only using the Social platforms/forums if data was shared". Participants stated that the policy was *unacceptable*, or they did not *trust* the provider, e.g., because the data would be stored abroad: "The US govt could access this data, and it is not trustworthy".

Some respondents stated that there was not enough information about why data was collected (*necessity, fairness, personal information collection*). A few answers were *emotionally* loaded, e.g., "The main reason is that the pictures spelled it out in clear form what would happen to my information. As a result it made me sceptical to share my information". Only a few responses hinted that *pictures help* or mentioned *usability*, e.g., "Also, the drawings definitely gave the impression the policy was unfair".

Agreeing. Seventeen reasons were identified among those who agreed. The main was the *lack of choice*: "If signing up for a service there is a little choice. It can't be changed. The only option is to not do so". Another reason was that the participants *wanted to use* the application: "if I wanted to use the website, I would have to consent to the privacy Policy. So I did not really considered disagreeing as an option".

Many respondents admitted that agreement is something they always do, a *habit*, e.g., "Honestly, it's automatic. I'm not sure I even saw a disagree button. It's like a next button". On the other hand, a few admitted that they *did not care* about privacy, e.g., "I did not provide much of personal information. My name and email are already accessible, why worry?", or stated that the policy was *not worse than others*. Some participants thought that the policy provided them with *control*, it was *somewhat clear* and *trustworthy* (e.g., "the transparency of the company made me believe they were slightly more trustworthy").

5 Discussion

Design Implications. We studied the relationship between the illustration type, affective framing and their impact on privacy awareness and willingness to disclose (*RQ1–3*). Our results show that the policy display alters affective states. Moreover, the combined illustration type and affective framing interact and influence arousal. Particularly, the negative anthropomorphic representation accompanying structured text increases arousal. Yet, the same illustration type has a lower influence on arousal, when framed positively.

We have not found a direct relationship between the anthropomorphic designs and information disclosure, as suggested by Monteleone et al. [25]. Although we did not find a significant effect of the illustration type on privacy awareness (*RQ1*), we identified that framing of the designs has a significant impact on awareness (*RQ3*). Our findings are similar to the results from past research—the implementation of a cartoon-like design may increase attention [36, 37]. However, we determined that in the context of privacy, such an effect is possible only when brought by affective framing. Perhaps emotions mediate the relationship between design and privacy awareness. Our qualitative results add to such a premise, as some of the participants mentioned in emotionally loaded statements, that they comprehended privacy information because of the illustrations. These results indicate that comic designs can convey emotional meaning and improve understanding, as it has been demonstrated by Noll Webb et al. [26]. Nevertheless, such assumption requires confirmation from future studies.

Considering our results about policy display, we infer that the structured text display combined with affective framing may improve transparency and clarity of the privacy information. Such findings may be implemented in the design of privacy policies to encourage more informed end-users' decisions, and service providers' legal compliance. For instance, negatively framed visual cues might be displayed next to a particular section of the privacy notice. The cues could emphasize specific data processing practices, which may result in potential risks to privacy (e.g., overexposure of sensitive personal information such as health-related data to undesirable third parties).

Users' Needs. Our qualitative analysis showed that the sign-up process requires improvements. Our participants expressed the need for more control and choice at an early-stage of interaction. Such findings align with past research, e.g., a lack of control as one of the privacy concerns, and call for "fine-grained" control mechanisms as shown in Sheth et al. [33]. Our participants were dissatisfied with the current designs, exhibiting desperation and indicating usability issues. Concurrently with the GDPR, this calls for granular and dynamic privacy policies. Policy designers should focus on identifying new ways, in which privacy policy could provide end-users with opt-in/opt-out functionality at the early stage of interaction. For instance, one of such solutions could allow users to entirely disconnect the newly installed application from their social network tracking, through a simple interaction method (e.g., enable/disable toggles). Yet, such functionality would have to be non-intrusive as privacy management is not a primary task during the sign-up process. Additionally, some of the past research shows that too much perceived control over disclosure might lead to increased risks to privacy [4]. Hence, the design of control mechanisms requires balanced solutions that provide controls in a simplified form, with only necessary options, perhaps only for the riskiest data processing practices.

Implications for the Research Community. We found arousal to be the most significant adjuster of the willingness to disclose, with lower arousal carrying the potential to reduce disclosure. According to our results, privacy concerns negatively correlated with willingness to disclose (*RQ4*), which may indicate that people with greater concerns manage their information more carefully. On the other hand, similar to the past research [10], we found no relationship between personality traits and privacy awareness or willingness to disclose.

Our work contributes to the research field by examination of factors acquired from the APCO framework. We demonstrated that concerns might impact willingness to disclose. These findings add to the existing knowledge on the relationship between concerns and disclosure, showing that in the context of early-stage interactions, these two constructs correlate, contradictory to the widely discussed phenomenon of the *privacy paradox*. We interpret this relationship as the demand for personalized systems recognizing and estimating the level of individuals' privacy concerns. Before mentioned systems could trigger affect and seemingly decrease information disclosure (e.g., presenting less concerned users with negatively framed policy to bring their attention to privacy issues). However, such a personalized approach might be challenging itself as it requires the collection of personal information.

Further, our results confirm the applicability of cognitive hypotheses, such as *affect-as-feeling*, for the models of privacy interactions [6]. According to our findings, negative affect appears to direct participants' attention towards new information, and through activation of *cognitive feelings*, possibly influences information recall. This finding could be used not only by the researchers interested in studying privacy-related decision-making but also by designers. Perhaps privacy policies could elicit—through visual and interaction design—negative emotions and shift people's attention towards information included in the policy.

Limitations and Future Work. The primary constraint of this study is the measurement of affect with self-reported measures. The research validity would increase, was it run in the lab, enabling additional measurements, e.g., eye-tracking or electroencephalogram. Such information could improve the measurement's accuracy. As future work, we consider replicating the research in the lab environment.

We ran the exploratory study, and the sampling method might have introduced bias as we gathered data only from participants interested in the research, reducing potential generalization of the results. Yet, participants gathered through a paid-for platform might be less engaged in the study, and provide answers solely to receive financial compensation.

Future work should expand beyond the scenario of well-being application. This could help to identify contextual dependencies of the role of visual design and affective states in the early-stage interactions.

6 Conclusion

Frequently, privacy policies leave us in a blind spot, unaware of what we agreed to. In this work, we have examined the role of visual displays in the acquisition of privacy information. We have investigated how the activation of affective states influences privacy awareness and willingness to disclose. To identify possible improvements in visual representations of privacy policies, we have examined why people decide to agree or disagree with the policies.

Our results show that affective framing and arousal carry the potential to alter privacy-related attitudes and behaviors. Further, our qualitative findings show that people feel hopeless during early-stage interactions, neither having control nor choice around their data. The results can be used to design granular and dynamic consents that enable better management of personal information. Such solutions could enhance an individual's privacy, as well as help companies to comply with new regulations, such as the GDPR. The knowledge gained in this study can be applied as a backbone for future research on predictive modelling, as well as to build personalized privacy solutions.

Acknowledgement. This work has received funding from the European Union's Horizon 2020 research and innovation programme under the Marie Skłodowska-Curie grant agreement No 675730.

References

1. Acquisti, A., Brandimarte, L., Loewenstein, G.: Privacy and human behavior in the age of information. Science **347**(6221), 509–514 (2015)
2. Angulo, J., Fischer-Hübner, S., Wästlund, E., Pulls, T.: Towards usable privacy policy display and management. Inf. Manag. Comput. Secur. **20**(1), 4–17 (2012)
3. Bente, G., Dratsch, T., Rehbach, S., Reyl, M., Lushaj, B.: Do you trust my avatar? Effects of photo-realistic seller avatars and reputation scores on trust in online transactions. In: Nah, F.F.H. (ed.) HCIB 2014. LNCS, vol. 8527, pp. 461–470. Springer, Cham (2014). https://doi.org/10.1007/978-3-319-07293-7_45
4. Brandimarte, L., Acquisti, A., Loewenstein, G.: Misplaced confidences: privacy and the control paradox. Soc. Psychol. Pers. Sci. **4**(3), 340–347 (2013)
5. Carmines, E., Zeller, R.: Reliability and Validity Assessment, vol. 17. Sage Publications (1979)
6. Clore, G., Gasper, K., Garvin, E.: Affect as information. In: Handbook of Affect and Social Cognition, pp. 121–144 (2001)
7. Coopamootoo, K.P., Groß, T.: Why privacy is all but forgotten: an empirical study of privacy & sharing attitude. Proc. Priv. Enhancing Technol. **2017**(4), 97–118 (2017)
8. Dinev, T., Mcconnell, A., Smith, H.: Informing privacy research through information systems, psychology, and behavioral economics: thinking outside the "APCO" box. Inf. Syst. Res. **26**(4), 639–655 (2015)
9. Donnellan, M., Oswald, F., Baird, B., Lucas, R.: The mini-IPIP scales: tiny-yet-effective measures of the big five factors of personality. Psychol. Assess. **18**(2), 192–203 (2006)

10. Egelman, S., Peer, E.: Predicting privacy and security attitudes. ACM SIGCAS Comput. Soc. Newsl. **45**(1), 22–28 (2015)
11. European Commission: Regulation (EU) 2016/679 Of The European Parliament and Of The Council of 27 April 2016. Official Journal of the European Union (2016)
12. Finucane, M., Alhakami, A., Slovic, P., Johnson, S.: The affect heuristic in judgments of risks and benefits. J. Behav. Decis. Mak. **13**(1), 1–17 (2000)
13. Gliem, J.A., Gliem, R.R.: Calculating, interpreting, and reporting Cronbach's alpha reliability coefficient for likert-type scales. In: Midwest Research-to-Practice Conference in Adult, Continuing, and Community Education (2003)
14. Hollenbaugh, E., Ferris, A.: Facebook self-disclosure: examining the role of traits, social cohesion, and motives. Comput. Hum. Behav. **30**, 50–58 (2014)
15. Jenkins, S., Brown, R., Rutterford, N.: Comparing thermographic, EEG, and subjective measures of affective experience during simulated product interactions. Int. J. Des. **3**(2), 53–65 (2009)
16. Joinson, A., Paine, C., Buchanan, T., Reips, U.: Measuring self-disclosure online: blurring and non-response to sensitive items in web-based surveys. Comput. Hum. Behav. **24**(5), 2158–2171 (2008)
17. Junglas, I., Spitzmüller, C.: Personality traits and privacy perceptions: an empirical study in the context of location-based services. In: International Conference on Mobile Business, ICMB 2006, pp. 387–402 (2006)
18. Kahneman, D.: A perspective on judgment and choice. Am. Psychol. **3**(4), 7–18 (2003)
19. Kehr, F., Kowatsch, T., Wentzel, D., Fleisch, E.: Blissfully ignorant: the effects of general privacy concerns, general institutional trust, and affect in the privacy calculus. Inf. Syst. J. **25**(6), 607–635 (2015)
20. Knijnenburg, B., Kobsa, A.: Making decisions about privacy: information disclosure in context-aware recommender systems. ACM Trans. Interact. Intell. Syst. **3**(3), 1–23 (2013)
21. Krasnova, H., Kolesnikova, E., Guenther, O.: "It won't happen to me!": self-disclosure in online social networks. In: AMCIS 2009 Proceedings, p. 343 (2009)
22. Li, H., Sarathy, R., Xu, H.: The role of affect and cognition on online consumers' decision to disclose personal information to unfamiliar online vendors. Decis. Support Syst. **51**(3), 434–445 (2011)
23. Malhotra, N., Kim, S., Agarwal, J.: Internet users' information privacy concerns (IUIPC): the construct, the scale, and a causal model. Inf. Syst. Res. **15**(4), 336–355 (2004)
24. Miltgen, C., Peyrat-Guillard, D.: Cultural and generational influences on privacy concerns: a qualitative study in seven European countries. Eur. J. Inf. Syst. **23**(2), 103–125 (2014)
25. Monteleone, S., van Bavel, R., Rodríguez-Priego, N., Esposito, G.: Nudges to privacy behaviour: exploring an alternative approach to privacy notices. Technical report, European Commission (2015)
26. Noll Webb, E., Balasubramanian, G., Ó'Broin, U., Webb, J.: Wham! pow! comics as user assistance. J. Usability Stud. **7**(3), 105–117 (2012)
27. Obar, J.A., Oeldorf-Hirsch, A.: The biggest lie on the Internet: ignoring the privacy policies and terms of service policies of social networking services. Inf. Commun. Soc. **23**(1), 128–147 (2018)
28. Preibusch, S., Krol, K., Beresford, A.R.: The privacy eonomics of voluntary over-disclosure in web forms. In: Böhme, R. (ed.) The Economics of Information Security and Privacy, pp. 183–209. Springer, Heidelberg (2013). https://doi.org/10.1007/978-3-642-39498-0_9

29. Reio, J., Thomas, G., Shuck, B.: Exploratory factor analysis: implications for theory, research, and practice. Adv. Dev. Hum. Resour. **17**(1), 12–25 (2015)
30. Schnotz, W., Kü, C.: External and internal representations in the acquisition and use of knowledge: visualization effects on mental model construction. Instr. Sci. **36**, 176–190 (2007)
31. Schwarz, N.: Feelings-as-information theory. Handb. Theor. Soc. Psychol. **1**(January), 289–308 (2012)
32. Shadish, W.R., Cook, T.D., Campbell, D.T.: Experimental and quasi-experimental designs for generalized causal inference (2002)
33. Sheth, S., Kaiser, G., Maalej, W.: Us and them: a study of privacy requirements across North America, Asia, and Europe. In: Proceedings of the 36th ICSE, pp. 859–870 (2014)
34. Slovic, P.: The affect heuristic. In: Heuristics and Biases; The Psychology of Intuitive Judgement, pp. 397–420. Cambridge University Press (2002)
35. Stanovich, K.E., West, R.F.: Individual differences in reasoning: implications for the rationality debate? Behav. Brain Sci. **23**(5), 645–665 (2000)
36. Sutcliffe, A., Namoune, A.: Getting the message across: visual attention, aesthetic design and what users remember. In: Proceedings of the 7th ACM Conference on Designing Interactive Systems, pp. 11–20. ACM (2008)
37. Tabassum, M., Alqhatani, A., Aldossari, M., Richter Lipford, H.: Increasing user attention with a comic-based policy. In: CHI 2018. ACM (2018)
38. Tasse, D., Ankolekar, A., Hailpern, J.: Getting users' attention in web apps in likable, minimally annoying ways. In: Proceedings of the 2016 CHI Conference on Human Factors in Computing Systems, pp. 3324–3334 (2016)
39. Waddell, T., Auriemma, J., Sundar, S.: Make it simple, or force users to read? paraphrased design improves comprehension of end user license agreements. In: CHI 2016, p. 4 (2016)
40. Zamanian, M., Heydari, P.: Readability of texts: state of the art. Theory Pract. Lang. Stud. **2**(1), 43–53 (2012)

Privacy CURE: Consent Comprehension Made Easy

Olha Drozd$^{(\boxtimes)}$ ⓘ and Sabrina Kirrane ⓘ

Vienna University of Economics and Business, Vienna, Austria
{olha.drozd,sabrina.kirrane}@wu.ac.at

Abstract. Although the General Data Protection Regulation (GDPR) defines several potential legal bases for personal data processing, in many cases data controllers, even when they are located outside the European Union (EU), will need to obtain consent from EU citizens for the processing of their personal data. Unfortunately, existing approaches for obtaining consent, such as pages of text followed by an agreement/disagreement mechanism, are neither specific nor informed. In order to address this challenge, we introduce our Consent reqUest useR intErface (CURE) prototype, which is based on the GDPR requirements and the interpretation of those requirements by the Article 29 Working Party (i.e., the predecessor of the European Data Protection Board). The CURE prototype provides transparency regarding personal data processing, more control via a customization, and, based on the results of our usability evaluation, improves user comprehension with respect to what data subjects actually consent to. Although the CURE prototype is based on the GDPR requirements, it could potentially be used in other jurisdictions also.

Keywords: Consent request · Informed consent · GDPR · Usable privacy

1 Introduction

In the European Union (EU) the General Data Protection Regulation (GDPR) came into force on May 25, 2018, modernizing the Data Protection Directive 95/46/EC of the European Parliament and of the Council of 24 October 1995 on the protection of individuals with regard to the processing of personal data and on the free movement of such data. Both of these documents, however, suggest obtaining consent for data processing from data subjects. Although the GDPR defines several potential legal bases[1] for the lawful personal data processing[2], for instance for the provision of a contract, in order to fulfill a legal obligation, in the case of vital interest, in the case of public interest, or for reasons of

---

[1] GDPR Art. 6(1)(b–f).

[2] For the lawful personal data processing data subject's consent is not required.

© IFIP International Federation for Information Processing 2020
Published by Springer Nature Switzerland AG 2020
M. Hölbl et al. (Eds.): SEC 2020, IFIP AICT 580, pp. 124–139, 2020.
https://doi.org/10.1007/978-3-030-58201-2_9

legitimate interest, in many cases data controllers and processors, will need to obtain consent from data subjects for the processing of their personal data[3], for example in order to deliver personalized recommendations or to improve their services. According to Art. 4(11)[4] of the GDPR, consent needs to be "freely given, specific, informed and unambiguous indication of the data subject's wishes by which he or she, by a statement or by a clear affirmative action, signifies agreement to the processing of personal data relating to him or her".

The de facto standard for consent requests is still ready-made, set in stone, static descriptions of current and future data processing in the form of privacy policies or terms and conditions. However, studies show that such policies and terms and conditions are rarely read and when they are, they are hard to digest [20]. Although there have been some attempts to give users more control and transparency regarding personal data processing [10,15], the cognitive limitation of data subjects in terms of understanding what exactly they consented to remains an open research challenge [1,6]. Considering that the GDPR in general, and GDPR Art. 4(11) in particular, is quite prescription when it comes to consent, we argue that consent request user interface (UI) designers should pay particular attention to consent requirements specified in the GDPR and the interpretation of said requirements, in the form of guidelines[5], by various expert groups, such as the European Data Protection Board, and its predecessor the Article 29 Working Party[6].

In this paper, we introduce our Consent reqUest useR intErface (CURE) prototype, based on said requirements and guidelines, which elicits greater involvement of data subjects when it comes to granting consent, affords them more control via customization, and provides high transparency with respect to personal data processing. Our evaluation results look very promising, not only in terms of usability, but also in terms of understandability. Our UI could be applied in different contexts, however, in this paper it is developed based on an exemplifying use case scenario, whereby an individual purchasing a new wearable appliance for fitness tracking needs to complete the consent request in order to activate the various features of the device. Also, although the requirements underpinning the design of the CURE prototype are based on the GDPR, the CURE prototype could potentially be used in other jurisdictions.

The remainder of the paper is structured as follows: we start by providing an overview of the state of the art; following on from this we highlight our exemplifying use case scenario, the general requirements and methodology that are used to guide our work; next we describe our CURE prototype and the corresponding usability evaluation; finally, we present our conclusions and describe future work.

---

[3] GDPR Art. 6(1)(a).

[4] Art. 4(11) is complemented by Art. 7 that provides information on conditions for consent.

[5] Article 29 Working Party Guidelines on consent under Regulation 2016/6791 are available at https://bit.ly/2BdQs08.

[6] Article 29 Working Party was an independent European working party that dealt with data protection issues. On 25.05.2018 it was replaced by the European Data Protection Board under the GDPR.

2   Related Work

Over the years there have been several papers tackling the problem of consent request design [21,27,28,30] and understandability of consent content [10,12,15, 17,20].

As for types and formats of consent requests, Steinsbekk et al. [30] distinguish the following consent models: (i) no consent (i.e., all data usage is prohibited), (ii) specific consent (i.e., consent is tightly coupled with the purpose), (iii) broad consent (i.e., a framework whereby data are categorized according to type), and (iv) blanket consent (i.e.,virtually unlimited (including future) use of the data). Schaub et al. [28] survey the literature on privacy notices and identify four design dimensions of privacy notices, namely timing (i.e., when the notice is shown); channel (i.e., medium that delivers the notice); modality (i.e., how the notice is communicated); and control (i.e., what control options are available). Utz et al. [32] describe common UI properties of consent requests and their influence on people's consent behavior. They found that privacy notices located in the bottom left part of the screen have higher interaction rates. Additionally, the researchers show that user choices can be strongly influenced by the nudging and highlight the need for clear consent requirements to ensure that consent is informed and freely given.

In terms of comprehension of the consent request content, much of the focus to date has been on privacy policy visualization. McDonald et al. [21] assessed three formats of privacy policies: layered policies, conventional human-readable policies, and Privacy Finder privacy report[7]. In contrast to Utz et al. [32], the authors do not recommend regulating privacy policies. The evaluation showed that users disliked all three formats of privacy policies similarly, however, the authors do not provide an explanation with respect to what could have caused such a result. Kumar [17], in turn, analyzed 23 privacy policies putting a particular focus on the lack of clarity. Automatic assessment of the privacy policy completeness is proposed by Costante et al. [10]. Though they group privacy policy content into categories, the text of the privacy policy still remains the same as in a typical privacy policy and, as a result, is incomprehensible for users. The same issue concerns the cookie-watch tool for cookie management, developed by Friedman et al. [12]. Although it was designed to improve users' understanding of cookies, it still uses verbose cookie descriptions similar to the text of classical privacy policies. The consent requests in such a format would not provide for an informed consent. Kelley et al. [15] describe a process for constructing privacy policies based on labels and argue that their approach improves users' performance, however, they fail to visualize the full data processing flow. Therefore, such policies would lack full transparency regarding data processing. Reeder et al. [27] test an expandable grid in the context of setting permissions in the

---

[7] A Privacy Finder is a search engine service that informs users whether the privacy policies of the displayed search results coincide with users' privacy preferences. It also generates a privacy report for each search result, providing users with the core information from the privacy policy.

Windows operating system. However, the amount of information presented to a user in such a context is much smaller than in the general context of obtaining consent, hence cannot be applied to consent requests. Other literature, related to obtaining consent from the data subjects, analyzes privacy control UIs, such as mobile application (app) permissions [18,35]. When compared to a consent request, app permissions only provide users with an overview of the type of access the app requires, whereas no details are provided about the data processing, which makes permission settings not sufficient for a valid informed consent.

In terms of specific or dynamic consent, Mont et al. [22] propose a dynamic consent, policy enforcement and accountable information sharing platform. However, the focus is primarily on the architecture as opposed to the design of a usable and understandable user interface. Consent, compliance, and transparency systems [16,24,34], tools[8] and dashboards [2,5,26] are a related topic in the privacy literature as well as in industry, however, in this paper we focus primarily on the UI aspects of a consent request. Although consent request design features offered by Railean et al. [25] have some promising results, the authors received inconsistent outcomes concerning the comprehension of their "privacy facts" labels which indicates a need for a reevaluation.

New approaches for obtaining consent, such as Usercentrics' consent request[9] (or any other cookie consent request), try to categorize data and give users customization options, as opposed to all or nothing approach in classical privacy policies. However, they still provide a lot of textual information that causes information overload according to our evaluation results, which are presented later in this paper. According to a Norwegian Consumer Council report[10], Google and Facebook trick users into providing consent for the processing of more information and intentionally make it harder to customize users' consent by employing dark patterns. The report states, that both companies: (i) preselect settings to the least privacy friendly options; (ii) hide/obscure preselected settings; (iii) use confusing wording; and (iv) design complicated paths to make it difficult to manage users' data processing.

Unlike most of the current consent requests, that employ an all or nothing approach or provide pages of incomprehensible information about the data processing, in our CURE prototype we provide users with: (i) transparency with respect to personal data processing, (ii) understandable information about the actual data processing, and (iii) control over the data processing with the help of customization feature.

3   Background and Methodology

Before describing the CURE prototype and its usability evaluation, we provide the necessary background information with respect to the use case, the consent requirements and the methodology used to guide our work.

---

[8] Compliance tools are offered by various companies, e.g., ShareThis Inc., eccenca GmbH, etc.

[9] Usercentrics' consent request can be viewed at https://usercentrics.com.

[10] Norwegian Consumer Council Report is available at https://bit.ly/2N1TRRC.

3.1 Exemplifying Use Case Scenario

The following exemplifying use case scenario guided the development of the CURE prototype. Sue buys a wearable appliance for fitness tracking from BeFit Inc. In order to use the device's features, she first needs to grant consent for the processing of her personal data. She browses to BeFit's website and is presented with a consent request that describes which data need to be gathered, how they will be processed and shared in order to provide her with fitness-related information. For example, the consent request says that the device records heart rate parameters such as resting heart rate and activity heart rate; these data are stored on the device without sharing them with anyone; and processed to provide Sue with information about her all day heart rate. For the purpose of our research the content for the consent request was derived from our analysis of four smart devices (Fitbit, Apple Watch, Garmin Vivomove, and Garmin ForRunner) and two cloud-based analytics services (Runkeeping and Strava).

3.2 Consent Request UI Requirements

The CURE prototype requirements were derived both from the text of the GDPR and its interpretation by the Article 29 Working Party, that examined how the GDPR might influence data controllers in terms of consent request modifications. According to the Article 29 Working Party Guidelines on consent under Regulation 2016/6791, consent should be: (i) freely given, (i.e., it provides real choice and control for data subjects); (ii) specific, (i.e., it is separate from information about other matters, is tied to a purpose, and provides separate opt-in for each purpose); (iii) informed, (i.e., it includes elements that are crucial to understand processing of personally identifiable information and make a choice); and (iv) unambiguous indication of the data subject's wishes by which they, by a statement or by a clear affirmative action, signify agreement to the processing of personal data relating to them.

3.3 Methodology

The Design Science Research (DSR) [23] methodology was the overarching methodology that guided the design of CURE prototype. DSR starts with the identification of the research problem and the justification of the solution necessity. Then the objectives are specified and the design and development of a research artefact begins. The evaluation of an artefact follows its development and the results of the evaluation are communicated to researchers and other stakeholders. DSR was complemented by Action Research (AR), as defined in [9], to allow for the iterative refinement of the prototype. AR is an iterative approach, that starts with a problem identification and a subsequent solution to it. In the end, the outcomes of the action taken to solve the problem are evaluated. The solution is improved if the evaluation outcomes are not satisfactory.

Given that we wanted to focus more on the why and how aspects of the user interaction, rather than on what, where, or when, an observational method was

Table 1. CURE prototype usability evaluation assignments.

Task #	Text of the task
T1	Give your consent to process your information to have health data on your device.
T2	Give your consent to process your information for your activities to be shown on a map.
T3	Give your consent to enable the fitness adviser.
T4	Give your consent to turn on the back-up of your data.
T5	Withdraw your consent to derive your cardio fitness score.
T6	Withdraw your consent to derive your race time predictions.
T7	Withdraw your consent to back up your data.
T8	Withdraw your consent to all the functionalities.
T9	Have a look at the detailed overview of the required data processing for the functionality "display route on map".

the methodology of choice for our usability testing [19]. The evaluation itself was done in an asynchronous remote way [3] using a think aloud method [8,29,33], where users recorded the video of their screen and the audio of their spoken thoughts. We combined the think aloud method with performance measurement (e.g., completion success rates, time spent on the tasks, errors, etc.) [14] and post-evaluation remote questionnaire[11] [13] containing single choice, multiple choice, rating scale and open-ended questions that provided us with participants' demographic data as well as their impression of the CURE prototype. In order to make our evaluation as realistic as possible (in contrast to usability evaluations performed in lab settings), we developed an online prototype, as it enabled the participants to give their consent from a place of their choosing. Additionally, we ensured ecological validity [7] by: (i) deriving the content for the consent from the popular wearable appliances for fitness tracking; (ii) developing a cross-platform prototype that allowed users to test it on any operating system and browser of their choice; and (iii) testing our prototype with broad segment of the population.

On commencement of the UI evaluation participants were asked to imagine themselves buying BeFit's wearable appliance for fitness tracking, and were presented with BeFit's information pertaining to activation and personal data processing practices. After the participants read this information, they were asked to activate the device, using the BeFit specific CURE prototype. During the usability evaluation, the participants first completed a set of predefined tasks (see Table 1) requiring them to grant and withdraw consent for specific features. After these predefined exercises, they were asked to simply give their own consent, as they would have done if they had bought the BeFit device. The former was used to enable us to assess the effectiveness of the UI, while, the latter was

---

[11] Our questionnaire is available at https://bit.ly/2DNOGC3.

used to assess the users' comprehension in terms of what they had consented to. Additionally, the participants were also asked to visit Usercentrics' website and provide their consent for the personal data processing there, so that they could compare and contrast our prototype and Usercentrics' consent request approach. We selected Usercentrics' consent request for a comparative evaluation in our usability testing because Usercentrics describes itself as the market leader in the area of enterprise consent management platforms and is often referred to by data protection experts.

Usercentrics' consent request is an on-demand pop-up located in the bottom left corner of the screen that provides users with a list of data processors, several clickable icons (history, id, help) and a checkbox near each processor, so users can provide their consent per data processor. When users click on a "help" icon, they are presented with a more detailed consent request. In its detailed consent request, Usercentrics again groups information regarding data processing by data controller and offers users a possibility to give and withdraw their consent for each data controller. The data processing information of each controller is presented in a textual format and is divided into the following categories: processing company, data purposes, technologies used, data collected, legal basis, location of processing, retention period, data recipients, further information/opt-out, and history. The tasks where the participants gave their own consent to BeFit and Usercentrics were assigned in a random order to rule out the influence of the order on participants' evaluations. In the post-evaluation questionnaire the respondents were also asked to compare the CURE prototype with a classical verbose consent request followed by an "agree" button.

4   The CURE Prototype

As the CURE prototype was developed in an iterative manner, in this paper we describe its third version that achieved the best evaluation results and is based on the usability evaluation outcomes of the first two versions. The first two prototypes and their evaluation results are presented in [11]. In contrast to the all-or-nothing approach, adopted by current consent requests, in the first version of the prototype we gave users *maximum control* over their data processing by providing them with an option to fully adjust their consent specifically to their needs. The results of the usability evaluation showed that the participants were overwhelmed with too much control over their data processing and there was a clear need to simplify the UI and to reduce the consent options. Based on the insights gained from the first usability evaluation, we developed a *simplified UI* prototype. This second version of the prototype reduced the customization options from full customization to just giving consent to data processing per device's functionality (i.e., purpose) with the possibility to customize third-party data sharing for each functionality. The evaluation of the second prototype indicated some improvement in terms of performance and comprehension. However, the users still complained about the amount of the information they had to digest and the lack of accelerators for giving and withdrawing consent.

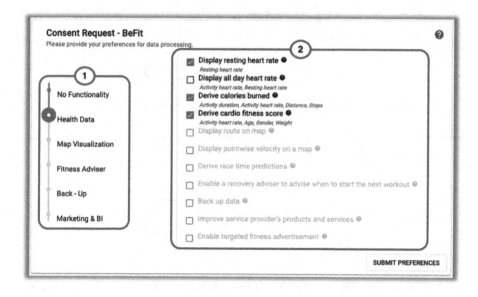

Fig. 1. The CURE prototype: (1) Slider. (2) Consent per purpose.

Figure 1, which is split into two components: (1) slider, (2) consent per purpose, depicts final BeFit's CURE prototype. The fully functional prototype[12], which was developed for more realistic usability testing, as well as its source code[13] are both available online. From a technology perspective, Angular and D3.js were used for the front-end development and Java and PostgreSQL for the server side.

4.1 The CURE Prototype Description

The CURE prototype offers the following features to the user. *Categorization.* The functionalities offered by the device equate to the purposes for personal data processing. We group these purposes into more general categories that can be browsed by just sliding the pointer up and down (see Fig. 1(1)). In the CURE prototype we order the categories in a way that when the pointer is at the top the users have maximum privacy with minimum device utility, and minimum privacy with maximum utility when the pointer is at the bottom. The ordering was done according to our own preferences. However, we envisage that companies will order those categories based on their device usage statistics. Additionally, the CURE prototype provides a detailed overview of the data processing separately for each purpose. This information is presented in a graphical form (see Fig. 2) and is classified according to five categories, namely (i) purpose (i.e., functionalities offered by a service), (ii) data (i.e., what data are collected from the data

---

[12] The prototype is available in two languages: English (http://cr-slider.soft.cafe/en/) and German (http://cr-slider.soft.cafe/de/).

[13] The source code is available at https://bit.ly/2GErFC7.

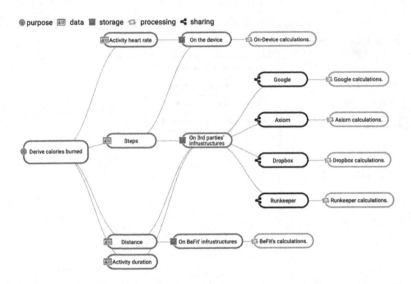

Fig. 2. Example of a detailed overview of the required data processing for the purpose "derive calories burned".

subject), (iii) storage (i.e., where the data are stored), (iv) processing (i.e., how the personal data are processed) and (v) sharing (i.e., with whom the data are shared). These categories were derived from questions that were routinely asked by our legal colleagues in the context of the SPECIAL[14] project, which aims to assess the lawfulness of personal data processing according to the GDPR. Since the amount of information regarding the data processing is usually large, categorization ensures that the interface is both clean and not overwhelming [31].

Customization. One of the most important aspects of the CURE prototype is the possibility to customize the consent. The CURE prototype allows users to consent to general categories using a slider. By selecting a category, users automatically preselect all purposes that belong to that category. For example, if users want to receive information about their health, they can just slide the pointer to the "Health" category. Four purposes for data processing, that fall under this category (i.e., display resting/all day heart rate; derive calories burned; derive cardio fitness score), are automatically selected. Additionally, the CURE prototype allows more granular customization (see Fig. 1(2)), where the preselected consent can be further adjusted by selecting or deselecting checkboxes corresponding to specific purposes. From a design perspective checkboxes were selected for their simplicity and immediate choice visibility [31].

Understandability. In our CURE prototype we use plain language and short phrases to improve the understandability of the consent request content. Addi-

---

[14] Scalable Policy-awarE linked data arChitecture for prIvacy, trAnsparency and compLiance (SPECIAL) project is described in detail on https://www.specialprivacy.eu/.

tionally, the CURE prototype provides feedback for every user action. For those users, who would prefer a detailed overview of the data processing, the CURE prototype contains the already mentioned comprehensive overview of the required data processing for each purpose. To reduce the amount of information that is shown immediately to the user, this comprehensive overview becomes available, on demand, upon clicking on a "?" symbol, placed after the description of each purpose. The understandability of this overview is enhanced with a graphical visualization of the data processing. Figure 2 shows an example of such an overview graph that provides details of the data processing required for the "derive calories burned" purpose. Additionally, we incorporated color-coding and icons into the graph. Different organizational models (e.g., treemap, sunburst, chord, circle packing, etc.) were applied to represent the detailed overview of the data processing. The graph, however, proved to be the most suitable for our content.

Revocation. According to GDPR Art. 7(3), the data subjects should be able to withdraw their consent at any time as easily as they gave it. In the CURE prototype, the consent revocation can be done in two ways, either by sliding up the pointer to withdraw the consent for multiple purposes at once or by deselecting a corresponding checkbox to withdraw the consent for each purpose separately. Although in our use case scenario the user is tasked with granting consent for the first time, the CURE prototype can be used as a control interface for the management of consent, which has already been given.

4.2   Results of the User Evaluations

In order to gain feedback regarding the effectiveness of our interface we conducted a usability evaluation of the CURE prototype. Thirty-five participants (69% - male, 31% - female) took part in our usability evaluation. The users belong to different age groups (51% - 16 to 25 years old, 23% - 26 to 35 years old, 17% - 36 to 45 years old, 6% - 46 to 55 years old, and 3% - 55 years old and over). Almost one third of the participants (31%) graduated from high school. The other 31% have bachelor's degrees. The rest have master's (14%) degrees, no degree with some college (12%), trade, technical or vocational training (6%), doctoral degrees (3%), and some high school education (3%). 63% of the participants come from Austria. Others come from Bosnia, Croatia, the United Kingdom, Italy, the Netherlands, Romania, and Serbia. The participants rated their Internet surfing skills as competent (43%), proficient (26%) and expert (28%). Most of them reported that they usually spend 3–6 h (43%) or 1–3 h (34%) on the Internet per day and preferably use a laptop (57%) or a desktop computer (23%) for the surfing. During the evaluation the participants, first, completed a set of predefined tasks that were outlined in the Methodology section. Then, they were instructed to imagine that they purchased BeFit's wearable appliance for fitness tracking and asked to give their own consent. The participants were also instructed to visit Usercentrics' website and provide their consent there. After finishing their assignments, the participants were asked to fill in a questionnaire about their experience with the CURE prototype.

Video Recordings. The analysis of the 35 video recordings provided by our participants showed that the UI was very easy to use and the participants were able to complete the tasks with ease and with almost no errors. We did not observe any major confusion or misunderstanding of the UI. The users immediately noticed the slider and understood the usage of checkboxes for the adjustment of consent. The participants required, on average, 1 s to complete each of the tasks. The average time needed to give their own consent was 20 s.

Comprehension Testing. We assessed the comprehension of the consent given to BeFit by presenting different possible consent variations in the questionnaire and asking the participants if they consented to that data processing. The answers of each user were compared with the actual consent given. More than a half of the participants answered all the questions correctly, and on average users got 86% of the questions correct.

Overall Satisfaction. When we asked users if they were satisfied overall with the consent request, 71% of the participants reported satisfaction (51% - somewhat satisfied, 20% - very satisfied) with the consent request. 20% of the users remained neutral towards the consent request (see Fig. 3(a)). There were no very dissatisfied users and only 9% were somewhat dissatisfied with our UI. The high overall satisfaction can also be reflected in the answers to the question about the recommendation of the websites with the CURE prototype to a friend. 40% said that it was very likely that they would recommend a website with such a consent request to a friend and 29% replied that it was moderately likely. 11% of the respondents would be slightly likely and 3% would be extremely likely to advise a friend to use a website with our consent request. 17% of the participants would not recommend it to a friend. Since only 9% of the users were somewhat dissatisfied with our UI, this was somewhat surprising. Unfortunately, it was not possible to determine why this was the case.

Ease of Use. It was very easy for the participants to use the CURE prototype (e.g., the respondents stated that "...it was very clear", "I did not face any major difficulties"). A lot of the users said that the slider on the left side was the easiest part about using the UI (e.g., "the easiest part of this consent form was definitely the slider...", "the slider is extremely easy to navigate"). The respondents also spoke positively about the way the UI is organized (e.g., "the easiest thing was to understand the logic behind how the different settings are divided", "I liked the structure very much").

Adjective Description. The users were asked to select adjectives that they would use to describe the UI they were testing. We used the list of adjectives from Microsoft Desirability Toolkit [4], which we adapted to our case. The adjectives that were selected support the results described above. The positive adjectives

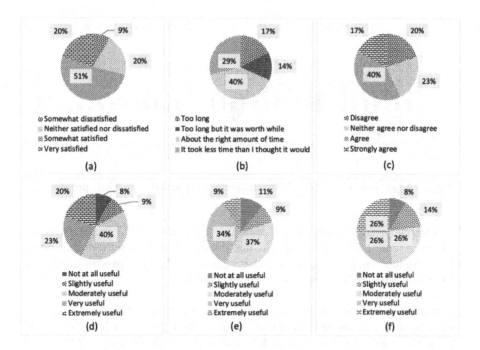

Fig. 3. (a) Overall satisfaction with the consent request. (b) Assessment of the time it took to give/withdraw the consent. (c) Perception of control over the data processing. (d) Usefulness of the detailed overview graph of the data processing. (e) Usefulness of the icons in the detailed overview graph of the data processing. (f) Usefulness of the color-coding in the detailed overview graph of the data processing.

received most of the participants' votes. The users found this UI easy to use (50%), useful (34%), clear (32%), helpful (32%), usable (32%), effective (29%), organized (29%), satisfying (23%), appealing (20%), efficient (20%), flexible (20%), and innovative (17%). Some of the participants described the prototype with the following negative adjectives: complex (17%), time-consuming (17%), and confusing (17%). Figure 4 provides a detailed overview of the adjectives chosen by the respondents.

Time Perception. When asked to provide their impression of the time it took to give or withdraw consent, 40% of the participants answered that it took them about the right amount of time (see Fig. 3(b)). 29% selected it took less time than they thought it would. 14% reported that it took too long, but it was worthwhile. For the rest of the users (17%), it took too long to give or withdraw the consent.

Being in Control. We asked the participants, if they felt that they were in control of the processing of their data when they used our consent request. Figure 3(c) depicts users' answers. More than a half of the participants agreed (40% - agree,

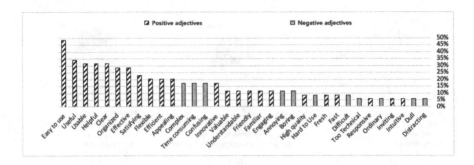

Fig. 4. Adjectives selected by the participants to describe the CURE prototype.

17% - strongly agree) that such a consent request gave them control over the data processing. 23% neither agreed nor disagreed that they were in control. 20% of the participants did not feel that they controlled the processing of their data. There were no users who strongly disagreed.

Overview Graph. The graph that provided an overview of the data processing related to each purpose was found to be useful to a greater or lesser extent by 92% of the users (see Fig. 3(d)). 20% found it extremely useful, 23% - very useful, 40% - moderately useful, 9% - slightly useful. Only 8% of the users did not find the graph useful. The participants were asked two questions regarding the design features of the overview graph to find out if they liked the color-coding and the icons used in the graph. 26% of the participants found the color-coding to work extremely well in the graph (see Fig. 3(f)). Another 26% reported the color-coding to be very useful. This feature was rated as moderately useful by 26% of the participants. 14% found it to be slightly useful. The rest (8%) did not find color-coding useful. The icons helped 89% of users (37% - moderately, 34% - very, 9% extremely, 9% slightly) to understand the graph better (see Fig. 3(e)). However, for 11% of participants the icons were not useful.

Prototype vs Existing Consent Requests. The CURE prototype was compared by the participants with two existing consent requests: (i) the classic consent request in the form of privacy policy and an "agree" button at the bottom of the web page, (ii) the consent request developed by Usercentrics. The respondents named four main reasons why they liked the CURE prototype better than traditional consent requests. Unlike classic consent requests, the CURE prototype provides: (i) choice (e.g., "...I have more opportunity to decide what happens with the data"), (ii) an understandable detailed overview of the data processing for each purpose (e.g., "...allows me to get a better image, especially with help of the diagrams for detailed overview, about who and how collects my personal data"), (iii) control over the data processing (e.g., "...helps control the way the data are used"), and (iv) usability (e.g., "it is very easy to use"). Although the consent request from Usercentrics is newly developed, the participants evaluated it similarly to the classic consent. Apart from appreciating customization, the users reported Usercentrics' consent request to be time consuming, overwhelming, not memorable and not user friendly. Only one out of thirty-five participants would choose this UI over the CURE prototype.

Prototype Improvement Suggestions. As users did not have any major problems while using the CURE prototype, they did not offer any improvements (e.g., "since I, literally, had no difficulties in navigating the UI, I do not have anything to say regarding the improvements", "I like the UI as it is"). One participant suggested to enhance the overview graph with links to third-party websites, wherever their names are mentioned.

5   Conclusion and Future Work

In this paper, we introduced our consent request user interface, which affords users more control over the processing of their personal data, by providing them with more transparency regarding personal data processing and giving them the opportunity to customize their consent. The UI was well received by the participants of our usability evaluation, who performed all tasks quickly, easily and almost without errors. Additionally, most of the adjectives used to describe the UI were very positive and the overall comprehension level of what the participants had consented to was very high. Our UI also performed better in a comparison task, where users compared it to a classical consent request in the form of privacy policy or terms and conditions, and one of the new solutions on the market offered by Usercentrics. All the materials used in the evaluations are available online, so that other consent UIs can be benchmarked against ours.

So far we have concentrated on the prototype development for laptops and desktop computers, because most of the users still use these devices to surf the Internet [11]. In the future we plan to adapt the CURE prototype for mobile devices and conduct the evaluation of the adapted prototype.

Acknowledgments. This paper is supported by the European Union's Horizon 2020 research and innovation programme under grant 731601. We would like to thank our colleagues from SPECIAL and WU for their legal support and help with the user studies.

References

1. Acquisti, A., Adjerid, I., Brandimarte, L.: Gone in 15 seconds: the limits of privacy transparency and control. IEEE Secur. Priv. **11**(4), 72–74 (2013)
2. Angulo, J., Fischer-Hübner, S., Pulls, T., Wästlund, E.: Usable transparency with the data track: a tool for visualizing data disclosures. In: Proceedings of the 33rd Annual ACM Conference Extended Abstracts on Human Factors in Computing Systems, pp. 1803–1808. ACM (2015)
3. Bastien, J.C.: Usability testing: a review of some methodological and technical aspects of the method. Int. J. Med. Inform. **79**, e18–e23 (2010)

4. Benedek, J., Miner, T.: Measuring desirability: new methods for evaluating desirability in a usability lab setting. Proc. Usability Prof. Assoc. **2003**(8–12), 57 (2002)
5. Bier, C., Kühne, K., Beyerer, J.: PrivacyInsight: the next generation privacy dashboard. In: Schiffner, S., Serna, J., Ikonomou, D., Rannenberg, K. (eds.) APF 2016. LNCS, vol. 9857, pp. 135–152. Springer, Cham (2016). https://doi.org/10.1007/978-3-319-44760-5_9
6. Borgesius, F.Z.: Informed consent: we can do better to defend privacy. IEEE Secur. Priv. **13**(2), 103–107 (2015)
7. Brewer, M.B., Crano, W.D.: Research design and issues of validity. In: Reis, H.T., Judd, C.M. (eds.) Handbook of Research Methods in Social and Personality Psychology, pp. 3–16. Cambridge University Press, Cambridge (2000)
8. Charters, E.: The use of think-aloud methods in qualitative research: an introduction to think-aloud methods. Brock Educ. J. **12**(2), 68–82 (2003)
9. Checkland, P., Holwell, S.: Action research. In: Kock, N. (ed.) Information Systems Action Research. Integrated Series in Information Systems, vol. 13, pp. 3–17. Springer, Boston (2007). https://doi.org/10.1007/978-0-387-36060-7_1
10. Costante, E., Sun, Y., Petković, M., den Hartog, J.: A machine learning solution to assess privacy policy completeness: (short paper). In: Proceedings of the 2012 ACM Workshop on Privacy in the Electronic Society, pp. 91–96. ACM (2012)
11. Drozd, O., Kirrane, S.: I agree: customize your personal data processing with the core user interface. In: Gritzalis, S., Weippl, E.R., Katsikas, S.K., Anderst-Kotsis, G., Tjoa, A.M., Khalil, I. (eds.) TrustBus 2019. LNCS, vol. 11711, pp. 17–32. Springer, Cham (2019). https://doi.org/10.1007/978-3-030-27813-7_2
12. Friedman, B., Howe, D.C., Felten, E.: Informed consent in the mozilla browser: implementing value-sensitive design. In: Proceedings of the 35th Annual Hawaii International Conference on System Sciences, p. 10. IEEE (2002)
13. Hartson, H.R., Castillo, J.C., Kelso, J., Neale, W.C.: Remote evaluation: the network as an extension of the usability laboratory. In: Proceedings of the SIGCHI. ACM (1996)
14. Ivory, M.Y., Hearst, M.A.: The state of the art in automating usability evaluation of user interfaces. ACM Comput. Surv. (CSUR) **33**(4), 470–516 (2001)
15. Kelley, P.G., Bresee, J., Cranor, L.F., Reeder, R.W.: A nutrition label for privacy. In: Proceedings of the 5th Symposium on Usable Privacy and Security, p. 4. ACM (2009)
16. Kirrane, S., et al.: A scalable consent, transparency and compliance architecture. In: Gangemi, A., et al. (eds.) ESWC 2018. LNCS, vol. 11155, pp. 131–136. Springer, Cham (2018). https://doi.org/10.1007/978-3-319-98192-5_25
17. Kumar, P.: Privacy policies and their lack of clear disclosure regarding the life cycle of user information. In: 2016 AAAI Fall Symposium Series (2016)
18. Liccardi, I., Pato, J., Weitzner, D.J.: Improving mobile app selection through transparency and better permission analysis. J. Priv. Confid. **5**(2), 1–55 (2014)
19. MacKenzie, I.S.: User studies and usability evaluations: from research to products. In: Proceedings of the 41st Graphics Interface Conference, pp. 1–8. CIPS (2015)
20. McDonald, A.M., Cranor, L.F.: The cost of reading privacy policies. ISJLP **4**, 543 (2008)
21. McDonald, A.M., Reeder, R.W., Kelley, P.G., Cranor, L.F.: A comparative study of online privacy policies and formats. In: Goldberg, I., Atallah, M.J. (eds.) PETS 2009. LNCS, vol. 5672, pp. 37–55. Springer, Heidelberg (2009). https://doi.org/10.1007/978-3-642-03168-7_3

22. Mont, M.C., Sharma, V., Pearson, S.: Encore: dynamic consent, policy enforcement and accountable information sharing within and across organisations. Technical report, HP Laboratories HPL-2012-36 (2012)
23. Peffers, K., Tuunanen, T., Rothenberger, M.A., Chatterjee, S.: A design science research methodology for information systems research. JMIS **24**(3), 45–77 (2007)
24. Piras, L., et al.: Defend architecture: a privacy by design platform for GDPR compliance. In: Gritzalis, S., et al. (eds.) TrustBus 2019. LNCS, vol. 11711, pp. 78–93. Springer, Cham (2019). https://doi.org/10.1007/978-3-030-27813-7_6
25. Railean, A., Reinhardt, D.: Let there be lite: design and evaluation of a label for IoT transparency enhancement. In: Proceedings of the 20th International Conference on Human-Computer Interaction with Mobile Devices and Services Adjunct, pp. 103–110. ACM (2018)
26. Raschke, P., Küpper, A., Drozd, O., Kirrane, S.: Designing a GDPR-compliant and usable privacy dashboard. In: Hansen, M., Kosta, E., Nai-Fovino, I., Fischer-Hübner, S. (eds.) Privacy and Identity 2017. IAICT, vol. 526, pp. 221–236. Springer, Cham (2018). https://doi.org/10.1007/978-3-319-92925-5_14
27. Reeder, R.W., et al.: Expandable grids for visualizing and authoring computer security policies. In: Proceedings of the SIGCHI Conference on Human Factors in Computing Systems, pp. 1473–1482. ACM (2008)
28. Schaub, F., Balebako, R., Durity, A.L., Cranor, L.F.: A design space for effective privacy notices. In: Eleventh Symposium on Usable Privacy and Security, pp. 1–17 (2015)
29. Seidman, I.: Interviewing as Qualitative Research: A Guide for Researchers in Education and the Social Sciences. Teachers College Press, New York (2013)
30. Steinsbekk, K.S., Myskja, B.K., Solberg, B.: Broad consent versus dynamic consent in biobank research: is passive participation an ethical problem? EJHG **21**(9), 897 (2013)
31. Tidwell, J.: Designing Interfaces: Patterns for Effective Interaction Design. O'Reilly Media, Inc., Sebastopol (2010)
32. Utz, C., Degeling, M., Fahl, S., Schaub, F., Holz, T.: (Un)informed consent: studying GDPR consent notices in the field. arXiv preprint arXiv:1909.02638 (2019)
33. Van Someren, M., Barnard, Y., Sandberg, J.: The Think Aloud Method: A Practical Approach to Modelling Cognitive Processes. Academic Press, London (1994)
34. Weitzner, D.J., et al.: Transparent accountable data mining: new strategies for privacy protection (2006)
35. Wijesekera, P., et al.: The feasibility of dynamically granted permissions: aligning mobile privacy with user preferences. In: 2017 IEEE Symposium on Security and Privacy (SP), pp. 1077–1093. IEEE (2017)

Detecting Malware and Software Weaknesses

JavaScript Malware Detection Using Locality Sensitive Hashing

Stefan Carl Peiser[1]([⊠]), Ludwig Friborg[1], and Riccardo Scandariato[2]

[1] Chalmers University of Technology, Gothenburg, Sweden
stefancarlpeiser@gmail.com, ludwig.friborg@gmail.com
[2] Chalmers and University of Gothenburg, Gothenburg, Sweden
riccardo.scandariato@cse.gu.se

Abstract. In this paper, we explore the idea of using locality sensitive hashes as input features to a feed-forward neural network with the goal of detecting JavaScript malware through static analysis. An experiment is conducted using a dataset containing 1.5M evenly distributed benign and malicious samples provided by the anti-malware company Cyren. Four different locality sensitive hashing algorithms are tested and evaluated: Nilsimsa, ssdeep, TLSH, and SDHASH. The results show a high prediction accuracy, as well as low false positive and negative rates. These results show that LSH based neural networks are a competitive option against other state-of-the-art JavaScript malware classification solutions.

Keywords: Malware · LSH · Neural network · JavaScript

1 Introduction

JavaScript is one of the most popular scripting languages in the world as it is the 'de facto' scripting language used by internet browsers. This means that JavaScript has become a popular attack vector to infect computers of internet users as these scripts are executed automatically by browsers. In this paper we focus on static techniques to detect malicious JavaScript code, as static approaches are simpler to apply and have a performance advantage. However, detecting malicious code statically has become difficult due to code obfuscation. On top of that, in the world of JavaScript, code obfuscation is not an indicator of maliciousness as most JavaScript code on benign websites is obfuscated as a side-effect of minimizing the size of production code and preserving intellectual property.

In this paper we present an approach that works on both clear-text and obfuscated scripts. In particular, we explore the use of locality sensitive hashing (LSH) as a means to extract features from the scripts. The features are fed to

---

S. C. Peiser and L. Friborg—These authors contributed equally to this work.

© IFIP International Federation for Information Processing 2020
Published by Springer Nature Switzerland AG 2020
M. Hölbl et al. (Eds.): SEC 2020, IFIP AICT 580, pp. 143–154, 2020.
https://doi.org/10.1007/978-3-030-58201-2_10

a neural network for the effective identification of malicious scripts. LSH is a family of dimensionality reducing algorithms, which previously has been used for document and code comparison and is used here in a novel way for malware detection.

In Sect. 2 we introduce background material and survey the related work. We present our approach in Sect. 3. In Sect. 4, we evaluate the approach on a large corpora of malware samples and compare the results to several alternative approaches from the state of the art (including Cujo and Zozzle). In Sect. 5 we discuss and investigate possible causes for false positives and false negatives during our experimentation. Finally, we present the concluding remarks in Sect. 6.

2   Background and Related Work

2.1   JavaScript Malware

Almost all web pages today utilize JavaScript in some form, whether to display fancy animations or to send data to web servers. Browsers have started to run JavaScript files automatically when loading websites, which has enabled many new attack vectors. JavaScript malware have various purposes. Many try to download other malware onto the victim's computer, e.g. remote access trojans (RATs), ransomware and more, these are commonly known as drive-by-downloads malware. Other common types of malware are bitcoin miners where the malware uses the infected computer's hardware to mine cryptocurrency. Facelikers are also common, as they try to "like" various posts and pages on Facebook using infected Facebook accounts.

Often, hackers obfuscate the code of malware in an attempt to make it harder to analyse and detect. However, obfuscation is not necessarily an indicator of maliciousness as it has become the norm in JavaScript development the last few years as a way of minimizing code, hide client-side code and more.

2.2   Identification of JavaScript Malware

There are several malware detection techniques that have been proposed in the state of the art. In this section we focus on the most prominent approaches, which are also used as comparison in Sect. 4.1. For a more complete coverage of malware identification, we refer the interested reader to the survey of Ye et al. [20].

Dynamic Analysis. Ratanaworabhan et al. [13] propose a runtime heap-spraying attack detector named Nozzle. The system has been used to analyse JavaScript-based malware. Nozzle uses emulation techniques to detect executable malicious code in objects allocated within the browser heap.

A drawback with using dynamic methods is that they are often resource intensive and thus expensive to use at runtime. Thus, it is prevalent among security vendors to use dynamic analysis methods to assess the scripts off-line and, at runtime, just compare script files with a collection of already classified samples.

Static Analysis. Ndichu et al. [11] proposes using Doc2Vec to extract features from malicious JavaScript files and then feed them into a support vector machine model. The performance of the classifier is promising but the validation dataset consists of only 80 files.

Curtsinger et al. [3] propose a method named Zozzle. They evaluate both a handpicked and a automated feature extraction method to then infer the maliciousness of a JavaScript file through a naive Bayesian classifier. It is important to note that their system is only able to function on unobfuscated code.

Xu et al. [19] propose a method named *JStill*, which operates on obfuscated code. This method works by analysing code and looking for blacklisted function calls. It is important to note that the approach relies on white/black lists. Therefore, the method is limited to cover only a subset of all JavaScript malware.

Likarish et al. [9] evaluate multiple different statistical learning methods together with a tokenized feature extraction method based on different keywords. Among the methods evaluated, the models with the lowest false positive rate are ADTree [5] and RBF SVM [2]. Wang et al. [18] later provide a more refined presentation of the results presented by Likarish. They also present a deep learning approach, called SdA-LR, based on the previously mentioned feature extraction method and a deep neural network for statistical inference.

Rieck et al. [14] propose a system called Cujo, which leverages three different methods of JavaScript malware analysis. One is static, one is dynamic and one is the combination of the previous two. The static method utilizes support vector machines to learn the patterns of malicious scripts. The dynamic method uses sandboxing. The work focuses on detecting one specific type of malware, namely the drive-by-download family.

Although not related to JavaScript, the work of Raff et al. [12] is worth mentioning. They train a deep learning model that consumes entire malware executable binaries. Thus, the model learns how the malware are structured internally. However, performance is a major drawback in this approach, as it takes a month to train the model on a dataset of 2M executable binaries.

2.3   Locality Sensitive Hashing

Raff et al. [12] show that using deep learning to learn structural properties of malware seems to be a powerful way of classifying them. However, the bottleneck is represented by the time and resources it takes to learn on entire malware files. Instead of processing whole files, our idea is to find a dense representation of the file contents and to infer characteristics from said representation. Hence this paper focuses on the use of locality sensitive hashing methods to provide concise input features for a neural network.

Locality Sensitive Hashing (LSH) is a relatively new family of dimensionality-reducing algorithms, including Nilsimsa [4], TLSH [10], ssdeep [8], and SDHASH [15], which are evaluated in this work. These algorithms produce condensed representations (hashes) of the given input data. By construction, the hashes of

Table 1. List of the most prevalent types of malicious scripts.

Malware type	Count	%
Redirector	166857	20.4
Trojan downloader	43505	5.3
CoinHive	6285	0.8
SEOHide	4394	0.5
IFrame	3629	0.4
FaceLiker	2285	0.3
Ramnit	1615	0.2
FakejQuery	1073	0.1
Crypted	938	0.1
Unknown type	588153	71.8
Total	818734	

similar files are also similar[1], hence the hashes can be used as proxies in order to compare the similarity of the original files. The benefit is that the hashes are much more concise and lend themselves to be used as features in learning algorithms.

3   Experimental Setup

3.1   Dataset

The dataset contains about 1.5M scripts, of which 54% are malicious. Table 1 describes the different malware types that are present in the dataset. The data is provided by Cyren (https://www.cyren.com), which is a large vendor in the field of cybersecurity and supplies, among other, the scanner for email attachments used by Google and Microsoft [1]. All JavaScript files in the dataset have been collected and labeled during the first half of 2019. The files originate from various sources, e.g. from web scrapers, customers sending in files for analysis, e-mail attachments, incoming files from VirusTotal [17] and more. Each of these files goes through Cyren's malware scanners (based on dynamic analysis) and the system assigns a label to the sample indicating whether it is clean or malicious. These labels represent our ground truth.

3.2   Feature Extraction

As shown in Fig. 1, the locality sensitive hashes are pre-processed before being used as input to the neural network. Thus we have to take into account the

---

[1] This contrasts to cryptographic hashing techniques, like SHA256, where the hashing algorithm minimizes the probability of collisions, i.e., two almost identical files yield two drastically different hashes.

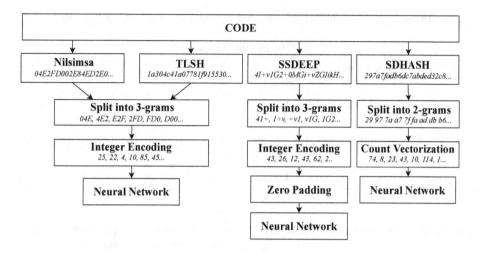

Fig. 1. Feature extraction and prediction pipeline.

different characteristics of the hashes. Both TLSH and Nilsimsa produce a fixed-length, hex-encoded strings of 70 and 64 characters respectively. SSDEEP produces a hash that is base64 encoded and its length is variable, but has a max size of 148 characters. Finally, SDHASH produces hex encoded hashes of variable length, but with no maximum limit.

To let the neural network find patterns in the substrings of the hashes we decided to split the hashes into n-grams by using a sliding window (of size n and sliding of 1 position at a time). As detailed later, the learning algorithm (namely, the embedding layer) uses a dictionary whose size is 16^n for TLSH and Nilsimsa (hex encoding), and 64^n for ssdeep (base64 encoding). A larger dictionary has an impact on the training time and the memory consumption. Therefore, after experimentation, the trade-off decision has been made to use tri-grams. During the experimentation, we also found that using $n \geq 4$ did not yield any noticeable classification improvements but a high increase in training time.

After splitting the hash into n-grams, each hash is then encoded as a sequence of integers, i.e., each n-gram is converted to its positional value. After the encoding, we are left with input vectors of different size for each LSH type. In the case of TLSH and Nilsimsa, the vectors are of fixed size and they are used as-is to train a neural network. In the case of SSDEEP, the vectors have variable length but, due to the nature of the output from this algorithm, there is an upper bound. In this case, we take the length of the longest vector and add zero-padding to the vectors so that they have the same length.

SDHASH produces output hashes with no definitive maximum length and no upper bound. Hence, for this hashing algorithm, the construction of the features is different. Starting from the hash, we split it into a vector of bi-grams (in place of tri-grams) and filter the vector through a count vectorizer, which returns a vector of frequencies for each unique bi-gram. We use the vector of frequencies

Table 2. Network model composition (where L is length of input vector).

Layer name	Output dimensions	
Embeddings	32 × L	
Flatten	1 × L	
BatchNormalization	1 × L	
Dense	1 × 256	Activation: relu
Dropout	1 × 256	Probability: 0.125
Dense	1 × 64	Activation: relu
Dense	1 × 1	Activation: sigmoid

as input vector for the neural network. Note that the ordering of bi-grams gets lost in the process, which might negatively affect the performance of the neural network performance. The choice of using bi-gram is justified by the fact that, in this way, the input vector is of similar size with respect to the other algorithms.

3.3   Neural Network Design and Implementation

A supervised learning approach with a normal deep feed-forward neural network is used to classify each locality sensitive hash. The input layer of the neural network takes the integers generated from each hash, and the output layer will return one single value, presented on a scale between 0 and 1, determining the likelihood of the input of being malicious. Table 2 provides an overview of the network structure. The embedding layer transforms positive integers into dense non-zero vectors. This was chosen to mitigate the problem of it having a high presence of sparse input-vectors in addition to some hashing methods producing hashes of an inconsistent length leading to a lot of 0-padding. Not embedding the input data resulted in worse performance and slower convergence rate for the learning model. We use both *Batch Normalization* [6] and *Dropout* [16] for regularization.

In terms of fitting the network to gain an accurate understanding of the given data *adam optimization* [7] was used together with binary cross-entropy as loss-function.

3.4   Experiments and Performance Indicators

By means of random sampling, we split the complete dataset into seven subsets of incrementally bigger sizes, namely 5k, 10k, 50k, 100k, 500k, 1M, 1.5M (i.e., the whole set). We use subsets of varying sizes in order to investigate the trade-off between prediction performance and training cost. Ultimately, we would like to understand how much data is necessary in order to generalize. Note that, as we use random sampling, the positive rate in the subsets is expected to be similar to the complete dataset.

Table 3. Results from the 5-fold cross-validation experiment.

LSH	ACC (%)	FPR (%)	FNR (%)
TLSH	97.79	1.01	3.25
Nilsimsa	98.05	1.09	2.69
ssdeep	97.97	0.94	2.98
SDHASH	95.06	1.83	7.63

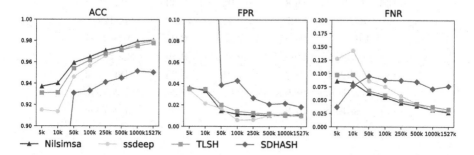

Fig. 2. Accuracy, false positive rate and false negative rate across the different experiments with increasingly larger dataset sizes.

For each subset and each LSH method, we run a 5-fold cross-validation experiment and measure the average performance of the prediction approach. As we use 5-fold cross-validation, the results we report are averaged over the performance obtained in the individual folds.

To assess the different prediction models, we rely on three performance indicators: accuracy (ACC), false positive rate (FPR), and false negative rate (FNR). The key performance indicators are FPR and FNR. However, we also include accuracy for comparison reasons, as this indicator is often reported by the other approaches we compare to (cf. Sect. 4.1). The performance indicators are calculated as follows:

- $ACC = \frac{TP+TN}{TP+TN+FP+FN}$
- $FPR = \frac{FP}{FP+TN}$
- $FNR = \frac{FN}{FN+TP}$

where TP, TN, FP and FN corresponds to the number True/False Positives/Negatives.

4 Results

Table 3 shows the results from the cross-validation experiment on 1.5M samples. Figure 2 shows the results for all the experiments with different dataset sizes. It is possible to observe that Nilsimsa has a slight advantage compared to the

Table 4. Comparison of the performance indicators between our models and the state of the art, where *M:C* corresponds to *Malware:Clean*, which is the amount of samples used.

Classifier	ACC (%)	FPR (%)	FNR (%)	M:C
Zozzle manual	98.2	1.50	1.20	900:8000
Zozzle auto	99.2	0.30	9.20	900:8000
JStill	97.3	17.5	0.53	30k:50k
RBF SVM	86.8	4.92	8.33	14k:12k
ADTree	82.7	2.42	14.92	14k:12k
SdA-LR	94.8	4.13	6.04	2959:2464
CUJO static	90.1	0.10	9.80	609:200k
Ours - TLSH	97.79	1.01	3.25	818k:709k
Ours - Nilsimsa	98.05	1.09	2.69	818k:709k
Ours - ssdeep	97.97	0.94	2.98	818k:709k

other methods. Interestingly, and contrary to expectations, the SDHASH model, which used a count-vectorized style of network input, also seems to produce good results, though falling short against the other LSH methods. The results also show that the models are more prone to making false negative predictions rather than false positives, which is a beneficial trait in the world of malware detection.

Observing the graphs in Fig. 2, it is possible to see that even in the smallest dataset of 5k samples, the best models (Nilsimsa, ssdeep, and TLSH) are already capable of yielding an accuracy of more than 90%. SDHASH, instead, requires a bigger dataset (50k samples and above) in order to produce stable results. In general, there is an expected trend of increased performance as the sample size grows, although with diminishing returns staring from a size of 500k samples.

4.1 Comparison to Alternative Approaches

In Table 4 we present a comparison between our models and other approaches that utilize static analysis. The performance values for the competing approaches are taken from the corresponding research papers.

In comparison to Zozzle, i.e., the best performing compared model we compare to, our model is quite close in performance but does not match it. However, our approach does support the classification of obfuscated JavaScript, which is not supported by Zozzle. This implies a wider range of applicability for our models. When comparing to the other models from the state of the art, our approach performs better when considering the accuracy (about 98%) and is more balanced when considering the FPR and the FNR jointly (e.g., with a threshold of about 3% for both).

In addition to this, due to the very large size of our dataset, we can reliably test the validity of our models and have confidence that a similar performance can

Table 5. Top 10 most common false negative categories, ordered by percentage of occurrences.

	TLSH	Nilsimsa	ssdeep	SDHASH
1st	Unknown	Unknown	Unknown	Unknown
2nd	Redirect	Redirect	Redirect	Redirect
3rd	Trojan	Trojan	Trojan	Trojan
4th	CoinHive	CoinHive	CoinHive	CoinHive
5th	SEOHide	SEOHide	SEOHide	SEOHide
6th	IFrame	IFrame	IFrame	IFrame
7th	Faceliker	Faceliker	Faceliker	Faceliker
8th	Crypted	FakejQuery	FakejQuery	Crypted
9th	FakejQuery	Crypted	Ramnit	FakejQuery
10th	Ramnit	Ramnit	Crypted	Ramnit

be achieved when used in real life circumstances. Making classifiers with small datasets might lead to less generic models. Since there exists a vast diversity of possible malware and clean files, a small dataset might give a skewed image of the performances of the methods, due to not being able to verify whether it works on new never-seen-before malware. In our case, we have 1.5M samples with a 54% positive rate. The only competitor that has a similarly sized dataset is Cujo, with roughly 201k samples, but very few samples of malware (0.3%). This can be further seen in Table 4, as the best performing classifiers all have very few samples of malware files compared to our dataset.

5 Discussion

In this section we discuss the possible causes of misclassifications, which might lead to false negatives and false positives.

5.1 False Negatives

False negatives are misclassified malware scripts, for which we have full access to the code. This section will focus on the models trained on the entire 1.5M dataset, as these are the best performing models and also the dataset that contains all malware files, giving a better view of the shortcomings of LSH. Table 5 shows the top 10 most common types of misclassified malware, for each LSH method. The detection names come from Cyren's labelling system. The most occurring category represents the most difficult class of malware for our models to generalise. The *unknown* category contains files that got flagged for malicious behaviour but where there was not enough information to sort the files into one of the more known malware families. One very likely scenario is that the *unknown* malware belong to smaller groups of malware types which might be less prevalent in the dataset.

Observing Table 5, it is possible to see that all LSH methods lead to almost the same false types of negatives: the top 7 misclassified categories are the same for all four methods. When inspecting these files, it can be seen that they have two common elements: either they are very similar to clean looking code, like in the case of Redirectors and FakejQuery, or the actual malicious part of the code is very small, making it easy to inject into otherwise clean code, like CoinHive.

In consequence, when these malware types are hashed, malicious information might get lost, e.g. if there is a single line of malicious code in an otherwise clean file it might result in that the hash looks more like a clean file rather than a malicious file, which is often the case with CoinHive or other cryptocurrency mining malware.

In the case of redirectors, we have malware that is not necessarily doing anything malicious, as redirecting users on websites is a very common thing, but it is the destination that is malicious. This is a similar problem with malware of the downloader type (in Table 5 are Trojan, Ramnit, FakejQuery, and Crypted) since the act of downloading is not malicious, but the file that is downloaded might be malicious. In that case, the JavaScript file itself does not actually hold any malicious code. In these cases, the destination/download URLs that are the malicious indicators might after locality sensitive hashing have a little to no difference from URLs that are benign. In other words when a locality sensitive hash is created, it might end up looking like other downloader/redirection programs that are benign.

5.2   False Positives

False positives are misclassified clean files. The clean files from Cyren were not directly available to us (only the file's SHA256 signature and its LSH hashes are stored in our dataset) as these files are more likely to contain personally identifiable information. Thus we have to rely on analysing the files that come from VirusTotal, which are publicly available. In comparison to false negatives, false positives are much harder to analyse because clean files do not carry a category label that we could use as a basis for generalization. By doing a manual inspection on 50 of the publicly available false positives, the following observations have been made:

- Due to malware like FakejQuery, there is a chance that other similar benign code gets detected, e.g., code that is a fork of jQuery or a jQuery plugin.
- Shorter files give hashes that carry less information, leading to higher false positives. This is the reason why the LSH methods have a recommended minimum file/length.
- Some obfuscation techniques are less common than others, for example, encoding JavaScript statements as a string which the program then interprets using the `eval` method is highly suspicious but is not always an indicator of maliciousness. It is sometimes used to hide sensitive data that should not be able to get scraped by web crawlers.

6   Conclusion

In this paper we have shown that utilising deep learning together with locality sensitive hashing as a form of feature extraction it is possible to classify JavaScript malware with a high accuracy and a low false positive rate. Our method works with obfuscated code and is completely static. When comparing our method to other methods of static JavaScript malware detection, our method provides competitive results without having drawbacks such as not being able to handle obfuscated code.

References

1. Cyren - Malware Attack Detection (2019). https://www.cyren.com/tl_files/down loads/resources/Cyren_Malware-Attack-Detection_Datasheet_20160915_ltr_EN_we b.pdf
2. Cortes, C., Vapnik, V.: Support-vector networks. Mach. Learn. **20**, 3 (1995). https://doi.org/10.1007/BF00994018
3. Curtsinger, C., Livshits, B., Zorn, B., Seifert, C.: Zozzle: low-overhead mostly static javascript malware detection. Technical report, MSR-TR-2010-156, November 2010
4. Damiani, E., De Capitani di Vimercati, S., Paraboschi, S., Samarati, P.: An open digest-based technique for spam detection, vol. 2004 (2004)
5. Freund, Y., Mason, L.: The alternating decision tree learning algorithm. In: Proceedings of the Sixteenth International Conference on Machine Learning (1999)
6. Ioffe, S., Szegedy, C.: Batch normalization: accelerating deep network training by reducing internal covariate shift. arXiv preprint arXiv:1502.03167 (2015)
7. Kingma, D.P., Ba, J.: Adam: a method for stochastic optimization (2014)
8. Kornblum, J.: VirusTotal (2018). https://ssdeep-project.github.io/ssdeep/index. html
9. Likarish, P., Jung, E., Jo, I.: Obfuscated malicious javascript detection using classification techniques. In: International Conference on Malicious and Unwanted Software (MALWARE) (2009)
10. Micro, T.: TLSH (2018). https://github.com/trendmicro/tlsh
11. Ndichu, S., Ozawa, S., Misu, T., Okada, K.: A machine learning approach to malicious javascript detection using fixed length vector representation, pp. 1–8, July 2018. https://doi.org/10.1109/IJCNN.2018.8489414
12. Raff, E., Barker, J., Sylvester, J., Brandon, R., Catanzaro, B., Nicholas, C.: Malware detection by eating a whole EXE. arXiv e-prints arXiv:1710.09435 (2017)
13. Ratanaworabhan, P., Livshits, B., Zorn, B.: Nozzle: a defense against heap-spraying code injection attacks. In: Proceedings of the Usenix Security Symposium (2009). https://www.microsoft.com/en-us/research/publication/nozzle-a-defense-against-heap-spraying-code-injection-attacks-2/
14. Rieck, K., Krueger, T., Dewald, A.: Cujo: efficient detection and prevention of drive-by-download attacks. In: Proceedings of the 26th Annual Computer Security Applications Conference (2010). https://doi.org/10.1145/1920261.1920267
15. sdhash@roussev.net: SDHash (2018). http://roussev.net/sdhash/sdhash.html
16. Srivastava, N., Hinton, G., Krizhevsky, A., Sutskever, I., Salakhutdinov, R.: Dropout: a simple way to prevent neural networks from overfitting. J. Mach. Learn. Res. (2014). http://jmlr.org/papers/v15/srivastava14a.html

17. VirusTotal: VirusTotal (2018). https://support.virustotal.com/hc/en-us/articles/115002126889-How-it-works
18. Wang, Y., Cai, W.D., Wei, P.C.: A deep learning approach for detecting malicious javascript code. Secur. Commun. Netw. (2016). https://doi.org/10.1002/sec.1441
19. Xu, W., Zhang, F., Zhu, S.: JStill: mostly static detection of obfuscated malicious javascript code. In: Proceedings of the Third ACM Conference on Data and Application Security and Privacy, CODASPY 2013 (2013). https://doi.org/10.1145/2435349.2435364
20. Ye, Y., Li, T., Adjeroh, D., Iyengar, S.S.: A survey on malware detection using data mining techniques. ACM Comput. Surv. (2017). https://doi.org/10.1145/3073559

RouAlign: Cross-Version Function Alignment and Routine Recovery with Graphlet Edge Embedding

Can Yang[1,2]([✉]), Jian Liu[1,2]([✉]), Mengxia Luo[1,2], Xiaorui Gong[1,2], and Baoxu Liu[1,2]

[1] Institute of Information Engineering, Chinese Academy of Sciences, Beijing, China
{yangcan,liujian6}@iie.ac.cn
[2] School of Cyber Security, University of Chinese Academy of Sciences, Beijing, China

Abstract. Reverse engineering is labor-intensive work to understand the inner implementation of a program, and is necessary for malware analysis, vulnerability hunting, etc. Cross-version function identification and subroutine matching would greatly release manpower by indicating the known parts coming from different binary programs. Existing approaches mainly focus on function recognition ignoring the recovery of the relationships between functions, which makes the researchers hard to locate the calling routine they are interested in.

In this paper, we propose a method using graphlet edge embedding to abstract high-level topology features of function call graphs and recover the relationships between functions. With the recovery of function relationships, we reconstruct the calling routine of the program and then infer the specific functions in it. We implement a prototype model called RouAlign, which can automatically align the trunk routine of assembly codes. We evaluated RouAlign on 65 groups of real-world programs, with over two million functions. RouAlign outperforms state-of-the-art binary comparing solutions by over 35% with a high precision of 92% on average in pairwise function recognition.

Keywords: Edge embedding · Calling routine recovery

1 Introduction

An essential purpose of reverse engineering is to pick out known calling routines from a new binary program. This analyzing task is generally used in malware family classification, reused component detection, patch comparison, and so on. But it could be a tedious job to find out every mutation of a program, especially when the main functionality stays the same but some calling routines added or removed. What's more, it would encounter plenty of difficulties in cross-architecture, cross-OS, cross-compiler, and cross-optimization programs routine cognition. This problem has now become more crucial while Internet-of-Things (IoTs) become massive and fragmentated.

For instance, Fig. 1.A shows a message processing routine of a printer with CVE-2017-2741. Now, if we have obtained the function call graph (Fig. 1.B) of another printer (with different architecture here), analyzing is needed to verify the vulnerability. In this case, traditional tools [9] could hardly help. A common way in practice is to locate the context functions by cross-references firstly. Then trace the calling routine to see whether a similar function exists in Fig. 1.B. We note that only a subset of functions in the routine are concerned by researchers, and the connectivity between functions is important in the analysis.

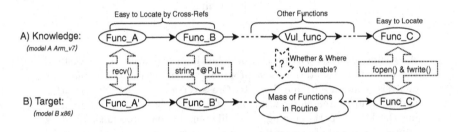

Fig. 1. Motivation: reuse knowledge of (A) to search vulnerabilities in (B)

Actually, the same vulnerability might be shared by dozens of binaries from different products. But automatically analyzing these cross-version binaries is complicated for many reasons. Generally speaking, difficulties are: 1) Different compilers prefer difference memory arrangements and inline hobbits. 2) Different compiler optimizations and obfuscators would greatly change the control flow [11, 19]. 3) Library and system functions vary a lot within different operating systems. 4) A software might change a lot after years of development, even if its main features were hardly modified.

Existing state-of-the-art solutions for cross-version binary analysis are not routine-sensitive. Approaches [7,14,15,21,26] are mainly trying hard to understand the semantics of functions for identification. These methods tend to identify functions directly, but isolated. Approaches [8,17,20,24] take the Function Call Graphs (FCG) into consideration. But these methods only utilize intuitive features like degrees of nodes, as assistance to the function internal features. However, considering in case cross-version analysis, internal features are not stable and reliable. We design a method to better utilize FCG than ever. By abstracting higher-order structural features into vectors and then modeling them via neural networks, we show that the FCG could play an important role in routine recovery and function alignment.

Our Approach: Alignment. In this paper, we aim at finding a way to recognize a common calling routine between cross-version binaries, and then identify functions in it. For the purpose of recognizing the calling routine, we must have abilities to recover the relationships between functions (mainly caller-callee relationship). With the recognized relationships, reverse engineers can pick out a calling routine from the FCG of an unknown program. Once the calling routine is aligned with a known routine, the functions in the same position can be viewed as functional equal. This method is what we called *Alignment* method because it infers a function by its position in a routine rather than investigate the inner implementation of the function. This method should be robust enough against variations such as function inline and addition function calls.

For relationships recovery, we propose a new algorithm based on Graphlet Edge Embedding (described in Sect. 3.3). This is inspired by the ideas of Graphlet Degree Signatures [22], which is a famous alignment algorithm in bioinformatics. Our method starts from a simple assumption that the similar functions in program have similar graph structures in the function call routine, and reasonable modifications (function inline, additional calls, etc., which could be introduced by programmers or compilers) to the graph structure is recognizable. For instance, a distributor function usually follows the input routines and has many subroutines for special tasks. In short, we used edge embeddings to abstract high-level features of functions in function call graphs, and then recover the caller-callee relationships between functions to reconstruct the function calling routine. With this method, we can tell a known routine from a new binary, thus functions in the routine can be recognized and an overall knowledge of the program can be achieved.

We have implemented a prototype tool called RouAlign. RouAlign utilized graphlet edge embeddings to align two calling routines automatically and then identified functions by the aligned positions in the routines. We evaluated RouAlign in 65 groups of cross-version binaries with over 200,000 functions. And we compared the function recognition results of RouAlign with the results of BinDiff and the results of Gemini. RouAlign performed better than both and showed a great potential of function call graphs in function recognition.

In summary, our contributions are as follows.

- **Routine Recovery.** We present a multistage approach to align FCGs where the calling routines are preserved as much as possible.
- **Edge Embedding Algorithm.** We propose a method to embedding edges in FCGs, and an algorithm to recover caller-callee relationships between functions with abilities to distinguish modifications like function inline.
- **Scalable Design.** Compared to existing algorithms, our algorithm is parallelable (the procedure can be speeded up via multi-processing) and incrementable (the results would be expanded when given extra knowledge) besides high precision.
- **Better Performance.** Compared to popular commercial binary diffing tools, our prototype can perform 35% better precision and 25% better recall on average within cross-version binaries.

2   Problems and Challenges

In this section, we address the problem to study, challenges facing, and reasonable ways to solve them. Some important symbols are defined as well.

2.1   Function Alignment

Existing function matching methods can be roughly classified into two categories. One is pairwise matching, which searches common functions in a pair of programs. The other is library matching, which represents functions in brief forms (i.e., embedding) and searches a new function from a pre-built representation library. *Function alignment* is a kind of pairwise matching, but differs from function matching methods. Function matching methods aim to find two functions exactly the same. In contrast, function alignment tries to find functions of the same use (namely, functionally equal).

Definition 1. *Functional Equal: If function F_a and F_b take the same responsibility in their individual calling routines, they are functional equal. Ideally, functional equal means F_a and F_b can be substituted with each other in their calling routines.*

Considering an example of algorithmic upgrade, suppose an old program A has a routine: "*Input $\rightarrow$ Encrypt $\rightarrow$ MD5 $\rightarrow$ Output*". And a new program B has a routine: "*Input $\rightarrow$ Encrypt $\rightarrow$ SHA1 $\rightarrow$ Output*". In both program A and B, the *Input*, *Output* and *Encrypt* are exactly the same. Usually, Function matching methods [7,15] will mark the $SHA1$ and $MD5$ as different and the relationships with both *Input* and *Output* are ignored. But function alignment should mark that $SHA1$ and $MD5$ are of the same use (both are hash functions) and the calling routine stays successive. This makes alignment methods robust when figuring out the main routine of a program, especially when some components were changed. We regard alignment as a relationships-defined procedure, and formally define the function alignment as follows.

Definition 2. *Function Alignment: given a target program P_{trgt} and a template program P_{tmpl}, function alignment aims to find a function mapping $A(F_{tmpl}) \rightarrow F_{trgt}$ between FCGs from P_{tmpl} to P_{trgt}, where F_{trgt} are functional equal to F_{tmpl}.*

In case the functions in P_{tmpl} were known, the function alignment procedure could be viewed as knowledge reasoning from P_{tmpl} to P_{trgt}. In Biological Network Alignments, it has been shown that aligned networks are functional similar [18]. Our experiments show that rule also worked for Function Call Graph Alignments.

2.2 Challenges

Directed Heterogeneous Network. Network alignment and graph alignment are also hot but tough topics in literature. In reverse engineering, FCG provides limited information. Data refers, syscalls and many attributes of function are not negligible. Taking this into consideration, the FCG becomes a heterogeneous network. This means, for reliable and convincing performance, our function alignment problem might be equivalent to heterogeneous network alignment problems. Although heterogeneous networks preserve richer information than homogeneous networks, they face more challenges [4]. In addition, the development of algorithms on heterogeneous networks is not mature enough now.

Low Recognizability of Sparse Network. The network alignment algorithms used in other fields, such as bioinformatics and graph theory, are usually designed for denser networks. However, in function call graphs, most functions only relate to other few functions. This means if we naively represent a function as its surrounding topologic, many functions might not be distinguishable. This is one of main reasons why embedding methods, like structure2vec [1,16], leave branch of functions as "similar". Low precision at one will significantly make the alignment methods not reliable because the mistakes would propagate via relationships.

Brief Solution. To overcome these challenges, we adapt two novel methods. Firstly, we separated the heterogeneous network into two layers. One contains the relationship between functions and other attributes; the other is a directed homogeneous network where nodes are functions. Secondly, instead of recognizing the nodes directly, we take a detour to recover edges among nodes, and design a new method to evaluate the similarity of these edges.

3 Function Alignment Method

In this section, we first show the overall workflow of RouAlign, which recover two informative structures from binary codes as necessary data. Then we introduce the core process of graphlet edge embedding method to extract higher-order graphic features. And finally, we describe the approach to aligning functions and recovering calling routines.

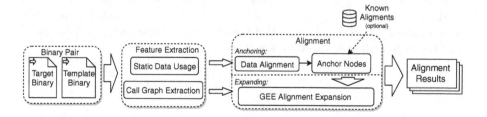

Fig. 2. Overview of RouAlign

3.1 Overview

The RouAlign is designed to align calling routines from the target binary to the template binary. Figure 2 shows the whole process of the tool. The first step is extracting necessary information from binaries, including static data references and function call graph. Static data includes string constants, numeric constants, etc. In experiments [12–14], they are proved to be reliable across versions. The function call graph preserves function nodes as well as caller-callee relationships between them. Thus, after extraction, our heterogeneous relation network has two layers with two different node types, one is func-data layer, the other is func-func layer.

The alignment stage can be separated into two phases—*anchoring* and *expanding*—for different layers of the relation network. The *anchoring* procedure tries to find some function nodes that are highly similar in the func-data layer. The *expanding* procedure trys to align more nodes from the anchored nodes in the func-func layer. They would be discussed later in Sect. 3.2 and 3.3. The basic idea of this method is to find some reliable nodes and then propagate the confidence as much as we can. This refers to the "seed and expand" idea of BLAST [3], and is also sort of simulation of the human analyzing procedure.

3.2 Anchor Nodes Searching

Many human researchers start to analyze a binary from limited entries, such as main functions, special library functions, functions with special and unique constants, etc. So inspired RouAlign. The reason behind is that, these features are the most likely to stay constant in the mutations [13]. These functions are naturally aligned and we call them anchor nodes.

We defined two kinds of anchor nodes. One comes from the running mechanism of executable binaries. In most situations, library calls and syscalls are explicit. For instance, Windows PE files use IAT to locate the library functions, and Linux ELF files use PLT. Many modern disassemble tools like IDA PRO can automatically indicate these calls in the binary. For this kind of anchor nodes, we directly take and use them. The other kind comes from human experiences. There are some unique constants in programs, such as s-Boxes in cryptography, magic bytes of protocols. Uses of unique constants can determine a function with high probability. Searching is needed for the second kind of anchor nodes.

Firstly, we match data nodes from different binaries, in order to find the constant data used by both two binaries. We extract some additional attributes for the data nodes, listing in the Table 1. We adapted SimHash [27] to resist slight changes to the constants. And then, we give these features to a linear classifier to tell whether two data are the same.

Table 1. Attributes for data nodes

Attribute name	Weights
Length of data	0.25
MD5 of data	0.48
SimHash of data	0.25
Offset in the segment	0.02

*Weights referred to [14]

Secondly, after the data nodes from different binaries are matched, we use the TF-IDF (Term Frequency-Inverse Document Frequency) model to tell whether the function nodes related to the matched data nodes should be anchored. The TF-IDF model, which is a well-studied algorithm, can reflect how important the data is to a function. We pick out the function nodes with high weights and calculate the cosine similarity between them. The function nodes with high similarity are the anchor nodes that we want.

3.3   Expanding with Graphlet Edge Embedding

Nodes anchoring can align very limited part of the program, in most case. The expanding stage starts from the anchor nodes and expands the alignment alone edges. We introduced a heuristic method to evaluate the similarity between different edges. With the ability to match edges, we could find out the relationships between functions, and the calling routine could be recovered.

Graphlet Edge Signature. Respectfully, we name our new design "Graphlet Edge Signature", a method to characterize edges in directed graphs. Our design refers to the Graphlet Degree Signature [22] (a.k.a. GSV), which has been proven to be a successful design to extract topology structure in bioinformatics [18]. However, GSV was designed for node identification in an undirected graph. The Function Call Graph is a directed graph, which means the GSV should be redesigned. In practice, a reverse engineer can easily infer the unknown functions near a known one by FCG, especially by caller-callee relationships. Thus, it's reasonable to pay attention to edges recovery than directly node identification.

Firstly, we use a node pair $\langle N_c, N_t \rangle$ to represent a directed edge between center node (N_c) and target node (N_t). Then, we pick out all 2nd order neighbors of N_c and N_t. A graphlet is then defined by these nodes. In our design, we only concern about the motifs that related to 1st order similarity and 2nd order similarity. Motifs are recurrent and statistically significant subgraphs [23]. Using motifs makes us can focus on specific commonality once in a time. In our design, we only concern about the motifs that related to 1st order similarity and 2nd order similarity. We pick out 45 basic motifs, denoted as $m_1, m_2, \ldots, m_{45}$ in Fig. 3. After that, we can count the motifs the target edge touches and get a vector V. Each dimension in the V stands for the number of times the motif m_i appearing in the graphlet. This vector is what we call the signature of the edge in the chosen graphlet (Graphlet Edge Signature, GES).

The policy of selecting these motifs in Fig. 3 is not to enumerate all isomorphism subgraphs in the extracted graphlet, but to focus on the special relationships between the center edge and its surrounding edges. In addition, the chosen motifs should be able to compose any other complex graphlets. We view the in-and-out edges pair between two nodes as a bi-directed edge. These bi-directed edges stand for some highly recognizable relationships between functions like iterations and loops. And when counting rings, we do not distinguish the source point and the destination point to reduce the complexity. We focus on surrounding nodes no more than 2nd order, although the edge signature vector will be defined more precisely with higher-order neighbors. This is because the complexity and time consumption will increase sharply while going into higher-order relationships [24].

Distance Measurement. Now we have managed to represent a directed edge into the numeric format. A measuring system is needed for further usage. For distance measurement, there is a simplified, intuitive mathematical solution adapting from GSV. We define the distance D between the target edge E_{trgt} and template edge E_{tmpl} as below. The D_i is the distance at the i_{th} motifs. The E^i is the i_{th} member of the signature vector, meaning the number of times edge E touches motif m_i.

$$D = \sum_{i=0}^{45} D_i(E_{trgt}, E_{tmpl}) = \sum_{i=0}^{45} \frac{|log(E_{trgt}^i + 1) - log(E_{tmpl}^i + 1)|}{log(max\{E_{trgt}^i, E_{tmpl}^i\} + 2)} \quad (1)$$

Obviously, the distance D results within range $[0, 1)$. A smaller distance indicates there is more similarity between two edges. However, in most FCGs, the induced graphlet is usually not dense enough to contain most motifs above, leaving a lot of zeroes in the signature vector and leading to the distribution of distances close to 0. We can remove the part that has no value to revise the weights and remap the distribution of distances into $[0, 1)$—to ignore the similarity comes from common deficiencies. The distance can be now defined as:

$$D = \frac{\sum_{i=0}^{45} D_i}{\sum_{i=0}^{45} B_i} \quad (2)$$

$$B_i = \begin{cases} 1, E_{trgt}^i \neq 0 \ and \ E_{tmpl}^i \neq 0 \\ 0, others \end{cases} \quad (3)$$

Embedding. The method introduced above is experience-based and only suitable for distance measurement. Additionally, we introduce an embedding representation not only suitable for similarity measurement but also semantic pre-

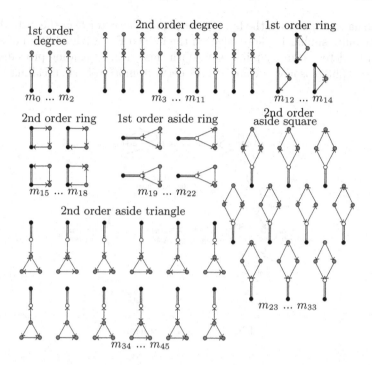

Fig. 3. Chosen basic motifs, in which central nodes, target nodes, and surrounding nodes are depicted as "black", "white" and "gray" vertexes respectively.

served. We use a neural network encoder with the Siamese architecture [2] to generate the embedding of an edge.

The Siamese architecture uses two identical embedding neural networks. In our case, a 3-layer neural network was used. Each embedding network takes a GES vector V as input and outputs what we call Graphlet Edge Embeddings (GEE). GES vector V is a 45-dimensional vector as mentioned above. The final output of the Siamese architecture is the Euclidean distance of the two embeddings. While training, distances of similar input pairs were set to 0, and distances of dissimilar input pairs were set to 1. We formulate the Siamese network output distance D' for each input pair as:

$$D' = \|Embed(V_1) - Embed(V_2)\| \qquad (4)$$

3.4   Inline Recognition

Our method is naturally suitable for inline recognition. Showing in Fig. 4, the function `ingroup` was inlined into `check_suid` due to compiled differences. However, in the origin FCG (at left), if we connect a virtual edge from the caller of the inlined function directly to the callee of the inlined function (depicted as two dotted lines from `check_suid` to `bb_internal_get_grgid` and `bb_internal_getpwnam` in the figure), the signature vector V of the virtual edges would be quite similar to those edges in the inlined FCG. An addition of a function can be detected in a similar way. With this trick, expanding procedure can step over slight reasonable changes and perform more robust in calling routine alignment.

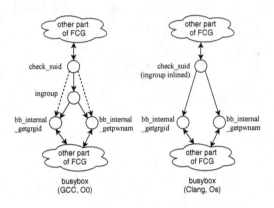

Fig. 4. Inline recognition

Algorithm 1. Expanding Routine

Require: Aligned pair: $\langle N_{trgt}, N_{tmpl} \rangle$
  $S_{tgrt} \leftarrow GES(Edge)$, for all Edge connected to N_{trgt}
  $S_{tmpl} \leftarrow GES(Edge)$, for all Edge connected to N_{tmpl}
  repeat
    for all V_1 in S_{tgrt}, V_2 in S_{tmpl} **do**
      if $D(V_1, V_2) <$ Threshold **then**
        mark the another two endpoints of the two edges as Aligned
      end if
    end for
    for all V_1 in S_{tgrt}, V_2 in S_{tmpl} without alignment **do**
      Perform inline search
    end for
  until All aligned nodes have been expanded.

The expanding procedure is now easy to explain: $1st$ choose an aligned node pair $\langle N_{trgt}, N_{tmpl} \rangle$. $2nd$ enumerate then embed edges of each node to obtain two sets of embeddings S_{tgrt} and S_{tmpl}. $3rd$ align edges pairwisely between the two sets by calculating the distances D (the average of both distances mentioned above). We leave edges "far from" any other edges alone, and then perform inline recognition on these isolated edges. The overall algorithm for expanding stage is summarized in Algorithm 1. Due to the space limit, we omit some details here, such as judgement of the closest distance and removal of duplications.

4 Evaluation

4.1 Implementation and Datasets

We had implemented a prototype of RouAlign. We used the IDA PRO as the tool to extract the necessary information (i.e., constant data, library functions, and the FCG) to construct the relation networks. We implemented the whole alignment stage with python, including isomorphic judgment and GEE algorithm. For embedding network training, we undersampled about 20 million edge pairs from the datasets. The embedding size was set to 20 empirically. Our experiments were conducted on a laptop with 8 GB memories and 4 cores at 2.6 GHz.

Our evaluation was base on two datasets: The first one was called the **horizontal dataset** where the binaries were compiled from the same source code but with different compilers and optimizations. This dataset contained 50 groups of binaries from 5 different programs. The second one was called the **longitudinal dataset** where the binaries were compiled from different source codes, and these source codes were referred to different versions during the development of the same software. This dataset contained 15 groups of binaries from 3 different generations of OpenSSL.

Each group needs at least 4 binaries: a tripped target, a stripped template, an unstripped target, and an unstripped template. The two unstripped binaries were used for ground truth extraction. With the debug symbols, the easiest way to get the ground truth of similar function pairs is comparing the function name. Some function name might change due to compiling definitions and developments. For example, The `OPENSSL_strlcpy` in OpenSSL 1.1.1 has a different name `BUF_strlcpy` in OpenSSL 0.9.8. We manually corrected these functions as a complement to the ground truth.

We use the Precision and the Recall metric. For every aligned function pair, if the pair is not in the ground truth, we count the precision as zero. For every function pair in the ground truth, if the pair is not in alignment results, we count the recall as zero. Therefore, the precision captures the ratio of function pairs that are correctly found, and the recall captures the ratio of function pairs that are supposed to be found.

4.2 Horizontal Comparison: Same Source, Different Compilation

Horizontal experiments were designed to simulate the circumstances where the same source code was reused in different environments. We implemented the horizontal experiment on 5 frequent-used real-world program projects. Each program was compiled into 5 different versions with different compile options. The compiler we used is `GCC` and `clang`. The options we used is O0 (without optimizations) Os (size-first optimization) and O3 (speed-first optimization). Binaries were aligned with each other by both RouAlign and BinDiff. BinDiff was used as the benchmark in our experiments. Table 2 shows the results of one-fifth of our horizontal experiments.

Table 2. Horizontal comparing result of BusyBox.

Binary pairs	Precision		Recall	
	RouAlign	BinDiff	RouAlign	BinDiff
G@O0 - G@O3	0.928	0.651	0.770	0.229
G@O0 - G@Os	0.946	0.546	0.792	0.456
G@O0 - C@O0	0.990	0.765	0.874	0.623
G@O0 - C@Os	0.913	0.452	0.703	0.344
G@O3 - G@Os	0.991	0.945	0.926	0.336
G@O3 - C@O0	0.918	0.617	0.707	0.217
G@O3 - C@Os	0.953	0.653	0.755	0.245
G@Os - C@O0	0.937	0.506	0.723	0.419
G@Os - C@Os	0.961	0.593	0.775	0.459
C@O0 - C@Os	0.933	0.524	0.756	0.404

G stands for the **GCC** compiler and **C** stands for **Clang**.
$^@*$ indicates the compiler optimizations.
For instance, **G$^@$O0** means a binary compiled using **GCC** with option "**-O0**".

A case study on results in Table 2 shows that the precision of RouAlign is much higher than that of BinDiff, and the performance is very stable. Generally, the O0-Os and O0-O3 shows the lowest performance, because the compiler would introduce a lot changes to the original FCG on specific purpose. An interesting phenomenon is that, the more the version varies from each other, the better RouAlign performs than BinDiff. This is because traditional matching methods rely much on internal function features, which change a lot during compiling procedures.

We made statistics on all results of 5 different binary sets, and cited some results of other state-of-art solutions, showing in Table 3. In the first part of the table, we presented some average numbers of some important indicators to describe the datasets. The number of functions and the number of ground truth showed the scale of the binary. The number of anchor nodes showed how efficient the expanding procedure was. It's easy to summarize from Table 3 that the RouAlign could perform better on larger and more complex binaries, where the FCGs are more tremendous and the graphlet features are more representative. All these horizontal comparing results proved that relationships are useful and our method could handle the problem correctly.

Table 3. Horizontal comparing results statistics.

	minigzip	BusyBox	ImageMagick	OpenSSL	Sqlite3
Average numbers					
Ground truth	162.5	4711.6	4571.8	8105.2	2657.4
Total functions	211.8	5200.0	5591.0	9054.6	3151.0
Extracted datas	75.2	7946.2	16407.8	12822.4	3491.8
Symbolic func	26.3	29.0	455.0	135.1	117.6
Anchor nodes	35.7	913.2	1254.7	546.3	346.0
Precision					
RouAlign	0.939	0.946	0.900	0.941	0.788
BinDiff	0.733	0.625	0.433	0.336	0.434
Gemini[a]	0.750	0.828	0.397	0.546	0.454
asm2vec[b]	-	0.856	0.837	0.792	0.776
αDiff[c]	0.546	0.546	0.546	0.546	0.546
Recall					
RouAlign	0.448	0.778	0.593	0.624	0.593
BinDiff	0.522	0.373	0.320	0.218	0.320
Gemini[a]	0.017	0.106	0.012	0.156	0.142

a: Gemini[1] here is a optimized version for the original program couldn't be accomplished in a 16GB memory machine. Gemini* was only tested on binary pair Clang-Os to GCC-O0)

b: Results of Asm2Vec[2] were cited (pairwise comparison on GCC-O0 and GCC-O3).

c: Results of αDiff is cited and then averaged of all their x86_64 results.

4.3   Longitudinal Comparison: Same Software, Different Versions

The longitudinal comparison was designed to simulate the circumstances where the same program itself varies a lot from version to version. We chose 3 different source code versions of OpenSSL, among which time spans nearly 10 years and 3 big generations, and then compiled them with 5 different options.

As shown in Table 4, RouAlign performed much more stable among different compiler optimizations with high precision. The recall was improved a little over that of BinDiff, because the calling routine did change quite a lot during long-term iterations. It should be noted that the results of RouAlign are continuous with high precision, providing more powerful assistant to human researchers. All these longitudinal comparing results proved that our methods are usable in detecting long-term changes to binary and can still recognize calling routines in a high precision.

5   Limitations

Major limitation of alignment methods is the missing of many internal function features. We designed so in order to show that the FCGs could provide much information for understanding binaries. A better way we advised in the future is to combine RouAlign with some function embedding methods that could nicely represent internal function feature cross-versions.

Table 4. Longitudinal comparing for cross-version OpenSSL.

Versions	Ver.100 to Ver.098		Ver.111 to Ver.100		Ver.111 to Ver.098	
	RouAlign	BinDiff	RouAlign	BinDiff	RouAlign	BinDiff
Precision						
GCC-O0	0.953	0.843	0.789	0.493	0.692	0.436
GCC-O3	0.944	0.794	0.602	0.332	0.501	0.296
GCC-Os	0.950	0.824	0.781	0.439	0.674	0.377
Clang-O0	0.959	0.822	0.775	0.496	0.697	0.423
Clang-Os	0.956	0.796	0.779	0.432	0.669	0.366
Recall						
GCC-O0	0.675	0.676	0.401	0.406	0.311	0.352
GCC-O3	0.618	0.544	0.231	0.228	0.185	0.200
GCC-Os	0.650	0.605	0.422	0.326	0.309	0.278
Clang-O0	0.671	0.584	0.385	0.357	0.304	0.305
Clang-Os	0.636	0.497	0.398	0.273	0.301	0.229

(Ver.111 Ver.100 and Ver.098 stand for OpenSSL Version 1.1.1, Version 1.0.0 and Version 0.9.8)

Another limitation is that the detection rate might be low in library-like binaries (.so files, etc.). This is unavoidable because functions in library binaries tend to be independent without caller-callee relationships to recover. But we won't regard this as a critical problem, because the original intention of RouAlign is an auxiliary tool to help researchers trace out the calling routine from a specified function node.

6   Related Works

Function alignment by FCGs is a long proposed topic, but poorly studied. [17] is about the first to introduce the Hungarian algorithm into binary analysis, e.g., malware classification. Further studies [25] use FCG merely on binary similarity discrimination rather than more detail analysis. Bindiff [9] introduces a MD index [8] to represent the topologic of function in FCG. But the MD index only counts the 1st order features like in-out degrees and could perform "medium" good in practice [10]. Recently, αdiff [20] uses FCG with DNN to detect cross-version binary code similarity and achieves some better results than Bindiff.

Cross-version function recognition is a hot topic recently. Dynamic analyzing methods assume that similar functions perform similar runtime behaviors. For example, Bingo [6], etc., capture behaviors of a function with various contexts. However, coverage and contexts generating are still problems for dynamic methods. Static methods utilize instructions and raw bytes to calculate the similarity between functions. They are not good at cross-version scenarios, and many researchers are trying to resolve this problem. For cross-platform problems, Gemini etc. [15,21], extract structure features and basic block features to calculate the similarity. For cross-optimization problems, Asm2vec [7] and InnerEye [26] map instructions and opcodes into high dimensional vector space, and then value the similarity by these mathematical representations.

7 Conclusion

In this paper, starting from the requirement of recognizing a calling routine from cross-version binaries, we proposed a novel method to learn high-level features of function call graphs to recover the caller-callee relationships between functions. We design a model to align routine and functions called RouAlign and series experiments to compare RouAlign with popular tools in real world. The evaluation results show that RouAlign outperforms the widely used commercial tools by over 35%s on average precision. We successfully reveal the great potential of function call graphs in function recognition and our Graphlet Edge Embedding method indicates a possible direction in the future.

Acknowledgments. We thank anonymous reviewers for their invaluable comments and suggestions. Can Yang and Jian Liu share the co-first authorship.

References

1. Le, S.: Structure2Vec: deep learning for security analytics over graphs (2018)
2. Bromley, J., et al.: Signature verification using a "siamese" time delay neural network. In: Advances in neural information processing systems (1994)
3. Altschul, S.F., et al.: Basic local alignment search tool. J. Mol. Biol. **215**(3), 403–410 (1990)
4. Shi, C., et al.: A survey of heterogeneous information network analysis. IEEE Trans. Knowl. Data Eng. **29**(1), 17–37 (2016)
5. Andriesse, D., et al.: An in-depth analysis of disassembly on full-scale x86/x64 binaries. In: 25th USENIX Security Symposium (USENIX Security 2016) (2016)
6. Chandramohan, M., et al.: BinGo: cross-architecture cross-OS binary search. In: Proceedings of the 2016 24th ACM SIGSOFT International Symposium on Foundations of Software Engineering. ACM (2016)
7. Ding, S., et al.: Asm2Vec: boosting static representation robustness for binary clone search against code obfuscation and compiler optimization. IEEE (2019)
8. Dullien, T., et al.: Automated attacker correlation for malicious code. Bochum University (Germany FR) (2010)
9. Dullien, T., Rolles, R.: Graph-based comparison of executable objects (English version). SSTIC **5**(1), 3 (2005)

10. BinDiff manual. https://www.zynamics.com/bindiff/manual/. Accessed 15 Sept 2019
11. Junod, P., et al.: Obfuscator-LLVM-software protection for the masses. In: 2015 IEEE/ACM 1st International Workshop on Software Protection, pp. 3–9. IEEE (2015)
12. Eschweiler, S, Yakdan, K., Gerhards-Padilla, E.: discovRE: efficient cross-architecture identification of bugs in binary code. In: NDSS (2016)
13. Feng, M., et al.: Open-source license violations of binary software at large scale. In: IEEE 26th International Conference on Software Analysis, Evolution and Reengineering (SANER) (2019)
14. Feng, Q., et al.: Scalable graph-based bug search for firmware images. In: Proceedings of the 2016 ACM SIGSAC Conference on Computer and Communications Security. ACM (2016)
15. Xu, X., et al.: Neural network-based graph embedding for cross-platform binary code similarity detection. In: Proceedings of the 2017 ACM SIGSAC Conference on Computer and Communications Security. ACM (2017)
16. Grover, A., Leskovec, J.: node2vec: scalable feature learning for networks. In: Proceedings of the 22nd ACM SIGKDD International Conference on Knowledge Discovery and Data Mining. ACM (2016)
17. Hu, X., et al.: Large-scale malware indexing using function-call graphs. In: Proceedings of the 16th ACM Conference on Computer and Communications Security. ACM (2009)
18. Kuchaiev, O., et al.: Topological network alignment uncovers biological function and phylogeny. J. R. Soc. Interface **7**(50), 1341–1354 (2010)
19. László, T., Kiss, Á.: Obfuscating C++ programs via control flow flattening. Annales Universitatis Scientarum Budapestinensis de Rolando Eötvös Nominatae, Sectio Computatorica **30**(1), 3–19 (2009)
20. Liu, B., et al.: αdiff: cross-version binary code similarity detection with DNN. In: Proceedings of the 33rd ACM/IEEE International Conference on Automated Software Engineering. ACM (2018)
21. Luo, M., Yang, C., Gong, X., Yu, L.: FuncNet: a Euclidean embedding approach for lightweight cross-platform binary recognition. In: Chen, S., Choo, K.-K.R., Fu, X., Lou, W., Mohaisen, A. (eds.) SecureComm 2019. LNICST, vol. 304, pp. 319–337. Springer, Cham (2019). https://doi.org/10.1007/978-3-030-37228-6_16
22. Milenković, T., Pržulj, N.: Uncovering biological network function via graphlet degree signatures. Cancer Inform. **6**, 257–273 (2008). CIN-S680
23. Milo, R., et al.: Network motifs: simple building blocks of complex networks. Science **298**(5594), 824–827 (2002)
24. Tang, J., et al.: LINE: large-scale information network embedding. In: Proceedings of the 24th International Conference on World Wide Web. International World Wide Web Conferences Steering Committee (2015)
25. Tang, Y., Wang, Y., Wei, S.N., Yu, B., Yang, Q.: Matching function-call graph of binary codes and its applications (Short Paper). In: Liu, J.K., Samarati, P. (eds.) ISPEC 2017. LNCS, vol. 10701, pp. 770–779. Springer, Cham (2017). https://doi.org/10.1007/978-3-319-72359-4_48
26. Zuo, F., Li, X., et al. Neural machine translation inspired binary code similarity comparison beyond function pairs. In: Proceedings of the 2019 Network and Distributed Systems Security Symposium (NDSS) (2019, in press)
27. SimHash wiki. https://en.wikipedia.org/wiki/SimHash. Accessed 3 Jan 2020

Code Between the Lines: Semantic Analysis of Android Applications

Johannes Feichtner[1,2(✉)] and Stefan Gruber[1]

[1] Institute of Applied Information Processing and Communications (IAIK),
Graz University of Technology, Inffeldgasse 16a, 8010 Graz, Austria
`johannes.feichtner@iaik.tugraz.at`
[2] Secure Information Technology Center – Austria (A-SIT),
Seidlgasse 22, 1030 Vienna, Austria

Abstract. Static and dynamic program analysis are the key concepts researchers apply to uncover security-critical implementation weaknesses in Android applications. As it is often not obvious in which context problematic statements occur, it is challenging to assess their practical impact. While some flaws may turn out to be bad practice but not undermine the overall security level, others could have a serious impact. Distinguishing them requires knowledge of the designated app purpose.

In this paper, we introduce a machine learning-based system that is capable of generating natural language text describing the purpose and core functionality of Android apps based on their actual code. We design a dense neural network that captures the semantic relationships of resource identifiers, string constants, and API calls contained in apps to derive a high-level picture of implemented program behavior. For arbitrary applications, our system can predict precise, human-readable keywords and short phrases that indicate the main use-cases apps are designed for.

We evaluate our solution on 67,040 real-world apps and find that with a precision between 69% and 84% we can identify keywords that also occur in the developer-provided description in Google Play. To avoid incomprehensible black box predictions, we apply a model explaining algorithm and demonstrate that our technique can substantially augment inspections of Android apps by contributing contextual information.

1 Introduction

As many Android applications perform security-critical tasks, it is crucial to validate their implementation security using static and dynamic program analysis. In recent years, researchers have elaborated various approaches to disclose possible leaks of private data, identify malware, or to uncover security deficiencies in Android apps. Typically, the results of these analyses fall into two categories: firstly, a classification into malevolent or harmless or, secondly, concrete results of specific aspects the inspection has been aiming for. While both types may be

© IFIP International Federation for Information Processing 2020
Published by Springer Nature Switzerland AG 2020
M. Hölbl et al. (Eds.): SEC 2020, IFIP AICT 580, pp. 171–186, 2020.
https://doi.org/10.1007/978-3-030-58201-2_12

adequate with regards to the particular objectives, they barely evolve to a superior level where the implemented behavior and context of program statements is also taken into account.

In practice, missing context awareness leads to situations where researchers disclose security flaws in execution traces but are unable to comprehend the impact or relevance of the finding in terms of the actual purpose of an application. E.g., basically, it is problematic if a constant, hard-coded key is used for encryption. However, if this happens within an advertisement library where encryption is only used for obfuscation, the impact of the finding needs to be assessed differently. Similarly, it depends on the use-case of an app whether supplying GPS information via HTTPS to an external entity, such as for assistance in traffic navigation, is a legitimate action or the undesirable leakage of sensitive data.

In a broader sense, these examples highlight what analyses are currently unable to cover: the *semantic understanding* of applications. Rather than gaining a high-level picture of the functionality and security of a program, common approaches for inspection focus on single instructions at the lowest possible level. While this is undoubtedly a legitimate level to determine the immediate effects on memory calls and registers, we are still missing a platform that enables us to reason about the effects of coherent code parts on the overall program state.

Augmenting app analysis by contextual information, such as the intended purpose and designated functionality, is of utmost importance to obtain a holistic picture of app behavior. However, currently no solutions exist that could relate the metadata of an app with their actual implementation. This situation is aggravated by the fact that developer-provided descriptions are often minimal, inaccurate, and miss key information. Within this context, we formulate the following problems: *(1) Which attributes of an application describe its behavior? (2) How to identify the main purpose of an app? (3) What keywords and phrases should be included in a description text to represent an app's functionality?*

In this paper, we introduce a solution that infers the main purpose of Android apps based on their implementation. Leveraging the recent advances in neural networks, our work attempts to capture and classify semantic relationships between apps. Our system works unsupervised, involves no labeling of data sets, and is trained with real-world app samples that are only coarsely pre-filtered, e.g., regarding the language of descriptions. The output is not only a prediction of what functionality our systems believes to be realized within an application. Using a model explanation algorithm, we also obtain an insight into what is relevant in apps, can explain the reasoning of predictions, and based on this knowledge, derive meaningful keywords and short phrases in natural language.

In summary, we make the following key contributions:

– To infer the functionality from Android app implementations, we propose a combination of three dense neural networks that combine knowledge extracted from resource identifiers, string constants, and API calls. Our system delivers concise keywords and short phrases that describe the main purpose of apps[1].

---

[1] Our implementation is available at: https://github.com/sg10/apk-verbalizer.

- We train, validate, and test our models with 67,040 apps from Google Play. In a case study, we demonstrate the practical relevance and plausibility of predictions by contrasting them with the developer-provided app description.
- To assess the quality of our system and to avoid incomprehensible black box predictions, we apply the model explaining algorithm SHAP [8]. It enables us to understand the influence of network input features on the derived output.

The outcome of this work represents a notable contribution towards a holistic analysis of Android applications. It helps researchers and users to foster an understanding of what functionality is actually implemented in Android apps.

2   Related Work

Aligning the description of Android apps with the alleged functionality and permission usage has become a growing field of research. In the following, we present related work on this topic and point out differences to our solution.

Behavior Modeling. Hamedani et al. [4] strive to find the most appropriate category for an app based on 14 implementation-related features that are processed using different classification algorithms. As shown in a case study by Kowalczyk et al. [6], using as many app attributes as possible for classification, tends to depict apps more accurately and improves the performance of all kinds of analysis tasks. Takahashi et al. [11] follow this principle and consider several thousand features. They combine permissions, API methods, categories, and presumed cluster assignments to identify malware based on Support Vector Machines. CLANdroid [12], in contrast, aims to identify similar apps by defining semantic anchors that refer to sensor information, permissions, intents, and identifiers. Based thereon, they use Latent Semantic Index to derive a matrix representation for every app. MalDozer [5] leverages a convolutional neural network to find harmful behavior by discretizing sequences of invoked API methods. FlowCog [9] adopts natural language processing to infer whether apps provide sufficient semantics for users to understand privacy risks emerging from the information flow.

App Descriptions. Among all related research, the work of Zhang et al. [15] comes closest to this paper. By extracting keywords contained in the call graph of permission-related API calls, the authors intend to derive a description of security-related app behavior. For instance, if the call graph contains the method `KeyguardManager.isKeyguardLocked()`, it is modeled as the words "the phone", "be", "locked". To assess the quality of app descriptions, Kuznetsov et al. [7] extract identifiers and strings from an app's XML definitions and semantically compare them with the developer-provided description text.

Sensitive APIs. In a combination of static code inspection and text analysis, Watanabe et al. [14] present a keyword-based technique to correlate access to privacy-relevant resources with app descriptions. AutoCog [10] correlates permission-related API calls with frequently occurring text fragments. As a result, semantic patterns are derived that can provide an insight into why Android apps request certain permissions. With a focus on potential abuse of sensitive APIs, Gorla et al. [3] derive app clusters based on pre-labeled description topics. Related to that, the approach of Gao et al. [2] infers expectable permissions by applying statistical correlation coefficients after mining topics from descriptions using NLP techniques and Latent Dirichlet Allocation (LDA).

3   Behavior Modeling of Android Apps

A naïve approach to identify functionality implemented in Android applications would be to statically define rules for classifying source code. However, the evolving nature of smartphone apps with constantly changing APIs and the usage of third-party libraries would make it cumbersome to spot and label specific behavior. As a remedy, our approach leverages modern methods of machine learning that work unsupervised and involve no prior labeling of data sets.

Before designing a neural network that predicts the main purpose of apps, we need to tackle a basic question: *Which attributes of an app describe its behavior?* Users can answer this question intuitively by installing and testing an application. Vendors would refer to the source code to derive similar conclusions. The approach presented in this paper is inspired by both perspectives and focuses on information sources that are included within the code and resources of Android app archives.

We attempt to model Android app behavior from two different angles. On the one hand, we consider static string resources that indicate what an app does from a user's and developer's perspective. On the other hand, we describe a program by the Android API calls it includes, e.g., to access sensitive information, draw UI effects, or implement event listeners. Based on the presence and co-occurrence of calls, we expect to see individual patterns that characterize different functionality.

In the following, we outline the features our neural network will use as an input to infer a semantic understanding of the purpose of apps:

- **App Resource Identifiers:** *Semantic information provided by developers.* In order to access resources, such as UI elements, graphics, or multilingual definitions from program code, Android uses IDs that unambiguously identify individual elements. Although these values can be chosen arbitrarily during development, they usually correspond semantically to the resource content.
- **String Constants:** *UI text and functional descriptions, shown to the user.* Static UI elements, language variables, and URLs are typically stored within app resources. When shown to the user, these constants provide valuable semantic information regarding the purpose of an app and actions users can perform. E.g., if an app includes UI elements containing the string values "new transaction", "account balance", and "money transfer", its implemented functionality most likely targets financial transactions.

- **API Calls:** *Define how an app interacts with the Android OS environment.* The widespread use of third-party libraries, code obfuscation techniques, and the multitude of possible usage scenarios make it challenging to identify the individual semantics for every code block. We, thus, postulate that the behavior of apps is not (only) determined by the interaction of individual code fragments, but especially by their interaction with the operating system and users. Consequently, to infer implementation behavior, we focus on calls to APIs of the Android framework. By their modus operandi, they, e.g., control access to sensitive user data, device sensors, visual effects, media processing, and networks and, thus, clearly define the functionality of apps.

As each of these three feature types is embedded within a different semantic context, it is not viable to simply collect all occurrences and use them as a combined input for a neural network. For a more accurate representation, we propose to train three separate neural networks that take different input features but share the same underlying architecture and produce the same type of output.

4 Semantic App Analysis

We design a dense neural architecture to infer the implemented functionality from real-world Android applications. Our goal is to develop a system that can process an unknown app archive and delivers keywords and short phrases that describe the main purpose. To remediate the "black box" usually associated with neural networks, we require that our solution provides an insight into which input features are decisive for predictions.

In the **training** phase, we train three separate neural networks with Android app archives and their developer-provided descriptions from Google Play. For each app, we first extract all relevant semantic features, weigh their importance using TF-IDF and use the resulting vector as input for the corresponding neural

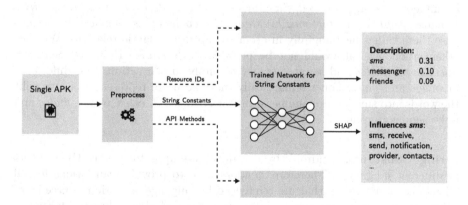

Fig. 1. Prediction of implemented app functionality using three dense neural networks.

network. In parallel, we build a TF-IDF model with app description texts that will be used to derive a neural network output in natural language.

In the **prediction** phase, our system receives an app not seen during training. After deriving and processing a TF-IDF vector representation of all features included in a given archive, each neural network will return a list of key words and short phrases that commonly occur in app descriptions when certain input features are used. As shown in Fig. 1, the output of the network for predicting description words based on given string constants may, e.g., consist of the words *sms*, *messenger*, and *friends*, with the adjacent decimal value expressing the relevance of the predictions. An algorithm for explaining neural networks called SHAP (see Sect. 4.4) is then applied to find out which input features contribute most to the prediction of these output tokens. Summarizing the outputs of all three models and sorting them regarding the shown relevance provides us with a ranked list of description fragments that describe the main purpose of an app.

4.1   Feature Preprocessing

Before training a neural network, it is essential to prepare the data for efficient learning. In the following, we cover the preprocessing steps that are applied to all developer-provided descriptions used in the training phase and the semantic input features processed by our networks after extracting them from app archives.

App Resource Identifiers. By parsing the XML files provided as resources in Android app archives, we obtain a list of identifiers consisting of alphanumeric characters and underscores. Unlike variable or function names in source code, identifiers are typically not obfuscated but stored in the way app vendors define them during development. The name, or identifier, usually reflects its purpose to some extent and can also give hints about the overall app. In practice, values are mostly made up of words or word combinations that are linked either by underscores or formatted via camel-case, e.g., *select_image_dialog*, *confirmRemove*, *pay_btn*, or *start_quiz_headline*. The challenge is therefore to decompose these values meaningfully in order to capture semantic relations. Without tokenization, e.g., it would not be possible to determine that the identifiers *select_image_dialog* and *select_video_dialog* imply similar actions that differ only in *image* and *video*. For a semantically more accurate representation, we split the words into smaller alphanumeric entities, i.e., *select*, *video*, *image*, *dialog* and link them as n-grams.

String Constants. Android, by design, allows apps to display UI elements in different languages. Therefore, vendors have to provide translations for all UI-related string values that are referenced by language-agnostic resource identifiers. In this work, we aim to infer keywords and short phrases in English only. To achieve this, we mimic the behavior of the Android operating system and try to match identifiers with constants by primarily searching them in language files that are supposed to include values in English, i.e., `values-en.xml` or `values-en-us.xml`. Only in the case of mismatch, we fallback to default definitions in `values.xml`. This simple resolution strategy ensures that the corpora of values subsequently trained in TF-IDF models consist mainly of English words.

After extracting all relevant string constants from an app, we iteratively decompose each value into substrings by splitting at non-alphanumeric characters, e.g., whitespaces, HTML tag brackets, dots, etc. While most resulting tokens are likely app-specific, others supposedly occur frequently across multiple apps. To estimate the relevance of individual tokens in relation to all apps, we use the tokens and their occurrence count to build a TF-IDF model. Thereby, we leverage the property of TF-IDF that rarely occurring and very frequent tokens are ignored to maintain a reasonable dictionary size. As a result, for each app, we obtain a TF-IDF vector that can be used as input for a neural network.

API Calls. Inspecting the call graph of Android apps enables us to identify and count invocations of Android APIs. We process the reverse-engineered source code of the app archive and build a call graph based on static, explicit code statements. We enrich the graph with additional edges by resolving inheritance relations and implicit data flows using EdgeMiner [1] by Cao et al. As Android apps have no predefined entry points, *Activities, Services,* and *Providers* defined in the `AndroidManifest.xml` of each app are used as the starting point for modeling the call graph. This approach ensures that we capture only calls of API methods that implement an app's main functionality.

Our goal is to count execution paths, i.e., connections, between app entry methods $E_{in,j}$ and API call methods $E_{out,k}$. Therefore, we use the Dijkstra algorithm to check for each node $E_{in,j}$ whether there is a connection to $E_{out,k}$ in the graph. If so, we increment a counter for API call k. We count all methods as a combination of their (fully qualified) class and their method name.

As with resource identifiers and string constants, we create a TF-IDF model for API methods. For each app, we now have a list of pairs that consist of method calls and how often it was found in the app's source code. By using the TF-IDF algorithm, we decide which method names end up in the dictionary, based on their frequency. TF-IDF then transforms this information and returns a 1-dimensional decimal vector for each app sample that we can use as neural network input.

App Descriptions. As the output of our machine learning model, we want to infer feature-related parts of the app description. Intuitively, we use $n = (1, 2, 3)$ to cover phrases that include one, two, and three words. With stopword removal and Porter stemming, we reduce the number of frequent word combinations that are of comparably minor importance beforehand, e.g., *take some photos* and *take a photo* both become *take photo*. By stemming tokens, removing stopwords, and windowing with three different window sizes, we aim to capture more meaning.

The tokens, regardless of whether the model finds frequent single occurrences or combinations, are stored in their stemmed form. Stemming removes parts of the word to subsume multiple word variations and facilitate computation. It often does not, however, reduce the words to a stem that can be easily read by humans. Since the stemming transformation is not a bidirectional transformation due to the loss of information, an accurate *un-stemming* method cannot exist. Stemmed tokens contrast our goal to provide human-readable description fragments.

As a solution, we use a greedy algorithm to recover original words from their stem. Therefore, we keep track of all the stemming transformations, i.e., whenever a token T is altered and results in its stemmed version $\widehat{T} = f_{\text{stem}}(T)$. The suffix removal of stemming leads to $\widehat{T}$ having multiple corresponding original tokens T, so we collect the number of times of: $T \rightarrow \widehat{T}$. After processing all descriptions, we obtain an association count table that lists how often $\widehat{T}$ was caused by each original T. E.g., if the stemming result of a token is *locat*, it will be replaced with *location*, regardless of whether the original token was *location*, *located*, *locating*, or *locate*. By counting how often an original token results in a particular stemmed token, we can replace the stemmed token by its most common origin.

Ultimately, each description is represented by a list of tokens that we want to transform via a TF-IDF model. The model has features that consist of single tokens, 2-grams, and 3-grams. Stemmed tokens are re-transformed to their most likely original, non-stemmed word to be more easily readable afterwards. Hence, for each app description, we obtain a 1-d vector with normalized decimal numbers between 0 and 1, which we can subsequently use as machine learning targets.

4.2 Model Architecture

We propose a combination of three models of dense neural networks to predict keywords and short phrases that characterize a given Android application. Each model produces n-grams as output and receives TF-IDF vectors with either resource identifiers, string constants, or method names as input. In this section,

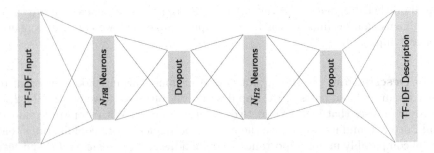

Fig. 2. Dense neural architecture to infer TF-IDF vectors with descriptive keywords from TF-IDF vectors of resource identifiers, string constants, and API calls.

we highlight the advantages of dense neural networks for our problem and present our network architecture regarding the set of chosen layers and hyperparameters.

Figure 2 illustrates our network architecture. The bag-of-words representation via TF-IDF vectors enforces positional constraints, i.e., the value for a particular word is always put into the same vector cell. This input property allows us to use a standard dense network structure in contrast to other convolutional or recurrent architectures that factor in positional and sequential information. Between dense layers, we apply dropout for regularization. As the output of each neuron consists of floating-point numbers, we have a regression task and use a linear activation function for the output layer and mean-squared error as a loss function.

The size of the input and output depend on the dictionary size of the TF-IDF models. Precisely, the dictionary sizes are limited by the minimum and the maximum document frequency, i.e., in how many apps a certain method call or resource identifier token occurs at all. Here, especially the lower boundary is crucial. If the minimum document frequency is too high, we miss information the neural network could use to infer the output more precisely. In case the minimum is too low, the model remembers too many tokens that rarely occur, and the dictionary becomes very large. The larger the input space, the more inputs and weight parameters are stored in memory, and the longer the training process takes. The selection of TF-IDF model parameters, thus, binds the training process. To find suitable network architectures, we used random search. For this non-exhaustive search, we trained networks with one to three hidden layers and 1,000 to 15,000 hidden neurons. Dropout was randomly set between 0% and 40%.

We choose the parameters empirically by trying different setups and observing the resulting dictionary sizes and model performances. Therefore, we set the minimum document frequency for each of the three input types to 2% of the total number of documents (apps), and the corresponding maximum frequency to 20%. This range means, e.g., if we have an app dataset of size N and a token occurs n times, it only ends up in the dictionary if it occurs in $0.02N \leq n \leq 0.2N$ apps. Table 1 lists our final network configurations and the TF-IDF dictionary sizes.

Table 1. Neural network configurations of the three models.

	Input TF-IDF # features	Network hidden layers	Description TF-IDF # features
Resource Identifiers	3315	2968, 3265, 1393 (3 Layers)	6140
String constants	6391	2898, 3105 (2 Layers)	6140
API methods	11735	5891 (1 Layer)	6140

4.3   Model Training

The three models are trained using the mean-squared error measure as a loss function. As a performance metric, however, it is not fit for the purpose. Unfortunately, it does not give any intuitive expression of how well the model performs. Thus, we discretize the description TF-IDF vectors by choosing a threshold θ, above which we set the vector element to 1, or 0 otherwise. We can then use standard performance metrics like F-score, precision, and recall on these binary vectors to compare an actual description's vector with a description prediction.

Our correlation-based learning approach tries to find similarities between apps and thus neglects app-specific terms in the description. From a performance point of view, this means that we can expect a lower recall than precision. For early stopping, we are required to choose a pivotal performance metric that measures whether training should stop or continue. We, thus, use a weighted F-score ($\beta = 0.5$) that rates precision higher than recall. Consequently, we apply the $F_{0.5}$ performance for early stopping to find a good final training state.

4.4   Explaining Predictions

The essence of machine learning is finding patterns via function approximations in a given set of data. Due to the complex inner working of networks, it is not always obvious how predictions are derived. To find out which input items contribute to the prediction of keywords, we apply the model explainer SHAP [8].

SHAP is a method proposed to estimate the importance of sample features. The algorithm behind it is based on Shapley values, a concept in cooperative game theory: of n potential players, several combinations of $k \leq n$ players are possible, i.e., can play together against the bank. Each combination of players achieves a different (monetary) result. The Shapley value shows the contribution of each player by incorporating different combinations. Lundberg et al. used this concept in combination with additive feature attribution. By masking out several parts of the input features, different model results per sample are obtained. The results can be united according to Shapley, but this is computationally expensive. SHAP provides several approximations, e.g., one for neural networks called Deep SHAP. By leveraging knowledge about the network's parameters and structure, and not treating it as a black box, Deep SHAP creates a simpler, approximated model. In this work, we apply Deep SHAP on our neural network models.

5   Evaluation

The goal of this evaluation is twofold. First, we investigate the performance of our neural network with real-world Android apps. Second, applying our solution on a hand-picked set of applications, we compare predictions about the presumed functionality of apps with the actual description text from Google Play.

5.1   Dataset

We evaluate our approach using real-world applications from the PlayDrone dataset [13]. We opted for this repository of apps as it does not only feature raw app archives but also makes the vendor-provided app description available.

After downloading 115,294 Android apps and their corresponding metadata, we removed cross-platform apps as they implement their core functionality with web technologies and lack the corresponding resource identifiers, string constants, and API calls. From the remaining set of 85,915 apps, we filtered apps that had no descriptions in English language and ensured that preprocessing each description text resulted in at least 20 TF-IDF vectors. This boundary was set to reduce the potential impact of insignificant samples on the training process.

Table 2 highlights the final set of apps we used to train, validate, and test each network input feature. 20% of apps used for training are randomly picked to be also part of the validation set. This partitioning scheme is required to prevent overfitting of our machine learning model and to ensure meaningful predictions. The test set includes 1,000 randomly chosen apps that are not used during training. We build the set such that it only includes apps with a reasonably good description. Therefore, we make the simplifying assumption that apps with a higher download count tend to have higher description quality and, thus, prefer samples from comparably popular apps. We sort all apps in the dataset by download count and take every third app until we obtain 1,000 test samples.

5.2   Results

We trained neural networks for resource identifiers, string constants, and API calls, each with a set of 66,040 apps. To ensure an unbiased evaluation, the three models were validated using 20% of training data and tested individually with 1.5% of previously unseen data to confirm their final performance.

Table 2. Subsets of Android apps used as neural network input.

	# Apps
Android apps crawled	115,294
Cross-platform apps	29,379
English descriptions and $\geq$ 20 TF-IDF tokens	67,040
Training set	66,040
Validation set (20%)	13,208
Test set	1,000

Table 3. Performance on the test set of the three neural network input types via discretized TF-IDF vectors. Discretization threshold: $\theta = 0.05$.

	Resource identifiers	String constants	API calls
Precision	79%	84%	69%
Recall	27%	19%	18%
$F_{0.5}$-Score	57%	50%	44%

The evaluation results on the test set are summarized in Table 3. The direct comparison of F-scores shows that resource identifiers yield the best results, while API calls perform significantly worse, with string constants in between. While precision values range between 69% and 84%, the recall column presents low values for all models. We attribute this mainly to two reasons. First, descriptions contain lots of words specific to the app that are hard to generalize. This makes reconstructing many of these rarely occurring words difficult. Second, the TF-IDF model for the description output does not take synonyms into account. E.g., if the description contains the word *image*, but the word *photo* is predicted, it counts as a mismatch and lowers the recall despite the semantic correctness.

In practice, these results mean that our trained neural networks can well predict keywords and short phrases that also occur in the developer-provided description. High precision and low recall imply that the rate of false negatives is higher than the rate of false positives. This is desirable in our setting because a lower false positive rate also produces fewer false attributions of app functionality.

5.3   Case Study

For a better understanding on the practical relevance of functionality predictions, in the following, we take a closer look at each model's output regarding two music-related apps that were not used during training. We visualize the top 8 predictions and relevance values via word clouds. The font size of each token is set with respect to the weight (relevance) the models assign to all outputs.

Figure 3 illustrates the top-ranked predictions of the three models for the music video streaming app *Vevo*. Apart from *video* being top-ranked, the nature of a video streaming and sharing platform is expressed by the phrases *tv show/tv channels, movies, subscription, music, live* and *content*. The tv-related phrases show that the models cannot distinguish between traditional television and online video streaming. As the predictions stem from many other apps, we reason that the neural networks understand the domain of the input and learn to cluster video-related applications internally. We also see that the inferred tokens based on API calls are much more general. The overall domain of the app becomes clear but, e.g., no n-grams, such as *tv channels* or *tv show* were learned. Overall, despite their independent reasoning, the three models each yield descriptive information and can correctly identify the app's main purpose.

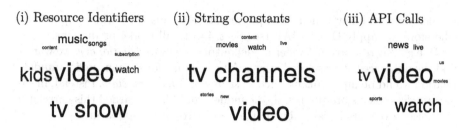

(i) Resource Identifiers   (ii) String Constants   (iii) API Calls

Fig. 3. Word clouds with each model's predictions for the video streaming app *Vevo*.

(i) Predicted Functionality | (ii) Actual Description

cloud playlist

music player

backup files   album

4shared Music was created for those, who can't live without music and don't want their attention to be attracted with anything else, but music while listening to it. Using your 'Search' menu item you can look for music files you like and add them to your playlist at 4shared Music. Moreover, you can upload tracks from your Android device to your 4shared Music. With 4shared Music you can enjoy 15GB of space for your music and nothing out of place. Upload and add all music files you like and make your life even more enjoyable with 4shared!

Fig. 4. Comparison of the real description of *4shared Music* and our models' predictions.

The app *4shared Music* is a music player that accesses audio files stored on the cloud storage provider 4shared. In Fig. 4, we contrast the developer-provided description with the summarized predictions of our three models. Our neural networks correctly found that the app is a *music player*, dealing with *playlists* and *albums*. They also identified the second domain of the app, the online storage platform, in terms of *cloud, backup,* and *files*. While all these tokens make sense, the actual app description text does not mention all of them, e.g., *player, cloud,* and *backup* are absent. In other words, since the description text does not cover these tokens literally, the measurable performance (see Sect. 5.2) decreases despite the good generalization. An accurate but abstracted word cloud that is intelligible to humans is, thus, difficult to measure.

5.4 Prediction Explanation

Each of our three machine learning models predicts a list of keywords and short phrases based on a given Android app archive. Apart from seeing this result, we also want to know which word predictions are caused by which input items. Therefore, we apply Deep SHAP (see Sect. 4.4) to all model predictions.

If, e.g., our resource identifier model outputs the word *dictionary*, we want to find the influences of these predictions. A reasonable, for humans understandable relation would be input tokens, such as *search*, *word*, or *translate*. Instead, in case meaningless tokens are predicted, the model would have learned this correlation as "noise" from similar apps but not from a particular app feature.

Table 4. SHAP algorithm applied on two predictions for the app *Slacker Radio*.

(i) Resource Identifiers

Description Token(s)	Input Tokens	SHAP
music player	artist	0.0122
	album	0.0107
	playlist	0.0071
	art	0.0034
	lyrics	0.0032

(ii) String Constants

Description Token(s)	Input Tokens	SHAP
music	playlist	0.0321
	song	0.0230
	stations	0.0125
	songs	0.0096
	tracks	0.0039

To assess network input-output relations, we take one sample and get the top prediction for it, i.e., we focus on the network's output with the highest numeric value. Then, we calculate the SHAP values for all inputs and list the corresponding input features and their SHAP values. Table 4 shows this result for the app *Slacker Radio*. The predicted keywords with the highest values were *music player* for resource identifiers and *music* for string constants. By looking at the top input influences, we can see that the two different network models make their decision based on reasonable inputs. These input tokens affect the output in a way that is easily comprehensible and verifiable by humans.

From applying SHAP to many samples, we noticed that for resource identifiers and string constants, found correlations are mostly self-evident. Although we also found many Android apps where the model based on API calls returned very accurate keywords, the associated SHAP values were not intuitively traceable. For instance, the *Vevo* app (see Fig. 3) has *video* as its top predicted term. The associated SHAP values refer to generic methods belonging to the `Activity` class from the Android API that, by their design, are unspecific to multimedia apps. We assume that in such cases, implementations make use of a specific set of methods that are then considered as a sort of fingerprint to identify video-related app purposes. In other cases, SHAP explanations for API calls show very obvious correlations. E.g., for the keyword *shake*, we found the `SensorManager` class of the Android API among the closest-related input features. Overall, our qualitative analysis using the SHAP model explanation algorithm confirmed that all our models could very well outline the main purpose of most real-world applications.

6 Conclusion

In this work, we presented a solution to describe the main purpose of Android apps in natural language by analyzing resource identifiers, string constants, and API calls contained in app archives. Based on a combination of three dense neural networks, our approach accurately captures semantic relationships among apps. We carefully evaluated our approach on 67,040 real-world Android apps and showed that with a precision between 69% and 84% our neural networks could predict keywords and short phrases that also occur in the developer-provided description in Google Play. Our solution provides an effective method to describe the behavior of unknown app implementations.

References

1. Cao, Y., et al.: EdgeMiner: automatically detecting implicit control flow transitions through the android framework. In: Network and Distributed System Security Symposium - NDSS 2015. The Internet Society (2015)
2. Gao, H., et al.: AutoPer: automatic recommender for runtime-permission in android applications. In: 43rd IEEE Annual Computer Software and Applications Conference, COMPSAC 2019, Milwaukee, WI, USA, 15–19 July 2019, vol. 1, pp. 107–116. IEEE (2019)
3. Gorla, A., Tavecchia, I., Gross, F., Zeller, A.: Checking app behavior against app descriptions. In: International Conference on Software Engineering - ICSE 2014, pp. 1025–1035. ACM (2014)
4. Hamedani, M.R., Shin, D., Lee, M., Cho, S., Hwang, C.: AndroClass: an effective method to classify android applications by applying deep neural networks to comprehensive features. Wirel. Commun. Mob. Comput. **2018**, 1250359:1–1250359:21 (2018)
5. Karbab, E.B., Debbabi, M., Derhab, A., Mouheb, D.: MalDozer: automatic framework for android malware detection using deep learning. Digital Invest. **24**, S48–S59 (2018)
6. Kowalczyk, E., Memon, A.M., Cohen, M.B.: Piecing together app behavior from multiple artifacts: a case study. In: Symposium on Software Reliability Engineering - ISSRE 2015, pp. 438–449. IEEE Computer Society (2015)
7. Kuznetsov, K., Avdiienko, V., Gorla, A., Zeller, A.: Checking app user interfaces against app descriptions. In: Workshop on App Market Analytics - WAMA, pp. 1–7. ACM (2016)
8. Lundberg, S.M., Lee, S.: A unified approach to interpreting model predictions. In: Neural Information Processing Systems - NIPS 2017, pp. 4765–4774 (2017)
9. Pan, X., et al.: FlowCog: context-aware semantics extraction and analysis of information flow leaks in android apps. In: USENIX Security 2018, pp. 1669–1685. USENIX Association (2018)
10. Qu, Z., Rastogi, V., Zhang, X., Chen, Y., Zhu, T., Chen, Z.: AutoCog: measuring the description-to-permission fidelity in android applications. In: Conference on Computer and Communications Security - CCS 2014, pp. 1354–1365. ACM (2014)
11. Takahashi, T., Ban, T.: Android application analysis using machine learning techniques. In: Sikos, L.F. (ed.) AI in Cybersecurity. ISRL, vol. 151, pp. 181–205. Springer, Cham (2019). https://doi.org/10.1007/978-3-319-98842-9_7

12. Vásquez, M.L., Holtzhauer, A., Poshyvanyk, D.: On automatically detecting similar Android apps. In: International Conference on Program Comprehension - ICPC 2016, pp. 1–10. IEEE Computer Society (2016)
13. Viennot, N., Garcia, E., Nieh, J.: A measurement study of Google Play. In: Measurement and Modeling of Computer Systems - SIGMETRICS 2014, pp. 221–233. ACM (2014)
14. Watanabe, T., Akiyama, M., Sakai, T., Mori, T.: Understanding the inconsistencies between text descriptions and the use of privacy-sensitive resources of mobile apps. In: Symposium On Usable Privacy and Security - SOUPS 2015, pp. 241–255. USENIX Association (2015)
15. Zhang, M., Duan, Y., Feng, Q., Yin, H.: Towards automatic generation of security-centric descriptions for Android apps. In: Conference on Computer and Communications Security - CCS 2015, pp. 518–529. ACM (2015)

System Security

IMShell-Dec: Pay More Attention to External Links in PowerShell

RuiDong Han[1]([⊠]), Chao Yang[1], JianFeng Ma[1], Siqi Ma[2], YunBo Wang[1],
and Feng Li[1]

[1] Xidian University, Shannxi, China
{hanruidong,robertwang,fli1996}@stu.xidian.edu.cn,
{chaoyang,jfma}@xidian.edu.cn
[2] CSIRO, Sydney, Australia
siqi.ma@csiro.au

Abstract. Windows proposes the POWERSHELL shell command line to substitute the traditional CMD. However, it is often utilized by the attacker to invade the victim because of its versatile functionality. In this paper, we investigate an attack combined POWERSHELL and image steganography. Compared with the traditional method, this attack can deceive the defender by hiding its malicious contents in benign images. To effectively detect this attack, we propose a framework IMSHELL-DEC, whose main target is to check external links before the execution of POWERSHELL script. IMSHELL-DEC trains a machine learning classifier with image examples, where the features are generated by merging histograms of three image color channels. Then IMSHELL-DEC examines the script through tracking and classifying the related images. The detector achieves more than 95% precision in 9,589 high-definition images.

Keywords: Intrusion detection · Powershell attack · Steganography detection

1 Introduction

Windows POWERSHELL is an adaptive and versatile command-line shell environment. It allows the user to take advantage of the .NET Framework [12,20], but it also provides additional functions for attackers to generate malicious scripts. Several open-source frameworks(e.g., *empire*[1], *nishang*[2], *PowerSploit*[3]) exploit it to attack victims. Traditional malicious scripts detection methods [1,5] rely on regular expression matching and complex rules. The regular expression is time-consuming to create while analyzing POWERSHELL script, and complex rules are

---

[1] https://github.com/EmpireProject/Empire.
[2] https://github.com/samratashok/nishang.
[3] https://github.com/PowerShellMafia/PowerSploit.

© IFIP International Federation for Information Processing 2020
Published by Springer Nature Switzerland AG 2020
M. Hölbl et al. (Eds.): SEC 2020, IFIP AICT 580, pp. 189–202, 2020.
https://doi.org/10.1007/978-3-030-58201-2_13

hard to derive and pose a maintenance burden as the attack method evolves. Recently, several automated solutions have proposed to address these issues. Hendler *et al.* [8] leverages deep neural networks to detect obfuscated malicious POWERSHELL script. They encode characters as features to train a classifier. And Zhenyuan *et al.* [15] design a novel subtree-based de-obfuscation method to detect obfuscation, since the attacker always uses obfuscation to conceal their malicious contents. They implement obfuscation detection and emulation-based recovery in the abstract syntax tree. PowerDrive [19], a de-obfuscator for PowerShell attacks, recursively de-obfuscates the code by processing multi-stage de-obfuscation.

Previous works assume the payload exists in the form of script, however, we discover that attacker can mount their malicious POWERSHELL payload on a harmless medium outside of the script. Specifically, attackers may attempt to hide POWERSHELL malicious content in an external resource and use another harmless script to recover it later, which eliminates the distinctive characteristic caused by excessive obfuscation. In this work, we focus on the POWERSHELL attack combines with image steganography, where the attacker injects POWERSHELL script's information into the image's color channels, then generates another POWERSHELL release script to decode the malicious contents from the image. Both the release script and image itself are harmless, and, to improve stealthiness, the release script is usually embedded into a file (e.g., Office, JavaScript, C#) before delivered to the victims. When they run the file, the latent POWERSHELL release script retrieves the image and releases the malicious script. The malicious script can download Web files with the framework plugin *WebClient*, establishes remote control by sending requests to remote service, sets a persistence mechanism by creating a scheduled task or uninstalls a local application forcefully.

To counter this attack, we propose a novel machine-learning-based detection method, named IMSHELL-DEC. Unlike previous researches, which only consider the security of script itself, we also consider the external link, since the attacker can conceal their real malicious script in the external resource. We locate the external resource in the script, then apply a machine-learning-based method to check these external resources. We integrate the color histogram as the feature and train a classifier to identify malicious script.

The contribution is summarized in two folds. First, we research a new type of POWERSHELL attack. It hides the malicious script into an image and generates a standard release script, which can not be detected by the existing detection method. To address this emerging threat, we propose IMSHELL-DEC, which locates and identify the potentially malicious content hiding in the external image. IMSHELL-DEC achieves more than 95% precision in 9,589 high-definition images.

The rest of this paper is organized as follows. In Sect. 2, threat model of POWERSHELL attack including victim setting is introduced. Then, the detailed process of the threat is reported in Sect. 3. In Sect. 4, the detection mechanism is illustrated, which combines the image color histogram feature and machine learning. In Sect. 5, we describe the way we generate data samples, and report the detection performance of our method. Finally, relevant researches and conclusion are shown respectively in Sect. 6 and Sect. 7.

2   Threat Model and Scope

In this paper, we explore a novel attack combine POWERSHELL attack with image steganography. In this attack, the attacker generates two parts of the resource, including an image and a trap file with a release script. Then, the attacker spread the trap file through Web document, Webmail or USB device, and attempt to fool potential victims to give the execution permissions for the release script. The release script then decodes the malicious script from the image, which is hosted on a website or send to the victim along with the trap file. The whole attack flow is shown in Fig. 1.

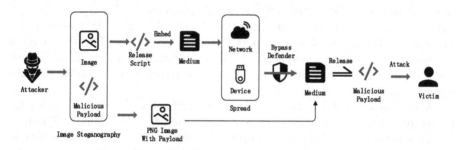

Fig. 1. System and threat model.

The scope of the attack is limited to the following scenarios. The target's system version is not older than Windows 7, since Microsoft developers set the POWERSHELL as a default application in the newer Windows version. The victim must be unaware or unfamiliar about the system security policy and proficiency of POWERSHELL. When victims get trap files, they accept to run it and granting necessary permission for the release script. For example, it is common for staff to download Office word documents from the Internet and open them with a local editor. When the document asks to allow update source or modify the file, the user often clicks sure button without paying attention to the prompts in the dialog box. Such action grants the file with specific permissions, allows the releasing script to retrieve a malicious payload and launch an attack.

3   Novel PowerShell Attack Through Image Steganography

In this section, we demonstrate the attack process through a concrete example and explain why the two parts of the attack can evade detection.

3.1   Principle of Attack

The conventional rule-based detection method mainly relies on the character form of POWERSHELL script to separate benign and malicious content. However, image steganography allows the attacker to conceal their malicious payload in an external image, thus bypassing existed script detection. The attacker can then use a release script, which has no difference from the common benign scripts, to recover the payload and execute the intended attack.

In this work, we assume the attacker use *Invoke-PSImage*[4], a commonly used tool in the POWERSHELL, to generate the steganography image. *Invoke-PSImage* embeds the bytes of a POWERSHELL script into pixels of a PNG image by utilizing the least significant 4 bits of 2 color values in each pixel to hold the payload, then generates a release script that can extract the original payload later. If treated separately, both the release script and the image are harmless: the image is a PNG file, and the script's content is no more than a benign POWERSHELL command. The diverse format of the release script further strengthened the stealthiness, as the script itself can be a drop-in Office, VBScript, JavaScript, BAT Script, or a base64 certificate. Once the attacker lures the user to opening/running the file with certain permission, an image decoding command is executed in the memory without any GUI activity. The malicious payload is then extracted from the image existed in local or remote storage, and launch the intended attack.

As our threat model mentioned, the release script is embedded in another file to ensure it can sneak into the user system environment. For example, Windows provides several methods for data transferring between applications. One method is to use the dynamic data exchange protocol [10]. The DDE protocol carries out macro-less code execution in Office documents. Although Microsoft has limited it in ADV170021(2017.12)[5], there are still users who are not installing this patch. We conduct a pilot experiment on a colleague's computer, which is installed with Office 2013(15.0.4.4569.1504), and found out that the older version Office can run POWERSHELL code execution under the default permissions. *Excel4-DCOM*[6] enable raw shellcode execution on a remote Excel(32Bit), which opens the possibility to combines shellcode attack with lateral movement. JavaScript is capable of running POWERSHELL script by utilizing component "child process", it can also start a process to execute local POWERSHELL.exe to run a script. And .Net Framework also manages applications through SCM(Services Control Manager), where we can interfere POWERSHELL scripts in C# with public API.

3.2   Threat Usage

We perform experiments to determine the ability of the attack with three different forms of samples POWERSHELL scripts. At the same time, we explain

---

[4] https://github.com/peewpw/Invoke-PSImage.

[5] https://portal.msrc.microsoft.com/en-US/security-guidance/advisory/ADV170021.

[6] https://github.com/outflanknl/Excel4-DCOM.

why release scripts can slip away from the victim's attention and why image steganography makes the attack payload harder to be detected.

To verify the sensitivity of different defenders to scripts. We collect a corpus of POWERSHELL scripts (i.e., 4,079 POWERSHELL scripts in total) from iocs[7], which containing 27 kinds of malicious POWERSHELL scripts. The most frequently appeared script is *Downloader DFSP*, which downloads file with Web-Client. To test the response of the defenders, we simulate a *Downloader DFSP* example as *iocs* provided, and process the example with different script forms, including an origin script, a base64 emending obfuscated script, and an image steganography script. In this simulation, we use this script to download the $7z$[8] application (and in the real attack, a malicious file) and execute it. More specifically, the origin script (see Fig. 2a) call WebClient to download the "7z.exe" into local directory "$HOME\Documents" and execute. The script is able to coding in Base64 (see Fig. 2b), which can directly be executed through POWER-SHELL with the option "-enc". For the image steganography attack, we encode the script into an image's color channels through *Invoke-PSImage*, then generates a lossless PNG image and a release script (see Fig. 2c). Figure 4 compared the original image with its steganography processed copy.

```
(New-Object System.Net.WebClient).DownloadFile('https://www.7-zip.org/a/7z1900-
x64.exe',"$HOME\Documents\7z.exe");
Start-Process ("$HOME\Documents\7z.exe")
```

(a) Downloader Script

```
JTI4TmV3LU9iamVjdCUyMFN5c3RlbS5OZXQuV2ViQ2xpZW50JTI5LkRvd25sb2FkRmlsZSUyOCUyN2h0
dHBzJTNBbLy93d3cuNy16aXAub3JnL2EvN3oxOTAwLTeVN3oxOTAwLXg2NC5leGU1MjJjJTJDJTIyTVDR
dw1lbnqlNuHJeiS1eGUlMjz1mjklWO3TdGFydC1Qcm9jZXNzJTIwJTI4JTIyJTIOSE9NRSU1QORvY3Vt
ZW50JTVDN3ouZXh1JTIyJTI5JTBB3TBB
```

(b) Coding Base64

```
sal a New-Object;Add-Type -A System.Drawing;
$g=a System.Drawing.Bitmap("xxx\evil-kiwi.png");
$o=a Byte[] 1600;(0..0)%{foreach($x in(0..1599)){$p=$g.GetPixel($x,$_);
$o[$_*1600+$x]=([math]::Floor(($p.B-band15)*16)-bor($p.G-band15))}};
$g.Dispose();
IEX([System.Text.Encoding]::ASCII.GetString($o[0..407]))
```

(c) Steganography Image Release Script

Fig. 2. Example of scripts.

Defender Name	Version	Origin	Base64	Release
360	12.0.0.2024	ignore	warning	ignore
Kaspersky	20.0.14.1085	ignore	warning	ignore
Huorong	5.0.28.1	ignore	warning	ignore
Tencent	2.0.6.27	ignore	warning	ignore
Kingsoft	8.29.18953	ignore	ignore	ignore
MS Defender	4.18.1907.4	ignore	ignore	ignore
Norton	5.16.1.3	ignore	warning	ignore
McAfee	4.0.127.1	ignore	ignore	ignore
AVAST	2.1.1286	ignore	ignore	ignore

Fig. 3. Reaction of defender.

3.3 Effect of Attack

We evaluate the stealthiness of methods by observing the defender's response during the execution of scripts. Before this experiment, we download the latest defenders from their official websites and install them on Windows 10(1903) with POWERSHELL's version 5.1.18362. Nine experience results about security

---

[7] https://github.com/pan-unit42/iocs/tree/master/psencmds.
[8] https://www.7-zip.org/.

defender are enumerated in Fig. 3. We observe that all tested defenders do not raise a warning to the original script, a natural result since the script itself doesn't contain any abnormal behavior. However, defenders can easily intercept a naked malicious URL download attempt. Even we obfuscate the original (malicious) script with deep embedding, half of the defenders report that the script is operating suspiciously. This observation conforms with the discovery in research [8,11]. Image steganography conceals the true payload into a legitimate medium, extract it later through another independent and benign-looking release script, thus bypass the conventional script detection method.

As for the image, both defender and firewall only examine the script itself but pay no attention to its external image. Besides, as Fig. 4 shows, it is challenging to notice the blemish in steganographic image by naked eyes.

(a) Original Image   (b) Steganography Image

Fig. 4. Comparison of original and steganographic image.

4   Our Proposed Defense Framework

To address the above POWERSHELL attacks, we proposed a machine-learning based defense framework, IMSHELL-DEC. In this section, we provide an overview of the proposed framework, and describe two key components of our framework: *feature extractor* and *detection model*.

4.1   Overview of IMShell-Dec

IMSHELL-DEC is a detection framework that aims to identify suspicious payload hiding in image. It starts by locating the external image links in POWERSHELL scripts. Once located, IMSHELL-DEC attempts to retrieve the image file, and determine whether there is a malicious payload in the image. The overview of IMSHELL-DEC is illustrated in Fig. 5.

When IMSHELL-DEC receives an unknown script, it starts by seeking for the external image links in POWERSHELL scripts and attempts to retrieve the

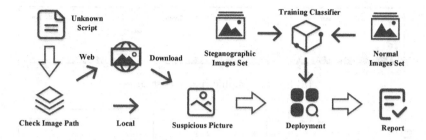

Fig. 5. Overview of IMSHELL-DEC

image for any link located. Once the image has successfully retrieved, the feature extractor will transform images into useful features, and then the detection model will determine the category of these images. If the detection model label the image as malicious, then IMSHELL-DEC will mark the source script as suspicious and raise a warning to the user. In the following subsections, we thoroughly describe the two key components of our proposed framework: *feature extractor*, and *detection model*.

4.2   Feature Extractor

Before calling the detection model, we use feature extractor to distill useful information from the raw images. A pixel in the typical RGB-colored image consists of three integers, where each integer represents a colored channel with a range between 0 to 255. If we plot the number of pixels for each possible value, we obtain a frequency graph that represents the tonal distribution in a digital image. Such a graph is called "histogram".

Usually, the distribution in an unmodified image histogram tends to be smooth in general. However, steganography tools like *Invoke-PSImage* will introduce additional offsets to pixels, which may break the smooth shape of the distribution.

To examine this conjecture, we record several image histograms and compare the smoothness of distribution before and after the steganographic process. As Fig. 6 shows, the steganographic process introduces numerous small yet obvious spikes in the image histogram. Hence, we leverage a filter with kernel $[-0.5, 1, -0.5]$ to process each color histograms, and transform the result of three channels into one feature vector, which reflected the smoothness of the transition between a particular value with its neighbor. To neutralize the influence of frequency scale, we further apply a min-max normalization and re-scale the feature vector to the range of $[-1, 1]$. The visualized image features are displayed in Fig. 7. It can be observed from the figure that the features extracted from a benign and malicious image are quite different.

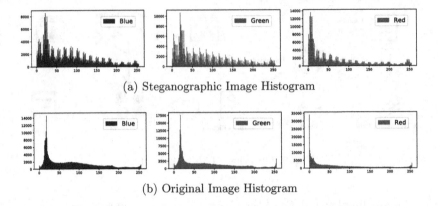

(a) Steganographic Image Histogram

(b) Original Image Histogram

Fig. 6. Image color histogram. (Color figure online)

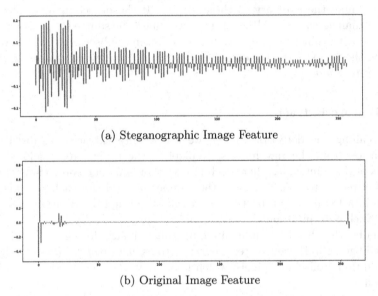

(a) Steganographic Image Feature

(b) Original Image Feature

Fig. 7. Visualization feature.

4.3 Detection Model

Once the image has processed into a feature, we can use a detection model to classify the images into two categories: benign or malicious. To obtain this model, we need to train it before the deployment with a training set.

A training set contains a set of images with a ground-truth label, where each image is processed forehand with feature extractor to generate corresponding feature vector. During the training process, these features are merged into one matrix, then the detection model takes the feature matrix as input and output the prediction. By comparing the prediction with ground-truth, the machine learning algorithm is able to correct and update the detection model, thus improving its classification performance. When the training is completed, we freeze the model parameter and deploy the discriminative model to predict unseen images.

The label prediction process takes as input the discriminative model and a feature vector that the label is to be predicted. The discriminative model would assign the likelihoods of the feature to belong to each of the two categories. The category with the highest likelihood would be outputted as the predicted label for the feature. The prediction result of the feature is the judgment of the image.

There are several machine learning algorithms able to perform the classification task. In this study, we select three algorithms, namely Linear Discriminant Analysis (LDA), Random Forest (RF), and Back-Propagation Networks (BPNs) as our experiment candidates. Their detection performance and time consumption will be evaluated in the next section.

5   Experiment of IMShell-Dec

5.1   Experiment Setting and Metrics

We implement our code in Python 3.7 and perform the experiment on a PC equipped with Intel i7-9700 CPU. We use *iocs*, a corpus contains 4079 POWERSHELL scripts as our malicious script database, which has an average size of 312 Bytes and can be divided into 27 categories by the attack behavior. Then, we collect 5,510 high-definition images from the Internet, and randomly select 4,079 of them to generate synthetic copies with malicious payloads. This image dataset(9,589 samples in total) is used for classifier training.

To ensure the fidelity and reproducibility of the experiment, we apply k-fold cross-validation to generate a diversified dataset for both training and evaluation. Specifically, the entire dataset is randomly split into $k(k = 10$ in our work) subsets, each subset contains approximately 958 images, with roughly 550 benign and 408 malicious. We then generate ten distinctive data groups by taking each unique subset as test data while the remaining subsets as training data. We train and evaluate models on each data groups, and report the average performance.

We use accuracy, precision, recall, and F1-score as the performance metrics, which are defined as follows:

$$Accuracy = \frac{TP + TN}{P + N} \tag{1}$$

$$Precision = \frac{TP}{TP + FP} \tag{2}$$

$$Recall = \frac{TP}{TP + FN} \tag{3}$$

$$F1 = \frac{2 \times Precision \times Recall}{Precision + Recall} \tag{4}$$

where P is the number of malicious image, N is the number of benign image, TP is the number of correctly identified malicious image, FP is the number of benign images that incorrectly labeled as malicious, and FN is the number of malicious image that wrongly classified as benign.

We also apply the receiver operating characteristic curve (ROC), area under curve (AUC) and precision/recall curve (PR) to assess the overall effectiveness of IMSHELL-DEC. ROC curve is a graphical plot that illustrates the diagnostic ability of a binary classifier system as its discrimination threshold is varied, and AUC, the size of the area under the ROC curve, represented the model's capability to distinguish between classes. Both indicators of the PR curve focus on positive examples in a binary classifier system. If the PR of one classifier is entirely covered another, it can be asserted that the classifier has better performance than another. In past studies, F1, accuracy, recall and precision scores of 0.8 or above are often considered reasonable (e.g., [3,13,17]).

5.2　Result

We implement and evaluate three classification algorithm, including linear discriminant analysis, back-propagation network, and random forest. Experiment results are shown in Table 1.

Table 1. Metrics of each classifiers.

Classifier	Accuracy	Precision	Recall	F1	AUC
LDA	0.918	0.898	0.943	0.920	0.972
RF	0.941	0.927	0.959	0.943	0.988
BPNs	0.961	0.954	0.968	0.961	0.993

Table 2. Average training time.

Classifier	Training (S)	Predicting (S)
LDA	0.31077	0.00151
RF	0.72302	0.01240
BPNs	5.67275	0.00747

We note that the results of these classifiers are reasonably good, which means our proposed scheme performs well in classifying images. Among the three machine learning algorithms, their F1 results achieve 0.920, 0.943, and 0.961 (out of 1) respectively. The result of LDA is lower than the other two algorithms. Through the ROC, AUC and PR results shown in Fig. 8 and Fig. 9, the result differences between these three algorithms are visible.

No matter which classifier is applied, we obtain a conclusion that our framework shows high performance in malicious image detection. Moreover, it represents that BPNs performs better than the other two algorithms, and we believe that BPNs is more suitable for our framework. The back-propagation network classifier has the following advantages:

- It can handle thousands of input features without feature deletion.
- It points out the important potential features for classification.
- It performs an internal unbiased estimate of the generalization error.

We also investigate the time consumption of each algorithm by measuring the time to process the entire training dataset and the time to predict 1000 images with malicious payloads. The result is illustrated in Table 2.

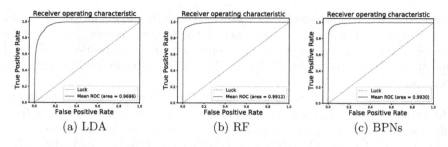

Fig. 8. ROC and AUC of algorithms.

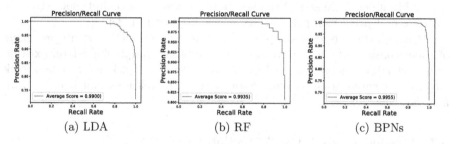

Fig. 9. Precision/Recall curve of algorithms.

5.3   Discussion

Limitation. We manually inspected some incorrectly classified images and identified the following issues that cannot be proceeded by IMSHELL-DEC.

- If a malicious image contains a sizeable pure color area, IMSHELL-DEC may predict the image as the wrong label.
- IMSHELL-DEC may incorrectly report a benign image with inferior quality.
- If the image path is deliberately obfuscated, our proposed scheme is unable to locate the image's position.

Future Work. To address the limitation mentioned above, we plan to find new feature extraction methods to solve the problem that some edges of the image may extract inaccurate features. Besides, we decide to design a better pattern matching method to locate the links of images more accurately.

6   Related Work

6.1   Malicious PowerShell Script Detection

Several works [6,8,11,16] has proposed their methods and algorithms to detect malicious scripts.

For example, Hendler *et al.* [8] extract features from malicious POWERSHELL scripts through the bag-of-words model, a natural language processing approach, where the system transform POWERSHELL commands into a multi-set of words, then calculate their frequency to generate the feature vectors. These feature vectors are further processed with Convolutional Neural Networks(CNNs) and Recurrent Neural Networks(RNNs) to identify the category of POWERSHELL commands.

Khan *et al.* [11] extract critical features through the wrapper approach to detect unseen malicious scripts. They collect malicious JavaScript codes from client sides, apply the wrapper method to distill an info-enriched feature subset, then feed this feature subset into the detection model. In this work, the author compared four supervised machine learning classifiers (Naive Bayes, Support Vector Machines, K-Nearest Neighbour and Decision Trees), and choose the one with the best prediction performance as the detection model.

Although these research apply different feature extraction strategies, none of them consider the attack vectors outside of the script. Therefore, existing script detection scheme can not identify our proposed attack, as the true attack payload is located in an external resource, and the release script itself is clean and harmless.

6.2 Steganography Image Detection

Due to the data structure of image, researchers has proposed several machine-learning based detection method [9,14,21–23] to recognize image processed with steganography tools. Wu *et al.* [21] leverage the residual network [7] to detect steganographic images. Ye *et al.* [22] promote a CNNs architecture to analyze steganography consisted of diverse activation modules. Ke *et al.* [9] proposed a hybrid deep learning framework, which combines the bottom hand-crafted convolutional kernels and threshold quantizers pairing with the upper compact deep-learning model.

For the adaptive pattern-based detection, Chen *et al.* [4] utilize local texture pattern (LTP) to detect binary image steganography, which LTP describes the texture distribution of areas and consist of pixels within the areas. Similarly, a feature selection approach [2] implemented adaptive inertia weight-based particle swarm optimization is proposed. Saman *et al.* [18] proposes a novel blind statistical analysis technique to detect the least significant bit flipping image steganography.

7   Conclusion

We investigate a new class of POWERSHELL attack combined with steganography, which allows an attacker to conceal their malicious payload in a medium outside of script, thus bypassing conventional intrusion detection methods. To examine the feasibility, we generate images hosted with script through a popular steganography tool, *Invoke-PSImage*, then retrieved and executed the payload successfully through another harmless release script. Pilot research shows that the synthesized image has no visual difference with the original, and multiple mainstream defenders failed to intercept the image nor the release script. Both results confirmed the stealthiness of this attack.

To address the emerging threat, in this paper, we propose a machine-learning-based defense framework, IMSHELL-DEC, to identify malicious POWERSHELL script that hiding their real payload in the external image. We train and evaluate our proposed framework on a synthesized dataset, in which our framework achieved high detection performance across multiple measurements. Our work can serve as an inspiration in designing a more robust and secure detection model against the proposed attack schemes.

Acknowledgments. This research has received funding from The Key Program of NSFC Grant (U140525), The National Nature Science Foundation of China (No. 61672415), Key Research and Development Program of Shaanxi Province (No. 2018ZDCXL-G-9-5), Open Foundation of Science and Technology on Communication Networks Laboratory (No. SXX18641X024), Key R&D Program of Shaanxi Province (No. 2019ZDLGY12-04), Scientific and Technical Innovation Plan of Shaanxi Province (No. 201809168CX9JC10) and National Key R&D Program of China(No. 2017YFB0801805).

References

1. Abadi, M., Xie, Y., Yu, F., John, J.P.: Identifying malicious queries, US Patent 8,495,742, 23 July 2013
2. Adeli, A., Broumandnia, A.: Image steganalysis using improved particle swarm optimization based feature selection. Appl. Intell. **48**(6), 1609–1622 (2017). https://doi.org/10.1007/s10489-017-0989-x
3. Antoniol, G., Ayari, K., Di Penta, M., Khomh, F., Guéhéneuc, Y.G.: Is it a bug or an enhancement?: a text-based approach to classify change requests. In: CASCON, vol. 8, pp. 304–318 (2008)
4. Chen, J., Lu, W., Fang, Y., Liu, X., Yeung, Y., Xue, Y.: Binary image steganalysis based on local texture pattern. J. Vis. Commun. Image Represent. **55**, 149–156 (2018)
5. Christodorescu, M., Jha, S.: Static analysis of executables to detect malicious patterns. Technical report, WISCONSIN UNIV-MADISON DEPT OF COMPUTER SCIENCES (2006)
6. Fass, A., Krawczyk, R.P., Backes, M., Stock, B.: JAST: fully syntactic detection of malicious (Obfuscated) JavaScript. In: Giuffrida, C., Bardin, S., Blanc, G. (eds.) DIMVA 2018. LNCS, vol. 10885, pp. 303–325. Springer, Cham (2018). https://doi.org/10.1007/978-3-319-93411-2_14
7. He, K., Zhang, X., Ren, S., Sun, J.: Deep residual learning for image recognition. In: Proceedings of the IEEE Conference on Computer Vision and Pattern Recognition, pp. 770–778 (2016)
8. Hendler, D., Kels, S., Rubin, A.: Detecting malicious PowerShell commands using deep neural networks. In: Proceedings of the 2018 on Asia Conference on Computer and Communications Security, pp. 187–197. ACM (2018)
9. Ke, Q., Ming, L.D., Daxing, Z.: Image steganalysis via multi-column convolutional neural network. In: 2018 14th IEEE International Conference on Signal Processing, pp. 550–553 (2018)

10. Kertesz, V., et al.: Dynamic data exchange server, US Patent 5,764,155 (1998)
11. Khan, N., Abdullah, J., Khan, A.S.: Defending malicious script attacks using machine learning classifiers. Wirel. Commun. Mob. Comput. **2017**, 9 (2017)
12. Lee, T., Mitschke, K., Schill, M.E., Tanasovski, T.: Windows PowerShell 2.0 Bible, vol. 725. Wiley, Hoboken (2011)
13. Lessmann, S., Baesens, B., Mues, C., Pietsch, S.: Benchmarking classification models for software defect prediction: a proposed framework and novel findings. IEEE Trans. Softw. Eng. **34**(4), 485–496 (2008)
14. Li, B., Wei, W., Ferreira, A., Tan, S.: ReST-Net: diverse activation modules and parallel subnets-based CNN for spatial image steganalysis. IEEE Signal Process. Lett. **25**(5), 650–654 (2018)
15. Li, Z., Chen, Q.A., Xiong, C., Chen, Y., Zhu, T., Yang, H.: Effective and lightweight deobfuscation and semantic-aware attack detection for PowerShell scripts. In: Proceedings of the 2019 ACM SIGSAC Conference on Computer and Communications Security, pp. 1831–1847. ACM (2019)
16. Milosevic, J., Sklavos, N., Koutsikou, K.: Malware in IoT software and hardware. In: Workshop on Trustworthy Manufacturing and Utilization of Secure Devices, pp. 14–16 (2016)
17. Moser, R., Pedrycz, W., Succi, G.: A comparative analysis of the efficiency of change metrics and static code attributes for defect prediction. In: Proceedings of the 30th International Conference on Software Engineering, pp. 181–190. ACM (2008)
18. Shojae Chaeikar, S., Zamani, M., Abdul Manaf, A.B., Zeki, A.M.: PSW statistical LSB image steganalysis. Multimedia Tools Appl. **77**(1), 805–835 (2018)
19. Ugarte, D., Maiorca, D., Cara, F., Giacinto, G.: PowerDrive: accurate deobfuscation and analysis of PowerShell malware. In: Perdisci, R., Maurice, C., Giacinto, G., Almgren, M. (eds.) DIMVA 2019. LNCS, vol. 11543, pp. 240–259. Springer, Cham (2019). https://doi.org/10.1007/978-3-030-22038-9_12
20. Wilson, E.: Windows PowerShell 3.0 First Steps. Pearson Education (2013)
21. Wu, S., Zhong, S., Liu, Y.: Deep residual learning for image steganalysis. Multimedia Tools Appl. **77**(9), 10437–10453 (2017). https://doi.org/10.1007/s11042-017-4440-4
22. Ye, J., Ni, J., Yi, Y.: Deep learning hierarchical representations for image steganalysis. IEEE Trans. Inf. Forensics Secur. **12**(11), 2545–2557 (2017)
23. Zeng, J., Tan, S., Li, B., Huang, J.: Large-scale JPEG image steganalysis using hybrid deep-learning framework. IEEE Trans. Inf. Forensics Secur. **13**(5), 1200–1214 (2018)

Secure Attestation of Virtualized Environments

Michael Eckel[1(✉)], Andreas Fuchs[1], Jürgen Repp[1], and Markus Springer[2]

[1] Fraunhofer SIT, Rheinstraße 75, 64295 Darmstadt, Germany
{michael.eckel,andreas.fuchs,Jurgen.Repp}@sit.fraunhofer.de
[2] Darmstadt, Germany

Abstract. Securing the integrity of virtualized environments like clouds is challenging yet feasible. Operators have discovered the advantages of virtualization technology in terms of flexibility, scalability, cost-effectiveness, and availability. Applications range from network and embedded devices to big data centers and cloud computing. Trusted Computing technology can be employed to protect the integrity of a system by leveraging a Trusted Platform Module (TPM) and remote attestation.

Existing research on remote attestation of virtualized environments differs in scalability, resource consumption, and provided security guarantees. While some approaches scale at large and use the TPM efficiently, they are way more intrusive, requiring changes to hypervisor and Virtual Machine (VMs). Others render entirely impractical with an increasing number of VMs, caused by the TPM being the bottleneck.

In this paper we analyze existing work on remote attestation for virtualized environments and discuss benefits as well as shortcomings. We identify an approach that provides adequate security and is easy to implement but is prone to relay attacks. We improve that approach by developing countermeasures, while maintaining existing security guarantees. Our contribution requires only minimal changes to the hypervisor system, keeping existing attestation protocols intact. We implement and evaluate on production-grade hardware, and compare our improved attestation approach with the most sophisticated alternative approach.

With performance measurements and further evaluations we show that our solution outperforms the other approach for a small number of VMs, as used in network devices and embedded systems.

Keywords: Virtualization · Remote attestation · Trusted computing

1 Introduction

Virtualization technology has paved the way for businesses to reduce infrastructure costs while also improving dependability and scalability. Being able to dynamically launch and tear down new VMs on demand, infrastructure costs are cut even further. Especially when handling huge amounts of data on the go, cloud services come in very handy. Based on virtualization technologies, they can

© IFIP International Federation for Information Processing 2020
Published by Springer Nature Switzerland AG 2020
M. Hölbl et al. (Eds.): SEC 2020, IFIP AICT 580, pp. 203–216, 2020.
https://doi.org/10.1007/978-3-030-58201-2_14

be hosted internally or externally, and be migrated back and forth. Depending on the use case, data and workloads handled by VMs may be of sensitive or confidential nature. Those can be protected against disclosure and manipulation by providing encryption and authenticated channels during transport. However, data can still leak if VMs or hypervisor hosts are manipulated.

To mitigate these threats, Trusted Computing technologies, such as the TPM and remote attestation, can be leveraged. Remote attestation is the process of a verifier making claims about the integrity of target systems, based on executed software. Hypervisors equipped with a TPM allow for this kind of remote attestation. Before data is to be processed on a VM, its trustworthiness could be verified using remote attestation.

Current technologies allow for both attestation of boot time and attestation of runtime. Boot time attestation encompasses all components that are executed in strictly sequential order during system boot, i.e. up to the kernel of an operating system (OS). From there, the runtime of a system begins, executing software applications in parallel in an unpredictable, non-deterministic order. A major problem is that software inside VMs is per se not considered in a remote attestation process. To make sure that VMs behave as expected, tools like Intel's Open Cloud Integrity Technology (Open CIT) implement features to measure the integrity of VM images prior to their execution. This approach turns out to be very time-consuming and inflexible since it supports only static images.

Hypervisor solutions like KVM support passing through the Physical TPM (pTPM) to VMs. That allows for identical attestation technologies to be used for VMs and hypervisor. However, forwarding the same pTPM to many VMs, makes the TPM a bottleneck and introduces race conditions. Virtual TPMs (vTPM) are software implementations of a TPM which can be assigned to VMs, conveying the impression to a VM of using a pTPM [2,3]. This way the same attestation technologies as for physical machines can be used. However, integrity of VMs depends on the integrity of the underlying hypervisor.

In this paper we analyze existing attestation approaches for virtualized environments. We improve the existing *separate attestation* approach to strengthen it against relay attacks. We implement the hypervisor-based attestation approach as proposed by Lauer and Kuntze [12] as well as our improved separate attestation approach. Eventually, we evaluate the feasibility of both approaches with performance measurements on production-grade hardware.

In Sect. 2 we analyze related work on attestation for virtualized environments. We present our target reference architecture in Sect. 3. Section 4 identifies attestation requirements which we consider vital. Section 5 then presents our main contribution, the strengthening of the separate attestation approach. In Sect. 6 we describe our implementation, followed by our evaluation in Sect. 7. Section 8 summarizes the paper and finishes with potential future work.

2   Related Work

Existing research on attesting virtualized environments focuses on either providing isolated attestations of the hypervisor or of single VMs [11,17]. Some propose more sophisticated solutions that attempt to build a trusted virtual machine monitor (VMM).

One of these approaches is Terra from Garfinkel et al. [10]. Terra protects VMs by isolating them from each other. It measures individual blocks of memory prior to loading them and enables remote attestation to external appraisers. This memory introspection approach is computing-intensive and requires a huge amount of main memory. However, Terra builds a basis for many other work which further elaborates on the idea of protecting VM memory, such as Cerberus [6] and TrustVisor [13].

Other approaches, such as the Hypervisor-Based Integrity Measurement Agent (HIMA) by Azab et al. [1], measure programs and services running inside a VM. Prior to execution by the hypervisor, VM system calls and hardware interrupts are intercepted and analyzed. It requires NX bit (no-execute bit) support on the hypervisor to mark measured memory pages prior to their execution. HIMA requires all memory pages of a program to be loaded into memory. As a consequence, changes to the OS are necessary. HIMA requires a large amount of computing power and its applicability must be carefully evaluated.

There exist CPU based attestation approaches to achieve software integrity protection, such as Bastion [5] and HyperWall [15]. These CPU extensions allow for measuring and verifying software modules prior to their execution and were analyzed by Zhang et al. in [18] regarding their applicability to cloud solutions.

Since memory verification techniques based on TPMs are slow, there was a desire to supply VMs with TPM functionality in a resource efficient manner. The work in [14] introduced an abstraction layer inside the VMM, adding context switching functionality in a pTPM. This provides VMs with the illusion of having exclusive access to a real pTPM. The problem with this approach is that sharing one physical TPM with many VMs makes the pTPM a bottleneck. With the introduction of vTPMs by Berger et al. [2], attestation of VMs changed to some extend. With vTPMs it is possible to supply every VM with its own TPM in software which is securely anchored in a pTPM. Since its introduction in 2006, Berger et al. have altered the vTPM implementation slightly, turning it into a hypervisor extension. Thus, eliminating the need for an additional management VM [3]. Due to its efficiency, many researchers now focus on the integration of vTPMs to attest software running inside VMs. Migration of VMs and associated vTPMs is another topic that is actively researched [17].

While the majority of existing research treats attestation of VMs and hypervisors separately, almost no research on binding these attestations together is conducted. A verifier may trust a VM after verifying its integrity, using remote attestation. However, if the underlying hypervisor is compromised, the integrity and trustworthiness of the VM may also be compromised. In case an attacker manages to compromise a hypervisor, she may be able to extract or manipulate sensitive information, e.g. by tampering with VM main memory.

The Virtualized Platform working group of the Trusted Computing Group (TCG) defined a deep attestation scheme [16] to link attestations of VMs and hypervisor. In [4], Celesti et al. describe how remote and deep attestation can be used to build federated cloud environments.

Lauer and Kuntze propose Hypervisor-based Attestation (HYPA) [12]. It adds an Attestation Manager (ATAMAN) to the hypervisor which directly reads the internal state of running vTPM instances. The approach falls into the category of bottom-up attestation approaches and aims at improving scalability of VM attestations, in cases where tens or hundreds of VMs are running.

In a HYPA process, the Verifier sends a single attestation request to the hypervisor (cf. Fig. 1, 1). In return, it receives a single attestation response (9), including attestations of all running VMs (2–7) as well as the hypervisor itself (8).

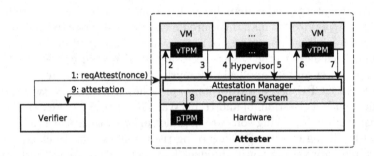

Fig. 1. Hypervisor-based attestation (based on [12])

The Attestation Manager directly accesses running vTPM instances to read their internal state, i.e. vPCRs. Furthermore, it reads the *virtual* Stored Measurement Log (vSML) from inside each VM. All vPCRs and vSMLs are compiled into a data structure, which is then hashed. The resulting digest is passed as qualifying data (nonce) to a *TPM Quote* operation of a hypervisor attestation, using the pTPM. The Attestation Manager runs within the bounds of the hypervisor, and as such, it is part of the hypervisor attestation. The overall attestation result includes the data structure with the vPCRs and vSMLs as well as the hypervisor attestation. The Verifier verifies both the hypervisor attestation and the VM attestations.

The main benefit of the hypervisor-based attestation approach is its huge scalability improvement compared to individual VM attestations. This is reflected by the reduction of attestation protocol overhead as well as reduced I/O operations. However, it is very intrusive, requiring access to currently running vTPM instances as well as access to VM internals, i.e. the vSMLs.

Separate Attestation (SEPA) of VMs and hypervisor is another approach described by Lauer and Kuntze in [12]. The Verifier sends an attestation request to a single VM (cf. Fig. 2, 1) and receives an attestation result (2). Then the Verifier sends an attestation request to the hypervisor (3), using the same nonce, and receives the attestation result (4). By using the same nonce, a weak layer linking is achieved between the VM and hypervisor.

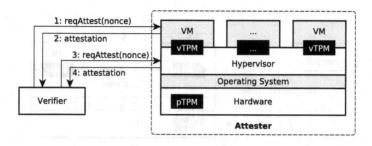

Fig. 2. Separate attestation (based on [12])

As stated by the authors, the SEPA approach is not resource-conserving and makes the pTPM the bottleneck during consecutive VM attestations. The fact that each individual VM attestation also requires an additional hypervisor attestation, reduces the scalability of this approach drastically. Another problem is that layer linking is not very strong and a Verifier requires constant up-to-date information on which hypervisor a VM is running. Since this kind of layer linking is neither enforced nor verifiable, it undermines the strong attestation statements of pTPM and vTPM. Lauer and Kuntze propose a way to improve the linking between VM and hypervisor by providing the VM with a secret value N which is used to generate remote attestation data. After the VM terminates, it provides the hypervisor with the secret value N over a secure channel between VM and hypervisor. The hypervisor then uses this secret value for attestation. The downside of this approach is that the Verifier does not treat VM and hypervisor equally. It requires changes to the guest OS and hypervisor. Thus, complicating the implementation and reducing scalability [12].

SEPA does not require changes to existing software components or protocols, and thus can be easily integrated into existing attestation solutions. It is possible to treat VMs and hypervisors equally from a Verifier point of view. In systems which only run a small number of VMs, this approach represents a feasible attestation solution. However, we observed that separate attestation as proposed by Lauer and Kuntze is subject to relay attacks.

There exist other cloud integrity verification techniques that are more complex but rely on previously described technologies. In the upcoming section we introduce our reference architecture, which we use to further evaluate the SEPA and HYPA approaches.

3 Reference System

Our reference architecture is based on the one presented by Intel and Hytrust in [8] which splits data into work packages to process them in parallel (cf. Fig. 3). We propose to use VMs for that purpose which can be flexibly spawned and teared down on current demands. The Workflow Orchestration handles distribution and scheduling of work packages to VMs. We assume host systems and VMs to be owned and operated by the same party.

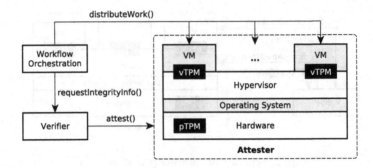

Fig. 3. vTPM-based reference architecture. The workflow Orchestration relies on the Verifier to verify the integrity of VMs and their hypervisor.

Before entrusting a VM with processing of potentially sensitive work packages, the Workflow Orchestration ensures the VM to be trustworthy. This process is complex and requires in-depth knowledge about the configuration of a particular VM. That is why a Verifier is dedicated to that task. It attests hosts and VMs to provide the Workflow Orchestration with up-to-date integrity information. The Verifier maintains a database of Reference Integrity Measurements (RIMs) which represent known good system configurations. By comparing them to the current operational state of a system, the Verifier decides whether or not hosts and VMs to be trustworthy.

Hosts are equipped with a pTPM and run Linux. They have a TPM-enabled BIOS and boot loader, and support Measured Boot for boot time integrity, and the Linux Integrity Measurement Architecture (IMA) for runtime integrity. The VM hypervisor supports vTPMs to be assigned to VM, such as QEMU/KVM. vTPMs are executed in the context of the hypervisor and one vTPM is assigned to exactly one VM [3]. vTPMs provide identical functionality as pTPMs. However, they lack a True Random Number Generator (TRNG) as well as an Endorsement Key Certificate (EK Cert) from the TPM manufacturer. Further, they cannot provide the same security guarantees as a pTPM as they are only software.

4   Attestation Requirements

Coker et al. [7] already postulate requirements for remote attestation based solutions. Lauer and Kuntze analyzed and extended them in [12]. The first of these requirements is the freshness of attestation information, which requires to keep the gap between the time of a measurement and the time of its use as small as possible to minimize the risk of using outdated information. The next requirement is the comprehensiveness of attestations to enable the verifier to deduct the state of a system in a replicable, accountable and comprehensive manner. The attestation information must also be presented in a logical form that helps the verifier to correlate multiple attestations over time to further improve the detection of misbehavior. Since attestations expose sensitive information about a target system, their disclosure must be constrained to valid verifiers. In order to build trust into an attestation, the verifier relies on the trustworthiness of delivery mechanisms which ensure authenticity and integrity of reported data.

In terms of cloud attestations, Lauer and Kuntze further require layer linking between VMs and hypervisor in order to trust VMs attestations [12]. Hence, there must be valid attestation information available for both VM and hypervisor. And it must be possible to correlate these in order to ensure a VM runs on its assigned hypervisor. Another requirement by Lauer and Kuntze is scalability of the attestation scheme, which targets systems with a large number of VMs. In terms of TPM-based attestations, that means to reduce the number of calls to the pTPM [12].

In addition, we propose implementation-specific requirements: *implementation complexity* and *guest independence*.

Implementation Complexity. Depending on the used attestation scheme and how attestation information is acquired, modifications to guest OS or vTPM are required, which increase development costs. This also applies to installation of additional software inside a guest system, even though these are not considered as critical as OS code changes. In a typical cloud environment, customers want to chose software and OS based on application needs, rather than whether an implementation for additional security tools exists. Impact and intrusiveness of these tools must be taken into account. The smaller and less intrusive tools are the better they can be ported. Huge code changes and dependencies to other software may yield a bigger obstacle in porting. Required system privileges for the software must also be taken into account.

Guest Independence. In order to reduce the attack surface, the attestation solution must rely on as little additional infrastructure as possible. Dependencies to additional infrastructure also influence the overall reliability of the solution. Increasing implementation complexity, results in systems becoming more error-prone. Less complex solutions are easier to maintain.

5   Secure Separate Attestation

During our analysis of the SEPA approach [12], we discovered a flaw in the layer linking mechanism between VM and hypervisor. An attacker could launch a relay attack to generate a verifiable VM attestation and thus fool the verifier into trusting a *Bad VM*.

We assume a threat model following the definitions of Dolev and Yao in [9]. The attacker has full control over the network, and thus can read, modify, insert, or block messages anywhere on the network. However, she is not able to break any underlying cryptographic primitives. Furthermore, the attacker is able to gain control over the system running inside a VM, but not the hypervisor.

To launch her attack the attacker operates her own hypervisor host (*Attacker-Controlled System*) outside the bounds of the target system, as depicted in Fig. 4.

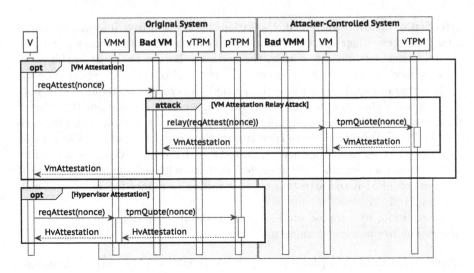

Fig. 4. Relay attack on separate attestation

On that system she runs a pristine copy of the VM alongside with the corresponding vTPM, including its configuration and keys. She further gains access to a VM on the *Original System*, in such a way that she can modify and run compromised software inside (cf. *Bad VM* in Fig. 4).

Figure 4 shows a time sequence diagram of the relay attack process. Whenever the Verifier (V) sends its attestation request to the VM, the *Bad VM* relays this request to the pristine VM on the Attacker-Controlled System. From there, the VM forwards the request to its vTPM which generates a *VmAttestation*. The VM returns this response to the Bad VM, which eventually forwards the VmAttestation to the Verifier. In a subsequent attestation of the hypervisor on the *Original System*, the pTPM is used. The Verifier in turn verifies both attestations, incorrectly considering the Bad VM trustworthy.

We solve the relay problem by using the vTPM itself as a trusted channel to the hypervisor. Whenever a VM receives an attestation request from the Verifier (V), it triggers a *TPM Quote* operation on the vTPM (cf. Fig. 5), as usual. At this point, as a matter of mitigation, we let the vTPM store a hash of the *vTPM Quote* result (VmAttestation$_{hash}$) on the hypervisor (3). Then, the usual flow continues, and the VM returns the VM attestation result to the Verifier.

Subsequently, the Verifier sends an attestation request to the hypervisor. The hypervisor uses the most recent VmAttestation$_{hash}$ for the VM and includes it in the hypervisor attestation. For that purpose, the hypervisor creates a compound nonce by hashing the concatenation of the nonce from the Verifier with the VmAttestation$_{hash}$. This compound nonce is used in the *TPM Quote* operation on the pTPM. The result is returned to the Verifier. The Verifier verifies that the VM attestation hashes match. For that purpose, it creates a hash of the VM attestation data (VmAttestation) it received from the VM attestation. The

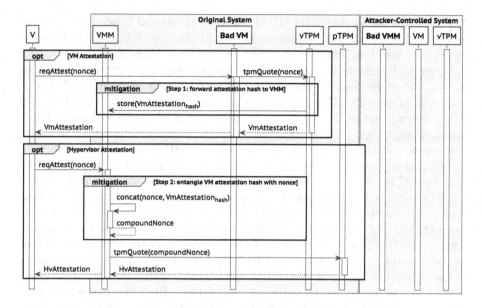

Fig. 5. Secure separate attestation

Verifier generates the nonce exactly as the hypervisor did, and compares it with the compound nonce from the hypervisor attestation data. Only if the compound nonces match, the Verifier can be certain it received the correct VM attestation. This way, layer linking between VM and hypervisor is significantly improved. After that, the Verifier continues, verifying VM and hypervisor attestations.

This approach introduces the risk of disclosing the nonce designated to a VM to other VMs or unauthorized third parties. We consider this risk to be minimal, as the attestation approach ensures that both VM and the underlying hypervisor host are trustworthy. Other security measures like encryption and access control mechanisms can be used to further secure the forwarded hashes. A hypervisor that is not trusted could potentially disclose forwarded information from the vTPM anyway, but would be detected using the SEPA scheme.

6   Implementation

Memory introspection approaches are computing-intensive, require a lot of main memory, and are not easy to implement. Intercepting system calls from VMs to the host OS requires changes to the hypervisor as well as the host OS. Because these violate many of our requirements, we do not consider them as candidates for our implementation. Layer-linking is vital and we choose SEPA and HYPA for our implementation, both of which are in accordance with our requirements.

We implement SEPA and HYPA as a single proof-of-concept, extending Intel's Open CIT 2.2. Open CIT features boot time attestation of host machines and uses Intel Trusted Execution Technology (TXT) to establish a hardware

Root of Trust for Measurement (RTM). It supports several hypervisors, such as VMware ESX, Citrix Xen, Kernel-based Virtual Machine (KVM), and Microsoft HyperV. Attestation information is presented via a web interface.

Open CIT consists of two main components: Attestation Server and Trust Agent. The Attestation Server acts as Verifier for remote attestations. It maintains a database with RIMs and attestation results, and exposes those via REST API to relying parties. Trust Agents run on any attested machine handling attestation requests from the Attestation Server. That is, performing *TPM Quote* operations, collecting Stored Measurement Logs (SMLs), and returning those.

We add support for attesting VMs to Open CIT, including HYPA and our improved SEPA layer binding mechanisms to associate VMs with their underlying hypervisor. This requires changes to both Trust Agent and Attestation Server. We develop a vTPM instance manager to provide VMs with vTPMs, using QEMU and Stefan Berger's vTPM implementation, adapted to our needs. That is, for HYPA we add Platform Configuration Register (PCR) read access to the hypervisor Trust Agent, and for SEPA we store VM attestation hashes in the hypervisor file system. For HYPA to access vSMLs inside VMs, we use *VirtIO* on the hypervisor to share a *tempfs* folder with VMs. Further, we add support for runtime integrity verification with IMA. This requires changes to Attestation Server, Trust Agents, and VM OS.

7   Evaluation

In this section we evaluate both SEPA and HYPA attestation approaches. The evaluation system is a Huawei RH5885 V2 server equipped with four Intel® Xeon® E7-8870 CPUs at 2.40 GHz, 10 cores per CPU and 2 threads per core. It provides 1 TiB of main memory and a plug-in physical TPM 2.0. It runs the customized Open CIT Attestation Server in a VM as well as ten distinct client VMs. The hypervisor host uses libvirt, KVM, and QEMU 2.6 for virtualization. All machines run Ubuntu 16.04. Client VMs and hypervisor run the customized Open CIT Trust Agents.

In order to compare performance measurements between SEPA and HYPA, we define evaluation scenarios based on typical actions which Open CIT performs to attest VMs and hypervisors: 1. Attest all VMs, 2. Attest a single VM, 3. Attest hypervisor only.

7.1   Evaluation Criteria

To evaluate our proof-of-concept implementation we define evaluation criteria. The following paragraphs explain them.

Execution Time. In order to compare the attestation schemes based on execution time, we measure the overall execution time of each scenario. This includes attestation request generation, response handling, verification, and transport over the network. Since Open CIT produces a lot of overhead in the backend in

Table 1. Execution time in ms

Scenario	Name	SEPA			HYPA		
		Min	Avg	Max	Min	Avg	Max
All VMs	Execution time	50097.25	50423.92	50751.25	12907.50	13152.17	13299.00
	Retrieve *TPM Quote*	1494.50	1513.35	1545.25	1594.50	1605.50	1617.00
	Verify *TPM Quote*	15.00	23.31	28.25	21.25	22.92	24.50
One VM	Execution time	4690.50	4790.75	4895.75	12890.50	13091.92	13231.75
	Retrieve *TPM Quote*	1509.25	1518.08	1525.75	1597.75	1610.83	1624.25
	Verify *TPM Quote*	21.25	24.92	28.25	21.25	22.42	23.75
Hypervisor	Execution time	2833.50	2857.00	2890.00	12815.00	13091.17	13258.00
	Retrieve *TPM Quote*	1497.50	1510.17	1521.50	1587.50	1605.17	1623.50
	Verify *TPM Quote*	24.50	25.84	26.50	21.00	21.83	23.00

order to generate and verify the *TPM Quote* response, we also measure the time these two events require to complete.

Network Usage. For each evaluation scenario we capture the entire network traffic for three subsequent attestations. For each connection from the Attestation Server to the hypervisor host or a VM, we compute the amount of received and transmitted data, the throughput rate, and the time between the first and last transmission. In our summary, we include only the accumulated amount of data for all connections.

CPU and Memory Usage. For three attestations per attempt, we measure the resident (non-swapped) physical memory consumption in megabytes as well as the percentage of CPU utilization. Depending on the scenario, the Attestation Server and the Trust Agent are measured every 100 ms with the Linux *top* command, computing average and peak values. Some tasks consume more than 100% of the CPU, which means they occupy more than one CPU core.

7.2 Evaluation Results

During evaluation, we observed the expected behavior for the schemes. Table 1 shows measured execution times for the scenarios. We generate ten measurements per scenario and accumulate them into a single table. That is, each value of a group is computed as the arithmetic mean of all measured execution times for a particular scenario.

As shown in Table 1, if all VMs are verified, HYPA is faster than SEPA, as it attests the hypervisor only once. In case only one VM, or only the hypervisor is verified, SEPA is a lot faster. An interesting observation is the time it takes to retrieve a TPM Quote response, and the time to verify it. This seems to be largely unaffected by the amount of attested VMs, with SEPA showing an exceptional maximum peak. In practice, however, HYPA will scale worse if fewer

Table 2. Network usage

Scenario	Type	SEPA Amount	HYPA Amount	Unit
All VMs	Send	0.64	0.06	KiB
	Receive	6317.20	2323.86	KiB
	Time	178.89	63.19	s
	Receive/s	43.11	36.81	KiB/s
One VM	Send	0.14	0.06	KiB
	Receive	592.56	2321.03	KiB
	Time	43.47	62.93	s
	Receive/s	13.64	36.93	KiB/s
Hypervisor	Send	0.06	0.06	KiB
	Receive	378.81	2320.77	KiB
	Time	15.07	62.84	s
	Receive/s	25.15	36.93	KiB/s

Table 3. CPU and memory usage

Scenario	Type	SEPA avg	SEPA peak	HYPA avg	HYPA peak
All VMs	%CPU	50.93	280.50	69.15	217.18
	RES/MB	966.48	1015.85	1045.48	1074.50
One VM	%CPU	58.82	202.43	70.20	225.63
	RES/MB	1146.65	1209.35	1055.06	1091.91
Hypervisor	%CPU	19.16	106.20	70.06	215.50
	RES/MB	1098.88	1105.92	1048.71	1086.60

attestations are requested, or if the IMA SMLs become very large in size. After a certain threshold of requested attestations is reached, which depends on the number of VMs, SEPA becomes less efficient than HYPA.

For CPU utilization, Table 3 shows that SEPA always has a smaller average and peak CPU usage, with the exception of verifying all VMs at once. HYPA requires less CPU time for attestation verifications as it performs fewer attestation operations than SEPA.

The memory consumption depicted in Table 3 shows unexpected behavior. HYPA is in most cases more efficient than SEPA. In theory, HYPA should require more memory at verification time, as it attests both hypervisor and VMs at the same time. We can only explain this behavior with JAVA's garbage collection, or the general OS memory management messing up our measurements.

Table 2 shows that SEPA utilizes the network more efficiently until the threshold of attestation requests is reached. If more client VMs were added to the hypervisor host, or more attestations were requested at once, HYPA would become more efficient.

We also tested whether or not the integrity of VMs or underlying hypervisor hosts, influence the results of our measurements. However, we could not find correlations or indicators that non-integer systems are more expensive. The results are so close and indistinguishable, that the differences are probably caused by different sources of noise, causing jitter on the measurements, such as network communication, host utilization by other applications and services, Java Just in Time (JIT) optimizations, garbage collection, or OS scheduling.

We also monitored the Trust Agent on the clients. We could not observe any apparent differences between the schemes. CPU utilization and memory consumption showed no difference between the schemes. This may again be caused by JAVA's overhead and garbage collection. Logically, there should be slightly more memory consumption when the Attestation Manager gathers attestation information in the form of SMLs and PCR values (which need to be loaded into memory).

Nonce generation time differs for both schemes. HYPA requires more time to gather and combine all attestation information. It is overall stable and has little only impact on the overall performance of the schemes. Nonce generation time for HYPA increases with the number of running VMs. Thus, HYPA may run into scalability issues on the hypervisor Trust Agent. But only if there are many guests and very big SMLs. SEPA only has scaling issues when many hosts need to be attested on the network, but not on a single Trust Agent.

We conclude that SEPA performs better than HYPA for a small number of VMs. Performance of SEPA decreases as the number of VM attestations increases. As expected, HYPA shows constant performance across all tests. Having support for both of the attestation schemes on target systems, efficient combinations can be defined.

8 Conclusions and Future Work

In this paper we analyzed existing Trusted Computing based attestation approaches for virtualized environments. We discovered a conceptual security weakness in the existing *separate attestation* approach.

By proposing *secure* separate attestation, we strengthened layer linking between hypervisor and VM layer. As a result, we improved security characteristics of the original separate attestation approach and provided an effective countermeasure against relay attacks. We implemented and evaluated the hypervisor-based attestation approach as well as our secure separate attestation approach on production-grade hardware. With performance measurements we underlined the feasibility of our approach for systems running a limited number of VMs. Further, we pointed out that our security improvement allows for keeping standard attestation protocols in place, by requiring only minimal changes to hypervisor software.

Future directions of work include the application of secure separate attestation in virtualized network equipment, fog, and edge computing. With the evolution of container technology the applicability of our approach beyond full-fledged machine virtualization is another interesting direction of research.

Acknowledgements. The work and results presented in this paper were developed in the scope of a technical research cooperation project on cloud integrity verification, together with the German Research Center of Huawei Technologies. We thank Huawei for giving us the opportunity to work and evaluate on production-grade hardware.

References

1. Azab, A.M., Ning, P., Sezer, E.C., Zhang, X.: Hima: a hypervisor-based integrity measurement agent. In: Computer Security Applications Conference, ACSAC 2009, Annual, pp. 461–470, December 2009
2. Berger, S., Cáceres, R., Goldman, K.A., Perez, R., Sailer, R., van Doorn, L.: vTPM: Virtualizing the trusted platform module. In: Proceedings of the 15th Conference on USENIX Security Symposium, USENIX-SS 2006, vol. 15. USENIX Association (2006)

3. Berger, S., Goldman, K.A., Pendarakis, D., Safford, D., Valdez, E., Zohar, M.: Scalable attestation: a step toward secure and trusted clouds. In: 2015 IEEE International Conference on Cloud Engineering (IC2E), pp. 185–194, March 2015

4. Celesti, A., Fazio, M., Villari, M., Puliafito, A., Mulfari, D.: Remote and deep attestations to mitigate threats in cloud mash-up services. In: 2013 World Congress on Computer and Information Technology (WCCIT), pp. 1–6, June 2013

5. Champagne, D., Lee, R.B.: Processor-based tailored attestation. Princeton University Department of Electrical Engineering, Technical Report (2010)

6. Chen, W.Z., Zhang, Z.P., Yang, J.H., He, Q.M.: Cerberus: a novel hypervisor to provide trusted and isolated code execution. In: 2010 International Conference of Information Science and Management Engineering (ISME), vol. 1, pp. 330–333, August 2010

7. Coker, G., et al.: Principles of remote attestation. Int. J. Inf. Secur. **10**(2), 63–81 (2011). https://doi.org/10.1007/s10207-011-0124-7

8. Cooperation, I.: Building trust and compliance in the cloud with intel trusted execution technology - the Taiwan Stock Exchange Corporation Develops a Secure Cloud Infrastructure. Technical report, Intel Cooperaion (2013). https://www.hytrust.com/uploads/2015/08/intel_txt.pdf

9. Dolev, D., Yao, A.: On the security of public key protocols. IEEE Trans. Inf. Theory **29**(2), 198–208 (1983)

10. Garfinkel, T., Pfaff, B., Chow, J., Rosenblum, M., Boneh, D.: Terra: a virtual machine-based platform for trusted computing. In: Proceedings of the Nineteenth ACM Symposium on Operating Systems Principles, SOSP 2003, pp. 193–206. ACM, New York (2003)

11. Ghosh, A., Sapello, A., Poylisher, A., Chiang, C.J., Kubota, A., Matsunaka, T.: On the feasibility of deploying software attestation in cloud environments. In: 2014 IEEE 7th International Conference on Cloud Computing, pp. 128–135, June 2014

12. Lauer, H., Kuntze, N.: Hypervisor-based attestation of virtual environments. In: The 13th IEEE International Conference on Advanced and Trusted Computing, July 2016

13. McCune, J.M., et al.: Trustvisor: efficient TCB reduction and attestation. In: 2010 IEEE Symposium on Security and Privacy, pp. 143–158, May 2010

14. Stumpf, F., Eckert, C.: Enhancing trusted platform modules with hardware-based virtualization techniques. In: 2008 Second International Conference on Emerging Security Information, Systems and Technologies, pp. 1–9, August 2008

15. Szefer, J., Lee, R.B.: Architectural support for hypervisor-secure virtualization. In: Proceedings of the Seventeenth International Conference on Architectural Support for Programming Languages and Operating Systems, pp. 437–450. ACM, New York (2012)

16. Trusted Computing Group: Virtualized Trusted Platform Architecture Specification, specification version 1.0, revision 0.26 edn., September 2011

17. Yu, A., Qin, Y., Wang, D.: Obtaining the integrity of your virtual machine in the cloud. In: 2011 IEEE Third International Conference on Cloud Computing Technology and Science (CloudCom), pp. 213–222, November 2011

18. Zhang, T., Szefer, J., Lee, R.B.: Security verification of hardware-enabled attestation protocols. In: 2012 45th Annual IEEE/ACM International Symposium on Microarchitecture Workshops (MICROW), pp. 47–54, December 2012

Network Security and Privacy

Security and Performance Implications of BGP Rerouting-Resistant Guard Selection Algorithms for Tor

Asya Mitseva[1(✉)], Marharyta Aleksandrova[1], Thomas Engel[1],
and Andriy Panchenko[2]

[1] University of Luxembourg, Esch-sur-Alzette, Luxembourg
{asya.mitseva,marharyta.aleksandrova,thomas.engel}@uni.lu
[2] Brandenburg University of Technology, Cottbus, Germany
andriy.panchenko@b-tu.de

Abstract. Tor is the most popular anonymization system with millions of daily users and, thus, an attractive target for attacks, e.g., by malicious autonomous systems (ASs) performing active routing attacks to become man in the middle and deanonymize users. It was shown that the number of such malicious ASs is significantly larger than previously expected due to the lack of security guarantees in the Border Gateway Protocol (BGP). In response, recent works suggest alternative Tor path selection methods prefering Tor nodes with higher resilience to active BGP attacks.

In this work, we analyze the implications of such proposals. We show that Counter-RAPTOR and DPSelect are not as secure as thought before: for particular users they allow for leakage of user's location. DPSelect is not as resilient as widely accepted as we show that it achieves only one third of its originally claimed resilience and, hence, does not protect users from routing attacks. We reveal the performance implications of both methods and identify scenarios where their usage leads to significant performance bottlenecks. Finally, we propose a new metric to quantify the user's location leakage by path selection. Using this metric and performing large-scale analysis, we show to which extent a malicious middle can fingerprint the user's location and what kind of confidence it can achieve. Our findings shed light on the implications of path selection methods on the users' anonymity and the need for further research.

Keywords: BGP routing attacks · Tor · Onion routing · Privacy

1 Introduction

In the age of mass surveillance and censorship, users rely on anonymization techniques to exercise their right to freedom of expression and to freely access information. Currently, Tor [7] is the most popular low-latency anonymization network designed to hide users' identities (i.e., IP addresses) from service providers

© IFIP International Federation for Information Processing 2020
Published by Springer Nature Switzerland AG 2020
M. Hölbl et al. (Eds.): SEC 2020, IFIP AICT 580, pp. 219–233, 2020.
https://doi.org/10.1007/978-3-030-58201-2_15

and to prevent third parties from exposing the relationship between communicating partners on the Internet. To accomplish this goal, the user traffic sent via Tor is encrypted in multiple layers and forwarded through three Tor nodes, known as *entry*, *middle*, and *exit*. Due to its popularity, it is an attractive target for adversaries aiming to compromise Tor users, e.g., by applying traffic analysis. An adversary who simultaneously observes the user traffic entering and exiting Tor can perform traffic correlation on packet sizes and timing and, thus, deanonymize user connections [15,23]. Website fingerprinting (WFP) is another type of traffic analysis, where the adversary aims to identify the website visited by a Tor user by observing patterns of data flows between the user and its entry node [14,22]. A common example of entities in the position to execute both types of attacks are autonomous systems (ASs), often called network-level adversaries, which lie on the path between the Tor user and its destination. Recent studies [23,25] have shown that natural Internet routing dynamics and active attacks against Border Gateway Protocol (BGP), the de-facto standard interdomain routing protocol, dramatically increase the number of ASs that are in a position to compromise Tor traffic by applying traffic correlation or WFP.

In response, several works have focused on developing sophisticated Tor path selection methods for choosing entry and exit nodes that consider not only the nodes' capacity but also the presence of asymmetric routing, potentially colluding ASs, and the robustness of network paths against active routing attacks [2,21]. The most recent proposals are Counter-RAPTOR [24] and DPSelect [11]. Counter-RAPTOR is an alternative path selection method preferring entries with higher resilience to BGP attacks, as estimated based on the network location of the Tor user. The hardened protection against active routing attacks provided by this method, though, negatively influences the randomness of entry node selection and leaks information about the user's location. This allows an attacker to link a user to its AS [11]. Such a leak can be further exploited to deanonymize users. DPSelect aims to overcome this drawback by using *differential privacy*.

Hanley et al. [11] have recently explored the privacy loss of both Counter-RAPTOR and DPSelect with respect to the fingerprintability of user ASs by using notions of entropy. However, their evaluation is based on a small dataset of 95 ASs only. Hence, the results cannot be generalized to all Tor users. Moreover, no existing work has examined the potential threats of malicious middle nodes to deanonymize Tor users utilizing rerouting-resistant path selection. Recent study has shown that traffic analysis from middle nodes can be as effective as from entry and exit positions in case of Tor onion services, although middles neither directly know the user nor its destination [14]. In this work, we show to which extent a malicious middle can close this gap and successfully mount a deanonymization attack by localizing a user. Our contributions are as follows:

1. We show that Counter-RAPTOR and DPSelect are not as secure as previously thought: about 20% of users that rely on these methods select an entry node from their country with five times higher probability than vanilla Tor. This exposes user location and seriously endangers user's anonymity. Our method allows users to assess their vulnerability.

2. DPSelect is not as resilient as widely accepted. We show that it achieves only one third of its originally claimed resilience and, hence, does not protect users from active routing attacks.
3. We identify scenarios where the usage of both path selection methods leads to serious performance bottlenecks, as they prefer poorly-performing entries.
4. We propose a new metric, *confidence increase*, to quantify the user's location leakage by Counter-RAPTOR and DPSelect. Using this metric, we show to which extent a malicious middle can fingerprint the location of a user and what kind of confidence it can achieve.

We perform a large-scale analysis and collect the most comprehensive set of ASs containing Tor users to analyze the security properties of Counter-RAPTOR and DPSelect. Our analysis allows to better understand the properties of these methods and warn vulnerable users about possible implications.

2   Background

Internet Routing: The Internet comprises a large set of interconnected ASs identified by unique AS numbers (ASNs) [18]. Each AS possesses a set of delegated IP addresses that are aggregated into blocks (i.e., IP prefixes) and is responsible for forwarding traffic to and from them. Some ASs, called transit ASs, are also able to forward traffic whose source and destination are not in their IP prefixes. ASs set up dedicated links between each other, based on confidential business agreements, and distribute reachability data using BGP. Since BGP does not provide any security guarantees, ASs can manipulate the global routing by distributing bogus data [18]. An AS is capable of claiming that it originates an IP prefix not delegated to it, known as a *prefix hijack*, and attract a fraction of Internet traffic to it. As this AS does not possess any valid route to the victim AS, the redirected traffic will be dropped and affected users will experience connectivity problems. A more sophisticated attack, BGP *interception* [18], is an improved version of prefix hijacks, where the malicious AS has a valid route to the victim AS. It can not only redirect traffic through itself, but also forward it via a detour to the real destination without disturbing the connectivity. These BGP attacks have been often exploited for country-level censorship [26] and tracking users of anonymization networks such as Tor [23].

Tor [7] is the most popular anonymization network designed for low-latency applications, e.g., web browsing. The traffic between a Tor user and its destination is sent via a virtual tunnel (i.e., *circuit*), over three nodes, known as *onion relays* (ORs). Information about identities and status of the available ORs is periodically distributed to Tor users in the form of a *consensus* document. Tor users select ORs for circuits probabilistically according to the ORs' bandwidth, availability, and exit policy to a given target. After negotiating a symmetric key between each OR in the circuit and the user, the user data is encrypted in multiple layers using these keys [7]. While forwarding the user data, each OR on the path removes (or adds, depending on the direction) one layer of encryption. Thus, none of the ORs in the circuit knows both the user and its destination at the same time. Each user also maintains a list of preselected entries, called *guard set*, to reduce the information leakage caused by the frequent selection of new entries for each new circuit. From its guard set, the user chooses a singe entry (i.e., *guard*) as the first hop for its circuits and continues using it for months [8]. Although the use of a guard reduces the probability of picking a malicious OR in a short time period, it does not prevent malicious ASs from being on the path between the Tor user and its guard and compromising user traffic.

Counter-RAPTOR: Sun et al. [24] proposed an enhancement to the original Tor path selection algorithm, called Counter-RAPTOR, aiming to decrease the probability of an AS actively putting itself on the path between a Tor user and its guard. According to the proposal, the user considers not only the available OR's bandwidth $B(i)$ but also the OR's resilience $R(i)$ to hijack attacks when choosing a guard. The OR's resilience value indicates the fraction of ASs that will not succeed in hijacking the user traffic sent to the OR by falsely claiming to originate the IP prefix containing that OR. In other words, the probability of a guard i being selected is proportional to its weight $W(i)$:

$$W(i) = \alpha \cdot R(i) + (1 - \alpha) \cdot \bar{B}(i), \tag{1}$$

where $\bar{B}(i)$ is the OR's bandwidth normalized in the range $[0, 1]$ and α is a configurable parameter to balance between the OR's resilience to hijack attacks and its bandwidth. To limit a user-specific guard selection, a random sampling is applied to the ORs' resilience values to produce a more uniform choice of guard. While not stated differently, in our work we use $\alpha = 0.5$ as recommended in [24].

DPSelect: Despite the use of random sampling to pick a guard from a set of ORs with high resilience values, Hanley et al. [11] showed that Counter-RAPTOR still leaks information about user locations. Consequently, the authors proposed DPSelect, which integrates a differential privacy metric into the weight function (1) of Counter-RAPTOR. This metric is intended to bound the difference between the largest probability of a user selecting a given guard and the least probability of another user choosing the same guard and, thus, prevents a statistical correlation between a guard selected by a user and the AS of that user. To ensure guard selection homogeneity among users, DPSelect relies on an exponential mechanism to compute the weight function $W(i)$ of a guard i:

$$W(i) = e^{\epsilon \cdot (\alpha \cdot R(i)^{x_1} + (1-\alpha) \cdot B(i)^{x_2})}, \tag{2}$$

where ϵ defines how private the guard selection should be and x_1 and x_2 are optimization parameters aiming to preserve the main goal of the original Counter-RAPTOR approach with respect to high bandwidth and resilience values of the considered OR. Hanley et al. apply a Monte-Carlo sampling-based method with equally-weighed resilience and bandwidth values (i.e., $\alpha = 0.5$) to tune x_1 and x_2 and, so, achieve a reasonable trade-off between OR's resilience and bandwidth.

3   Related Work

Threat of Network-Level Attackers: The threat of an AS simultaneously observing both ends of Tor user connections was first examined by Feamster and Dingledine [10], who detected that up to 30% of randomly generated Tor circuits are vulnerable to an AS adversary. Due to the increased number of ASs carrying Tor traffic over the years, the natural intuition was that the likelihood of a single AS being able to observe user traffic entering and exiting Tor reduced. In [9], this assumption was verified by using an updated model for Tor and showed that the risk of deanonymization by a single AS is not reduced. Another work [20] explored the threat to Tor users posed by Internet eXchange points (IXP) – a shared physical infrastructure in a single location connecting several ASs. The authors showed that an attacker, who is positioned at an IXP and observes the traffic passing through any AS co-located at that IXP, can correlate high-speed network flows even at low rates of sampling and compromise users' anonymity.

Juen et al. [17] questioned the accuracy of the AS path inference methods used to evaluate the vulnerability of Tor to AS attackers. Wacek et al. [27] used traceroute data from the Center for Applied Internet Data Analysis (CAIDA) [6] to reconstruct the AS interconnectivity and showed that the same AS may still appear in both ends of 27.4% of randomly created Tor circuits. Johnson et al. [15] explored the amount of time needed by an attacker controlling a set of ASs or IXPs to compromise Tor circuits. Although the user's security strongly depends on its location, they showed that an attacker possessing several ASs or IXPs has a much greater compromise speed, even against users in safer locations. Sun et al. [23] showed that traffic correlation attacks succeed even when an AS observes paths in different directions on both ends of a Tor circuit. In response, Nithyanand et al. [21] reevaluated the threat posed by these attacks and discovered that up to 40% of Tor circuits are vulnerable to traffic correlation by single ASs, 42% by colluding ASs, and 85% by state-level (i.e., the set of ASs located in a single country) attackers. In [23], the authors also showed that BGP hijack and interception attacks used to redirect Tor traffic can dramatically increase the likelihood of an AS eavesdropping on both ends of Tor connections. Tan et al. [25] extended this analysis and detected that more than 90% of the total bandwidth available in Tor is vulnerable to BGP hijack attacks.

Defenses Against Network-Level Attackers: The idea of avoiding a single AS that appears on both ends of a Tor circuit when choosing entry and exit was first proposed by Feamster and Dingledine [10] and developed by Edman and Syverson [9] by using a snapshot of the current AS topology. *LASTor* [1] is another alternative path selection method, which predicts the ASs through which the user traffic entering and exiting Tor is highly likely to be routed. However, Wacek et al. [27] showed that almost 25% of LASTor circuits remain vulnerable to network-level adversaries. To limit the effectiveness of hijack attacks used to redirect Tor traffic, Tan et al. [25] relied on periodical traceroute measurements to detect guards under active BGP attack and prevent users from selecting them.

However, this method can neither detect short-lived BGP attacks nor protect already established circuits [23,24]. *DeNASA* [2] is another Tor path selection method that avoids a predefined set of large ASs often appearing on both sides of Tor circuits. *Astoria* [21] considers OR capacity, asymmetric routing, and potential colluding ASs during circuit creation. Contrary to Counter-RAPTOR and DPSelect, DeNASA and Astoria only focus on passive AS-level attackers. Both methods have also been shown to be user location-dependent and vulnerable to network-level attackers who can exploit user behavior over time to compromise anonymity [16,28]. Wails et al. [28] raised the further criticism that none of the proposed location-aware approaches, including Counter-RAPTOR and DPSelect, consider user mobility, which dramatically reduces the anonymity provided by these methods over time. Wan et al. [29] showed that an attacker can exploit the location awareness of the methods and strategically launch ORs in locations that increase their likelihood of being selected as guards by target users.

4 Datasets

To throughly analyze the impact of the modified path selection schemes Counter-RAPTOR and DPSelect on privacy of the users, there is a need to use representative real-world data. To this end, we gathered information about (*i*) available guards and the ASs they are located in, (*ii*) the set of all possible user ASs, and (*iii*) existing AS relationships. To obtain Tor network data, we downloaded consensus from CollecTor[1] for March 1, 2017 and extracted guards, whose IP addresses were mapped to ASs using Maxmind GeoIP database[2]. In total, we obtained 2,451 guards belonging to 475 unique ASs in 50 countries.

To acquire all possible user ASs, we collected all known ASs from CAIDA [3] during March 2017, comprising 57,015 unique ASNs, and filtered out transit and content hosting ASs (as these do not contain end-users). In total, we obtained 30,848 possible user ASs. As we are interested to know the estimated number of end-users in a given AS for our analysis, we also collected the number of IP addresses delegated to each of the ASs by using CAIDA AS Ranking dataset [5]. From our set of user ASs, we excluded 2,361 ASs for which we could not infer any data about delegated IP addresses and 2,606 ASs for which Counter-RAPTOR and DPSelect cannot compute a network path between these ASs and the collected guard ASs (breadth-first search of these methods may discard unprofitable AS relationship and yield no valid path). Finally, we obtained 25,881 possible user ASs distributed in 223 countries, where 81.4% of them were located in countries containing guard nodes too. We refer to this dataset as D.

For further analysis, we applied the method proposed in [27] to construct a reduced map of the Internet including latency measurements between hosts. We were able to extract latency values for a fully-connected graph of ASs containing 333 guard ASs and 7,052 user ASs from our initial sets of guard and user ASs. We refer to this dataset as D_{lat}. The guard ASs in D_{lat} cover 88.9% of all available

[1] https://metrics.torproject.org/collector.html.
[2] https://dev.maxmind.com/geoip/geoip2/geolite2/.

guards in D and are located in 48 countries. The user ASs in D_{lat} contain 91% of all IP addresses delegated to the set of user ASs in D and are distributed in 187 countries. Moreover, 80.6% of the user ASs in D_{lat} are located in countries containing guards from D_{lat}. Table 1 summarizes the statistics for the sets of collected user and guard ASs.

Like [11,24], we used CAIDA AS Relationship dataset [4] to acquire data about existing commercial AS relationships and inferred network paths between ASs necessary to compute the resilience values between user and guard ASs.

DPSelect Parameters for D and D_{lat}: DPSelect weight function (2) contains two parameters, x_1 and x_2, that need to be tuned with regard to the set of possible user ASs and the current Internet topology. In [11], the authors showed that $x_1 = 2$ and $x_2 = 0.75$ are optimal for the set of top-93 Tor user ASs and $\alpha = 0.175$ achieves a reasonable trade-off between OR's resilience and bandwidth. As the number of user ASs in our dataset is larger by several orders of magnitude, we repeated the optimization procedure proposed in [11] before analyzing the security properties of DPSelect. However, we did not observe any appreciable impact of the newly obtained parameters on the average user resilience and bandwidth. Thus, we sticked to the optimal values as proposed in [11].

Table 1. Statistics for collected user and guard ASs.

Description	Number	Countries	Guards	Dataset
Total number of collected ASs	57,015	230	–	–
Total number of possible user ASs	25,881	223	2,451	D
Total number of guard ASs	475	50	2,451	
Number of user ASs with latency	7,052	187	2,180	D_{lat}
Number of guard ASs with latency	333	48	2,180	

5 Vulnerabilities in Counter-RAPTOR and DPSelect

In this section, we analyze information leakage in Counter-RAPTOR and DPSelect and summarize our key findings. In particular, we show that DPSelect is not as secure concerning active routing attacks as widely accepted as it achieves only one third of its originally claimed resilience. Then, we show that for 20% of the users both methods select a guard from their country with five times higher probability than vanilla Tor and propose a method allowing users to assess their vulnerability. We also identify scenarios where the usage of both path selection methods leads to significant performance bottlenecks. Finally, we propose a new metric that allows users to assess their location leakage with respect to a malicious middle node and bound its confidence.

Comprehensive Revision of DPSelect: The main goal of DPSelect is to prevent information leakage concerning user locations while achieving resilience to hijack attacks as by Counter-RAPTOR. Hanley et al. [11] evaluated the performance of DPSelect in terms of user resilience for the set of top-93 Tor user ASs and showed that DPSelect achieves very similar average user resilience to Counter-RAPTOR. Our analysis reveals that these results cannot be generalized for all Tor users. As shown in Fig. 1, the user resilience achieved by DPSelect (densely dotted line) degrades significantly compared to Counter-RAPTOR (dash-dotted line). While for 57% of Tor users Counter-RAPTOR provides up to a 70% probability of being resilient to hijack attacks, this probability reduces by 10% for DPSelect. Compared to vanilla Tor, DPSelect is able to improve the average user resilience only by 12.5% while Counter-RAPTOR achieves an increase of up to 30.5%.

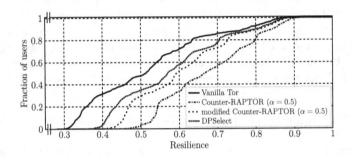

Fig. 1. CDF of the average user resilience for different guard selection algorithms.

To identify the reason for the significant difference in user resilience obtained by Counter-RAPTOR and DPSelect, we revisited the implementations of both methods provided by the authors. To compute the weight function (2), DPSelect relies on a resilience probability $R_{prob}(i) = \frac{R(i)}{\sum_i R(i)}$ and a bandwidth probability $B_{prob}(i) = \frac{B(i)}{\sum_i B(i)}$ instead of a resilience value $R(i)$ and a normalized bandwidth $\bar{B}(i)$ used by Counter-RAPTOR. To see the impact of the adjusted values, we modified the original code of Counter-RAPTOR to use resilience and bandwidth probabilities. Figure 1 shows that DPSelect (densely dotted line) and the modified Counter-RAPTOR (loosely dotted line) produce very similar user resilience.

To sum up, we showed that DPSelect does not provide a user resilience as high as the original Counter-RAPTOR method. Hence, Counter-RAPTOR still remains the only alternative for keeping Tor users resilient against hijack attacks.

Information Leaks in Counter-RAPTOR and DPSelect: To evaluate whether Tor users relying on Counter-RAPTOR and DPSelect increase their probability of selecting a guard from the same country as the user, denoted by p_C, we consider all guards and only those user ASs that are located in countries containing at least one guard from our dataset D. We obtained 21,064 user ASs comprising 81% of all user ASs in D. We computed how many times p_C increases compared to p_C for vanilla Tor. Figure 2 shows that for 80% of our users utilizing the location-aware methods, the probability of selecting a guard located in the same country as the user increases. For roughly 20% of users relying on Counter-RAPTOR ($\alpha = 0.5$), p_C increases by more than five times and for around 10% of DPSelect users, p_C increases by nine times. Moreover, the higher values of α in case of Counter-RAPTOR (i.e., the user is paying more attention to its resilience to hijack attacks than to the performance of its circuits) result in significantly higher probability of choosing a guard from the same country as the user.

We also examined information leaks in Counter-RAPTOR and DPSelect using the number of ASs between a Tor user and its guard and geographical distance between a Tor user and its guard (using GeoIP data). However, we did not observe any significant correlation when applying both methods.

In summary, Counter-RAPTOR and DPSelect users are more likely to choose a guard from the same country as the user, in contrast to vanilla Tor users. For 20% of the users, this probability is five times higher. This information leak can be further exploited to improve guard placement attacks, as proposed in [29].

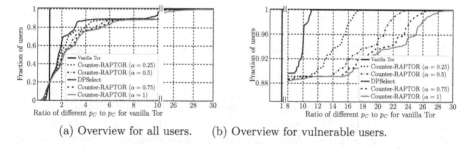

(a) Overview for all users.   (b) Overview for vulnerable users.

Fig. 2. CDF of the ratio of p_C for location-aware methods to p_C for vanilla Tor.

Fingerprinting User Locations: As shown above, Counter-RAPTOR and DPSelect usually leak information about a user by allowing an attacker to link a user to its location. To quantify this information leak, we propose a new metric, *confidence increase*, and we use it to measure the increase of the attacker's confidence from a middle position[3] about the location of Tor users. Our metric shows the ratio of the cumulative probability of users in the top-N most probable ASs selecting a guard to the cumulative fraction of IP addresses delegated to those ASs. The larger is the fraction of IP addresses delegated to the user ASs and the lower is the cumulative probability of those ASs, the smaller is the confidence increase achieved by the attacker for the user location.

---

[3] This metric can be used for other scenarios as well, not only from a middle position.

Inspired by Gini index, confidence increase allows to account for small values of probabilities due to the large number of possible user ASs and to focus on inequality of distribution among the top most preferable ASs. A traditional metric, i.e., *decrease in entropy*, as compared to the baseline (when the probability is uniformly distributed among all user ASs), depends on the total number of available user ASs. As opposite, if the number of IP addresses between user ASs is uniformly distributed, the value of confidence increase will be constant. In case of non-uniform distribution of the number of IP addresses, confidence increase allows to additionally capture the information leak related to the association of high probability values with ASs that have a small number of potential users.

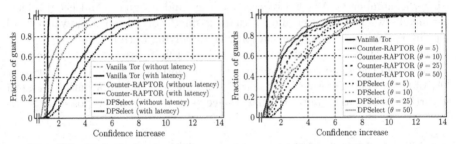

(a) Influence of latency measures ($\theta = 5$).   (b) Varying accuracy of latency measures.

Fig. 3. CDF of the confidence increase for different guard selection algorithms.

By using our dataset D, we first computed the Gini index for both location-aware methods and observed deviations from the uniform distribution of guards in case of vanilla Tor. Thus, we focus on the top of the inequality of the distributions for both methods, where our metric is more illustrative. We established $N = 25\%$ (inequality of distribution in the first quarter of top ASs) as a reasonable threshold for the efficiency of our metric. Figure 3a shows that the confidence increase for vanilla Tor (dashed gray line) always equals one as the probability of a user being located in a given AS is distributed uniformly among all user ASs and the cumulative probability of the first quarter of user ASs is always 0.25. As the cumulative fraction of IP addresses delegated to these user ASs changes depending on the chosen subset of user ASs, we take the mean of all combinations, which is equal to 0.25. Contrariwise, Counter-RAPTOR (dash-dotted gray line) and DPSelect (densely dotted gray line) leak a considerable amount of user-specific information. For more than 40% of guards selected by Counter-RAPTOR users and more than 20% of guards chosen by DPSelect users, the confidence increase of a middle connected to these guards is 100% higher than for vanilla Tor. Even worse, the confidence of the middle increases by 300% for 15% of guards connected to Counter-RAPTOR users and almost 10% of guards chosen by DPSelect users. Although the overall confidence increase for DPSelect is less than for Counter-RAPTOR, the protection provided by DPSelect is far smaller than originally claimed.

Next, we examine if the use of latency-based attacks proposed in [12] can further increase the attacker's confidence about the location of Tor users. In 2007, Hopper et al. showed that an attacker, who has access to a web server, a network coordinate system, and an OR, can estimate the latency between a Tor user connected to the adversarial web server and its guard and localize the user. To do this, the authors apply the Tor circuit clogging attack suggested by Murdoch and Danezis [19] to detect the ORs utilized by the user in its circuit. Then, the attacker creates its own circuit via the same ORs to estimate the latency between the guard and the exit. The latency between the user and its exit is also easily measured as the user is connected to the adversarial web server. By subtracting both latency estimates, the attacker obtains the latency between the user and its guard. The adversary further utilizes the network coordinate system to compute a set of possible latencies between potential users and guards and localize the user based on the estimated latency. In our work, we assume even a weaker attacker model where the adversary controls only at least one middle node. For all user connections traversing an adversarial middle, the attacker knows the identities of the guards and exits utilized by these users. This allows an estimation of the latency between the guard and the middle and between the user and the middle and a computation of the latency between the user and its guard. The rest of the attack remains identical to [12].

For our evaluation, we used the dataset D_{lat} containing latency measures for each pair of ASs. We assume that each user AS contains at least one victim user that the attacker is attempting to compromise, and iterate through each user AS as a potential adversarial target. As the latency estimates measured by the attacker are not precise, we consider a reduced set of potential user ASs whose estimated latency to a guard is in the interval $r \in [lat_{meas} - \theta, lat_{meas} + \theta]$ where lat_{meas} is the real latency between the target user and its guard and θ is a configurable parameter indicating the inaccuracy of estimated latency measured by the attacker. Once the adversary measured the latency between all candidate user ASs and a guard, user ASs whose latencies are significantly different from the estimated latency of the target user (i.e., those outside the interval r) can be excluded from consideration. For the reduced number of user ASs, the attacker computes the confidence increase as described above. As shown in Fig. 3a, for more than 40% of guards selected by Counter-RAPTOR users (dash-dotted black line) and more than 20% of guards chosen by DPSelect users (densely dotted black line), the confidence increase of a middle is nearly 200% higher when the attacker relies on latency estimates, compared to the confidence increase obtained for these methods without any latency measures, and almost 400% higher compared to vanilla Tor. Hence, taking into account latencies allows to further narrow down the possible location of the user.

Lastly, we examine the confidence increase of an adversarial middle when the accuracy of attacker's latency measurements vary. We computed the confidence increase of the middle for different values of θ. As the change of the confidence increase for vanilla Tor was negligible for $\theta \in \{0, 5, 10, 25, 50\}$, for this method we present only $\theta = 0$ for simplicity. Figure 3b shows that, as expected, the attacker gains less information about the user location when the latency estimates are less precise. Still, even in the worst case scenario ($\theta = 50$) the confidence increase is doubled for nearly 50% of guards chosen by Counter-RAPTOR and DPSelect users compared to vanilla Tor. Hence, even imprecise latency measurements help to significantly boost the confidence increase in identifying a user location.

To sum up, we proposed a new metric for quantifying information leakage about user's location when using Counter-RAPTOR and DPSelect. Using this metric, we showed that both location-aware methods strengthen the attacker's ability to fingerprint user locations from a middle node. The impact becomes considerably higher when our approach is enhanced with the latency information.

Performance Analysis: In [11, 24], the authors examined the performance of Counter-RAPTOR and DPSelect and showed that both methods achieve very similar average bandwidth in guard selections for the top-93 Tor user ASs to vanilla Tor. We verify if these results can be generalized for all Tor users. To do this, we recompute the average bandwidth of selected guards for our dataset D. We observe that the average bandwidth of guards chosen by Counter-RAPTOR users reduces by 52% compared to the average bandwidth of guards selected by vanilla Tor users. This drop is by 30% for DPSelect. Thus, we can conclude that – when considering all users – both location-aware methods have significantly lower average bandwidth of selected guards than previously expected. In the rest, we elaborate on the reasons for this and describe our performance analysis.

A major shortcoming of the previous analysis in [11, 24] is the fact that all guards in the simulated Tor network are highly-performing ORs (i.e., middles were the bottleneck for Tor circuits). Such analysis cannot capture the real impact of both methods on Tor performance, as the guards (in the case of saturated middles) do not have major influence on the performance of the circuits. The described situation in the previous analysis is a particular case and can change with the evolution of Tor. Thus, we revisit the performance of both methods by using Shadow [13] with the same number of simulated Tor users and ORs as in [11, 24] but a slightly modified configuration of the Tor network as follows. First, the bandwidth of each middle and exit is higher than the maximum bandwidth available to each guard in order to avoid network bottlenecks created by middle or exit ORs. Second, the latency between each pair of users and ORs is equal in order to eliminate the impact of latency on the speed and quality of user connections. As Counter-RAPTOR and DPSelect require meaningful IP addresses for their operation, we assigned randomly chosen user IP addresses from our set of user ASs in D. As shown in Fig. 4, while the download time for users relying on DPSelect and Counter-RAPTOR with $\alpha = 0.5$ to browse the web is similar to that of web users utilizing vanilla Tor, the download time for Counter-RAPTOR users paying more attention on their resilience to hijack attacks ($\alpha = 1$) increases substantially. In the case of bulk users (i.e., users downloading files of large size), the increase in the download time for users utilizing Counter-RAPTOR with $\alpha = 1$ is by nearly 10%. Moreover, the average sender and receiver throughput for all Tor nodes reduces significantly for DPSelect.

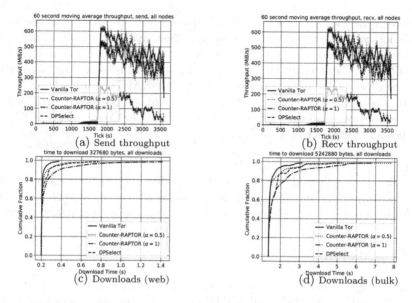

Fig. 4. Average throughput and download time for the first experiment.

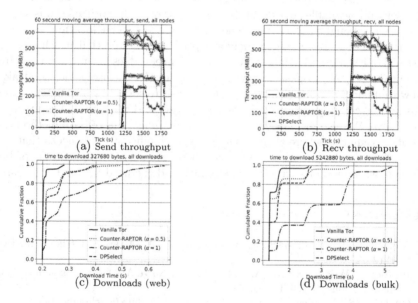

Fig. 5. Average throughput and download time for the second experiment.

We modify the experiment presented above such that our simulated Tor network contains highly resilient low-bandwidth guards and highly-performing low-resilient guards. To this end, we assigned IP addresses to our users belonging to a single AS and distributed the guards in two other ASs, whose network paths with the user AS are low- and high-resiliently, respectively. The rest of the simulation configuration is the same as described above. As shown in Fig. 5, we observe a significant increase of the download time for both, Counter-RAPTOR and DPSelect, users. While the download time for web users utilizing vanilla Tor does not exceed 0.3 s, only nearly 60% of Counter-RAPTOR users for $\alpha = 1$ are able to load a website within this time period. This drop is even worse for bulk users, whose download time increases by almost 20% for Counter-RAPTOR with $\alpha = 0.5$ and DPSelect and to almost 80% for Counter-RAPTOR with $\alpha = 1$. Like the previous experiment, the average sender and receiver throughput for all Tor nodes drops dramatically for DPSelect.

To sum up, we showed that Counter-RAPTOR and DPSelect negatively influence the Tor performance. We identified scenarios where the usage of both methods leads to significant bottlenecks, as users prefer poorly-performing guards.

6 Conclusion

We analyzed the susceptibility of the most recent location-aware Tor path selection methods Counter-RAPTOR and DPSelect with regard to malicious middle ORs. To do this, we collected comprehensive set of ASs containing at least one Tor user and available guards in Tor. We showed that both methods are not as secure as thought before: for some users they leak their location. Moreover, DPSelect is not as resilient as widely accepted. We showed that it achieves only one third of its originally claimed resilience. Hence, it does not protect users from routing attacks. We proposed a new metric to quantify the user's location leakage and with its help performed a large-scale analysis to show to which extent a malicious middle can fingerprint the location of a user and what kind of confidence it can achieve. We also revealed the performance implications of both methods and identified scenarios where their usage leads to significant bottlenecks that were not originally anticipated. Our findings shed light on the implications of both location-aware methods on users' anonymity and the need for further research.

References

1. Akhoondi, M., et al.: LASTor: A Low-Latency AS-Aware Tor Client. In: IEEE S&P (2012)
2. Barton, A., Wright, M.: DeNASA: Destination-Naive AS-Awareness in anonymous communications. In: PETS (2016)
3. CAIDA: AS Classification. https://www.caida.org/data/as-classification/
4. CAIDA: AS Relationships. http://www.caida.org/data/as-relationships/
5. CAIDA: ASRank. https://asrank.caida.org/
6. CAIDA: The IPv4 Routed/24 Topology Dataset. https://www.caida.org/data/active/ipv4_routed_24_topology_dataset.xml
7. Dingledine, R., et al.: Tor: the second-generation onion router. In: USENIX Security (2004)
8. Dingledine, R., et al.: One fast guard for life (or 9 months). In: HotPETs (2009)
9. Edman, M., Syverson, P.: AS-awareness in Tor path selection. In: ACM CCS (2009)

10. Feamster, N., Dingledine, R.: Location diversity in anonymity networks. In: ACM WPES (2004)
11. Hanley, H., et al.: DPSelect: a differential privacy based guard relay selection algorithm for Tor. In: PETS (2019)
12. Hopper, N., et al.: How much anonymity does network latency leak? In: ACM CCS (2007)
13. Jansen, R., Hopper, N.: Shadow: running Tor in a box for accurate and efficient experimentation. In: NDSS (2012)
14. Jansen, R., et al.: Inside job: applying traffic analysis to measure tor from within. In: NDSS (2018)
15. Johnson, A., et al.: Users get routed: traffic correlation on tor by realistic adversaries. In: ACM CCS (2013)
16. Johnson, A., et al.: Avoiding the man on the wire: improving Tor's security with trust-aware path selection. In: NDSS (2017)
17. Juen, J., et al.: Defending Tor from network adversaries: a case study of network path prediction. In: PETS (2015)
18. Mitseva, A., et al.: The state of affairs in BGP security: a survey of attacks and defenses. Comput. Commun. **124**, 45–60 (2018)
19. Murdoch, S.J., Danezis, G.: Low-cost traffic analysis of Tor. In: IEEE S&P (2005)
20. Murdoch, S.J., Zieliński, P.: Sampled traffic analysis by internet-exchange-level adversaries. In: Borisov, N., Golle, P. (eds.) PET 2007. LNCS, vol. 4776, pp. 167–183. Springer, Heidelberg (2007). https://doi.org/10.1007/978-3-540-75551-7_11
21. Nithyanand, R., et al.: Measuring and mitigating AS-level adversaries against Tor. In: NDSS (2016)
22. Panchenko, A., et al.: Website fingerprinting at internet scale. In: NDSS (2016)
23. Sun, Y., et al.: RAPTOR: routing attacks on privacy in Tor. In: USENIX Security (2015)
24. Sun, Y., et al.: Counter-RAPTOR: safeguarding Tor against active routing attacks. In: IEEE S&P (2017)
25. Tan, H., et al.: Data-plane defenses against routing attacks on Tor. In: PETS (2016)
26. Tschantz, M.C., et al.: SoK: towards grounding censorship circumvention in empiricism. In: IEEE S&P (2016)
27. Wacek, C., et al.: An empirical evaluation of relay selection in Tor. In: NDSS (2013)
28. Wails, R., et al.: Tempest: temporal dynamics in anonymity systems. In: PETS (2018)
29. Wan, G., et al.: Guard placement attacks on path selection algorithms for Tor. In: PETS (2019)

Actively Probing Routes for Tor AS-Level Adversaries with RIPE Atlas

Wilfried Mayer[1]([✉]), Georg Merzdovnik[1], and Edgar Weippl[2]

[1] SBA Research, Vienna, Austria
{wmayer,gmerzdovnik}@sba-research.org
[2] University of Vienna, Vienna, Austria
edgar.weippl@univie.ac.at

Abstract. Tor provides anonymity to millions of users around the globe, which has made it a valuable target for malicious actors. As a low-latency anonymity system, it is vulnerable to traffic correlation attacks from strong passive adversaries, such as large autonomous systems. Estimations of the risk posed by such attackers as well as the evaluation of defense strategies are mostly based on simulations and data retrieved from BGP updates. However, this might only provide an incomplete view of the network and thereby influence the results of such analyses. It has already been acknowledged in previous studies that direct path measurements, e.g. with traceroute, could provide valuable information. But in the past, such measurements were thought to be impossible, because they require the placement of measurement nodes in the same ASes as the respective Tor network nodes. With the rise of new technologies and methodologies, this assumption needs to be re-evaluated.

In this paper we present a novel methodology to utilize the RIPE Atlas framework, a network of more than 10,000 probes worldwide, to actively perform traceroute commands from and to Tor guard and exit relays to clients and destinations. Based on multiple global scans our results validate previous results and show the large influence on Tor posed by a limited set of ASes. These are in a strong position to carry out effective correlation attacks on Tor traffic. With this work, we provide an additional source of information that can be used together with BGP route information to increase the accuracy of future models and simulations of Tor and ultimately improve anonymity on the Internet.

Keywords: Tor · Ripe Atlas · Traceroute measurements

1 Introduction

Tor is the most notable anonymity network, used by 2 to 3 million people on a daily basis and advertising up to 400 Gbit/s of bandwidth by utilizing around 6,500 voluntarily operated Tor relays. It provides anonymity by routing traffic via three different Tor nodes. As a low latency network, due to its design, it is not capable of guaranteeing anonymity in the case of a global passive observer. This

© IFIP International Federation for Information Processing 2020
Published by Springer Nature Switzerland AG 2020
M. Hölbl et al. (Eds.): SEC 2020, IFIP AICT 580, pp. 234–247, 2020.
https://doi.org/10.1007/978-3-030-58201-2_16

form of attacker is explicitly excluded from the threat model, assuming that such a global passive observer does not exist. Although not global, powerful observers exist, potentially threatening the anonymity of Tor users. However, their capabilities are not exactly clear. One reason for this is the theoretical assumption, that the underlying Internet hierarchy is flat and evenly distributed. Trivially, this is not the case, as the Internet is shaped in different tiers and various entities with different levels of control, e.g., Internet Exchange Points (IXP) with a high level of control, and small ISPs with a low level of control. Also, the Tor network does not utilize the Internet in an evenly distributed manner, as the location of Tor relays is depending on various parameters, e.g., economical (the price of bandwidth) or political (censorship, prosecution) reasons. Prior work [9,11,19] has shown that traffic through the Tor network only takes a limited set of routes on the Internet, making the threat of a powerful passive observer far more likely. They point out that few AS-level entities provide a high proportion of the Tor bandwidth, thus making them powerful entities for traffic correlation attacks. These studies rely on BGP updates and a prediction of routes taken. While they also describe that a traceroute-based approach could potentially yield better results, they also argue that it would not be feasible for measuring AS-level adversaries in the Tor network, because of the need to have measurement nodes placed on the same ASes as Tor nodes and destinations. However, with the introduction of the RIPE Atlas network [21] this assumption can no longer be taken for granted. The RIPE Atlas network is a global measurement network, which can be used by researchers to measure Internet connectivity and reachability. It has already been used for several studies [4] concerning network routing [10] as well as censorship measurements [3].

Our work presents a novel method of measuring the routes that traffic takes from and to the Tor network by utilizing active network probing, in contrast to estimations via BGP updates. We do this by utilizing probes that are placed in autonomous systems (AS) also in use by Tor relays, Tor users or Tor connection recipients. For this purpose, we utilize the RIPE Atlas network, which consists of more than 10,000 globally distributed probes connected to many different autonomous systems. To measure the routes a packet takes from and to the Tor network, we execute traceroute commands on these probes and collect information on the ASes observed on the respective paths. With this method, we gather data to create better predictions of powerful adversaries existing on the Internet and thus to improve the anonymity of Tor users. More specifically, the contributions of this paper are as follows:

Active Measurements of AS Interconnections: Using *traceroute* based measurements we estimate the capabilities of AS-level adversaries and show the influence of only a few ASes on a large amount of traffic.

Open-Source Active Measurement Tool: To improve the evaluation of future attacks and defenses against Tor, we provide an open-source framework to perform active measurement to acquire routing information for Tor nodes.

2   Related Work

Tor, described originally by Dingledine et al. in 2004 [8], grew to the most important anonymity system online nowadays. As a low-latency overlay network, it is inherently vulnerable to passive attacks by global observers, which is already described in the original specification. Instead, they work with a threat model that includes attackers that can only observe fractions of the network traffic.

Feamster and Dingledine [11] provided the first analysis of location diversity in the Tor network for independently operated autonomous systems based on BGP routing tables. They analyzed the probability of an entry path to the network and an exit path from the network will cross through the same AS. Their analysis shows that previous methods of choosing paths/nodes based on IP prefixes are not sufficient to guarantee a diverse set of ASes, since in about 10% to 30% of the time both the entry and exit path to the mix network will cross through the same AS. A refinement of this approach by Edman and Syverson in 2009 [9] shows that the previous study even underestimated the potential threat. A study of Tor security properties against traffic correlation attacks was presented by Johnson et al. [16]. Their results show that, depending on location, a user's chance of compromise can be at 95% within 3 months of monitoring against a single AS. One mitigation they propose is to carefully select which entry and exit nodes to use. Wacek et al. [25] built a graph of the Tor network to capture the networks AS boundaries. Using this graph they provide an evaluation of a set of proposed relay selection methods and quantify their respective anonymity properties. Their results show that bandwidth is an important property for the performance of such algorithms, and should not be neglected.

The importance of location diversity in the Tor network has been shown by several attacks proposed in recent years. Vanbever et al. [24] provide a study of the capabilities of AS level adversaries. Sun et al. [23] describe a set of advanced routing attacks on Tor, named *Raptor*. They also describe the feasibility of asymmetric AS-level attacks by observing not only data traffic from exit relay to the server but also TCP acknowledgment traffic on other routes which increases the capabilities of AS-level adversaries. In 2016, Nithyanand et al. [19] also use data on the Internet's topology [13] in a combination with AS-topology simulations [12] to estimate the threat posed by adversaries to Tor users. While previous attempts at the correlation of traffic [15,17] had very limited performance or required a large amount of captured traffic or time, *DeepCorr* [18], developed by Nasr et al. greatly improves the feasibility of such attacks. By leveraging emerging learning mechanisms they manage to achieve drastically higher performance compared to existing state-of-the-art systems.

To mitigate the threat posed by an AS to be able to monitor Tor users, various kinds of protection mechanisms have been proposed [2]. Nithyanand et al. proposed *Astoria* [19], an AS-aware Tor client. While similar in functionality to *LASTor* [1], it provides improved protection with concern to threat models and attacker capabilities. Sun et al. [22] presented a measurement study on the security of Tor against BGP hijacking attacks and presented a new relay selection mechanism to mitigate such attacks on Tor. In contrast to previous approaches

DeNASA from Barton et al. [5] provides a mechanism for AS-aware path selection independently of the destination. Additionally, they propose another system for the creation of efficient and anonymous Tor circuits [6]. Hanley et al. [14] proposed an extension to the work presented by Sun et al. [22] to increase the provided privacy and anonymity guarantees. Wan et al. [26] showed that several attacks against a set of the proposed protections are still possible, but they also proposed simple solutions, which allow mitigating the threat posed by their developed methods.

3   Active Acquisition of Routing Information

In the following section, we describe a novel method to measure strong AS-level observers, which are in a good position to conduct correlation attacks. As an overlay network, Tor depends on the underlying structure of the Internet. While often a flat hierarchy is assumed, it is clear that this is not the case. We can model the structure of the Internet by looking at autonomous systems identified by a unique AS number (ASN). One AS can be seen as an administrative entity that is responsible for a defined routing policy. Some AS are large and include a lot of Tor users, destinations or relays, others do not contain users and destinations but are used for routing Tor traffic through the Internet and others are not important for Tor routing at all. Thus, some entities can observe more traffic than others. With our measurements, we find a way to quantify which entities are in a stronger position. Figure 1 illustrates the basic idea of a standard traffic correlation attack, where one adversary (AS2) is placed on the incoming route to Tor as well as on the outgoing route to the destination. Sun et al. [23] showed that it is also possible to correlate reverse-path traffic. Other work already quantified strong adversaries with the help of BGP route updates. In contrast, we develop a method that utilizes the RIPE Atlas framework to actively acquire routing information.

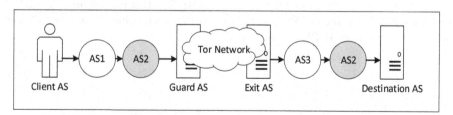

Fig. 1. AS2 in a possible position for a traffic correlation attack

3.1   Relay as Diversity

As shown in Table 1 the Tor network currently consists of 6,509 relays (January 5th, 2020). Only relays with the *Guard* flag (stable and reliable relays after a ramp-up phase [7]), are used as entry relay. Only relays configured to allow exiting traffic are potential exit relays in a Tor circuit. Because of the more stringent requirements, the number of guard and exit relays (with guard/exit probability >0) is a lot smaller than 6,509. This also affects the AS diversity, which is the number of different ASes these relays are placed in. Current numbers are shown in Table 1. Tor relays are chosen based on their flags and consensus weight. In Fig. 3 we show the AS diversity relation to guard and exit probability. We see that a small number of AS has a large share of exit (a) and guard (b) probability. Eight ASes have more than 50% exit probability and 48 ASes have more than 90%. We also see that only four AS have more than 50% guard probability and 122 have more than 90%. So although all Tor relays are distributed over more than 1,100 ASes, the majority of entry and exit routing endpoints are placed in a few ASes.

Table 1. Tor Relay overview

	Relays	Diff. AS	BW (Gbit/s)
All Relays	6,509	1,104	418.07
Exit Relays	1,000	275	112.90
Guard Relays	2,415	470	254.61

3.2 The RIPE Atlas Framework

The RIPE Atlas framework is a highly distributed measurement network consisting of more than 10,000 available probes, deployed in over 3,500 different ASes. It allows us to execute various low-level commands, e.g., ping or traceroute, on these probes and further process the results. We will utilize this to execute traceroute commands from RIPE Atlas probes that are deployed in the same ASes as Tor guard or exit relays as well as clients and popular destinations. Figure 2 illustrates the global distribution of RIPE Atlas probes and the global distribution of Tor relays. We see that countries with a higher number of Tor relays also run more RIPE Atlas probes.

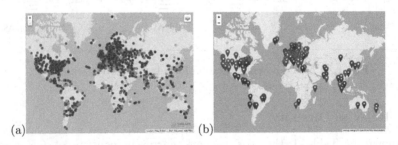

(a)   (b)

Fig. 2. (a) Worldwide RIPE Atlas Coverage (https://atlas.ripe.net/.) (b) Visualization of Tor Relays (https://tormap.void.gr/.)

Figure 3 also shows the cumulated guard and exit probability for autonomous systems that contain RIPE Atlas probes. From 275 ASes that contain exit relays, only 112 also contain a probe (419 relays out of 1,000). Still, that makes approx. 41% of the total exit probability (35% with only 17 ASes). This differs from the cumulated guard probability. From 470 ASes that contain 2,415 relays, 238 ASes (with 1,848 relays) also include a RIPE Atlas probe, which represent guard relays with a sum of 83% guard probability (80% with 98 ASes). Especially for exit relays, these numbers could be drastically increased if only a few, exit-focused ASes would also host RIPE Atlas probes. Table 2 identifies ASes, that are currently not hosting any RIPE probes. By adding only 5 probes we could measure ASes with 76% exit probability in total and 10 probes would gain up to 87% probability in total.

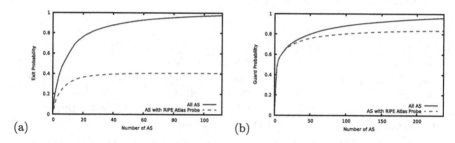

Fig. 3. Accumulated percentage of (a) exit, and (b) guard probability with the number of autonomous systems

Table 2. AS with Tor relays currently not hosting a RIPE Atlas probe

AS Name	Relays	Gbit/s BW	P_{exit}	P_{guard}
200052 FERAL	54	17.01	.158	.004
208323 APPLIEDPRIVACY	16	7.28	.082	.001
53667 FRANTECH	94	8.78	.048	.011
8972 HOSTEUROPE	23	2.60	.000	.010
63949 LINODE-AP	162	3.71	.001	.008

3.3 Active *traceroute* Probing with RIPE Atlas

As illustrated in Fig. 4 we perform *traceroute* measurements to identify routes taken for four different directions: (1) all client ASes to all guard ASes, (2) exit ASes with probes installed to the destination ASes, (3) destination ASes to all exit ASes, and (4) guard ASes with probes installed to the client ASes. With these measurements, we do not cover all possible routes since not all ASes have probes installed. In the different directions we measure (1) 1s00% (2) ~40% (3) 100% (4) ~83% in terms of route probability.

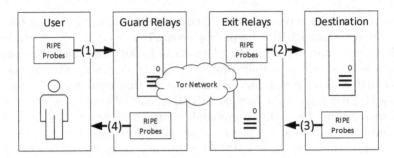

Fig. 4. Four different directions of active RIPE Atlas *traceroute* scans

In detail, this process works as follows:

1. Create the following sets:
   i. AS_{client} ... ASes of the clients
   ii. AS_{guard} ... all ASes with guard relays
   iii. $AS_{guard+probe}$ ... all ASes with guard relays and RIPE atlas probes
   iv. AS_{exit} ... all ASes with exit relays
   v. $AS_{exit+probe}$ ... all ASes with exit relays and RIPE atlas probes
   vi. $AS_{destination}$ ... ASes of the destinations

2. Generate ICMP traceroute measurement definitions for the following directions:

   (1) $AS_{client} \xrightarrow{traceroute} AS_{guard}$

   (2) $AS_{exit+probe} \xrightarrow{traceroute} AS_{destination}$

   (3) $AS_{destination} \xrightarrow{traceroute} AS_{exit}$

   (4) $AS_{guard+probe} \xrightarrow{traceroute} AS_{client}$

3. Execute the *traceroute* with the RIPE Atlas measurement API. (`"protocol"`: `"ICMP"`, `"response_timeout"`: 20000, `"packets"`: 1). Every RIPE Atlas measurement is charged with credits, obtained by hosting RIPE Atlas probes. For the current deployment that estimates to $20 \cdot 1230 = 24600$ credits for one client and one destination.

4. Process all results and look up the corresponding AS from the *ip2asn* database.

5. For every *traceroute*, mark all included ASes with the probability of that path being chosen, i.e., the corresponding guard/ exit probability.

6. Combine the values for the directions 1 and 4 for the entry side, and 2 and 3 for the exit side, s.t., if an AS appears on either the forward or the reverse path it is assigned with the probability of that path being chosen. For multiple destinations, all traceroutes are combined.

7. Point out the top ASes, that appear on entry and exit side by looking at $P_{guard} \cap P_{exit}$.

3.4   Origin and Destination AS

The sets of guard and exit relays can be derived by combining the Tor consensus with the RIPE Atlas probe overview. However, a client set and a destination set has to be chosen to conduct a measurement. A single client and a single destination are easily scannable, but it doesn't give us a full picture. However, executing traceroutes for all possible client and destination ASes is not feasible. Thus, we have to choose client and destination AS sets for our measurements. In 2008, Edman and Syverson [9] captured traffic from Tor relays to determine top autonomous systems. We are choosing a different approach using popular destinations and large client ASes. For the client set, we choose different countries and pick the 10 ASes containing the most RIPE Atlas probes. Then, we pick one probe thereof. E.g., Germany has 1,485 probes installed, in 343 different ASes, and we pick the ASes with most probes installed[1]. For the US we do the same[2]. For the most common destinations, we derive a list of top destinations from the Tranco [20] top sites list[3]. We take the 100 most popular domains, resolve the domain, and match the corresponding ASes. From the 100 top sites in 44 different ASes, ten ASes also have a RIPE Atlas probe installed[4] and will be used as our destination ASes.

3.5   Data Sources

To facilitate reproducibility and encourage openness, all used data files are publicly available at the project website[5]. In particular, our work relies on following data sources:

1. The Tor consensus that contains all Tor relays with their IP address, associated flags (particularly "Guard" and "Exit"), advertised bandwidth and guard and exit probability. We collect this information via the Tor network status protocol *onionoo*[6].
2. Statistical data about the *RIPE Atlas probes*[7]. We use different data (e.g., id, number and AS of the probes) to find all probes connected to the same ASes as guard and exit relays.
3. Freely accessible *ip2asn*[8] databases to match IP addresses with the corresponding AS number.
4. Active RIPE Atlas *traceroute* results[9]. The measurements used for this paper are accessible at the projects website.

---

[1] Client ASes Germany: 3320, 6830, 31334, 8881, 3209, 6805, 553, 680, 8422, 9145.
[2] Client ASes USA: 7922, 701, 7018, 209, 20115, 22773, 5650, 20001, 10796, 11427.
[3] Available at https://tranco-list.eu/list/YL6G.
[4] Destination ASes: 3, 15169, 4837, 24940, 36351, 14618, 16509, 14907, 3356, 794.
[5] Project website: https://github.com/sbaresearch/ripe-tor.
[6] onionoo: https://metrics.torproject.org/onionoo.html.
[7] probes: https://atlas.ripe.net/probes/.
[8] ip2asn: https://iptoasn.com/.
[9] measurements: https://atlas.ripe.net/measurements.

4   Evaluation

In the following section, we evaluate our traceroute scans and show results. We start with an evaluation of a basic scan. Then, we present a larger measurement with multiple clients and destinations. We assess both directions on the guard and the exit side separately and also look at the combined results.

4.1   Measurment with a Single Client and a Single Destination

As an illustration of the capabilities of our methodology, we evaluate the results of measurements with one fixed client AS and one fixed destination AS. Therefore, we choose the AS of our research center as $AS_{client} = \{AS1764\}$, and the AS of one mirror of the torproject.org website as $AS_{destination} = \{AS24940\}$. We choose RIPE Atlas probes deployed in these ASes (id: 26895, 50609). We then execute 1,240 traceroute commands as defined in Sect. 3.3. Thereof, 269 only contain the client and destination AS, while 971 contain additional ASes on the path. In Table 3 we show various results. As expected, the client and destination AS (Hetzner, Nextlayer) are found on all traceroutes. ASes with a high guard or exit probability (Feral, Applied Privacy, OVH) also have a great share, although they are not intermediary and only found on the single traceroute to/from their AS. Large transit ASes, that appear on many routes are more interesting. In our measurement, we identified AS6939, AS47147, AS1200, and AS174 to be in a powerful position, as they appear on many routes and gain probability of up to 18%. Table 4 shows that for this single measurement only few ASes have a probability higher than 1% to appear on both sides.

Table 3. Results for a single client and single destination

AS Name	Dir	P	P_{relays}	P_{routes}	Routes
24940 HETZNER-AS	exit	.988	.004	.984	269
200052 FERAL	exit	.161	.161	–	1
6939 HURRICANE	exit	.158	.001	.157	20
47147 AS-ANX	exit	.116	–	.116	4
1200 AMS-IX1	exit	.068	–	.068	17
1764 NEXTLAYER	guard	.992	–	.992	454
24940 HETZNER-AS	guard	.202	.202	–	1
16276 OVH	guard	.152	.152	–	1
1200 AMS-IX1	guard	.180	-	.180	55
174 COGENT-174	guard	.095	.007	.088	87

As described in Sect. 3.2, not all ASes have RIPE Atlas probes installed, $AS_{exit+probes} \rightarrow AS_{destination}$ only represents around 38% of total exit probability and $AS_{guard+probes} \rightarrow AS_{client}$ only represents around 83% of total guard probability. This means real values are estimated to be even higher.

Table 4. Combined results for a single destination and a single client

AS Name	P_{guard}	P_{exit}	$P_{combined}$
24940 HETZNER-AS	.202	.988	.199
1200 AMS-IX1	.180	.068	.012
16276 OVH	.152	.065	.010

4.2   Measurements with Multiple Clients and Multiple Destinations

We conducted the scans on the guard side and exit side separately, and afterward combined the results. We conducted 15,160 successful traceroutes for the 10 entry side ASes originating in the US and Germany. On the destination side, we gathered 4,270 successful traceroute results. The scans were performed around 31.12.2019.

Client to Guard Relays. We found ASes that have a high probability to appear on the route to/from guard relays. Figure 7 shows the probability of different ASes to be on a route to/from a guard relay in the US and Germany. The different data points represent the different originating ASes, and the line the min and max values. We identify ASes in good positions for both countries. AS3356 (LEVEL 3) will be traversed with a high probability for all originating ASes and has also a high probability for the set of German probes. We identify AS1200 and AS1273 and AS6830 only in German ASes. AS1299 (TELIANET), AS2914 (NTT-COMMUNICATIONS-2), AS174 (COGENT) and AS9002 (RETN) are strong for both client sets (Fig. 5).

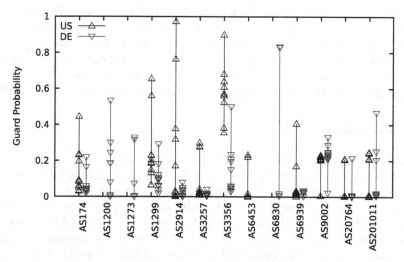

Fig. 5. Summarized guard probability for ASes that appear on a route from the originating client AS to all guard ASes

Destination Results. For the destination set, we are using probes of ten different autonomous systems, derived from the Tranco Top pages list, as explained in Sect. 3.4. We identified all ASes that were located on the routes for every destination AS. We then combined these values to represent the possibility of a client connecting to all destinations. Table 5 shows all ASes that have a probability over 20%. Figure 6 additionally shows the data points for every single destination AS. We excluded all destination ASes, because they appear with certainty, and excluded ASes that only appear because exit relays are hosted (AS200052, AS208323 - Applied Privacy).

Table 5. Results on the exit side, with a summarized exit probability over 20%

AS Name	P
6939 HURRICANE	0.808
6461 ZAYO-6461	0.510
174 COGENT-174	0.415
1299 TELIANET	0.377
1200 AMS-IX1	0.370
2914 NTT-COMMUN	0.362
10578 GIGAPOP-NE	0.359
3257 GTT-BACKBO	0.290

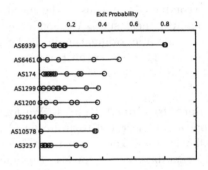

Fig. 6. Summarized probability with single data points representing the different destination ASes

Combined Results. Combining all results, we identify ASes that have a high probability to be on the guard side as well as on the exit side. We investigate combinations of single client ASes with all ASes on the exit side, because users connect from one client AS to different destinations. In Fig. 7, we can identify strong ASes for our measurement setup. AS3356 (LEVEL3) has a combined value of up to 67.1% ($P_{guard} = .681 \cdot P_{exit} = .985$) for the client AS7018. Other notable ASes are AS6939, AS1299 and AS2914 with combined values > 20%.

5 Discussion

We presented a methodology to utilize the RIPE Atlas network to gather valuable routing data from and to Tor relays. Related work already quantified AS-level adversaries' capabilities for traffic correlation attacks. Thus, our work will not provide any surprising insights. However, our methods can be used to refine existing models with timely and actively gathered routing data. While the result set of this paper is rather limited with only 16,500 executed traceroute commands and a small number of probes utilized, the methodology is highly scalable. For future work, we plan to scale up the number of measurements performed in various ways. First, we want to enlarge the measured client and destination sets.

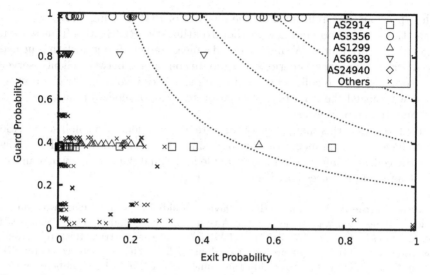

Fig. 7. Combined probability of ASes appearing on the client and destination path

Second, we think about reoccurring scans in contrast to *oneoff* measurements conducted in this paper. Last, a more fine-grained measurement, using probes in the same IP subnets as the relays could improve the results. We publish our source code openly available as free software. This enables other entities, such as large relay operators, to also perform measurements. All measurement results gathered with RIPE Atlas are also openly available and could include valuable results for the Tor network. We argue that large relay operators should deploy RIPE Atlas probes in their networks, not only to further improve our future results but also to enable other measurements. Only a few more probes would increase the coverage significantly. In Sect. 3.2 we identified the largest relay operators (AS-wise) without RIPE probes. The evaluation illustrates the possibilities of our methodology. However, it is limited in various ways. We currently do not consider various factors that are important to accurately quantify the threat of AS-level observers. This includes user behavior, Tor circuit creation algorithms, and others. Hence, a combination of our data acquisition method with other simulations is necessary to correctly quantify the traffic correlation threat.

Finally, we argue for increased AS diversity in the Tor network. Even with simple measurements, we see that the distribution of Tor relays is skewed. We hope that our measurements can improve the informed decision how this diversity should be achieved.

6   Conclusion

To address Tor traffic correlation attacks through ASes we presented a novel way to analyze the network routes taken by traffic from and to the Tor network.

While previous research relied on the analysis of BGP routing information and simulations, we proposed a new method to utilize the RIPE Atlas framework to measure network routes. We implemented a measurement framework that utilizes the RIPE Atlas probes to perform traceroute commands between clients, servers and Tor endpoints to collect information on the ASes involved in traffic routing. Next, we utilized the collected information to create a model of paths to locate and quantify strong observers.

By leveraging this methodology we were able to identify a small set of ASes which have a great influence on the total amount of Tor bandwidth. This shows that the collected information is a valuable additional data source when analyzing attacks and defenses based on AS topology.

Acknowledgment. We want to thank David Schmidt for his preliminary work on this topic. This research was funded by the Austrian Science Fund (FWF): P30637-N31, the Josef Ressel Center (JRC) project TARGET and the Austrian Research Promotion Agency (FFG) through project AutoHoney(I)IoT. The competence center SBA Research (SBA-K1) is funded within the framework of COMET – Competence Centers for Excellent Technologies by BMVIT, BMDW, and the federal state of Vienna, managed by the FFG.

References

1. Akhoondi, M., Yu, C., Madhyastha, H.V.: LASTor: a low-latency AS-aware Tor client. In: Symposium on Security and Privacy. IEEE (2012)
2. AlSabah, M., Goldberg, I.: Performance and security improvements for Tor: a survey. ACM Comput. Surv. (CSUR) **49**(2), 1–36 (2016)
3. Anderson, C., et al.: Global network interference detection over the RIPE atlas network. In: USENIX Workshop on Free and Open Communications on the Internet (FOCI) (2014)
4. Bajpai, V., Eravuchira, S.J., Schönwälder, J.: Lessons learned from using the RIPE atlas platform for measurement research. ACM SIGCOMM Comput. Commun. Rev. **45**(3), 35–42 (2015)
5. Barton, A., Wright, M.: DeNASA: Destination-Naive AS-awareness in anonymous communications. In: Proceedings on Privacy Enhancing Technologies (2016)
6. Barton, A., Wright, M., Ming, J., Imani, M.: Towards predicting efficient and anonymous Tor circuits. In: USENIX Security Symposium (2018)
7. Dingledine, R.: The lifecycle of a new relay (2013)
8. Dingledine, R., Mathewson, N., Syverson, P.: The second-generation onion router. In: USENIX Security Symposium, Tor (2004)
9. Edman, M., Syverson, P.: AS-awareness in Tor path selection. In: Conference on Computer and Communications Security. ACM (2009)
10. Fanou, R., Francois, P., Aben, E.: On the diversity of interdomain routing in Africa. In: Passive and Active Network Measurement Conference (2015)
11. Feamster, N., Dingledine, R.: Location diversity in anonymity networks. In: Workshop on Privacy in the Electronic Society. ACM (2004)
12. Gill, P., Schapira, M., Goldberg, S.: Modeling on quicksand: dealing with the scarcity of ground truth in interdomain routing data. ACM SIGCOMM Comput. Commun. Rev. **42**(1), 40–46 (2012)

13. Giotsas, V., Luckie, M., Huffaker, B., Claffy, K.C.: Inferring complex AS relationships. In: Internet Measurement Conference. ACM (2014)
14. Hanley, H., Sun, Y., Wagh, S., Mittal, P.: DPSelect: a differential privacy based Guard relay selection algorithm for Tor. In: Proceedings on Privacy Enhancing Technologies (2019)
15. Hopper, N., Vasserman, E.Y., Chan-Tin, E.: How much anonymity does network latency leak? ACM Trans. Inf. Syst. Secur. (TISSEC) **13**(2), 1–28 (2010)
16. Johnson, A., Wacek, C., Jansen, R., Sherr, M., Syverson, P.: Users get routed: traffic correlation on Tor by realistic adversaries. In: Conference on Computer and Communications Security. ACM (2013)
17. Mittal, P., Khurshid, A., Juen, J., Caesar, M., Borisov, N.: Stealthy traffic analysis of low-latency anonymous communication using throughput fingerprinting. In: Conference on Computer and Communications Security. ACM (2011)
18. Nasr, M., Bahramali, A., Houmansadr, A.: DeepCorr: strong flow correlation attacks on Tor using deep learning. In: Conference on Computer and Communications Security. ACM (2018)
19. Nithyanand, R., Starov, O., Zair, A., Gill, P., Schapira, M.: Measuring and mitigating AS-level adversaries against Tor. In: Network and Distributed System Security Symposium (NDSS) (2016)
20. Pochat, V.L., Van Goethem, T., Tajalizadehkhoob, S., Korczynski, M., Joosen, W.: Tranco: a research-oriented top sites ranking hardened against manipulation. In: Network and Distributed System Security Symposium (2019)
21. Staff, R.N.: RIPE atlas: a global internet measurement network. Internet Protoc. J. **18**(3), (2015)
22. Sun, Y., Edmundson, A., Feamster, N., Chiang, M., Mittal, P.: Counter-RAPTOR: safeguarding Tor against active routing attacks. In: Symposium on Security and Privacy. IEEE (2017)
23. Sun, Y., et al.: Routing attacks on privacy in Tor. In: USENIX Security Symposium, RAPTOR (2015)
24. Vanbever, L., Li, O., Rexford, J., Mittal, P.: Anonymity on QuickSand: using BGP to compromise Tor. In: Proceedings of the 13th ACM Workshop on Hot Topics in Networks. ACM (2014)
25. Wacek, C., Tan, H., Bauer, K.S., Sherr, M.: An empirical evaluation of relay selection in Tor. In: Network and Distributed System Security Symposium (2013)
26. Wan, G., Johnson, A., Wails, R., Wagh, S., Mittal, P.: Guard placement attacks on path selection algorithms for Tor. In: Proceedings on Privacy Enhancing Technologies (2019)

Zeek-Osquery: Host-Network Correlation for Advanced Monitoring and Intrusion Detection

Steffen Haas[1]([⊠]), Robin Sommer[2], and Mathias Fischer[1]

[1] Universität Hamburg, Hamburg, Germany
{haas,mfischer}@informatik.uni-hamburg.de
[2] Corelight, Inc., San Francisco, CA, USA
robin@corelight.com

Abstract. Intrusion Detection Systems (IDSs) can analyze network traffic for signs of attacks and intrusions. However, encrypted communication limits their visibility and sophisticated attackers additionally try to evade their detection. To overcome these limitations, we extend the scope of Network IDSs (NIDSs) with additional data from the hosts. For that, we propose the integrated open-source *zeek-osquery* platform that combines the Zeek IDS with the osquery host monitor. Our platform can collect, process, and correlate host and network data at large scale, e.g., to attribute network flows to processes and users. The platform can be flexibly extended with own detection scripts using already correlated, but also additional and dynamically retrieved host data. A distributed deployment enables it to scale with an arbitrary number of osquery hosts. Our evaluation results indicate that a single Zeek instance can manage more than 870 osquery hosts and can attribute more than 96% of TCP connections to host-side applications and users in real-time.

Keywords: Intrusion detection · Network monitoring · Host-network correlation · Zeek · Osquery

1 Introduction

Computer networks need a second line of defense against cyber-attacks, in which network devices and connected systems are monitored to detect signs of intrusions. NIDSs can fill this gap and allow to collect extensive information about a monitored network. They can detect ongoing attacks and compromised hosts. However, the (definitely positive) ongoing trend towards secure and encrypted communication, turns an IDS partially blind. It cannot analyze the encrypted data anymore and thus might miss signs of intrusions. Furthermore, the complete reconstruction of sophisticated attacks, e.g., Advanced Persistent Threats (APTs) [7], is almost impossible based on network data only. Especially the detection of multi-step attacks across multiple hosts [13] that requires to identify related or similar flows, e.g., the Command and Control channel after a

© IFIP International Federation for Information Processing 2020
Published by Springer Nature Switzerland AG 2020
M. Hölbl et al. (Eds.): SEC 2020, IFIP AICT 580, pp. 248–262, 2020.
https://doi.org/10.1007/978-3-030-58201-2_17

Trojan download and the following lateral movement in the network, can only be correlated with uncertainty without any insights into host data [19].

Host context on network flows can improve the accuracy of NIDSs [1,5,14]. The combination of host and network monitoring leads to an increased visibility on attacks and requires to jointly analyze host and network data. However, while an NIDS can protect a complete network, a Host IDS (HIDS) has to run on every device in the network. Moreover, this induces a high correlation load when correlating host with network data. Furthermore, to be applicable for intrusion detection, such a system must be able to process the data of the monitored hosts close to real-time and thus need to scale with the number of HIDSs. Security Information and Event Management (SIEM) systems have been designed for this task [3]. They are centralized systems that usually read in log files collected from NIDSs and HIDSs and perform high-level correlation and aggregations across them. In contrast to their coarse-grained data that lacks detailed network data, our fine-grained correlation system makes use of causal relations in the data for the purpose of real-time intrusion detection in the network.

The main contribution of this paper is the novel open-source platform *zeek-osquery*[1] for the scalable and joint monitoring of networks and their hosts. For that, we combine the network monitor and IDS Zeek [12] (formerly known as Bro) with the host monitor osquery [6]. Our solution correlates data from the Operating System (OS) level with network information in real-time. Furthermore, it allows to dynamically select from a great variety of OS data available for processing. This way, we provide the fundamentals for a new class of detection algorithms that operate on a much broader visibility. We extend the context of network flows, for example to attribute them to the originating processes and the users that started them. Zeek-osquery can be flexibly adapted to different detection scenarios, as osquery-hosts are directly managed from Zeek scripts and all data processing can be implemented in Zeek. Examples are the detection of executed files downloaded from the Internet, the detection of lateral movement of attackers via SSH hopping [18], or to provide Zeek with Kernel-TLS keys obtained at hosts for the decryption and inspection of network traffic.

We extensively evaluated zeek-osquery in a small-scale real-world deployment and conducted additional experiments to investigate its scalability with an increasing number of osquery hosts. Our evaluation results indicate that we can attribute more than 96% of all TCP connections to their originating processes and the responsible users on monitored hosts, contrary to less than 0.1% attributed connections when using Zeek alone. Moreover, our system seems to scale with an increasing number of osquery hosts, enabling one Zeek instance to handle more than 870 osquery hosts in our evaluation setting. For larger deployments, we also propose a distributed setup with multiple Zeek instances that enable zeek-osquery to scale to arbitrarily large networks.

The remainder of this paper is structured as follows: Sect. 2 presents related work. Section 3 highlights the concept of host-network correlation and shows how to link host and network data for network attribution. Section 4 introduces our

---

[1] https://github.com/zeek/zeek-osquery.

open-source platform *zeek-osquery* to monitor both hosts and network and to correlate monitoring data in real-time. The evaluation of zeek-osquery in Sect. 5 is done in a real-world deployment for insights and in a stress test to highlight the scalability of our solution. We conclude with Sect. 6.

2   Related Work

We identified four groups of related work that is relevant for our work in the following: (1) Collaborative IDS (CIDS), (2) host context for network intrusion detection, (3) host activity to describe communication behavior, and (4) SIEM systems that can correlate logs from several sources.

CIDSs consist of several host or network IDSs that collect, exchange, and analyze data to create a holistic view of a network. However, these CIDS either do not scale, are built for a very specific purpose, e.g., to detect worm outbreaks [4], or offer a poor detection accuracy [17].

From the perspective of a NIDS, the inclusion of *environmental context* can increase the detection accuracy [15]. An early work from Snapp et al. [14] combines a NIDS with remote login events from hosts to identify login chains across multiple hosts for the same user. More recently, the context directly comes from the communicating application. Almgren et al. [1] instruct a NIDS to verify that the application processed the network messages correctly and to retrieve decrypted message payloads. Dreger et al. [5] compare how the NIDS and the application decode network messages. This allows to detect attackers that obfuscate their traffic for IDS evasion. However, these approaches require modifications to all applications and do not systematically correlate host and network data to increase the network visibility in general.

To gain more insight into *host activities* related to network communication, dependency graphs with processes, files, and sockets are utilized to link host activities [8]. The objects in the dependency graph are usually created from OS audit data [2]. For example, Ma et al. [11] taint objects in these graphs to propagate provenance in audit logs. This allows to enrich network-related activities on a single host, but it is not incorporated into network intrusion detection. For the usage of dependency graphs in intrusion detection [10], King et al. [9] extend these graphs across hosts to argue for causal relationships between attack steps. Sun et al. [16] incorporate IDS alerts into dependency graphs linked across hosts to find the most likely attack path through the network. However, to the best of our knowledge, no approach systematically leverages host context similar to dependency graphs for network intrusion detection in real-time.

SIEM systems [3] store logs from various sources, including host monitors, host applications, and network monitors in a central storage. They correlate host and network data to detect and investigate security incidents. However, SIEM systems fail to detect sophisticated attacks, because they miss detailed network data and their capabilities for analysis are usually limited to data aggregation, thresholding, and pattern detection. In contrast, our work provides additional host context specifically for particular network flows. It is used flexibly in Zeek scripts for network intrusion detection in real-time. Analysis results can be written to log files, be processed by SIEM systems, or induce an alert.

3   Refining the Network Visibility

To increase the accuracy of intrusion detection, we highlight network-related host activity that links between network and host monitoring. More generally, we refine the network visibility by incorporating host context into network monitoring. For all network traffic, we identify related properties that come from the hosts, e.g., user or process information. In particular, we explain how to attribute traffic in the network to applications and users on the respective hosts.

Network-Related Activities on Hosts. Throughout this paper, we use the term *flow* to describe the communication between two hosts with a 5-tuple of IP address and port of the hosts, and the protocol. We denote the flow initiator as *originator* and the other host as *responder*. *Processes*, identified by a process ID (*pid*), use sockets to abstract flows. A socket is identified by a unique socket ID, i.e., the combination of a file descriptor (*fd*) and pid, and additionally includes the attributes of the respective flow 5-tuple. Processes and sockets are retrieved by monitoring the system calls (*syscalls*) to the kernel, e.g., as provided by the kernel audit in Linux. Several syscalls exist for the interaction of processes with the kernel, including `execve` to spawn processes as well as `bind` and `connect` to establish incoming and outgoing flows, respectively. Another way to retrieve processes and sockets is to probe the current kernel status of Windows, Mac, and in particular the `procfs` in Linux. Kernel status data holds all attributes about current processes and sockets.

The data from both *kernel audit* and *kernel status* come along with different properties. While the audit allows for an asynchronous pushing of new processes and sockets, the status has to be frequently probed and compared with the previous one to detect any changes. Despite this probing overhead, it outperforms the audit variant when looking at the available attributes (data *soundness*). This is because audit monitors syscalls and consequently can only record actual parameters of these calls. For example, in case of a `connect`, only the destination IP address and port are part of the call. The local IP address and port remain unknown, even when combining several socket-related syscalls. However, relying on the status variant alone is error prone regarding retrieving all objects (data *completeness*), as a short-living process or socket might start and end between two status probes. Consequently, such processes or sockets would be missed. Therefore, a combination of both audit and status variants is elaborated next to achieve both full data soundness and completeness.

Attributing Network Flows. Both the originator and the responder of a network flow can be attributed by identifying the respective socket on either host, where applicable. For simplicity, we assume that the socket identification

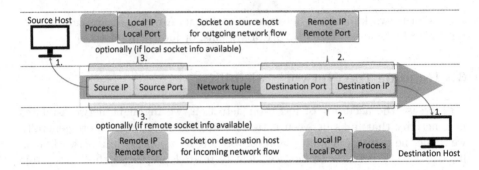

Fig. 1. Attributing a network flow to a process on source and destination host by matching the network tuple to the socket information on each of the hosts.

is sufficient, as this is the missing link to other host activity like processes and files [2]. The identification of the respective socket for a network flow requires a match on the flow 5-tuple. On the originator, this is a socket representing an outgoing flow, and an incoming flow on the responder. This is relevant as the 5-tuple for sockets reflects the IP address and port of the local and remote hosts, while it reflects originator and responder host for network flow. Thus, the incoming socket actually requires to match the inverse 5-tuple as the destination in the network flow is required to match the local host on the responder. Figure 1 illustrates the originator with its outgoing socket (top left), the responder with its incoming socket (bottom right), and the network flow with its full 5-tuple (middle).

In contrast to kernel status data, the incomplete data soundness from kernel audit results in unavailable socket attributes to match the source of a network flow. To account for that, we correlate sockets and network flows for attribution as following in three steps:

(1) Identify originator and responder hosts by the IP addresses in the network flow. This requires a maintained list of IP addresses and hosts in the network.
(2) On the originator and responder, identify the socket(s) for which the flow destination equals the remote or local socket info, respectively.
(3) Also require the flow source to equal local or remote socket info, respectively.

The correlation is unambiguous when the socket attributes for Step 3 are available. Otherwise, the correlation might be *vague*. In case of two hosts with a connect syscall to the same destination IP address and port, our correlation is still unambiguous because of Step 1. However, it is vague for the same host with multiple flows to the same remote IP and port (from different source ports). Ideally, the correlation outcome is exactly one socket for the originator and the responder. However, in case of vague correlation we list all candidate hosts, processes, and users that might be responsible for the flow.

Validity of Activities. Processes and sockets that already terminated some time ago must not be considered for attribution of a currently ongoing network flow. For that, we hold *state* about host activities and remove them from the state when the respective process terminated or socket is closed. Thus, with maintaining the host activities according to their *validity* in our state, we aim to follow the life-cycle of processes and sockets from their creation to termination.

Data from kernel status is easy to incorporate into the state, as the status reflects a current snapshot and comparing it to the previous snapshot allows to explicitly identify new or removed processes and sockets, respectively. For the kernel audit, the life-cycle for processes and sockets can be followed by syscalls like `execve`, `socket`, or `close`. This works as long as the process decides on its own to terminate or to close a socket. But there will not be such an audit event when the process crashes or the TCP connection breaks. To prevent our state to be polluted in such cases, we regularly perform a *verification* of it. We do so by probing the host if all the processes (pid) and sockets (pid, fd) in our state are still present by the current kernel status.

4 Monitoring and Event Correlation with Zeek-Osquery

In the following, we will describe zeek-osquery, a system for the collection, analysis, and correlation of host and network data that follows the approach from Sect. 3. After introducing the existing monitoring tools Zeek and osquery, we explain how our system *zeek-osquery* combines these two tools for the purpose of advanced monitoring and event correlation.

4.1 Monitoring Tools and Overview

The network monitoring and intrusion detection is performed by *Zeek* [12] (formerly known as Bro). It captures and parses network traffic in its core and provides a powerful scripting language to further analyze the traffic with custom scripts. The Zeek publish-subscribe (pub-sub) library Broker[2] dispatches events internally even among remote machines. We have enhanced Zeek to retrieve host events from osquery hosts and to natively process them analogous to network events in Zeek. Based on this, Zeek exposes itself as a platform with the ability to correlate various information from both host and network events.

Osquery [6] is an OS instrumentation framework. It provides an SQL-like interface to query the OS as a relational database, including from kernel audit and status. SQL tables represent abstract concepts such as running processes, open network flows, browser plugins, or file hashes. When running in background as host sensor, osquery regularly executes SQL queries as defined in its schedule. We extended osquery to communicate with Zeek via Broker to retrieve SQL requests from Zeek and report matching host events. The flexible pub-sub communication enables osquery hosts to join and leave the Broker overlay at any

---

[2] https://docs.zeek.org/projects/broker.

Fig. 2. Communication among osquery and zeek.

time. The seamless integration of host events from osquery into the Zeek processing pipeline allows for efficient processing of host events and their correlation with network events directly in Zeek scripts.

In zeek-osquery, the hosts are continuously monitored by osquery, which send host events to Zeek via the Broker overlay that connects osquery hosts and Zeek among each other. Added or removed entries in an osquery table are retrieved as a continuous stream of host events. Alternatively, osquery tables can be also queried on demand to retrieve a snapshot of an osquery table, e.g., to gather all running processes at a certain time. This allows for an interactive analysis of hosts, e.g., to investigate a specific security issue. Zeek acts as a correlation platform that analyzes and correlates both, the network events for the traffic captured by Zeek and the host events retrieved from all osquery hosts. For that, we extended Zeek by a new Zeek framework to define custom queries and result handling. For large deployments, our Zeek correlation platform can be set up in a distributed manner with multiple, communicating Zeek instances.

4.2   System Architecture

We implemented a novel Zeek *framework*, i.e., a collection of Zeek scripts, to control osquery hosts. This way, Zeek is capable of: (1) requesting complete results to a one-time query immediately and (2) scheduling queries that are regularly executed. We address specific osquery hosts or groups of them in the pub-sub overlay by distinct topic names, labeled as `groups` throughout this paper. Apart from some default *groups*, custom ones can either be pre-configured at the hosts or dynamically controlled by Zeek. It uses the group labels to control the SQL queries for specific selections of osquery hosts. An `interest` denotes the binding of a query to a *group*. It contains additional information, e.g., whether the query is executed regularly or just once and how to send the results back to Zeek. This way, Zeek can publish an *interest* over Broker to osquery hosts in a particular *group*, e.g., for logged in users on all monitored servers.

When an *interest* is published, the currently connected osquery hosts will receive it, but others that join the overlay later missed previous but valid *interests*. Thus, they would not execute the scheduled queries. For that, Zeek instances can take over the following roles as illustrated in Fig. 2:

– An `Authoritative` Zeek is the origin of an *interest*. This role defines queries and retrieves query results, i.e., host events, from the osquery hosts.

– A `Proxy` Zeek collects and holds all interests from `Authoritative` Zeek instances. It forwards only applicable queries to its directly connected osquery hosts. The `Proxy` Zeek maintains the query schedule and *group* assignments of hosts, both when they join and later when their interests change.

Our overlay design with respect to the Zeek roles, enables a scalable deployment with multiple Zeek instances that run in a distributed fashion for load balancing and availability reasons. Distributing the load among multiple Zeek instances can be achieved in three ways:

– Resource intensive correlation tasks can run exclusively on an additional *Authoritative* Zeek instance. For that, another Zeek joins the overlay and publishes *interests* for events that are required for detection. The resources of this instance are completely available to the detection and all other instances can continue using their resources to perform their tasks.
– If large amounts of osquery hosts would overwhelm a single *Authoritative* Zeek instance, the osquery hosts are organized in *groups*, with one out of multiple Zeek instances being responsible for one *group*. All Zeek instances are then interested in the same query that they publish to a specific *group*.
– To reduce the load on a single *Proxy* Zeek instance, multiple instances can be deployed. Then, each one needs to handle a lower number of directly connected hosts that still receive the same *interests* as before.

After an osquery host joined the Broker overlay, it is controlled by its *Proxy* Zeek and now accepts and executes any forwarded *interest*. However, note that *interests* originally come from *Authoritative* Zeeks and query results should also be routed back to them via the pub-sub overlay. For that, the originating *Authoritative* Zeek by default sets the response topic to its own topic when publishing *interests*. If the same *interest* query originates from multiple Zeeks, we suggest to choose the same response topic across Zeek instances for the same *interest*. This way, *interests* can be consolidated on osquery hosts and the query results are sent efficiently over Broker to multiple *Authoritative* Zeek instances.

4.3 Event Correlation for Network Attribution

We developed a processing pipeline as part of our Zeek framework to process and correlate host and network events. We implemented it in the Zeek-typical event-based fashion to allow custom scripts to reuse events emitted by our pipeline for further analysis. The three different stages in the processing pipeline are illustrated in Fig. 3, follow the concept as described in Sect. 3, and are detailed in the remainder of this section.

In the `Querying` stage *interests* are defined, i.e., SQL queries, that are sent to and scheduled on osquery hosts. Events on this stage are a continuous stream of raw host events that directly come from osquery. Incoming events reflect updates of an osquery table, e.g., processes or sockets.

The `State` stage assembles raw host events from osquery to a state in real-time and reflects the current host status, e.g., a process is added upon creation

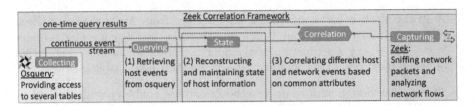

Fig. 3. Architecture of the processing pipeline.

and removed upon termination. Tables in osquery based on Linux kernel audit (cf. Sect. 3) report only new processes and sockets, so we verify the state periodically against the kernel status utilizing one-time queries. The same mechanism is used to retrieve a snapshot for initial state before continuously updating it with audit events. The state consolidates raw host events from different tables in case they describe the same class of data, e.g., the socket state is built based on the osquery tables *socket_events*, *listening_ports*, and *process_open_sockets*. While state of Windows and Mac hosts is reconstructed solely from tables reflecting kernel status, state of Linux hosts is additionally based on kernel audit and therefore more accurate because of data completeness (cf. Sect. 3).

In the `Correlation` stage, the data base for correlations encompasses the triggering event and any state that is available both natively in Zeek and about osquery hosts. As an example, we implemented the attribution of network flows by linking them with the respective application and user in real-time. To demonstrate the effect, we extended the statistics about every network flow in Zeek (`conn.log`) to additionally list the respective host, application, and user.

4.4   Examples for Scenario Detection

Building on the network attribution (cf. Sect. 4.3), we implemented the detection of three particular scenarios using our processing pipeline in Zeek scripts.

Execution of Mail Attachments. Once an email campaign with malware is recognized and its mail recipients identified, it must be reconstructed who of them executed the attachment and on which machines. Zeek-osquery tracks the execution of mail attachments as follows: First, Zeek notices a file download from the Internet as mail attachment and remembers the file hash associated with the attachment. Second, in parallel Zeek interactively requests the file hash of unknown binaries upon process creations. A match among the download hashes and the binary hashes reveals the execution of an Internet download.

Stepping Stone Detection. Attackers often hide their identify by using an infected machine in the network as proxy to reach the actual target. An example for such an attack is SSH chaining and zeek-osquery detects it as follows: First, Zeek identifies all hosts that have both an incoming and outgoing SSH connection, i.e., which is an indication for a SSH proxy. To verify the relation between incoming and outgoing connection, Zeek interactively requests the *pids* of all children under the process with the incoming connection. If this list contains the *pid* of the process with the outgoing connection, a stepping stone is detected.

TLS Decryption. TLS proxies often actively break the end-to-end encryption for traffic analysis. With zeek-osquery, we provide the ability to selectively request cryptographic material from hosts such that Zeek can passively decrypt the traffic. As proof-of-concept, we extended osquery to capture the respective system call used in Kernel-TLS (KTLS), when the application forwards the keys to delegate the symmetric de- and encryption after the TLS handshake to the kernel. Osquery then provides a tables with the obtained keys to Zeek.

5 Evaluation

In this section, we evaluate zeek-osquery. First, Sect. 5.1 gives insights into a real-world deployment. Afterwards, we stress-test the system with more hosts and host events in Sect. 5.2 to evaluate its scalability properties.

5.1 Real-World Evaluation

We deployed zeek-osquery to monitor eleven office machines of a working group in the computer science department on a university campus for three working days. The machines were running different Linux distributions, including Ubuntu, Linux Mint, Fedora, and Arch Linux. To monitor their network traffic and to correlate it with host events, we tunnel the traffic through a VPN on the campus site that is monitored by a Zeek instance. Note, that the correlation is performed in real-time during this experiment.

The data processed by zeek-osquery in this setup is characterized in Table 1. It reports characteristics of the flows that our zeek-osquery ideally correlated with host data. Furthermore, the table reports the number of received host events. On average, each of the eleven machines was monitored for 6 h and 21 min per day. An individual host on average reported 20.22 process, 5.63 socket, and 0.37 user events per minute that go into state (cf. Sect. 4.3). Note, that also the initial state that is retrieved from hosts upon their (re-)connects goes into the average event rate. The following provides results and experiences on how zeek-osquery enhances the visibility and accuracy of monitoring.

Table 1. Characteristics of the real-world dataset.

Network flows				Host events for state			
Total	TCP	UDP	ICMP	Process	Socket	User	Interface
344,366	273,241	70,929	196	2,793,406	776,910	51,719	7,919

Table 2. Attributing of network flows.

(a) Attribution rate		
All	UDP	TCP
86.61%	50.43%	96.05%

(b) Attribution uniqueness			
	Host	Process	User
Unique attributions	100%	88.53%	98.14%
Average candidates	1.00	1.17	1.02

Attribution. Table 2a shows the success rate of our attribution for the 344,366 network flows in our dataset. For 96.05% of TCP connections and 86.61% of all flows we identify the responsible processes and users. False negatives are caused when: First, the host data is not retrieved in time for real-time correlation with short-lived flows. Second, applications like Skype use Stateless IP/ICMP Translation (SIIT) to embed the actual IPv4 destination address into an IPv6 address. But as the host sends an IPv4 message, this causes a mismatch between IPv4 (in network flow) and IPv6 addresses (in host events). Third, remote hosts continue a flow although the monitored host already left the VPN and a new host joined the VPN reusing the same IP address. These packets cannot be attributed to a process on the new host. The attribution rate for UDP flows is only about 50% because Zeek retrieves host events about UDP sockets from the audit status only (cf. Sect. 3), which is provided at discrete time slots only. Thus, short-living sockets might be missed out. This holds especially true for DNS requests that are responsible for 89% of the UDP flows.

We further evaluate the attributed flows with respect to a unique host, process, and user. In Table 2b, we count the number of flows that have been attributed to a single entity and furthermore calculate the average number of candidate entries per attribution. Apart from the vague correlation (cf. Sect. 3), a fast re-usage on hosts of the same process ID or socket, i.e., file descriptor, can be a reason for multiple attribution candidates. The effects of the vague correlation become visible, especially for DNS flows. Usually applications use the DNS server defined by the OS and therefore many processes establish flows to the same server and port combinations. If we skip attributing flows to the DNS servers, the unique attribution of processes increases from 88.53% to 93.15%. Although a single user was logged in on the monitored machines, in some cases the user attribution overlaps with a system account, e.g., in case of parallel DNS requests by the system and an user application.

Network Applications. To identify communicating applications, the state-of-the-art is to inspect network packets for application specific indicators like the HTTP user agent. Zeek already analyses such indicators and derives the respective application, where applicable. If Zeek itself cannot derive the application from the network packets, zeek-osquery can still verify the application via the correlation with host data. Table 3 lists the top 10 network applications ranked by their number of attributed flows. We observed two outcomes when comparing both methods for identifying communicating applications: First, zeek-osquery is

Table 3. Top 10 attributed applications among all network flows.

Rank	Zeek		Zeek-osquery	
	Attributed flows	0.06%	Attributed flows	86.61%
1	Chrome	(0.01%)	Firefox	(23.17%)
2	Firefox	(0.01%)	Thunderbird	(12.30%)
3	Spotify	(0.01%)	Spotify	(6.11%)
4	Thunderbird	(0.01%)	Opera	(5.41%)
5	Debian APT-HTTP	(<0.01%)	Syncthing	(5.39%)
6	libdnf	(<0.01%)	Chromium	(4.55%)
7	Wget	(<0.01%)	Skype	(3.87%)
8	<unknown browser>	(<0.01%)	Seafile	(3.80%)
9	OpenSSH	(<0.01%)	Chrome	(3.56%)
10	gvfs	(<0.01%)	Qutebrowser	(3.33%)
Total	33 applications		88 applications	

able to attribute significantly more flows compared to Zeek, i.e., 298255 (86.61%) compared to 212 (0.06%). Specifically for the Firefox browser, zeek-osquery was able to attribute flows 2971 times more often than Zeek. Second, zeek-osquery is able to identify applications that were not identified by Zeek. This includes user applications such as Syncthing, Seafile, and Skype, but also system-related components such as the network time synchronization daemon NTPD and the Dynamic Host Configuration Protocol (DHCP) client dhclient.

However, we have also seen limitations of zeek-osquery, especially when a process launches another application that immediately starts a network flow. Because the flow could have happened before or after the parent process with the same pid transferred control with the execve syscall to the new child, both parent and child application are candidates for the attribution. In our experiment, applications that are known to never communicate directly are candidates for 0.18% of attributed flows. Also, some monitored hosts were running NATed Virtual Machines (VMs) with a Windows guest system. While osquery runs on the Linux hypervisor host only, it attributes any traffic of the VM to the virtualization application (2.29%). However, Zeek might still identify the Windows application inside the VM based on identifiers in the network packets (0.01%).

Zeek-osquery significantly increases the identification rate of communicating applications. This enables to enforce the use of allowed applications and assists threat hunters in detecting malware that covers its communication in well-known protocols, e.g., HTTPS, that is usually allowed to pass the firewall.

5.2   Zeek Performance Analysis

In this section, we provide evaluation results to assess the scalability and efficiency of zeek-osquery (cf. Sect. 4) with an increasing number of osquery hosts and an increasing number of events. For that, we implemented a simplified prototype of our actual Zeek-enhanced osquery implementation in Python that simulates new processes and sockets. Each host continuously sends four events per second to Zeek, which is more then in our real-world evaluation.

We distribute the total amount of the lightweight osquery instances equally among ten bare-metal machines. Zeek takes over the role of both Proxy and Authoritative Zeek and is running on another bare-metal machine. This comes close to a real-world deployment, in which Zeek runs on a single machine and osquery instances are distributed on different machines in the network. All of the machines are equipped with an Intel(R) Core(TM) i5-2400 CPU @ 3.10 GHz and 8 GB of RAM. We run each configuration setup for a specific number of hosts for 20 min, measuring the average overhead of Zeek in terms of CPU and RAM utilization for handling osquery hosts and processing host events in Fig. 4. During the experiment, Zeek retrieves, logs, reconstructs state, and correlates process, socket, and user events from hosts as it is done for the attribution of network flows. The resources scale linearly with an increasing number of osquery hosts. A single host causes 0.11% CPU and 0.45 MB RAM at the Zeek instance during real-time correlation. Theoretically, to achieve 100% CPU utilization, about 870 osquery hosts would be required, each sending four events per second.

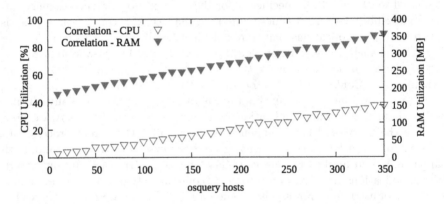

Fig. 4. Resource utilization of Zeek for hosts with four host events per second.

6   Conclusion

In this paper, we introduced *zeek-osquery* as a novel approach to enrich network intrusion detection with host data. For that, zeek-osquery leverages existing OS instrumentation to collect processes and users and correlates them with network flows. Our open-source implementation performs efficiently in real-time and in a scalable fashion, as different roles in the platform can be distributed. Our system gives broader network visibility and attributes network flows to users and applications at large scale. Compared to a network-based IDS only, e.g., Zeek, the ratio of attributed network flows to applications increases by orders of magnitudes. Zeek-osquery can attribute more than 96% of the TCP connections to the originating process and the respective users in real-time. On that basis, we can detect malware that encrypt its communication in protocols such as HTTPS, which usually passes a NIDS without detection. Future work can include more host data, e.g., opened files, and can develop more correlation algorithms on top of zeek-osquery, e.g., to detect distributed and multi-step attacks.

References

1. Almgren, M., Lindqvist, U.: Application-integrated data collection for security monitoring. In: Lee, W., Mé, L., Wespi, A. (eds.) RAID 2001. LNCS, vol. 2212, pp. 22–36. Springer, Heidelberg (2001). https://doi.org/10.1007/3-540-45474-8_2
2. Bates, A., Tian, D., Butler, K.R.B., Moyer, T.: Trustworthy whole-system provenance for the Linux Kernel. In: Proceedings of the 24th USENIX Conference on Security Symposium, pp. 319–334. USENIX Association (2015)
3. Bhatt, S., Manadhata, P.K., Zomlot, L.: The operational role of security information and event management systems. IEEE Secur. Priv. **12**(5), 35–41 (2014). https://doi.org/10.1109/MSP.2014.103
4. Cai, M., Hwang, K., Kwok, Y.K., Song, S., Chen, Y.: Collaborative internet worm containment. IEEE Secur. Priv. **3**(3), 25–33 (2005). https://doi.org/10.1109/MSP.2005.63
5. Dreger, H., Kreibich, C., Paxson, V., Sommer, R.: Enhancing the accuracy of network-based intrusion detection with host-based context. In: Julisch, K., Kruegel, C. (eds.) DIMVA 2005. LNCS, vol. 3548, pp. 206–221. Springer, Heidelberg (2005). https://doi.org/10.1007/11506881_13
6. Facebook: osquery — Easily ask questions about your Linux, Windows, and macOS infrastructure. https://osquery.io/. Accessed 21 Feb 2020
7. Friedberg, I., Skopik, F., Settanni, G., Fiedler, R.: Combating advanced persistent threats: from network event correlation to incident detection. Comput. Secur. **48**, 35–57 (2015). https://doi.org/10.1016/j.cose.2014.09.006
8. King, S.T., Chen, P.M.: Backtracking intrusions. In: Proceedings of the Nineteenth ACM Symposium on Operating Systems Principles, pp. 223–236 (2003). https://doi.org/10.1145/945445.945467
9. King, S.T., Mao, Z.M., Lucchetti, D.G., Chen, P.M.: Enriching intrusion alerts through multi-host causality. In: Proceedings of the Network and Distributed System Security Symposium. The Internet Society (2005)
10. Liu, M., Xue, Z., Xu, X., Zhong, C., Chen, J.: Host-based intrusion detection system with system calls: review and future trends. ACM Comput. Surv. (CSUR) **51**(5) (2018). https://doi.org/10.1145/3214304
11. Ma, S., Zhang, X., Xu, D.: ProTracer: Tt and distributed system security symposium. The Internet Society (2016)
12. Paxson, V.: Bro: a system for detecting network intruders in real-time. Comput. Netw. **31**(23), 2435–2463 (1999). https://doi.org/10.1016/S1389-1286(99)00112-7
13. Shin, J., Choi, S.H., Liu, P., Choi, Y.H.: Unsupervised multi-stage attack detection framework without details on single-stage attacks. Future Gener. Comput. Syst. **100**, 811–825 (2019). https://doi.org/10.1016/j.future.2019.05.032
14. Snapp, S.R., et al.: DIDS (distributed intrusion detection system) - motivation, architecture, and an early prototype. In: Proceedings of the 14th National Computer Security Conference, vol. 1, pp. 167–176 (1991)

15. Sommer, R., Paxson, V.: Enhancing byte-level network intrusion detection signatures with context. In: Proceedings of the 10th ACM Conference on Computer and Communications Security, pp. 262–271 (2003). https://doi.org/10.1145/948109.948145
16. Sun, X., Dai, J., Liu, P., Singhal, A., Yen, J.: Towards probabilistic identification of zero-day attack paths. In: 2016 IEEE Conference on Communications and Network Security (CNS), pp. 64–72 (2016). https://doi.org/10.1109/CNS.2016.7860471
17. Vasilomanolakis, E., Karuppayah, S., Mühlhäuser, M., Fischer, M.: Taxonomy and survey of collaborative intrusion detection. ACM Comput. Surv. (CSUR) **47**(4) (2015). https://doi.org/10.1145/2716260
18. Wang, L., Yang, J.: A research survey in stepping-stone intrusion detection. EURASIP J. Wirele. Commun. Netw. **2018**(1) (2018). https://doi.org/10.1186/s13638-018-1303-2
19. Wilkens, F., Haas, S., Kaaser, D., Kling, P., Fischer, M.: Towards efficient reconstruction of attacker lateral movement. In: Proceedings of the 14th International Conference on Availability, Reliability and Security. ACM, New York (2019). https://doi.org/10.1145/3339252.3339254

Access Control and Authentication

Revisiting Security Vulnerabilities in Commercial Password Managers

Michael Carr[1] and Siamak F. Shahandashti[2([envelope])]

[1] Piksel, York Science Park, York YO10 5ZD, UK
mikey.carr@piksel.com
[2] Department of Computer Science,
University of York, York YO10 5GH, UK
siamak.shahandashti@york.ac.uk

Abstract. In this work we analyse five popular commercial password managers for security vulnerabilities. Our analysis is twofold. First, we compile a list of previously disclosed vulnerabilities through a comprehensive review of the academic and non-academic sources and test each password manager against all the previously disclosed vulnerabilities. We find a mixed picture of fixed and persisting vulnerabilities. Then we carry out systematic functionality tests on the considered password managers and find four new vulnerabilities. Notably, one of the new vulnerabilities we identified allows a malicious app to impersonate a legitimate app to two out of five widely-used password managers we tested and as a result steal the user's password for the targeted service. We implement a proof-of-concept attack to show the feasibility of this vulnerability in a real-life scenario. Finally, we report and reflect on our experience of responsible disclosure of the newly discovered vulnerabilities to the corresponding password manager vendors.

Keywords: Vulnerability testing · Password managers · Password manager security · Authentication

1 Introduction

Passwords remain the dominant authentication mechanism in the digital realm despite their shortcomings. Furthermore, they are expected to persist as a primary authentication mechanism for the some time [6]. Among the tools that can greatly reduce the cognitive burden of remembering multiple passwords for multiple services are password managers. Hence, their use is strongly advocated by security experts, including the UK's National Cyber Security Centre [13].

A password manager is an encrypted vault that stores any number of credentials for the user and is accessed by a single master password. In this context, a credential is a username-password pair that authenticates the user to a web-based service. Over and above individual use, a commercial password manager

© IFIP International Federation for Information Processing 2020
Published by Springer Nature Switzerland AG 2020
M. Hölbl et al. (Eds.): SEC 2020, IFIP AICT 580, pp. 265–279, 2020.
https://doi.org/10.1007/978-3-030-58201-2_18

usually provides extra features, e.g. credential sharing and admin interfaces, and aims to increase enterprise security. Obviously, vulnerabilities in such an application provide opportunities for malicious actors to extract credentials, compromise commercial information, or violate employee privacy. Therefore, rigorous security analysis of password managers is crucial.

Analyses focusing specifically on the security of password managers appear within academic literature and other less formal publications such as blogs as early as 2003. Each work usually reports one or more discovered vulnerabilities and how they could be exploited in an attack against certain password managers in the hope that password manager vendors eventually rectify these issues. However, it is not clear to what extent reported issues apply to other password managers and to what extent they are mitigated by corresponding vendors. In fact, there does not seem to be any reference that aggregates the major security vulnerabilities reported in the literature, and existing reports remain fragmented in multiple sources. In this work we attempt to address this gap as well as reporting new vulnerabilities we discovered in our analyses.

We report the results of our work on analysing the security of the enterprise editions of five major password managers: LastPass, Dashlane, Keeper, 1Password, and RoboForm. These password managers were chosen after a rigorous selection process which considered popularity and features of the individual and commercial offerings of 19 password managers. Our contributions are threefold:

1) We carried out a survey of both formally and informally published vulnerabilities of password managers, identified six main vulnerabilities, tested current versions of the five considered password managers against each vulnerability, and report our results whether each password manager is susceptible to each previously disclosed vulnerability.
2) Through comprehensive systematic testing of mobile, desktop, and web applications (including browser extensions) of the considered password managers, we discovered four new issues that can lead to exploitable vulnerabilities, developed a proof-of-concept Android application to demonstrate how the most serious issue might be used in a real-world phishing attack, and report on whether each password manager is susceptible to each discovered vulnerability.
3) Following the principle of responsible disclosure, we engaged with the corresponding password manager vendors and informed them of the newly discovered vulnerabilities. We report and reflect on our experience of interacting with these vendors.

Many modern browsers provide password management services on the side. However, we focus on stand-alone password managers that provide a commercial offering for organisations and do not consider browser password managers.

The rest of this paper is organised as follows: in Sect. 2 we review the literature on password manager security; Sect. 3 specifies our method for selecting and analysing the password managers considered; Sect. 4 reports on our results on both previously disclosed and newly discovered vulnerabilities and discusses their feasibility and impact; Sect. 5 reports on our responsible disclosure to the corresponding vendors; and concluding remarks come in Sect. 6.

2 Related Work

In recent years password managers have been analysed a multitude of times, both within and outside academia. Here we review the major reported vulnerabilities.

2.1 Autofill Vulnerabilities

An area that has been of substantial interest to researchers is the autofill feature that password managers implement to increase their usability. A number of works have exploited poor implementation of autofill to extract user's credentials, in some cases automatically [1,5,11]. In [11], a minimal survey implemented as an HTML form was sent to users of multiple webmail services. The form contained a visible question along with invisible email and password input boxes. The idea was that the password managers would see the email as a login form with the webmail domain as origin and autofill the credentials for the webmail service. With auto-login enabled, merely opening the email would automatically fill in the credentials and submit the form in some webmail services, and in others the user was warned that a form is about to be submitted but would still be vulnerable if they clicked through the warning.

2.2 Web-Based Vulnerabilities

A rigorous analysis of the security of five web-based password managers (including two we consider here, LastPass and RoboForm) was performed by Li et al. [8]. The authors found a diverse range of vulnerabilities ranging from classic web vulnerabilities such as cross-site scripting (XSS) and request forgery (CSRF) to more specific authorisation and user interface vulnerabilities. Notably the authors found that in some cases only authentication was carried out and not authorisation. This allowed an attacker registered with the password manager to successfully request a victim's password to be shared with another party.

Bookmarklets were extensively used by password managers to provide browser integration when extensions (a.k.a. add-ons) were not available, e.g. in many mobile browsers. With the extended functionality of native APIs, and in view of the inherent vulnerability of bookmarklet code execution, password managers have moved on to providing separate applications on multiple operating systems, and either have already discontinued bookmarklet support or discourage its use.

The vault encryption methods used in the enterprise versions of RoboForm and LastPass have been analysed in [14] where the authors define a threat model that takes into account two forms of attackers with different capabilities: outsider attackers and insider attackers. The authors focus specifically on three forms of attack: brute force attacks, local decryption attacks, and request monitoring attacks. In LastPass, local decryption by outsider, brute force by outsider, and brute force by insider attacks were all capable of retrieving a user's master password. In RoboForm, vulnerabilities were found in local decoding by outsider, brute force by outsider, and server-side request monitoring by insider attacks.

Dashlane was the subject of a security analysis in 2016 [4]. When attempting to log on, if an invalid username is entered, a message stating 'Incorrect login' is shown, whereas if an incorrect password is entered, a message stating 'Incorrect password' is shown. This indicates that a username is registered with Dashlane and would aid an attacker when attempting a brute force attack on usernames and passwords. Although an attacker would need access to the victim's devices as Dashlane uses two-factor authentication (2FA) for any new devices, a device authentication vulnerability meant that 2FA could be bypassed. This allows an unauthorised device to access passwords.

2.3 Non-academic Sources

In 2017, a vulnerability in the implementation of 2FA (via a QR code) in Last-Pass [12] was found. The issue was that the URL where the QR code was stored was a predictable hash of the user's master password. An attacker that is hoping to bypass 2FA will already know the victim's password and, therefore, is capable of accessing the QR code, which is needed to generate the valid temporary codes. The vulnerability was likened to a safe within a building that can be opened with the same key as that of the building door [12]. However, for the request to access the QR code to be valid, a user has to be authenticated, but it was shown that this could be defeated using a cross site request forgery vulnerability. LastPass have since patched this vulnerability.

In 2016 a vulnerability was discovered in the LastPass extension URL parsing code used to decide on whether to autofill a website [7]. In short, it meant that a specially crafted URL was able to extract the credentials for arbitrary websites. Browsers treat a URL like `example.com/@twitter.com/@xyz.php` as from `example.com` while the extension treated it as from `twitter.com` since only the last occurrence of the @ was considered. Hence, it was possible to confuse the extension and allow an attacker to identify the credentials for a targeted website. LastPass have since patched this vulnerability.

There does not seem to be a survey of password manager security analyses bringing together an aggregated list of reported vulnerabilities. In this work, we address this issue. Note that there is a related line of research on the security of encrypted database formats used in password managers (see e.g. [3]) which considers the threat model in which an adversary gets direct access to the password manager vault. We do not consider this threat model here.

3   Method

We specify the methods we used in each step of this work in the following.

3.1 Identification of Password Managers

To ensure a wide range of password managers were considered, a comprehensive survey of individual and commercial password managers was undertaken.

This took into account the number of users documented by the password manager vendors, install counts in application stores and recommendations by reputable websites such as PCMag.com. Further, less publicised products were identified by inputting terms such as 'password manager' into web search engines.

Once the search reached saturation, identified by a lack of new products appearing, each of the password managers listed was investigated and their features compared. To make our final selection, we considered two characteristics: popularity of the tool as an indicator of the number of users affected by a potential vulnerability, and richness of features, as an indicator of both desirability for companies as customers and at the same time diversity of attack vectors.

3.2 Identification of Previously Disclosed Vulnerabilities

A comprehensive review of the literature on password managers was carried out. Besides, we examined general and tech news sources for any security issues reported for password managers. We limit our presentation to vulnerabilities that lend themselves to feasible and impactful attacks.

To keep our survey focused on password manager specific vulnerabilities, we do not consider general web vulnerabilities such as XSS or CSRF for which there are standard recommended solutions. Furthermore, given the gradual phaseout and the inherent vulnerability of bookmarklets, we leave bookmarklet-specific vulnerabilities out of the presented results here. Ultimately, the results of our survey needs to be considered alongside the vulnerabilities listed by Li et al. [8], and those considered by the literature on database format security (e.g. [3]) for a more comprehensive view of password manager security.

3.3 Testing for Identified and New Vulnerabilities

After selecting the products for testing, a two-week enterprise trial was started with each of the products consecutively. To begin, the systems were tested under normal operation to identify any abnormalities. This involved completing a large number of tasks using features that are available (to users as well as admins) in the enterprise editions of the software. A comprehensive list of all the operations that were performed is not presented here, but included the following:

- logging in as a user and an administrator;
- adding a password through the vault and automatic capture features;
- sharing passwords between users;
- updating shared passwords and individual passwords on multiple devices;
- linking a personal account to the corporate account;
- analysing activity reports and their accuracy; and
- adding and removing users from groups and roles.

Following the initial testing of standard features, all of the password managers were tested against the identified previously disclosed vulnerabilities. Through checking previously disclosed vulnerabilities across all of the password managers in the sample, it is possible to establish whether patches have been correctly applied and whether the issues are common across password managers. The abnormalities discovered through the initial testing were then capitalised on through the development of proof of concept exploits.

Ethical Considerations: Throughout this work, ethical considerations have been paramount. No live user account was used or attacked. All testing was carried out using accounts that belong to the investigators. All vulnerabilities have been responsibly disclosed to the vendors at least six months before publication.

4   Results

In this section we first give the detailed specifications of our test settings and then provide our results on testing the selected password managers against previously disclosed vulnerabilities and our discovery of new vulnerabilities.

Our search for password managers identified 19 applications supporting most of the features that can be considered basic features for password managers, e.g. password capture and encrypted storage, password generation, mobile app, and autofill. Overall, we identified 27 features, including a number of desirable additional security features, e.g. two-factor and biometric authentication, and some that are especially desirable in a professional environment, e.g. password sharing, security breach alerts, admin console, and API provision. The full list of password managers and features we considered can be found in Appendix A.

From the 19 password managers identified, those with the greatest popularity and richness of features were selected for testing. These password managers are LastPass, Dashlane, Keeper, 1Password, and RoboForm.

The desktop components of the password managers were tested using a laptop running Windows 10 Enterprise version `10.0.14393` build `14393` and Chrome version `59.0.3071.115` where extensions were used. Any mobile components were tested using an Android 7.0 phone. Note that Windows, Android, and Chrome are respectively the current most widely-used OS, mobile OS, and browser worldwide. Tested password manager versions are shown in Table 1.

Table 1. Version numbers of the password managers tested.

OS	Password manager				
	Dashlane	LastPass	Keeper	1Password	RoboForm
Windows	4.8.2	4.1.60	10.8.1	6.6.439	8.3.7.7
Android	4.17.0.1995	4.2.762	10.7.0	6.5.3	8.0.9

4.1   Previously Disclosed Vulnerabilities

Our survey resulted in the identification of six main issues that we list in this section. Our initial tests indicated that authorisation vulnerabilities discussed by

Li et al. [8] appear to have been patched in all password managers we considered. Hence, we do not list those vulnerabilities here in the interest of conciseness.

Two-Factor Authentication Seed Vulnerability: Disclosed for LastPass in which the seed for enabling 2FA was stored at a predictable URL [12]. This was tested on the password managers by initiating the 2FA set-up process and identifying whether the seed URL appear predictable based on any user information.

Element Inspection Vulnerability: Leakage of shared passwords through DOM element inspector tools such as Chrome's `Inspect Element`, as shown in the Dashlane security analysis [4]. This can be tested by sharing limited access to a password with another user, which allows them to use the password but not see it. Following this, logging in as the other user and then using an element inspector on the shared password exposes the password.

Registration Discovery Vulnerability: An indication of whether a username is registered with the service through UI prompts, as shown in the Dashlane security analysis [4]. This is tested through attempting to log in with an incorrect username and then incorrect password.

URL Mismatch Vulnerability: Log in fields being filled with a username and password, despite the source and destination URLs not matching [1].

HTTP(S) Autofill Vulnerability: Autofill policies do not distinguish between HTTP and HTTPS when attempting to fill a credential that has been stored with HTTPS on an HTTP version of the site [1]. This would enable a man-in-the-middle attacker to impersonate an HTTP version of a popular website and steal user credentials originally stored for the HTTPS version.

Ignoring Subdomains Vulnerability: Subdomains are ignored when filling passwords [1]. This is tested with the university websites: `york.ac.uk` and `cs.york.ac.uk`. An attacker in a subdomain can hence steal user credentials for the parent domain or other subdomains. This is an issue in many websites such as forums and blogs where different subdomains host different services.

Summary: Table 2 shows the results of testing the five password managers against the vulnerabilities listed above. These vulnerabilities were tested using the same processes and resources for all the password managers. As can be seen from the table, at least one of the password managers is vulnerable to every single issue apart from 2FA Seed vulnerability. The tested password managers are most vulnerable to URL Mismatch, HTTP(S) Autofill, and Ignoring Subdomains vulnerabilities, with all but one of the managers being susceptible to URL Mismatch and all to HTTP(S) Autofill and Ignoring Subdomains vulnerabilities. All of these vulnerabilities concern the web interfaces, and more specifically the autofill feature, which has been an area of focus for previous works. Hence, it was hoped that vendors had responded by making their software resilient to such attacks. However, this appears not to be always the case.

Table 2. Previously disclosed vulnerabilities analysed against the password managers tested. A ● indicates the application is vulnerable, a ○ indicates it is not.

Vulnerability	Password manager				
	Dashlane	LastPass	Keeper	1Password	RoboForm
2FA Seed	○	○	○	○	○
Element Inspection	●	●	●	○	○
Registration Discovery	●	○	○	○	○
URL Mismatch	●	○	●	●	●
HTTP(S) Autofill	●	●	●	●	●
Ignoring Subdomains	●	●	●	●	●

4.2   Discovered Vulnerabilities

Our extensive feature testing flagged some issues which we investigated further. Here we present a developed proof-of-concept attack and three other vulnerabilities of the tested password managers. Unlike previously disclosed vulnerabilities, the ones we discuss here do not only concern web interfaces and some are related to mobile or desktop applications.

Phishing Attack: Both the 1Password and LastPass Android applications were found vulnerable to a phishing attack. The issue discovered was that both applications use weak matching criteria for identifying which stored credentials to suggest for autofill. This allowed for a rogue application to impersonate a legitimate one simply by crafting the package name to be identical. A developed proof-of-concept attack is described in detail below for LastPass but essentially the same attack applies to 1Password.

To identify the process used when matching an application and credentials, a blank login screen was created. After selecting the `Add Login` option in the LastPass pop-up, the URL shown in the LastPass application is the package name of the application developed. This indicated that the matching criteria employed by LastPass is based on the package name of the application only.

After discovering how LastPass matches applications and credentials, a malicious app was developed with the package name of `com.google`. Again, this app had a login screen; this can be seen in Fig. 1. This login screen was designed to mimic that of the official Google login screen and thereby be hard to distinguish. The weak matching employed by LastPass means that if the malicious app is launched, LastPass will offer to autofill the login page with Google credentials stored in a user's vault. This can be seen in Fig. 2. In our proof-of-concept attack, after a victim has selected their credentials from the LastPass pop-up and tapped the `Next` button, the credentials are sent across to a server and stored in a file. Hence, as long as the victim is tricked into installing and launching a malicious application, their credential can be stolen easily leveraging the weak matching used by 1Password and LastPass.

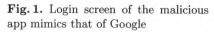

Fig. 1. Login screen of the malicious app mimics that of Google

Fig. 2. LastPass showing Google credentials for the malicious app

The attack developed here succeeds if the following conditions are met. Firstly, the malicious app needs to be installed on the victim's device. Attackers might achieve this by either getting around app store security mechanisms (see e.g. [10] in the case of Google Play Store) or otherwise fooling the victim into sideloading the app onto their device. This could be done in combination with another phishing attack, for example, sending an email stating the targeted service's application requires an upgrade. Secondly, the victim needs to be a user of the vulnerable password managers and using the LastPass or 1Password autofill prompt, although other users may be fooled and enter their password manually. Finally, the user needs to have credentials for the target application, in this case, Google, in their vault. Having said these, if an organisation is identified as a commercial user of a vulnerable password manager along with other services (e.g. Google email service), the latter two conditions are met and a large-scale phishing campaign may be launched against the organisation employees which one expects to have some degree of success in stealing employee credentials and thereby potentially compromising organisation security. The suggested mitigation for this vulnerability is for password managers to apply more strict matching criteria that is not merely based on an app's purported package name.

Clipboard Vulnerability: A crucial usability feature of password managers is the ability to autofill credentials on a website. While autofill performs as expected on an overwhelming majority of websites across all the password managers tested, occasionally it would not. When the autofill feature does not work, password managers often provide the option to copy credentials to the clipboard.

It was discovered during the initial testing phase that the tested password managers do not provide enough protection surrounding copying sensitive items to the clipboard, except 1Password. Standard computer security advice recommends that a user locks their machine as soon as they leave it unattended and if a user was to follow this advice, the risk associated with leaving passwords in the clipboard should be reduced in theory. However, Windows 10 allows access to the clipboard of a locked machine [9]. This allows pasting in the value of the clipboard in cleartext by an adversary that may be a person with physical access to the machine or an application running on the machine. Although the attack will not be aware as to what account this password is associated with, they can try the credentials with a precompiled list of websites for which autofill is known not to work. The suggested mitigation for this issue would be for the password managers to provide an option to clear the clipboard after a set amount of time.

PIN Brute Force Vulnerability: To ease authentication to the Android applications, some password managers allow for a user to set a four digit PIN to access the application. This removes the need for a user to enter a long, complex master password every time they wish to enter their vault.

It was discovered during testing, that the RoboForm and Dashlane Android applications do not correctly implement a persistent counter on the number of times an incorrect PIN can be entered when trying to access the application. It is possible to attempt two PINs consecutively, remove the application from the recent application drawer, then try a further two PINs. Both PINs were four digits long and therefore, have 10,000 combinations. Through extrapolation of manual testing, it is estimated that even a manual random guessing attack is on average expected to find a randomly selected PIN in 2.5 h. If the attacker was to factor in common PINs the results in [2] suggest that the attack time would reduce to approximately 1.5 h, and if the birth date of the victim is known, around 8% of the PINs are expected to be found within the first six guesses. We did not fully automate this attack, but we expect an automated attack to take considerably less time to brute force the PIN.

This attack has the potential to be catastrophic for the victim. A malicious attacker would have full access to the application, providing there is no prompt for the user to re-authenticate using something other than the PIN. Access to the application in both Dashlane and RoboForm enables the user to view, modify, or delete records within the password manager's vault.

The suggested mitigation for this issue is to implement a persistent counter that is not reset when the application is removed from recent applications.

Possible Brute Force via Extension: All password managers tested have web-based extensions that can be used to access the respective vaults. When logging into the application after it has initially been locked, the user only needs to enter their master password.

Our tests suggested that Keeper, Dashlane and 1Password were vulnerable to a UI driven brute force attack when entering the master password. This was because there appear to be no measures in place to halt multiple attempts when logging into the extension. This suggested that it would be possible to mount a dictionary attack against a user's account.

Technically, the attack should be identified and halted by the password manager vendors. When testing, ten incorrect passwords were attempted against accounts with each of the password managers with no indication that a count on the number of incorrect attempts was being kept in any of the five. RoboForm implements a five second time delay after three incorrect passwords and in Last-Pass, there are multiple clicks required between entering successive passwords. These measures slow down a possible attack, but do not prevent it.

Due to ethical reasons, the number of passwords attempted was considerably less than would be required in a dictionary or brute force attack, and it is possible that the vendors implement measures to identify larger number of login attempts. Hence, we regard this as a possible vulnerability requiring further investigation. The standard mitigation would be to lock the a user's account following a number of incorrect login attempts.

Summary: Table 3 shows a summary of the susceptibility of five tested password managers to the discovered vulnerabilities. The reported issues are categorised as an (implemented) attack, two vulnerabilities, and a potential vulnerability.

Table 3. Summary of new vulnerabilities discovered. A ● indicates the application is vulnerable, a ◖ indicates it is partially vulnerable, a ○ indicates it is not vulnerable.

	Password manager				
	Dashlane	LastPass	Keeper	1Password	RoboForm
Attack:					
Phishing	○	●	○	●	○
Vulnerabilities:					
Clipboard	●	●	●	○	●
PIN Brute Force	●	○	○	○	●
Possible vulnerability:					
Extension Brute Force	●	◖	●	●	◖

Discussion on Feasibility and Impact: To further contextualise the discovered attacks and vulnerabilities here, we discuss their feasibility and potential impact. In our analysis, we adopt an approach similar to that of the Common Vulnerability Scoring System (CVSS) industry standard (see www.first.org/cvss) to make it easier to translate our discussions here to CVSS scores if necessary.

The phishing attack discovered and developed here is a highly feasible attack. It does not require any physical or privileged access to the device, but it does require user interaction. As long as a victim is tricked into installing a malicious app it will be able to present itself as a legitimate and rather indistinguishable option on the autofill prompt and have a high chance of success. The impact of the attack is limited to the loss of a single credential at a time, although this may be a highly valuable credential (such as an email password) that could possibly enable access to further accounts. The loss of a single credential enables the attacker to get access to the compromised account, change content, and make content unavailable by changing the credential, so the account is potentially affected on all three aspects of confidentiality, integrity, and availability.

The clipboard vulnerability is limited to an attacker with physical access to the device, however it does not require any privilege. This is an opportunistic attack that requires a specific uncommon user action, i.e. copying credentials to the clipboard. The impact is loss of the credential, hence affecting confidentiality, integrity, and availability for the compromised account.

The PIN brute force vulnerability may also enable an opportunistic attack. It requires physical access to the victim's device. Although it does not require any further privilege of user interaction. The impact of the attack is much more severe than the previous two attacks since a successful attacker gets access to the entire password manager vault and any services whose passwords are managed by the password manager. This means that a successful attacker may freely access and modify the contents and credentials of all the managed accounts and hence it amounts to severe possible loss of confidentiality, integrity, and availability.

Finally, the possible brute force via extension vulnerability would only require network access to the victim's device and no specific privilege or user interaction. However, since a password is being brute forced, the probability of success is typically less than the case where a PIN is targeted. Nevertheless, the low complexity and remote executability of this attack make it a highly feasible attack which if not mitigated can be exploited rather comfortably. The attack also has the potential of a severe impact in the form of loss of the master password that enables the attacker to access all the accounts managed by the password manager. Hence, confidentiality, integrity, and availability may be all severely impacted. Perhaps the only limitation of this attack is that it can be, at least in theory, easily identified through detecting higher than usual frequency of attempts to gain access to the targeted password manager account(s).

5   Responsible Disclosure

In this section we go through our disclosure of the vulnerabilities to the vendors and their responses. We started discovering the vulnerabilities discussed here in 2017. After confirming the persistence of issues and developing and successfully testing our proof-of-concept attack, we started notifying the five vendors in 2018. For more severe vulnerabilities, we emailed the technical team and in some cases were asked to follow up the conversations through dedicated vulnerability reporting programs. For less severe issues, vendors were contacted through support tickets on their website. We continued our disclosure until late 2018 when we notified the vendors of our intention to publish our results in the form of an academic paper after a further public non-disclosure period of six months.

In general we found all the five vendors quite responsive. However, only a few disclosures resulted in a fix to be rolled out. This was due to many of the disclosed issues being classified as low priority. In the following we discuss some of the more notable interactions we had with the vendors.

The phishing vulnerability was disclosed to LastPass via their vulnerability reporting system and to 1Password via email. At LastPass, it was marked as

'External Behaviour > Browser Feature > Autocomplete Enabled' which has a priority of 5 (lowest priority) according the Bugcrowd Vulnerability Rating Taxonomy (https://bugcrowd.com/vulnerability-rating-taxonomy) and therefore was assigned a response of 'Won't Fix'. LastPass had no further comment.

The clipboard vulnerability was communicated to all vendors affected. Dashlane stated that unlike mobile OSs such as Android, Windows does not provide any expiration mechanism for partial removal of data on clipboard and hence the only way to remove data from clipboard would be to delete all data on it. This would make such a solution quite invasive. Keeper responded that clipboard expiration was supported on iOS devices only. RoboForm told us that "if you are using copy/paste actions for inserting some passwords from the RoboForm Editor, you will need to clear the clipboard manually."

The PIN brute force vulnerability was disclosed to the affected vendors including 1Password via their reporting system. 1Password fixed the issue within 11 days of reporting and emphasised that this vulnerability requires access to an unlocked Android device to be exploited. Dashlane told us they will add a persistent counter and later added that "this issue requires access to an unlocked android device to be exploited", implying a low priority.

The extension brute force vulnerability was disclosed to all vendors. 1Password responded that it would be infeasible to guess a user's master credentials.

6   Conclusions

This work has analysed and reported on vulnerabilities in commercial password managers through two distinct avenues: testing previously disclosed vulnerabilities and developing exploits for newly discovered vulnerabilities. Many of the previously reported vulnerabilities have been found to persist in popular password managers. Furthermore, four new vulnerabilities were found through extensive testing and responsibly disclosed to the corresponding vendors. Some were fixed immediately while others were deemed low priority.

In our correspondence with password manager vendors we saw both positive and negative sides to how they deal with vulnerability disclosure. On the positive side, vendors appear to be quite responsive and issues deemed high priority or easily rectifiable are fixed promptly. On the negative side, issues assessed as low priority appear to be considered non-issues and rather too easily dismissed.

We acknowledge that some issues, e.g. the clipboard vulnerability, do not have an easy fix and vendors faced with a choice between leaving a low priority issue and applying a fix that has side effects may choose the former.

A possible future direction would be developing rigorous security models and canonical security tests for password managers. The newly discovered vulnerabilities is this work were all user interface related vulnerabilities, as in they were discovered by testing the applications under typical operation scenarios. Such functionality tests along with further analyses focusing on architecture and processes may serve as a basis for standard tests.

A   Full List of Password Managers and Features

The 19 password managers we considered are (alphabetically): 1Password, Dashlane, EnPass, KeePass, Keeper, LastPass, LogMeOnce, mSecure, Password Boss, Password Manager Pro, Password Safe, PasswordState, RoboForm, SplashID, Sticky Password, TeamPassword Manager, TeamsID, TrueKey, and Zoho Vault.

The 27 features considered are as follows (in no specific order): Mobile Applications, Extension Support, Bookmarklet, AutoFill, Form Fill, Password Capture (automatically saving entered passwords), Password Generation (generating new strong passwords), Multi Device Sync, Biometric Authentication, AES-256 Encryption, Vault Backup/Export Functionality, Password Sharing (with other users), Two Factor Authentication, Store data types other than passwords, Automatic Password Changes (e.g. on a regular basis), Portable App, Security Breach Alerts, Password Change Listener, Commercial Offering (for organisations), Admin Console (for organisation admins), Active Directory Integration, Reports and Auditing, Personal and Business Password segmentation (on the same app), Group Password Sharing, Manage User Account and Roles (for organisation admins), Custom Password Policies, and API Provision.

References

1. Blanchou, M., Youn, P.: Password managers: exposing passwords everywhere. White paper, iSEC Partners (2013)
2. Bonneau, J., Preibusch, S., Anderson, R.: A birthday present every eleven wallets? The security of customer-chosen banking PINs. In: Keromytis, A.D. (ed.) FC 2012. LNCS, vol. 7397, pp. 25–40. Springer, Heidelberg (2012). https://doi.org/10.1007/978-3-642-32946-3_3
3. Gasti, P., Rasmussen, K.B.: On the security of password manager database formats. In: Foresti, S., Yung, M., Martinelli, F. (eds.) ESORICS 2012. LNCS, vol. 7459, pp. 770–787. Springer, Heidelberg (2012). https://doi.org/10.1007/978-3-642-33167-1_44
4. Gentili, P., Shader, S., Yip, R., Zeng, B.: Security analysis of Dashlane (2016). https://courses.csail.mit.edu/6.857/2016/files/25.pdf
5. Gonzalez, R., Chen, E.Y., Jackson, C.: Automated password extraction attack on modern password managers. ArXiv e-print arXiv:1309.1416 (2013)
6. Herley, C., Van Oorschot, P.: A research agenda acknowledging the persistence of passwords. IEEE Secur. Priv. 10(1), 28–36 (2011)
7. Karlsson, M.: How I made LastPass give me all your passwords, July 2016. https://labs.detectify.com/2016/07/27
8. Li, Z., He, W., Akhawe, D., Song, D.: The emperor's new password manager: security analysis of web-based password managers. In: 23rd USENIX Security Symposium, San Diego, CA, pp. 465–479 (2014)
9. Moe, O.: Accessing clipboard from the lock screen in Windows 10, January 2017. https://msitpros.com/?p=3746
10. Oberheide, J., Miller, C.: Dissecting the Android bouncer. In: SummerCon2012, New York 95, 110 (2012)
11. Silver, D., Jana, S., Boneh, D., Chen, E.Y., Jackson, C.: Password managers: attacks and defenses. In: Usenix Security, pp. 449–464 (2014)

12. Vigo, M.: Design flaws in Lastpass 2FA implementation (2017). www.martinvigo.com/design-flaws-lastpass-2fa-implementation
13. Emma, W.: What does the NCSC think of password managers? (2017). www.ncsc.gov.uk/blog-post/what-does-ncsc-think-password-managers
14. Zhao, R., Yue, C., Sun, K.: A security analysis of two commercial browser and cloud based password managers. In: SocialCom, vol. 2013, pp. 448–453 (2013)

Evaluation of Risk-Based Re-Authentication Methods

Stephan Wiefling[1,3(✉)] ⓘ, Tanvi Patil[2] ⓘ, Markus Dürmuth[3],
and Luigi Lo Iacono[1] ⓘ

[1] H-BRS University of Applied Sciences, Sankt Augustin, Germany
{stephan.wiefling,luigi.lo_iacono}@h-brs.de
[2] University of North Carolina at Charlotte, Charlotte, NC, USA
tpatil@uncc.edu
[3] Ruhr University Bochum, Bochum, Germany
{stephan.wiefling,markus.duermuth}@rub.de

Abstract. Risk-based Authentication (RBA) is an adaptive security measure that improves the security of password-based authentication by protecting against credential stuffing, password guessing, or phishing attacks. RBA monitors extra features during login and requests for an additional authentication step if the observed feature values deviate from the usual ones in the login history. In state-of-the-art RBA re-authentication deployments, users receive an email with a numerical code in its body, which must be entered on the online service. Although this procedure has a major impact on RBA's time exposure and usability, these aspects were not studied so far. We introduce two RBA re-authentication variants supplementing the de facto standard with a link-based and another code-based approach. Then, we present the results of a between-group study (N = 592) to evaluate these three approaches. Our observations show with significant results that there is potential to speed up the RBA re-authentication process without reducing neither its security properties nor its security perception. The link-based re-authentication via "magic links", however, makes users significantly more anxious than the code-based approaches when perceived for the first time. Our evaluations underline the fact that RBA re-authentication is not a uniform procedure. We summarize our findings and provide recommendations.

Keywords: Risk-based Authentication (RBA) · Re-authentication · Usable security

1 Introduction

Passwords were and continue to be the predominant authentication mechanism of online services [23]. However, threats to password-based authentication are increasing, e.g, by large-scale password database leaks and credential stuffing [26]. Therefore, website operators have to provide additional or alternative

© IFIP International Federation for Information Processing 2020
Published by Springer Nature Switzerland AG 2020
M. Hölbl et al. (Eds.): SEC 2020, IFIP AICT 580, pp. 280–294, 2020.
https://doi.org/10.1007/978-3-030-58201-2_19

authentication mechanisms to adequately protect their users. Two-factor authentication (2FA) is one such measure which is widely used but has proven to be unpopular among users [19]. Biometric authentication is considered impractical for large-scale online services since it requires special hardware and active participation from the user [9]. For these reasons, several large online services deployed risk-based authentication (RBA) to protect their users [27]. RBA is an adaptive authentication measure that provides high security with minimal impact on user interaction, and thus has the potential to be more accepted by users than 2FA. Moreover, RBA is recommended in the NIST digital identity guidelines to mitigate account takeover [12].

During password entry, RBA monitors additional features, e.g., IP address or user agent, and requests for re-authentication when a particular risk is detected [8]. In state-of-the-art deployments, the re-authentication is mostly based on email address verification [27]. Here, the user receives an email with a multi-digit code in the email body that has to be entered on the online service.

Despite its clear presence in RBA deployments, there are, to the best of our knowledge, no studies that evaluate this state-of-the-art re-authentication method. Investigating different devices is important for RBA because push notifications from mobile email apps can make it possible to check emails on mobile devices faster than on desktop devices. Furthermore, using the website on a desktop PC and checking email on a mobile device can slow down the re-authentication process since the code has to be typed in manually. We also discovered that online services using RBA offer different email verification methods for account registration than for RBA re-authentication. When registering an account, the user received either an email with a digit code in the email subject and body, or a verification link. Thus, we wondered why these verification methods are not being used in the RBA re-authentication context so far and whether they have the potential to improve the RBA experience while maintaining the same level of security. To close this gap, we formulated the following research questions.

Research Questions. With these questions, we aim to give answers as to whether the widespread email-based re-authentication method can be improved by other approaches and how all of these methods are perceived by users.

RQ1: a) How does link-based re-authentication affect the authentication time compared to the state-of-the-art with code-based re-authentication?

b) How does showing the authentication code inside the email subject line and body affect the authentication time compared to showing the authentication code only inside the email body?

RQ2: a) Does the re-authentication method (e.g., code or link-based) affect the user behavior?

b) Do the devices used for re-authentication (e.g., desktop or mobile) affect the user behavior?

RQ3: How do users perceive different re-authentication methods?

Contributions. We designed and conducted a between-group study with 592 participants recruited from the online service Mechanical Turk (MTurk) [17] and evaluated the usability and perception of email-based re-authentication methods. Since there is still only one method used in practical deployments, we introduce two alternative RBA re-authentication methods, both of which have not yet been seen in the RBA context: a code-based and a link-based re-authentication scheme. We compared these approaches with the state-of-the-art RBA re-authentication method based on prior findings [27].

Our results show that code-based methods have the potential to significantly speed up the re-authentication process while keeping the security properties at a similar level. We also identify significant differences in the perception of the re-authentication methods and provide recommendations.

Our work helps developers and website owners decide whether they should consider alternative re-authentication methods for RBA in their use case scenarios. Researchers obtain first insights on the perception of different email-based RBA re-authentication methods.

2   Study

To compare different RBA re-authentication methods, we designed a between-group usability study based on a specifically developed website. On this website, the participants registered a user account, providing a username and password as login credentials. After registering, participants were prompted to log in. When submitting the login credentials, the participants were asked for re-authentication through an email associated with the user account. Each participant perceived one of three different re-authentication methods, depending on the three study conditions below:

(i) **State of the Art** (SOTA): The email had a six-digit authentication code in the body, which needed to be entered on the online service.
(ii) **Subject** (SUBJ): The email contained the authentication code in both subject line and body, which had to be entered on the online service.
(iii) **Link** (LINK): The email body contained an URL link, which had to be opened to confirm the authentication.

We chose these re-authentication methods based on state-of-the-art RBA deployments [27] and email based verification methods known from popular online services. For the evaluation, we also subdivided the devices into three combinations, which we found realistic for practical RBA use case scenarios:

(i) **Desktop/Desktop**: The participants used a desktop PC on the website and also checked the email with this device.
(ii) **Desktop/Mobile**: The participants used a desktop PC on the website and checked the email with a mobile device.
(iii) **Mobile/Mobile**: The participants used a mobile device on the website and also checked the email with this device.

We did not test Mobile/Desktop since we considered it to be an unrealistic use case scenario for RBA. We assume that most mobile devices have a pre-installed email app, making it unnecessary for users to check their email on a desktop PC while using a mobile device for the website.

2.1 Design Decisions

The dialogs and email contents for re-authentication differed in each condition. We outline the differences and design criteria in the following (see Fig. 1).

State of the Art (SOTA). In previous work, we measured how RBA is used on popular online services [27]. We analyzed the Alexa Top 50 for RBA properties and extracted the RBA dialogs, if RBA was in use. Based on these observations on state-of-the-art RBA deployments, we designed a generic RBA dialog and confirmation email that we used in the study. We put text characteristics of dialogs and emails into categories and took the characteristics with the highest occurrences into the final dialog and email (see Fig. 1a).

Subject (SUBJ). Authentication codes in the email subject line have been unknown in terms of RBA so far. However, we see potential in improving authentication speed and usability since the code is visible before opening the email, e.g., via push notifications on mobile devices. Codes in both subject line and email body are often used in email verification when registering a new user on a website. Both re-authentication dialog and email body are similar to those presented in SOTA. For the subject line, we collected account registration emails of popular online services that were using authentication codes in both subject line and body. Based on emails of LinkedIn, Facebook, and Slack, we created a generic subject line.

Link (LINK). The link re-authentication method has not been seen in the context of RBA yet. We based this method on similar methods using a link for signing in (*"magic links"*), used by the popular online services Tumblr, Medium,

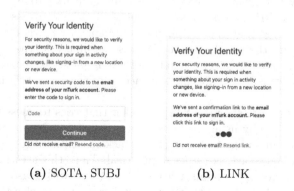

(a) SOTA, SUBJ   (b) LINK

Fig. 1. Presented dialog types for the different study conditions

(a) Confirmation dialog

(b) After confirming the desktop device on a mobile device in the Desktop/Mobile scenario

Fig. 2. Re-authentication dialogs for the access confirmation in the LINK condition

and Slack [3]. We adjusted the workflow for the RBA use case as follows: After entering the correct login credentials, the user received an email containing a link. The link contained a random verification string only known to the online service. We slightly changed the confirmation dialog to match the link confirmation use case (see Fig. 1b). When opening this link, the user was asked to confirm the device for signing in (see Fig. 2a). We based the dialog on Google's Android device confirmation dialog [11]. After the user confirmed the device, this confirmed device was signed in. If the device that confirmed the login differed from the confirmed device, e.g., mobile device in the Desktop/Mobile use case, the user was advised to check the signed in device to proceed (see Fig. 2b). We did the additional confirmation to prevent that link prefetching via GET requests [18] would cause the confirmation to be successful, i.e., we required an additional POST request to confirm the device. We tested this re-authentication method since the lack of entering a code has the potential to improve authentication speed and usability.

2.2   Attacker Models

In order to analyze our re-authentication methods in terms of usability metrics, their security properties have to be comparable with state-of-the-art deployments. Thus, we compare their online guessing security properties with three attacker models derived from known attacks on password-based authentication [8]. We assume that the victim uses different passwords for the targeted online service and the email account. We also assume that the email provider blocks access to accounts after a number of wrong password entries (rate limiting). The attacker does not have physical access or eye contact with the victim's devices.

The **password guesser** is a weak attacker that tries to guess the password of the victim, either by using brute-force or a list of popular passwords. When guessing the victim's password correctly, attackers still need to guess the email password, making the attack rather impractical. Thus, this attacker will not be able to bypass all targeted re-authentication methods with reasonable effort.

The **credential stuffing attacker** is a rather strong attacker that has access to login credentials of the victim. The credentials are sourced from a password database leak of a different online service but are identical to the targeted one. Assuming that the password of the email account is not leaked, this attacker will not be able to bypass all targeted re-authentication methods.

The **phishing attacker** is a very strong attacker that tricks the victim to reveal the correct login credentials. The attacker sets up a website on a phishing domain imitating the appearance of the targeted online service. The degree of imitation varies from simply copying the HTML code of the targeted online service to forwarding the complete traffic between victim and online service (man in the middle, MITM). On success, attackers obtain the victim's login credentials. For MITM, attackers can even forward the entered authentication code to the online service, bypassing the re-authentication. However, attackers cannot bypass email verification links, since the phishing domain is not included in the email verification link. Thus, the link verification is conducted at the real online service. Assuming that the email password is not leaked, a phishing attacker could bypass SOTA and SUBJ but not LINK.

2.3   Study Design

We decided to conduct a two-part between-group study to compare different re-authentication methods of RBA in terms of authentication time and user perception, and to measure the behavior when perceiving this re-authentication on the website for the first time. The study consisted of two parts:

Login. First, the participants registered on the study website with username and password. The website was reachable via HTTPS via an internet domain not linked to our university to mitigate social desirability bias [22]. After registering, the participants tried logging into the website. After submitting the correct login credentials, the website asked for re-authentication, which differed between the three conditions SOTA, SUBJ, and LINK.

Exit Survey. After completing the re-authentication, the participants answered a short survey. The questions were presented in random order to randomly distribute ordering effects [15]. The order of response options were also randomized in each question to randomly distribute response order bias [4,14].

In the survey, the participants stated in a free text answer the device on which they opened the identity verification email on, to determine if the device used for verification is a desktop or a mobile device. They also listed in free text answers three feelings they had when they were asked to verify their identity. This question was inspired by Golla et al. [10]. We used it to discover the user perceptions of the re-authentication. The participants also answered, by ticking checkboxes, which online services they used in the last month. The list of online services included the response option *MTurk* as an attention check to verify the quality of our results [1]. The survey concluded with demographic questions.

2.4   Data Collection

To answer our research questions, we collected the following data: (i) **Timing and event information**: We collected timestamps of when certain events occurred on the website. We used the timestamps to calculate durations for parts of the re-authentication process. In addition, we used the recorded events to analyze the participants' behavior during re-authentication. (ii) **Device information**: We collected the user agent string of the device that the participant used to log in on the website. On the LINK condition, we also collected the user agent string of the device that opened the verification link. We used this information to determine the devices as mobile or desktop devices. We also used this information to verify in the LINK condition if the survey answer regarding the used device was correct. This enabled us to increase the quality of the collected data. (iii) **Survey answers**: We stored the survey responses digitally and analyzed them after the study.

2.5   Data Processing

After collecting the data, we processed the data as follows:

Devices. We subdivided our data set into the three different device combinations Desktop/Desktop, Desktop/Mobile, and Mobile/Mobile. We determined the device used for logging in with the recorded user agent string. Due to the different properties of the code and link-based conditions, we determined the email checking device as follows. For the code based conditions SOTA and SUBJ, we checked the corresponding free text responses given by the participants and classified them into the categories mobile or desktop device. For LINK, we also checked the user agent string of the device that clicked the link.

In the Desktop/Mobile use case, we furthermore analyzed the recorded browser events to verify the given answer of the participant. If the event log showed that the participant copied and pasted the code, which is not possible for all setups except for those using the macOS Universal Clipboard feature, we assumed that the participant gave an invalid response and filtered this response.

Times. We calculated different types of times from the timestamp information. We measured the times to find out whether one of the re-authentication methods is completed faster in parts of the re-authentication process than the other.

(i) **Challenge Completion Time**: We measured the time needed to complete the re-authentication challenge. In the code-based challenges (SOTA and SUBJ), the time was calculated as the timestamp differences between submitting the code and the last focus event before entering the code. We decided to take the last focus event since we needed to consider the delay between understanding the user interface and conducting the code entering action. Also, when opening the link in the LINK condition, the window is focused in that moment as well, making LINK comparable to SOTA and SUBJ. In the Desktop/Mobile case, we took the timestamp differences between submitting the code and the beginning of the code entering. Though we took a different timestamp in this case, we expect the overall time for Desktop/Mobile to be higher than for Desktop/Desktop and Mobile/Mobile anyway since the code has to be entered manually. By doing this, we aimed to ensure comparability between the code and link-based re-authentication methods in any use case scenario. (ii) **Re-Authentication Duration**: We also measured the time needed for the re-authentication in total. We calculated this time as the difference between finishing the re-authentication challenge and loading the identity confirmation dialog for the first time.

Feelings. From the feelings provided in the open ended question, we corrected the grammar, and converted nouns and verbs to adjectives with the WordNet [20] database where applicable. We did this to correct misspellings and differences in tenses. We also clustered the feelings with Emolex [21] into the categories positive, neutral, and negative, to analyze the sentiment towards the perceived re-authentication method. This approach was similar to Golla et al. [10].

2.6   Piloting

We did a pilot study with 10 participants to test and verify our study procedure. After the pilot study, we added additional measurements and slightly changed some dialogs on the website as a result of piloting. Participants involved in the pilot study were excluded from the final study to avoid bias.

2.7   Recruiting

We recruited participants via the crowdworker platform MTurk, which has shown to be applicable for usability studies involving short reactional tasks [17]. We required the participants to be 18 years or older, and have a 95% task approval rate. The study was advertised as a website testing study that is expected to take 10 min. We did not mention that we test authentication schemes to avoid bias. Each participant was compensated with $1.64 after study completion.

Each participant was randomly assigned to one of the three conditions while keeping the group size of each condition as equal as possible.

2.8   Ethical Considerations

We made sure to meet the needs of the MTurk participants (clickworkers) for ethical issues and to improve our data quality. We offered the clickworkers more flexibility by increasing the task time to 24 h since it has shown to both speeding up task completion and improving the result quality [28]. Rejected work on MTurk can result in clickworkers losing qualifications on the platform, affecting their monthly income. Thus, we communicated to the workers that we do not reject any work to make them feel comfortable [13]. We followed the paying recommendations by Hara et al. [13], having in mind that workers are not paid

Table 1. Number of participants in each condition and device use case scenario

Website/Email	SOTA	SUBJ	LINK
Desktop/Desktop	67	67	72
Desktop/Mobile	50	45	48
Mobile/Mobile	30	36	36

between MTurk tasks. In order for the clickworkers to make a living, we set the compensation so high that it is possible for them to earn more than the hourly minimum wage of their home country, i.e., \$7.25/hr in the US. We did not collect any email addresses, as this is against MTurk's acceptable use policy. Instead, the MTurk service sent the emails out to the participants. All participants gave informed consent. All questions offered a "don't know" option.

We do not have a formal IRB process at TH Köln, where we conducted this study, but besides our ethical considerations above, we made sure to minimize potential harm by complying with the ethics code of the German Sociological Association (DGS) as well as the standards of good scientific practice of the German Research Foundation (DFG). We also made sure to comply with the terms of the EU General Data Protection Regulation.

3   Results

The study took place between July and October 2019 and a total of 592 users participated. 499 participants completed the study. From these participants, 48 were excluded from the set for the following reasons: (i) They copied and pasted the authentication code while stating that they used a specific Desktop/Mobile setup in which this is technically not feasible (n = 19). (ii) They failed the attention check (n = 13). (iii) They used a mobile device on the website and checked the email with a desktop PC, which we did not test in our study (n = 11). (iv) We were unable to determine the device based on the participant's free text answer (n = 5). The dropouts were similarly distributed across all conditions.

At the end, we retained 451 participants for the analysis. Table 1 shows how these were distributed among the different conditions and device combinations. The participants completed the study in four minutes on median average.

Our participants were 53.6% female, 45.0% male, and 0.2% non-binary. The age of the participants ranged from 18 to 74. The majority of participants were between 25 and 34 years old (41.9%), while 11.3% were younger and 46.4% were older. The remaining percentages preferred not to answer the corresponding demographical question. The majority of participants had an associate degree or higher (62.8%) and did not have a computer science background (75.4%).

For statistical analysis of the timing data, we used Kruskal-Wallis tests for the omnibus case and Dunn's multiple comparison test with Bonferroni correction for post-hoc analysis. For categorical data, i.e., the feelings and number of login

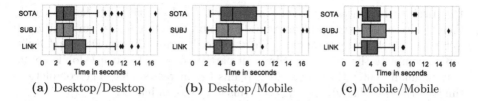

Fig. 3. Challenge completion times for the conditions and device combinations. There are significant differences in Desktop/Desktop and Desktop/Mobile.

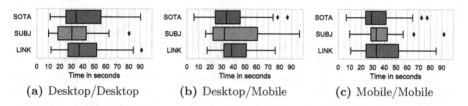

Fig. 4. Re-authentication duration for the conditions and device combinations. The difference between LINK and SUBJ in Desktop/Desktop is significant.

attempts, we used Pearson's chi-square test for contingency table analysis (χ^2). We set 0.05 as the threshold for statistical significance, i.e., $p < 0.05$ is significant. In the following, we outline the results ordered by the research questions given in Sect. 1. A discussion follows after the results of each research question.

3.1   Authentication Times (RQ1)

Challenge Completion Time. The participants completed the re-authentication challenge with median times between three and six seconds (see Fig. 3). There were significant differences in some conditions and device combinations.

For Desktop/Desktop, the challenge completion time for LINK was significantly higher than those for SOTA and SUBJ (LINK/ SOTA: p = 0.0024; LINK/SUBJ: p = 0.0009). For Desktop/Mobile, the challenge completion time for LINK was significantly lower than for SOTA (p = 0.0038). For Mobile/Mobile, there were no significant differences between all three conditions.

Completing the re-authentication challenge took significantly more time on Desktop/Mobile than on Desktop/Desktop for the code-based conditions (SOTA: p<0.0001; SUBJ: p = 0.0002). For SOTA in addition, challenge completion took significantly more time on Desktop/Mobile than on Mobile/Mobile (p = 0.0069).

Concluding the results, link-based authentication challenges were solved faster than the code-based ones when they were not solved on the same device that they used for the login attempt. In the other cases, they were either solved slower (Desktop/Desktop) or with similar speed (Mobile/Mobile). Showing the authentication code inside the email subject did not have a significant effect on the challenge completion time.

Discussion: In contrast to SOTA and SUBJ, LINK participants had to check their device in an extra confirmation dialog and therefore loaded an additional web page, which is why we assume that they needed more time on Desktop/Desktop to complete the challenge. Since all participants on Desktop/Mobile could only manually enter the code, this explains the increased challenge completion time for the code-based challenges on this device combination.

Re-Authentication Duration. In summary for all participants, it took a median of 33.82 seconds to re-authenticate (mean: 71.89s, std: 398.22s). For the Desktop/Desktop combination (see Fig. 4a), the overall re-authentication time for SUBJ was significantly lower than for LINK ($p = 0.0226$). For all the other conditions, we could not find any significant differences.

Concluding the results, showing the authentication code inside the email subject decreased the re-authentication time compared to link-based authentication. However, it did not significantly affect the re-authentication time compared to showing the authentication code only inside the email body. Also, link-based authentication did not significantly affect the authentication time compared to the state-of-the-art code-based authentication.

Discussion: Since there were significant differences, we assume that showing the code in the subject line affected the login duration in total. Opening a link introduces a delay to load the target website. Some email providers also introduce additional delays when clicking on a link, mostly to advise their users that they are redirected to another website. As a result, participants using login links will always experience a constant delay. This explains the significantly longer login duration for LINK. We assume that the faster login duration for SUBJ with Desktop/Desktop combination lies in the fact that the participants saw the authentication code earlier and thus did not have to open the email to receive it. In summary, the email delivery and opening is the biggest factor affecting the login duration. Thus, we suggest that this email based re-authentication should not be asked too often, which is the case with RBA.

3.2   Behavior During Authentication (RQ2)

Most SUBJ and SOTA users and all LINK users passed the re-authentication challenge on the first attempt (SOTA: 95.2%, SUBJ: 98.0%, LINK: 100%). The remaining participants passed the challenge on the second attempt.

The majority of participants in the code-based conditions copied and pasted the code into the code entering form when the device combination allowed it (Desktop/Desktop: 88.1%; Mobile/Mobile: 59.1%). Concluding these results, code-based re-authentication schemes have the tendency to cause users to copy and paste the code when conducted on the same device.

Discussion: We assume that copying and pasting the code was the main reason why the code-based challenges were solved faster than the link-based challenges when solved on the same device. Our results reflect findings of Doerfler et al. [7] regarding a high success rate for email-based re-authentication.

3.3 Perceptions (RQ3)

All participants listed three feelings they had after they were asked to verify their identity. Figure 5 shows the 25 most mentioned feelings ordered by the number of occurrences. The re-authentication methods resulted in mixed emotions. While there was no clear tendency for positive or negative feelings in SOTA and LINK, the top 25 feelings in SUBJ were more negative. The feelings *security* and *annoying* were the most mentioned ones in all three conditions. We discovered significant differences between the three conditions for anxious, nervous and neutral (see Table 2).

The other feelings were mentioned in similar occurrences across all categories. The most mentioned positive feelings were curiosity, happy, safe, calm, and good. For the neutral direction, these were security, concerned, relaxed, substitute, and accept. The most mentioned negative feelings were annoying, confuse, nervous, anxious, and worried.

Discussion: Due to phishing awareness campaigns and trainings, users are trained not to open links in emails [25]. Being asked to click on a link in an email for authentication contradicts the trained behavior, resulting in an insecure feeling. We assume that this explains why participants named the anxious feeling significantly more often in LINK . However, it is possible that this anxious feeling declines when repeating the link-based re-authentication procedure multiple times [29]. There are differences between re-authentication emails and phishing emails that support this assumption. First, the website accessed by the link does not require login credentials. Second, we assume that users expect this re-authentication email to appear in their email inbox shortly.

SUBJ participants did not need to open the email to get the authentication code. SOTA and LINK participants had to open an email whose contents they had never seen before, i.e., the code or link. We assume that this is why SUBJ participants named a nervous feeling less often than those of SOTA and LINK.

4 Limitations

The results are limited to a part of a population of a specific country. We assume that the self-reported answers were typical for participants from the US with college education that are younger than 50 years [24]. Due to the restrictions of

Table 2. Significant χ^2 results for the mentioned feelings in each condition and the percentage of mentions in each condition.

Feeling	χ^2	p	SOTA	SUBJ	LINK
Anxious	7.8053	0.0202	7.5%	6.8%	15.4%
Nervous	6.9677	0.0307	15.6%	6.1%	10.9%
Neutral	6.6667	0.0357	4.1%	0.7%	0.6%

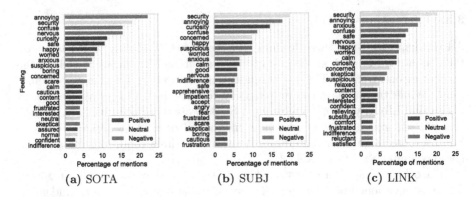

Fig. 5. Feelings the participants had when asked to verify their identity

MTurk, we could only test email address verification for plain text emails. It is possible that HTML emails are perceived differently by participants [16].

Since the participants were only authenticating once, we assume that they expected the re-authentication for every login attempt when reporting the feelings. Following that, we assume that the results were more related to 2FA than for RBA. Since users tend to disable re-authentication when asked too often [5], we assume that the feelings results would be more positive in the real world.

5   Related Work

RBA re-authentication challenges were not evaluated in literature so far. There are related studies evaluating other authentication methods. De Cristofaro et al. [6] compared three 2FA solutions with a study involving MTurk participants. In contrast to our study, their participants were not exposed to RBA solutions. Agarwal et al. [2] evaluated four re-authentication methods for smartphones. Similar to our study, they introduced new re-authentication methods and exposed their participants to them. However, these re-authentication methods were only applicable for mobile apps and thus were not suitable for RBA in general.

Doerfler et al. [7] evaluated the effectiveness of Google's re-authentication challenges by analyzing login attempt data. Their results showed that code-based re-authentication protected against more than 90% of all phishing attempts. Although this shows the effectiveness of RBA against phishing, no usability metrics are examined in their work that study its characteristic and potentials.

6   Conclusion

As long as online services continue to use password-based authentication, RBA is becoming increasingly important as a complementary protection measure. This is further underlined by the fact that RBA is explicitly recommended by NIST [12].

However, there is little scientific research focused on RBA so far. Its development is mainly driven by online services that already use RBA. Since these are popular online services, they have a major impact on the state-of-the-art deployment as can be derived from the single re-authentication method. No scientific evaluation indicates that this is the most appropriate approach to use for implementation.

Our study closes this gap and compares the state-of-the-art email-based RBA re-authentication method with two introduced alternatives regarding their time exposure, security, and user-perceived security. Our results indicate that link-based re-authentication results in higher time requirements and anxiety when perceived for the first time. Code-based re-authentication has proven to be more advantageous in this respect. More specifically, showing the authentication code in the subject line has the potential to reduce re-authentication time with perceptions comparable to the state-of-the-art deployment. Following that, website owners should carefully adjust their RBA re-authentication design to be appropriate for their applications. In general, our research suggests that further research should study RBA more consistently so that all services can benefit from reliable scientific results while hardening password authentication with RBA.

Acknowledgments. This research was supported by NERD.NRW sponsored by the state of North Rhine-Westphalia. The research was also supported by a RISE Germany scholarship granted by the German Academic Exchange Service (DAAD) and sponsored by the German Federal Foreign Office.

References

1. Abbey, J.D., Meloy, M.G.: Attention by design: using attention checks to detect inattentive respondents and improve data quality. JOM **53–56**(1), 63–70 (2017)
2. Agarwal, L., Khan, H., Hengartner, U.: Ask me again but don't annoy me: evaluating re-authentication strategies for smartphones. In: SOUPS 2016 (2016)
3. van Amstel, K.: Should we embrace magic links and leave passwords alone?, January 2018. https://medium.com/@kelvinvanamstel/c73db7007fc4
4. Chan, J.C.: Response-order effects in Likert-type scales. Educ. Psychol. Measur. **51**(3), 531–540 (1991)
5. Crawford, H., Renaud, K.: Understanding user perceptions of transparent authentication on a mobile device. J. Trust Manag. **1**(1), 1–28 (2014). https://doi.org/10.1186/2196-064X-1-7
6. De Cristofaro, E., Du, H., Freudiger, J., Norcie, G.: A comparative usability study of two-factor authentication. In: USEC 2014, February 2014
7. Doerfler, P., et al.: Evaluating login challenges as a defense against account takeover. In: WWW 2019 (2019)
8. Freeman, D., Jain, S., Dürmuth, M., Biggio, B., Giacinto, G.: Who are you? A statistical approach to measuring user authenticity. In: NDSS 2016, February 2016
9. Gaddam, A.: Usage of behavioral biometric technologies to defend against bots. In: Enigma 2019, January 2019
10. Golla, M., et al.: "What was that site doing with my Facebook password?": designing password-reuse notifications. In: CCS 2018 (2018)
11. Google: Sign in faster with 2-Step Verification phone prompts, October 2019. https://support.google.com/accounts/answer/7026266

12. Grassi, P.A., et al.: Digital identity guidelines. Technical report NIST SP 800–63b (2017)
13. Hara, K., et al.: A data-driven analysis of workers' earnings on Amazon mechanical turk. In: CHI 2018 (2018)
14. Hartley, J.: Some thoughts on Likert-type scales. Int. J. Clin. Health Psychol. **14**(1), 83–86 (2014)
15. Kalton, G., Schuman, H.: The effect of the question on survey responses. J. Roy. Stat. Soc. Ser. A (Gen.) **145**(1), 42 (1982)
16. Karakasiliotis, A., Furnell, S.M., Papadaki, M.: Assessing end-user awareness of social engineering and phishing. In: AIWSC 2006 (2006)
17. Kelley, P.G.: Conducting usable privacy & security studies with Amazon's mechanical turk. In: SOUPS 2010, July 2010
18. Komoroske, A.: Prerendering in Chrome, June 2011. https://blog.chromium.org/2011/06/prerendering-in-chrome.html
19. Milka, G.: Anatomy of account takeover. In: Enigma 2018, January 2018
20. Miller, G.A.: WordNet. Commun. ACM **38**(11), 39–41 (1995)
21. Mohammad, S.M., Turney, P.D.: Crowdsourcing a word-emotion association lexicon. Computat. Intell. **29**(3), 436–465 (2013)
22. Nederhof, A.J.: Methods of coping with social desirability bias: a review. Eur. J. Soc. Psychol. **15**(3), 263–280 (1985)
23. Quermann, N., Harbach, M., Dürmuth, M.: The state of user authentication in the wild. In: WAY 2018, August 2018
24. Redmiles, E.M., Kross, S., Mazurek, M.L.: How well do my results generalize? In: SP 2019, May 2019
25. Sheng, S., et al.: Who falls for phish?: a demographic analysis of phishing susceptibility and effectiveness of interventions. In: CHI 2010 (2010)
26. Thomas, K., et al.: Protecting accounts from credential stuffing with password breach alerting. In: USENIX Security 2019, August 2019
27. Wiefling, S., Lo Iacono, L., Dürmuth, M.: Is this really you? An empirical study on risk-based authentication applied in the wild. In: Dhillon, G., Karlsson, F., Hedström, K., Zúquete, A. (eds.) SEC 2019. IAICT, vol. 562, pp. 134–148. Springer, Cham (2019). https://doi.org/10.1007/978-3-030-22312-0_10
28. Yin, M., Suri, S., Gray, M.L.: Running out of time: the impact and value of flexibility in on-demand crowdwork. In: CHI 2018 (2018)
29. Zajonc, R.B.: Attitudinal effects of mere exposure. JPSP **9**(2, Pt.2), 1–27 (1968)

Fuzzy Vault for Behavioral Authentication System

Md Morshedul Islam[(✉)] and Reihaneh Safavi-Naini

University of Calgary, Calgary, Canada
{mdmorshedul.islam,rei}@ucalgary.ca

Abstract. A fuzzy vault encrypts a message using fuzzy data such as user's biometric data as the vault key. Fuzzy vault can be used to protect users' cryptographic keys in smart cards and inside applications. We consider fuzzy vault based on behavioral data. A behavioral profile of a user consists of a set of features that collectively authenticates the user. Compared to biometric vault behavioral vault has the advantages of being revocable and less privacy sensitive. Fuzzy vaults for behavioral data, however, introduces significant challenges including feature representation, and feature matching algorithms that can provide the required correctness, security, and efficiency. We design and analyze a fuzzy vault based on the user's behavioral data that employs a novel soft-decision decoding algorithm and implement our design for two behavioral authentication (BA) systems. Our approach is general and can be used for other BA systems. We discuss our results and directions for future research.

Keywords: Fuzzy vault · BA system · BAVault

1 Introduction

Fuzzy vault was proposed by Juels and Sudan [12] to encrypt (*lock*) a sensitive value into a cryptographic *vault* such that unlocking needs a decryption key that is "close" to the encryption key. In a fuzzy vault, the sensitive data (e.g., a cryptographic key) defines a polynomial $f(x)$ of degree k over a finite field $\mathbb{F}_q$, that will be evaluated for each element of a "locking" set $A \subset \mathbb{F}_q$, to form a set of "legitimate points", $L = \{a_i, f(a_i) : a_i \in A\}$. The set L is then combined with a set Ch of *chaff points* that are randomly selected from $\mathbb{F}_q^2$ and used to hide the elements of L in the vault (ciphertext) $V = L \cup Ch$. The vault can be "opened" (and the sensitive message recovered) by using an unlocking set B, where B has a large overlap with A. Biometric-based fuzzy vault uses a user's biometric features for the locking and unlocking sets. Fuzzy vaults have been implemented using fingerprint, iris, and face data [6,14,15,17,21], and for higher security, using multimodal biometric systems [13]. Fuzzy vaults have been used for biometric-based protection of cryptographic keys in smart cards [6] and online authentication systems [24]. In these applications, the secret key is stored in the

© IFIP International Federation for Information Processing 2020
Published by Springer Nature Switzerland AG 2020
M. Hölbl et al. (Eds.): SEC 2020, IFIP AICT 580, pp. 295–310, 2020.
https://doi.org/10.1007/978-3-030-58201-2_20

fuzzy vault and becomes available to the system when the user presents their correct biometric. Fuzzy vault provides an attractive solution for the protection of keys in mobile apps and electronic wallets.

Juels et al. proved that recovering the correct polynomial without knowing the set A, has exponential computation in the number of chaff points. Biometric implementations of fuzzy vault, however, introduce new attacks due to imperfect selection of chaff points, and for the attacks on the underlying authentication systems. Protection against these attacks together with providing efficiency has been widely studied [6,21,22]. Using biometric-based fuzzy vaults in multiple applications introduces a new threat: if multiple vaults of the same user are leaked, the user biometric data will be compromised [19]. This will allow all the previous vaults to be opened, and also the future usage of the fuzzy vault for that user becomes insecure. So, it is important to make the bio-data of the user changeable (*revocable*). We achieved this goal by using behavioral data and referred to such vaults as BAVault. A Behavioral Authentication (BA) system [3, 8,10] constructs a profile for the users by identifying and capturing a number of behavioral features during well-designed activities. A behavioral profile consists of a set of d features, each represented by a set of n samples, forming a $n \times d$ matrix. A BAVault will use a user's profile to lock a secret, and its *unlocking algorithm* will "match" the profile of a verification claim to unlock the vault.

Advantages of BAVaults compared to biomteric based systems are less linkability of behavioral data, revocability by replacing the underlying BA system with a similar system, and no requirement for additional hardware.

Challenges of Implementing a BAVault. The main challenge of BAVaults is the high dimensionality of feature data that results in inefficient implementations. In a BA system, a feature consists of n sample vectors and direct mapping of a behavioral feature to a finite field results in a high degree extension field (e.g. in DAC[10] a sample feature vector has dimension 40–120). Generating (chaff points), locking and unlocking over a field of this size result in an extremely inefficient system (see Section 4).

Our Work. In BA systems, a feature corresponds to a probability distribution. We represent a feature with its first and the second moments (mean and variance). We use the samples in the profile and the verification claim to construct estimates of these moments. The task of feature matching is to decide if the two pairs of estimates correspond to the same underlying distribution. This allows us to represent a feature as a tuple of two elements of $\mathbb{F}_q$, and will result in a vault that is as efficient as a fingerprint vault (i.e. using a field extension of degree 2 or 3) [6,17,21]. It, however, requires a well-designed decoding approach to reduce the error in matching. A major challenge in using this compact representation is generating chaff points. In a BAVault, a feature is mapped to a point $(a_i, f(a_i))$, where a_i is obtained from the mean and variance of the feature. A chaff point is of the form $(a_i, \bar{a}_i)$ where a_i represents the mean and variance of a hypothetical distribution, and $\bar{a}_i \neq f(a_i)$. The value of a_i in chaff point must be chosen such that its corresponding distribution will be distinguishable for the distributions of all features using the chosen statistical tests. Additionally, the set of chaff points should not "separable" from the set of vault points $(a_i, f(a_i))$ which correspond to true features.

Figures 1a and 1b are the block diagrams of the proposed locking and unlocking algorithms of the BAVault, respectively. The algorithms follow the structure of biometric vault (e.g., Fig. 2 in [21]), with the new components indicated with dashed lines. In a BAVault, the secret message is first encoded using Cyclic Redundancy Check (CRC) and used to define a polynomial $f(x)$. The features are preprocessed using a *random projection (RP)* algorithm that transforms the feature set into a smaller set of features, each a random linear combination of the original features. Each projected feature is then represented by a pair $a_i = (\mu_i, \sigma_i^2)$ of the mean and variance of the transformed feature which will be used as the evaluation points for $f(x)$. A *chaff point* $(a_i, \bar{a}_i)$ is generated through a multi-step process such that a_i corresponds to a hypothetical distribution with mean and variance (μ, σ^2), which is not "close" to real feature where closeness is measured by using statistical tests for mean (tTest [16]) and variance (fTest [9]). The *unlocking algorithm* is a novel *soft-decision decoding* algorithm (details is in Sect. 4).

We evaluate the security of the vault in protecting, (i) the secret message, and (ii) the privacy of the profile. We consider the following attacks that have been used to evaluate the security of biometric vault systems: (i) *chaff point recovery attack* that uses uneven distribution of vault points in the vault space allowing the attacker to infer the correct feature points, (ii) using multiple vaults with the same user profile that allows the attacker to recover the true features by comparing the set of vault points, and (iii) impersonation through mimicry attack against the underlying BA system.

BAVault Implementation and Experiments. We implemented and evaluated our design on two BA systems. The first system is *Touchalytics* [8] that uses touch behavior such as up-down and left-right scrolling to verify the user's identity. The second system, *DAC (Draw A Circle)* [10], is a challenge and response system that verifies the users' identity using their behavior in drawing challenge circles. We designed a feature-based verification algorithm and tuned the parameters to ensure a lower error rate. The collected data was also used to implement and evaluate the BAVault. We used the published data for Touchalytics, and collected new data for the redesigned DAC. Through extensive experiments, we show that (i) both BAVaults have acceptable error rate; (ii) a random invalid claim can recover a very small number of legitimate points, while a mimicry attack can recover more feature points. However, in both cases, the recovered features are not sufficient to unlock the vault. We also show that RP prevents the multi-vault attack, and ensures that in a compromised vault user's profile will not be leaked. We estimate the number of polynomials that a brute force attacker must check to achieve success. The secret message sizes in Touchalytics and DAC based *BAVault* are 192–208 bits and 448–480 bits, respectively.

Ethics Approval. We obtained ethics approval from the Research Ethics Board of our institution and performed our experiments in accordance with ethics guidelines governing user personal data privacy and security.

Paper Organization. Section 2 is background and related works. Section 3 defines BAVault and Sect. 4 gives the design of our BAVault. Section 5 is implementation and experimental results and Sect. 6 concludes the paper.

2   Preliminaries and Related Works

We recall definitions and results that are used in the remainder of the paper.

BA System. A BA system constructs a *behavioral profile* for a user, which consists of a set of features measurements, and uses it to verify verification request, a second set of measurements of the features. A BA profile $\mathbf{X} = (F_1, F_2, \cdots, F_d)$ consists of d features, and can also be represented by a set $\{\mathbf{x_i}, i = 1, \cdots, n\}$ of n vectors of dimension d over $\mathbb{R}^d$. The set $\{x_{i,j}, i = 1, \cdots, n\}$ grips n samples of a feature F_j, represents intrinsic behavioral characteristics of a user.

Matching Algorithm. A matching algorithm $M(\mathbf{X}, \mathbf{Y})$ compares *verification data* $\mathbf{Y}$ with the stored profile $\mathbf{X}$ of the claimed user u, and returns 1 (accept), or 0 (reject). *Feature-based matching algorithms* [3,10] compare each feature in the profile against the corresponding feature in the claim, and produces a matching score that will be compared against a predefined threshold to accept or reject the claim. A BA system has (δ_1, δ_2)-*correctness*, if it satisfies $Pr[M(\mathbf{X}, \mathbf{Y}) = 0 \mid u = v] \leq \delta_1 \, \& \, Pr[M(\mathbf{X}, \mathbf{Y}) = 1 \mid u \neq v] \leq \delta_2$. False Acceptance Rate (FAR) and False Rejection Rate (FRR) are used to estimate the value of δ_1 and δ_2, respectively. One can combine two parameters into a single one, δ_E Equal Error Rate (EER), where FAR and FRR are equal. BA systems may use *vector-based* matching algorithm [8] too. For the BAVault, we need to use feature-based matching.

Attacks on BA Systems. Attacks on BA systems aim to fool the matching algorithm to accept the verification data of an invalid user. In a *mimicry attack* [25] the attacker attempts to mimic a user u by learning and mimicking u's behavior. An impersonation attack may use mimicry to claim a victim's identity. The success of this attack depends on the design of the BA system and the choice of features. We do not consider network-based attacks where the attacker eavesdrops communication of the valid user and uses their data as the verification data in an attacked session. Such attacks can be prevented by securing the communication channel using protocols such as Transport Layer Security (TLS) [18].

Random Projection (RP). RP is a distance preserving transformation that projects vectors in a high-dimensional space to a lower-dimensional space using a random projection matrix. The projection matrix $\mathbf{R}^{t \times d}, t < d$, projects a vector $\mathbf{x} \in \mathbb{R}^d$ to a vector $\mathbf{x}' = \mathbf{Rx}, \mathbf{x}' \in \mathbb{R}^t$, and (approximately) preserves the relative Euclidean distances between the vectors in the projected space. Elements of $\mathbf{R}$ are sampled from a standard normal distribution $N(0, 1)$ (see Lemma 1.3 of [23]). For faster computation we use discretized form of $N(0, 1)$ given by $Pr(x = +1) = \frac{1}{2\phi}, \, Pr(x = +0) = 1 - \frac{1}{\phi}, \, Pr(x = -1) = \frac{1}{2\phi}$. Distance preserving property of the resulting RP is shown in [1] for $\phi = 3$. It was shown in [20] that applying RP in the BA system will maintain correctness property of the system, and will also provide privacy for the profile.

Definition 1 (Fuzzy Vault [12]). *A fuzzy vault* V_A *is specified by a 4-tuple of parameters* $(\mathbb{F}_q, r, t, k)$ *and works as follows.*

1. *To encrypt a uniformly random secret message* $m = (m_0 \cdots m_k) \in \mathbb{F}_q^{k+1}$, *a polynomial* $f(x)$ *of degree* k *is constructed:* $f(x) = \sum_{i=0}^{k} m_i x^i$.
2. *The polynomial is then evaluated on a set of points* $A = \{a_i \in \mathbb{F}_q : i = 1, \cdots, t\}$, *called the* locking set. *The set* $L = \{(a_i, f(a_i)) \in \mathbb{F}_q^2 : i = 1, \cdots, t\}$ *forms the set of* legitimate points *in the vault.*
3. *To hide* L, *a random set of* $r - t$ *chaff points* $Ch = \{(a_i, \bar{a}_i) \in \mathbb{F}_q^2 : i = 1, .., r - t\}$ *are selected with the property that* $\bar{a}_i \neq f(a_i)$, *to get spurious polynomials.*
4. *The fuzzy vault is obtained by permuting the elements of* $V_A = L \cup Ch$, *and is published together with the parameters* $(\mathbb{F}_q, r, t, k)$.
5. *To unlock* V_A *(decrypt the secret) using an* unlocking set B, *a decoding algorithm is used to find the best estimate of the legitimate points, which will be used to recover the message.*

The output of the decoding algorithm may contain legitimate and chaff points. To recover m, one can use Reed-Solomon (RS) decoder to correct the errors in the recovered set [12], or append a CRC to the secret message and use the pair $(m, CRC(m))$ in $f(x)$. The CRC will be used to identify the correct polynomial [17,21,22]. We will use this latter method that results in better error recovery.

Attacks on Fuzzy Vaults. Attacks can be grouped into, (i) algebraic attacks, and (ii) implementation attacks. In an algebraic attack, also called brute force attack, an attacker examines all candidate polynomials to find $f(x)$. In implementation attacks, the weaknesses of the vault implementation are used to recover the secret message. Lemma 1 of [6] gives the relation between the success probability of brute force attack and the number of spurious polynomials that the attacker must examine in biometric fuzzy vaults. In CRC-based biometric fuzzy vault, a brute force attacker must check on average $\binom{r}{k+1}\binom{t}{k+1}^{-1}$ polynomials [6]. Chang et al. [5] showed how to distinguish chaff points if they are not evenly distributed in vault space. Scheirer et al. [19] considered a number of attack scenarios including multiple vaults attack where the attacker knows multiple vaults (different m) with the same user biometric. This will allow the attacker to relate the data from different vaults to recover the secret. They also considered the loss of biometric privacy if the attacker learns the secret of a published vault.

3   BAVault

A BAVault uses a (δ_1, δ_2)-correct BA system (see Sect. 2) and profile data X of the BA system to lock the vault. The BAVault will open only by using the verification data Y of the BA system of the same user. The feature-based matching algorithm of the BA system employs a similarity function Sim $(.,.)$ to decide if two sets of samples have the same underlying distribution and output a confidence value $p_{i,j}$. A larger $p_{i,j}$ corresponds to higher confidence about the "sameness" of the distributions of the two sets. BAVault uses Sim $(.,.)$ function to measure the similarity of elements of B and V_A.

Definition 2. *A BAVault is defined by the tuple* $(\mathbb{F}_q, r, t, k, aux)$, *where the first four parameters are the same as Definition 1, and aux is the auxiliary data that can be provided with the vault. BAVault has a pair of algorithms* (VLOCK, VUNLOCK) *to lock and unlock the vault.*

1. *VLOCK works the same as Steps 1–4 in Definition 1 using the profile data* $\mathbf{X}$. *Locking algorithm uses the feature set of* $\mathbf{X}$ *to construct the* legitimate point set *for the secret value* $m \in \mathbb{F}_q^{k+1}$. *We use A, L, and Ch to denote the locking set, sets of legitimate points and chaff points, respectively. Points in Ch must each, (i) have a minimum "distance" from any legitimate point (to remain distinguishable by the BA matching algorithm), and (ii) should not satisfy the polynomial* $f(x)$.
2. *VUNLOCK has a* soft-decision *decoding algorithm* CGen *which uses the* Sim $(.,.)$ *function of the BA system to construct a* $r \times t$ *confidence matrix* $[p_{i,j}]$, *that will be used to recover the* $f(x)$.

(Δ_1, Δ_2)**-correctness:** Consider a (δ_1, δ_2)-BA system that uses a feature matching function Sim $(.,.)$, a matching algorithm $M(.,.)$. Let $\mathbf{X}$ and $\mathbf{Y}$ be two BA profiles (or claims). For a uniformly distributed secret m, a BAVault $V_A \leftarrow$ VLOCK$(\mathbf{X}, m)$ is (Δ_1, Δ_2)-correct if the conditions: (i) $Pr[\text{VUNLOCK}(V_A, \mathbf{Y}) \neq m | M(\mathbf{X}, \mathbf{Y}) = 1] \leq \Delta_1$, and (ii) $Pr[\text{VUNLOCK}(V_A, \mathbf{Y}) = m | M(\mathbf{X}, \mathbf{Y}) = 0] \leq \Delta_2$ hold. The correctness property[1] of the BAVault is also referred to as Δ_1-FRR and Δ_2-FAR.

Security. We evaluate the security of a BAVault in (a) protecting the secret m, and (b) ensuring the privacy of X. Following Kirckoff's principle, we assume the details of the vault system is public. For (a) we consider a number of attacks, including when the attacker has access to multiple vaults. To evaluate (b), we assume the attacker knows a vault V_A and its corresponding message m.

Attacker strategies. For (a), that is message recovery, we consider (i) algebraic attacks, and (ii) system (implementation) attacks, including attacks that exploit non-uniform distribution of vault points, attack using multiple vaults of the same user, and using impersonation attack on the BA system. For (b), that is profile privacy, the attacker knows the secret message of a published vault that allows them to find the points in the vault that correspond to true features.

---

[1] We used FAR and FRR to evaluate BAVault correctness.

4   A Secure BAVault

Let the locking and unlocking sets be of the same size, that is $|A| = |B|$. Figure 1a and 1b are the block diagrams of the BAVault locking and unlocking algorithms. They are shown in the Appendix, Algorithm 1 and Algorithm 2.

4.1   Locking

The locking algorithm takes m and $\mathbf{X}$ and does the following.

Message m. The message is appended with a CRC (preprocessing) and is used to construct the polynomial $f(x)$.

Profile Data. The profile $\mathbf{X}$ will be transformed to $\mathbf{X}' = \mathbf{RX}$ by using an RP (preprocessing). Because of the distance-preserving property of RP, the relative distances among profile vectors will be maintained and so the correctness of the feature matching algorithm will not be affected. Assuming that the distribution of the features F_i in the profile are normal[2], the distribution of the projected features F_i' will also be normal. We thus represent F_i' with its mean and variance, $a_i = (\mu_i, \sigma_i^2)$. To map (μ_i, σ_i^2) to an element of $\mathbb{F}_q$ (locking set generation), we write μ_i and σ_i^2 as binary strings, and concatenate them. The number of binary digits for each component is determined by the required correctness parameters (Δ_1, Δ_2), and will determine the finite field size. The set A consists of $\mathbb{F}_q$ values of all transformed features. The mapping of (μ_i, σ_i^2) to an element of $\mathbb{F}_q$ is one-to-one and invertible. The polynomial $f(x)$ is then evaluated on elements of $A = \{a_i\}_{i=1}^{t}$ to form the *legitimate points set* $L = \{(a_i, f(a_i)) \in \mathbb{F}_q^2\}_{i=1}^{t}$.

Generating chaff point needs feature similarity evaluation. A *feature similarity function* $\texttt{Sim}^{MV}(.,.)$ measures the closeness (sameness) of two distributions whose estimated[3] means and variances are $a_i = (\mu_i, \sigma_i^2)$ and $b_j = (\mu_j, \sigma_j^2)$, respectively. The function uses (i) $\texttt{tTest}$- test for the sameness of μ_i and μ_j, and (ii) $\texttt{fTest}$- test for the sameness of σ_i^2 and σ_j^2, to obtain two confidence values $p_{i,j}^m$ and $p_{i,j}^v$, respectively, and combines them by a metadata analyzer $\texttt{FMethod}$ [4] (Fisher's method) to obtain a final confidence value.

Available Chaff Points. Chaff points of the form $(a_i, \bar{a}_i)$ must be chosen such that (i) a_i does not correspond to the parameters of a distribution that is close to the distributions of the true features, and (ii) $\bar{a}_i \neq f(a_i)$. For given ranges R_1, R_2 of mean and variance, each a subinterval of $\mathbb{R}$, we first find D_F the number of distinct variances in R_2 that can be distinguished using $\texttt{fTest}$ test. For this, we start with the lowest value of the variance R_2, σ_0^2, and find smallest σ_1^2 for which $\texttt{Sim}^{MV}(a_0, a_1) = 0$ for a chosen significance value α. That is the variance test will consider σ_1^2 not similar to σ_0^2. We repeat this starting from σ_1^2, and continue until the next σ_i^2 is outside the upper limit of the range R_2. For each found value of σ_i^2, we find $D_{T,i}$, the number of distinguishable means using a similar approach (now using $\texttt{tTest}$) within the range R_1. This gives an estimate of the number of available X-coordinates for chaff points.

---

[2] This is true for features of BA systems that have been used in our experiments.
[3] From the corresponding sample sets.

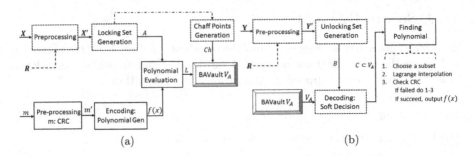

Fig. 1. Block diagram of BAVault (a) locking and, (b) unlocking.

Lemma 1. *The available X-coordinate for chaff points is upper bounded by* $Q_X = \sum_{\sigma_i^2 \in D_F} |D_{T,i}|$.

Generating Chaff Points. To provide even distribution for vault points, we use algorithm ChaffGen (see Algorithm 3 in Appendix) for chaff point generation. It divides $\mathbb{F}_q^2$ into ν^2 subareas and attempts to put almost the same number of vault points in each subarea. The algorithm generates random chaff points $(a_i, \bar{a}_i)$ (that satisfy, a_i distinguishable from all feature values, and $\bar{a}_i \neq f(a_i)$), and place them in ν if they satisfy the bound on corresponding subarea, and reject otherwise. The algorithm first obtains an estimate of the vault size r by taking into account the required security against brute force attack, determines r/ν^2, the number of allowable points in a subarea. It then obtains the number of chaff points in a subarea by subtracting the number of true feature points in a subarea from r/ν^2. To evaluate ChaffGen, we used Kolmogorov-Smirnov (KS) test [11] to estimate the uniformity of vault points, and also the distribution of their X-coordinates. The vault V_A is obtained by permuting the points in each subarea.

4.2 Unlocking

The unlocking algorithm takes a V_A and the verification data $\mathbf{Y}$ of a user as input. It uses the published helper data (aux) to generate $\mathbf{R}$ that is used to transform $\mathbf{Y}$, resulting in the unlocking set B.

Soft Decision Decoding CGen. For an unlocking set B, we find a matching subset of V_A in two steps: (i) a feature matching algorithm FMatch, and (ii) a set matching algorithm SMatch. Feature matching FMatch uses $\text{Sim}^{MV}(.,.)$ to construct an $r \times t$ matrix $\text{ConF} = [P_{i,j}]$ of confidence values, by comparing each element of B against each element of V_A. The set matching algorithm finds a subset of V_A that is the *best match*. We define the best matching subset of the vault points as a subset that maximizes the total confidence value. The set matching SMatch must find a subset of r columns of ConF, and in each column chooses exactly one element, such that no two elements are in the same row. We formulate this as a Linear Assignment Problem (LAP) [2] by augmenting ConF to CônF, a $r \times r$ square matrix with zeros in all new entries. LAP is a fundamental combinatorial optimization problem that minimizes the total cost of assigning agents to tasks when all agent-task pairs are possible but have different costs. There are efficient algorithms for solving the LAP. The output of CGen is a set C (see Algorithm 4 in Appendix).

Theorem 1. *Algorithm* CGen *outputs a set C that has the highest total confidence of matching B, in $O(r^3)$ number of steps.*

The final step is the polynomial reconstruction from C, and uses the CRC of the secret message to recover the correct polynomial.

4.3   Security Analysis

Message recovery by brute force attack needs searching among at least $\frac{\psi}{3} q^{k-t} (r/t)^t$ spurious polynomials for every $\psi > 0$ with probability $1 - \psi$ (see Lemma 1 of [6]) that go through t vault points, or $\binom{r}{k+1}\binom{t}{k+1}^{-1}$ polynomials that go through $k + 1$ vault points. The chaff points generation algorithm will ensure the chaff points are evenly distributed and cannot be distinguished from true feature points.

Multi-vault Attack. Consider two vaults V_A^i and V_A^j for a profile $\mathbf{X}$. Using two different random matrices $\mathbf{R}_i$ and $\mathbf{R}_j$ ensures that the projected profiles $\mathbf{X}_i' = \mathbf{R}_i \mathbf{X}$ and $\mathbf{X}_j' = \mathbf{R}_j \mathbf{X}$ are independent and will not leak any information about $\mathbf{X}$. *Impersonation (mimicry) attack* on the underlying BA system will also break the BAVault. This is similar to the attack on the biometric-based vault. A careful selection of the behavioral features will protect against this attack.

Profile privacy requires profile data to be protected even if the attacker knows the secret message of a vault. Using m and the vault, an attacker will only be able to recover the projected profile $\mathbf{X}'$. However, as shown in [20], recovering $\mathbf{X}$ from $\mathbf{X}'$ using the *minimum-norm* solution to $\mathbf{R}$, which is the best-known estimator of $\mathbf{X}$ from $\mathbf{X}'$, cannot recover the original $\mathbf{X}$.

5   BAVault Implementation

We implemented and evaluated our proposed BAVault using Touchalytics [8] and DAC [10] data.

Touchalytics uses users' touch data (up-down and left-right scrolling) when interacting with an app, and uses a vector-based matching algorithm to achieve an EER of less than 3.0%. The system uses 30 behavioral features and data from 41 users.

DAC uses the behavioral features of users that are collected while drawing random challenge circles that are presented to them, to verify their verification claims. We extended DAC [10] and added a new set of features. This results in 65 features and reduces the EER of DAC from 5.0% to 1.05%.

Experiment Setup. We downloaded and cleaned[4] Touchalytics data before using them. There are 41 profiles and 41 valid verification claims. For DAC, we collected data from 199 Amazon Mechanical Turks (AMT). Suitability of AMT for cognitive behavioral experiments has been confirmed in [7]. After removing outlier data (around 2.66%), we obtained 195 profiles and 891 valid verification claims (each Turk had multiple verification attempts).

To obtain reliable features distributions from the collected data, we combined all user data, shuffled them, and divided them into two halves: the first half was used for vault locking and the second half was used for vault unlocking. Every profile (unlocking claim) has 93–615 vectors of dimension 30 in Touchalytics BAVault, and 40–120 vectors of dimension 65 in DAC BAVault. Against each vault, there were one valid unlock attempt and 5 invalids unlock attempts from 5 randomly chosen users. The locking and unlocking of Touchalytics and DAC based BAVault takes (10.78 and 1.66 seconds) and (26.89 and 3.37 seconds), respectively, on a desktop that uses Intel Core(TM)i5-2400 CPU (3.10 GHz), 8 GB RAM.

Feature Encoding. For RP, the dimension of projected spaces for Touchalytics and DAC are $t = 25$ and $t = 45$, respectively. We generated **R** from the discrete distribution uses in [1] and normalized profile data after RP. To measure distinctiveness and normality of BA features we used $\text{Sim}^{MV}(.,.)$ function, and Chi-square goodness-of-fit test. Touchalytics and DAC profiles had 97.37% and 92.81% distinct features before RP, and 99.82% and 97.73%, after RP, respectively. The normality test results for the two systems before and after RP are 2.32% and 53.4%, and 65.56%, 54.83%, respectively. EER of both BA systems after RP remained almost the same; 1.20% in Touchalytics and 4.66% in DAC.

To encode (μ, σ^2) as an element of $\mathbb{F}_q$, we remove the decimal points of μ_i and σ_i^2, take the three most significant digits of each, and concatenate them. For σ^2 we only consider two digits because the first digit after the decimal place is always zero. In Touchalytics profiles all $a_i \in A$ are in the range [15400, 84600], and in DAC profiles they are in [15000, 80500]. We bring all the data to the range [0,65535] by subtracting the lowest value, and cutting off all the values above 65535[5] and then represented them as a binary string in $\mathbb{F}_{2^{16}}$.

Generate Chaff Points. We estimated Q_X for both BAVaults. The mean and variance range for the features in Touchalytics is between [230.0, 820.0] and $[1.0^2, 52.0^2]$, respectively. For DAC, the corresponding values are [108.0, 875.0] and $[1.0^2, 98.0^2]$, respectively. For $N_i = N_j = 300$ (average samples in a features) in Touchalytics BAVault, D_F allows 24 distinct σ^2, and for each $\sigma_i^2 \in D_F$ the size of all D_T are $1896, 884, \cdots, 42$, respectively. In DAC BAVault for $N_i = N_j = 80$ the set size $|D_F| = 21$ and all $|D_T|$ are $2464, 1039, \cdots, 33$, respectively.

To distribute vault points evenly, we divided the range of both X and Y-axis of both vaults into equal size segments which produce $\nu^2 = 25$ subareas. We

---

[4] We replace 'NaN' and 'Infinity' by zero and dropped the 'doc id', 'phone id', and 'change of finger orientation' columns.

[5] In Touchalytics there are around 3.70% of a_i that are out of the range [0, 65535] and in DAC it is only 0.32%. This rounding slightly affects BAVault correctness.

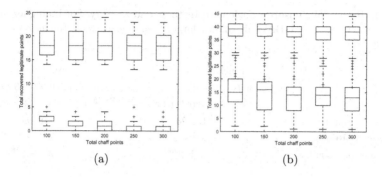

(a)   (b)

Fig. 2. The distribution of recovered legitimate points for both valid and invalid claims for the different number of chaff points. Figure (a) for Touchalytics based BAVault and (b) for DAC based BAVault.

chose $|V|$ =125–325 for Touchalytics and $|V|$ =145–345 for DAC based BAVault. ChaffGen algorithm counts the number of legitimate points in each subarea and added random points to each subarea when possible, taking into account the total vault size $|V|$. The KS-test gives average confidence value for the uniformity of Touchalytics and DAC based BAVault as 0.69 and 0.66, respectively. The average confidence values of KS-test for uniformity of X-components of the two vaults are 0.89 and 0.78, respectively.

Recovering Legitimate Points. The CGen algorithm of the BAVault outputs a set $C \subset V_A$ that has $\hat{t} \leq t$ legitimate points out of t recovered points. The value of $\hat{t}$ depends on the unlocking claim. In our experiments, we added 100–300 chaff points to each vault. This number can be increased at the cost of increased encoding and decoding time. Figure 2 is the recovered legitimate points in a Box-plot for both valid and invalid claims. The valid and invalid claims can recover 15–22 and 0–3 (Touchalytics) and 33–41 and 7–20 (DAC), legitimate points. A valid user may not be able to recover all legitimate points because of the variability of the user's behavior, and an attacker may be able to recover some of the legitimate points of a target vault by using attacker's profile and public data $\mathbf{R}$. The Box-plots show that the gap between the first quartile corresponding to the valid claims and the third quartile corresponding to the invalid claims is large and both BAVaults work correctly. The gap increases with the number of chaff points.

BAVault Correctness and Security. Table 1 summarizes correctness and security of the two BAVaults. The values are inline with existing fuzzy vault systems. The degree of the polynomials in Touchalytics and DAC based BAVaults are 12–13, and 28–30 respectively, resulting in FAR and FRR to be 0.0% and 2.43%, and 2.56% and 4.65%, respectively. The secret sizes in the two cases are 192–208 bits, and 448–480 bits, respectively. For a valid polynomial that goes through t or $k + 1$ valid vault points, the brute force attacker will

Table 1. Both vaults ensure sufficient correctness and security. For its higher number of features, DAC based BAVault allows larger secret size than Touchalytics based BAVault.

	Touchalytics		DAC	
FAR	degree of $f(x)$:	0.0%	degree of $f(x)$:	0.0%-2.56%
FRR	$k = 12\text{-}13$	0.0%-2.43%	$k = 28\text{-}30$	3.89%-4.65%
Size of m (bits)		192-208		448-480
$f_{cand}(x)$(CRC)		$2^{54} - 2^{58}$		$2^{101} - 2^{110}$
Spurious polynomials		$2^{20}\text{-}2^{26}$		$2^{41} - 2^{56}$

need to check 2^{20}-2^{26} and 2^{41}-2^{56} spurious polynomials, or 2^{54}-2^{58} and 2^{101}-2^{110} candidate polynomials in both BAVaults, respectively.

Multi-vault security. Two vaults of a user will have two different vault point sets. To investigate possible residual relation between the two vaults that share true features, we used a modification of CGen algorithm which takes V_A^i and V_A^j and matches each X-element of the first set against all X-elements of the second set, and returns a subset C that has the highest total confidence value. This recovers only 3.0% and 7.0% legitimate points in Touchalytics and DAC based BAVault, respectively.

Protection Against Impersonation Attack. We considered a pair of profiles $\mathbf{X}_i$ and $\mathbf{X}_j$, that have 5.0%–16.0% overlapping features (e.g. from a mimicry attack). We then used $\mathbf{X}_i$ to construct a BAVaultand used $\mathbf{X}_j$ to recover the legitimate points from the vault. This can recover around 2.0%–9.0% more legitimate points compared to an invalid claim. This is, however, not sufficient to open the vault.

6   Concluding Remarks

BAVault offers significant advantages over biometric-based fuzzy vaults. We outlined challenges of implementing an efficient and secure BAVault, proposed a design that addresses these challenges, and validated our design analytically and experimentally. Our work can be extended to use higher-order statistics for representing features. Another direction is to employ *ranked assignment problem* to use the top t highest ranking sets to improve reliability.

A   Appendix

Algorithm 1: $V_A \leftarrow$ **VLock**$(\mathbf{X}, m)$

1: *Construct a polynomial.* For a secret message m, appends CRC to m to obtain $m' = [m_0, m_1, \cdots, m_k] \in \mathbb{F}_q^{k+1}$; define $f(x) = \sum_{i=0}^{k} m_i x^i$.

2: *Profile projection.* Use RP to transform $\mathbf{X} \in \mathbb{R}^{n \times d}$ to $\mathbf{X}' \in \mathbb{R}^{n \times t}$ $(t \leq d)$. The random seed that is used to generate $\mathbf{R}$ is the *helper data (aux)*.

3: *Locking set generation.* Each feature $F_i' \subset \mathbf{X}'$ will be represented by its *mean* and *variance*, (μ_i, σ_i^2), and encoded to $a_i \in \mathbb{F}_q$ to form a set $A = \{a_i\}_{i=1}^{t}$.

4: *Polynomial evaluation.* The polynomial $f(x)$ is evaluated on the elements of A to obtain the set of legitimate points $L = \{(a_i, f(a_i)) \in \mathbb{F}_q^2\}_{i=1}^{t}$.

5: *Chaff point generation.* Generate $Ch = \{(a_i, \bar{a}_i) \in \mathbb{F}_q^2, i = 1, \cdots, r - t, \bar{a}_i \neq f(a_i)\}$ by using **ChaffGen** algorithm, taking into account t points in L, and polynomial $f(x)$. Chaff points must satisfy the required properties.

6: *The vault.* Permute the elements of $V_A = L \cup Ch$ to obtain V_A.

Algorithm 2: $\{m, \perp\} \leftarrow$ **VUNLOCK**$(V_A, \mathbf{Y})$

1: *Claim projection.* The claim $\mathbf{Y}$ will be transformed to $\mathbf{Y}'$, using $\mathbf{R}$ that can be reconstructed using aux.

2: *Unlocking set generation.* Each sample set $F_j' \in \mathbf{Y}'$ will be summarized to a pair $b_j = (\mu_j, \sigma_j^2) \in \mathbb{R}^2$; the set of t pairs will form the set $B = \{b_j\}_{j=1}^{t}$.

3: *Recovering the legitimate points.* The soft-decision decoding algorithm **CGen** recovers the legitimate points from V_A. The algorithm **CGen**(V_A, B) has two steps: Step 1: **FMatch** uses $\text{Sim}^{\text{MV}}(.,.)$ for each pair of elements of B and V_A; Step 2: **SMatch** uses an optimization algorithm to find the "best" matching subset $C \subset V_A$.

4: *Recover the secret.* A candidate polynomial $f_{cand}(x) = \sum_{i=0}^{k} m_i^* x^i$ of degree k is constructed from $k + 1$ points of C. If the coefficients of $f_{cand}(x)$ do not satisfy the CRC, $f_{cand}(x)$ is rejected, and a new set is chosen. The process will be repeated until m is found, or $\perp$ is outputted, indicating no polynomial was found.

Algorithm 3: $V_A \leftarrow$ ChaffGen($\mathbb{F}_q, L, r$)

INPUT/OUTPUT:
 $\mathbb{F}_q^2$: Vault space
 L: Legitimate points set
 r: Total vault points
 V_A: A set of r points.

1: Divide $\mathbb{F}_q^2$ in ν^2 subareas
2: $|\nu_{max}| = \lceil \frac{r}{\nu^2} \rceil$
      ▷ max allowable-points in a subarea
3: **for each** ν_i **do**
4:     $|\nu_i| \leftarrow$ number of $(a_i, f(a_i)) \in L$
5:     **if** $|\nu_i| < |\nu_{max}|$ **then**
6:         $w(\nu_i) = [\frac{1}{\nu^2}(1 - \frac{|\nu_i|}{|\nu_{max}|})]$
              ▷ calculate the weight
7:     **else**
8:         $w(\nu_i) = 0$
9:     **end if**
10: **end for**

11: **for each** $k \leq r - |L|$ **do**
                        ▷ for each chaff point
12:     pick a ν_i based on $w(\nu_i)$
13:     choose a_i for ν_i from X-axis of V_A
            where $\forall b_j \in V_A$, $\text{Sim}^{MV}(a_i, b_j) = 0$
            ▷ X-component of the chaff point
14:     choose $\bar{a}_i$ for ν_i from Y-axis of V_A
            where $\bar{a}_i \neq f(a_i)$
            ▷ Y-component of the chaff point
15:     $Ch \leftarrow \{(a_i, \bar{a}_i)\}$
            ▷ add chaff point in Ch
16:     Update $V_A \leftarrow L \cup Ch$
17:     $|\nu_i| \leftarrow |\nu_i| + 1$
18:     $w(\nu_i) = [\frac{1}{\nu^2}(1 - \frac{|\nu_i|}{|\nu_{max}|})]$
            ▷ update weight
19: **end for**
20: **return** V_A

Algorithm 4: $C \leftarrow$ CGen(V_A, B)

INPUT/ OUTPUT:
 $V_A = \{(a_1, a_1^*), .., (a_r, a_r^*)\}$
 $B = \{b_1, b_2, \cdots, b_t\}$
 $C \subset V_A$: t pairs of points

1: ConF = FMatch(V_A, B)
2: Φ = SMatch(ConF)
3: **for each** $i \leq r$ **do**
4:     **for each** $j \leq t$ **do**
5:         **if** $\Phi[i, j] = 1$ **then**
6:             $C \leftarrow (a_i, a_i^*)$
7:         **end if**
8:     **end for**
9: **end for**
10: **return** C
    //Pseudocode of FMatch
11: move $\forall a_i \in \mathbb{F}_q$ to $a_i = (\mu_i, \sigma_i^2) \in \mathbb{R}^2$
12: **for each** $a_i \in V_A$ **do**
13:     **for each** $b_j \in B$ **do**
14:         $p_{i,j}^m \leftarrow$ tTest(μ_i, μ_j);
                $\mu_i \in a_i$ and $\mu_j \in b_j$
15:         $p_{i,j}^v \leftarrow$ fTest(σ_i^2, σ_j^2);

                $\sigma_i^2 \in a_i$ and $\sigma_j^2 \in b_j$
16:         $p_{i,j} \leftarrow$ FMethod($p_{i,j}^m, p_{i,j}^v$)
17:         ConF$[i, j] \leftarrow p_{i,j}$
18:     **end for**
19: **end for**
20: **return** ConF
    //Pseudocode of SMatch
21: add $r - t$ pseudo points
     $\hat{B} = \{b_1, b_2, \cdots, b_t, \hat{b}_{t+1}, \cdots, \hat{b}_r\}$
22: **for each** $i \leq r$ **do**
23:     **for each** $j \leq r$ **do**
24:         **if** $j > t$ **then**
25:             $\bar{\text{ConF}}[i, j] \leftarrow 0$
26:         **else**
27:             $\bar{\text{ConF}}[i, j] \leftarrow$ ConF$[i, j]$
28:         **end if**
29:     **end for**
30: **end for**
31: $\Phi \leftarrow$ LAP($\bar{\text{ConF}}$)
        ▷ assign 1 for optimal subset or 0
32: **return** Φ

References

1. Achlioptas, D.: Database-friendly random projections: Johnson-Lindenstrauss with binary coins. JCSS **66**(4), 671–687 (2003)
2. Akgül, M.: The linear assignment problem. In: Akgül, M., Hamacher, H.W., Tüfekçi, S. (eds.) Combinatorial Optimization. NATO ASI Series (Series F: Computer and Systems Sciences), vol. 82, pp. 85–122. Springer, Heidelberg (1992). https://doi.org/10.1007/978-3-642-77489-8_5
3. Alimomeni, M., Safavi-Naini, R.: How *to prevent* to delegate authentication. In: Thuraisingham, B., Wang, X.F., Yegneswaran, V. (eds.) SecureComm 2015. LNICST, vol. 164, pp. 477–499. Springer, Cham (2015). https://doi.org/10.1007/978-3-319-28865-9_26
4. Brown, M.B.: A method for combining non-independent, one-sided tests of significance. Biometrics **31**, 987–992 (1975)
5. Chang, E.C., et al.: Finding the original point set hidden among chaff. In: Proceedings of the ASIACCS 2006, pp. 182–188. ACM (2006)
6. Clancy, T.C., et al.: Secure smartcardbased fingerprint authentication. In: Proceedings of the ACM SIGMM WBMA 2003, pp. 45–52. ACM (2003)
7. Crump, M.J., et al.: Evaluating Amazon's mechanical turk as a tool for experimental behavioral research. PLoS One **8**(3), e57410 (2013)
8. Frank, M., et al.: Touchalytics: on the applicability of touchscreen input as a behavioral biometric for continuous authentication. IEEE Trans. Inf. Forensics Secur. **8**(1), 136–148 (2013)
9. Hahs-Vaughn, D.L., et al.: Statistical Concepts: A Second Course. Routledge, Abingdon (2013)
10. Islam, M.M., et al.: Poster: a behavioural authentication system for mobile users. In: Proceedings of the ACM CCS 2016, pp. 1742–1744. ACM (2016)
11. Massey, Jr., Frank, J., et al.: The Kolmogorov-Smirnov test for goodness of fit. JASA **46**(253), 68–78 (1951)
12. Juels, A., et al.: A fuzzy vault scheme. Des. Codes Crypt. **38**(2), 237–257 (2006). https://doi.org/10.1007/s10623-005-6343-z
13. Kaur, M., et al.: Fuzzy vault template protection for multimodal biometric system. In: Proceedings of the ICCCA 2017, pp. 1131–1135. IEEE (2017)
14. Lee, Y.J., Bae, K., Lee, S.J., Park, K.R., Kim, J.: Biometric key binding: fuzzy vault based on iris images. In: Lee, S.-W., Li, S.Z. (eds.) ICB 2007. LNCS, vol. 4642, pp. 800–808. Springer, Heidelberg (2007). https://doi.org/10.1007/978-3-540-74549-5_84
15. Li, C., et al.: A security-enhanced alignment-free fuzzy vault-based fingerprint cryptosystem using pair-polar minutiae structures. IEEE Trans. Inf. Forensics Secur. **11**(3), 543–555 (2015)
16. Mankiewicz, R.: The Story of Mathematics. Cassell, London (2000)
17. Nandakumar, K., et al.: Fingerprint-based fuzzy vault: implementation and performance. IEEE TIFS **2**(4), 744–757 (2007)
18. Salowey, J.A., et al.: TLS 1.3, 10 August 2018. https://www.ietf.org/blog/tls13/. Accessed 22 Apr 2019
19. Scheirer, W.J., et al.: Cracking fuzzy vaults and biometric encryption. In: Biometrics Symposium 2007, pp. 1–6. IEEE (2007)
20. Taheri, S., Islam, M.M., Safavi-Naini, R.: Privacy-enhanced profile-based authentication using sparse random projection. In: De Capitani di Vimercati, S., Martinelli, F. (eds.) SEC 2017. IAICT, vol. 502, pp. 474–490. Springer, Cham (2017). https://doi.org/10.1007/978-3-319-58469-0_32

21. Uludag, U., Pankanti, S., Jain, A.K.: Fuzzy vault for fingerprints. In: Kanade, T., Jain, A., Ratha, N.K. (eds.) AVBPA 2005. LNCS, vol. 3546, pp. 310–319. Springer, Heidelberg (2005). https://doi.org/10.1007/11527923_32
22. Uludag, U., et al.: Securing fingerprint template: fuzzy vault with helper data. In: Proceedings of the CVPRW 2006. pp, 163–163. IEEE (2006)
23. Vempala, S.S.: The Random Projection Method, vol. 65. American Mathematical Society, Providence (2005)
24. Wu, L., et al.: A face based fuzzy vault scheme for secure online authentication. In: Proceedings of the ISDPE 2010, pp. 45–49. IEEE (2010)
25. Yampolskiy, R.V.: Mimicry attack on strategy-based behavioral biometric. In: Proceedings of the ITNG 2008, pp. 916–921. IEEE (2008)

Crypto Currencies

Improvements of the Balance Discovery Attack on Lightning Network Payment Channels

Gijs van Dam$^{(\boxtimes)}$ ⓘ, Rabiah Abdul Kadir ⓘ, Puteri N. E. Nohuddin ⓘ,
and Halimah Badioze Zaman ⓘ

Institute of Visual Informatics, The National University of Malaysia (UKM),
43600 Bangi, Selangor, Malaysia
p95677@siswa.ukm.edu.my
http://www.ivi.ukm.my/en/

Abstract. The Lighting Network (LN) is a network of micropayment channels that runs on top of Bitcoin. The balances of payment channels are not broadcasted to the LN network to preserve the privacy of the nodes participating in the network. A balance disclosure attack (BDA) has been proven to be successful in determining the balance of large amounts of channels in the network. In this paper we propose an improved algorithm for the BDA as well as a new type of attack that leverages the differences between LN client software implementations. Our improved algorithm extends the original BDA by performing payments from both sides of the channel. The new attack uses malformed payments to shutdown payment channels an adversary is not part of.

Keywords: Bitcoin · Lightning Network · Network security

1 Introduction

Bitcoin, the cryptocurrency with the largest market capitalization, has inherently limited scalability. Bitcoin generates 1 block of transactions every 10 min and the size of that block is limited to 1 MB. With a basic transaction taking up 250 bytes and an average transaction size of 500 bytes the network has a maximum capacity of 4000 transactions per block and an average capacity of 2000 transactions per block. This boils down to 3–7 transactions per second. Increasing this capacity by either increasing the block size or the rate at which blocks are generated reduces the security of the Bitcoin network [1]. Increasing scalability of Bitcoin without abandoning security remains desirable. Firstly because if the amount of transactions being broadcasted exceeds the capacity of the network, the law of supply and demand dictates that the transaction fees will increase [2] Secondly, if we want to achieve a viable alternative to current centralized payment networks we need to achieve comparable throughput which is in the order of magnitude of several thousand transactions per second.

© IFIP International Federation for Information Processing 2020
Published by Springer Nature Switzerland AG 2020
M. Hölbl et al. (Eds.): SEC 2020, IFIP AICT 580, pp. 313–323, 2020.
https://doi.org/10.1007/978-3-030-58201-2_21

It was Satoshi Nakamoto, the mysterious pseudonymous person or group of persons famous for developing Bitcoin, who suggested the use of transaction replacement for something he called high frequency trading [3]. In Nakamoto's proposal a group of parties could keep updating a transaction that had yet to be committed. The order of the updates was kept by a sequence number. Only the last agreed upon transaction needed to be broadcast. By doing so all the transactions prior to the final transaction were kept off-chain. Nakamato's approach couldn't operate in a trustless environment and was never seriously considered.

LN is a peer-to-peer (P2P) network of connected nodes that uses Poon-Dryja [4] payment channels. Two connected nodes can open up a payment channel between them. A transaction from node A to node B can only happen if there is enough balance on the side of node A. Likewise, a transaction from node B to node A can only happen if there is enough balance on the side of node B. Both balances added together define the capacity of the channel. To create a transaction between two nodes that don't have a payment channel between them, multiple payment channels can be connected to form a route, as long as the balances along that route allow for the payment. This is known as a multi-hop payment. To participate in LN you have to run LN client software. Each LN client follows the LN specifications, set out in the Basis of Lightning Technology (BOLT) [5] documents.

Balances on the other hand are kept private and are never broadcasted on the network. The only balances known to a node are the balances of the channels that node participates in. Because of this it is impossible to know upfront whether a multi-hop payment will succeed, and there is only one way to find out: executing the payment. By executing multiple (fake) payments it is possible to probe the unknown balance of a payment channel. Disclosing balances this way has been dubbed the balance discovery attack (BDA) [6]. LN uses an onion routing [7] scheme called Sphinx [8] for the routing of payments.

In this study we analyzed potential BDA algorithm improvements and the role of LN client software in BDA. We propose an improvement to the basic algorithm for BDA that achieves a two-fold increase of the upper limit of balances that can be disclosed. Furthermore, we found that in certain situations LN client software can be leveraged to remove the upper limit of BDA completely. Finally we describe a specific situation where the interplay between different LN client software types leads to the permanent shutdown of a payment channel. This new attack, dubbed Payment of Death (POD), makes it possible to remotely shut down channels. We will show that POD is a threat to the integrity of LN, as it has the potential for a malicious party to shutdown 17.5% of the network capacity.

2   Background

A formal analysis of privacy in the context of PCNs has been hindered by a lack of a rigorous definition of the PCN protocols, the absence of a threat model, and the ambivalent interpretations of the concept of anonymity [9].

A threat model is necessary to perform a formal analysis of privacy in the setting of trustless PCNs. Malavolta [9] describes a threat model with four notions of interest:

- Balance security: participants don't run the risk of losing coins to a malevolent adversary.
- Serializability: executions of a PCN are serializable as understood in concurrency control of transaction processing, i.e. for every concurrent processing of payments there exists an equivalent sequential execution.
- (Off-path) value privacy: malicious participants in the network cannot learn information about payments they are not part of.
- (On-path) relationship anonymity: given at least one honest intermediary, corrupted intermediaries cannot determine the sender and the receiver of a transaction better than just by guessing.

2.1 Balance Discovery Attack

In the basic scenario for channel balance discovery [6] it is assumed that there is an open payment channel AB between Alice, A, and Bob, B, with capacity C_{AB}. The goal of the adversary, Mallory, M, is to discover the balances of each node in channel AB: $balance_{AB}$ and $balance_{BA}$. To do so Mallory opens up a channel with Alice (see Fig. 1).

Fig. 1. Basic BDA were the adversary Mallory tries to disclose the balance between Alice and Bob

Mallory tries to disclose $balance_{AB}$ by routing invalid payments through $M \leftrightarrow A \leftrightarrow B$, using the basic BDA algorithm. The inputs for the algorithm are the target node B, the route to the target node, the value range to search in, given by 0 and C_{AB}, and the required accuracy for the algorithm. The algorithm creates invalid payments by using random, invalid payment hashes for each payment. The value for each payment follows a binary search pattern for which the initial lower and upper bounds are given by the value range input.

Bob, the recipient of the payment, is the only one who can determine that a payment from Mallory is invalid. Therefore, receiving an error stating the payment hash is invalid, means that $balance_{AB}$ was sufficient to route the payment, because if it was not, Alice would have returned an error stating insufficient funds and Bob would never have known about the payment. This fact is leveraged by updating the lower bound of the binary search to the value of the last payment. If however the failure message states insufficient funds, the upper bound is updated with the value of the last payment. This process repeats itself recursively until the difference between the upper bound and the lower bound of the binary search is within the threshold set by the accuracy input. The algorithm returns a tuple that gives the range within which $balance_{AB}$ sits. Since the capacity of the channel C_{AB} is known, the $balance_{BA}$ can be calculated with $balance_{BA} = C_{BA} - balance_{AB}$.

By periodically executing a BDA, an adversary can monitor balances over time. This allows for tracing transactions. Therefore, this type of attack poses a threat for the value privacy as described in the threat model above.

3   Method

In order to research the role of LN client software in BDA we must first determine which LN clients are available. We used 1ML Lightning Network Search and Analysis Engine[1] to estimate respective proportions of each client in LN. 1ML is a website that publishes the current state of the LN graph and allows for node owners to self-report on a voluntary basis the type of client they use.

We chose the three LN clients with the largest network share to run a local cluster of LN nodes, each node running one of three supported clients. All LN nodes used Bitcoin Core's Bitcoind implementation as the Bitcoin backend. Bitcoind ran in regression testing mode, known as regtest mode. This is a local test mode, making it possible to almost instantly create blocks with no real-world value. Using regtest mode, the different implementations could be tested without incurring transaction fees for the on-chain transactions and without having to wait for blocks to be mined.

On this cluster we analyzed the basic and improved algorithm having the LN nodes in each possible permutation of supported clients. This helped us determine if the new algorithm was to be considered an improvement and whether client differences could play a role in BDA.

3.1   Two-Way Channel Probing

The original algorithm [6] is bound by an upper limit set by MAX_PAYMENT_ ALLOWED. This limit makes it impossible to probe balances that are higher than $2^{32} - 1 \, msat$. This paper proposes an improved algorithm.

Consider a channel AB with capacity C_{AB}. Since $C_{AB} = C_{BA} = balance_{AB} + balance_{BA}$, the following holds

$$C_{AB} < 2^{33} \implies min\{balance_{AB}, balance_{BA}\} < 2^{32}$$

For all channels with a capacity $C_{AB} < 2^{33}$ there's always a balance lower than $\frac{2^{33}}{2} = 2^{32}$ on one end of the channel. With this knowledge we can extend the algorithm by letting it probe the channel from the other side, once we assess that the balance is higher than MAX_PAYMENT_ALLOWED on the initial probing side. This setup requires an optional second channel from the adversary Node M to Node B, to be able to probe the channel between Node A and Node B from the side of Node B (See Fig. 2).

---

[1] https://1ml.com/.

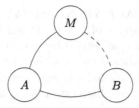

Fig. 2. Basic scenario with an optional second channel for two-way probing

Algorithm 1 describes BDA with optional two-way probing for channels with a capacity above MAX_PAYMENT_ALLOWED. Algorithm 1 takes the same input parameters as the basic algorithm and returns the same tuple.

Algorithm 1. Two-way Probing

Data: route, target, maxFlow, minFlow, accuracy_treshold
Result: bwidth, an array of tuples that gives the range of bandwidth discovered for each channel

1: $missingTests \leftarrow True$
2: $bwidth.max \leftarrow maxFlow$
3: $bwidth.min \leftarrow minFlow$
4: $channelCapacity \leftarrow getInfo(target).capacity$
5: **while** missingTests **do**
6:     **if** $bwidth.max - bwidth.min \leq accuracy\_threshold$ **then**
7:         $missingTests \leftarrow False$
8:     **end if**
9:     **if** $bwidth.max \geq 2^{32}$ **then**
10:         $flow \leftarrow 2^{32} - 1$
11:     **else**
12:         $flow \leftarrow (bwidth.min + bwidth.max)/2$
13:     **end if**
14:     $h(x) \leftarrow RandomValue$
15:     $response \leftarrow sendFakePayment(route = [route, target], h(x), flow)$
16:     **if** $response = UnknownPaymentHash$ **then**
17:         **if** $bwidth.min < flow$ **then**
18:             $bwidth.min \leftarrow flow$
19:         **end if**
20:     **else if** $response = InsufficientFunds$ **then**
21:         **if** $bwidth.max > flow$ **then**
22:             $bwidth.max \leftarrow flow$
23:         **end if**
24:     **end if**
25:     **if** $bwidth.min = 2^{32} - 1$ **then**
26:         $newTarget \leftarrow route.pop()$
27:         $route \leftarrow route.push(target)$
28:         $bwidthBA \leftarrow twowayProbing(route, newTarget, bwidth.min, 0, accuracy\_treshold)$
29:         $bwidth.min \leftarrow channelCapacity - bwidthBA.max$
30:         $bwidth.max \leftarrow channelCapacity - bwidthBA.min$
31:         $missingTests \leftarrow False$
32:     **end if**
33: **end while**
34: **return** $bwidth$

If C_{AB} is higher than MAX_PAYMENT_ALLOWED, the algorithm will try to send a fake payment with a size of exactly MAX_PAYMENT_ALLOWED. If that payment is possible, we have assessed that we are on the wrong end of the channel for probing the balance. The algorithm now calls itself with the target node and the final node of the route switched. The algorithm assumes that there is a route from the adversary to this new target node. The return value of that call is $balance_{BA}$, for calculating $balance_{AB}$ we use the following formula:

$$balance_{AB} = C_{BA} - balance_{BA}$$

If C_{AB} > MAX_PAYMENT_ALLOWED and C_{AB} < 2 × MAX_PAYMENT_ALLOWED, the value of the first payment will not be exactly in the middle of the value range for the binary search, since it will use the fixed value of MAX_PAYMENT_ALLOWED for the first payment. That makes this algorithm slightly less computationally efficient then a perfect binary search, but it minimizes the use of the optional second channel.

4 Results

We confirmed the improvements provided by the two-way probing algorithm in two ways. Firstly we confirmed the feasibility of the algorithm in our local testing cluster. Secondly we analyzed LN running on top of Bitcoin mainnet, to estimate the number of channels that can have their balances disclosed by this algorithm and compare this to the earlier version of this attack.

4.1 Local Network Evaluation

We ran the Two-way Probing algorithm with every possible permutation of clients. By analyzing the responses from the clients, and analyzing the code of the respective clients on GitHub, we found that not every client implemented the MAX_PAYMENT_ALLOWED the same way.

On May 23rd, 2017 the BOLT specification was changed[2] by Paul "Rusty" Russel, who authored the majority of the BOLT documents. The variable containing the payment amount, amount_msat, was changed from a 32 bit unsigned integer to a 64 bit unsigned integer. This meant that before that change it was impossible to create a payment bigger than $2^{32} - 1$ whatsoever, but after that change in theory it was possible to create bigger payments. Additional specifications required the sending node to set the four most significant bytes of amount_msat to 0. But those additional requirements aren't implemented equally by the three main clients.

C-lightning is the only client that fully adheres to the requirements. Eclair has a limit of $5 \cdot 10^9 msat$. LND doesn't verify the amount for certain RPC's. By using the unverified RPC in our algorithm we could send fake payments up to the

[2] https://github.com/lightningnetwork/lightning-rfc/commit/068b0bccf94e8cdaf5f29 8dade0fcc8cc8421ef6#diff-3369c5aa1774fef2ff1e246979f223eaR590.

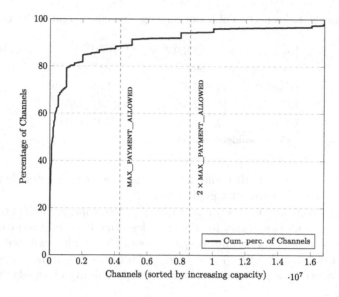

Fig. 3. Cumulative percentage graph of payment channels ordered by increasing capacity. MAX_PAYMENT_ALLOWED shows the percentage of channels with disclosable balances using the basic BDA algorithm. 2× MAX_PAYMENT_ALLOWED shows the percentage of channels with disclosable balances using the two-way probing algorithm.

maximal channel capacity. This meant that we can disclose any balance between two LND Nodes, even if the balance is above the upper limit of the two-way probing algorithm. In the scenarios where Alice is a LND node and Bob is an Eclair node or both are Eclair nodes, balances up to $5 \cdot 10^9 msat$ can be disclosed without making use of two-way probing.

4.2 Channels Affected

The two-way probing algorithm works regardless of the client software. So we can look at the channel capacity of all public channels in the LN graph and determine the proportion of channels that are now susceptible to this type of attack based on a snapshot of the network taken on the 3rd of October, 2019 (see Fig. 3).

To estimate the number of channels susceptible for BDA above the 2^{33} limit set by the Two-way algorithm, we need to know the type of client on either side of a channel. There's no known way of figuring out what kind of client is installed, but if you know the proportion of each client type in the LN, it is possible to estimate the amount of channels for each specific combination of clients.

We queried 1ML for each node in our snapshot of the LN. We identified the client type for 273 nodes out of 3608 and estimated the proportion of nodes running different clients based on that data (See Table 1).

The LN is a graph G, with the number of vertices $n = |G(V)|$ and the number of edges $m = |G(E)|$. Our analysis yielded the following values for n and m:

Table 1. Proportion of nodes running different Lightning clients

Client	n	Proportion (%)	CI[a] (%)
LND	220	80.59	(79.35–81.83)
c-lightning	40	14.65	(13.54–15.76)
Eclair	11	4.03	(3.41–4.65)
Other	2	0.73	(0.47–1.00)

[a] 95% Confidence interval

$n = 3608$ $m = 9438$ with 1086 channels having a capacity greater than 2^{32} and 540 channels having a capacity greater than 2^{33}.

The client software defines the type of the vertex. $type_l$ for LND nodes, $type_c$ for c-lightning nodes and $type_e$ for Eclair nodes. An edge is said to be of $type_{(l,c)}$ if it connects a $type_l$ vertex and a $type_c$ vertex. The graph is without self-loops and undirected, so edge $type_{(l,c)} \equiv type_{(c,l)}$. Since we know the proportions of the different vertex types we can calculate the probability of an edge being of a specific type.

- $P(type_{(l,l)}) = 0.8059^2$
- $P(type_{(c,c)}) = 0.1465^2$
- $P(type_{(e,e)}) = 0.0403^2$
- $P(type_{(l,c)}) = 2 \times 0.8059 \times 0.1465$
- $P(type_{(l,e)}) = 2 \times 0.8059 \times 0.0403$
- $P(type_{(c,e)}) = 2 \times 0.1465 \times 0.0403$

Assuming vertex type and channel capacity have a covariance of zero, the number of edges of each edge type, having a capacity greater than 2^{33} is calculated as follows: $P(type_{([c,e,l],[c,e,l])}) \times 540$. We are interested in the $type_{(l,l)}$ and $type_{(l,e)}$ channels, because the $type_{(l,c)}$ channels are susceptible to the Payment of Death explained below, which doesn't allow for discovering the balance. So the amount of channels with a capacity above 2^{32} is $540 \times P(type_{(l,l)}) + 540 \times P(type_{(l,e)}) = 386$ channels. So a total of $9438 - 540 + 386 = 9284$ channels have balances that can be disclosed. This is 98.4% of all channels.

4.3 Payment of Death

In the case where Alice is a LND node and Bob is a C-lightning node, we saw interesting behavior of the C-lightning node which turned out to be a vulnerability of the current LN that can be exploited.

If a C-lightning node is being requested to route a payment to another node, or is the receiver of a payment, with an amount that his higher than MAX_PAYMENT_ALLOWED, it decides to fail the channel with the requesting node and close down that channel. Since LN uses onion routing, the requesting node from the perspective of the c-lightning node, is the one that comes just before it in the route. But that isn't necessarily the node from which the payment originated.

Consider the basic scenario (see Fig. 1), where Mallory and Alice run LND, and Bob runs c-lightning. Both channels between Mallory and Alice and between Alice and Bob have balances that allow for payments bigger than the MAX_PAYMENT_ALLOWED limit. If Mallory would create a fake payment with an amount above that limit, Bob would close down it's channel with Alice, without Alice being able to mitigate this in any way. We coined the term Payment of Death (POD) for this attack, after the infamous Ping of Death.

For the amount of channels affected by the POD we are interested in all $type_{(l,c)}$ channels, with a balance above MAX_PAYMENT_ALLOWED. This is $1086 \times P(type_{(l,c)}) = 256$ channels, meaning that 2.7% of all channels can be shutdown by using malformed payments.

We have notified the developers of the LN implementations by means of a responsible disclosure.

5 Discussion

Herrera-Joancomarti [6] reported that 89.10% of all channels could have their balances exactly disclosed. Our research showed that we can improve this to 98.37% of all channels, a 9.27% point increase (See Table 2). The basic BDA performed slightly less in our snapshot of the LN network because in the period between the two snapshots of the 8th of January, 2019 and the 3rd of October, 2019, the percentage of channels with a capacity C of $C > 2^{32}$ slightly increased.

Table 2. Percentage of channels susceptible for the basic BDA and the two-way probing BDA

Disclosable channels	Basic BDA (%)	Two-way probing BDA (%)
$C \leq 2^{32}$	89.10	88.49
$C > 2^{32} \wedge C \leq 2^{33}$	0	5.79
$C \leq 2^{33}$	0	4.09
TOTAL	89.10	98.37

5.1 Impact of Payment of Death

The properties of the vulnerability make it so that the highly capitalized nodes are more vulnerable, since it are these nodes that have channels with a balance above MAX_PAYMENT_ALLOWED limit. The average capacity of those 1086 channels is 10196116 $msat$. Using that average combined with the estimated proportions of affected channels, 17.5% of the total capacity of the network could be taken down with an organized attack. These proportions align with proportions earlier found through alternative methods [10]. It's reasonable to assume that these channels are responsible for routing a disproportionate amount of the payments on the network. Such an attack could have substantial impact on the ability to route payments of the network as a whole.

The closing of channels comes at a cost to the victim nodes, since you have to broadcast on-chain transactions for closing a channel and again for reopening it. Those transactions have transaction fees attached to it. Furthermore, channel age is used as heuristic for determining the reliability of a node for routing payments, so routing nodes have an incentive to keep channels open as long as possible.

5.2   Countermeasures

Clients should adhere to the BOLT specification, making it impossible to create payments with a value higher than MAX_PAYMENT_ALLOWED and deny to consider payments with a value above the MAX_PAYMENT_ALLOWED for routing. The latter would make it impossible to disclose balances above $2^{33}\,msat$. Secondly, clients should not consider a malformed payment a reason for permanently closing down a channel. This would make it impossible to mount a POD attack.

Limiting the number of payment requests per unit of time or randomly deny payment requests following a configurable *dropping rate* [6] are unfeasible. These countermeasures, implemented generically, come at a high cost for usability of the network as a whole. So a selective approach is preferable, identifying nodes that are the source of suspicious payment requests, and limit or deny requests from these nodes. But this selective approach could quite easily be circumvented by inserting different non-malicious nodes with known balances in the route in subsequent payment requests. This way the source of the attack from the point of view of the attacked node is not determinable and each non-malicious node itself doesn't see a pattern that resembles an attack.

6   Conclusion

This paper presented an improvement to the algorithm of the original BDA. We showed that by approaching a payment channel from both sides instead of from one side, payment channels with a higher capacity than in the original BDA are now also susceptible to this attack. Since monitoring balances over time makes it possible to detect payments, it can be used to learn information about payments an adversary isn't part of [9]. We exposed differences in the implementation of the BOLT specification by the main three clients. These differences led us to develop a new attack that closes down remote payment channels. We estimated the proportions of each client in LN, by using self-reported information. Based on these proportions we estimated that this attack can be used to take down an important part of LN's entire network capacity.

Acknowledgements. We would like to thank the National University of Malaysia, which has funded the publication of this paper with grant ZG-2018-001.

References

1. Sompolinsky, Y., Zohar, A.: Secure high-rate transaction processing in bitcoin. In: Böhme, R., Okamoto, T. (eds.) FC 2015. LNCS, vol. 8975, pp. 507–527. Springer, Heidelberg (2015). https://doi.org/10.1007/978-3-662-47854-7_32
2. Easley, D., O'Hara, M., Basu, S.: From mining to markets: the evolution of bitcoin transaction fees. J. Financ. Econ. **134**, 91–109 (2019). https://doi.org/10.1016/j.jfineco.2019.03.004
3. Hearn, M.: Anti DoS for tx replacement (2013). https://lists.linuxfoundation.org/pipermail/bitcoin-dev/2013-April/002417.html
4. Poon, J., Dryja, T.: The Bitcoin Lightning Network: Scalable Off-Chain Instant Payments (2016). https://www.bitcoinlightning.com/wp-content/uploads/2018/03/lightning-network-paper.pdf
5. Basis of Lightning Technology. https://github.com/lightningnetwork/lightning-rfc/blob/master/00-introduction.md
6. Herrera-Joancomartí, J., Navarro-Arribas, G., Ranchal-Pedrosa, A., Pérez-Solà, C., Garcia-Alfaro, J.: On the difficulty of hiding the balance of lightning network channels, pp. 602–612 (2019). https://doi.org/10.1145/3321705.3329812
7. Reed, M.G., Syverson, P.F., Goldschlag, D.M.: Anonymous connections and onion routing. IEEE J. Sel. Areas Commun. **16**, 482–493 (1998). https://doi.org/10.1109/49.668972
8. Danezis, G., Goldberg, I.: Sphinx: a compact and provably secure mix format. In: Proceedings of the IEEE Symposium on Security and Privacy, pp. 269–282 (2009). https://doi.org/10.1109/SP.2009.15
9. Malavolta, G., Moreno-Sanchez, P., Kate, A., Maffei, M., Ravi, S.: Concurrency and privacy with payment-channel networks. In: Proceedings of the 2017 ACM SIGSAC Conference on Computer and Communications Security - CCS 2017, pp. 455–471. ACM Press, New York (2017). https://doi.org/10.1145/3133956.3134096
10. Pérez-Solà, C., Ranchal-Pedrosa, A., Herrera-Joancomartí, J., Navarro-Arribas, G., Garcia-Alfaro, J.: LockDown: Balance Availability Attack against Lightning Network Channels (2019). https://eprint.iacr.org/2019/1149

CCBRSN: A System with High Embedding Capacity for Covert Communication in Bitcoin

Weizheng Wang and Chunhua Su$^{(\boxtimes)}$

Division of Computer Science, University of Aizu, Aizuwakamatsu, Japan
chsu@u-aizu.ac.jp

Abstract. Covert communication has been using to prevent confidential information from being leaked to an unintended receiver. In this paper, we present a general purpose novel methodology for blockchain-based covert communication system design to be used in Bitcoin environment. Blockchain is a distributed system which combines P2P network, consensus protocol, encryption algorithm to complete the first reliable cryptocurrency system Bitcoin. According to the high security and convenient access of this technology, many applications based on Blockchain such as smart contracts, distributed cloud storage have been developed. However, in the field of covert communication, there are few researches are applied in Blockchain. Therefore in this paper, we propose a system called Covert Communication based on Bitcoin Regtest Self-built Network (CCBRSN), which takes Blockchain as a covert communication channel and embeds encrypted messages into Blockchain's addresses to transmit. In this model, users can transmit covert messages via Blockchain mutually and fast. Finally, we provide experimental analysis for our proposal to show that it is suitable for practical application.

Keywords: Blockchain · Bitcoin · Cryptography · Covert communication

1 Introduction

Covert communication targets at hiding wireless transmissions, which meets the ever-increasing desire of strong security and privacy. In a typical covert communication system, a transmitter (Alice) intends to communicate with a legitimate receiver (Bob) without being detected with a warden (Willie), who is observing this communication [1]. Hence a reliable communication channel is the most important thing for covert communication, which can level up the security of critical communication or be confidential during the transmitting process.

Covert communication has two important parts—Cryptography and Steganography. Cryptography encrypts the plaintext to ciphertext, which can protect users' privacy. The method of steganography conceals the existence of

© IFIP International Federation for Information Processing 2020
Published by Springer Nature Switzerland AG 2020
M. Hölbl et al. (Eds.): SEC 2020, IFIP AICT 580, pp. 324–337, 2020.
https://doi.org/10.1007/978-3-030-58201-2_22

the message, to make them unintelligible. Simultaneously, channel is crucial for steganography. In practical use, many channels have been tried as covert channels for steganography, for example, Covert Channels in the HTTP Network Protocol [2], Covert Channels in IPv6 [3], A novel covert channel based on length of messages [4] and so on. Whereas, most of them are not stable, such as HTTP, if we meet an error during communication, maybe the transferring message is lost forever. Meanwhile, with the advance of decryption technology, the security of these channels can not be ensured in the future. All in all, it is still hard for us to find a high-quality and securable medium for steganography.

On the other hand, Blockchain is becoming more and more popular. As a highly decentralized, open and transparent distributed database structure, Blockchain was first introduced in the paper [5] which was published by Nakamoto in 2008. Blocks which are in a sequential order consist of the Blockchain. Every list of the transaction which is traded and packed is all recorded in a block. To maintain the runtime of Blockchain, every main node in the Blockchain real-time updates a separate global ledger. At the same time, all the main nodes are also competitors, they use their computing power to calculate a puzzle. In this race, the faster one will be the winner and get the authority of bookkeeping. If a winner in a mining race tries to tamper the data of one block or one transaction to get more profit, then the hash value of this block and the subsequent blocks will be changed immediately. After receiving this new-generated block, the honest nodes will compare the new ledger with owns and perceive the falsity of the chain. At last, they will refuse this published ledge and rollback. Based on security and openness, many applications choose to build up on the Blockchain, for example, smart contracts in the Ethereum [6], intelligent transport system [7], e-voting system [8]. In consideration of the above advantages of Blockchain, we also take Blockchain as a tentative covert communication channel.

There are plenty types of Blockchains in the world. Why do we select the Bitcoin as our experiment communication medium? There are the following four reasons: (1) huge computing power in the Bitcoin's network ensures the safety of Bitcoin, and until now the hash rate has already reached 92,468,911 (TH/s) [9]. If an attacker attempts to take control of Bitcoin's network and do some bad things, it means he must get the 51% resource of the computing power. However, a regular GPU of PC can just provide 50–60 (MH/s). Therefore, as a communication channel, Bitcoin is relatively reliable. (2) no matter where you are and what you have, as long as you can get access to the Internet, then you can use tens of thousands of applications that serve as light nodes in the Bitcoin to conduct transactions. Compared with other Blockchains, Bitcoin is more convenient as a channel. (3) cheap—you can deliver a million dollars' transaction with only a few dollars' transaction fees. (4) everyone can join or leave the network as they will, and this is an anonymous mode, you needn't concern about the disclosure of your privacy [10].

1.1 Related Works

Covert communication can be traced back to the steganography which was proposed in the 16th century's book—"Steganographia". With the development of the Internet, covert communication began to spring up in the late 20th century and now is widely used in the field of digital communication and network security. Covert communication can be generally divided into two sides—Steganography and digital watermarking.

In terms of Steganography, there are many mature technologies, such as in the paper [11] suggested a way that uses a class of new distortion functions known as uniform embedding distortion function (UED) for both side-informed and non side-informed secure JPEG steganography, and in paper [12] also proposed an enhanced least significant bit modification technique for audio steganography, finally paper [13] proposed method creates an index for the secret information and the index is placed in a frame of the video itself.

On the other side, the digital watermarking means capable of carrying such information as authentication or authorisation codes or a legend essential for image interpretation, which is also an efficient way for covert communication. In 1997, Ingemar J. Cox et al. proposed a NEC algorithm [14] that combines the author's identification code with the image hash value to generate a key as a seed generation sequence, and then DCT transforms the image. This algorithm not only reduces the redundancy of the video signal, but also guarantees the robustness and security of the algorithm. Bender W suggested a digital watermark based on statistics [15], which selects a certain number of arbitrary pairs of image points in the image. When the brightness of one point in each pair of image points increases, the brightness of the corresponding other point decreases. To achieve the loading of the watermark, this method has good concealment and strong resistance but is not suitable for images with only a small amount of arbitrary texture.

1.2 Motivation

Although there are many methods for covert communication, however, we can only find a few experiments and applications on the Blockchain. In paper [16], Juha Partala et al. firstly suggested a method of submitting covert messages through a Blockchain considered as a payment platform. The overview of his ideal is to separate the message into unit bit and use the LSB (Least Significant Bit) of the address to match the unit bit, if the unit bit accords with the LSB then we use this address to do a transaction, repeat previous steps after this transaction is recorded into a block, finally the receiver can restore the message in a specific order.

This is an innovative way for covert communication in Blockchain, but it still exists some problems as follows:

1. In paper [16], they only provide a simplified Blockchain model hypothetically and discuss their scheme all in theory, in practical use it is hard to verify the feasibility of their named BLOCCE scheme.

2. A block is produced in Blockchain will cost users several minutes, if you want to transmit all bits of the message but one block only has one transaction, the whole process will need a long time to be finished. The timeliness of the message can't be promised.
3. Every transaction needs transaction fee, if the number of transaction is huge, you should pay a colossal sum of money. The Performance-to-Price ratio of this communication may be low. Although there are some Blockchains which don't need transaction fee, it seems this problem could be solved. In fact, most of them are not the mainstream, we can't ensure their security.

Hence, we try to find a more practical and efficient way for covert communication on Blockchain.

1.3 Our Contributions

In this paper, we propose a scheme—CCBRSN which realizes covert communication on the Bitcoin's Regtest network. We also base on this scheme to develop a visualized operating system for the users. The users who join this network and use our devised tools can exchange messages safely, efficiently, conveniently. The main procedure of our ideal is to use DES and Base58 to encrypt and code the message successively, then we embed the ciphertext into a set of addresses in order, finally, we employ this set as output to conduct a transaction. After a transaction, a file for decryption will be produced. When the transaction is recorded into the Bitcoin ledger, the opponent can import the above-mentioned file into our tool to track this particular transaction and decrypt the ciphertext automatically. There are two remarking characteristics of our measures. One is we increase the embedded rate of address, which means one address can be embedded more information. The other feature is a message needn't be separated into multiple transactions, we can only use one transaction to transmit the whole address set(message) in most of the time. Although this system is proposed for Bitcoin, while other Blockchain only if which adopts address can also use this model to construct a covert communication system.

1.4 The Organization of Remaining Paper

The rest of the paper is organized as follows. Section 2 explains the preliminaries for the rest of the paper, such as the structure of Blockchain we use, the configuration of Regtest Network, the method of encryption, coding and threat model. Section 3 describes the detail of our proposed CCBRSN Scheme. The experiment environment and evaluation are presented in Sect. 4. Finally, we conclude and propose future work in Sect. 5.

2 Preliminaries

2.1 The Structure of Blockchain

The birth of Bitcoin creates the conception of Blockchain. All the nodes in the Blockchain maintain a public ledger. When each transaction is produced, it will be verified by all nodes to ensure no error. After checking, this transaction will be packed into a block in the structure of the Merkle tree and added into a decentralized ledger. The relation between transaction and block is illustrated in Fig. 1.

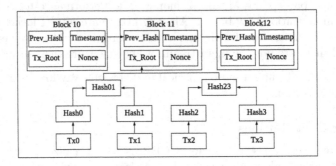

Fig. 1. The structure of Block.

The biggest difference between Bitcoin and other systems is whether or not exists a central trusted authority. Blockchain is a decentralized system, in this network trust is achieved by every participated node. If there is an attacker who attempts to take charge of the system, firstly he must occupy the 51% computing power of the entire Blockchain. However, it is difficult for common people to get enormous computing power. For this reason, Blockchain is quite safe, people can feel free to do the transaction on them.

Blockchain technology has attracted enormous investors and researchers from fields of healthcare, finance, transportation, government and so on. Until now, there are various applications that are built on the Blockchain, such as smart contracts, intelligent transportation, and identity verifying, etc. Bitcoin is a "first-generation" Blockchain, Ethereum broke the mold by becoming the first-ever second-generation Blockchain. Ethereum revolutionized the crypto-space by bringing in smart contracts on the Blockchain. Smart contracts were first conceptualized by Nick Szabo. The idea is simple, have a set of self-executing instructions between two parties that don't need to be supervised or enforced by a third-party. The idea seems pretty straightforward. However, smart contracts enabled Ethereum to create an environment wherein developers from around the world could create their decentralized application aka Dapps [17].

2.2   The Configuration of Regtest Network

Bitcoin and most other cryptocurrencies have 3 modes of operation. Mainnet is the network which is used as the official version, and it has value. All real transactions happen on this network, people get paid or pay using Mainnet.

Testnet, a network which has almost the same rules (some opcodes are forbidden on Mainnet, while this restriction is lifted on Testnet) as Mainnet. It has peer discovery, that is it can find peers on the Testnet network, similar to Mainnet, and a peer-to-peer (P2P) network is running it.

Regtest is a private Blockchain which has the same rules and address format as Testnet, but there is no global p2p network to connect to [18]. It is convenient because this feature makes us easily to build Bitcoin network in local. After dowloading the Bitcoin core client, only one thing we need do configuring Bitcoin.conf file to change network from Mainnet to local Regtest network.

```
E:\bitcoin-0.17.1\bin>bitcoind
2019-11-01T15:51:06Z Bitcoin Core version v0.17.1 (release build)
2019-11-01T15:51:06Z InitParameterInteraction: parameter interaction: -whitelistforcerelay=1 -> setting
-whitelistrelay=1
2019-11-01T15:51:06Z Warning: Config setting for -rpcbind only applied on regtest network when in
[regtest] section.
2019-11-01T15:51:06Z Validating signatures for all blocks.
2019-11-01T15:51:06Z Setting
nMinimumChainWork=0000000000000000000000000000000000000000000000000000000000000000
2019-11-01T15:51:06Z Using the 'sse4(1way),sse41(4way),avx2(8way)' SHA256 implementation
2019-11-01T15:51:06Z Using RdRand as an additional entropy source
2019-11-01T15:51:06Z Default data directory C:\Users\lifewwz\AppData\Roaming\Bitcoin
2019-11-01T15:51:06Z Using data directory C:\Users\lifewwz\AppData\Roaming\Bitcoin\regtest
2019-11-01T15:51:06Z Using config file C:\Users\lifewwz\AppData\Roaming\Bitcoin\bitcoin.conf
2019-11-01T15:51:06Z Using at most 125 automatic connections (2048 file descriptors available)
2019-11-01T15:51:06Z Using 16 MiB out of 32/2 requested for signature cache, able to store 524288
elements
2019-11-01T15:51:06Z Using 16 MiB out of 32/2 requested for script execution cache, able to store
524288 elements
2019-11-01T15:51:06Z Using 8 threads for script verification
2019-11-01T15:51:06Z scheduler thread start
2019-11-01T15:51:06Z libevent: getaddrinfo: nodename nor servname provided, or not known
2019-11-01T15:51:06Z Binding RPC on address :: port 18443 failed.
2019-11-01T15:51:06Z HTTP: creating work queue of depth 16
```

Fig. 2. The successful execution of Regtest network.

From the Fig. 2, we can see the program shows Bitcoin client version and the information of network creation. It means the local network have been established successfully. Then we can use bitcoin-cli commands to execute some operations in the Bitcoin network, such as send transactions or get block information.

2.3   The Method of Encryption and Coding

In this model, we do two operations on original message, one is DES encryption, the other one is Base58 encoding.

In the covert communication, it is necessary for us to encrypt the message firstly in case of disclosure. At present, maybe the encryption of DES are not strong enough very safe, an attacker who attempts to use brute-force can crack the ciphertext. As a result, many corporations and individuals tend to choose other encryption such as AES, RSA. In the consideration of achieving a balance between simplicity and security, the DES encryption is better. Because the outcome of DES encryption is shorter than AES or 3DES, and the security of message can be ensured in some ways. The length of ciphertext is of great importance for transaction. In theory, the shorter one needs less addresses to match.

Hence, we select DES as our encryption scheme, which can increase the huge efficiency of embedded rate.

After encrypting, then we should use Base58 to encode our encrypted message. In Bitcoin, the adaptation of coding scheme is Base58, if we want to embed ciphertext into addresses, the absolutely necessary thing is to unit the coded system. Then we can make some matches.

Finally, the system will produce a decrypt file for receivers to find the original message. We put another DES encryption to this decrypt file again, which can resist the cryptoanalysis from the leakage of the this file.

2.4   Threat Model

Here, we assume there are some attackers in our model who attempt to tamper or intercept message, cryptoanalyse transaction.

If attackers attempt to tamper data on the Bitcoin, it means they should create enough fake identities, which can repel real nodes on the network by a majority of votes. Then fake nodes can reject the receive or transfer blocks, effectively preventing other users from accessing the network. In the relatively large-scale Sybil attack, the premise is that when the attackers have controlled most of the computer network or hash rate, they can carry out the system attack covering 51%. In this case, they can easily change the order of the trades and prevent the trades from being confirmed. They can even take over and reverse transactions, leading to a double payout problem. But Bitcoin mining is intense and highly rewarding, most of the miners are keen on legitimate mining methods instead of trying to conduct Sybil attack. Bitcoin as a covert communication medium, which can guarantees the truth of the data [19].

All the transactions in the Blockchain are transparent, the attackers also can witness the generation of these transactions. If a user continues to transmit overlong length of messages, the attackers may notice the continuous transactions with multiple output addresses. Maybe they will analyse these transactions, even if they distinguish some transactions from the same sender, they still can't understand how to restore the addresses to the ciphertext. Because our model CCBRSN takes a special rules to embed messages into addresses and use DES to encrypt the decrypt file again. The only way to crack the ciphertext is to intercept the decrypt file the model produced and get access to our tool at the same time. In fact, it seems very impossible unless the user reveals initiatively.

3   The Proposed CCBRSN Scheme

In this section, we give an exhaustive description of our scheme called CCBRSN. Firstly we introduce the configuration of the Regtest network in Bitcoin. Then we describe the overview of our method. At last, we will talk about the process of embedding and restore in detail.

3.1   General Overview of CCBRSN

In our scheme, User A wants to send an encrypted message to User B through the Bitcoin, however, User A doesn't expect this message is revealed or decrypted to anyone other than User B. Due to consensus algorithm in Bitcoin, if User A completes all the process of sending, anyone even User A himself can't change the content of the message. For malicious guys, they also have no ability to tamper the text of the message because of this feature in Bitcoin. The general procedure of our scheme is as follows:

1. User A inputs a message m that he wants to send.
2. User A enters a password k for DES encryption, the outcome of encrypting m is $DES_k(m)$. Then $DES_k(m)$ is encoded into $Base58(b)$ by $Base58$.
3. User A applies $ECDSA$ to generate a pair of private and public key$(s_k^{(1)}, p_k^{(1)})$
4. User A starts with the $p_k^{(1)}$, computes the SHA256 hash and then computes the RIPEMD160 hash of the result, finally uses $Base58$ to produce an address $a^{(1)}$.
5. User A compares each bit of $Base58(b)$ with each bit of $a^{(1)}$. If the match is successful, then User A will record the corresponding indexes of $Base58(b)$ and $a^{(1)} set^m[[1, 2, ..., n], ..., [1, 2, ..., n]]$ and $set^a[[1, 2, ..., n], ..., [1, 2, ..., n]]$.
6. User A replaces the corresponded bits in $Base58(b)$ with *, then $Base58(b)$ will be transformed into $Base58(b1)$. User A continues to use $Base58(b1)$ to repeat the above steps until all bits in $Base58(b1)$ are matched.
7. User A submits a transaction whose output addresses are $a^{(1)}, a^{(2)}$, $a^{(3)}, ..., a^{(n)}$. Transaction fee of each address are in a address generated time order. After sending process, a file $File$ will be produced.
8. For the protection of information in the file, we should use DES encryption with a defined key in advance to encrypt the $File$ to $encFile$ again.
9. Until this transaction is packed into a block, User B can import file $encFile$ to restore the message.

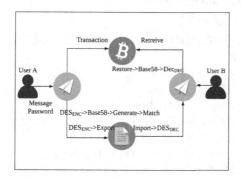

Fig. 3. The process of execution.

During the entire transaction, User A only pays a little money for transaction fee. Because all pairs of private and public key are all in User A's charge, he can transfer back the money. Although we base this system on Bitcoin, other Blockchains who accept address can also use this model to build a new covert communication system on their own. The detailed steps have been illustrated in the Fig. 3.

3.2   Messages Embedment

In this section, we explain the detailed steps of the embedding algorithm. Firstly, we assume that User A can transmit encrypt file to User B in a public channel. Although somebody could intercept this file, however, it is hardly possible for him to find our tool for decryption. In the initial stage, we use DES to encode the original messages. Now DES is not safe which can be cracked by some analysis. Considering the length of the outcome, we still choose this encryption algorithm. Like $Base64$, $Base58$ is also a specific coding scheme that is employed in the Bitcoin system. To make our ciphertext correspond with address, we take the same way to encode text.

In our model, we build our test experiment on the Bitcoin Regtest network. Even though, Regtest is developed in local and doesn't have all the abilities of Mainnet. It still can satisfy most of the requirements it needs, for example, the generation of public and private keys, generate address, transaction and so on.

The following Algorithm 1 is our embedding procedures.

Algorithm 1. Messages Embedding Algorithm

1: **procedure** EMBED(k, m)
2:     $c \leftarrow DES(k, m)$
3:     $b \leftarrow Base64(c)$
4:     $n \leftarrow 0$
5:     **while** $b \; != \; ' **...**'$ **do**
6:         $n \leftarrow n + 1$
7:         $s_k^{(n)} \leftarrow Random(2^0, 2^{256})$
8:         $p_k^{(n)} \leftarrow KeyGen(s_k^{(n)})$
9:         $a_k^{(n)} \leftarrow BASE58(RIPEMD160(SHA256(p_k^{(n)})))$
10:         $Flag \leftarrow False$
11:         **for** each bit_1 in $a_k^{(n)}$ **do**
12:             **for** each bit_2 in b **do**
13:                 **if** $bit_1 == bit_2$ **then**
14:                     $Flag \leftarrow True$
15:                     $setAddr_{index} \leftarrow IndexOf(bit_1)$
16:                     $setMsg_{index} \leftarrow IndexOf(bit_2)$
17:                 **end if**
18:             **end for**
19:         **end for**
20:         **if** $Flag == True$ **then**

21:          $setAddr_{addr} \leftarrow a_k^{(n)}$
22:       **end if**
23:    **end while**
24:    **if** $setAddr_{addr} \mathrel{!}= NULL$ **then**
25:       $TxID \leftarrow$ Transaction($setAddr_{addr}$)
26:       $encFile \leftarrow$ Write($Enc('wwz12345')$,
27:               $setAddr_{index}, setMsg_{index}, TxID$)
28:    **end if**
29: **end procedure**

3.3 Messages Extraction

Extraction is the reverse process of embedment. User B will import the received file into the system to restore some important parameters. Then User B uses the value of $TxID$ to locate the corresponding transaction information and find all the addresses. Finally, User B can decode and decrypt the ciphertext to plaintext. The detailed procedure of extraction is described in Algorithm 2.

Algorithm 2. Messages Extraction Algorithm

1: **procedure** EXTRACT($File$)
2:    $File \leftarrow Dec('wwz12345', encFile)$
3:    $TxId \leftarrow Restore(File)$
4:    $setAddr_{index} \leftarrow Restore(File)$
5:    $setMsg_{index} \leftarrow Restore(File)$
6:    $k \leftarrow Restore(File)$
7:    $setAdd_{addr} \leftarrow FindTx(TxID)$
8:    $b \leftarrow Match(setAddr_{index}, setMsg_{index},$
9:        $setAddr_{addr})$
10:   $c \leftarrow deBase64(b)$
11:   $m \leftarrow Dec(c, k)$
12: **end procedure**

---

4 Experiment and Evaluation

4.1 Experiment Environment

Our model is deployed in Windows 10. The main used tools are Bitcoin Core 0.18.1 client and python 3.6. Based on the scheme we proposed, we use python and the package of bitcoinlib to develop a covert communication system which connects to the Bitcoin Regtest Network. Users can use this system to transmit messages in this self-built network at any time. For the evaluation of our model, we choose 10 different length of text from 5 bits to 50 bits. Then inputting random generated data to the tool we developed, every type of text is tested 100 times for the accuracy of the experiment. Then we calculate the average value for our experiment.

4.2 Evaluation Results

We are from three aspects to build experiments for the evaluation of our model.

1. Embeded Rate: Firstly, we use our dataset to analyse the embed rate of generated addresses. As we can see from Fig. 4, although there is a fluctuation during the whole process, overall the reuse rate of address becomes higher with the increment of text length. The increment is very apparent, at last, the embed rate even reaches to 11.08%.

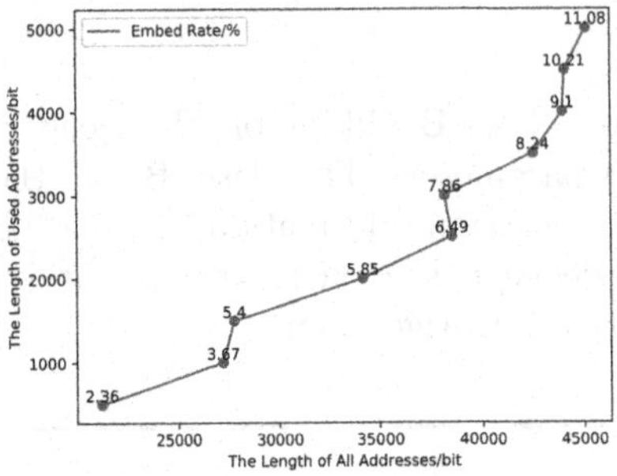

Fig. 4. The embed rate in CCBRSN

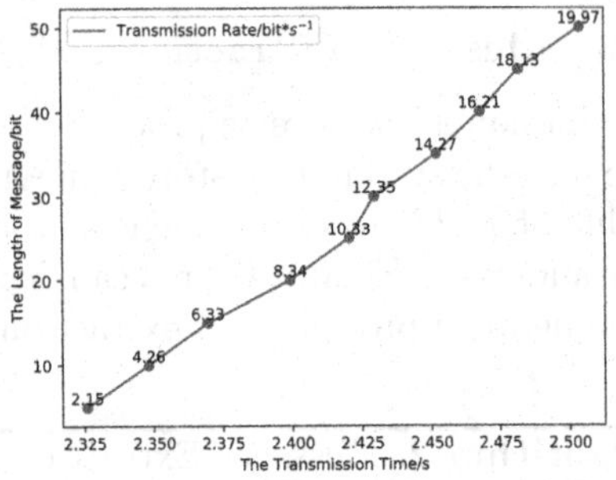

Fig. 5. The encrypt rate in CCBRSN

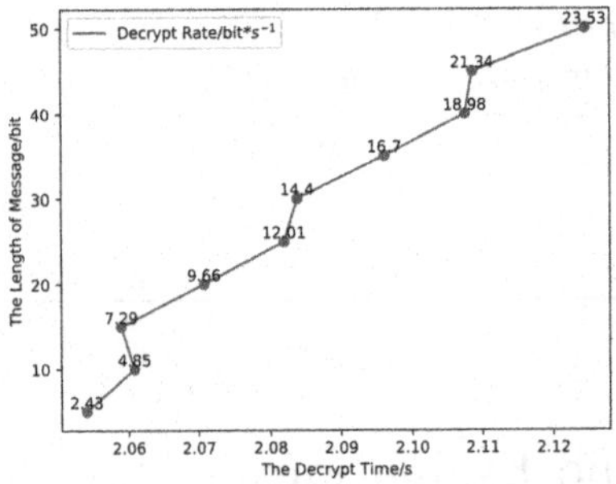

Fig. 6. The decrypt rate in CCBRSN

2. Transmission Rate: We record all the time from inputting data to the generation of decrypt file. Figure 5 describes the transmission rate between the length of messages and the transmission times. At the beginning, the encrypt rate is a little low which is just around 2.15 bit/s. Because there are 34 bits text in address, whereas, some bits in an address are also repetition. If we attempt to pair address and text, the short length of sending text need the same number of addresses like long ones. Hence the first step will cost fixed

time, then the processing time will slow down and have a little difference. Once the length of text increases a lot, the rate of address utilization will be raised, then the embed rate will have a huge gap. As we can see from the figure, the fastest transmission rate can be up to 19.97 bit/s. Therefore, at first, the transmission rate is very low, but as length increases, the transmission rate is getting faster. In conclusion, the increment of bits corresponds with the trend of the time, and the transmission time is in the tolerance interval.

3. Decryption Rate: Figure 6 shows the decrypt rate in CCBRSN. We can see decrypt rate is the same as encrypt rate, which is very low at the beginning, then high at the ending. The reason for explaining this phenomenon is the same as embed rate. However, in this stage, the difference is restoring message dominates the main time, other things only have a small effect on it. Hence, the tiny increment of text size leads to enormous improvement in decrypt rate, which even achieves 23.56 bit/s. Although the decrypt rate is not fast at the beginning, but there are always some delays in communication, decrypt time is around 2 s which is also considered as acceptable.

4.3   Compared with Other Schemes

Few related papers also take blockchain as a covert channel medium. In the paper [16], they proposed a pioneering concept attempts to conduct covert communication in Blockchain and give us a simple example. BlBasuki et al. [20] suggested joint steganography by utilizing blockchain-based transaction steganography and image steganography to achieve a secure and secret communication medium. We try to use the following tables to analyze the pros and cons of these methods.

Table 1. Transaction steganography comparison

Method	Capacity/transaction	Security	Blockchain networks
BLOCCE	2000 bits	+	Any
JTISHCC	29 bits	++	Ethereum
CCBRSN	68000 bits	++	Any(default: Bitcoin)

As we can see from Table 1, in the aspect of capacity, our scheme-CCBRSN has the overwhelming advantages of the other methods. Due to the reuse features of the addresses, if possible CCBRSN can make use of every bit in an address(most of the addresses have 34 bits). The max number of addresses in a transaction is usually between 2000 and 3000. When it refers to security, our scheme uses Des encryption and special coding rules to ensure the privacy of our content. Simultaneously, only if the blockchain who has addresses for the transaction, our schemes can be applied to, therefore the appliance is rarely widespread. Based on the above analysis, CCBRSN is suitable for covert communication.

5   Conclusions and Future Work

In this paper, we present a method which is called CCBRSN. This method firstly encrypts and encode plaintext into a specific type, then embed this type of message into Bitcoin's addresses, finally construct a transaction that includes these addresses to transmit information. If this transaction is finished successfully, a decrypt file will be produced. If a user who owns the decrypt file can input it into the same system, then the plaintext will be restored.

Although our way has successfully implement covert communication on Bitcoin, It still needs further improvement. For example: 1) Our model is just based on local network, so we don't take deeply consideration of the crowd of transaction, the latency of the block generation and so on which really exists in public network. 2) We use multiple match to greatly improve the efficiency of transmission. However if a user attempts to send a huge size of message such as document, the number of address may reach thousand or even ten thousand, then the size of a transaction will exceed the rated value. As a result, this transaction can't be generated. 3) Decrypt file is significant for receivers, users will use this specific file to restore message. Nonetheless, we don't know people how to transmit it, maybe in a public communication way. If an attacker intercepts this file and just right has access to this tool, the security of transmission can't be ensured. 4) In the future research, we can attempt to apply our model to other Blockchain systems.

For the improvement of our scheme, we will attempt to take some countermeasures to solve the above mentioned problems in our future research.

Acknowledgement. This work is partly supported by JSPS Kiban(B) 18H03240 and JSPS Kiban(C) 18K11298.

References

1. Zhang, W., Zhao, N., Zhang, S., Yu, F.R.: Multi-antenna covert communications with random access protocol. arXiv preprint arXiv:1907.07481 (2019)
2. Brown, E., Yuan, B., Johnson, D., Lutz, P.: Covert channels in the HTTP network protocol: Channel characterization and detecting man-in-the-middle attacks. In: 5th European Conference on Information Management and Evaluation, ECIME 2011 (2011)
3. Lucena, N.B., Lewandowski, G., Chapin, S.J.: Covert channels in IPv6. In: Danezis, G., Martin, D. (eds.) PET 2005. LNCS, vol. 3856, pp. 147–166. Springer, Heidelberg (2006). https://doi.org/10.1007/11767831_10
4. Ji, L., Jiang, W., Dai, B., Niu, X.: Novel covert channel based on length of messages. In: Proceedings of International Symposium on Information Engineering and Electronic Commerce. IEEC 2009, vol. 2009 (2009)
5. Nakamoto, S.: Bitcoin: a peer-to-peer electronic cash system—Satoshi Nakamoto Institute. Technical report, bitcoin.org (2008)
6. Wood, G.: Ethereum: a secure decentralised generalised transaction ledger. Ethereum Project Yellow Paper (2014)

7. Yuan, Y., Wang, F.Y.: Towards blockchain-based intelligent transportation systems. In: IEEE Conference on Intelligent Transportation Systems, Proceedings, ITSC (2016)
8. Pawlak, M., Poniszewska-Marańda, A., Kryvinska, N.: Towards the intelligent agents for blockchain e-voting system. Procedia Comput. Sci. **141**, 239–246 (2018)
9. The number of tera hashes per second in the bitcoin network. https://www.blockchain.com/zh-cn/charts/hash-rate. Accessed 17 Oct 2019
10. Zhou, Q., Huang, H., Zheng, Z., Bian, J.: Solutions to scalability of blockchain: a survey. IEEE Access **8**, 1–10 (2020)
11. Guo, L., Ni, J., Shi, Y.Q.: Uniform embedding for efficient JPEG steganography. IEEE Trans. Inf. Forensics Secur. **9**(5), 814–825 (2014)
12. Asad, M., Gilani, J., Khalid, A.: An enhanced least significant bit modification technique for audio steganography. In: International Conference on Computer Networks and Information Technology, pp. 143–147. IEEE (2011)
13. Balaji, R., Naveen, G.: Secure data transmission using video steganography. In: 2011 IEEE International Conference on Electro/Information Technology, pp. 1–5. IEEE (2011)
14. Cox, I.J., Kilian, J., Leighton, F.T., Shamoon, T.: Secure spread spectrum watermarking for multimedia. IEEE Trans. Image Process. **6**(12), 1673–1687 (1997)
15. Bender, W., Gruhl, D., Morimoto, N., Lu, A.: Techniques for data hiding. IBM Syst. J. **35**(3.4), 313–336 (1996)
16. Partala, J.: Provably secure covert communication on blockchain. Cryptography **2**(3), 18 (2018)
17. Different Blockchains: Ethereum vs cosmos vs hyperledger and more! https://blockgeeks.com/guides/different-blockchains/. Accessed 20 Oct 2019
18. How to set up a bitcoin regtest environment. https://bisq.network/blog/how-to-set-up-bitcoin-regtest. Accessed 19 Oct 2019
19. Huang, H., et al.: Real-time fault-detection for IIoT facilities using GBRBM-based DNN. IEEE Internet Things J. (2019)
20. Basuki, A.I., Rosiyadi, D.: Joint transaction-image steganography for high capacity covert communication. In: 2019 International Conference on Computer, Control, Informatics and its Applications (IC3INA), pp. 41–46. IEEE (2019)

Privacy-Friendly Monero Transaction Signing on a Hardware Wallet

Dusan Klinec[✉] and Vashek Matyas

Masaryk University, Brno, Czech Republic
{xklinec,matyas}@fi.muni.cz

Abstract. Keeping cryptocurrency spending keys safe and being able to use them when signing a transaction is a well-known problem, addressed by hardware wallets. Our work focuses on a transaction signing process for privacy-centric cryptocurrency Monero, in the hardware wallets. We designed, implemented, and analyzed a privacy-preserving transaction signing protocol that runs on a hardware wallet and protects the spending keys. Moreover, we also implemented a privacy-preserving multi-party version of the Bulletproof zero-knowledge prover algorithm, which runs on a hardware wallet with constant memory. We present the protocols and evaluate their performance on a real hardware wallet.

Keywords: Monero · Transaction signing · Bulletproofs ·
Zero-knowledge system · Multi-party computation · Hardware wallets

1 Introduction

Cryptocurrencies gained popularity and increased adoption by general public in the recent years. They became a valuable asset worth protecting. In the vast majority of the cryptocurrency designs, the only thing needed to transact (spend) the coins is a cryptographic key (master key). Recently, we have seen several attacks on the software wallets storing the master keys and leading to coin thefts [4,11].

Software wallets are inherently vulnerable to malware threats, so users seek better ways to protect their cryptographic assets. One option is to use a dedicated hardware device, the hardware wallet, that stores the master key securely and performs the signature on the transactions specified by the user. The device can be equipped with a display to show the transaction details to the user (e.g., destination and the amount) and buttons to confirm the transaction information. As the hardware wallet (HW) is a special-purpose device, it has a much smaller attack surface than a PC. The HW is limited and usually needs a PC client for operation, e.g., transaction construction, transaction scanning.

Bitcoin, the first massively used cryptocurrency, does not provide much privacy to its users. i.e., the whole transaction history is stored in a public

© IFIP International Federation for Information Processing 2020
Published by Springer Nature Switzerland AG 2020
M. Hölbl et al. (Eds.): SEC 2020, IFIP AICT 580, pp. 338–351, 2020.
https://doi.org/10.1007/978-3-030-58201-2_23

blockchain (append-only ledger), it contains source, destination addresses (cryptographic keys, pseudonymous identifiers), and transacted amounts in a clear form so the attacker can mount several chain analysis techniques to trace the financial flow between the users. On the other hand, creating the signature and implementing the logic in the HW is usually straightforward as it requires just transaction serialization logic and ECDSA signature over the data.

We focus on a privacy-centric cryptocurrency, *Monero* [1], which is the most used privacy-centric cryptocurrency[1]. In Monero, all destination addresses are unique, and the amounts being transacted are hidden using Pedersen commitments [9]. The secure implementation of the Monero transaction signing is thus a more challenging task. Moreover, HWs are resource-constrained devices with limited memory and computational power.

For the practical testing, we choose a Trezor HW model T^2 (Trezor for short) as it represents a class of HWs with generally available processors used in the embedded devices, with around 100 kB of RAM. It runs Micropython[3], a Python version for resource-constrained devices.

Contribution: This work builds on our previous technical report [5] and for an extended version of this paper please refer to the [6]. We designed and implemented a Monero transaction signing protocol for HWs. The protocol is simple, which helps with the security analysis. Moreover, it mimics the already deployed cold-signing protocol [5] used with offline Monero wallets. We implemented the protocol to Trezor and Monero codebases, and it is being used in practice. Moreover, we designed and implemented a secure multi-party protocol (MPC) version of a zero-knowledge proving system called Bulletproof [3], which uses constant memory and works on HWs. The MPC version protects private values, from PC-based attacker. To the best of our knowledge, this is the first MPC implementation of the Bulletproof runnable on HWs.

General Methods: As the HW is a resource-limited device, the general methods for converting arbitrary protocols into MPC, such as Garbled circuits [10], are not applicable, as those usually require significantly more memory and running time than we have available. We thus resort to a more effective protocol offloading design tailored specifically to the application domain, to preserve the practical usability of the resulting protocol.

1.1 Cryptocurrency Primer

The elementary operation of transacting a particular amount from a sender to a receiver is called *transaction*. The transaction is an atomic state transition. Transactions are stored in the blocks, the block contains a hash of a previously generated block, thus forming a ledger of blocks, a blockchain. A new block is created every 10 min.

---

[1] By the market value https://coinmarketcap.com, accessed on 5. 1. 2020.

[2] https://wiki.trezor.io/Trezor_Model_T.

[3] https://micropython.org.

Transaction has $|\mathcal{T}^{\text{in}}| = m$ inputs $\mathcal{T}_j^{\text{in}}$, $|\mathcal{T}^{\text{out}}| = p$ outputs $\mathcal{T}_t^{\text{out}}$ and a fee. The amounts values in the input and the output side have to be equal, i.e., $\sum_{j=1}^{m} v_j^{\text{in}} = \sum_{t=1}^{p} v_t^o + \text{fee}$, so the transaction is a valid state transition (and no value is lost or created). Let's denote transaction outputs TXOs. Transaction inputs are also called unspent transaction outputs (UTXOs). UTXOs are addresses that have a non-zero balance that can be spent. A balance can be trivially computed by replaying all transactions recorded in the blockchain. Blockchain clients usually track all UTXOs and update the state with each new block.

Transaction construction is controlled from the PC client as it scans the blockchain for UTXOs that can be spent. A user enters the transaction recipient addresses and amounts on the PC. The client then performs the transaction signing protocol with an HW to obtain a signed transaction. The signed transaction is then broadcasted to the cryptocurrency network and eventually added to a block.

The Monero user wallet has two key-pairs, (k^v, K^v) and (k^s, K^s), the *view-key*, and *spend-key*, respectively. The view-key is used to scan the blockchain for incoming transactions to the user wallet; the spend-key is required to create a signature for spending the incoming coins.

1.2 Attacker Model

HWs are considered as trusted in all attacker models in this paper, i.e., HW securely stores master keys, and an attacker can gain no knowledge by observing and tampering the HW device. We only focus on an attacker controlling the PC client. The *honest-but-curious* attacker model is defined by an attacker that obeys the protocol precisely but tries to learn new information observing the protocol transcripts. The *malicious* attacker model is stronger, an attacker can arbitrarily deviate from the protocol. He can start multiple instances of protocols, interleave protocol runs, send, replay, delay, or drop any protocol messages.

1.3 Notation

We use a standard notation used in the related literature, such as [1,3]. Due to the paper application domain in the Monero transactions, we use the elliptic curve (EC) *Ed25519* [2] as a specialization of the cyclic group $\mathbb{G}$ of the prime order l, let's denote $\mathbb{Z}_l$ the ring of integers modulo l. The $\mathbb{Z}_l^*$ denotes $\mathbb{Z}_l \backslash \{0\}$. The $x \xleftarrow{\$} \mathbb{Z}_l^*$ denotes a uniform sampling of an element from $\mathbb{Z}_l^*$. Capital letters represent points on the curve $\mathbb{G}$, lower-case letters represent scalars from $\mathbb{Z}_l^*$ unless said otherwise. We use the EC additive notation for $\mathbb{G}$, e.g., $P+Q$ is a point addition, $aP = (P + \cdots + P)$ is a scalar multiplication, $0P = O$, i.e., neutral element, point in infinity. Let $\mathbb{F}^n$ denote a vector space over $\mathbb{F}$, the $\boldsymbol{a} \in \mathbb{F}^n$ is a vector from the vector space with elements $a_0, \ldots, a_{n-1} \in \mathbb{F}$. The $\boldsymbol{a} \cdot \boldsymbol{b} = \sum_{i=0}^{n-1} a_i b_i$ denotes a dot-product of $\boldsymbol{a}, \boldsymbol{b} \in \mathbb{F}^n$, the $\boldsymbol{a} \circ \boldsymbol{b} = \{(a_i b_i)\}_i$ is element product. We also use Python notation for vector slicing, i.e., $\boldsymbol{a}_{[:l]} = (a_0, \ldots, a_{l-1})$, $\boldsymbol{a}_{[l:]} = (a_l, \ldots, a_n)$. For $k \in \mathbb{Z}_l^*$, the $\boldsymbol{k}^n \in \mathbb{F}^n$ denotes the vector $k_{|i|} = k^i$. The G is a generator of the

$\mathbb{G}$, i.e., a base point. Let's define a cryptographic hash function $\mathcal{H} : \{0,1\}^* \to \{0,1\}^{256}$, the $\mathcal{H}_p : \{0,1\}^* \to \mathbb{G}$ is a cryptographic hash function to curve points, $\mathcal{H}_s : \{0,1\}^* \to \mathbb{Z}_l^*$ is a cryptographic hash function to scalars. Moreover, let's define $H = \mathcal{H}_p(G)$, a point of unknown logarithm. Binary format of the scalars and points is 256 bits long. Let's denote the binary concatenation as $||$ and a key derivation function as $\text{KDF}(x) = \mathcal{H}(\mathcal{H}(x))$.

2   Transaction Signing Protocol

Ring signatures are signatures generated by a single private key k_π corresponding to the public key K_π which is in the ring of unrelated public keys $\mathcal{R} = \{K_0, \ldots, K_\pi, \ldots, K_n\}$. The verifier is not able to tell which $K_i \in \mathcal{R}$ generated the signature. This provides n-anonymity for the signer. Keys $K_i, i \neq \pi$ are called decoy keys. Let's define $n = |\mathcal{R}|$, i.e., the ring size.

Monero uses Schnorr-style multilayered linkable spontaneous anonymous group signatures (MLSAG) [8]. The linkability is a property that links signatures generated with the same private keys. The linked signatures have the same *key image* (explained later). Signatures with already seen key images are considered as invalid to protect from double-spending the same UTXO.

Monero uses the *Pedersen commitment* to conceal the transacted amounts and to prove that transaction input amounts are equal to transaction output amounts. A Monero *range proof* is a zero-knowledge proof that the TXO amount encoded in the scalar value $v \in \mathbb{Z}_l^*$ lies[4] in the interval of allowed values $[0, 2^N]$, $N = 64$. The range proof is an essential part of the confidential transactions as it protects from overflows and new coin generation.

The *transaction generator* takes $\mathcal{T}^{\text{in}}$ and set of destination addresses and amounts $\mathcal{T}^{\text{out}}$ and produces a transaction with signature. The value $|\mathcal{T}^{\text{in}}|$ can be quite high and is limited by the fee the user is willing to spend for the transaction to be added to the blockchain and the current block size. The current Monero protocol version (0.15.0.1), i.e. hard-fork, specifies that for a valid transaction it holds that $2 \leq |\mathcal{T}^{\text{out}}| \leq 16$. Thus the $|\mathcal{T}^{\text{in}}|$ is the main limiting factor for the transaction generator with respect to the memory. The ring size n is fixed to 11 at the current version, but it is likely to increase in the future.

It is not feasible to construct a transaction in the HW in one pass. Thus the building process has to be separated into several steps so it can be computed with limited memory. We designed, implemented, and tested the transaction generation protocol that runs in the HW with unlimited $\mathcal{T}^{\text{in}}$ (the protocol).

Transaction Signing Protocol with State Offloading: *The offloaded signing protocol is described fully in the extended paper* [6]. *Here we explain only key ideas of the protocol construction.*

A *state offloading* is required to build the transaction incrementally. Some parts of the state are sent to the host for later retrieval during the transaction construction. The protocol uses HMAC to protect the public state

---

[4] v in Pedersen commitment $\gamma G + vH$, $\gamma \xleftarrow{\$} \mathbb{Z}_l^*$. Refer to Sect. 3 for more details.

parts, e.g., parts of the final transaction, and an authenticated encryption (Chacha20Poly1305) for private state information, e.g., T^{in} private spending keys.

All MLSAG signatures are generated in the HW, the k^s never leaves the device, while the k^v is exported to the host so it can scan all blockchain transactions to determine whether the funds were sent to the recipient wallet keys. Performing the blockchain scanning with the device would be inefficient.

The transaction is built on the host incrementally, from the information provided by the HW. In general, the host sends initial transaction information to the HW. The user is asked to confirm transaction details on the HW screen, such as destination address, amounts, and transaction fee. If confirmed, the HW generates HMACs for transaction input elements so they cannot be changed later (commitment to values).

Then all T^{in} are sent to the HW one by one; the HW derives required signing keys, serializes T^{in} to blockchain format, incrementally hashes information required for later MLSAG construction. Then destination information is sent one by one; the HW generates T^{out} related information, serializes T^{out} to the blockchain format, range proof generation (see Sect. 3) is handled. Finally, the MLSAG is generated per T^{in}.

Key Construction Scheme: Let's describe HMAC key construction on the T^{out} example, generated after user confirmation. HW returns to the host T^{out}: $\{T_i^{out}$, HMAC(T_i^{out}, key= KDF(k^{mac} ||"txdest"||i))$\}_i$, where k^{mac} is a random HMAC master key generated per-transaction. The HMAC keys construction prevents from changing destination specification later in the protocol by an attacker. All the offloading keys used in the protocol are generated correspondingly, i.e., the keys are unique per offloaded element to make the protocol strictly commit to the offloaded values and their ordering. The key is derived from the master keys, the domain separator, e.g., "txdest", and the item index.

Encrypt-then-Reveal: In order to limit the attacker's reactivity, MLSAG signatures are returned encrypted to the host. The encryption key is returned to the host after the protocol finishes successfully.

Analysis: The protocol is based on the cold-signing protocol [5] implemented in Monero codebase, which takes all transaction inputs T^{in}, transaction outputs T^{out}, asks the user to confirm transaction outputs, and a fee and generates a valid Monero transaction. Cold-signing protocol is trivially secure as it is evaluated in a secure environment (offline Monero wallet), and the user confirms all transaction outputs. Our offloaded protocol mimics the cold-signing protocol. It is evaluated in a HW, which is considered a secure environment. The transaction is constructed incrementally, from the basic input blocks T^{in}, T^{out} sent one by one to the HW. The user confirms the T^{out} on the HW, as it has a display and touch screen. After the confirmation is done, the HW generates HMAC for confirmed T^{out}. Thus it cannot be later modified by an attacker.

Each call is guarded by a state automaton, set up in step 1 by the parameters of the transaction. This prevents from calling protocol methods in a different than expected order. Moreover, due to HMAC and encryption key construction, it is not possible to modify, reorder, reply, or drop the offloaded state elements. Protocol aborts if invalid input is provided.

The only place where the k^s is used is during spend key computation, during $\mathcal{T}^{in}$ construction. The result of the computation is offloaded in an encrypted form, which could only be used as input in the last protocol step, during MLSAG generation per each $\mathcal{T}^{in}$. MLSAG signature is generated over hash commitment $\mathfrak{m}$, which hashes the entire transaction specification $(\mathcal{T}^{in}, \mathcal{T}^{out})$. The protocol is thus secure in the malicious attacker model as cheating in each protocol step is detected by HMAC, auth tag, or state transition failure.

The only information the attacker can obtain from the protocol runs (without a need to finish the protocol) is key images corresponding to the $\mathcal{T}_j^{in}$. The key images are part of the constructed transaction. As we need the host to sort key images so some kind of order-preserving encryption would have to be used to protect key images from leaking before the protocol finish. However, we do not consider this as a required measure as the key images are computed during the blockchain scanning once the transaction sent to our wallet has been found.

Performance and Space Complexity: The space complexity is determined by $O(n + p)$, i.e., by a ring size and the number of the transaction outputs, i.e., $n = 11$ and $p \leq 16$ in the current Monero version. The whole ring is needed only for the MLSAG signature, which can be easily extended to support large rings. If the p is increased later, the protocol can be easily changed to offload all output-related values. The transaction signing protocol implemented in Micropython

Table 1. Performance of the transaction signing protocol on Trezor HW. The algorithm was tested on the emulator and Trezor T HW. Configuration is a tuple (#inputs, #outputs). The first metric, "Time emu", is a runtime in an emulator, other statistics are from runs on the real hardware. "$\sum$ Steps" is protocol computation time without communication overhead, "rounds" is a total number of message round-trips. Rows with "State" show a maximal state size over the protocol, where "real" is the real size measured in the implementation, "min" is the minimal space required, without Micropython objects overhead. Note that the range-proof is not included in the statistics as it is measured separately in Sect. 3. It is visible that the state size is constant, and timing is linear to the number of inputs.

Configuration	2-2	16-2	32-2	64-2	128-2	2-16
Time Emu [s]	9.31	29.93	58.13	106.32	209.88	21.45
Time [s]	16.90	83.22	156.82	306.74	604.09	46.13
$\sum$ Steps	12.49	56.30	106.69	207.33	408.42	36.62
Rounds	14	56	104	200	392	28
RAM [B]	41 264	42 176	42 208	42 048	58 512	41 376
State min [B]	2 385	2 385	2 385	2 385	2 385	4 406
State real [B]	5 315	5 315	5 315	5 315	5 315	9 224

for Trezor HW was tested with various input transactions. Refer to Table 1 for performance overview data.

3   Range Proof

A range proof is a zero-knowledge proof that the amount encoded in a scalar $v \in \mathbb{Z}_l^*$ (256-bit number for Ed25519), lies in the interval $[0, 2^{64})$, without revealing the amount value. Range proof computations are the most resource expensive operations in the transaction construction (time and memory). Thus it makes sense to offload the computation to the host.

The range proofs make use of commitments $V = \gamma G + vH$, where $\gamma \xleftarrow{\$} \mathbb{Z}_l^*$ is a mask, and the V is part of the publicly stored information. If the attacker generates the masks in a special way, he can exfiltrate information about the keys or the transaction. From the binding property of the commitment scheme which relies on the discrete logarithm problem, it is infeasible to find a different v', γ', s.t. $\gamma'G + v'H = \gamma G + vH$. The attacker already knows the amount as he observes the transaction construction, but knowing the masks enables the attacker to prove the amount to a third party (e.g., court). This poses a privacy risk as the attacker can prove that he has seen the transaction construction or knows the amount keys.

The *Bulletproof* [3] (BP) is the range proof system used in Monero. The proof size increases logarithmically with respect to the number of statements (transaction outputs). BP can prove statement of the form $M = 2^x$. We implemented the memory-optimized prover version for the Trezor HW, described in Algorithm 1.

Space Complexity: Up to the while-loop on line 29, all vectors can be evaluated on-the-fly with a constant memory and low CPU overhead with just v, γ stored. Vector foldings on lines 36–39 dominate the space complexity. Overall the space complexity is $O(MN)$. Please refer to full paper [6] for detailed analysis.

Implementation: We implemented the in-memory Bulletproof prover as specified in the Algorithm 1 and the verifier in Micropython and tested on the Trezor HW. The memory usage is $32(128M + 12log(M)) + O(max(log(N), M))$ B. The verification algorithm runs with $O(max(log(N), M))$ memory. Table 2 shows the performance of the prover and the verifier implemented on the Trezor.

3.1   Offloaded Bulletproofs

Due to increasing space complexity, it is not possible to generate BPs with $M \geq 4$ on the Trezor. We thus designed a new privacy-preserving secure multi-party computation protocol (MPC) to compute Bulletproofs jointly with the PC host and an HW with a constant memory on the HW side. We do not consider the time and memory requirements of the protocol running on the host in the following[5].

---

[5] Multiplying by 8^{-1} protects from small subgroup addition https://www.getmonero.org/2017/05/17/disclosure-of-a-major-bug-in-cryptonote-based-currencies.html.

Algorithm 1. Bulletproof prover. $N = 64, M = |\boldsymbol{v}|, \boldsymbol{v}$ is a vector of amounts

---

1 **function** BULLETPROOFPROVER$(\boldsymbol{v}, \boldsymbol{\gamma})$ ▷ Input: Amounts and masks
2   $(\boldsymbol{V}, A, S, T1, T2, \tau_x, \mu, x, h, l_{0,i}, l_{1,i}, r_{0,i}, r_{1,i}) \leftarrow$ BULLETPROOFPREFIX$(\boldsymbol{v}, \boldsymbol{\gamma})$
3   $l_i \leftarrow l_{0,i} + x l_{1,i}$ ▷ Vector $\boldsymbol{l}$
4   $r_i \leftarrow r_{0,i} + x r_{1,i}$ ▷ Vector $\boldsymbol{r}$
5   $t \leftarrow \boldsymbol{l} \cdot \boldsymbol{r}; x' \leftarrow \mathcal{H}_s(x||x||\tau_x||\mu||t)$ ▷ Evaluated with const. memory up to here
6   $(\boldsymbol{L}, \boldsymbol{R}, a'_0, b'_0) \leftarrow$ BULLETPROOFLOOP$(\boldsymbol{l}, \boldsymbol{r}, \mathring{\boldsymbol{G}}, \boldsymbol{y}^{-|\mathring{H}|} \circ \mathring{\boldsymbol{H}}, MN, -1, x', x')$
7   **return** $(\boldsymbol{V}, A, S, T1, T2, \tau_x, \mu, \boldsymbol{L}, \boldsymbol{R}, a'_0, b'_0, t)$
8 **function** BULLETPROOFPREFIX$(\boldsymbol{v}, \boldsymbol{\gamma})$ ▷ varint encodes integer to bytes
9   $\mathring{G}_{i\in[0,...,MN)} \leftarrow \mathcal{H}_p(\mathcal{H}(\text{``bulletproof''}||H||\text{varint}(2i+1)))$
10   $\mathring{H}_{i\in[0,...,MN)} \leftarrow \mathcal{H}_p(\mathcal{H}(\text{``bulletproof''}||H||\text{varint}(2i)))$
11   $V_j \leftarrow \gamma_j G + v_j H$ ▷ Compute commitment vector $\boldsymbol{V}$ used on line 18

12   $\alpha \xleftarrow{\$} \mathbb{Z}_l^*$ ▷ expand$(\boldsymbol{v})=\boldsymbol{x}$: $\sum_{i=0}^{63} 2^i x_{64j+i} = v_j, j \in [0, |\boldsymbol{v}|), x_i \in \{0,1\}$
13   $\boldsymbol{a}_L \leftarrow$ expand$(\boldsymbol{v}); \boldsymbol{a}_R = \boldsymbol{a}_L - \boldsymbol{1}^{MN}$
14   $A \leftarrow 8^{-1}\left(\alpha G + \sum_{i=0}^{MN-1} a_{L,i} \mathring{G}_i + a_{R,i} \mathring{H}_i\right)$ ▷ Commitment over values

15   $\rho, R \xleftarrow{\$} (\mathbb{Z}_l^*)^2$ ▷ randVct$(j) = \boldsymbol{x} : |\boldsymbol{x}| = MN, x_i = H_s(\text{"mask"}||R||i||j)$
16   $\boldsymbol{s}_L \leftarrow$ randVct$(0), \boldsymbol{s}_R \leftarrow$ randVct(1)
17   $S \leftarrow 8^{-1}\left(\rho G + \sum_{i=0}^{MN-1} s_{L,i} \mathring{G}_i + s_{R,i} \mathring{H}_i\right)$ ▷ Commitment over random masks
18   $y \leftarrow \mathcal{H}_s(\mathcal{H}_s(\boldsymbol{V})||A||S); z \leftarrow \mathcal{H}_s(y)$ ▷ Compute commitments over inputs
19   $\boldsymbol{l}_0 \leftarrow \boldsymbol{a}_L - z\boldsymbol{1}^{MN}; \boldsymbol{l}_1 \leftarrow \boldsymbol{s}_L$ ▷ Evaluated with const. memory, with $\boldsymbol{v}$
20   $\zeta_i \leftarrow z^{2+\lfloor i/N \rfloor} 2^{i\%N}$ ▷ Evaluated with const. memory and time
21   $\boldsymbol{r}_0 \leftarrow ((\boldsymbol{a}_R + z) \circ \boldsymbol{y}^{MN}) + \boldsymbol{\zeta}; \boldsymbol{r}_1 \leftarrow \boldsymbol{s}_R \circ \boldsymbol{y}^{MN}$
22   $t_1 \leftarrow \boldsymbol{l}_0 \cdot \boldsymbol{r}_1 + \boldsymbol{l}_1 \cdot \boldsymbol{r}_0; t_2 \leftarrow \boldsymbol{l}_1 \cdot \boldsymbol{r}_1$

23   $\tau_1, \tau_2 \xleftarrow{\$} (\mathbb{Z}_l^*)^2$
24   $T_1 = 8^{-1}(\tau_1 G + t_1 H); T_2 = 8^{-1}(\tau_2 G + t_2 H)$
25   $x \leftarrow \mathcal{H}_s(z||z||T1||T2)$
26   $\tau_x \leftarrow \tau_1 x + \tau_2 x^2 + \sum_{i=0}^{M} \gamma_i z^{i+2}; \mu \leftarrow \rho x + \alpha$
27   **return** $(\boldsymbol{V}, A, S, T1, T2, \tau_x, \mu, x, h, l_{0,i}, l_{1,i}, r_{0,i}, r_{1,i})$
28 **function** BULLETPROOFLOOP$(\boldsymbol{a}', \boldsymbol{b}', \boldsymbol{G}', \boldsymbol{H}', n', c, w, x')$
29   **while** $n' > 1$ **do**
30    $\bar{n} \leftarrow n'; n' \leftarrow n'/2; c \leftarrow c+1$
31    $c_L \leftarrow \boldsymbol{a}'_{[0,...,n')} \cdot \boldsymbol{b}'_{[n',...,\bar{n})}$
32    $c_R \leftarrow \boldsymbol{a}'_{[n',...,\bar{n})} \cdot \boldsymbol{b}'_{[0,...,n')}$
33    $L_c \leftarrow 8^{-1}\left(\left(\sum_{i=0}^{n'} a'_i \ G'_{i+n'} + b'_{i+n'} H'_i\right) + (c_L x') H\right)$
34    $R_c \leftarrow 8^{-1}\left(\left(\sum_{i=0}^{n'} a'_{i+n'} G'_i \ + b'_i \ H'_{i+n'}\right) + (c_R x') H\right)$
35    $w \leftarrow \mathcal{H}(w, L_c, R_c)$
36    $a'_{i\in[0,...,n')} \leftarrow w \ a'_i + w^{-1} a'_{i+n'}$ ▷ Scalar vector folding
37    $b'_{i\in[0,...,n')} \leftarrow w^{-1} b'_i + w \ b'_{i+n'}$ ▷ Folding reduces vector size by 2
38    $G'_{i\in[0,...,n')} \leftarrow w^{-1} G'_i + w \ G'_{i+n'}$ ▷ Hadamard folding
39    $H'_{i\in[0,...,n')} \leftarrow w \ H'_i + w^{-1} H'_{i+n'}$ ▷ Folding reduces vector size by 2
40   **return** $(\boldsymbol{L}, \boldsymbol{R}, a'_0, b'_0)$ ▷ vector $\boldsymbol{L}$ composed from L_c

Table 2. BP performance on the Trezor T HW. Verifier is faster than prover and requires significantly lower memory. Prover time and space complexity increase linearly to the input size. The *RAM min* shows the minimal amount of RAM required to cover the BP generation w.r.t. dominating cost - vectors, excluding the constants and state required for on-the-fly evaluation. The difference between Total RAM and minimal RAM is due to memory handling mechanisms in Micropython and constant memory overhead for on-the-fly vector evaluation.

Prover outputs	1	2	4	8	16
Time [s]	16.88	30.55	57.40	121.21	246.57
RAM min [B]	4 480	8 640	16 896	33 344	66 176
RAM total [B]	9 648	13 536	22 224	39 696	74 400
Verifier outputs	1	2	4	8	16
Time [s]	5.12	9.58	18.56	39.00	80.40
RAM total [B]	5 664	6 256	6 912	7 616	8 512
Proof size [B]	704	800	928	1120	1440

A naïve offloading protocol computes all vector-related operations by chunking, i.e., exporting encrypted vectors to a host, then asks for vector chunks to compute the intermediate results. The vectors l, r and dot-products c_L, c_R, t can be computed incrementally as $t = \sum l_i r_i$. This yields a constant memory protocol, but with high communication overhead.

We present basic offloading techniques in the following paragraphs, which are used to transform the in-memory prover to the privacy-preserving MPC prover with constant memory.

Dot-Product Offloading: We can evaluate dot-products and foldings on the host privately, using homomorphic property of a *blinding*. We export the vectors $\pi_{a'} a', \pi_{b'} b'$ to the host, where $\pi_{a'}, \pi_{b'} \xleftarrow{\$} \mathbb{Z}_l^{*2}$ are random blinding scalars known only to the HW. The host computes the dot-product of blinded vectors $\bar{r} = \pi_{a'} a' \cdot \pi_{b'} b' = \sum \pi_{a'} a'_i \pi_{b'} b'_i = \pi_{a'} \pi_{b'} \sum a'_i b'_i$ and returns $\bar{r}$, i.e., blinded value r, to the HW. The HW then unblinds the $\bar{r}$ as $\pi_{a'}^{-1} \pi_{b'}^{-1} \bar{r} = r = a' \cdot b'$ to get the dot-product.

As the scalars are from $\mathbb{Z}_l^*$ and vector elements are essentially random, the attacker cannot infer a' from $\pi_{a'} a'$. The $\pi_{a'} a'_0 = z$ does not have a unique factorization, i.e., $\forall z, x \ \exists y : xy = z; \ y = zx^{-1}$. Thus, a blinded vector is indistinguishable from an unblinded one for an attacker. Moreover, each element is divisor of 1 in $\mathbb{Z}_l^*$ so we cannot extract the blinding masks by $\text{GCD}(\pi l_0, \pi l_1)$ as it is undefined.

Folding Offloading: A vector folding is defined as $a'_{i \in (0,...,n']} = w a'_i + w^{-1} a'_{i+n'}$, before folding it holds $|a'| = 2n'$, after the fold $|a'| = n'$. Computing the folding on the host saves CPU and communication round-trips. Only the w is needed for the host to compute the folding, but it is desired to keep internal constants secret to preserve the privacy-preserving property of the offloading. Thus $\{w, w^{-1}\}$ are incorporated into blinding masks.

We have two distinct blinding constants for one vector. One for the lower half (LO), the other for the higher half (HI): $\{\pi_{a'_{LO}}, \pi_{a'_{HI}}\}$. The folding is then computed in two parts, as we preserve the LO/HI blinding also for the folding result vector, as shown in Eq. 1, so this blinding scheme is composable.

Let's thus define $\boldsymbol{x}_{LO} = \boldsymbol{x}_{[:\frac{n}{2}]}$ and $\boldsymbol{x}_{HI} = \boldsymbol{x}_{[\frac{n}{2}:]}$ for vector $\boldsymbol{x}$ of length n, $Lh(0)=$LO, $Lh(1)=$HI, then define folding constants as $\phi_{\boldsymbol{x},j}, \boldsymbol{x} \in \{\boldsymbol{a'}, \boldsymbol{b'}, \boldsymbol{G'}, \boldsymbol{H'}\}$, $j \in [0,3]$, $\phi_{\boldsymbol{x},j} = \theta_{\boldsymbol{x}_{Lh(\lfloor j/2 \rfloor)}} w^{1-(2j\%4)} \pi_{\boldsymbol{x}_{Lh(j\%2)}}^{-1}$, e.g., $\phi_{\boldsymbol{a'},0} = \theta_{a'_{LO}} w \pi_{a'_{LO}}^{-1}$, where $\boldsymbol{\theta}$ are randomly generated blinding masks from $\mathbb{Z}_l^*$ for the next round. The ϕ is constructed so it cancels the blinding mask π, multiplies by $w^{\{1,-1\}}$, and multiplies by a new blinding mask θ. It is also easy to observe that folding offloading is compatible with the dot-product offloading, as $c_L = \boldsymbol{a'}_{LO} \cdot \boldsymbol{b'}_{HI}, c_R = \boldsymbol{a'}_{HI} \cdot \boldsymbol{b'}_{LO}$.

The blinding technique differs from the dot-product offloading due to constants $\{w, w^{-1}\}$ being used. We need to have distinct blinding masks for each term in the folding sum, so an attacker cannot extract the w from the blinding masks. The folding offloading works in the following way:

$$\theta_{a'_{LO}} \boldsymbol{a'}_{[:\frac{n'}{2}]} \leftarrow \overbrace{\left(\theta_{a'_{LO}} w \pi_{a'_{LO}}^{-1}\right)}^{\phi_{a',0}} \left(\pi_{a'_{LO}} \boldsymbol{a'}_{[:n']}\right) + \overbrace{\left(\theta_{a'_{LO}} w^{-1} \pi_{a'_{HI}}^{-1}\right)}^{\phi_{a',1}} \left(\pi_{a'_{HI}} \boldsymbol{a'}_{[n':]}\right)$$

$$\theta_{a'_{HI}} \boldsymbol{a'}_{[\frac{n'}{2}:]} \leftarrow \underbrace{\left(\theta_{a'_{HI}} w \pi_{a'_{LO}}^{-1}\right)}_{\phi_{a',2}} \left(\pi_{a'_{LO}} \boldsymbol{a'}_{[:n']}\right) + \underbrace{\left(\theta_{a'_{HI}} w^{-1} \pi_{a'_{HI}}^{-1}\right)}_{\phi_{a',3}} \left(\pi_{a'_{HI}} \boldsymbol{a'}_{[n':]}\right) \quad (1)$$

High half of new $\boldsymbol{a'}$ Low half of $\boldsymbol{a'}$ High half of $\boldsymbol{a'}$
blinded by $\theta_{a'_{HI}}$ blinded by $\pi_{a'_{LO}}$ blinded by $\pi_{a'_{HI}}$

Initial $\boldsymbol{G'}, \boldsymbol{H'}$ Folding: The folding of the $\boldsymbol{G'}, \boldsymbol{H'}$ cannot be performed as defined above as the vectors are protocol constants in the first round (known to attacker), i.e., $\pi_{G'} = \pi_{H'} = 1$. Thus the attacker could extract w from the ϕ and unblind the folded vectors. We define folding constants $\phi^{(0)}$ for the first round as in the Eq. 2: $\phi_{\boldsymbol{x},j}^{(0)}, \boldsymbol{x} \in \{\boldsymbol{G'}, \boldsymbol{H'}\}, j \in [0,3]$, $\phi_{\boldsymbol{x},j}^{(0)} = \theta_{\boldsymbol{x}_{Lh(\lfloor j/2 \rfloor)}} w^{(2j\%4)-1} + (1 - j\%2)\pi_{\boldsymbol{x}_{LO}}$, e.g., $\phi_{\boldsymbol{G'},0}^{(0)} = \theta_{G'_{LO}} w^{-1} + \pi_{G'_{LO}}$.

The host computes the folding with the $\boldsymbol{G'}, \boldsymbol{H'}, \phi^{(0)}$, the HW then generates a vector of correction points $\pi_{G'_{LO}} \boldsymbol{G'}_{LO}$ and returns it to the host so the host can remove extraneous component caused by the additive blinding mask $\pi_{G'_{LO}}$.

$$\theta_{G'_{LO}} \boldsymbol{G'}_{[:\frac{n'}{2}]} + \pi_{G'_{LO}} \boldsymbol{G'}_{LO} \leftarrow \left(\theta_{G'_{LO}} w^{-1} + \pi_{G'_{LO}}\right) \boldsymbol{G'}_{[:n']} + \left(\theta_{G'_{LO}} w\right) \boldsymbol{G'}_{[n':]}$$

$$\theta_{G'_{HI}} \boldsymbol{G'}_{[\frac{n'}{2}:]} + \pi_{G'_{LO}} \boldsymbol{G'}_{LO} \leftarrow \left(\theta_{G'_{HI}} w^{-1} + \pi_{G'_{LO}}\right) \boldsymbol{G'}_{[:n']} + \left(\theta_{G'_{HI}} w\right) \boldsymbol{G'}_{[n':]} \quad (2)$$

L_c, R_c Offloading: Observe that L_c from line 33 contains 3 independent components: $L_c = 8^{-1} \left(\left(\left(\sum_{i=0}^{n'} a'_i G'_{i+n'} \right) + \left(\sum_{i=0}^{n'} b'_{i+n'} H'_i \right) \right) + (c_L x') H \right)$. Each component can be computed by the host with blinded vectors. The c_L is offloaded dot-product, host returns $\pi_{a'_{LO}}\pi_{b'_{HI}}c_L$. The sum $\sum_{i=0}^{n'} a'_i G'_{i+n'}$ is computed from the blinded vectors in a similar way, the host returns: $\overline{L_{cA}} = \pi_{a'_{LO}}\pi_{G'_{HI}}\sum_{i=0}^{n'} a'_i G'_{i+n'}$, the other sum is analogical. The HW unblinds the components and computes L_c.

Analysis: The offloaded Bulletproof prover as defined in Algorithm 2 was implemented in the Micropython for the Trezor and performance of the implementation was evaluated. Please refer to Table 3 and Fig. 1 for performance metrics. *Attacker Constraints:* As we transformed the Algorithm 1 to the Algorithm 2

using offloading steps that preserve the privacy of the computation, the protocol remains secure in the honest-but-curious attacker model. The malicious attacker could tamper the intermediate results to learn new information or break the security properties of the protocol. However, such manipulation leads to an invalid proof with overwhelming probability due to the use of a cryptographic hash function on line 16. Rejection of an invalid proof leads to attack being detected. We could also run a Bulletproof verifier on the generated proofs, abort the transaction signing, and alert the user on the invalid proof. As in-memory verifier runs in constant memory, the protocol becomes malicious attacker resistant; however, the running time increases. There might be more effective methods to verify intermediate results or catch attacker cheating with high probability. Such extensions are left for future work.

Table 3. Offloaded BP performance on the Trezor emulator and Trezor, parameters: $b_{tch} = 32, n_{thr} = 32$. Offloaded version is faster and requires only constant memory compared to in-memory prover. The table shows a total time and memory consumption for the HW PC-based emulator and the HW. The performance statistics for previous in-memory implementation is included for comparison. The HW part contains maximum RAM needed for all steps of the algorithm, which gives minimal RAM needed for the offloaded algorithm. Real total RAM usage is higher due to Micropython memory management, message recoding, serialization, etc.

Prover outputs	1	2	4	8	16
Time Emu [s]	6.97	9.69	14.75	25.48	44.81
Total RAM Emu [B]	24 896	25 056	25 120	25 408	25 632
Time HW [s]	25.10	37.49	59.03	99.96	184.02
Total RAM HW [B]	8 768	8 928	9 488	10 656	12 816
Max state RAM used [B]	5 576	7 720	7 848	8 040	8 360
Time HW in-mem [s]	16.88	30.55	57.40	121.21	246.57
RAM HW in-mem [B]	9 648	13 536	22 224	39 696	74 400

4   Related Work

The work in [7] presents a signature protocol for a Ledger[6] HW (Ledger for short). Ledger is an HW with a secure element (SE). Using the SE and the overall architecture limits the usable RAM to a few tens kB. Thus they had to implement a more low-level protocol with basic operations such as: generate key image, $\mathcal{H}_s(x)$, xP, get sub-address secret key, etc.

Low-level cryptographic operations are computed in the device, acting as crypto proxy. The protocol is tightly integrated into the Monero codebase, and it imposes maintainability challenges as a Monero algorithm change usually requires an HW signing protocol change. The low-level protocol design makes the security analysis difficult as the information flow is quite complicated, and the attacker can call several methods in an arbitrary order, which can lead to information leak and potential vulnerability.

Algorithm 2. Bulletproof prover with offloading. b_{tch} is a number of elements to offload in one batch, n_{thr} is a n' threshold for in-memory finish

---

1 **function** BULLETPROOFPROVEROFFLOADED(v, γ)
2      $(V, A, S, T1, T2, \tau_x, \mu, x, h, l_{0,i}, l_{1,i}, r_{0,i}, r_{1,i}) \leftarrow$ BULLETPROOFPREFIX(v, γ)
3      $t \leftarrow 0; c \leftarrow -1; n' \leftarrow MN; \boldsymbol{\pi} \xleftarrow{\$} (\mathbb{Z}_l^*)^8$ ▷ New random blinding masks $\boldsymbol{\pi}$
4   **for** $i \in \left[0, \ldots, \frac{MN}{b_{tch}}\right)$ **do**   ▷ Compute t, export blinded $\boldsymbol{l}, \boldsymbol{r}$ vectors
5          $\boldsymbol{l}_c \leftarrow l_{0,j} + x l_{1,j}; \boldsymbol{r}_c \leftarrow r_{0,j} + x r_{1,j}, \; j \in [i b_{tch}, (i+1) b_{tch})$
6          $\bar{\boldsymbol{l}}_c \leftarrow \pi_{a'_{\delta(i)}} \boldsymbol{l}_c$ ▷ $\delta(x) = x < n' \; ? \; \text{LO} : \text{HI}, \; \bar{\boldsymbol{l}}_c$ means blinded $\boldsymbol{l}_c$
7          $\bar{\boldsymbol{r}}_c \leftarrow \pi_{b'_{\delta(i)}} \boldsymbol{r}_c; t \leftarrow t + \boldsymbol{l}_c \cdot \boldsymbol{r}_c$
8   Send$(\bar{\boldsymbol{l}}_c, \bar{\boldsymbol{r}}_c)$ ▷ $\bar{\boldsymbol{l}}_c, \bar{\boldsymbol{r}}_c$ are $\bar{\boldsymbol{a}}', \bar{\boldsymbol{b}}'$ for the first while iteration
9      $w \leftarrow x' \leftarrow \mathcal{H}_s(x||x||\tau_x||\mu||t)$ ▷ $t = \boldsymbol{l} \cdot \boldsymbol{r}$
10   Send(y) ▷ The host needs y to compute $\boldsymbol{H}'$ and L_c, R_c related sums
11   **while** $n' > 1$ **do**   ▷ The y is public, computable from the final proof
12         $\bar{n} \leftarrow n'; n' \leftarrow n'/2; c \leftarrow c + 1$
13   Receive$(\overline{cL}, \overline{cR}, \overline{L_{cA}}, \overline{L_{cB}}, \overline{R_{cA}}, \overline{R_{cB}})$ ▷ $\overline{L_{cA}}$ is first blinded sum from the L_c
14         $L_c \leftarrow 8^{-1} \left(\pi_{a'_{LO}}^{-1} \pi_{G'_{HI}}^{-1} \overline{L_{cA}} + \pi_{b'_{HI}}^{-1} \pi_{H'_{LO}}^{-1} \overline{L_{cB}} + x' \pi_{a'_{LO}}^{-1} \pi_{b'_{HI}}^{-1} \overline{cL} H \right)$
15         $R_c \leftarrow 8^{-1} \left(\pi_{a'_{HI}}^{-1} \pi_{G'_{LO}}^{-1} \overline{R_{cA}} + \pi_{b'_{LO}}^{-1} \pi_{H'_{HI}}^{-1} \overline{R_{cB}} + x' \pi_{a'_{HI}}^{-1} \pi_{b'_{LO}}^{-1} \overline{cR} H \right)$
16         $w \leftarrow \mathcal{H}(w||L_c||R_c); \boldsymbol{\theta} \xleftarrow{\$} (\mathbb{Z}_l^*)^8$ ▷ Compute w, generate blindings $\boldsymbol{\theta}$
17   **if** $n' \leq n_{thr}$ **then**   ▷ Finish in-memory with original algorithm
18   Receive$(\bar{\boldsymbol{a}}', \bar{\boldsymbol{b}}', \bar{\boldsymbol{G}}', \bar{\boldsymbol{H}}')$; Unblind to obtain $\{\boldsymbol{a}', \boldsymbol{b}', \boldsymbol{G}', \boldsymbol{H}'\}$
19             $(\boldsymbol{L}, \boldsymbol{R}, a'_0, b'_0) \leftarrow$ BULLETPROOFLOOP$(\boldsymbol{a}', \boldsymbol{b}', \boldsymbol{G}', \boldsymbol{H}', n', c, w, x')$
20   **return** $(V, A, S, T1, T2, \tau_x, \mu, \boldsymbol{L}, \boldsymbol{R}, a'_0, b'_0, t)$ ▷ Combine $\boldsymbol{L}, \boldsymbol{R}$
21   Send$\left(\phi_{x,l}^{(c)} : x \in \{\boldsymbol{a}', \boldsymbol{b}', \boldsymbol{G}', \boldsymbol{H}'\}, l \in [0, 3] \right)$ ▷ Compute and send blindings
22   **if** $c = 0$ **then**
23   Compute and send folding correction points for $\boldsymbol{G}', \boldsymbol{H}'$, by chunks
24         $\boldsymbol{\pi} \leftarrow \boldsymbol{\theta}$ ▷ Update blinding masks for the next round

---

[6] https://www.ledger.com.

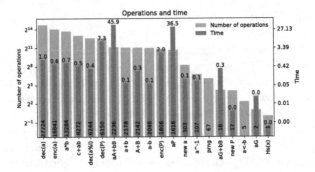

Fig. 1. Privacy-preserving multi-party BP with $M = 16$ cryptographic operations and timing breakdown. The most expensive operations are aP and point recodings.

To the best of our knowledge, the overall protocol is not documented nor analyzed. The low-level commands are documented in [7] only. The protocol does not use a state machine to guard the command calls.

To the best of our knowledge, there is no other Monero transaction signing protocol published nor used. Our protocol addresses issues with the security analysis, works on higher abstraction level, has very simple interface and thus reduced attack surface, it is more stable over protocol changes, easy to maintain, and needs less message round trips. Moreover, we compute the Bulletproofs in HW thus protecting blinding masks.

5   Conclusion

We designed, implemented, and tested a secure Monero transaction signing protocol for HWs. We designed and analyzed the memory and time complexity of the zero-knowledge proofs (range-proofs, Bulletproofs [3]), algorithms focused on low-memory consumption so they can be computed in HW. The memory consumption is linear in the number of inputs/UTXOs. The results can be easily applied to other protocols based on ring signatures, Pedersen commitments, and Bulletproof range proofs.

We also designed, implemented, and tested a privacy-preserving two-party Bulletproofs computation protocol with constant memory, enabling the computation of large input instances securely and in a reasonable time. This is the first privacy-preserving Bulletproof prover implementation running on an HW in constant memory. Techniques used in the protocol are applicable to similar protocols like Bulletproof, and Bulletproof also has several applications outside of Monero.

The implemented protocols are practically usable. The transaction signing protocol has been deployed since Nov. 7, 2018, integrated both to Trezor and Monero codebases. All implemented sources are available online under a permissive open source license at: https://github.com/ph4r05/monero-tx-paper.

Acknowledgement. We thank our colleagues Petr Švenda and Marek Sýs, who provided valuable insights and ideas that helped to improve the protocols. Thanks also go to SatoshiLabs employees, Tomáš Sušánka, Jan Pochyla and Ondřej Vejpustek who did the security review of the design and implementation and helped significantly with simplifying the protocol implementation. We also thank the anonymous reviewers for their feedback and suggestions for improvement, and to Daniel Slamanig for shepherding the final revisions of our submission. This work was partly supported by the Czech Science Foundation project 20-03426S. For an extended paper please refer to the [6].

References

1. Alonso, K.M.: Zero to monero: first edition (2018). https://www.getmonero.org/library/Zero-to-Monero-1-0-0.pdf. Accessed 20 Feb 2020
2. Bernstein, D.J., Duif, N., Lange, T., Schwabe, P., Yang, B.Y.: High-speed high-security signatures. J. Cryptograph. Eng. **2**(2), 77–89 (2012). https://doi.org/10.1007/s13389-012-0027-1
3. Bunz, B., Bootle, J., Boneh, D., Poelstra, A., Wuille, P., Maxwell, G.: Bulletproofs: short proofs for confidential transactions and more, pp. 315–334, May 2018. https://doi.org/10.1109/SP.2018.00020
4. Goodin, D.: Official monero website is hacked to deliver currency-stealing malware (2019). https://arstechnica.com/information-technology/2019/11/official-monero-website-is-hacked-to-deliver-currency-stealing-malware. Accessed 26 Feb 2020
5. Klinec, D.: Monero wallet trezor integration (2018). https://github.com/ph4r05/monero-trezor-doc. Accessed 26 Feb 2020
6. Klinec, D., Matyas, V.: Privacy-friendly monero transaction signing on a hardware wallet, extended version. Cryptology ePrint Archive, Report 2020/281 (2020). https://ia.cr/2020/281
7. Mesnil, C.: Ledger device for Monero. Online (2019). https://github.com/LedgerHQ/ledger-app-monero. Accessed 20 Feb 2020
8. Noether, S.: Ring signature confidential transactions for monero. Cryptology ePrint Archive, Report 2015/1098 (2015). https://eprint.iacr.org/2015/1098
9. Pedersen, T.P.: Non-interactive and information-theoretic secure verifiable secret sharing. In: Feigenbaum, J. (ed.) CRYPTO 1991. LNCS, vol. 576, pp. 129–140. Springer, Heidelberg (1992). https://doi.org/10.1007/3-540-46766-1_9
10. Yao, A.C.: Protocols for secure computations. In: 23rd Annual Symposium on Foundations of Computer Science, pp. 160–164. IEEE (1982). https://doi.org/10.1109/SFCS.1982.88
11. Young, J.: Malware steals user funds & bitcoin wallet keys from PCs (2017). https://cointelegraph.com/news/malware-steals-user-funds-bitcoin-wallet-keys-from-pcs-bitcoin-altcoins-targeted. Accessed 26 Feb 2020

Privacy and Security Management

A Matter of Life and Death: Analyzing the Security of Healthcare Networks

Guillaume Dupont[1]([⊠]), Daniel Ricardo dos Santos[2], Elisa Costante[2],
Jerry den Hartog[1], and Sandro Etalle[1]

[1] Eindhoven University of Technology, Eindhoven, The Netherlands
g.f.c.dupont@tue.nl
[2] Forescout Technologies, Eindhoven, The Netherlands

Abstract. Healthcare Delivery Organizations (HDOs) are complex institutions where a broad range of devices are interconnected. This interconnectivity brings security concerns and we are observing an increase in the number and sophistication of cyberattacks on hospitals. In this paper, we explore the current status of network security in HDOs and identify security gaps via a literature study and two observational studies. We first use the literature study to derive a typical network architecture and the threats relevant to HDOs. Then we analyze in the first observational study data from 67 HDOs to highlight the challenges they face with regards to device security and management. The second study leverages the network traffic from 5 HDOs in order to point out a number of concrete observations which depict how patient data can be exposed and how cyber-physical attacks could impact patient health. Finally we offer in this paper a starting point for securing HDOs' network.

Keywords: Healthcare · Network security · Medical devices

1 Introduction

Healthcare Delivery Organizations (HDOs), such as hospitals and clinics, are complex institutions where a broad range of Information Technology (IT), Operational Technology (OT), and Internet of Things (IoT) devices are increasingly interconnected [28]. IT devices and enterprise systems process and exchange highly sensitive data (e.g., patients' health records and financial information), whereas OT and IoT devices are used for diverse functions such as building automation, and guest entertainment. Specialized IoT devices, refers to as Internet of Medical Things (IoMT) [11], are connected medical devices supporting clinical care and can generate and exchange patient data with other devices,

S. Etalle—This work was supported by ECSEL joint undertaking SECREDAS (783119-2), EU-H2020-SAFECARE (no. 787002) and SunRISE (PENT181005).

© IFIP International Federation for Information Processing 2020
Published by Springer Nature Switzerland AG 2020
M. Hölbl et al. (Eds.): SEC 2020, IFIP AICT 580, pp. 355–369, 2020.
https://doi.org/10.1007/978-3-030-58201-2_24

such as Electronic Health Records (EHR) systems [20]. These new technologies and increased connectivity can help improve the efficiency and quality of care.

However, this reliance on such technologies can also introduce new privacy and security risks [1,16]. We are witnessing an increase in the number and sophistication of cyberattacks on hospitals [14]. So far, these attacks are mainly in the form of ransomware [21], targeting mostly the IT part of the network. But the increased connectivity is not restricted to the IT systems as it also applies to the OT systems. Does this raise security and compliance risks for HDOs that have not been (sufficiently) considered so far?

Targeted attacks against life-supporting devices may have devastating consequences for patients and HDOs. Attacks already seen in different domains like Building Automation Systems (BAS) [27,32] show that OT may be targeted. Specialized tools (e.g., Shodan) for finding exposed OT devices and potential exploits can aid attackers in launching such attacks. All of this makes it essential to be prepared for attacks that exploit the complexity of HDO ecosystems.

Security assessment for IT infrastructures is a well covered topic [24], and work like [17] looks at the human factor in HDOs. Here we aim to establish the current technical state of readiness of HDOs with respect to cyberattacks targeting their networks and aiming at, for example, stealing or altering patients' data or even harming their health.

To achieve this aim, we address the following Research Questions (RQs):

RQ1 How is an HDO's network organized?
RQ2 What are some potential threats to an HDO's network?
RQ3 What kinds of devices and software are present in an HDO's network?
RQ4 What security vulnerabilities are linked to HDO's network protocols?

We answer RQ1 and RQ2 by investigating existing literature to give an overview of the network architecture and examples of threats on typical HDOs (Sect. 2). To answer RQ3, we conduct a large-scale investigation of 67 HDO networks (Sect. 3). To answer RQ4, we perform a network security assessment of 5 of these HDO networks (Sect. 4). Finally, we conclude the paper with a discussion on the results, a description of related work and an outlook on future research (Sect. 5). Our key findings are:

1. **HDO networks are very diverse:** the diversity of connected medical devices, including different vendors and operating systems, make it increasingly difficult to secure networks.
2. **Common services and legacy operating systems leave the network vulnerable:** Certain devices found in HDOs are not only running network services often exploited by malware and malicious actors (e.g., SMB and RDP) but also legacy operating systems no longer supported by vendors, thus providing potential access to attackers.
3. **Insecure protocols and communications are common:** these flaws in network security in healthcare organizations can expose sensitive data and create the potential to harm patients by tampering with the network communication of connected medical devices.

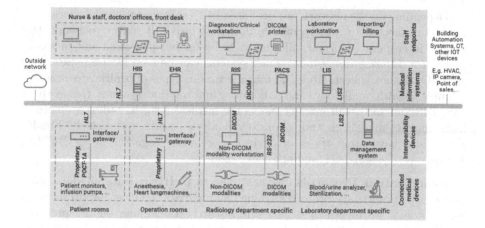

Fig. 1. Simplified network architecture of a typical HDO

2 Network Model and Threats

In this section we conduct a literature study to answer the first and a second research questions, namely "How is an HDO's network organized?" (RQ1) and "What are some potential threats to an HDO's network?" (RQ2). We address RQ1 by providing a network model of a typical HDO and RQ2 by listing examples of threats to HDOs. In addition we validate the attacks in a laboratory setting.

Organization of HDO's Network. The major distinction between HDO networks and typical enterprise networks comes from (i) the type of devices deployed and (ii) the communication protocols used, both of which are described below.

Network Devices. HDOs are generally divided into several departments, delivering specific clinical care (e.g., radiology) or organizational services (e.g., administration). We represent on Fig. 1 a simplified model of typical HDO networks, including two departments in the plain-line boxes, as well as some of the IT, OT, and IoMT devices commonly found. While some departments can have specialized equipment related to their operations (e.g., imaging modalities in radiology department), there also are certain devices that can be found in multiple departments. In addition, there are systems that can be found ubiquitously across an HDO such as IT devices, as depicted in the upper left side of the figure.

We classify HDO's networked devices into 4 categories. The *connected medical devices* support clinical care, while *interoperability devices* assure communication for some devices on the network. Then *medical information systems* store and manage clinical data and finally *staff endpoints* provide human interfaces to information systems. *Connected medical devices* can be further divided into active or passive devices [15]. Active medical devices are meant to deliver medical treatment and sustain patient life (e.g., drug pumps). Passive devices monitor patient information such as vital signs or test results, and report events or need for treatment to clinical staff (e.g., patient monitors and laboratory equipment).

Depending on the network protocol used by the aforementioned devices, they may be connected to *interoperability devices*, which will convert network data into an interoperable format, allowing it to be further processed and/or stored by *medical information systems*. Such systems can be seen as the backbone of an HDO, as they collect, store and manage various types of healthcare data. For example, health, radiology, and laboratory information systems (respectively HIS, RIS and LIS), will manage electronic medical records, radiology pictures from imaging modalities and laboratory analysis results, respectively. Finally, HDOs also have other types of devices represented together under Building Automation Systems, OT and other IoT devices.

Communication Protocols. Medical devices in HDOs transmit data using standard or proprietary protocols. Table 1 summarizes the most important medical protocols we identified during our research. Depending on the protocol, specific information about the device can be found in packets' payload such as the firmware version and hardware version for that device.

HL7v2 is the most widely used interoperability and data exchange protocol in medical networks. This messaging standard allows the exchange of patient, clinical and administrative information. DICOM defines both the format for storing medical images and the communication protocols used to exchange them. As de-facto standard, it is implemented by all major vendors of devices involved in medical imaging processes (e.g., modalities and diagnostic workstations). POCT1-A and LIS2-A2 are used for point-of-care and laboratory devices, respectively. These protocols can issue test orders with patient information and transfer the results of tests to a Data Management System (DMS). The proprietary protocols Philips Data Export [29] and GE RWHAT [23] are used to control patient monitors of their respective vendors. They allow patient monitors to communicate the vital readings of patients to a central monitoring system.

While supporting critical operations in HDOs, these medical protocols support neither encryption nor authentication (or support them without enforcing their usage, in the case of DICOM), a situation similar to what is found in other cyber-physical systems, e.g., Industrial Control Systems (ICS) [4] and Building Automation Systems (BAS) [5]. We also identified other protocols such as HL7 FHIR, as well as other proprietary protocols. However we choose to ignore them in this paper as they are not as widely deployed as the ones in Table 1.

Table 1. Main medical protocols identified

Protocol	Type	Devices
DICOM	Standard	Imaging modalities, PACS
HL7v2	Standard	Connected Medical Devices, Medical Information Systems, Interoperability Gateways
POCT1-A	Standard	Point of Care Testing
LIS2-A2	Standard	Laboratory devices
Data Export	Prop. (Philips)	Patient monitors
RWHAT	Prop. (GE)	Patient monitors

Potential Threats to an HDO's Network. Malicious actors may have various motivations to attack HDOs [14,15]. All reported attacks on HDOs (see, e.g., [8,36,37]) seem to have been motivated by financial gains directly via ransomware and cryptomining, or indirectly via stolen information and use of infected computers in botnets.

However in the light of the security research done on medical devices and their protocols [3,6,13,23,25,30,31,42], one can wonder how an attacker could leverage vulnerabilities on such devices. We provide below some examples of attacks, considering an attacker on the network. Such foothold can be established in various ways [14]. These attacks can be the final step in a multi-step attack [15].

Attack Examples. Security research in healthcare focuses either on devices or network protocols. Vulnerabilities in specific medical devices have been found over the past years (see, e.g., [12,30,31]), and the number of security advisories in the medical space has been growing [39,42]. Currently, there is a trend of research into protocol insecurity [7,10]. Vulnerabilities of the protocols below have been demonstrated.

HL7 standards, which are used to exchange patient data between systems, can be abused in several ways and are often insecurely implemented [3,6,13]. As HL7 data is sent over unauthenticated communications, attackers can intercept and modify information in transit, which may lead to life threatening consequences.

Similarly, unauthenticated and unencrypted DICOM communications also allow attackers to tamper with medical images, misleading medical staff to wrong diagnostics. The DICOM standard supports user authentication and message encryption, however while their implementations and usage are left to product vendors and HDOs, we observe in a number of HDOs that these security mechanisms are not implemented. To demonstrate the possible consequences of this situation, researchers implemented a proof-of-concept to add or remove tumors from CT scan images being transferred over the network, leading to dramatic consequences for patients [25].

Proprietary protocols have also caught the attention of security researchers, who have shown [23] how one could intercept a patient's vital signs sent by a GE patient monitor over their RWHAT protocol. Once intercepted, a malicious actor could modify the patient signs arbitrarily. In the same fashion, we reproduced in our lab a similar attack with a Philips patient monitor. Such monitors send information over the Data Export protocol, which can be intercepted, decoded and modified on the fly.

Attacks against unprotected protocols such as POCT1-A and LIS2-A2 have not yet been demonstrated but can follow the same procedure. In Table 2, we summarize seven example attacks against these protocols.

3   Large-Scale Study

In this section we answer the third research question, "What kinds of devices and software are present in an HDO's network?" To this end we leverage data from

Table 2. Potential attacks on the main medical protocols identified

ID	Protocol	Target	Attack	Description
A1	HL7v2	Patient data	Data theft	An attacker can retrieve sensitive patient data such as clinical and financial information as the data is sent unencrypted
A2	HL7v2	Patient health	Tamper with EHR	An attacker can modify arbitrarily the electronic health records of patients (e.g., change the allergies or medication prescription)
A3	DICOM	Patient health	Tamper with test results	An attacker can tamper with medical images by virtually adding or removing tumors for respectively healthy or sick patients
A4	POCT1-A	Patient health	Tamper with test results	An attacker can change the results of point of care equipment (e.g., blood glucose analysis)
A5	LIS2-A2	Patient health	Tamper with test results	An attacker can modify the test results of laboratory equipment (e.g., blood analysis)
A6	Data Export	Patient health	Tamper with vitals	An attacker can tamper with patients' vital signs read by Philips patient monitors
A7	RWHAT	Patient health	Tamper with vitals	An attacker can tamper with patients' vital signs read by GE patient monitors

various HDOs, providing us insights into the devices connected on their networks. We present the charts resulting from our analysis, alongside our conclusions.

Methodology. We collected data in 67 HDOs, consisting in traffic gathered and analysed by network monitoring appliances connected to network switches in each HDO. The appliances collect data both by passively listening and actively interacting with the devices on the network (e.g., using Nmap and other network scanning tools). The data is then analyzed by the appliance to find *attributes* of devices (e.g., MAC address or operating system).

Some of these attributes, called *raw attributes*, can be directly obtained from the network traffic, like the MAC address. Other attributes we refer to as *Classified attributes* are obtained by classifying devices using a *Device Profile Library*. It is a set of rules which assign a profile to a device once a given combination of raw attributes have been detected for that device. A profile is a triple of attributes (*vendor, OS, function*), where the first two elements are self-explanatory and the third element represents the function of a device in the network (e.g., 'OT/Healthcare/X-ray machine' or 'IT/Printer'). The classification of devices is not the focus of this work and we assume that the Device

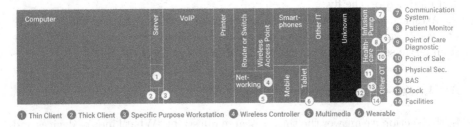

Fig. 2. Average distribution of IT and OT devices found on HDOs' networks

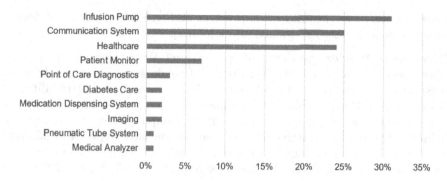

Fig. 3. Top-10 connected medical devices on HDO networks

Profile Library is correct. We comment on that assumption in Sect. 5. The data is anonymized and sent to a data lake which aggregates the data collected in all HDOs. We further analyze the data retrieved by executing a number of queries.

Sample Description. The dataset comprises a total of 2.3 million devices. The amount of unique devices per HDO, regardless of their type, ranges from 597 to 234305 with an average of 50078 and a median value of 12766. We see a wide range of sizes across the sample, but most are in the thousands to tens of thousands of devices. To help better understand the composition of HDO networks we provide below different perspectives through our data analysis.

High-Level Device Overview. Figure 2 represents the three main classes of device found in HDOs, namely IT, OT and unknown devices. On average, these classes correspond to respectively 84%, 7% and 9% of the total number of devices. *IT devices* include personal computers, VoIP devices, network printers, mobile devices, and various networking equipment among other things. *OT devices* are comprised of not only healthcare devices and infusion pumps, but also BAS devices, points of sale, physical security and other facilities-related devices such as IP security cameras. Finally, the devices that were not possible to be classified are referred to as *unknown devices*.

Figure 2 also shows the average distribution of device types in HDOs. One can observe that more than roughly a third of the connected devices are computers (36.4%), followed by VoIP devices (13.8%) and smartphones (5.7%). Understanding the distribution of devices is important because many networks still operate in organizational silos, where different departments are responsible for different sections of the network. This situation tend to leave gaps in security [22].

Types of Medical Devices. Since connected medical devices are especially critical for HDOs, it is important to understand the distribution of these devices in a finer granularity. Figure 3 shows the most common types of connected medical devices. Per-patient devices, such as infusion pumps and patient monitors represent the majority of healthcare devices on HDO networks, as well as per-personnel devices like communication systems. This makes sense as they are the devices deployed mostly on a 1:1 ratio. Devices such as those used in laboratory diagnostics or medical imaging represent a smaller number because they are shared devices. The "healthcare" device type on Fig. 3 refers to medical devices that cannot be further categorized into a more specific type.

Diversity of Vendors and Operating Systems. We now look at the diversity of the device ecosystem in HDOs in terms of vendors and Operating Systems (OS). Our analysis shows that on average, HDOs have a total of 152 different device vendors. When looking at the number of unique vendors for specific device types in HDOs, we observe for example that IT computers have on average 51.5 unique vendors and networking and VoIP equipment have respectively 25.5 and 7.2 unique vendors. Regarding medical devices, infusion pumps, patient monitors and point of care diagnostics devices have respectively 2.5, 2.2 and 2.6 unique vendors on average.

The complexity of device management is linked to the number of unique vendors whose devices are deployed on a network. Vendors have different support, maintenance, and patching programs, which can affect the time between the disclosure of a vulnerability and the patching of the related systems. As an example, consider the recently disclosed set of vulnerabilities on the IP stack of the VxWorks real-time OS [34]. Some medical devices run this particular OS, but it is not immediately clear to the users whether a particular device is affected, if there is a patch available and how it can be applied. Contacting each vendor for inquiry would be very time consuming.

Additionally, it is important to consider the diversity in OS as it can bring some security concerns as well. Figure 4 shows the OS variants of devices on HDO networks. For each OS, its proportion relative to the others is given and, for some of them, a breakdown of the version in use. Windows is the most common OS across HDO's devices (41%). Windows 7, 10 and Windows Server 2012 represent respectively 11%, 8% and 1% of the OS, while we still observe a non-negligible amount of other variants such as Windows XP, Windows Server 2008 and 2003.

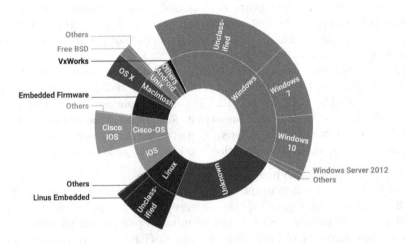

Fig. 4. Distribution of OS variants in devices on HDO networks

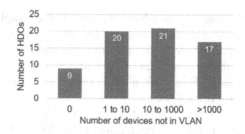

Fig. 5. Occurrences of HDOs with devices not in VLAN

Our analysis revealed that 40% of networks have more than 20 different OS. We see that 0.4% of devices are running an unsupported version of Windows and 70% of devices a version of Windows for which Microsoft support is planned to expire by January 14, 2020[1], such as Windows 7, Windows 2008 and Windows Mobile. Running unsupported OS is a well known security issue. HDOs' networks will most likely continue to have medical devices running legacy OS since updating can be too costly or even infeasible, due to unacceptable downtime required or (software) compatibility issues. Consequently many devices would have to keep operating while remaining potentially vulnerable. This situation calls for additional protections, such as appropriate segmentation of systems, which can be achieved through Virtual Local Area Networks (VLAN) for example.

VLAN Analysis. Network segmentation is a commonly advised security measure [24]. VLANs can segment the network by effectively isolating critical systems, segregating similar devices by function, and limit access to data and other assets in a segment. In this context, isolating medical devices in VLANs could help to keep them separated from the rest of the network.

However, our study shows that, on average less than 20% of the medical devices are deployed in a VLAN and, as Fig. 5 shows, 86.5% of the HDOs have medical devices outside of VLANs.

In addition we also found that 61 of these HDOs have at least one VLAN with a combination of medical devices and other OT devices, thus undermining the segmentation that use of a VLAN may provide. Examples of such cases that we saw in the data are VLANs containing both medical imaging modalities and IP cameras or HVAC systems, or even blood glucose monitors with points of sale.

This observation confirms the statement of the ISE regarding HDO's network being improperly segmented [15].

Enabled Common Services. Some common network services are often targeted by recent malware and malicious actors [26]. Table 3 shows the amount of devices that have the given service's port open.

Server Message Block Protocol (SMB) is the transport protocol used by Windows machines for a variety of purposes such as file sharing and access to remote

---

[1] https://bit.ly/38e9QXc.

Windows services. WannaCry and NotPetya are two examples of ransomware that exploit vulnerabilities in SMB. Remote Desktop Protocol (RDP) is another common protocol exploited by modern automated threats. Secure Shell (SSH) may be abused by brute-force attacks to log remotely onto machines. Telnet and File Transfer Protocol (FTP) are often-exploited vectors: these protocols do not secure nor encrypt network sessions.

Overall, after analyzing the kinds of devices and software present in an HDO's network, we can conclude that a large number of devices on HDO networks have high-risk services turned on. The access requirements of medical vendors and outsourced suppliers often require devices to have services like RDP enabled. Other times, the network ports are left open by default without the knowledge of IT and security staff. In the next section we look closer at HDO networks to better understand the security vulnerabilities linked to network protocols.

4   In-Depth Study

The in-depth study described in this section aims at answering our fourth research question, "What security vulnerabilities are linked to HDO's network protocols?" We analyze network traffic of HDOs in order to provide a detailed view on their network security posture, identify insecure protocols and susceptibility to attacks.

Methodology. We captured raw network traffic and perform various analyses, looking at network activities and communication protocols among other things. Collecting all network data from all HDOs is clearly not feasible. Instead, the study leverages datasets from five HDOs captured at key locations in their network. These HDOs are referred to as HDO_{1-5}.

The network traffic is analyzed using Forescout's SilentDefense[2] solution, enhanced with our *Protocol Dissectors* for the key medical protocols presented earlier in Table 1. For each of those protocols, we created a dissector which allows us to identify its presence in traffic and parse the contents of network packets.

Sample Description. The datasets used in this study correspond to raw network traffic of five different HDOs. For HDO_1 and HDO_2 the data was captured

Table 3. Common enabled network services

Network service (port number)	Devices (%)	Devices (absolute)
SMB (445)	26%	573,455
RDP (3389)	14%	318,634
SSH (22)	8%	187,135
Telnet (23)	5%	113,071
FTP (21)	5%	107,719

---

[2] https://www.forescout.com/platform/silentdefense/.

over a period of 2 days and it comprises a total of respectively 2207 and 1513 devices. For HDO$_3$ the capture lasted one day and it collected data from 12289 devices. Finally for HDO$_4$ and HDO$_5$ the captures ran over four days and account for 11051 and 4423 devices respectively.

Overview and Network Activities. In the datasets, we found the healthcare network protocols presented on the left side of Table 4. Recall that these protocols are used by diverse device types in HDOs as described previously in Sect. 2.

The presence of these protocols indicates that these HDOs are susceptible to some of the attacks described in Sect. 2. We propose in Table 2 a list of attacks leveraging these protocols' weaknesses that an attacker could execute once having access to the HDO's network. As one can see in Table 4, all five HDOs in our analysis are susceptible to be vulnerable to at least two attacks on medical device protocols. We also found obsolete versions of other protocols such as SNMPv1 and v2 and NTPv1 and v2. We do not elaborate on those findings because they do not fit the attack examples that we defined in Sect. 2.

Weak Encryption. As presented on the right side of Table 4, we found that SSLv3, TLSv1.0 and TLSv1.1 are still used. Secure Sockets Layer (SSL) and Transport Layer Security (TLS) are cryptographic protocols used to secure network communications of higher-level protocols, such as HTTPS or FTPS. SSLv3, TLSv1.0/1.1 are known to be insecure. They are impacted, for instance, by the POODLE and BEAST attacks [35], in which an attacker can downgrade a connection and decrypt the traffic. Our analysis shows that these weak protocols are used internally in HDOs, where one could still argue that other additional security measures could compensate. However, they are also used externally, even to connect to organizations such as Microsoft and Google.

Additionally, our analysis revealed issues with the SSL/TLS certificates used in HDOs. Such certificates play a critical role in authentication and data encryption. We found that all HDOs use certificates with non-whitelisted issuers. For security purposes, it is usually recommended to only use certificates delivered by trusted issuers (i.e., whitelisted issuers). Also two of the HDOs displayed

Table 4. Findings of network traffic analyses in five HDOs

| Dataset | Healthcare protocols | | | | | | Susceptible to attacks | | | | | | | Weak protocols | | | Certificates | |
	HL7v2	DICOM	POCT1-A	LIS2-A2	Data Export	RWHAT	A1	A2	A3	A4	A5	A6	A7	SSLv3	TLSv1.0	TLSv1.1	Issuer not whitelisted	Expired
HDO$_1$	✓	✓				✓	✓	✓	✓				✓		✓	✓	✓	
HDO$_2$		✓			✓				✓			✓			✓		✓	
HDO$_3$	✓	✓		✓			✓	✓	✓		✓			✓	✓		✓	✓
HDO$_4$	✓	✓	✓				✓	✓	✓	✓				✓	✓	✓	✓	✓
HDO$_5$	✓	✓		✓			✓	✓	✓		✓				✓	✓	✓	

are still using expired certificates, both for healthcare applications and network equipment.

External Interfaces and Communication. As discussed, HDO networks are complex and use many different protocols, including ones dedicated to healthcare. For operational reasons, some medical applications can be reached from the outside of the network, sometimes using healthcare protocols. This adds to the complexity of managing such systems and increases the probability of sensitive information or systems being exposed. For example we found in one HDO a system containing an EHR application exposed on the public Internet.

In addition, in all HDOs except for HDO$_2$, we observed communications between public and private IP addresses using HL7v2. As these communications are unencrypted, they can be easily read, and leak sensitive patient information such as names and addresses, employment status, phone number, allergies and also test results. Other information regarding the care provider can also be found such as the doctor's name in charge of the patient, with his or her license number.

Moreover, there were also in two HDOs medical devices communicating over non-medical protocols with external servers. For example, a medical information system was seen to communicate over SSH, and another to reach a web server over HTTP. In one instance, a communication with an external file server over FTP was observed, and we confirmed (using Shodan) that this external machine contains up to 25 vulnerabilities. If exploited, it could potentially lead to the compromise of such a server and create an entry point into the HDO's network.

Additionally, we also observed in an HDO a machine behaving suspiciously. In our sample, this computer was trying to reach a number of public IP addresses over various ports. We noted a number of port scans executed and other host discovery attempts. Finally, it was communicating internally with 11 other machines over Telnet. These signs of compromise require further investigation, and we are validating our hypothesis with the network's owners.

Firmware Versions and Vulnerabilities. Certain firmware are known to be vulnerable, as reported in *ICS Medical Advisories* [39]. To determine whether HDOs have medical devices running known vulnerable firmware, we employ the protocol dissectors we developed (see Sect. 2). We find that in HDO$_2$ Philips IntelliVue patient monitors deployed in intensive care units have a firmware which could potentially be abused. If successfully exploited, the vulnerabilities could allow an attacker to read and write the memory of the device, and force it to restart, potentially leading to delays in diagnosis and treatment of patients[3].

In HDO$_4$, we find vulnerable Roche Accu-Chek Inform II blood glucose meters. This model, popular and commonly found in HDOs, presents multiple vulnerabilities in which attackers could execute arbitrary code on the device by crafting POCT1-A packets and change the instrument configuration. This could lead to false analysis results and inaccurate diagnosis[4].

---

[3] https://bit.ly/2E8wCC2 and https://bit.ly/2YFCwnE.
[4] https://www.us-cert.gov/ics/advisories/ICSMA-18-310-01.

5   Conclusion

We explore the technical state of readiness of HDOs through studies across 67 organizations. The key findings, given in Sect. 1 indicate gaps such as insecure protocols, weak encryption, and private-to-public network communications which can directly expose patient data to attackers. Filling these gaps is challenging: HDOs are large diverse ecosystems of devices, including legacy and safety critical systems, processing sensitive data. They are also difficult to manage and secure because they comprise a variety of software, vendors, and protocols. Solutions that address the combination of these characteristics will be needed.

Related Work. Most work on cybersecurity in healthcare focuses on connected medical devices (e.g. [2, 18, 38, 41]), with special attention on implantable devices because of their potential direct harm to patients [33]. These works mostly ignore other kinds of devices present in an HDO's network and that can be used during cyberattacks. Some works discuss the security threats not only to medical devices, but also to medical data (see, e.g., [19]). Jaigirdar et al. [16] analyzed the trust that physician's place in secure end-to-end communication of healthcare data. Kune et al. [9] surveyed medical and non-medical protocols used in HDOs and analyzed their security properties. Wood et al. [40] introduced a method to capture network traffic from medical IoT devices and automatically detect cleartext information that may reveal sensitive medical conditions.

Limitations and Future Work. We were not in control of the traffic captured in the HDOs and the location of the appliances has an impact on the traffic they see. Device classification is based on a set of heuristics that is continually improved, but which can contain errors (see Sect. 3). We plan to work on improving the device classification heuristics and vulnerability matching for medical devices.

References

1. Alsubaei, F., Abuhussein, A., Shiva, S.: Security and privacy in the Internet of medical things: taxonomy and risk assessment. In: LCN (2017)
2. Altawy, R., Youssef, A.: Security tradeoffs in cyber physical systems: a case study survey on implantable medical devices. IEEE Access **4**, 959–979 (2016)
3. Bland, M., Dameff, C., Tully, J.: Pestilential protocol: how unsecure HL-7 messages threaten patient lives (2018)
4. Bodungen, C., Singer, B., Shbeeb, A., Wilhoit, K., Hilt, S.: Hacking Exposed Industrial Control Systems. McGraw-Hill, New York City (2016)
5. Ciholas, P., Lennie, A., Sadigova, P., Such, J.: The security of smart buildings: a systematic literature review. arXiv e-prints (2019)
6. Duggal, A.: Understanding HL7 2.X standards, pen testing, and defending HL7 2.X messages. Black Hat US 2016 (2016). https://youtu.be/MR7cH44fjrc
7. Fiebig, T., et al.: SoK: an analysis of protocol design: avoiding traps for implementation and deployment. arXiv e-prints (2016)
8. FireEye: Double dragon (2019). https://bit.ly/38nj6bU

9. Foo Kune, D., Venkatasubramanian, K., Vasserman, E., Lee, I., Kim, Y.: Toward a safe integrated clinical environment: a communication security perspective. In: MedCOMM (2012)
10. Forshaw, J.: Attacking Network Protocols. No Starch Press, San Francisco (2017)
11. Gatouillat, A., Badr, Y., Massot, B., Sejdic, E.: Internet of medical things: a review of recent contributions dealing with cyber-physical systems in medicine. IEEE IoT J. **5**(5), 3810–3822 (2018)
12. Hanna, S., Rolles, R., Molina-Markham, A., Poosankam, P., Fu, K., Song, D.: Take two software updates and see me in the morning: the case for software security evaluations of medical devices. In: HealthSec (2011)
13. Haselhorst, D.: HL7 data interfaces in medical environments: attacking and defending the achille's heel of healthcare. Technical report, SANS (2017)
14. HIMSS: 2019 HIMSS cybersecurity survey. Technical report (2019)
15. ISE: Securing hospitals: a research study and blueprint. Technical report (2016)
16. Jaigirdar, F., Rudolph, C., Bain, C.: Can I trust the data I see?: A physician's concern on medical data in IoT health architectures. In: ACSW (2019)
17. Koppel, R., Smith, S.W., Blythe, J., Kothari, V.H.: Workarounds to computer access in healthcare organizations: you want my password or a dead patient? ITCH **15**(4), 215–220 (2015)
18. Kramer, D., Baker, M., Ransford, B., Molina-Markham, A., Stewart, Q., Fu, K.: Security and privacy qualities of medical devices: an analysis of FDA postmarket surveillance. PLoS ONE **7**(7) (2012)
19. Kumar, C.: New dangers in the new world: cyber attacks in the healthcare industry. Intersect **10**(3), 3–4 (2017)
20. Lee, I., et al.: Challenges and research directions in medical cyber-physical systems. Proc. IEEE **100**(1), 75–90 (2011)
21. Mansfield-Devine, S.: Ransomware: taking businesses hostage. Netw. Secur. **2016**, 8–17 (2016)
22. McAdams, A.: Security and risk management: a fundamental business issue. Inf. Manag. **38**(4), 36 (2004)
23. McKee, D.: 80 to 0 in under 5 seconds: falsifying a medical patient's vitals (2018). https://bit.ly/2LJI8bB
24. McNab, C.: Network Security Assessment. O'Reilly Media, Newton (2016)
25. Mirsky, Y., Mahler, T., Shelef, I., Elovici, Y.: CT-GAN: malicious tampering of 3D medical imagery using deep learning. In: USENIX Security (2019)
26. MITRE: ATT&CK tactic: lateral movement (2019). https://bit.ly/2qwuUaE
27. Mundt, T., Wickboldt, P.: Security in building automation systems - a first analysis. In: Cyber Security (2016)
28. O'Brien, G., Edwards, S., Littlefield, K., McNab, N., Wang, S., Zheng, K.: Securing wireless infusion pumps. In: Healthcare Delivery Organizations (2017)
29. Philips: Data export interface programming guide (2015)
30. Regalado, D.: Inside the alaris infusion pump, not too much medicine, plz. DEF CON 25 IoT Village (2017). https://youtu.be/w4sChnS4DrI
31. Rios, B.: Infusion pump teardown. S4x16 (2016). https://youtu.be/pq9sCaoBVOw
32. Roberts, P.: Let's get cyberphysical: Internet attack shuts off the heat in Finland. https://bit.ly/33XQgeK
33. Rushanan, M., Rubin, A., Kune, D., Swanson, C.: SoK: security and privacy in implantable medical devices and body area networks. In: IEEE S&P (2014)
34. Seri, B., Vishnepolsky, G., Zusman, D.: Critical vulnerabilities to remotely compromise VxWorks, the most popular RTOS. Technical report, Armis (2019)

35. Sheefer, Y., Porticor, Holz, R., Munchen, T.U., Saint-Andre, P.: Summarizing known attacks on Transport Layer Security (TLS) and Datagram TLS (DTLS) (2015)
36. Symantec: New orangeworm attack group targets the healthcare sector in the U.S., Europe, and Asia (2019). https://symc.ly/33Rpp3S
37. Symantec: Whitefly: Espionage group has Singapore in its sights. https://symc.ly/2qoF3WG (2019)
38. Taylor, C., Venkatasubramanian, K., Shue, C.: Understanding the security of interoperable medical devices using attack graphs. In: HiCoNS (2014)
39. US DoH CISA: ICS-CERT advisories (2019). https://bit.ly/369pLnZ
40. Wood, D., Apthorpe, N., Feamster, N.: Cleartext data transmissions in consumer IoT medical devices. In: IoTS&P (2017)
41. Xu, J., Venkatasubramanian, K., Sfyrla, V.: A methodology for systematic attack trees generation for interoperable medical devices. In: SysCon (2016)
42. Xu, Y., Tran, D., Tian, Y., Alemzadeh, H.: Poster: analysis of cyber-security vulnerabilities of interconnected medical devices. In: CHASE (2019)

Establishing a Strong Baseline for Privacy Policy Classification

Najmeh Mousavi Nejad[1,2(✉)], Pablo Jabat[3], Rostislav Nedelchev[1],
Simon Scerri[2], and Damien Graux[4]

[1] Smart Data Analytics (SDA), University of Bonn, Bonn, Germany
nejad@cs.uni-bonn.de, rostislav.nedelchev@uni-bonn.de
[2] Fraunhofer Intelligent Analysis and Information Systems (IAIS),
Sankt Augustin, Germany
simon.scerri@iais.fraunhofer.de
[3] Company Watch Ltd., London, England
pjabat@companywatch.net
[4] ADAPT Centre, Trinity College Dublin, Dublin, Ireland
damien.graux@adaptcentre.ie, https://sda.tech/,
https://www.iais.fraunhofer.de/, https://www.companywatch.net/,
https://www.adaptcentre.ie/

Abstract. Digital service users are routinely exposed to Privacy Policy
consent forms, through which they enter contractual agreements con-
senting to the specifics of how their personal data is managed and used.
Nevertheless, despite renewed importance following legislation such as
the European GDPR, a majority of people still ignore policies due to
their length and complexity. To counteract this potentially dangerous
reality, in this paper we present three different models that are able to
assign pre-defined categories to privacy policy paragraphs, using supervised machine learning. In order to train our neural networks, we exploit
a dataset containing 115 privacy policies defined by US companies. An
evaluation shows that our approach outperforms state-of-the-art by 5%
over comparable and previously-reported F1 values. In addition, our
method is completely reproducible since we provide open access to all
resources. Given these two contributions, our approach can be considered
as a strong baseline for privacy policy classification.

Keywords: Privacy policy · Multi-label classification · Deep learning

1 Introduction

Various studies indicate that, despite their proliferation, a majority of consumers
still skip privacy policy consent forms due to the difficulty required for lay users
to comprehend their contents. In fact, a recent study called "The Biggest Lie
on the Internet" reported that only around a fourth of participants read privacy
policies, and they only invest just over a minute to do so [15]. Moreover, these
statistics are probably lower outside of laboratory conditions. Another survey

© IFIP International Federation for Information Processing 2020
Published by Springer Nature Switzerland AG 2020
M. Hölbl et al. (Eds.): SEC 2020, IFIP AICT 580, pp. 370–383, 2020.
https://doi.org/10.1007/978-3-030-58201-2_25

showed that if users were to read the privacy policies of all services they visit on the Internet, they would need on average 244 h each year which is almost more than half of the average time a user spends on the Internet [12].

To assist end-users with consciously agreeing to the conditions, we consider Natural Language Processing (NLP) and Machine Learning (ML) methods and apply them to classify privacy policy paragraphs into pre-defined categories for easier comprehension. Our efforts seek to build on the results of two earlier dominant studies in the literature. The first is the OPP-115 dataset, which contains 115 privacy policies at paragraph level, each of which includes fine-grained annotations from 3 experts [22]; e.g., the paragraph in Fig. 1 from the Amazon policy[1] is annotated with two classes: *User Access, Edit & Deletion* and *Data Retention*. The second study which inspired our research is the effort by *Polisis* to build a Convolutional Neural Network (CNN) model exploiting OPP-115 [5]. Despite the valuable contribution of these earlier studies, they exhibit one major weakness: reproducibility. Due to a lack of information on the exact ML dataset splits used, and the lack of a common gold standard in the literature, subsequent studies have created their own. This makes it difficult to collectively interpret and compare the different results. A major contribution of the efforts presented here is our provision of a strong and reproducible baseline for future research.

> " [...] You can add or update certain information on pages such as those referenced in the *Which Information Can I Access?* section. When you update information, we usually keep a copy of the prior version for our records. [...] "
>
> – *User Access, Edit and Deletion*
> – *Data Retention*

Fig. 1. Excerpt from Amazon privacy notice

More concretely, our contributions are the following:

- A comprehensive set of experiments based on two different gold standards;
- A presentation of a strong baseline for privacy policy classification using NLP and ML that successfully reproduces state-of-the-art findings (though with our self-created data splits and gold standards) and furthermore improves the results by employing the *BERT* framework [3] for the two gold standards;
- Ensuring the reproducibility of our results by providing all resources utilised to generate our conclusions.

Central to our efforts is a multi-label classification problem with 12 classes, which can be used to predict one or more classes for each paragraph of a given privacy policy, based on a neural network and the OPP-115 dataset. We first

---

[1] To retrieve the exact source used: <https://www.amazon.com/gp/help/customer/display.html?nodeId=468496> (Sub-entry *What Choices Do I Have?*) – last accessed March.2nd.2020.

compiled two gold standards from OPP-115: one based on majority votes (i.e., two or more experts agree on a label); and the other with the union of all expert annotations. The dataset creators [22] considered the majority-vote-based standard, whereas *Polisis* used the union-based, with the rationale that disagreements are a result of the experts' high understanding of legal texts and that therefore, none of their annotations should be deemed incorrect.

In order to establish a strong baseline, we compare three models with both gold standards. The first model is a CNN, whose generation is directly comparable to the earlier *Polisis* efforts. The second and third models are based on the *BERT* transformer, a model that has recently gained a lot of attention as a potential superior alternative. To the best of our knowledge, our efforts are the first attempt to produce a reliable and completely reproducible result on privacy policy classification. The results attained demonstrate consistency and significant improvement over the baseline and indicate good reliability: A 77% micro-average F1 on the union-based gold standard, and a 85% micro-average F1 on the majority-based gold standard.

The rest of the paper is divided as follows: in Sect. 2 we compare our approach to the existing studies on privacy policies. Section 3 provides details of the three models. In Sects. 4 and 5, an extensive set of experiments is presented and discussed. Finally, Sect. 6 concludes this study and suggests future directions towards privacy policy analysis.

2   Related Work

In light of the, now enforced EU-wide, General Data Protection Regulation (GDPR), there has been an increasing interest toward privacy policy analysis. Some studies investigated the essential regulatory model, *notice and choice* [9] in web privacy principles [10,16]. Libert monitored data flows on websites and identified third parties who collect and use personal data [10]. Afterward, over 200,000 websites' privacy policies are scanned to determine whether the parties identified, are explicitly mentioned in the page's privacy policy. Furthermore, privacy policies are additionally analyzed to check whether they respect the "Do Not Track" browser setting[2]. In another study, the authors applied NLP and supervised ML to automatically extract control choice excerpts and opt-out hyperlinks from privacy policy documents [16]. In order to evaluate their work, OPP-115 was used and the results showed that ML is feasible, even with the small number of samples for *'User Choice/Control'* category in OPP-115. In contrast to our problem, these approaches have addressed only a specific feature of privacy policies, whereas our method processes the whole document for the benefit of regular end-users.

A few approaches developed a model with supervised ML to measure completeness of privacy policies [2,4]. The dataset used in training, contains a set of pre-defined categories based on privacy regulations and guidelines. Finally the trained model predicts a category for an unseen paragraph. According to the

---

[2] https://en.wikipedia.org/wiki/Do_Not_Track.

papers, this structure helps users to examine privacy policies faster and allows them to focus on those categories in which they are interested. However, based on our observation, most of online privacy policies use rich HTML representations and therefore offer a basic level of structural view to the end-users. Moreover, to the best of our knowledge none of the corpora were created with the full support of experts, which is an essential prerequisite in legal text processing.

A prominent group on privacy policy analysis is *Usable Privacy Policy Project*[3], they provided OPP-115, the first comprehensive dataset with fine-grained annotations on paragraph level [22]. The project aims to extract important information for the benefit of regular and expert end users. To do so, a corpus containing 115 privacy policies from 115 US companies was annotated by 3 experts on paragraph level (10 experts in total and 3 experts per document). The annotations in OPP-115 dataset are in two levels: 10 high level categories and 22 distinct attributes. For instance, the high level category *First Party Collection* has 9 low level attributes, some of which are: *Collection Mode, Information Type, Purpose*. Along with the creation of dataset, the authors built different ML models for prediction of high level categories. The gold standard for evaluating the methods was compiled based on majority votes: if two or more experts agreed on a single category, it was considered in the final gold standard. The best reported micro-average F1 is 66% that was achieved with Support Vector Machine.

Leveraging OPP-115 and deep learning, *Polisis* extracts segments from privacy policies and presents them to users in a visualized format [5]. According to the paper, the union-based gold standard is used for experiments; 65 privacy policies were considered for training and 50 policies were kept for the test set. The authors claim that a successful multi-label classifier should not only predict the presence of a label, but also its absence[4]. They report only macro-averages and further compute the average of F1 and F1-absence and yield 81% average on the test set. Despite the encouraging work done in *Polisis*, we believe that the paper lacks two fundamental elements: there is no validation set involved in training phase; and there is no information on micro-averages.

It is worth to mention that none of the above studies provided their dataset splits and therefore there is no standardized benchmark for privacy policy classification. As a result, in the following sections, first we show how we successfully reproduce *Polisis* results (though with different data splits) and further present two transformer models that significantly outperform *Polisis*.

3 Approach

In order to establish a firm foundation, we attempt to reproduce the work of [5] with additional improvements. To do that, we conduct experiments using word

---

[3] https://usableprivacy.org/.

[4] They also claim that a model that predicts that all labels are present would have 100% precision and recall, which is obviously wrong.

embeddings and a Convolutional Neural Network (CNN). Furthermore, we evaluate Bidirectional Encoder Representations from Transformers (*BERT*) [3] that has state-of-the-art performance on many other text classification tasks.

3.1   Convolutional Neural Network

Pre-trained Word-Embeddings. Traditionally, text classifiers have taken advantage of vector representations like bag of words or term-frequency inverse-document-frequency (TF-IDF). However, it is clear that this method has the disadvantage of not retaining the semantic information depicted by the order of words, as well as the meaning of the single words as independent units and be purely dependent on the context. Thus, we investigate word embeddings.

Word embeddings were initially proposed by [1,14] and were later popularized by [13]. The continuous bag of words method, which is a variant of word2vec, creates a numeric representation of words by attempting to predict a given word by considering its neighbors as seen in text. A huge benefit such an algorithm is that, no labeled data is necessary, but only great amounts of correct text.

While word2vec is effective at storing some semantic meaning in a vector representation, it treats words as atomic units and thus, it does not consider the internal structure of words. Such information can be useful for less frequent or compound words like rainfall or greenhouse. FastText uses a bag of character n-grams to represent words, where each character n-gram is a vector and all the constituents are summed up to create a representation for the word [6,25].

The aforementioned properties can be useful for the context of privacy policies. Since most openly available word embeddings are trained on news or Wikipedia corpora [25], we utilize fastText to create vector representations that are more suitable for the current task. For that purpose, we used a big corpus of 130k privacy policies scraped from an application store for smart phones. In app stores, applications are required to provide privacy policies. After tokenizing the text with NLTK [18], there are 132 595 084 tokens in total and 173 588 unique ones. We compared the vocabulary between this corpus and two version of OPP-115 that we utilize. We saw that there are 1 072 words which are seen only in OPP-115 majority-vote version, but not in the corpus used for drafting the word vectors. Similarly, for the gold standard containing union of all classes, there were 1 119 out-of-vocabulary (OOV) words. The difference in the amount of OOVs is due to the fact that the majority vote dataset has less paragraphs (when there was no agreement on a single category) and thus, it is less likely that there are unseen words. More details regarding the size of the dataset versions are provided in Sect. 4. After manual inspection, we concluded that most of the OOV words are names of brands, products, services or their web-addresses. These are completely omitted, since from an intuitive perspective they should not be decisive for the correct detection of a policy class. Hence, the vocabulary is sufficient.

Architecture. To tackle the multi-label classification problem, we follow the work of [5] by using a CNN (displayed in Fig. 2). The previously explained word embeddings are provided as input to the neural network. A convolutional operation is applied with a context window of 3 words, whose output then passes through a Rectified Linear Activation (ReLU) function. Then, from each context output, only the strongest features are selected by a max-pooling layer, resulting in a single vector that contains the most informative properties of each context, thus the neural network is forced to focus only on certain features that are specific to the current goal. Furthermore, a linear layer followed by a ReLU are applied to create a higher level representation of the collected information. Finally, a linear layer with as many nodes as classes is applied to provide an output in the target dimensions and passed through a sigmoid function to obtain per label probability scores.

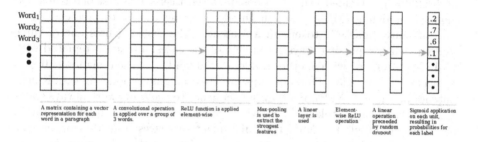

Fig. 2. CNN architecture

The proposed architecture shares a strong resemblance with the work of [7], where a CNN is used for multi-class classification of sentences. However, it lacks a random dropout just before the last linear layer. We conduct experiments with 50% dropout. Additionally, we used Adam [8] optimization algorithm combined with early stopping. The convolutional neural network is optimized using binary cross entropy loss:

$$\ell(x, y) = L = \{l_1, \ldots, l_N\}^{\top} \tag{1}$$

$$l_n = -w_n \left[y_n \cdot \log x_n + (1 - y_n) \cdot \log(1 - x_n) \right] \tag{2}$$

where $l_1, \ldots, l_N$ specify the 12 loss values for each of the 12 possible labels that we have in the dataset. It is being calculated for each, since this is a multi-label classification and we could have any combinations of those. After we have the 12 losses, we take the mean of those 12 to get one scalar number. Furthermore, x is the model prediction, y is the true label, w is the class specific weight which in our case are all 1. For instance, if we consider that our current model assigns probability p to observation o for the *Data Retention* label, the loss function for this specific label will be:

$$loss(DataRetention) = y \cdot \log p + (1 - y) \cdot \log(1 - p) \tag{3}$$

where y is 1 if observation o is labeled with *Data Retention* in the gold standard and 0 if not.

3.2   Bidirectional Encoder Representations from Transformers

The *BERT* framework [3] uses several layers of transformer encoders [20] to create a bidirectional representation of the tokens in the sequence. The approach operates in two stages: first, the model is pre-trained on large amounts of unlabelled data; second, it is fine-tuned on specific labeled data to solve a downstream problem, which in our case is multi-label classification.

To handle various domains and tasks, *BERT* is using WordPiece [23] tokenization. It provides a reasonable balance between character and subword level information. For example, a model using it, can detect similar suffixes or roots among words. This way, the vocabulary stays within a reasonable size, without having too many entries. The chosen vocabulary size is 30 000 [3].

BERT is pre-trained using two unsupervised tasks. The first one is masked language modeling (MLM), i.e., the model is being taught to predict 15% of the randomly "masked" tokens in a sentence. The masking uses one of three randomly chosen possible ways: 1) in 80% of the cases, a token is replaced with $[MASK]$; 2) in 10% with another random word; and 3) in the remaining 10% no replacement is done [3]. The other unsupervised language modeling task is next sentence prediction (NSP). Every input sequence to the framework always starts with the classification token $[CLS]$, which provides a fixed-length representation for the whole input. For NSP, two subsequent sentences from the corpora are concatenated with another separator token, $[SEP]$, so that the model is aware of the separation between the two. In 50% of the cases, the second sentence is replaced by another one. Thus, *BERT* is trained to recognize when a pair of sentences appear together in the corpora (or they don't), using the CLS token [3].

We use a pre-trained version of $BERT_{BASE}$[5, 6] which has 12 encoder layers, a hidden state size of 768, and 12 attention heads, totaling in 110M parameters. Additionally, we also prepare another fine-tuned version of the language model with our 130 K privacy policy corpus[7]. Ninety percent of those were used for training while the remaining ten for validation. We fine-tune the model for three epochs and achieved a cross-entropy loss on the mask languaged model task of 0.1151 and perplexity, 1.1220. Finally, both versions of the approach are trained on the privacy policy classification task and evaluated. For more detail on *BERT*, we would forward the reader to the relevant references [3, 20].

4   Evaluation

In pursuance of providing a reliable baseline for privacy policy classification, two gold standards were compiled out of OPP-115 dataset. OPP-115 high-level annotations are divided into 10 classes:

---

[5] https://github.com/huggingface/transformers.

[6] https://github.com/kaushaltrivedi/fast-bert.

[7] The `BertLMDataBunch` class contains `from_raw_corpus` method that takes a list of raw texts and creates `DataBunch` for the language model learner.

1. *First Party Collection/Use*: how and why the information is collected.
2. *Third Party Sharing/Collection*: how the information may be used or collected by third parties.
3. *User Choice/Control*: choices and controls available to to users.
4. *User Access/Edit/Deletion*: if users can modify their information and how.
5. *Data Retention*: how long the information is stored.
6. *Data Security*: how is users' data secured.
7. *Policy Change*: if the service provider will change their policy and how the users are informed.
8. *Do Not Track*: if and how Do Not Track signals is honored.
9. *International/Specific Audiences*: practices that target a specific group of users (e.g., children, Europeans, etc.)
10. *Other*: additional practices not covered by the other categories.

Ten experts were hired to create fine-grained annotations and each privacy policy was randomly assigned to 3 of them. OPP-115 comprises 3 792 paragraphs, 10 high-level classes and 22 distinct attributes[8]. Each paragraph was labeled with one or more classes (out of 10). According to the dataset creators, the best agreement was achieved on *Do Not Track* class with Fleiss' Kappa equal to 91%, whereas the most controversial class was *Other*, with only 49% of agreement [22]. The latter category was further decomposed into its attributes: *Introductory/Generic*, *Privacy Contact Information* and *Practice Not Covered*. Therefore, we face a multi-label classification problem with 12 classes. It should be clarified here that computing Fleiss' kappa considering all categories together is not feasible for OPP-115, as annotators differ per policy. Aforementioned, there were 10 experts and each policy was randomly assigned to 3 of them. If 3 experts were the same experts for the whole dataset, it was rational to compute an overall Fleiss's kappa for all 10 categories and between 3 annotators. For this reason, [22] reported Fleiss' kappa per category.

To evaluate our three models, we compiled two gold standards: union-based, which contains all expert annotations; and the majority-vote-based gold standard, where only annotations with an agreement between at least 2 experts were retained. Label distributions in both gold standards are shown in table 1. Following conventional ML practices, dataset splits are randomly partitioned into a ratio of 3:1:1 for training, validation and testing respectively; while maintaining a stratified set of labels. In total, the union-based dataset contains 3 788 unique segments and the majority-based one comprises 3 571 unique segments[9]. The latter has less segments due the 217 paragraphs that were eliminated because no expert agreement was reached.

In total, 6 experiments were carried out. The scores obtained (micro-averages ranging from 70–85% and macro-average in range of 65–76% for both gold standards) are considered very accurate, especially in the context of the Fleiss expert agreements, reported in [22], which showed human agreement between 49–91% for the same classes here considered. As expected, for all 6 experiments,

---

[8] Here, we only consider high-level categories.
[9] All splits are available for further experiments. See footnote 13.

Table 1. Label distribution in gold standards; Tr: Train; V: Validation; T: Test

Labels	Union						Majority votes					
	Tr	V	T	Tr(%)	V(%)	T(%)	Tr	V	T	Tr(%)	V(%)	T(%)
First party collection & Use	988	243	288	40.8	40.1	38	781	176	250	34.2	30.9	35
Third party sharing & collection	755	204	227	31.1	33.7	30	584	158	203	25.5	27.7	28.4
User access, edit and deletion	155	29	46	6.4	4.8	6.1	101	24	24	4.4	4.2	3.4
Data retention	111	21	24	4.6	3.5	3.2	50	14	14	2.2	2.4	2
Data security	251	65	59	10.3	10.7	7.8	139	31	40	6.1	5.4	5.6
International/specific audiences	225	67	61	9.3	11.1	8.1	204	41	56	9	7.2	7.8
Do not track	22	3	7	1	0.5	0.9	22	6	3	1	1	0.4
Policy change	118	27	47	4.9	4.4	6.2	73	25	21	3.2	4.4	3
User choice/control	405	97	130	16.7	16	17.2	233	48	77	10.2	8.4	10.8
Introductory/generic	514	137	162	21.2	22.6	21.4	240	72	78	10.5	12.6	11
Practice not covered	402	102	138	16.6	16.8	18.2	83	21	25	3.6	3.7	3.5
Privacy contact information	207	44	72	8.5	7.3	9.5	129	32	42	5.6	5.6	5.9

Table 2. F1 for three models on the two gold standards in (%) with tuned epochs on validation; V: Validation; T: Test; Threshold = 0.5

Labels	Majority-vote gold standard						Union-based gold standard					
	CNN		BERT		BERT-fine-tuned		CNN		BERT		BERT-fine-tuned	
	V	T	V	T	V	T	V	T	V	T	V	T
First party collection/use	83	82	87	88	88	91	83	81	83	84	87	86
Third party sharing/collection	84	82	86	85	87	90	80	79	79	82	83	86
User access, edit & deletion	80	70	82	63	77	73	56	45	54	49	56	65
Data Retention	43	40	42	33	54	56	36	48	36	68	62	71
Data security	76	75	87	82	87	80	66	72	71	80	73	76
International/specific audiences	96	82	94	81	95	83	89	92	87	93	92	92
Do not track	91	100	80	100	80	100	80	60	80	60	100	92
Policy change	80	88	80	88	85	90	69	77	75	78	77	80
User choice & Control	77	72	75	81	78	81	66	64	64	63	66	65
Introductory/Generic	63	73	75	76	78	79	63	65	74	68	73	67
Practice not covered	8	13	18	32	35	35	41	37	44	46	45	48
Privacy contact information	86	84	79	80	79	78	79	71	75	71	83	78
Macro averages	72	71	74	74	77	79	67	65	68	70	75	76
Micro averages	79	78	81	82	83	85	72	70	73	74	77	77

micro- outperform macro-averages, because for a few labels, the model is not able to learn the class weights properly due to sample scarcity. For instance, *Data Retention* corresponds to only 2–3% of dataset, and yet this class has 1/12 weight in macro-average calculation; whereas micro-average considers dataset heterogeneity and decreases the impact of scarce categories on the final result. Furthermore, the category *Practice Not Covered* shows low F1 on both gold standards. This category refers to all practices that are not covered by other 11 categories and therefore represents a broad range of topics. Consequently, due to diversity of vocabulary, it is difficult for the model to learn this specific class.

Table 2 shows that even $BERT_{BASE}$ achieves state-of-the-art and further improves the results (without domain-specific embeddings). This is due to the facts that 1) transformers scale much better on longer text sequences because they operate in a concurrent manner; 2) *BERT* is using WordPiece encoding and therefore it has a dictionary which is hard to have an OOV case with it; and 3) it has been trained on massive amounts of data. Moreover, the fine-tuned $BERT_{BASE}$ with 130 K corpus privacy policy has significantly enhanced F1 average on both gold standards[10]. Interestingly, fine-tuned *BERT* has improved macro-average more than micro. It is a proof that exploiting a good language model enables the classification model to learn the weights more properly, even with the scarce number of samples.

In order to compare our result to *Polisis*, we present table 3 which provides macro-averages on the union-based gold standard. As mentioned in Sect. 2, *Polisis* used the union-based dataset to report their results. The average lines in the table represent the macro-average of the metric (precision, recall or F1) in predicting the presence of each label and predicting its absence (the 7th line in the table - F1 - is also included in table 2).

As shown in table 3, we successfully reproduce *Polisis* findings (although with different splits, which remain unavailable) and further improve the result by 5% compared to the state-of-the-art. However, we believe this type of average is not a fair measure for multi-label classification. As shown in table 2, the fine-tuned *BERT* model has nevertheless significantly enhanced macro-averages (from 65% to 76%) which is not visible in table 3, where the enhancement is limited to 5%.

Table 3. Macro averages on the union-based gold standard in (%) with tuned epochs on validation; V:Validation; T:Test; Threshold=0.5

Measure	CNN		BERT		BERT-fine-tuned	
	V	T	V	T	V	T
Precision	81	81	81	84	81	83
Precision-absence	94	94	94	95	95	95
average	**86**	**86**	**86**	**89**	**88**	**89**
Recall	58	57	60	62	70	71
Recall-absence	97	97	97	97	97	97
average	**78**	**77**	**79**	**80**	**84**	**84**
F1	67	65	68	70	75	76
F1-absence	95	95	95	96	96	96
average	**81**	**80**	**82**	**83**	**86**	**86**

In case of multi-label classification, it is not clear which average (macro or micro) best defines a model's performance. As Sebastiani argues, there is no agreement to choose between micro- and macro-averages in literature [17]. Some studies claim that macro-average is fair in case of class imbalance, since all the categories have the same weight, whereas micro-average favours methods that just correctly predict the most frequent categories [21]. However, others (the majority) believe that when the label distribution is not balanced, computation

---

[10] Fine-tuning BERT took 33 h for 3 epochs on a single GPU. Once it is completed, training the classification model takes only a few hours, depending on the number of epochs.

of micro-average is preferable, because a micro-average aggregates the contributions of all classes to compute the average metric [11,19]. In order to establish a firm foundation, we report both averages.

Table 2 presents F1 scores across all labels with a threshold equal to 0.5 for the two gold standards. For CNN, we applied Adam with default parameters and with 50% dropout just before the last linear layer (learning rate = 0.001, decay rates: $\beta_1 = 0.9$, $\beta_2 = 0.999$). *BERT* is optimized with the default configuration and LAMB optimizer [24].

5   Discussion

This paper considers notoriously cumbersome privacy policies and investigates automatic methods to assist end-users in comprehending these contractual agreements. The conducted experiments confirm the feasibility of our approach in reaching this objective. Since we are benefiting from supervised ML, the performance of the generated model highly depends on the training dataset quality. As shown in table 1, there is a huge difference between the two gold standards for the *Practice Not Covered* class. In the union-based dataset 642 segments are categorized as *Practice Not Covered*, whereas the majority-based gold standard only records 129 occurrences. Unsurprisingly, for this specific label, all models trained with the union-based dataset outperform the models which were trained by the majority-based one. In addition, 513 variation for the *Practice Not Covered* category between the two gold standards shows high expert disagreement. This was not evident in the original paper [22], because the authors reported Fleiss' Kappa on the parent category (*Other*) and there is no information on annotator agreement for its subcategories.

Figure 3 shows an example of disagreement on *Practice Not Covered* category in two gold standards. The shown paragraph explains Amazon's policy on treating children's data. In the union-based dataset this segment is annotated with *International and Specific Audiences* and *Practice Not Covered* classes, whereas in the majority-based, it is only labeled with *International & Specific Audiences*.

> " [...] Amazon.com does not sell products for purchase by children. We sell children's products for purchase by adults. If you are under 18, you may use Amazon.com only with the involvement of a parent or guardian. [...] "
>
> – *International and Specific Audiences*
> – *Practice Not Covered*

Fig. 3. Disagreement example for the Amazon privacy notice

Regarding label-specific performance, almost all models perform quite well on *Do Not Track* class in spite of the low sample occurrence. This is probably due to a smaller set of terminology that is often used in such paragraphs, including specifically the word *track*. Furthermore, as mentioned earlier, the best human agreement was also achieved on *Do Not Track* class with Fleiss' Kappa equal to 91%, which indicates that our ML models simulate human thinking fairly.

In summary, OPP-115 has proven to be a small, yet reliable dataset for supervised privacy policy classification. However, our experiments confirmed legal text subjectivity for a few classes. One possible solution is decomposing those categories into less controversial subclasses with higher experts agreement. In Fig. 3, breaking the *Specific Audiences* segment into more specific classes will make annotations less subjective, for human experts and machines alike.

To the extent of our knowledge, this is the first effort to establish a standard benchmark on privacy policy classification. In the light of recently enforced data protection laws in the EU, all parties that use and collect personal information must ensure their compliance with GDPR. Although OPP-115 consists of policies defined by American companies, most of the top-level categories can still be largely mapped to GDPR articles[11]. For instance, the category *First Party Collection/Use* can reflect many practices stated in the Article 13, 'Information to be provided where personal data are collected' and *User Access, Edit & Deletion* can be linked to Articles 16 & 17 ('Right to Rectification/Erasure')[12]. The OPP-115 dataset also contains annotations at attribute level. By extracting these values from an arbitrary privacy policy, it is possible to perform an in-depth analysis and assist experts to check compliance of privacy policies text based on GDPR.

6   Conclusion and Future Work

In this paper we investigate the potential of automatic classification of consent agreements in privacy policy consent forms that are frequently faced by lay users. Our findings are based on the compilation of two gold standards, thus providing a reference privacy policy classification baseline for the relevant research community. To the best of our knowledge, this is the first effort towards a standardized benchmark for privacy policies experiments. The evaluation shows that our best model yields F1 score highs of 77–85% (micro-avg) and 76–79% (macro-avg) for union-based and majority-based gold standards, respectively. Both metrics outperform the reported state-of-the-art. In light of human annotator agreement levels achieved for the same data and classes (ranging from 49%–91%), the results can safely be considered as successful.

The approach and method presented are completely reproducible and all resources and data splits are openly accessible[13]. Since the context surrounding our methods (including the data splits) are available, they can be used as a

---

[11] Website privacy policies in EU depend also on Directive 2002/58/CE.

[12] Website privacy policies in European union depend also on Directive 2002/58/CE.

[13] A *supplementary archive* is available online for download: <https://github.com/SmartDataAnalytics/Polisis_Benchmark>. The archive contains *inter alia* the source-code required to reproduce all the experiments, some useful documentation and necessary datasets.

benchmark for other approaches exploring machine-assisted privacy policy classification for improved human understanding.

To further improve the F1 scores achieved, the imbalanced label distribution of OPP-115 (see table 1) could be addressed. A possible solution is to use a weighted objective function with respect to the frequency of the labels. Another approach in consideration is to use sampling techniques to improve the balance. Finally, alternative novel methods can be investigated to take fuller advantage of the three different expert annotations available. In this regard, we will examine the usage of methods that take the varying labels collectively into consideration.

In conclusion, we intend to continue building upon the baseline achieved and the positive results presented in this paper. As demonstrated by the EU-wide GDPR implementation, data regulation is increasingly recognized as a critical area at a political and governance level, whose impact is felt by all digitally-enabled world citizens. Therefore, although not novel, the application of AI techniques to this area has renewed relevance, and there is great value in exploring automation to support private users entering contractual agreements to have a clearer and more secure understanding of their rights, risks and implications.

Acknowledgment. This work has been partly supported by the European H2020 project "DAPSI" under the Grant Agreement 871498.

References

1. Collobert, R., Weston, J.: A unified architecture for natural language processing: deep neural networks with multitask learning. In: Proceedings of the 25th International Conference on Machine Learning, ICML 2008, pp. 160–167. ACM, New York (2008). https://doi.org/10.1145/1390156.1390177, http://doi.acm.org/10.1145/1390156.1390177
2. Costante, E., Sun, Y., Petković, M., den Hartog, J.: A machine learning solution to assess privacy policy completeness: (short paper). In: Proceedings of the 2012 ACM Workshop on Privacy in the Electronic Society, WPES 2012. ACM, New York, pp. 91–96 (2012). https://doi.org/10.1145/2381966.2381979, http://doi.acm.org/10.1145/2381966.2381979
3. Devlin, J., Chang, M.W., Lee, K., Toutanova, K.: BERT: pre-training of deep bidirectional transformers for language understanding. arXiv preprint (2018). arXiv:1810.04805
4. Guntamukkala, N., Dara, R., Grewal, G.W.: A machine-learning based approach for measuring the completeness of online privacy policies. In: 2015 IEEE 14th International Conference on Machine Learning and Applications (ICMLA), pp. 289–294 (2015)
5. Harkous, H., Fawaz, K., Lebret, R., Schaub, F., Shin, K.G., Aberer, K.: Polisis: automated analysis and presentation of privacy policies using deep learning. In: Proceedings of the 27th USENIX Security Symposium (2018)
6. Joulin, A., Grave, E., Bojanowski, P., Mikolov, T.: Bag of tricks for efficient text classification. arXiv preprint (2016). arXiv:1607.01759
7. Kim, Y.: Convolutional neural networks for sentence classification. In: Proceedings of the 2014 Conference on Empirical Methods in Natural Language Processing (EMNLP), pp. 1746–1751. Association for Computational Linguistics (2014). https://doi.org/10.3115/v1/D14-1181, http://aclweb.org/anthology/D14-1181

8. Kingma, D.P., Ba, J.: Adam: a method for stochastic optimization. CoRR abs/1412.6980 (2015)
9. Landesberg, M.K., Levin, T.M., Curtin, C.G., Lev, O.: Privacy online: a report to congress. NASA (19990008264) (1998)
10. Libert, T.: An automated approach to auditing disclosure of third-party data collection in website privacy policies. In: Proceedings of the 2018 World Wide Web Conference, WWW 2018, International World Wide Web Conferences Steering Committee, Republic and Canton of Geneva, Switzerland, pp. 207–216 (2018). https://doi.org/10.1145/3178876.3186087
11. Manning, C.D., Raghavan, P., Schütze, H.: Introduction to Information Retrieval. Cambridge University Press, New York, NY, USA (2008)
12. McDonald, A.M., Cranor, L.F.: The cost of reading privacy policies. ISJLP **4**, 543 (2008)
13. Mikolov, T., Sutskever, I., Chen, K., Corrado, G., Dean, J.: Distributed representations of words and phrases and their compositionality. In: Proceedings of the 26th International Conference on Neural Information Processing Systems, NIPS 2013, vol. 2, pp. 3111–3119. Curran Associates Inc., USA (2013). http://dl.acm.org/citation.cfm?id=2999792.2999959
14. Mnih, A., Hinton, G.: Three new graphical models for statistical language modelling. In: Proceedings of the 24th International Conference on Machine Learning, ICML 2007, pp. 641–648. ACM, New York (2007). https://doi.org/10.1145/1273496.1273577, http://doi.acm.org/10.1145/1273496.1273577
15. Obar, J.A., Oeldorf-Hirsch, A.: The biggest lie on the Internet: ignoring the privacy policies and terms of service policies of social networking services. Inf. Commun. Soc. **23**, 1–20 (2018)
16. Sathyendra, K.M., Schaub, F., Wilson, S., Sadeh, N.M.: Automatic extraction of opt-out choices from privacy policies. In: AAAI Fall Symposia (2016)
17. Sebastiani, F.: Machine learning in automated text categorization. ACM Comput. Surv. **34**(1), 1–47 (2002). https://doi.org/10.1145/505282.505283, http://doi.acm.org/10.1145/505282.505283
18. Tang, D., Wei, F., Yang, N., Zhou, M., Liu, T., Qin, B.: Learning sentiment-specific word embedding for twitter sentiment classification. In: Proceedings of the 52nd Annual Meeting of the Association for Computational Linguistics (Volume 1: Long Papers), pp. 1555–1565. Association for Computational Linguistics (2014). https://doi.org/10.3115/v1/P14-1146, http://aclweb.org/anthology/P14-1146
19. Van Asch, V.: Macro-and Micro-Averaged Evaluation Measures (Basic Draft). CLiPS, Belgium (2013)
20. Vaswani, A., et al.: Attention is all you need. In: Advances in Neural Information Processing Systems, pp. 5998–6008 (2017)
21. Wiener, E., Pedersen, J.O., Weigend, A.S.: A neural network approach to topic spotting (1995)
22. Wilson, S., et al.: The creation and analysis of a website privacy policy corpus. In: Proceedings of the 54th Annual Meeting of the Association for Computational Linguistics (Volume 1: Long Papers), vol. 1, pp. 1330–1340 (2016)
23. Wu, Y., et al.: Google's neural machine translation system: bridging the gap between human and machine translation. arXiv preprint (2016). arXiv:1609.08144
24. You, Y., Li, J., Hseu, J., Song, X., Demmel, J., Hsieh, C.J.: Reducing BERT pre-training time from 3 days to 76 minutes. arXiv abs/1904.00962 (2019)
25. https://code.google.com/archive/p/word2vec/

Cross-Platform File System Activity Monitoring and Forensics – A Semantic Approach

Kabul Kurniawan[1,3]([⊠]) [iD], Andreas Ekelhart[1,2] [iD], Fajar Ekaputra[1] [iD],
and Elmar Kiesling[1] [iD]

[1] TU Wien, Favoritenstraße 9–11, Vienna, Austria
kabul.kurniawan@tuwien.ac.at
[2] SBA Research, Floragasse 7, Vienna, Austria
[3] University of Vienna, Währingerstraße 29, Vienna, Austria

Abstract. Ensuring data confidentiality and integrity are key concerns for information security professionals, who typically have to obtain and integrate information from multiple sources to detect unauthorized data modifications and transmissions. The instrumentation that operating systems provide for the monitoring of file system level activity can yield important clues on possible data tampering and exfiltration activity but the raw data that these tools provide is difficult to interpret, contextualize and query. In this paper, we propose and implement an architecture for file system activity log acquisition, extraction, linking and storage that leverages semantic techniques to tackle limitations of existing monitoring approaches in terms of integration, contextualization, and cross-platform interoperability. We illustrate the applicability of the proposed approach in both forensic and monitoring scenarios and conduct a performance evaluation in a virtual setting.

Keywords: Semantic log analysis · Digital forensics · File system monitoring · Exfiltration detection

1 Introduction

In our increasingly digitized world, Information and Communication Technologies pervade all areas of modern life. Consequently, organizations face difficult challenges in protecting the confidentiality and integrity of the data they control, and theft of corporate information – i.e., data breaches or data leakage – have become a critical concern [7].

In the face of increasingly comprehensive collection of sensitive data, such incidents can become an existential threat that severely impacts the affected organization, e.g., in terms of reputation loss, decreased trustworthiness, and direct consequence that affect their bottom line. Fines and legal fees, either due to contractual obligations or laws and regulations (e.g., the General Data

© IFIP International Federation for Information Processing 2020
Published by Springer Nature Switzerland AG 2020
M. Hölbl et al. (Eds.): SEC 2020, IFIP AICT 580, pp. 384–397, 2020.
https://doi.org/10.1007/978-3-030-58201-2_26

Protection Regulation in the EU), have become another critical risk. Overall, the number and size of data breaches have been on the rise in recent years[1].

On a technical level, exfiltration of sensitive data is often difficult to detect. In this context, we distinguish two main types of adversaries and associated threat models: *(i)* an insider with legitimate access to data, who either purposely or accidentally exfiltrates data, and *(ii)* an external attacker who obtains access illegitimately. Insiders typically have multiple channels for exfiltration at their disposal, including conventional protocols (e.g., ftp, sftp, ssh, scp), cloud storage services (e.g., dropbox, onedrive, google drive, WeTransfer), physical media (e.g., USB, laptop, mobile phone), messaging and email applications, and dns tunneling [11]. Whereas an insider may leverage legitimate access permissions directly or at least internal resources as a starting point, an external attacker must first infiltrate the organization network and obtain access to the data (e.g., by spreading malware or spyware, stealing credentials, eavesdropping, brute forcing employee passwords, etc.).

State-of-the-art perimeter security solutions such as intrusion detection and prevention systems (IDS/IPS), firewalls, and network traffic anomaly detection are per se generally not capable of detecting insider attacks [20]. However, such activities typically leave traces in the network and on the involved systems, which can be used to spot potential misuse in real time or to reconstruct and document the sequence of events associated with an exfiltration and its scope ex-post. This examination, interpretation, and reconstruction of trace evidence in the computing environment is part of digital forensics. Upon detection of security violations, forensic analysts attempt to investigate the relevant causes and effects, frequently following the hypothesis-based approach to digital forensics [6]. Although there are a variety of tools and techniques available that are employed during a digital investigation, the lack of integration and interoperability between them, as well as the formats of their sources and resulting data hinder the analysis process [8].

In this paper, we introduce a novel approach that leverages semantic web technologies to address these challenges in the context of file system activity analysis. This approach can harmonize heterogeneous file and process information across operating systems and log sources. Furthermore, it provides contextualization through interlinking with relevant information and background knowledge.

The research question we address in this article is: *How can semantic technologies support digital file activity investigations?* Addressing this question resulted in the following main contributions: *(i)* a set of log and file event vocabularies (Sect. 3); *(ii)* an architecture and prototypical implementation for file system log acquisition, event extraction, and interlinking across heterogeneous systems and with background knowledge (Sect. 4); *(iii)* a set of demonstration scenarios for continuous monitoring and forensic investigations (Sect. 5); and *(iv)* a performance evaluation in a virtual setting (Sect. 6).

---

[1] https://www.informationisbeautiful.net/visualizations/worlds-biggest-data-breaches-hacks/.

2   Related Work

Our approach builds upon and integrates multiple strands of work, which we will review in the following: *(i)* approaches for file activity monitoring, both in the academic literature and commercial tools; *(ii)* file system ontologies; and *(iii)* semantic file monitoring & forensics.

File Activity Monitoring. In contrast to the approach presented in this paper, prior work in this category does not involve semantic or graph-based modeling, which facilitates interoperability and integration, contextualization through interlinking with background knowledge, and reasoning.

The authors in [12] focus on data exfiltration by insiders. They first apply statistical analyses to characterize legitimate file access patterns and compare those to file access patterns of recent activities to identify anomalies. The authors mention that the approach can result in a high number of suspicious activities, which can be impractical for individual investigation. [4] aims to predict insider threats by monitoring various parameters such as file access activity, USB storage activity, application usage, and sessions. In their evaluation, they train a deep learning model on legitimate user activity and then use the model to assign threat scores to unseen activities. In [3], the authors introduce a policy-based system for data leakage detection that utilizes operating system call provenance. They facilitate real-time detection of data leakage by tracking operations performed on sensitive files. This approach is similar to the one presented in this paper in its objectives, i.e., it also aims to monitor file activities (copy, rename, move), but it does not cover contextualization and linking to background knowledge. [9] proposes an approach that leverages data provenance information from OS kernel messages to detect exfiltration of data returned to users from a database. The proposed system builds profiles of users' actions to determine whether actions are consistent with the tasks of the users. While it has similar goals, the focus is limited on data exfiltration from databases via files.

Apart from the academic research on various techniques for file activity monitoring, a wide range of tools is available commercially, such as Solarwind Server and Application Monitor, ManageEngine DataSecurity Plus, PA File Insight, STEALTHbits File Activity Monitor, and Decision File Audit. These tools cover varying scopes of leakage detection and typically provide a simple alerting mechanism upon suspicious activity. Another category of existing tools are Security Information and Event Management systems (e.g., LogDNA, Splunk, ElasticSearch). Their purpose is to manage and analyze logs and they do not specifically tackle the problem of tracking file activity life-cycles.

File System Ontologies. Ontological representation of file system information has been explored, e.g., in [18], in which the authors propose TripFS, a lightweight framework that applies Linked Data principles for file systems in order to expose their content via dereferenceable HTTP URIs. The authors model file systems with their published vocabulary that is aligned with the NEPOMUK File Ontology (NFO)[2]. Similar to TripFS, [19] proposes VDB-

---

[2] http://oscaf.sourceforge.net/nfo.html.

FilePub to expose file systems as Linked Data and to publish user-defined content metadata. With focus on end-user access, [17] provide an extension to TripFS which enables users to navigate the published files, and to annotate and download them via common web browsers without the need to install special software packages.

In recent work, the authors of [16] proposed a Semantic File System (SFS) Ontology[3] which extends terms from the NEPOMUK ontology. They further provide technical definitions of terms and a class hierarchy with persistent URIs and content negotiation capabilities. In our approach, we use the basic concepts for files, such as file names and file properties as proposed in the related work, but our approach integrates additional concepts, such as, e.g., file activities, source and target locations, and file classification.

Semantic Approaches to File Access Monitoring & Forensics. The application of semantics for digital forensics has been the topic of multiple research publications. While they are motivated by similar challenges, such as heterogeneity, variety and volume of data, they do not focus on file activity monitoring and life-cycle construction in particular, but on the digital evidence process in general.

Early work on using semantic web technology in the context of forensics includes [13], which introduces an evidence management methodology to semantically encode why evidence is considered important. An ontology is used to describe the metadata file contents and events in a uniform and application-independent manner. In [1], the authors propose a similar ontology-based framework to assist investigators in analyzing digital evidence. They motivate the use of semantic technologies in general and discuss the advantage of ontological linking, annotations, and entity extraction. A broader architecture to lift the phases of a digital forensic investigations to a knowledge-driven setting is proposed in [8]. This results in an integrated platform for forensic investigation that deals with a variety of unstructured information (e.g., network traffic, firewall logs, and files) and builds a knowledge base that can be consulted to gain insights from previous cases via SPARQL queries.

Finally, in a recent contribution [2], the authors propose a framework that supports forensic investigators during the analysis process. This framework extracts and models individual pieces of evidence, integrates and correlates them using a SWRL rule engine, and persists them in a triplestore. Compared to our approach, their focus is on text processing while file activity analysis is not considered.

The approach presented in this paper extends preliminary work published in [15] by introducing cross-platform interoperability, scenarios that demonstrate the approach, linking to background knowledge and a performance evaluation.

---

[3] https://w3id.org/sfs-ontology#.

388 K. Kurniawan et al.

3 Conceptualization

Operating systems typically provide mechanisms and instrumentation to obtain information on system-level file system operations, typically on the level of kernel calls. Reconstructing the corresponding user activities, such as editing, moving, copying or deleting a file from these low-level signals can be challenging. In particular, the sequence of micro-operations triggered by a file system operation varies across operating systems and applications, which complicates the analysis. On Windows systems, for instance, file operations such as `Create` generate a number of access operations including `ReadAttributes`, `WriteData`, `ObjectClosed`, etc.

To construct our vocabularies, we analyzed the structure, format, and access patterns of the different file activity log sources on both Windows and Linux. Furthermore, as contextualization is a key requirement for the interpretation of file activity in forensic analyses, we also include sources of *(i)* process activity information, and *(ii)* authentication events (login, logout, etc.). The scenarios in Sect. 5 illustrate how we make use of process information and authentication information. Due to space restrictions, we will not cover the process and authentication vocabulary in full detail and refer the interested reader to the source[4].

3.1 Vocabulary

As existing ontologies (reviewed in Sect. 2) do not fully cover the requirements of our approach, we developed a custom ontology. We followed a bottom-up approach starting from low-level information from log sources with the goal to choose and collect appropriate terms directly from the sources of evidence (e.g. users, hosts, files). We organize our semantic model into two levels, i.e., *log entry* level and *file operation* level. On the *log entry* level, we define a vocabulary to represent information on micro-level operations for both Windows and Linux OS log sources which is based on a previously developed vocabulary [10] for generic log data. On the *file operation* level, we model a generic vocabulary to express higher-level events such as actual file event activity (e.g., created, modified, copied, rename, delete) derived from micro-level operations (Fig. 1).

Log Entry Vocabularies. The Windows Log Event (wle) vocabulary[5] represents Windows file access events using `wle:WindowsEventLogEntry`, a subclass of `cl:LogEntry` from the SEPSES core log[6]. The `wle:Subject` class represents account information such as `wle:accountName` and `wle:logonID`; the `wle:AccessRequest` class represents file access information such as `wle:access-Mask` and `wle:accesses`; the `wle:Process` class represents running processes and the `wle:Object` class represents object file information such as `wle:objectName`, `wle:objectType`, and `wle:handleID`. To cover Linux file

---

[4] https://w3id.org/sepses/vocab/event/process-event.
[5] https://w3id.org/sepses/vocab/log/win-event.
[6] https://w3id.org/sepses/vocab/log/core.

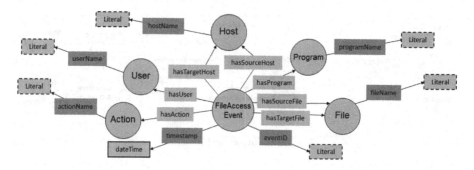

Fig. 1. High-Level event vocabularies (File Access Event)

access events, we developed the Linux Log Event (lle)[7] vocabulary that comprises five main classes: `lle:LinuxEventLogEntry`, a subclass of `cl:LogEntry` from the SEPSES core vocabulary, `lle:Event` class, which covers information on file access events such as `lle:eventType`, `lle:eventId`, `lle:eventCategory`, and `lle:eventAction`; the `lle:File` class represents information about file objects such as `lle:fileName` and `lle:filePath`; the `lle:User` class covers information on users who perform the file event activities such as `lle:userName` and `lle:userGroup`; the `lle:Host` class represents `lle:hostArchitecture`, `lle:hostOS`, `lle:hostName`, `lle:hostId`, etc.

The **File Operation vocabulary**[8] describes `fae:FileAccessEvents` by means of the following properties: `fae:hasAction` reflects the type of access (e.g., created, modified, copied, renamed, deleted); `fae:hasUser` links the file event to the user accessing the file; `fae:hasProgram` represents the executable used to access the file, and `fae:timestamp` captures the time of access. The properties `fae:hasSourceFile` and `fae:hasTargetFile` model the relation between an original and copied instance of a file. Finally, property `fae:hasSourceHost` and `fae:hasTargetHost` represent the hosts where the source and target files are located.

3.2 Background Knowledge

To support contextualization and enrichment, we leverage several existing sources of internal and external background knowledge.

Internal background knowledge can be developed by manually or automatically collecting an organization's persistent information (e.g. IT Assets, Network Infrastructure, Users). In our scenarios, we use predefined internal background knowledge to contextualize and create linking with file access events during event extraction.

---

[7] https://w3id.org/sepses/vocab/log/linux-event.
[8] https://w3id.org/sepses/vocab/event/file-access.

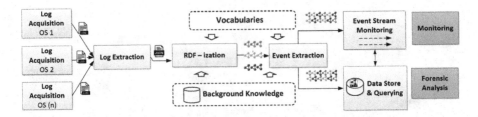

Fig. 2. Solution architecture

Furthermore, it is possible to leverage existing external knowledge, such as the SEPSES cybersecurity knowledge graph (CSKG)[9], to link external information with system events.

4   Architecture and Prototype Implementation

In this section, we describe our architecture and prototypical implementation for semantic integration, monitoring, and analysis of file system activity as depicted in Fig. 2.

The *Log Acquisition* component deals with the acquisition of log information and is installed as an agent on clients or servers. We implement our Log Acquisition component on *Filebeat*[10], an open-source log data acquisition tool that ships log data from a host for further processing. Using Filebeat, we can easily select and configure and add log sources from both Windows and Linux machines. Furthermore, we use the Filebeat Audit module to ship process and authentication information from the log sources.

The *Log Extraction* component handles the parsing of various log data provided by the Log Acquisition component and can act as a filter that keeps only relevant parts. We use *Logstash*[11], an open source log processing tool that provides options for developing processing pipelines to distinguish and handle different types of log sources. Furthermore, it provides different output options such as a web socket protocol that supports data streaming.

The *RDF-ization* component transforms data into RDF by mapping structured log data produced by the Log Extraction component to a set of predefined ontologies (cf. Sect. 3). This produces an RDF graph as the basis of file operation events extraction. We use TripleWave[12] to publish RDF streaming data through specified mappings (e.g. RML[13]). Furthermore, TripleWave supports the web socket protocol to publish the output.

The *Event Extraction* component generates file operation events by identifying a sequence of low level (e.g., kernel-level) file system events. Furthermore,

---

[9] http://sepses.ifs.tuwien.ac.at.
[10] https://www.elastic.co/products/beats/filebeat.
[11] https://www.elastic.co/products/logstash.
[12] https://streamreasoning.github.io/TripleWave/.
[13] http://rml.io.

it enriches the events by creating links between file operation events and existing internal (hosts, users, etc.) and external (e.g., the SEPSES cybersecurity knowledge graph [14]) background knowledge. We developed a Java-based event extractor[14] and use the C-Sprite [5] engine to implement the event extraction process. C-Sprite is an RDF stream processing engine that allows us to register a set of continuous SPARQL-Construct queries against the low level RDF graph of file system events to generate a graph of file operation events.

Finally, the **Data Storage, Querying, and Visualization** component stores the extracted RDF graph of file operation events in a persistent storage (e.g., a triplestore) and facilitates querying and further analysis. We choose the widely-used Virtuoso[15] triple store, which provides a SPARQL endpoint, for our prototypical implementation. Furthermore, we developed a simple web-based graph visualization interface[16] that helps analysts to interpret file access lifecycles (cf. Sect. 5 for an example).

5 Application Scenarios

In this section, we demonstrate the feasibility of our approach by means of two application scenarios. For both scenarios, we set up a virtual lab with several Windows and Linux machines, users, groups, and shared folders.

5.1 Scenario 1: Data Exfiltration

In the first scenario, we assume that an organization has learned that confidential information was leaked. The task in this scenario is to investigate how and by whom this information has been transferred out of the organizational network.

Figure 3 depicts an excerpt of the company network, including Linux and Windows workstations and a Linux file server that stores company-wide shared data as well as confidential data with restricted access permissions (e.g., customer and financial data). The organization's access model distinguishes two groups: *manager* and *office users*. Both groups are authorized to log in to the company workstations and access the internal file shares. Access to the confidential data is restricted to the *manager* group.

As a starting point, the analyst has the name of a file that contains the leaked sensitive information and starts to investigate its history. Listing 1.2 depicts the SPARQL query to obtain lifecycle information for this file. The result is given in Table 1 and shows that the file *cstcp001.xls* was accessed and modified multiple times. Inspecting the timeline, we can see that a file *customer.xls* was modified on *FileServer1* with the IP *193.168.1.2*. It thereafter was copied, renamed and modified on the file server. Then, the file appeared on *Workstation2* and got deleted from the file server. Finally, the file was renamed to *cstcp001.xls* and copied to another folder on *Workstation2* with the name *Dropbox* in its file path. Figure 4 visualizes the file history.

---

[14] https://github.com/kabulkurniawan/fileAccessExtractor.

[15] https://virtuoso.openlinksw.com/.

[16] https://w3id.org/sepses/sparqlplus.

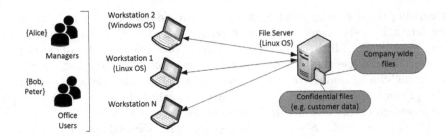

Fig. 3. Scenario 1 network excerpt

```
SELECT distinct ?time ?accessType ?sourceFile ?targetFile ?hostIP ?hostType
    WHERE {
        ?y fae:timestamp ?timestamp.
        ?y fae:hasAction/fae:actionName ?accessType.
        ?y fae:hasSourceFile/fae:pathName ?sourceFile.
        ?y fae:hasTargetFile/fae:pathName ?targetFile.
        ?y fae:hasTargetHost ?h.
        ?h cl:IpAddress ?hostIp.?h fae:hasSourceHost ?hostName.
        ?y fae:hasSourceFile/fae:fileName "cstcp001.xls".
        ?x fae:relatedTo* ?y .
    } ORDER BY ASC(?time)
```

Listing 1.1. SPARQL query to retrieve the history of a file

Table 1. File history results

timestamp	accessType	sourceFile	TargetFile	hostIP	hostName
11:06:55	Modified	/home/alc/secdt/customer.xls	/home/alc/secdt/customer.xls	193.168.1.2	FileServer1
13:39:01	Copied	/home/alc/secdt/customer.xls	/home/alc/customer.xls	193.168.1.2	FileServer1
13:39:35	Renamed	/home/alc/customer.xls	/home/alc/customer-cp.xls	193.168.1.2	FileServer1
13:40:23	Modified	/home/alc/customer-cp.xls	/home/alc/customer-cp.xls	193.168.1.2	FileServer1
13:43:17	Created	C:\Work\customer-cp.xls	C:\Work\customer-cp.xls	193.168.2.2	Workstation2
13:43:52	Deleted	/home/alc/customer-cp.xls	/.trash/customer-cp.xls	193.168.1.2	FileServer1
15:50:57	Renamed	C:\Work\customer-cp.xls	C:\Work\cstcp001.xls	193.168.2.2	Workstation2
15:53:52	Copied	C:\Work\cstcp001.xls	C:\DropBox\cstcp001.xls	193.168.2.2	Workstation2

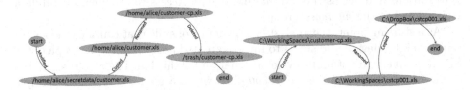

Fig. 4. Graph visualization of the file history

Table 2. Potential exfiltration process – results

timestamp	eventType	hostIP	hostName	programName	pid	userName	groupName
13:43:17	ProcessStopped	193.168.1.2	FileServer1	/usr/bin/scp	223	Alice	Manager
13:43:17	ProcessStopped	193.168.1.2	FileServer1	/usr/bin/ssh	224	Alice	Manager
13:43:17	ProcessStarted	193.168.2.2	Workstation2	C:\ ... nsshd.exe	1988	-	-
13:43:18	ProcessStopped	193.168.2.2	Workstation2	C:\ ... nsshd.exe	1988	-	-

Next the analyst wants to know how the file was transferred from *FileServer1* to *Workstation2*. A SPARQL query[17] lists the running processes and user names in the time period of the suspicious activities. Potential exfiltration processes are modeled in the background knowledge with the concept *sys:potentialExfiltration-Processes*, which includes channels such as FTP, SCP, SSH, etc. This illustrates how queries can automatically make use of modeled background knowledge. Table 2 shows the results of the query. From this, the analyst learns that a secure copy event */usr/bin/scp* was started on *FileServer1* prior to the file copy and also on the Windows host *Workstation2*. The processes on the file server were performed by user *Alice* from the manager group. The analyst concludes that the *customer-cp.xls* file was successfully transferred via SCP (SSH service) by the user *Alice*.

Next, the analyst wants to collect more information about this file transfer and the users involved in those steps. Therefore, a LoginProcess[18] query is executed to retrieve a list of users logged in to these hosts in the time period of interest, including `userName`, `sourceIp`, `targetIp`, `hostName`, and the `timestamp`. The query result depicted in Table 3 shows that *Alice* was not logged in to *Workstation1* during this time. Instead, *Bob* shows up several times in the login list of Workstation1. From *Workstation1*, a login event was performed on *FileServer1* with Alice's credentials. At the time the file copy to the Dropbox folder happened on *Workstation2*, only Bob was logged in on this computer. Concluding from this evidence, the analysts suspects that Bob logged in to *Workstation1*, then accessed the confidential file on *FileServer1* with the credentials of Alice. Finally, he copied the file to *Workstation2* and exfiltrated the data via Dropbox.

Table 3. Login process results

timestamp	eventType	sourceHost	sourceIp	targetHost	targetIp	userName
13:30:23	Login	-	172.24.66.19	Workstation1	192.168.2.1	Bob
13:33:31	Login	-	172.24.66.19	Workstation1	192.168.2.1	Bob
13:38:16	Login	Workstation1	192.168.2.1	FileServer1	192.168.1.2	Alice
14:53:06	Login	-	172.24.66.19	Workstation2	192.168.2.2	Bob

5.2 Scenario 2: Sensitive Data on Vulnerable Hosts

In the second scenario, we illustrate how the semantic monitoring approach can be used to protect confidential information by combining public vulnerability information with file activity information from inside the company network. We assume a policy that restricts handling of confidential files on hosts with known vulnerabilities. The objective in this scenario is to automatically detect violations of this policy. More precisely, the goal is to spot whenever files flagged as *confidential*[19] are copied or created on an internal host with a known vulnerability.

---

[17] https://w3id.org/sepses/IFIP2020/queries/potentialExfitrationProcesses.sparql.

[18] https://w3id.org/sepses/IFIP2020/queries/loginProcess.sparql.

[19] Using a classification schema of confidential, private, protected, public.

```
SELECT * WHERE {
    ?s rdf:type fae:FileAccessEvent;
        fae:hasFileAccessType sys:Created;
        fae:hasSourceFile/fae:fileName ?filename;
        asset:hasDataClassification sys:Private;
        fae:hasSourceHost/fae:hostName ?hostName;
    {SELECT ?hostName ?OSName ?hostIP ?cveId ?conf ?score WHERE {
        ?t rdf:type sys:Host. ?t sys:hostName ?hostName.
        ?t sys:OSName ?OSName. ?t sys:IPAddress ?hostIP.
        ?t sys:hasProduct ?p.
        SERVICE <http://sepses.ifs.tuwien.ac.at/sparql> {
            ?cve cve:hasCPE ?p. ?cve cve:id ?cveId.
            ?cve cve:hasCVSS2BaseMetric ?cvss2. ?cvss2 cvss:confidentialityImpact ?conf.
            ?cvss2 cvss:baseScore ?cvssScore. }}}}
```

Listing 1.2. Query to check vulnerable host

Table 4. Vulnerability assessment results excerpt

fileName	hostName	OSName	hostIP	cveId	conf	score
C:\nDocuments\nCustomer.xls	Workstation2	Windows	192.168.2.1	2016-1653	COMPLETE	9.3
/home/docs/employee.xls	Workstation3	Linux	192.168.2.1	2016-1583	COMPLETE	7.2

As background knowledge, we import information on installed software on each host. This information is represented in the Common Platform Enumeration (CPE) format and can be collected automatically by means of software inventory tools. To link this information to known vulnerabilities, we rely on Common Vulnerabilities and Exposures (CVE), a well-established enumeration of publicly known cybersecurity vulnerabilities. We take advantage of our recent work on transforming this structured knowledge into a knowledge graph [14] available via various semantic endpoints. This allows us to directly integrate this information and use it in our scenario.

To implement the monitoring in this scenario, we set up a federated continuous SPARQL query at Listing 1.2 to identify whether a sensitive file shows up on a vulnerable workstation. To restrict the query to confidential files, we use the property `asset:hasDataClassification` and restrict our query to `sys:Private` files. Table 4 shows the query results and reveals that *Workstation2* and *Workstation3* have critical vulnerabilities, but store confidential files. The results include the `fileName`, `hostName`, `hostIP`, `cveId`, etc. As a next step, an analyst can inspect the life-cycle of the files to understand where they came from, who accessed them and explore information on the vulnerabilities and potential mitigations. Taking automated actions based on the results, such as blocking the access or alerting the user, is a further option.

6   Evaluation

In this section, we present our empirical evaluation setup and discuss the results.

6.1   Experimental Setup

We ran the experiments on an Intel Core i7 processor with 2,70 GHz, 16 GB RAM, and 64-bit Microsoft Windows 10 Professional and emulate hosts as docker containers. We used C-Sprite as event extraction engine with a 3 seconds time window that slides every second. In order to simulate user activity, we developed a java-based event generator[20] to generate scripts for random file activities and use weighted random choices to select activities.

6.2   Experiments and Results

To measure the correctness and the completeness of the event extraction and detection using RDF stream processing with C-Sprite, we define a set of metrics, including *(i)* Actual Events (AE) – number of the events executed in the simulation (ground truth), and *(ii)* Returned Events (RE) – number of events correctly detected by the RDF-Stream processing (C-Sprite). We get detection (%D) by dividing RE by AE.

$$Detection(\%D) = \frac{ReturnedEvents(RE)}{ActualEventsGenerated(AE)} * 100\%$$

On each target OS (Linux and Windows), we test a varying number of events per second, i.e. 1, 10, 20, 50, 80, 100, 125 and 200 events/sec. In the results, we report the mean of detected events over 5 runs with 480 simulated events each.

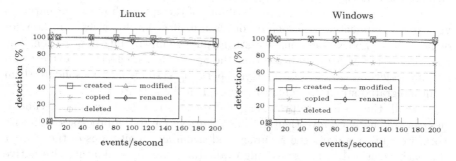

Fig. 5. Detection rate on Linux (l) and Windows (r)

As shown for Linux in Fig. 5, all events can be detected close to 100% for all frequencies (1 event/sec up to 200 events/sec) except the copy event, which reached a maximum of 91,89%. At 200 events/sec, we observe that the detection of copy events decreases to approx. 70%, which is mainly caused by incorrect pairings of *readAttribute* and *create* events when these micro operations generated by two or more sequential copy events appear together in the same window. Furthermore, we noticed that low-level events sometimes do not arrive in sequence and hence, are not detected by our queries.

---

[20] https://github.com/sepses/fileAccessExtractor/tree/master/eventGenerator.

For Windows, the event detection performance for *created, modified, renamed* and *deleted* events is higher with almost 100% of detected events for all frequencies. However, the copy event detection in Windows achieves a lower detection with a maximum of 75,46%.

Finally, considering scalability we can make an estimation based on [5], which shows that C-Sprite achieves a throughput of more than 300000 triples/s. Consequently, it should be able to handle up to 23000 events/s (an individual event consists of at least 13 triples). For forensic scenarios, the Virtuoso triple store can load more than 500 million triples per 16 GB RAM[21], which means that it should be possible to handle more than 38 million events per 16 GB RAM.

7   Conclusions

In this paper, we tackled current challenges in file activity monitoring and analysis, such as the lack of interoperability, contextualization and uniform querying capability, by means of an architecture based on Semantic Web technologies. We introduced a set of vocabularies to model and harmonize heterogeneous file activity log sources and implemented a prototype. We illustrate how this prototype can monitor file system activities, trace file life cycles, and enrich them with information to understand their context (e.g., internal and external background knowledge). The integrated data can then be queried, visualized, and dynamically explored by security analysts, as well as be used to facilitate detection and alerting by utilizing stream processing engines.

Finally, we demonstrate the applicability of the approach in two scenarios in virtual environments – one focused on data exfiltration forensics, and another on monitoring policy violations integrating public vulnerability information. The results of our evaluation indicate that the approach can effectively extract and link micro-level operations of multiple operating systems and consolidate them in an integrated stream of semantically explicit file activities.

Overall, the results are promising and demonstrate how semantic technologies can enrich digital investigations and security monitoring processes. In future work, we aim to address the accuracy and scalability limitations of the current approach identified in the streaming evaluation, e.g., by evaluating alternative streaming engines and alternative approaches (e.g. complex event processing) based on big data technologies. Furthermore, we will investigate the integration of our approach into existing standards (e.g., STIX and CASE) to increase interoperability for forensic investigation.

Acknowledgments. This work was sponsored by the Austrian Science Fund (FWF) and netidee SCIENCE under grant P30437-N31, and the COMET K1 program by the Austrian Research Promotion Agency. The authors thank the funders for their generous support.

---

[21] http://docs.openlinksw.com/virtuoso/virtuosofaq11/.

References

1. Alzaabi, M., Jones, A.: An ontology-based forensic analysis tool. In: Annual ADFSL Conference on Digital Forensics, Security and Law (2013)
2. Amato, F., Cozzolino, G., Mazzeo, A., Moscato, F.: An application of semantic techniques for forensic analysis. In: 32nd WAINA (2018)
3. Awad, A., Kadry, S., Maddodi, G., Gill, S., Lee, B.: Data leakage detection using system call provenance. In: International Conference on INCoS (2016)
4. Bhavsar, K., Trivedi, B.: Predicting insider threats by behavioural analysis using deep learning. In: International Conference on SAM (2018)
5. Bonte, P., Tommasini, R., De Turck, F., Ongenae, F., Valle, E.D.: C-sprite: efficient hierarchical reasoning for rapid RDF stream processing. In: 13th ACM International Conference on DEBS, pp. 103–114. ACM (2019)
6. Carrier, B.D.: A hypothesis-based approach to digital forensic investigations. Ph.D. thesis, Purdue University (2006)
7. Cheng, L., Liu, F., Yao, D.D.: Enterprise data breach: causes, challenges, prevention, and future directions. Wiley Interdisc. Rev.: Data Min. Knowl. Discov. **7**(5), e1211 (2017)
8. Cuzzocrea, A., Pirró, G.: A semantic-web-technology-based framework for supporting knowledge-driven digital forensics. In: 8th MEDES Conference (2016)
9. Daren Fadolalkarim, E.B.: PANDDE: provenance-based anomaly detection of data exfiltration. J. Comput. Secur. **84**, 276–278 (2019)
10. Ekelhart, A., Kiesling, E., Kurniawan, K.: Taming the logs - vocabularies for semantic security analysis. In: 14th SEMANTiCS Conference (2018)
11. Gordon, P.: Data leakage - threats and mitigation. Report, SANS Institute (2007)
12. Hu, Y., Frank, C., Walden, J., Crawford, E., Kasturiratna, D.: Profiling file repository access patterns for identifying data exfiltration activities. In: IEEE Symposium on CICS, April 2011
13. Kahvedžić, D., Kechadi, T.: Semantic modelling of digital forensic evidence. In: 2nd ICDF2C (2010)
14. Kiesling, E., Ekelhart, A., Kurniawan, K., Ekaputra, F.: The SEPSES knowledge graph: an integrated resource for cybersecurity. In: Ghidini, C., et al. (eds.) ISWC 2019. LNCS, vol. 11779, pp. 198–214. Springer, Cham (2019). https://doi.org/10.1007/978-3-030-30796-7_13
15. Kurniawan, K., Ekelhart, A., Kiesling, E., Froschl, A., Ekaputra, F.: Semantic integration and monitoring of file system activity. In: 15th SEMANTiCS (2019)
16. Mashwani, S.R., Khusro, S.: The design and development of a semantic file system ontology. J. Eng. Technol. Appl. Sci. Res. **8**, 2827–2833 (2018)
17. Popitsch, N., Schandl, B.: Ad-hoc file sharing using linked data technologies. In: International Workshop on PSD 2010 (2010)
18. Schand, B., Popitsch, N.: Lifting file systems into the linked data cloud with TripFs. In: WWW2010 Workshop on Linked Data on the Web (2010)
19. Shen, Z., Hou, Y., Li, J.: Publishing distributed files as linked data. In: 8th International Conference on FSKD (2011)
20. Suresh, N.R., Malhotra, N., Kumar, R., Thanudas, B.: An integrated data exfiltration monitoring tool for a large organization with highly confidential data source. In: 4th CEEC, September 2012

Machine Learning and Security

A Correlation-Preserving Fingerprinting Technique for Categorical Data in Relational Databases

Tanja Sarcevic$^{(\boxtimes)}$ and Rudolf Mayer

SBA Research, Vienna, Austria
{TSarcevic,RMayer}@sba-research.org

Abstract. Fingerprinting is a method of embedding a traceable mark into digital data, to verify the owner and identify the recipient a certain copy of a data set has been released to. This is crucial when releasing data to third parties, especially if it involves a fee, or if the data is of sensitive nature, due to which further sharing and leaks should be discouraged and deterred from. Fingerprinting and watermarking are well explored in the domain of multimedia content, such as images, video, or audio.

The domain of relational databases is explored specifically for numerical data types, for which most state-of-art techniques are designed. However, many datasets also, or even exclusively, contain categorical data.

We, therefore, propose a novel approach for fingerprinting categorical type of data, focusing on preserving the semantic relations between attributes, and thus limiting the perceptibility of marks, and the effects of the fingerprinting on the data quality and utility. We evaluate the utility, especially for machine learning tasks, as well as the robustness of the fingerprinting scheme, by experiments on benchmark data sets.

Keywords: Fingerprinting · Relational database · Categorical data · Data utility analysis · Robustness analysis

1 Introduction

Digital watermarking is a method that helps protecting intellectual property for various types of data. It embeds a piece of information into the data to provide an identification of the data owner. Since it does not control access to data, watermarking is a *passive* protection tool. Applications include copyright protection, fraud or tamper detection. *Fingerprinting* is used for data leakage source tracking. It is a special application of watermarking, where different recipients of the data obtain differently watermarked content. This property allows identifying the authorised recipient of the information. First techniques were developed for the multimedia domain (images, audio, video). The generally large amount of data required to represent this content offers space to embed the marks,

© IFIP International Federation for Information Processing 2020
Published by Springer Nature Switzerland AG 2020
M. Hölbl et al. (Eds.): SEC 2020, IFIP AICT 580, pp. 401–415, 2020.
https://doi.org/10.1007/978-3-030-58201-2_27

without significantly affecting the actual content. The application domain was later extended to other types of digital data such as text, software, or relational databases. The effects caused by marking this type of data is a bigger concern.

In the domain of fingerprinting relational data, most state-of-the-art techniques address only numerical type of data. It is important to address the problem of fingerprinting categorical values, as many real world datasets contain some or exclusively categorical attributes. Limitations are the discrete nature of categorical values, where the required modifications for embedding the marks cause a discrete (and not minor) alteration, as well as mutual correlations between attributes. Therefore, any change to the categorical value is more perceptible than a (minor) change to the numerical.

Our approach addresses the problem of semantic relations between categorical attributes in a relational database that can be disturbed by fingerprinting. Considering attributes independently of each other and embedding a random mark into a categorical value might lead to non-consistent records, by introducing an uncommon or impossible combination of values in the data. For example, in a database containing attributes such as *sex* and *numberOfPregnancies*, these attributes intuitively contain an impossible combination of values: (*sex*:male, *numberOfPregnancies*:1). A very uncommon combination of values could be in a medical database containing information about the patients suffering from Alzheimer's disease: (*alzheimersStage*:middle, *employed*:yes), but this might be introduced by a random fingerprint mark. With database domain knowledge, these examples would be rather suspicious and thus perceptible. In our approach, we therefore aim to take into account the correlation between the values of different attributes and avoid uncommon combinations.

The remainder of this paper is organised as follows. In Sect. 2 we describe the related work in the area of watermarking and fingerprinting relational databases. In Sect. 3 we describe our scheme for fingerprinting categorical attributes. In Sect. 4 we present the analysis of the scheme's robustness against malicious attacks and data utility. We provide conclusions in Sect. 5.

2   Related Work

The technique pioneering **watermarking relational data** by Agrawal et al. [1] allows watermarking datasets containing numerical data. Minor alterations to the data are made in specific positions, creating a pseudo-random pattern. If the pattern is known, it is possible to extract the watermark from the data, and thus prove the ownership. The technique relies on a key property of one-way hash functions – it is easy to calculate an output (hash value) for a given input, but computationally difficult to do the inverse. This means that only by knowing the key that was used in the embedding process of watermarking (which is kept by the owner of data), one can extract the watermark from the data. The technique has been extended in later approaches. They differ by the patterns of embedding the watermark, or the type of information used as a watermark. For instance, a watermark in a form of a binary image [2], owner's speech compressed and converted into a bit-stream as watermark information [3], etc.

Categorical data types require different techniques for watermarking purposes than numerical ones, due to their discrete nature. This is a major the reason for considerably fewer watermarking and fingerprinting techniques proposed for categorical data types. Sion et al. [4] propose a watermarking scheme for categorical data in relational databases, and later extend it [5]. The scheme in its simplest form applies a pseudo-random mark to the categorical value based on the primary key of the relation by changing it to another value from the attribute domain. The authors further address the malicious attack of vertical data partitioning where even the primary key is potentially removed. The extended version of the scheme applies a pseudo-random mark to the categorical value based on other categorical values from the relation and repeats the process for every pair of categorical attributes in the dataset. It utilises correlation and discreteness of the categorical attributes as a strength to avoid the scheme's dependence on the primary key, instead of it being a weakness in terms of lack of data redundancy for mark embedding. However, the scheme quickly gets too complex for dataset with many categorical attributes. Furthermore, it does not address semantic correlation between categorical attributes.

One of the earliest **fingerprinting** schemes for relational data [6] is based on Agrawal et al. [1]. Other fingerprinting schemes propose different patterns for marking the data. In [7], the owner's unique fingerprinting is embedded into previously partitioned blocks of data. In [8] the fingerprint is embedded in two-layers - the first of which identifies the owner. Once the verification is successful, the recipient can be detected from the second layer. The watermarking and fingerprinting system Watermill [9] extends the methods by considering the constraints of data alteration and treating fingerprinting as an optimisation problem.

Fingerprinting techniques for categorical data are less researched, compared to techniques for numerical. The fingerprinting technique from [10] can be applied on relational database containing any type of data. It exploits the fact that different sets of equivalence classes can be created in the data when making it k-anonymous [11]. However, the scheme has several limitations, such as a limited number of available fingerprints, diverging utility of different fingerprinted data copies and needing to keep each recipient's fingerprint in a separate data storage which associates additional security risk. In our previous work [12], we introduced a simplistic scheme for fingerprinting categorical values. In this approach, all categorical values are firstly encoded to numerical. The scheme for fingerprinting numerical values from [6] is then applied to the dataset, and the values are decoded back to categorical. This scheme is essentially altering a categorical value to a random one from the domain of the attribute. One limitation is that the scheme does not consider any relation between the attributes of the dataset. However, the scheme may serve as a robust solution for fingerprinting datasets with semantically independent and non-highly correlated attributes.

All the above schemes claim to satisfy the *blindness* property – the original dataset is not needed for the successful watermark/fingerprint extraction.

3   Fingerprinting Categorical Data

Fingerprinting consists of two main processes: *insertion (embedding)* and *detection (extraction)*. The insertion process comprises fingerprint creation and embedding to the data. It embeds a different mark for each distributed copy, specific for each recipient. The output is the marked copy of the data that can be distributed. The detection process extracts the fingerprint from the data. It reports the existence of a fingerprint in the data given as the input, and identifies the recipient. We describe these two processes in detail below for our proposed scheme.

3.1   Prerequisites and Notation

A *Cryptographic Hash function* is a deterministic function that takes a string input of any length and returns a fixed-size string value called *hash value*. A hash function has three main properties: (i) it is easy to calculate a hash value for any given input string, (ii) it is computationally difficult to calculate an input that has given a certain hash value and (iii) it is extremely unlikely that two different inputs, even remotely different, have the same hash value.

A *Pseudo-random number sequence generator (PRNG)* is an algorithm for generating a sequence of numbers whose properties approximate the properties of sequences of random numbers. The PRNG-generated sequence is not truly random, because it is completely determined by an initial value, called the *seed*.

k-nearest neighbours algorithm (k-NN) is a method that (in classification task) classifies the object by a plurality vote of its neighbours, with the object being assigned to the class most common among its k nearest neighbours. The neighbourhood of an object can be determined in multiple ways, frequently for discrete variables a form of the *Hamming distance* (overlapping measure) is used. We use an adaptation of k-NN with Hamming distance as a step in the insertion algorithm. k-NN is, as well, used as one of the classifiers for our data utility analysis in Sect. 4.2. Table 1 shows the notation used in the remainder of the paper.

Table 1. The notions of the most common parameters and functions

Notation	Meaning	Notation	Meaning
$\mathcal{R}$	database relation	$\mathcal{K}$	owner's secret key
P	primary key attribute	$1/\gamma$	Ratio of tuples to be marked
A_i	i^{th} attribute	L	length of a fingerprint
v	number of attributes	|	concatenation function
N	number of tuples	$\mathcal{H}$	hash function

3.2   Insertion

The insertion algorithm introduces modifications to the original data on the pseudo-randomly selected positions in the dataset. The main outline of the algorithm is modelled on the fingerprinting algorithm from [6]. Namely, the legitimate owner of the data holds her secret key which is used to verify the ownership of the data and detect the potential malicious users. For each data user that is authorised to use the fingerprinted data (recipient), a distinct fingerprint is generated. The fingerprint defines the pattern of applying the modifications on the data, and ultimately, this pattern identifies the specific data recipient.

The insertion algorithm is designed with the aim of preserving the correlations between categorical attributes in a relational database. This is resulting in zero occurrences of value combinations that were not initially in the original database, and low frequency occurrences of value combinations that were already rare in the original database. This insertion algorithm reduces perceptibility of a fingerprint mark in a relational database.

Algorithm 1.1: Insertion

Input: database $\mathcal{R}$ with scheme $(P, A_0, ..., A_{v-1})$, buyer n's ID id
Output: fingerprinted database $\mathcal{R}'$

1 fingerprint of buyer n: $\mathcal{F}(\mathcal{K}, id) = \mathcal{H}(\mathcal{K}|id)$
2 **foreach** *tuple* $r \in \mathcal{R}$ **do**
3   **if** $(\mathcal{S}_1(\mathcal{K}|r.P) \; mod \; \gamma == 0)$ **then**
4   attribute_index $i = \mathcal{S}_2(\mathcal{K}|r.P) \bmod v$
5   fingerprint_index $l = \mathcal{S}_3(\mathcal{K}|r.P) \bmod L$
6   fingerprint_bit $f = f_l$
7   mask_bit $x = 0$ if $\mathcal{S}_4(\mathcal{K}|r.P)$ is even; $x = 1$ otherwise
8   mark_bit $m = x \oplus f$
9   **if** $m == 1$ **then**
10   neighbourhood $= select\_neighbours()$
11   target_values, freq $= get\_frequencies$(neighbourhood)
12             $r.A_i = random$(target_values, $weight =$ freq)
13   **else**
14   no marking
15   **end**
16 **end**
17 **return** $\mathcal{R}'$

The insertion algorithm of our fingerprinting scheme is shown in Algorithm 1.1. The algorithm starts with creating a distinct fingerprint for an authorised data receiver. A user's fingerprint $\mathcal{F}$ is a bit-string of length L generated as a hash value of the owner's secret key $\mathcal{K}$ and user's identification id (which may be available publicly).

In lines 2–15 of Algorithm 1.1, the fingerprint is embedded in the data. For each tuple (row) r in the database $\mathcal{R}$, a pseudo-random number sequence generator S is seeded with a concatenation of the owner's secret key $\mathcal{K}$ and the primary key of the tuple, $r.P$. This step allows the creation of a distinct sequence of numbers for each of the database's tuples. Furthermore, seeding the generator with the owner's secret key ensures that the sequence cannot be generated without knowing the secret key. Using the modulo value of the first number from the pseudo-random sequence with the parameter γ, the algorithm decides if the observed tuple is selected for introducing a modification (line 3). Due to the uniform distribution of the output of a pseudo-random sequence generator, approximately N/γ tuples will be selected for marking. Therefore, with parameter γ, we control the amount of modifications in a fingerprinted copy of the data. In the line 4, the next pseudo-random number is generated, which is used to select the attribute A_i for marking. In lines 5–6, the next pseudo-random number from the sequence is used to select the fingerprint bit f_l that will mark the value $r.A_i$. The purpose of lines 7 and 8 is to obtain a uniform distribution of marks that are modifying the data. We can see in lines 9–14 that the marking is performed only if the mark value is 1. If fingerprint bits are directly used as marking bits, they can heavily influence the amount of modifications in the data, as it is not expected that ones and zeroes will be equally represented in a fingerprint. Fingerprint bits are, thus, subjected to an *xor* function with uniformly distributed mask bits x, in the line 8. Finally, if the mark value is 1, the data value is modified.

In the process of marking the data we do not only consider the value $r.A_i$ selected for marking, but the entire tuple r. The goal is to modify the value $r.A_i$ to a value that is *likely to occur in the original database*, considering the other values of the same tuple. To achieve this, the algorithm searches in the database for the tuples most similar to the one observed, i.e the most similar "neighbours" (cf. line 10). Once the neighbours are selected, the algorithm extracts the values of the attribute A_i from the neighbouring tuples, *target_values*, and calculates their frequencies (line 11). The value $r.A_i$ will be changed to one of the values appearing in the attribute A_i of the neighbourhood. The calculated frequencies of these values correspond to the probability for a specific value being selected. The line 12 shows the selection of the new value: it is randomly chosen from the neighbourhood values, weighted by the frequency of their occurrences. This technique is known in genetic algorithms as a fitness proportionate selection, or roulette wheel selection, a genetic operator used for selecting potentially useful solutions for recombination. The analogy to a roulette wheel can be drawn as follows: each candidate value represents a pocket on the roulette wheel; the size of the pockets are proportionate to the frequency of the values among the neighbours. Thus, the most common value is the most likely to be drawn, but any value with a non-zero frequency can be chosen.

Once all the tuples are examined, the output of the algorithm is a fingerprinted copy of the data, $\mathcal{R}'$.

3.3 Detection

The detection algorithm extracts a fingerprint from a fingerprinted copy of the data by searching for the specific pattern embedded by the insertion algorithm. The pseudo-code for the detection algorithm is shown in Algorithm 1.2.

Algorithm 1.2: Detection

Input: fingerprinted database $\mathcal{R}'$ with scheme $(P, A_0, ..., A_{v-1})$, original database $\mathcal{R}$ with scheme $(P, A_0, ..., A_{v-1})$

Output: suspected buyer's ID id

1 fingerprint template $\mathcal{F} = (f_0, ..., f_{L-1}) = (?, ..., ?)$
2 $count[i][0] = count[i][1] = 0$ for $i = 0$ to $L - 1$
3 **foreach** tuple $r \in R'$ **do**
4 $\quad$ **if** $\mathcal{S}_1(\mathcal{K}, r.P) \ mod \ \gamma == 0$ **then**
5 $\quad\quad$ attribute_index $i = \mathcal{S}_2(\mathcal{K}, r.P) \ mod \ v$
6 $\quad\quad$ fingerprint_index $l = \mathcal{S}_3(\mathcal{K}, r.P) \ mod \ L$
7 $\quad\quad$ mask_bit $x = 0$ if $\mathcal{S}_4(\mathcal{K}, r.P)$ is even; $x = 1$ otherwise
8 $\quad\quad$ **if** $r.A_i$ is different from the original **then**
9 $\quad\quad\quad$ mark_bit $m = 1$
10 $\quad\quad$ **else**
11 $\quad\quad\quad$ mark_bit $m = 0$
12 $\quad\quad$ fingerprint_bit $f = m \oplus x$
13 $\quad\quad$ $count[l][f] + +$
14 $\quad$ **end**
15 **end**
16 //recover the fingerprint
17 **for** $l = 0$ to $L - 1$ **do**
18 $\quad$ **if** $count[l][0] + count[l][1] == 0$ **then**
19 $\quad\quad$ **return** none suspected
20 $\quad$ **end**
21 $\quad$ $f_l = 0$ if $count[l][0]/(count[l][0] + count[l][1]) > \tau$
22 $\quad$ $f_l = 1$ if $count[l][1]/(count[l][0] + count[l][1]) > \tau$
23 $\quad$ **return** none suspected otherwise
24 **end**
25 $\mathcal{F} = (f_0, ..., f_{L-1})$
26 $id = detect(\mathcal{F}$
27 **if** $id \geq 0$ **then**
28 $\quad$ **return** id
29 **else**
30 $\quad$ **return** none suspected
31 **end**

Each fingerprint bit might be embedded multiple times in the data, so the detection algorithm searches for all the occurrences and counts the detected values. The algorithm starts by initialising the empty fingerprint template of length L, and the votes for fingerprint bit values, all set to zero. The next step is to find the tuples and attributes that should have been fingerprinting according to the pseudo-random number sequence (lines 3–5). Note that the concatenation of the owner's secret key and dataset primary key values is used as a seed to generate exactly the same number sequences as in the insertion algorithm. We retrieve the fingerprint bit index l and the mask bit x in the same manner (lines 6 and 7). Next, to find the value of the mask bit m, it is necessary to compare the suspected fingerprinted database to the original. If the corresponding value is different from the original, meaning it was modified by the insertion algorithm, then the value m was 1 in the insertion algorithm, otherwise 0. This step is performed in the lines 8–11. In line 12, we obtain the fingerprint bit value f from the mark bit m and mask bit x^1. The line 13 represents the vote that the fingerprint bit on position l is value f.

After all votes are collected, the algorithm attempts to recover the fingerprint. In case the votes for some fingerprint bit on position l do not exist (all remained zero), then the fingerprint can not be recovered and it is not possible to identify the authorised user who owns the given fingerprinted copy (lines 18–20). Otherwise, the value for every fingerprint bit is decided by a *majority voting*, i.e. the most frequent value is chosen. The quorum for the majority can, besides the simple absolute majority described above, also be a user-specified setting, with the parameter $\tau \in [0.5, 1)$, i.e. a larger consensus among the votes can be required.

The extracted fingerprint template is compared to fingerprints of authorised recipients of the data (cf. line 26 in Algorithm 1.2). In case of a perfect match, a user is identified.

3.4   Discussion

In the Sect. 3.2 we propose an insertion algorithm that can be applied to categorical attributes in the relational data and keep it as the main focus of the study. Indeed, the insertion algorithm, Algorithm 1.1, assumes a database $\mathcal{R}$ with attributes $A_0, ... A_{v-1}$ of a only categorical variables as its input. Following our claims from above, real-world databases are oftentimes containing attributes of various data types. For the purpose of fingerprinting such databases, one may select either numerical or categorical attributes, depending on what makes the majority and apply a corresponding fingerprinting scheme, as one solution. The other solution would be to combine schemes for each data type and perform them separately. This way, all of the attributes may be selected for marking, and therefore harder to attack compared to the first solution. On the other hand, dealing with multiple secret keys and parameters in the fingerprinting process might not be convenient for a practical use.

The proposed scheme relies on the existence of database's primary key attribute. Li et. al. [6] proposed a technique for creating a virtual primary key for relational databases in case one does not exist in the original database.

---

[1] If $m = x \oplus f$, then $f = m \oplus x$.

In the data marking phase of Algorithm 1.1, we need to select the neighbourhood of the observed tuple. We find the neighbours using the nearest neighbours algorithm with a form of the Hamming distance and let the user define the parameter k and the attributes that will be included in calculating the nearest neighbours.

Due to the requirement to preserve semantic relations in the fingerprinted copy of the dataset, the modified values are calculated from the data itself, instead of some external deterministic method. As a result, for fingerprint extraction, it is necessary to have access to the original dataset (line 8 of Algorithm 1.2). Therefore, our scheme is a *non-blind* scheme.

4 Evaluation

For our experiments, we choose two datasets from the UCI Machine Learning repository[2] that feature categorical data: Breast Cancer[3] and Nursery[4]. The Breast Cancer dataset describes breast cancer features and whether or not the cancer reoccurred. The dataset has ten columns (including the target attribute) and 286 rows. The Nursery dataset contains data for ranking applications for nursery schools. It contains 12,980 rows and nine columns (including the target attribute). In this section we present our analyses on the scheme's robustness and the utility of the fingerprinted data.

4.1 Attacks and Robustness Analysis

Fingerprinting techniques are vulnerable to operations that potentially erase the fingerprint from the database. These operations can be either a result of benign updates of the database, or malicious attacks by an adversary. In either case, a fingerprint should be robust enough to be recognisable by the owner even from the altered data.

For our evaluation of the scheme for categorical data, we consider the following attacks on the fingerprinted database:

- **Subset attack:** The attacker releases only a subset of the fingerprinted database. We differentiate two cases: In a **horizontal** attack, a subset of complete tuples (rows) is removed from the original copy of the dataset. In a **vertical** attack, one or more columns are removed from the database.
- **Flipping attack:** The attacker flips a selected value to a random, valid one, and repeats this for multiple data values. This attack is the adapted version of the *bit-flipping attack* from the domain of fingerprinting numerical values, where the attacker flips a least significant bit of a chosen set of values.

In the following, we present our empirical evaluation of the robustness of the proposed fingerprinting techniques against the attacks described above. We use the following robustness measures [6] in our experiments:

---

[2] http://archive.ics.uci.edu/ml.
[3] https://archive.ics.uci.edu/ml/datasets/breast+cancer.
[4] https://archive.ics.uci.edu/ml/datasets/nursery.

- **Misattribution false hit** (fh^A): The probability of *detection of an incorrect,* but existing fingerprint from fingerprinted data.
- **False negative** (fn): The probability of *not detecting* a valid fingerprint from fingerprinted data.
- **False miss** (fm): The probability of failing to detect an embedded fingerprint correctly. False miss rate is the sum of the false negative and misattribution false hit rates, i.e. $fm = fh^A + fn$.

In our scheme for fingerprinting categorical data, the exact positions of fingerprint marks are known only with the knowledge of the owner's secret key. Assuming the key being protected, we thus model the attacker such that her choice of positions within the database to attack is random. We further assume the attacker knows the algorithmic steps of insertion and detection processes, and its parameters – in fact, the only unknown is the owner's secret key.

We choose the values for γ for the Breast Cancer dataset: (1, 2, 3, 5) and length of fingerprints is $L = 8$. Parameter γ is expected to contribute the most to the robustness level of the scheme, since it defines the number of fingerprint marks in the data. For the Nursery dataset, due to its bigger size, we experiment with the larger values for γ: (5, 10, 20, 30). The length of the fingerprint is set to $L = 64$.

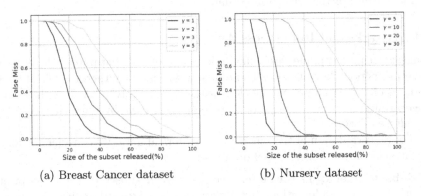

(a) Breast Cancer dataset   (b) Nursery dataset

Fig. 1. Robustness against horizontal subset attack

Horizontal Subset Attack. We simulate the horizontal subset attack, and over a number of runs measure the attacker's success via the False Miss rate depending on the amount of data she chooses to publish.

As can be seen in Figs. 1a and 1b, the false miss rate shows a decreasing trend for more data released. A robust scheme should minimise the false miss rate. Choosing smaller values for γ, i.e. more marks in the data, results in lower false miss rates.

The analysis shows the best robustness for the scheme with $\gamma = 1$ (i.e. each row will be fingerprinted) for fingerprinting Breast Cancer data. The false miss rate is close to zero for approximately 40% of published rows, i.e. the attacker needs to delete more than 60% of the data to increase her chances of destroying a fingerprint. Choosing the value $\gamma = 5$ for the same dataset gives the attacker better chances for success. Similar results are presented in Figs. 1b for the Nursery dataset, where schemes with smaller data show better robustness. Interestingly, the scheme with $\gamma = 5$ for Nursery dataset outperforms even the most robust scheme (the one with $\gamma = 1$) for Breast Cancer data. Furthermore, it even more outperforms the scheme for Breast Cancer with the same value $\gamma = 5$. This is because the size of the fingerprinted dataset plays an important role in the robustness of the scheme. Fingerprinted using the same value for the parameter γ, larger dataset will count more marks than the smaller, therefore making the fingerprint harder to erase.

fh^A was zero in all of the experiments, therefore the recorded fm was contained of false negatives only (fn).

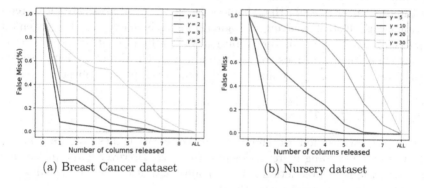

(a) Breast Cancer dataset   (b) Nursery dataset

Fig. 2. Robustness against vertical subset attack

Vertical Subset Attack. Datasets with few columns may be very susceptible to a vertical attack. The results of our analysis are shown in Figs. 2a and 2 for Breast Cancer and Nursery datasets, respectively. The false miss rate is larger for cases where the attacker releases fewer columns. The most robust scheme for Breast Cancer with $\gamma = 1$ shows the fm of only 0.1 for only one released column. In the Fig. 2b, the trend of decrease of the false miss rate is slower than in the previous case due to fewer columns in the Nursery data. Erasing one column in the Nursery data shows more negative effect on robustness than erasing a column in the Breast Cancer dataset. fh^A was zero in all of the experiments.

Flipping Attack. We show the results of the flipping attack simulation in Fig. 3a and Fig. 3b. The false miss rate is recorded in dependence on the percentage of data values *not* affected by the attacker. The false miss rate is generally bigger if the attacker altered more data. We show the results for 40% and more unchanged values. Modifying more than 60% of the data values seriously affects the dataset

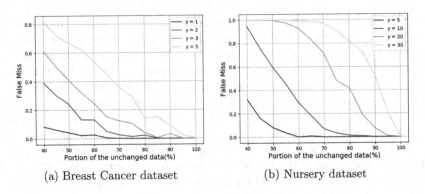

(a) Breast Cancer dataset   (b) Nursery dataset

Fig. 3. Robustness against flipping attack

credibility, therefore we assume such data is not usable. The most robust scheme for Breast Cancer is again the scheme with $\gamma = 1$; false miss rate measured on datasets with 40% of unchanged(original) values is about 0.1. The scheme for Nursery data with $\gamma = 5$ is very robust against a flipping attack; the false miss rate is close to zero in most of the experiments. On the other hand, schemes with larger γ values, $\gamma = 20$ and $\gamma = 30$, show much poorer robustness results.

4.2 Data Utility Effects

In the previous section we showed that better robustness of the scheme is achieved by embedding more marks into the data. However, more marks imply more alterations and reduction of data quality and utility, e.g. for the data mining tasks we want to perform on the data.

We thus measure utility of the fingerprinted data. To this end, we compare the performance of a predictive classifier trained with that data, to one trained on the original, not modified dataset.

Table 2. Parameter settings

	Decision tree	Logistic regression	k-NN	Gradient boosting
Breast Cancer	max_depth: 2 criterion: 'entropy'	solver: 'saga' C: 90	n_neighbors: 19 algorithm: 'kd_tree'	n_estimators: 200 loss: 'exponential' criterion: 'mae'
Nursery	max_depth: 13 criterion: 'entropy'	solver: 'lbfgs' C: 20	n_neighbors: 8 algorithm: 'kd_tree'	n_estimators: 100 loss: 'deviance' criterion: 'friedman_mse'

Specifically, we measure the micro-averaged classification accuracy, which is the percentage of correctly classified data samples, using a 10-fold cross-validation. The classification accuracy is measured in the interval [0,100]%. We use the following classification models: Decision Tree, Logistic Regression, k Nearest Neighbours (k-NN) and Gradient Boosting, with the hyper-parameter settings in Table 2 obtained from a random search with 10 iterations over the following search domain[5]:

- Decision Tree: **max_depth**:(1, 30), **criterion**:['gini', 'entropy']
- Logistic Regression: **solver**:['liblinear', 'newton-cg', 'lbfgs', 'saga'], **C**:(10, 100)
- k-NN: **n_neighbors**:(1, 20), **algorithm**:['auto', 'ball_tree', 'kd_tree', 'brute']
- Gradient Boosting: **n_estimators**:(50, 200), **loss**:['deviance', 'exponential'], **criterion**:['friedman_mse', 'mse', 'mae']

For each of the models, we first obtained the result on the original dataset (equivalent to $\gamma = 0$). We then trained the models on the fingerprinted datasets, using the same hyper-parameters. For clarity of the results, we report the *differences in classification accuracy* when training these two settings.

Table 3 shows the results for the Breast Cancer dataset. We can observe that there is a general trend that the lower the value is for γ, the lower is also the impact on the classification accuracy, though the trend is not linear, and some deviations from this trend occur for specific settings. Specifically Logistic Regression is affected only marginally. While Decision Trees show a larger degradation, k-NN and even better Gradient Boosting are not degrading significantly.

In Table 4, we see that the general trend, i.e. that the impact on the classification accuracy is lower for bigger γ, is present in the Nursery dataset as well. We can see that the loss in accuracy for $\gamma = 1$ and $\gamma = 3$ is significantly bigger compared to other cases and is in the same magnitude as the results with Breast Cancer data and the same γ values. However, in this case with the low γ values, Gradient Boosting is the worst classifier, and Logistic Regression has a significantly higher degradation for small γ values than on the Breast Cancer dataset. For higher values of γ, Decision Trees and Gradient Boosting are affected the most. Logistic Regression and k-NN show a smaller degradation in this case.

Overall, the choice of the parameter γ should lean towards larger values because the impact on the classification accuracy is in that case lower. However, an acceptable trade-off with the desired robustness settings needs to be found.

---

[5] Other parameters are set to default values from the *scikit-learn* Python library.

Table 3. Impact on classification accuracy on the Breast Cancer dataset

γ	Decision tree	Logistic regression	k-NN	Gradient boosting
0	71.68%	66.78%	75.17%	67.83%
1	−3.15%	−0.15%	−1.86%	−1.14%
2	−1.75%	−0.08%	−1.29%	−0.40%
3	−5.24%	−0.70%	−1.18%	−0.61%
5	−1.74%	−0.35%	−0.77%	−0.30%

Table 4. Impact on classification accuracy on the Nursery dataset

γ	Decision tree	Logistic regression	k-NN	Gradient boosting
0	77.99%	84.50%	77.30%	98.38%
1	−1.84%	−2.22%	−2.94%	−5.82%
3	−0.66%	−0.78%	−1.02%	−2.05%
5	−0.85%	−0.42%	−0.41%	−1.30%
10	−0.59%	−0.21%	−0.21%	−0.64%
20	−0.83%	−0.10%	−0.10%	−0.33%
30	−0.40%	−0.08%	−0.18%	−0.25%

5   Conclusion and Future Work

We present a novel scheme for fingerprinting categorical attributes in relational databases. The scheme is designed such that it minimises the occurrence of non-existing and rare combinations of values in the fingerprinted dataset, preserving that way the semantic coherence of the dataset. Furthermore, we presented two types of analysis for our scheme: (i) robustness analysis that measures scheme's vulnerability to malicious attacks, and (ii) the data utility analysis that measures the effects that the fingerprint has on a classification accuracy.

The most important parameter γ, defining the amount of marks in the data, has a dual effect on the scheme. We showed in Sect. 4.1 that a smaller γ values make the scheme more robust against all types of mentioned attacks. On the other hand, the analysis in Sect. 4.2 shows that smaller γ values lead to larger effect on the data classification accuracy. Therefore, γ should be selected in a trade-off between scheme's robustness and data utility.

Future work will be focused towards designing a scheme that unifies the processes of fingerprinting different types of data and, therefore, enhance the applicability of fingerprinting to real-life, mixed-type relational datasets.

Acknowledgement. This work was partially funded by the EU Horizon 2020 research and innovation programme under grant agreement No 732907 (project "MyHealthMy-Data") and the "Industrienahe Dissertationen" program (No 878786) of the Austrian Research Promotion Agency (FFG) (project "IPP4ML")

References

1. Das, S., Dingman, A., Camp, L.J.: Why Johnny doesn't use two factor a two-phase usability study of the FIDO U2F security key. In: Meiklejohn, S., Sako, K. (eds.) FC 2018. LNCS, vol. 10957, pp. 160–179. Springer, Heidelberg (2018). https://doi.org/10.1007/978-3-662-58387-6_9

2. Wang, C., Wang, J., Zhou, M., Chen, G., Li, D.: Atbam: an Arnold transform based method on watermarking relational data. In: International Conference on Multimedia and Ubiquitous Engineering (MUE), Busan, Korea, pp. 263–270. IEEE (2008)

3. Wang, H., Cui, X., Cao, Z.: A speech based algorithm for watermarking relational databases. In: International Symposiums on Information Processing, Moscow, Russia, pp. 603–606. IEEE (2008)

4. Sion, R.: Proving ownership over categorical data. In: Proceedings of the International Conference on Data Engineering, Boston, MA, USA, pp. 584–595. IEEE (2004)

5. Sion, R., Atallah, M., Prabhakar, S.: Rights protection for relational data. IEEE Trans. Knowl. Data Eng. **16**(12), 1509–1525 (2004)

6. Li, Y., Swarup, V., Jajodia, S.: Fingerprinting relational databases: schemes and specialties. Trans. Dependable Secure Comput. **2**(1), 34–45 (2005)

7. Liu, S., Wang, S., Deng, R.H., Shao, W.: A block oriented fingerprinting scheme in relational database. In: Park, C., Chee, S. (eds.) ICISC 2004. LNCS, vol. 3506, pp. 455–466. Springer, Heidelberg (2005). https://doi.org/10.1007/11496618_33

8. Guo, F., Wang, J., Li, D.: Fingerprinting relational databases. In: ACM Symposium on Applied Computing (SAC), Dijon, France, pp. 487–492. ACM (2006)

9. Lafaye, J., Gross-Amblard, D., Constantin, C., Guerrouani, M.: Watermill: an optimized fingerprinting system for databases under constraints. IEEE Trans. Knowl. Data Eng. **20**(4), 532–546 (2008)

10. Kieseberg, P., Schrittwieser, S., Mulazzani, M., Echizen, I., Weippl, E.: An algorithm for collusion-resistant anonymization and fingerprinting of sensitive microdata. Electron. Markets **24**(2), 113–124 (2014). https://doi.org/10.1007/s12525-014-0154-x

11. Sweeney, L.: k-anonymity: a model for protecting privacy. Int. J. Uncertainty Fuzziness Knowl. Based Syst. **10**(5), 557–570 (2002)

12. Šarčević, T., Mayer, R.: An evaluation on robustness and utility of fingerprinting schemes. In: Holzinger, A., Kieseberg, P., Tjoa, A.M., Weippl, E. (eds.) CD-MAKE 2019. LNCS, vol. 11713, pp. 209–228. Springer, Cham (2019). https://doi.org/10.1007/978-3-030-29726-8_14

FDFtNet: Facing Off Fake Images Using Fake Detection Fine-Tuning Network

Hyeonseong Jeon[1], Youngoh Bang[1], and Simon S. Woo[2(✉)]

[1] Department of Artificial Intelligence,
Sungkyunkwan University, Suwon, South Korea
{cutz,byo7000}@g.skku.edu
[2] Department of Applied Data Science,
Sungkyunkwan University, Suwon, South Korea
swoo@g.skku.edu

Abstract. Creating fake images and videos such as "Deepfake" has become much easier these days due to the advancement in Generative Adversarial Networks (GANs). Moreover, recent research such as the few-shot learning can create highly realistic personalized fake images with only a few images. Therefore, the threat of Deepfake to be used for a variety of malicious intents such as propagating fake images and videos becomes prevalent. And detecting these machine-generated fake images has been more challenging than ever.

In this work, we propose a light-weight robust fine-tuning neural network-based classifier architecture called *Fake Detection Fine-tuning Network (FDFtNet)*, which is capable of detecting many of the new fake face image generation models, and can be easily combined with existing image classification networks and fine-tuned on a few datasets. In contrast to many existing methods, our approach aims to reuse popular pre-trained models with only a few images for fine-tuning to effectively detect fake images. The core of our approach is to introduce an image-based self-attention module called *Fine-Tune Transformer* that uses only the attention module and the down-sampling layer. This module is added to the pre-trained model and fine-tuned on a few data to search for new sets of feature space to detect fake images. We experiment with our FDFtNet on the GANs-based dataset (*Progressive Growing GAN*) and Deepfake-based dataset (*Deepfake* and *Face2Face*) with a small input image resolution of 64×64 that complicates detection. Our FDFtNet achieves an overall accuracy of 90.29% in detecting fake images generated from the GANs-based dataset, outperforming the state-of-the-art.

Keywords: Fake image detection · Neural networks · Fine-tuning

1 Introduction

The emergence of Generative Adversarial Networks (GANs) [6], which produces high-quality images through a generator and a discriminator that is trained adversely and competitively, enables the generated outputs to be highly realistic

© IFIP International Federation for Information Processing 2020
Published by Springer Nature Switzerland AG 2020
M. Hölbl et al. (Eds.): SEC 2020, IFIP AICT 580, pp. 416–430, 2020.
https://doi.org/10.1007/978-3-030-58201-2_28

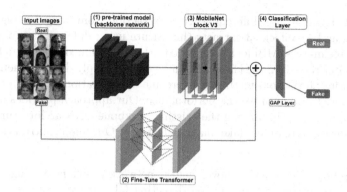

Fig. 1. Overview of our FDFtNet. FDFtNet modules are shown in yellow and green: (2) Fine-Tune Transformer to an input image and, (3) MobileNet block V3 is attached to (1) pre-trained model (backbone network), where details of each block is shown in Sect. 3. (4) Classification layer, which consists of a global average pooling layer (GAP layer), predicts the real and fake. (Color figure online)

and sophisticated [17,18,34,38]. However, such high-quality images and videos generated by machines have been abused and harmed the general public (e.g., DeepFake [33]). Furthermore, a recent study using the few-shot learning technique [28] in GAN allows Deep Learning models to produce high-quality outputs with only a small amount of training data. Zakharov et al. [38] demonstrated that models capable of generating highly realistic personalized talking head faces could be constructed using few-shot learning techniques, where the training inputs provide attention to the generator as a compressed form of feature landmarks, extracted through embedding layers. Leveraging this method, DeepFake can easily be generated even with only a small amount of training data. Recently reported incidents [36] related to DeepFake [33] and DeepNude show that these technologies are an imminent threat to the public.

Most of the previous approaches have focused on exploiting metadata information or handcrafted characteristics of images to detect fake images. However, these approaches fail to detect GAN-based fake images, because they are created from scratch and metadata can be also forged; handcrafted features are no longer useful for detection. Recent models, such as *ShallowNet* [30] and *FakeTalkerDetect* [16], used neural networks to detect GANs-generated fake images Yu et al. [37] used patterns from GAN generated fake to show improvement in detection. *FaceForensics* [23] showed various forgery detection techniques. However, they lack generalization and will thus have difficulties coping with newly developed DeepFake generation techniques.

In this paper, we propose *Fake Detection Fine-tuning Network* (*FDFtNet*), a new robust fine-tuning neural network-based architecture for fake image detection. FDFtNet combines *Fine-Tune Transformer* (FTT), with a pre-trained Convolutional Neural Network (CNN) as a backbone, and *MobileNet block V3* (MBblockV3). Figure 1 shows an overview of our approach, where we utilize well-known, existing CNN architectures [7,11–13,27,29] for fake image detection. Our

FTT is designed to use different feature extraction from images using the self-attention, and MBblockV3 extracts the feature using different convolution and structure techniques. MBblockV3 is added to the pre-trained model as a backbone network after removing the classification layers. We apply data augmentation by implementing the Cutout method to overcome the limitation of using a small fine-tuning dataset and improve the performance. Our approach provides a reusable fine-tuning network, improving the existing backbone CNN architectures, which were not designed to detect fake images effectively. Our main contributions are as follows:

- We propose FDFtNet, a novel neural network-based fake image detector, showing superior performance on detecting fake images compared to previous approaches by achieving 97.02% accuracy, improving the baseline model accuracy from 4% to 45% through our methods.
- We provide a robust fine-tuning neural network-based classifier, which requires only a small amount of data for fine-tuning and can be easily integrated with popular CNN architectures.

2   Related Work

Traditional Image Forgery Detection. Many researchers [5,19,21,35,37] have investigated various digital forensics algorithms to detect forged images. One way to detect forged images is to analyze them in the frequency domain. However, it is difficult to analyze images with refined, smooth edges, thus giving rise to a different method. In JPEG Ghost [5], the forged part is regularly copied from different real images. The normalized pixel distance of the reproduced image differs from the original image, causing a difference in JPEG quality. However, this method will not work if the original image and the forged image have the same quality level. Another approach is Error Level Analysis (ELA) [19], which checks the error level of the images. However, with GANs-generated fake images, ELA cannot classify the error level between the real and generated images. Another algorithm called the Copy-move Forgery detection [21] is based on Pixel Based approach. Firstly, the dyadic wavelet transform (DWT) is applied to the input image. This transforms the original image to an image of a reduced dimension representation, i.e., the LL1 sub-band. Then this LL1 sub-band is divided into sub-images. To compute the spatial offset between the Copy-move regions, the phase correlation is adopted. The Copy-Move regions can easily be located by pixel matching, which shifts the input image according to the offset and calculates the difference between its shifted version and the original image. In the final step, the Mathematical Morphological Operations (MMO) are used to remove isolated points to improve the location. Traditional digital forensic tools fail to detect GANs-generated images because they are generated as a single image. For this reason, these approaches are not effective.

Image Forgery Detection with Neural Network. Various CNN-based models have been used to detect forged images. ShallowNet [30] outperformed previous architectures in detecting real vs. PGGAN with a shallow layer architecture. However, their approach showed limitations when detecting other types of DeepFake images. FaceForensic++ [24] proposed a forgery detection method tailored to facial manipulations and provided an extensive evaluation in a supervised manner. In addition, they introduced an automatic metric that takes into account the four forms of distortion in realistic scenarios (i.e., random encoding and random dimensions). Using these benchmarks, they analyzed various methods of forgery detection pipeline. However, transfer learning or fine-tuning capabilities were not explored. Recent research by Yu et al. [37] proposed a method by learning the metadata, mentioned as GAN fingerprints, to effectively detect GANs-generated images. However, our method includes deepfake datasets as well as GANs for detection without the usage of metadata.

Self-attention and Transformer. To achieve long-term dependencies on image data, CNN needs to increase the amount of computation via deeper layers, because one-time convolution computation sees only the convolution kernel size. In contrast, self-attention solves this long-term dependency issue by using the softmax outputs of the entire sequence that provide attention to CNN. Zhang et al. [39] used self-attention modules to generate images with GANs. Our FTT is different in that we build only self-attention modules, such as Transformer, during the feature extraction in the classification tasks. We apply FTT for the image feature extractor and not for the generator. This approach is similar to the *Multi-head Attention Module* [32] (Query, key, and Value), but the difference is that FTT is suitable for the image to be applied to the 1×1 convolution.

3   Fake Detection Fine-Tuning Network (FDFtNet)

3.1   Dataset Description

CelebA. CelebFaces Attributes Dataset (CelebA) [20] is a large-scale face attributes dataset with more than 200,000 celebrity images. It is widely used for benchmarking and as inputs for generating training and test datasets for various GAN and VAE approaches. We use CelebA as an input to generate PGGAN [17] fake images.

PGGAN. For the GAN-generated image, we used Progressive Growing GANs Dataset (PGGAN) [17], consisting of 100,000 GAN-generated fake celebrity images at 1024×1024 resolution using the CelebA dataset. The key idea in PGGAN is to grow both the generator and discriminator progressively. The training starts with both the generator and the discriminator having a low resolution. New layers are added as the training process advances, thus increasing the resolution of the generated images.

Deepfakes. Deepfakes [33] was the first publicly available method, which anyone can download and use to produce fake images and videos. The code is based on two autoencoders with a shared encoder. The trained encoder and decoder of the source image are applied to the target image face to produce a forged image. The output of the autoencoder is then blended with the target image. For our experiment, we used the dataset provided by Google/Jigsaw (Fig. 2).

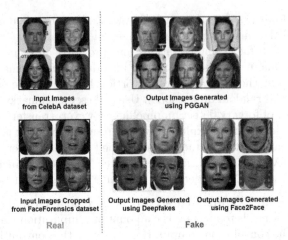

Input Images
from CelebA dataset

Output Images Generated
using PGGAN

Input Images Cropped
from FaceForensics dataset

Output Images Generated
using Deepfakes

Output Images Generated
using Face2Face

Real

Fake

Fig. 2. Illustration of our datasets. CelebA [20] images are used as inputs for PGGAN [17] fake image generation. Images from the FaceForensics [23] dataset are cropped and used as input images for Deepfakes [33] and Face2Face [31] fake image generation.

FaceForensics. FaceForensics [23] is a video dataset comprised of more than 500,000 frames, containing faces from 1004 videos that can be used to study image or video forgeries. An automated version of Face2Face [31] approach is used to create the videos. The goal is to animate the facial expressions of the target video by a source actor and re-render the manipulated output video in a photo-realistic fashion. Face2Face re-renders the synthesized target face on top of the corresponding video stream such that it seamlessly blends with the real-world illumination. Since our goal is to detect fake images, we use each frame from the generated output.

3.2 Description of Pre-trained Backbone CNN Networks

We used the following CNN networks as our backbone networks, as shown in Fig. 1, as well as our baselines (backbone networks): SqueezeNet, ShallowNetV3, ResNetV2, and Xception. Each network is pre-trained from each dataset (i.e., PGGAN, Deepfakes, and Face2Face).

SqueezeNet. SqueezeNet [14] has an AlexNet-level accuracy with fewer parameters and would generally have poor performance in fake detection tasks because SqueezeNet is not designed for fake detection. We chose SqueezeNet as the baseline because our FDFtNet can provide a huge improvement.

ShallowNetV3. ShallowNetV3 [30] has the highest area under the receiver operating characteristic (AUROC) (93.99%) on 64 × 64 resolution images from the CelebA and PGGAN datasets. However, ShallowNetV3 has burdensome fully-connected layers (FC layer) for binary classification. Convolution layers have 115,490 parameters, while FC layers have 4,725,762 parameters.

Table 1. Specification for the self-attention module. Conv denotes convolution, W, H, and C define the input size for the previous layer, and b denotes the bottleneck ratio in the block. The number of parameters are simulated with the following hyperparameters: $W = H = C = 64$ and $b = 8$.

Input size	Operation	Num. parameters	Output dim	Stride
$W \times H \times C$	1×1 Conv	16	C / b	1
$W \times H \times C$	1×1 Conv	16	C / b	1
$W \times H \times C$	1×1 Conv	16	C	1
$W \times H \times C / b$	Matmul	0	$W \times H$	–
$WH \times WH$	Softmax	0	$W \times H$	–
$WH \times WH$	Batchdot	0	C	–
$W \times H \times C$	Multiply	1	C	–
$W \times H \times C$	Add	0	C	–

In addition, since this approach has not been tested on deepfakes other than those generated by PGGAN, we aim to investigate the performance.

ResNetV2. ResNetV2 has been widely adopted in many image classification tasks. We chose ResNetV2 [8] as one of the baselines, because ResNetV2 has an opposing characteristic to ShallowNetV3 in terms of the model depth, i.e., ResNetV2 has 50 layers, while ShallowNetV3 has only 8 layers. We believe that these two architectures would show complementary results, and we plan to see the effect of our approach on such deep and shallow CNN architectures.

Xception. Xception [2] has been served as the baseline for fake image detection in [24,30]. For FaceForenscis++, Xception showed the highest accuracy, i.e., 96.36% in Deepfake and 86.86% in Face2Face, justifying our choice of it as a baseline. Xception has no FC layers, but extracts various image feature spaces thanks to *depthwise separable convolutions*, compared to the burdensome FC layers in the ShallowNetV3. We cut the classification layers in a pre-trained model, and add our FTT and MBblockV3 modules.

3.3 Fine-Tune Transformer (FTT)

Fine-Tune Transformer (FTT) consists of several self-attention modules, as shown in Fig. 3, where each attention module has $f(x)$, $g(x)$, and $h(x)$ using a 1×1 convolution filter. We iterate M times from the image inputs. M is a hyper-parameter, and we empirically determined that $M = 3$ yields the highest performance.

$$f(x) = W_f x, \quad g(x) = W_g x, \quad h(x) = W_h x,$$
$$\beta_{j,i} = Softmax\left(f(x_i)^T g(x_j) \right). \tag{1}$$

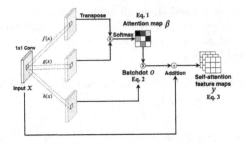

Fig. 3. Self-attention module in the Fine-Tune Transformer. The input x (the image or the output from the previous layer) is divided by a 1×1 convolution into f, g, and h. The attention map β is the softmax output from f and g. The batchdot o multiplies h and the attention map β. The input image x is added to o. The final output y is the self-attention feature maps.

Table 2. Specification for Fine-Tune Transformer (FTT). Conv, BN, DConv, and GAP denote convolution, batch normalization, depth-wise separable convolution, and global average pooling operation, respectively. The "Attention" operation in bold indicates the end of one transformer block. We repeat FTT three times ($M = 3$) to maximize the performance.

Input size	Operation	Num. parameters	Output dim.	Stride
$64 \times 64 \times 3$	3×3 DConv	123	32	2
$32 \times 32 \times 32$	BN	128	32	–
$32 \times 32 \times 32$	ReLU	0	32	–
$32 \times 32 \times 32$	**1st Stage self-attention**	1,321	**32**	–
$32 \times 32 \times 32$	3×3 DConv	2,336	64	2
$16 \times 16 \times 64$	BN	256	64	–
$16 \times 16 \times 64$	ReLU	0	64	–
$16 \times 16 \times 64$	**2nd Stage self-attention**	5,201	**64**	–
$16 \times 16 \times 64$	3×3 DConv	8,768	128	2
$8 \times 8 \times 128$	BN	512	128	–
$8 \times 8 \times 128$	ReLU	0	128	–
$8 \times 8 \times 128$	**3rd Stage self-attention**	20,641	**128**	–
$8 \times 8 \times 128$	1×1 Conv	73,728	576	1
$8 \times 8 \times 576$	BN	2,304	576	–
$8 \times 8 \times 576$	ReLU	0	576	–
$8 \times 8 \times 576$	GAP	0	576	–

In Fig. 3, the input x of the previous layers or the input image is divided into three feature spaces $f(x)$, $g(x)$, and $h(x)$. As shown in Eq. 1, all of them are obtained through the 1×1 convolution, where W_f, W_g, and W_h are the respective filter weights of each space. $f(x)$ and $g(x)$ have b channel bottleneck ratio parameter, $\frac{C}{b}$, where C is the number of channels. In this study, we choose $b = 8$ as suggested by Zhang et al. [39]. In particular, we use the dot-product attention to produce the attention map β in Fig. 3, synthesizing the ith and j^{th} locations after the $Softmax$ operation as shown in the above equation.

$$o_j = Batchdot\left(\beta_{j,i}\,,\,h\left(x\right)\right) \qquad (2)$$

$$y_i = \gamma o_j + x_i. \qquad (3)$$

After obtaining the attention map β, we apply the $Batchdot$ operation to multiply the attention map $\beta_{j,i}$ with $h(x)$, as shown in Eq. 2, and produce output o_j. After the $Batchdot$ multiplication, o_j is added to the input x_i. Finally, the self-attention feature map, y_i, is obtained via multiplying γ and adding the input x_i, as shown in Eq. 3. In particular, γ is a learnable parameter initialized as 0 at the early stage of learning. This is favorable since the softmax function equally provides attention to all the feature spaces at the early stage of learning.

Table 3. Specification for MBblockV3 with $W = H = 8$ and $C = 256$. Conv, BN, DConv and GAP denote convolution, batch normalization, depth-wise separable convolution, and global average pooling. W, H and C indicate input size. If the stride of 3×3 DConv is 2, the addition operation is skipped, and W and H are divided by 2. Bold operations represent the Squeeze-and-Excitation block.

Input size	Operation	Num. parameters	Output dim.	Stride
$W \times H \times C$	1×1 Conv	294,912	576	1
$W \times H \times 576$	BN	2,304	576	–
$W \times H \times 576$	h-swish	0	576	–
$W \times H \times 576$	3×3 DConv	5,184	576	1 or 2
$W \times H \times 576$	BN	2,304	576	–
$W \times H \times 576$	**GAP**	0	576	–
$1 \times 1 \times 576$	**1×1 Conv**	82,944	144	1
$1 \times 1 \times 144$	**ReLU**	0	144	–
$1 \times 1 \times 144$	**1×1 Conv**	82,944	576	1
$1 \times 1 \times 576$	**hard-sigmoid**	0	576	-
$1 \times 1 \times 576$	**Multiply**	0	576	–
$W \times H \times 576$	h-swish	0	576	–
$W \times H \times 576$	1×1 Conv	73,728	128	1
$W \times H \times 128$	Linear	0	128	–
$W \times H \times 128$	BN	2,304	128	–
$W \times H \times 128$	Add	0	128	–

Next, in our FTT, we apply the self-attention module three times ($M = 3$) with an input size of $64 \times 64 \times 3$, as shown in Table 2. The first layer is a 3×3 separable convolution with 32 filters and 2 strides followed by Batch Normalization (BN) [15] and ReLU. The dimension of the output feature map from the self-attention module is 32, 64, and 128, respectively; the width (the number of channels) is doubled when the resolution is down-sampled, as shown in Table 2. After that, self-attention is performed three times ($M = 3$), followed by SeparableConv3 $\times$ 3, BN, and ReLU. The main reason we apply self-attention modules in FTT is to overcome the limitations of CNN in achieving long-term dependencies, caused by the use of numerous Conv filters with a small size. On the other hand, only one-time use of the FTT is necessary to achieve the long-term dependencies, avoiding the construction of deep CNN layers. Also, a three-time application of self-attention modules allows us to explore and learn diverse deep features of the input images via fine-tuning.

3.4   MobileNet Block V3

We chose MobileNet block V3 (MBblockV3) to explore the image feature space through inverted residual structure and linear bottleneck [25]. Depthwise separable convolutions, as in Xception and MobileNetV1 [11], are also included in MBblockV3. Comprehensively, MobileNet is an architecture that has already proven its efficiency by using a small number of parameters, drastically increasing computational efficiency. We chose MBblockV3, because it is a suitable module for the efficient extraction of the feature space over the pre-trained feature space. FTT and MBblockV3 are repeatedly used M and N times, respectively. Each of them is added before the final classification layer. MBblockV3 has the parameter N after the pre-trained model. In our experiment, we use $N = 4$, determined empirically, yielding the best performance for fine-tuning. In particular, we use the modified *h-swish* [10] and the ReLU6 as activation functions. This non-linearity [4,9,22] significantly improves the performance of neural networks and is defined as follows:

$$\text{h-swish}[\text{x}] = x \frac{\text{ReLU6}\,(x+3)}{6}, \text{ where ReLU6}[\text{x}] = min\,(max\,(0,x)\,,6)\,. \quad (4)$$

Since clipping the input values at the bottom layers may have a side effect of distorting the data distribution [26], we apply these activation functions at the top layers to reduce distortion and extract different signals from ReLU. Next, the *Squeeze-and-Excitation blocks* (SE block) in Squeeze and Excitation networks [12] are applied in the bottleneck layer. Global information on the image resolution is embedded in the squeeze stage, and information aggregation is used to capture channel dependencies and is re-calibrated through the gated computation (element-wise multiplication), similar to the attention mechanism in the excitation stage. Details of the SE block parameters are summarized in Table 3.

4   Experimental Results

4.1   Training Details

All datasets have train, validation, test, and fine-tune sets. The size of each dataset is shown in Table 4. Our FDFtNet is trained with Stochastic Gradient Descent (SGD) with momentum for 300 epochs on all datasets. The learning rate is initialized at 0.3 and annealed using a cosine function. The momentum rate is set to 0.9, and the mini-batch size is set to 128. Early stopping is applied, when the validation loss ceases to decrease for 20 epochs. To reenact the most challenging scenario in detecting fake images, all input images are resized to 64×64 resolution.

Data Augmentation. Input images are translated into a width and height range of $[-2, 2]$ with the nearest-padding on empty pixels generated after translation. Zoom and rotation are also applied to a degree range of $[-0.2, 0.2]$. We also perform random horizontal flipping. These data augmentations are applied to all fine-tune sets. For validation and test sets, only a $1/255$ scaling augmentation to the input image is applied.

Cutout. Cutout method applies squared zero masks on a random location of each input image. Figure 4 presents an example of a Cutout data augmentation. DeVries et al. [3] used random zero masks of 16 pixels for CIFAR-10 (32×32 pixels images), 5 random iteration parameters α for cutting, and 16 random size multipliers β for the cutting masks. We use 4×4 pixels mask, 3 iterations, and 5-size multipliers for cutting masks for 64×64 images ($\alpha = 3$ and $\beta = 5$). Since we use random translation, we do not use random center cropping, which was used in the original paper. When we conducted with the original setting, we faced severe underfitting with no convergence of losses. We observed

Table 4. The respective size of the train, validation, test, and fine-tune sets. We use only 1,000 real and fake images, respectively, for fine-tuning.

Dataset	Train	Validation	Test	Fine-tune
PGGAN	128,404	32,100	37,566	**1,000 (real), 1,000 (fake)**
Deepfake	60,000	18,000	20,000	**1,000 (real), 1,000 (fake)**
Face2Face	60,000	18,000	20,000	**1,000 (real), 1,000 (fake)**

Fig. 4. Example of a Cutout data augmentation. Random regions of the original image (left) are masked out by black rectangles. Every epoch, the rectangular mask changes in form and all images are resized to 64×64 resolution.

higher performance with a setting of low Cutout parameters ($\alpha = 3$ and $\beta = 5$) as compared to the implementation without Cutout, which showed strong overfitting. Because we fine-tune with a small amount of data, we apply this non-aggressive parameter setting.

4.2 Performance Evaluation

We present our overall performance results in Table 5. In Table 5, we use the accuracy (ACC) and AUROC as evaluation metrics. We experimented with all four baseline models on each dataset with similar training strategies. The experimental results show that our FDFtNet has superior detection performance in both ACC and AUROC, compared to all the baselines. In terms of training data size, our model shows high performance using 1,000 images for real and fake, respectively.

PGGAN. To yield the best detection performance, we freeze the weight parameters of all layers of the pre-trained models. FTT with parameter $M = 3$ is used, and MBblockV3 with parameter $N = 2$ is added; the same data augmentation is applied. Table 5 shows the results of our models compared with the baseline models. Our results show that Xception, among all baseline models, achieved the highest performance (87.12% ACC and 94.96% AUROC). Our model showed a performance of 90.29% ACC and 95.98% AUROC, which is higher than that of ShallowNetV3 with an ensemble [30]. ShallowNetV3 is improved from 85.73% and 92.90% ACC to 88.03% and 94.53% AUROC, respectively, similar to the ensemble version. SqueezeNet baseline shows the lowest baseline performance, but it is significantly improved to a similar level to that of ShallowNetV3, from 50.00% to 92.76%, by applying our model.

Table 5. Overall performance evaluation results. The evaluation metrics used are ACC (%) and AUROC (%). The underlined results are improved performance compared to the baseline and the best detection results among all are highlighted in bold.

Model	Dataset	PGGAN		Deepfake		Face2Face	
	Backbone	ACC (%)	AUROC	ACC (%)	AUROC	ACC (%)	AUROC
SqueezeNet	baseline	50.00	50.00	50.00	50.00	50.00	50.00
FDFtNet (Ours)	SqueezeNet	88.89	92.76	92.82	97.61	87.73	94.20
ShallowNetV3†	baseline	85.73	92.90	89.77	92.81	83.35	88.49
FDFtNet (Ours)	ShallowNetV3	88.03	94.53	94.29	97.83	84.55	93.28
ResNetV2	baseline	84.80	88.58	81.52	89.72	58.83	62.47
FDFtNet (Ours)	ResNetV2	84.83	94.05	91.03	96.08	85.15	92.91
Xception	baseline	87.12	94.96	95.10	98.92	85.78	93.67
FDFtNet (Ours)	Xception	**90.29**	**95.98**	**97.02**	**99.37**	**96.67**	**98.23**

Table 6. Ablation study for Fine-Tune Transformer (FTT). Our model with FTT has 2.46% higher accuracy (ACC) than those without FTT, increasing the ACC from 94.56% to 97.02%.

Method	Backbone	Dataset	Acc	AUROC
With FTT	Xception	Deepfake	**97.02%**	**99.37%**
Without FTT	Xception	Deepfake	94.56%	98.89%

Deepfake. Here also, the same data augmentation techniques are applied. For FTT, we use $M = 3$ and $N = 4$ for MBblockV3. Cutout has $\alpha = 3$ iteration parameters and $\beta = 10$ multiplier parameters. The results show that all models achieve significant improvement in performance. Table 5 indicates that Xception has the highest performance of 95.10% ACC and 98.92% AUROC. Using our approach, this baseline model is also improved to 97.02% ACC and 99.37% AUROC. ShallowNetV3 has 89.77% ACC and 92.81% AUROC. They increased to 94.29% ACC and 97.83% AUROC, respectively. ResNetV2 is also improved from 81.52% ACC and 89.72% AUROC to 91.03% ACC and 96.08% AUROC. SqueezeNet baseline shows the lowest performance, 50.00% ACC and AUROC, but is improved to 92.82% ACC and 97.61% AUROC.

Face2Face. The training strategies for Face2Face are very similar to those of the Deepfake dataset. Data augmentation is also applied. M, N, α, and β are set to 3, 4, 3, and 10, respectively. The interesting point is that ResNetV2 baseline performed poorly (58.83% ACC and 62.47% AUROC), but significant improvements are made using our methods (85.15% ACC and 92.91% AUROC). Our results demonstrate the generalization ability of our approach, improving the poorly performing baseline above 90% across all models and datasets. Compared to *FaceForensics Benchmark Results* [1], the highest state-of-the-art method is Xception, which shows 96.4% ACC in Deepfake and 86.9% ACC in Face2Face. Our FDFtNet achieves higher performance (97.02% and 96.67%) than the current state-of-the-art method for the same dataset.

5   Ablation Study, Discussions, and Limitations

In this section, we validate each module and technique through an ablation study. In Table 6, we choose the Xception model and the Deepfake dataset to compare our model with and without the FTT, while all other settings remain the same. With FTT, we can achieve about 2.5% higher performance than without FTT, as shown in Table 6. Our current work has the following limitations: First, we used both real and fake data for training and fine-tuning, but we have constrained resources in practice. In FakeTalkerDetect [16] for fake detection, researchers used Siamese networks for training only on real data. However, in our implementation, few-shot learning and unbalanced learning are major obstacles to achieving high performance. Second, transfer learning is required to improve performance. We trained each model on each dataset. For future work, we plan to research the transfer learning ability to further generalize our model.

6   Conclusion

We propose FDFtNet, which is a robust fine-tuning neural network-based architecture, to detect fake images and significantly improve the baseline CNN architectures. Our model achieves the state-of-the-art accuracy in fake image detection on the GAN-based dataset and the Deepfake-based dataset. Our experimental results with the use of a limited amount of data show the exploration and exploitation of image feature space beyond the pre-trained models. Our results show that FDFtNet is a promising method for detecting fake images generated by powerful deep learning methods, requiring only a small amount of images for re-training. Therefore, FDFtNet can be a viable option even for detecting new fake images in a real-world scenario, where available datasets are extremely limited. Further, we offer open source versions of our work for it to be widely leveraged by the research community[1].

Acknowledgements. We thank Siho Han for providing his expertise to greatly improve this work. This work was partly supported by Institute of Information communications Technology Planning & Evaluation (IITP) grant funded by the Korea government (MSIT) (No. 2019-0-00421, AI Graduate School Support Program (Sungkyunkwan University)). Also, this research was supported by Energy Cloud R&D Program through the National Research Foundation (NRF) of Korea funded by the Ministry of Science, ICT (No. 2019M3F2A1072217), and was supported by the National Research Foundation of Korea (NRF) grant funded by the Korea government (MSIT) (No. 2017R1C1B5076474, and 2020R1C1C1006004).

References

1. Rössler, A., Cozzolino, D., Verdoliva, L., Riess, C., Thies, J., Nießner, M.: This table lists the benchmark results for the binary classification scenario. (2019). http://kaldir.vc.in.tum.de/faceforensics_benchmark/
2. Chollet, F.: Xception: deep learning with depthwise separable convolutions. In: Proceedings of the IEEE Conference On Computer Vision and Pattern Recognition, pp. 1251–1258 (2017)
3. DeVries, T., Taylor, G.W.: Improved regularization of convolutional neural networks with cutout (2017). arXiv preprint arXiv:1708.04552
4. Elfwing, S., Uchibe, E., Doya, K.: Sigmoid-weighted linear units for neural network function approximation in reinforcement learning. Neural Netw. **107**, 3–11 (2018)
5. Farid, H.: Exposing digital forgeries from jpeg ghosts. IEEE Trans. Inf. Forensics Secur. **4**(1), 154–160 (2009)
6. Goodfellow, I., et al.: Generative adversarial nets. In: Advances in Neural Information Processing Systems, pp. 2672–2680 (2014)

---

[1] https://github.com/cutz-j/FDFtNet.

7. He, K., Zhang, X., Ren, S., Sun, J.: Deep residual learning for image recognition. In: Proceedings of the IEEE Conference On Computer Vision and Pattern Recognition, pp. 770–778 (2016)
8. He, K., Zhang, X., Ren, S., Sun, J.: Identity mappings in deep residual networks. In: Leibe, B., Matas, J., Sebe, N., Welling, M. (eds.) ECCV 2016. LNCS, vol. 9908, pp. 630–645. Springer, Cham (2016). https://doi.org/10.1007/978-3-319-46493-0_38
9. Hendrycks, D., Gimpel, K.: Bridging nonlinearities and stochastic regularizers with gaussian error linear units. ArXiv abs/1606.08415 (2017)
10. Howard, A., et al.: Searching for mobilenetv3. arXiv preprint arXiv:1905.02244 (2019)
11. Howard, A.G., et al.: Mobilenets: efficient convolutional neural networks for mobile vision applications (2017). arXiv preprint arXiv:1704.04861
12. Hu, J., Shen, L., Sun, G.: Squeeze-and-excitation networks. In: Proceedings of the IEEE Conference on Computer Vision and Pattern Recognition, pp. 7132–7141 (2018)
13. Iandola, F., Moskewicz, M., Karayev, S., Girshick, R., Darrell, T., Keutzer, K.: Densenet: implementing efficient convnet descriptor pyramids (2014). arXiv preprint arXiv:1404.1869
14. Iandola, F.N., Han, S., Moskewicz, M.W., Ashraf, K., Dally, W.J., Keutzer, K.: Squeezenet: alexnet-level accuracy with 50x fewer parameters and< 0.5 mb model size (2016). arXiv preprint arXiv:1602.07360
15. Ioffe, S., Szegedy, C.: Batch normalization: accelerating deep network training by reducing internal covariate shift (2015). arXiv preprint arXiv:1502.03167
16. Jeon, H., Bang, Y., Woo, S.S.: Faketalkerdetect: effective and practical realistic neural talking head detection with a highly unbalanced dataset. In: Proceedings of the IEEE International Conference on Computer Vision Workshops (2019)
17. Karras, T., Aila, T., Laine, S., Lehtinen, J.: Progressive growing of gans for improved quality, stability, and variation (2017). arXiv preprint arXiv:1710.10196
18. Karras, T., Laine, S., Aila, T.: A style-based generator architecture for generative adversarial networks. In: Proceedings of the IEEE Conference on Computer Vision and Pattern Recognition, pp. 4401–4410 (2019)
19. Krawetz, N., Solutions, H.F.: A picture's worth. Hacker Factor Solutions 6, 2 (2007)
20. Liu, Z., Luo, P., Wang, X., Tang, X.: Deep learning face attributes in the wild. In: Proceedings of the IEEE International Conference on Computer Vision, pp. 3730–3738 (2015)
21. Mankar, S.K., Gurjar, A.A.: Image forgery types and their detection: a review. Int. J. Adv. Res. Comput. Sci. Softw. Eng. 5(4), 174–178 (2015)
22. Ramachandran, P., Zoph, B., Le, Q.V.: Swish: a self-gated activation function 7 (2017). arXiv preprint arXiv:1710.05941
23. Rössler, A., Cozzolino, D., Verdoliva, L., Riess, C., Thies, J., Nießner, M.: Faceforensics: a large-scale video dataset for forgery detection in human faces (2018). arXiv preprint arXiv:1803.09179
24. Rössler, A., Cozzolino, D., Verdoliva, L., Riess, C., Thies, J., Nießner, M.: Faceforensics++: learning to detect manipulated facial images (2019). arXiv preprint arXiv:1901.08971
25. Sandler, M., Howard, A., Zhu, M., Zhmoginov, A., Chen, L.C.: Mobilenetv 2: inverted residuals and linear bottlenecks. In: Proceedings of the IEEE Conference on Computer Vision and Pattern Recognition, pp. 4510–4520 (2018)

26. Sheng, T., Feng, C., Zhuo, S., Zhang, X., Shen, L., Aleksic, M.: A quantization-friendly separable convolution for mobilenets. In: 2018 1st Workshop on Energy Efficient Machine Learning and Cognitive Computing for Embedded Applications (EMC2), pp. 14–18. IEEE (2018)
27. Simonyan, K., Zisserman, A.: Very deep convolutional networks for large-scale image recognition (2014). arXiv preprint arXiv:1409.1556
28. Sun, Q., Liu, Y., Chua, T.S., Schiele, B.: Meta-transfer learning for few-shot learning. In: Proceedings of the IEEE Conference on Computer Vision and Pattern Recognition, pp. 403–412 (2019)
29. Szegedy, C., et al.: Going deeper with convolutions. In: Proceedings of the IEEE Conference on Computer Vision and Pattern Recognition, pp. 1–9 (2015)
30. Tariq, S., Lee, S., Kim, H., Shin, Y., Woo, S.S.: Gan is a friend or foe?: a framework to detect various fake face images. In: Proceedings of the 34th ACM/SIGAPP Symposium on Applied Computing, pp. 1296–1303. ACM (2019)
31. Thies, J., Zollhöfer, M., Stamminger, M., Theobalt, C., Nießner, M.: Face2Face: real-time Face Capture and Reenactment of RGB Videos. In: Proceedings of the Computer Vision and Pattern Recognition (CVPR). IEEE (2016)
32. Vaswani, A., et al.: Attention is all you need. In: Advances in neural information processing systems, pp. 5998–6008 (2017)
33. Wikipedia: Deepfake. https://en.wikipedia.org/wiki/Deepfake (2019). Accessed 15 July 2019
34. Wu, J., et al.: Sliced wasserstein generative models. In: The IEEE Conference on Computer Vision and Pattern Recognition (CVPR) (2019). https://arxiv.org/pdf/1706.02631.pdf
35. Yang, X.: Estimating distribution costs with the e aton-k ortum model. Rev. Dev. Econ. **19**(3), 653–665 (2015)
36. Yin, C.: Altering faces via ai deepfake may be outlawed. China Daily, April 2019. http://global.chinadaily.com.cn/a/201904/22/WS5cbd15c4a3104842260b76c8.html
37. Yu, N., Davis, L.S., Fritz, M.: Attributing fake images to GANs: learning and analyzing Gan fingerprints. In: Proceedings of the IEEE International Conference on Computer Vision, pp. 7556–7566 (2019)
38. Zakharov, E., Shysheya, A., Burkov, E., Lempitsky, V.: Few-shot adversarial learning of realistic neural talking head models (2019). arXiv preprint arXiv:1905.08233
39. Zhang, H., Goodfellow, I., Metaxas, D., Odena, A.: Self-attention generative adversarial networks (2018). arXiv preprint arXiv:1805.08318

Escaping Backdoor Attack Detection
of Deep Learning

Yayuan Xiong[1], Fengyuan Xu[1(✉)], Sheng Zhong[1], and Qun Li[2]

[1] State Key Lab for Novel Software Technology,
Nanjing University, Nanjing, China
yayuan.xiong@smail.nju.edu.cn,
{fengyuan.xu,zhongsheng}@nju.edu.cn
[2] Department of Computer Science,
College of William and Mary, Williamsburg, USA
liqun@cs.wm.edu

Abstract. Malicious attacks become a top concern in the field of deep learning (DL) because they have kept threatening the security and safety of applications where DL models are deployed. The backdoor attack, an emerging one among these malicious attacks, attracts a lot of research attentions in detecting it because of its severe consequences. Latest backdoor detections have made great progress by reconstructing backdoor triggers and performing the corresponding outlier detection. Although they are effective on existing triggers, they still fall short of detecting stealthy ones which are proposed in this work. New triggers of our backdoor attack can be generally inserted into DL models through a hidden and reconstruction-resistant manner. We evaluate our attack against two state-of-the-art detections on three different data sets, and demonstrate that our attack is able to successfully insert target backdoors and also escape the detections. We hope our design is able to shed some light on how the backdoor detection should be advanced along this line in future.

Keywords: Backdoor attack · Trigger reconstruction · Evading detection

1 Introduction

Currently deep neural networks (DNN) are used in every field of machine learning tasks, such as the image classification [10], the face recognition [17], and the autonomous driving [16]. DL models have shown significant performance improvements compared to traditional methods.

Usually the user and the trainer of a DL model are different for the following reasons. First, the training of DL models is an end-to-end procedure consuming the huge computational resources and training data, which is unaffordable to a user. Second, a good-quality DL model needs a lot of tuning experience and

© IFIP International Federation for Information Processing 2020
Published by Springer Nature Switzerland AG 2020
M. Hölbl et al. (Eds.): SEC 2020, IFIP AICT 580, pp. 431–445, 2020.
https://doi.org/10.1007/978-3-030-58201-2_29

domain expertise, which is impossible for a user to do. Therefore, users frequently utilize DL models from third-party trainers, which could be honest or malicious.

When a trainer is malicious, he can manipulate his DL models during the training procedure and cause dangerous consequences or even life-threatening situations after the models are utilized. Among all attacking methods available, the backdoor attack [6,9,11,14] is uniquely hard to be detected due to its stealthy malicious behaviors which can only be triggered by certain rare inputs. In order to launch a backdoor attack, a malicious trainer needs to insert a backdoor into the target model, just like making a Trojan, during the training procedure. It is achieved by deliberately poisoning the training data which is totally controlled by the trainer. After the poisoned training, this model is able to perform the inference tasks like classification honestly and normally except the case when there is a special trigger appearing in the inference input. This trigger, usually a rare visual content like a special sunglasses, will activate malicious actions of the poisoned model and lead to severe outcomes.

A vast number of detection methods have been proposed [4,7,8,12,15,18] to address this dangerous backdoor attack. Some of them want to detect if the pre-trained model contains a backdoor while others aim to detect if the input data to the target model contains a trigger. Neural Cleanse [18], for example, is one of the state-of-the-art methods of detecting the backdoor in a pre-trained model, and it shows a new direction of detection. It proposes "reverse-engineer" to find the potential backdoor trigger for each class and then identifies the victim class via the outlier detection.

Although this new direction is promising as it works well on existing triggers. However, we show that a malicious trainer is able to escape such detection like Neural Cleanse (NC) if he conducts either of two concealed backdoor attacks proposed in this paper. The first proposed attack is a basic one which utilizes the trigger reconstruction in NC for attacking. The second proposed attack is an advanced one which scatters a trigger like randomly generated noises on a poisoned image. This trigger scattering is independent of any specific trigger reconstruction. Moreover, we also show that both basic and advanced backdoor attacks proposed are also able to escape the detection of another trigger-reconstruction based detection method called DeepInspect [5]. Therefore, our attack design is generic and might shed light on how the detection along this line should be developed in the future.

Our Contributions. First, we proposed two new backdoor attacks, both of which can successfully insert the backdoor and escape the state-of-the-art detections based on the trigger reconstruction [5,18]. Second, we further raise our attack ability as well as the detection difficulty by reducing the ratio of our trigger size. In our evaluation, the trigger size is only 5% of MNIST image size, 3% of GTSRB image size, and 0.6% of YouTube-Faces image size, respectively. Last, we implement our two attacks for the MNIST, GTSRB and YouTube Faces data sets, and evaluate them against the Neural Cleanse [18] and DeepInspect [5] to demonstrate their effectiveness and concealment.

2   Related Work

2.1   Backdoor Attack

There have been a number of backdoor attacks. Gu et al. proposed Badnets [9], which inserts the backdoor into models by poisoning training data. These models will classify the input data with the trigger into the target class, while the clean input will be classified normally. Chen et al. further proposed an attack in which the attacker only needs to poison a very small amount of data to complete the attack [6].

The attacker may also use perturbation-based method to achieve data poisoning. Liao et al. proposed two methods of data poisoning based on perturbation for backdoor attack [11], static perturbation and dynamic perturbation. The former has a fixed perturbation pattern, while the latter will adjust the perturbation pattern according to the difference between the original class and the target class, which is more stealthy and dangerous.

In addition to directly poisoning the training data, Liu et al. proposed a backdoor attack that does not require access to the training data [14]. In this scenario, the target model is a pre-trained model, the attacker looks at neurons inside the model and designs trigger based on neurons that are more sensitive to the changes in input.

2.2   Backdoor Detection

There are already some defenses to mitigate the backdoor attack. Fine-Pruning combines pruning and fine-tuning to mitigate the impact of the backdoor [12], while this method will affect the performance of the model [18]. Liu et al. suggested three ways to defend the attack [15], input anomaly detection, re-training, and input preprocessing, which bring significant computing overhead [13].

Some work tries to defend against the backdoor attack by detecting whether the input contains the trigger. STRIP [8] determines if an input contains a trigger by adding a strong perturbation to the input, they argue that the trigger would be disrupted by the strong perturbation added. However, this can disrupt the normal input and lead to misclassification [13].

Neural Cleanse [18] is one of the most powerful and representative methods. It provides an advanced and promising method for detecting the backdoor attack. For a pre-trained model, it reconstructs the trigger for each class with some clean data as input. Then it applies outlier detection on these reconstructed triggers. Since the mask of true trigger performs differently from other generated triggers, the outlier is marked as the true trigger. According to their experiment, the trigger of size up to 18% of the whole image can be detected on MNIST, and the trigger of size up to 39% of the whole image can be detected on YouTube Faces. Chen et al. proposed another detecting method against backdoor attack called DeepInspect [5], in which the trigger is reconstructed by a generative neural network.

3   Concealed Backdoor Attacks

In this section, we introduce our concealed backdoor design, including the reconstructed trigger approach and the randomly-generated trigger approach. We first provide our threat model, and describe how to conduct such two backdoor attacks respectively.

3.1   Threat Model

In our proposed attack, the attacker has the ability to manipulate the training data and to train the model. The attacker aims to make the trained model to classify the data with the trigger into the target class while classifying the clean data correctly. At the same time, the backdoor inserted in the trained model can not be detected by Neural Cleanse.

One of the most important challenges is that the trigger reconstructed by Neural Cleanse has been trained by neural network, which is different from the original trigger we added at the beginning [18]. The reconstructed trigger then seems like just the characteristics of the original trigger, which is still relatively small and easy to be detected by outlier detection naturally. That is to say, even the original trigger injected into the model seems normal, the reconstructed one can still be detected through the shrinking. In order to overcome this challenge, we proposed the countermeasure of adding noise to clean data, which can be found in the following section in detail.

3.2   Reconstructed Trigger Approach

In this section, we describe the first attack, which is intuitively inspired by the result of trigger reconstruction [18].

In the backdoor attack, the attacker can manipulate part of the training data, inserts the trigger into the data and modifies their labels to the target class. Then through neural network learning enables the trained model to learn the trigger and connect it to the target class. In Neural Cleanse [18], the trigger that needs to be added if the clean data is misclassified into each class is recovered by reverse reconstruction. It is based on the assumption that the trigger is often small so that the real trigger could be identified by outlier detection. The paper also mentions that the detection effect on the larger trigger would decrease, so we tried to find a way to construct the trigger without significantly increasing its size but being able to evade the detection.

We note that the trigger used for attack in Neural Cleanse [18] is a square placed in the corner of an image. And we wonder if a more complicated trigger will have a more shady effect.

Intuitively we tried to carry out the attack directly using the trigger reconstructed from the clean model. As such the reconstructed trigger will not be recognized as outlier if Neural Cleanse can restore the trigger as the original one. Next, we will describe the process of the attack in detail, which can also be found in Algorithm 1.

Algorithm 1: Reconstructed trigger attack

Input: i: the target class

$label_{img}$: the label of img

S: the whole training set

S_p: training set that needs to be poisoned, $S_p \subseteq S$

S_n: training set that needs data argumentation, $S_n \subseteq S$

S_c: the rest clean data set

α: sampling rate of adding noise

Output: the poisoned model

1 $M_{clean} \leftarrow$ Train on S

2 $Set_{mask}, Set_{pattern} \leftarrow$ Neural Cleanse(M_{clean})

3 $mask, pattern \leftarrow$ mask and pattern that belongs to class i

4 **for** $img \subseteq S_p$ **do**

5 $\quad$ $img \leftarrow (1 - mask) \times img + mask \times pattern$

6 $\quad$ $label_{img} \leftarrow i$

7 **for** $img \subseteq S_n$ **do**

8 $\quad$ $mask' \leftarrow RandomSample_\alpha(mask)$

9 $\quad$ $pattern' \leftarrow pattern$

10 $\quad$ $img \leftarrow (1 - mask') \times img + mask' \times pattern'$

11 $S' \leftarrow S_p \cup S_n \cup S_c$

12 $M_{poisoned} \leftarrow$ Train on S'

Data Poisoning. First, we train a clean model M with the original training set, then trigger of each class can be reconstructed by Neural Cleanse on M. We set the target label as l, so we select the corresponding mask and pattern for the attack. Then we manipulate part of the training data as the carrier of the trigger. Specifically, we do the following with these data, and change their label to be l.

$$img = (1 - mask) \times img + mask \times pattern \tag{1}$$

Data Argumentation. In order to prevent the trained model from being detected by Neural Cleanse, that is to say, the mask reconstructed by the target class l can not be too small to seem quite different from others. The model we trained should be able to learn the whole picture of trigger as much as possible, instead of only extracting part of the features. However, as we mentioned before, the trigger reconstructed from Neural Cleanse is not exactly the same as the original trigger, usually smaller.

To overcome this challenge, we select part of the clean training data which haven't been poisoned in the previous step, and add noise to them, also we need to ensure the accuracy of model classification at the same time. The purpose of adding noise is to enable the model to learn a more complete trigger, so the noise we add to the clean data is a random selection of the subset of the trigger, and keep the label of these data unchanged. Set the data set that needs to add noise as S and the sampling rate of mask as α. For each image img belonging to

S, first we generate a subset of mask with the sampling rate α as $mask'$, while the pattern keeps unchanged, and do the following:

$$img = (1 - mask') \times img + mask' \times pattern \tag{2}$$

Model Training. After the above two steps, the training data is divided into three parts, the poisoned data which has been injected with the trigger, the data with noise and the clean data. We train the model on these data to obtain the poisoned model inserted with a backdoor. We will demonstrate that the trained model can not only achieve the purpose of injecting backdoor, but also can evade the detection of Neural Cleanse.

3.3 Randomly-Generated Trigger Approach

Although the proposed attack can evade the detection of Neural Cleanse, the shape of the generated trigger is determined by the reconstruction process, which brings inconvenience. Therefore, in this section we consider a more general case, in which we only qualify the size of the trigger so that the shape of the trigger can be designed by the attacker. In this attack, no reconstruction result of Neural Cleanse is needed to make up the trigger, instead, we can generate the mask and pattern of the trigger randomly to achieve the same effect with smaller mask size. The main process of this attack is shown in Algorithm 2.

Algorithm 2: Randomly-generated trigger attack

Input: i: the target class
$label_{img}$: the label of img
S: the whole training set
S_p: training set that needs to be poisoned, $S_p \subseteq S$
S_n: training set that needs data argumentation, $S_n \subseteq S$
S_c: the rest clean data set
α: sampling rate of adding noise
z: the size of mask
$m \times n$: the shape of input image
Output: the poisoned model

1 $mask \leftarrow Zeros_{m \times n}$
2 randomly select z elements and set them to 1 in $mask$
3 $pattern \leftarrow$ vector of shape $m \times n$
4 each element in $pattern$ is set randomly from 0 to 255
5 **for** $img \subseteq S_p$ **do**
6      $img \leftarrow (1 - mask) \times img + mask \times pattern$
7      $label_{img} \leftarrow i$

8 **for** $img \subseteq S_n$ **do**
9      $mask' \leftarrow RandomSample_\alpha(mask)$
10     $pattern' \leftarrow pattern$
11     $img \leftarrow (1 - mask') \times img + mask' \times pattern'$

12 $S' \leftarrow S_p \cup S_n \cup S_c$
13 $M_{poisoned} \leftarrow$ Train on S'

Fig. 1. Poisoned images and noisy images in reconstructed trigger attack

Data Poisoning. In this attack, the mask and pattern of the trigger are randomly generated, and both of their shapes are the same as the input image. The mask represents the coverage of the trigger, while the pattern represents the content of the trigger. Set the size of mask to z, and the shape of input image to $m \times n$. The mask is a vector of shape $m \times n$, we randomly select z pixels of mask and set them to 1, keep the rest pixels of mask as 0. The pattern is a randomly generated vector of shape $m \times n$, with the value of each pixel ranging from 0 to 255. For the mask and pattern we obtained, a part of the data is selected to inject the trigger as Eq. 1, and their labels will be changed to the target class l.

Data Argumentation. This step is the same as before. For each image that needs to add noise, we sample the mask randomly with sampling rate α, and keep the pattern unchanged. The image then being manipulated as defined in Eq. 2.

Model Training. We train the model on the data that has been manipulated in the previous steps. The results of experiments show that mask of size 36 (up to 5%) in MNIST can successfully inject the backdoor and evade the detection, while in Neural Cleanse, the threshold for effective detection is 18%. In YouTube Faces, the mask of size 16 (up to 0.6%) can achieve the same effect, and the threshold in Neural Cleanse is 39% [18].

4   Attack Performance Evaluation

We show the attack performance of our two attack approaches against the detection of NC. We adopt the experiment designs and detection codes from the NC work [18]. Attacks are conducted on top of the Keras, a Python library for DL.

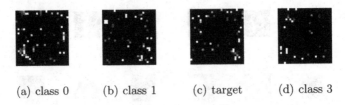

(a) class 0   (b) class 1   (c) target   (d) class 3

Fig. 2. Neural Cleanse reconstructed results in reconstructed trigger attack on MNIST

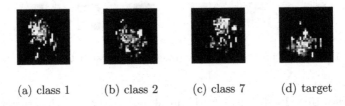

(a) class 1   (b) class 2   (c) class 7   (d) target

Fig. 3. Neural Cleanse reconstructed results in reconstructed trigger attack on GTSRB

4.1   Experiment Settings

We use in our experiments the following three widely-used data sets.

- **MNIST.** The MNIST data set [2] contains handwritten numbers, ranging from 0 to 9. Each image is 28×28 pixels. It contains 10 classes, 60000 images for training and 10000 images for testing.
- **GTSRB.** The GTSRB data set [1] contains traffic signs. Each image is 32×32 pixels. It contains 43 classes, 19604 images for training and 19605 images for testing.
- **YouTube Faces.** The YouTube Faces is a data set [3] of face videos designed for face recognition in videos. Each image is 55×47 pixels. It contains 1595 classes, i.e 1595 different people. We follow the setting in [18] to only select classes that contain more than 100 images. However, the number of images is still too large to process, so we select 100 classes from them. The final data set contains 52148 images for training and 2000 images for testing.

We conduct extensive experiments to determine the appropriate parameter values in the experiment. For the sampling rate used in both reconstructed trigger attack and randomly-generated trigger attack, which is between 0 and 1, we test multiple sets with a step size of 0.1. While in randomly-generated trigger attack, we conduct the experiments by gradually reducing the size of the mask to find a suitable size, so that the size of mask is small enough to evade detection. The reference value for size can be the size of mask in the previous attack.

In MNIST case, we select 6000 samples for data poisoning and all training set for data argumentation. The sampling rate of adding noise is 0.6. Specifically to the randomly-generated trigger attack, we set the mask size to 36. The target label is 2 for both attacks.

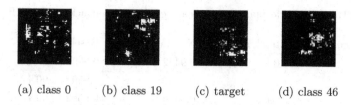

(a) class 0   (b) class 19   (c) target   (d) class 46

Fig. 4. Neural Cleanse reconstructed results in reconstructed trigger attack on YouTube Faces

In GTSRB case, we select 1960 samples for data poisoning and 10000 samples for data argumentation. In the reconstructed trigger attack, we set the sampling rate of adding noise to 0.6. In the randomly-generated trigger attack, we set the sampling rate to 0.8 and mask size to 30. Label 33 is used as the target label in both attacks.

In YouTube case, we select 5500 samples for data poisoning and 40000 samples for data argumentation. The sampling rate of adding noise is 0.6. Specifically to the randomly-generated trigger attack, we set the mask size to 16. The target label is 21 for both attacks.

Table 1. Performance of reconstructed trigger attack on MNIST

Sampling rate	Attack accuracy	Normal accuracy	Baseline	Against NC
0.5	0.999	0.9858	0.9869	80%
0.6	0.999	0.9847	0.9869	90%
0.7	0.994	0.9833	0.9869	90%

4.2 Experimental Results

We designed experiments on MNIST, GTSRB and YouTube Faces data sets. Reconstructed trigger attack and randomly-generated trigger attack were applied

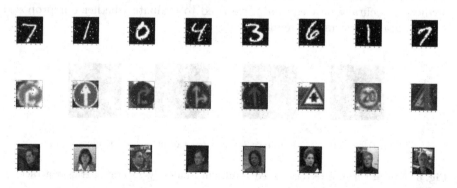

Fig. 5. Poisoned images and noisy images in randomly-generated trigger attack

Table 2. Performance of reconstructed trigger attack on GTSRB

Sampling rate	Attack accuracy	Normal accuracy	Baseline	Against NC
0.5	1.0	0.9452	0.9592	80%
0.6	1.0	0.942	0.9592	90%
0.7	0.99	0.9386	0.9592	90%

Table 3. Performance of reconstructed trigger attack on YouTube Faces

Sampling rate	Attack accuracy	Normal accuracy	Baseline	Against NC
0.5	0.9997	0.9828	0.98	100%
0.6	0.9997	0.9777	0.98	100%
0.7	1.0	0.9796	0.98	100%

to the data sets respectively. We will show images poisoned with the trigger, and images added with noise. We used the open source code of [18] for outlier detection. The detection results showed that all of our attacks mentioned before can evade the detection. We will also show recovered triggers for each class reconstructed by Neural Cleanse to demonstrate that this detection can not detect the trigger injected by our proposed attacks. Moreover, we changed the sampling rate used in data argumentation and mask size used in randomly-generated trigger attack, and list the prediction accuracy in the case of different parameter values on clean data (the data without the trigger) and poisoned data (the data with the trigger). The former means poisoned model's performance on normal data, and the latter means accuracy to the target class on poisoned data. Specifically, we repeated the attack 10 times, calculated the prediction accuracy on clean data and poisoned data, and counted the percentage of attack instances which can successfully evade detection against NC under each case. These will measure the model's performance on clean data and the effectiveness of backdoor attack. We will also list the prediction accuracy of the original model which has not been injected with the backdoor, by comparing with the poisoned model's prediction accuracy on clean data, we tried to evaluate whether our proposed attack caused performance reduction.

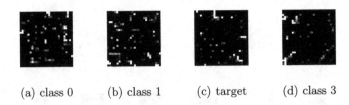

(a) class 0   (b) class 1   (c) target   (d) class 3

Fig. 6. Neural Cleanse reconstructed results in randomly-generated trigger attack on MNIST

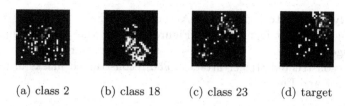

(a) class 2   (b) class 18   (c) class 23   (d) target

Fig. 7. Neural Cleanse reconstructed results in randomly-generated trigger attack on GTSRB

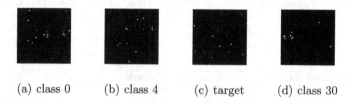

(a) class 0   (b) class 4   (c) target   (d) class 30

Fig. 8. Neural Cleanse reconstructed results in randomly-generated trigger attack on YouTube Faces

Reconstructed Trigger Attack. In this part, we deployed the reconstructed trigger attack. Figure 1 shows the poisoned images and noisy images, the left four columns of images in each figure are poisoned images, while the right four columns of images are noisy images. We can see that the injected triggers are not salient.

The reconstructed masks of the target label and other three masks of clean class reconstructed by Neural Cleanse are shown in Fig. 2, Fig. 3 and Fig. 4. In Fig. 2, the target label is 2 and other three classes are 0, 1 and 3 on MNIST. We can find that the sizes of the four masks are similar which means our backdoor attack cannot be detected by Neural Cleanse. We can find the similar results on GTSRB and YouTube Faces which are shown in Fig. 3 and Fig. 4.

Table 1, Table 2 and Table 3 show the performance of the reconstructed trigger attack on three data sets. We list the attack success rates, model's performance on clean data and the percentage of attack instances that can evade detection against NC when the sampling rate changed. The performance of clean model is also shown in the tables as the baseline. Compared with the baseline, we can see that the performance of the attacked model remains high. When the sampling rate is 0.5, 80% attack instances can evade the detection of Neural Cleanse. This rate rises to 90% when the sampling rate becomes 0.6. We also notice that the performance of model on clean data decreases slightly when the sampling rate increases, which means the noise added in data argumentation becomes larger. We can find that the prediction accuracy of poisoned model on both poisoned data and clean data are high. And the attack does not cause significant performance reduction. We can also find that most of the attacks can evade the detection.

Randomly-Generated Trigger Attack. We here show the results of randomly-generated trigger attack. Figure 5 shows the poisoned images and noisy images. We can see that noises in these images are much smaller than those in reconstructed trigger attacks. The reconstructed masks are shown in Fig. 6, Fig. 7 and Fig. 8.

Table 4. Performance of randomly-generated trigger attack on MNIST

Mask size	Sampling rate	Attack accuracy	Normal accuracy	Baseline	Against NC
	0.6	0.999	0.9858	0.9869	40%
36	0.7	0.9857	0.9832	0.9869	40%
	0.8	0.9807	0.981	0.9869	20%

Sampling rate	Mask size	Attack accuracy	Normal accuracy	Baseline	Against NC
	30	0.9987	0.9872	0.9869	30%
	36	0.999	0.9858	0.9869	40%
0.6	42	0.999	0.9856	0.9869	40%
	48	0.999	0.9852	0.9869	50%

Table 5. Performance of randomly-generated trigger attack on GTSRB

Mask size	Sampling rate	Attack accuracy	Normal accuracy	Baseline	Against NC
	0.6	0.9897	0.9616	0.9592	60%
30	0.7	0.9911	0.9512	0.9592	80%
	0.8	0.9493	0.9528	0.9592	90%

Sampling rate	Mask size	Attack accuracy	Normal accuracy	Baseline	Against NC
	20	0.9184	0.9561	0.9592	60%
	30	0.9493	0.9528	0.9592	80%
0.8	40	0.9498	0.9551	0.9592	100%
	50	0.9488	0.9521	0.9592	100%

The attack success rate, the prediction accuracy of clean data and the percentage of attack instances that can evade detection are listed respectively in Table 4, Table 5 and Table 6 for cases of three data sets. We can find that in this attack, the size of mask is much smaller than reconstructed trigger attack. In MNIST, the size of mask changes from 48 in reconstructed trigger attack to 36 in randomly-generated trigger attack. In GTSRB, the size of mask changes from 96 to 30. In YouTube Faces, the size of mask changes from 270 to 16.

Additionally, tables show that, even when requiring models to achieve a high success rate and prediction accuracy in the randomly-generated trigger case, it is still possible to find attack instances that can evade the detection with a small mask size. We also observe that the performance of models on clean data decreases slightly when the sampling rate increases. In order to make the attack

Table 6. Performance of randomly-generated trigger attack on YouTube Faces

Mask size	Sampling rate	Attack accuracy	Normal accuracy	Baseline	Against NC
16	0.6	0.9681	0.9904	0.98	100%
	0.7	0.9068	0.9919	0.98	100%
	0.8	0.7565	0.9897	0.98	100%

Sampling rate	Mask size	Attack accuracy	Normal accuracy	Baseline	Against NC
0.6	8	0.8729	0.9934	0.98	100%
	12	0.9467	0.9932	0.98	100%
	16	0.9681	0.9904	0.98	100%
	20	0.9769	0.9919	0.98	100%

and normal classification both achieve a good effect, We choose the sampling rate of 0.6 for MNIST, YouTube Faces and 0.8 for GTSRB. When sampling rates were set as that, the percentage of attack instances that can evade detection against NC also increases with the mask size increases.

5   Attack Generalization Evaluation

In this section, we tried to evaluate whether the proposed attacks could evade the detection by other detection tools. DeepInspect [5] is proposed by Chen et al. which can detect backdoor attacks in the black box scenario. DeepInspect is also based on the trigger reconstruction like Neural Cleanse. The difference is that DeepInspect utilizes the conditional GAN to reconstruct the trigger. Both approaches utilize the similar idea to detect potential backdoor in a model, that is, to reconstruct possible triggers and apply outlier detection which is based on the size of the trigger.

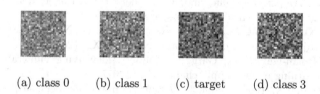

(a) class 0   (b) class 1   (c) target   (d) class 3

Fig. 9. DeepInspect reconstructed results in reconstructed trigger attack on MNIST

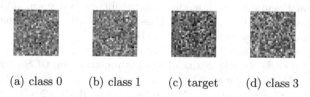

(a) class 0   (b) class 1   (c) target   (d) class 3

Fig. 10. DeepInspect reconstructed results in randomly-generated trigger attack on MNIST

We designed the experiment of backdoor detection according to the algorithm description in [5] on MNIST, GTSRB and YouTube Faces. We utilized the conditional GAN to reconstruct triggers and applied DMAD [5] on them for outlier detection. The results demonstrate that DeepInspect can not detect the backdoor inserted by our proposed attacks as well. Part of reconstructed results by DeepInspect are shown in Fig. 9 and Fig. 10.

6 Conclusion

In summary, we proposed two concealed backdoor attacks which can bypass recently-proposed reconstruction based defenses. We demonstrate the effectiveness of both attacks over different datasets and various attack conditions.

Acknowledgements. The work is supported in part by NSFC-61872180, Jiangsu "Shuang-Chuang" Program, Jiangsu "Six-Talent-Peaks" Program, Ant Financial through the Ant Financial Science Funds for Security Research, NSFC-61872176, and US NSF grant CNS-1816399.

References

1. GTSRB data. http://benchmark.ini.rub.de/?section=gtsrb&subsection=dataset
2. MNIST data. http://yann.lecun.com/exdb/mnist/
3. Youtube faces data. https://www.cs.tau.ac.il/~wolf/ytfaces/
4. Chen, B., et al.: Detecting backdoor attacks on deep neural networks by activation clustering. arXiv (2018)
5. Chen, H., Fu, C., Zhao, J., Koushanfar, F.: Deepinspect: A black-box trojan detection and mitigation framework for deep neural networks. In: IJCAI (2019)
6. Chen, X., Liu, C., Li, B., Lu, K., Song, D.: Targeted backdoor attacks on deep learning systems using data poisoning. arXiv (2017)
7. Chou, E., Tramèr, F., Pellegrino, G., Boneh, D.: Sentinet: detecting physical attacks against deep learning systems. arXiv (2018)
8. Gao, Y., Xu, C., Wang, D., Chen, S., Ranasinghe, D.C., Nepal, S.: Strip: a defence against trojan attacks on deep neural networks. arXiv (2019)
9. Gu, T., Dolan-Gavitt, B., Garg, S.: Badnets: identifying vulnerabilities in the machine learning model supply chain. arXiv (2017)
10. He, K., Zhang, X., Ren, S., Sun, J.: Delving deep into rectifiers: surpassing human-level performance on imagenet classification. In: ICCV (2015)
11. Liao, C., Zhong, H., Squicciarini, A., Zhu, S., Miller, D.: Backdoor embedding in convolutional neural network models via invisible perturbation. arXiv (2018)
12. Liu, K., Dolan-Gavitt, B., Garg, S.: Fine-pruning: defending against backdooring attacks on deep neural networks. In: RAID (2018)
13. Liu, Y., Lee, W.C., Tao, G., Ma, S., Aafer, Y., Zhang, X.: ABS: scanning neural networks for back-doors by artificial brain stimulation. In: CCS (2019)
14. Liu, Y., et al.: Trojaning attack on neural networks. In: NDSS (2018)
15. Liu, Y., Xie, Y., Srivastava, A.: Neural trojans. In: ICCD (2017)

16. Redmon, J., Divvala, S., Girshick, R., Farhadi, A.: You only look once: unified, real-time object detection. In: CVPR (2016)
17. Taigman, Y., Yang, M., Ranzato, M., Wolf, L.: Deepface: closing the gap to human-level performance in face verification. In: CVPR (2014)
18. Wang, B., et al.: Neural cleanse: identifying and mitigating backdoor attacks in neural networks. In: S&P (2019)

Author Index

Akram, Raja Naeem 3
Aleksandrova, Marharyta 219

Bang, Youngoh 416
Bangui, Hind 78
Beneš, Tomáš 49
Bhatti, Muhammad Khurram 32
Buhnova, Barbora 78

Carr, Michael 265
Čejka, Tomáš 49
Correia, Miguel 64
Costante, Elisa 355

den Hartog, Jerry 355
dos Santos, Daniel Ricardo 355
Drozd, Olha 124
Dupont, Guillaume 355
Dürmuth, Markus 280

Eckel, Michael 203
Ekaputra, Fajar 384
Ekelhart, Andreas 384
Engel, Thomas 219
Etalle, Sandro 355

Feichtner, Johannes 171
Fischer, Mathias 248
Friborg, Ludwig 143
Fuchs, Andreas 203

Ge, Mouzhi 78
Gogniat, Guy 32
Gong, Xiaorui 155
Graux, Damien 370
Gruber, Stefan 171

Haas, Steffen 248
Han, RuiDong 189
Hynek, Karel 49

Islam, Md Morshedul 295

Jabat, Pablo 370
Jaskolka, Jason 17
Jeon, Hyeonseong 416

Kadir, Rabiah Abdul 313
Kalbantner, Jan 3
Kävrestad, Joakim 95
Kiesling, Elmar 384
Kirrane, Sabrina 124
Kitkowska, Agnieszka 109
Klinec, Dusan 338
Kubátová, Hana 49
Kurniawan, Kabul 384

Li, Feng 189
Li, Qun 431
Liu, Baoxu 155
Liu, Jian 155
Lo Iacono, Luigi 280
Luo, Mengxia 155

Ma, JianFeng 189
Ma, Siqi 189
Markantonakis, Konstantinos 3
Martucci, Leonardo A. 109
Matos, David R. 64
Matyas, Vashek 338
Mayer, Rudolf 401
Mayer, Wilfried 234
Merzdovnik, Georg 234
Mitseva, Asya 219
Moura, Ricardo 64
Mousavi Nejad, Najmeh 370
Mukhtar, Muhammad Asim 32

Nedelchev, Rostislav 370
Nohlberg, Marcus 95
Nohuddin, Puteri N. E. 313

Panchenko, Andriy 219
Pardal, Miguel L. 64
Patil, Tanvi 280
Peiser, Stefan Carl 143

Repp, Jürgen   203

Safavi-Naini, Reihaneh   295
Sarcevic, Tanja   401
Sattolo, Thomas A. V.   17
Scandariato, Riccardo   143
Scerri, Simon   370
Semal, Benjamin   3
Shahandashti, Siamak F.   265
Shulman, Yefim   109
Sommer, Robin   248
Springer, Markus   203
Su, Chunhua   324

van Dam, Gijs   313

Wang, Weizheng   324
Wang, YunBo   189
Wästlund, Erik   109
Weippl, Edgar   234
Wiefling, Stephan   280
Woo, Simon S.   416

Xiong, Yayuan   431
Xu, Fengyuan   431

Yang, Can   155
Yang, Chao   189

Zaman, Halimah Badioze   313
Zhong, Sheng   431

Printed in the United States
by Baker & Taylor Publisher Services